1

2

Operation, Lubrication, Maintenance and Tune-up 3

Lay-up and Fitting Out 4

Single-Cylinder Engines 5

Multicylinder Engines 6

Fuel Injection and Governor Systems 7

Cooling System 8

Electrical System 9

Transmission—KM Series 10

Transmission—KBW Series 11

Index 12

Wiring Diagrams 13

Common spark plug conditions

NORMAL

Symptoms: Brown to grayish-tan color and slight electrode wear. Correct heat range for engine and operating conditions.
Recommendation: When new spark plugs are installed, replace with plugs of the same heat range.

WORN

Symptoms: Rounded electrodes with a small amount of deposits on the firing end. Normal color. Causes hard starting in damp or cold weather and poor fuel economy.
Recommendation: Plugs have been left in the engine too long. Replace with new plugs of the same heat range. Follow the recommended maintenance schedule.

CARBON DEPOSITS

Symptoms: Dry sooty deposits indicate a rich mixture or weak ignition. Causes misfiring, hard starting and hesitation.
Recommendation: Make sure the plug has the correct heat range. Check for a clogged air filter or problem in the fuel system or engine management system. Also check for ignition system problems.

ASH DEPOSITS

Symptoms: Light brown deposits encrusted on the side or center electrodes or both. Derived from oil and/or fuel additives. Excessive amounts may mask the spark, causing misfiring and hesitation during acceleration.
Recommendation: If excessive deposits accumulate over a short time or low mileage, install new valve guide seals to prevent seepage of oil into the combustion chambers. Also try changing gasoline brands.

OIL DEPOSITS

Symptoms: Oily coating caused by poor oil control. Oil is leaking past worn valve guides or piston rings into the combustion chamber. Causes hard starting, misfiring and hesitation.
Recommendation: Correct the mechanical condition with necessary repairs and install new plugs.

GAP BRIDGING

Symptoms: Combustion deposits lodge between the electrodes. Heavy deposits accumulate and bridge the electrode gap. The plug ceases to fire, resulting in a dead cylinder.
Recommendation: Locate the faulty plug and remove the deposits from between the electrodes.

TOO HOT

Symptoms: Blistered, white insulator, eroded electrode and absence of deposits. Results in shortened plug life.
Recommendation: Check for the correct plug heat range, over-advanced ignition timing, lean fuel mixture, intake manifold vacuum leaks, sticking valves and insufficient engine cooling.

PREIGNITION

Symptoms: Melted electrodes. Insulators are white, but may be dirty due to misfiring or flying debris in the combustion chamber. Can lead to engine damage.
Recommendation: Check for the correct plug heat range, over-advanced ignition timing, lean fuel mixture, insufficient engine cooling and lack of lubrication.

HIGH SPEED GLAZING

Symptoms: Insulator has yellowish, glazed appearance. Indicates that combustion chamber temperatures have risen suddenly during hard acceleration. Normal deposits melt to form a conductive coating. Causes misfiring at high speeds.
Recommendation: Install new plugs. Consider using a colder plug if driving habits warrant.

DETONATION

Symptoms: Insulators may be cracked or chipped. Improper gap setting techniques can also result in a fractured insulator tip. Can lead to piston damage.
Recommendation: Make sure the fuel anti-knock values meet engine requirements. Use care when setting the gaps on new plugs. Avoid lugging the engine.

MECHANICAL DAMAGE

Symptoms: May be caused by a foreign object in the combustion chamber or the piston striking an incorrect reach (too long) plug. Causes a dead cylinder and could result in piston damage.
Recommendation: Repair the mechanical damage. Remove the foreign object from the engine and/or install the correct reach plug.

YANMAR

DIESEL INBOARD SHOP MANUAL

ONE, TWO & THREE CYLINDER ENGINES • 1980-2009

WHAT'S IN YOUR TOOLBOX?

YouTube™

More information available at Clymer.com

Phone: 805-498-6703

Haynes Publishing Group
Sparkford Nr Yeovil
Somerset BA22 7JJ England

Haynes North America, Inc
859 Lawrence Drive
Newbury Park
California 91320 USA

ISBN-10: 1-59969-457-3
ISBN-13: 978-1-59969-457-3
Library of Congress: 2011931885

Technical Illustrations: *Michael Rose and Robert Caldwell*
Cover: *Courtesy of Hunter Marine Corporation, Alachua, Florida*

Printed in the UK

B800-2, 10U1, 16-248

ABCDEFGHIJKLMNOPQRS

Contents

QUICK REFERENCE DATA IX

CHAPTER ONE
GENERAL INFORMATION 1

Manual organization 1
Notes, cautions and warnings 2
Safety first 2
Service hints 3
Parts replacement 4
Torque specifications 4
Fasteners 4
Lubricants 8
RTV gasket sealant 9
Threadlock 9
Basic hand tools 9
Precision measuring tools 13
Mechanic's tips 16
Bearing replacement 18
Seals 23

CHAPTER TWO
TROUBLESHOOTING 26

Starting system 27
Charging system 31
Charging system tests 31
Fuel system 32
Cooling system 34
Engine exhaust smoke 35
Engine noises 35
Engine troubleshooting 36
Cooling system 36
Lubrication system 36

CHAPTER THREE
OPERATION, LUBRICATION, MAINTENANCE AND TUNE-UP 42

Fuel requirements 42
Preoperational checks 42
Starting checklist 43
Stopping the engine 44
Emergency engine stopping 44
Post-operational checks 44
Engine maintenance and lubrication 44
Cooling system 52
Battery 56
Engine tune-up 57
Transmission 60

CHAPTER FOUR
LAY-UP AND FITTING OUT 63

Lay-up 63
Cooling system draining 64
Fitting out 66

CHAPTER FIVE
SINGLE-CYLINDER ENGINES 68

Diesel engine fundamentals 68
Engine serial number and code 70
Replacement parts 70
Engine removal precautions 70
Valve cover 71
Breather assembly 71
Decompression mechanism 73
Cylinder head 73
Rocker shaft assembly 76
Valves and valve seats 77
Push rods 79
Piston/connecting rod assembly 79
Timing gearcase 85
Lubrication system 86
Flywheel 89
Drive disc 91
Crankshaft 91
Main bearings 93
Camshaft 93
Cylinder block 95

CHAPTER SIX
MULTICYLINDER ENGINES 99

Engine serial number and code 99
Replacement parts 100
Engine 100
Valve cover 101
Breather assembly 101
Decompression mechanism 102
Exhaust manifold 103
Cylinder head 105
Rocker shaft assembly 109
Valves and valve seats 110
Push rods 113
Piston/connecting rod assembly 113
Timing gearcase 118
Lubrication system 120
Flywheel 122
Drive disc 123
Crankshaft 123
Main bearings 126
Camshaft 127
Cylinder block 128

CHAPTER SEVEN
FUEL INJECTION AND GOVERNOR SYSTEMS 138

Fuel injection fundamentals 138
Fuel injection system bleeding 142
Fuel injection timing 144
Fuel injector 146
Fuel injection pump 149
Fuel transfer pump 150
Fuel lines 151
Governor system 152

CHAPTER EIGHT

COOLING SYTEM ... 159

Cooling systems ... 159
Thermostat ... 165
Hose replacement ... 168
Drive belts ... 169
Seawater pump ... 170
Freshwater pump ... 177
Freshwater cooling system maintenance ... 177
Seawater cooling system maintenance ... 181

CHAPTER NINE

ELECTRICAL SYSTEM ... 183

Battery ... 183
Electrical protection ... 188
Charging system ... 189
Starting system ... 190
Switches ... 195
Senders ... 195
Warning lamps ... 197
Alarm buzzer ... 197
Tachometer ... 197

CHAPTER TEN

TRANSMISSION—KM SERIES ... 199

Operation ... 199
Removal/installation ... 201
Overhaul ... 202
Reassembly ... 208
Bearing adjustment ... 211
Drive disc ... 213

CHAPTER ELEVEN

TRANSMISSION—KBW SERIES ... 216

Operation ... 216
Removal/installation ... 217
Overhaul ... 217
Bearing adjustment ... 224
Drive disc ... 225

INDEX ... 227

WIRING DIAGRAMS ... 231

Quick Reference Data

TUNE-UP SPECIFICATIONS

Model	Idle rpm (no-load)	Full throttle rpm (no-load)	Fuel injection timing	Value clearance all models
1GM	850	3750	15° BTDC	0.2 m (0.008 in.)
1GM10	850	3825	15° BTDC	0.2 m (0.008 in.)
2GM	850	3750	15° BTDC	0.2 m (0.008 in.)
2GMF	850	3750	15° BTDC	0.2 m (0.008 in.)
2GM20	850	3825	15° BTDC	0.2 m (0.008 in.)
2GM20F	850	3825	15° BTDC	0.2 m (0.008 in.)
3GM	850	3750	18° BTDC	0.2 m (0.008 in.)
3GMF	850	3750	18° BTDC	0.2 m (0.008 in.)
3GMD	850	3750	18° BTDC	0.2 m (0.008 in.)
3GM30	850	3825	18° BTDC	0.2 m (0.008 in.)
3GM30F	850	3825	18° BTDC	0.2 m (0.008 in.)
3HM	850	3600	21° BTDC	0.2 m (0.008 in.)
3HMF	850	3600	21° BTDC	0.2 m (0.008 in.)
3HM35	850	3625	21° BTDC	0.2 m (0.008 in.)
3HM35F	850	3625	21° BTDC	0.2 m (0.008 in.)

APPROXIMATE ENGINE OIL CAPACITIES

Model	Oil capacity
1GM, 1GM10	1.4 qt. (1.3 L)
2GM, 2GM20	2.1 qt. (2.0 L)
3GM, 3GM30	2.8 qt. (2.6 L)
3HM, 3HM35	5.7 qt. (5.4 L)

FRESHWATER (CLOSED) COOLING SYSTEM CAPACITY

Model	Capacity
2GM20F	2.9 L (0.77 gal.)
3GM30F	3.4 L (0.9 gal.)
3HM35F	4.9 L (1.3 gal.)

ENGINE MODELS

Model	Number of cylinders	Displacement	Horsepower/ rpm	Gearbox	Gearbox ratio (forward gear)
1GM	1	293 cc (17.9 cu. in.)	6.5 hp/3400 rpm	KM2A	2.21, 2.62 or 3.22
1GM10	1	318 cc (19.4 cu. in.)	8 hp/3400 rpm	KM2C or KM2P	2.21, 2.62 or 3.22
2GM	2	586 cc (35.7 cu. in.)	13 hp/3400 rpm	KM2A	2.21, 2.62 or 3.22
2GMF	2	586 cc (35.7 cu. in.)	13 hp/3400 rpm	KM2A	2.21, 2.62 or 3.22
2GM20	2	636 cc (38.8 cu. in.)	16 hp/3400 rpm	KM2C or KM2P	2.21, 2.62 or 3.22

(continued)

ENGINE MODELS (continued)

Model	Number of cylinders	Displacement	Horsepower/ rpm	Gearbox	Gearbox ratio (forward gear)
2GM20F	2	636 cc (38.8 cu. in.)	16 hp/3400 rpm	KM2C or KM2P	2.21, 2.62 or 3.22
3GM	3	879 cc (53.6 cu. in.)	20 hp/3400 rpm	KBW10D	2.14, 2.63 or 2.83
3GMF	3	879 cc (53.6 cu. in.)	20 hp/3400 rpm	KBW10D	2.14, 2.63 or 2.83
3GMD	3	879 cc (53.6 cu. in.)	20 hp/3400 rpm	KM3A	2.36, 2.61 or 3.20
3GM30	3	954 cc (58.2 cu. in.)	24 hp/3400 rpm	KM3A or KM3P	2.36, 2.61 or 3.20
3GM30F	3	954 cc (58.2 cu. in.)	24 hp/3400 rpm	KM3A or KM3P	2.36, 2.61 or 3.20
3HM	3	1126 cc (68.7 cu. in.)	27 hp/3200 rpm	KBW10E	2.14 or 2.83
3HMF	3	1126 cc (68.7 cu. in.)	27 hp/3200 rpm	KBW10E	2.14 or 2.83
3HM35	3	1282 cc (78.2 cu. in.)	30 hp/3200 rpm	KBW10E	2.14 or 2.83
3HM35F	3	1282 cc (78.2 cu. In.)	30 hp/3200 rpm	KBW10E	2.14 or 2.83

GENERAL TORQUE SPECIFICATIONS

Thread diameter	N•m	ft.-lb.	in.-lb.
M6	8-10	–	71-88
M8	23-27	17-20	204-240
M10	44-50	32-37	–
M12	75-85	55-63	–
M14	125-135	92-100	–
M16	200-210	147-155	–

Chapter One

General Information

This Clymer shop manual covers the GM Yanmar marine diesel engine series identified in **Table 1**.

Troubleshooting, tune-up, maintenance and repair are not difficult, if you know what tools and equipment to use and what to do. Step-by-step instructions guide you through jobs ranging from simple maintenance to complete engine overhaul.

This manual can be used by anyone from a first-time do-it-yourselfer to a professional mechanic. Detailed drawings and clear photographs provide all the information needed to do the work right.

Some of the procedures in this manual require the use of special tools. The resourceful mechanic can, in many cases, think of acceptable substitutes for special tools. However, using a substitute for a special tool is not recommended, as it can be dangerous and may damage the part. If a tool can be designed and safely made, but will require some type of machine work, contact a local community college or high school that has a machine shop curriculum. Shop teachers sometimes welcome outside work that can be used as practical shop applications for students.

Each Yanmar marine diesel can be identified by its individual model number. The model numbers for all Yanmar marine diesel engines covered in this manual are listed in **Table 1**.

Some engine model numbers end with the letters F or D, such as 2GMF or 3GMD. Suffix letter F indicates the engine is equipped with a freshwater (closed) cooling system. Suffix letter D indicates the engine is equipped with a Kanzaki KBW10D transmission.

Except where specified, F and D series engines are included when a basic model number is specified. For example, if model 3GM is called out in a procedure, the procedure also applies to 3GMD and 3GMF.

NOTE
Engine models ending with the letters C (sail drive) or V (V-drive transmission) are not covered in this manual.

Metric and U.S. standards are used throughout this manual. U.S. to metric conversions are in **Table 2**.

Critical torque specifications are provided at the end of each chapter (as required). Use the general torque specifications listed in **Table 3** if a torque specification is not listed for a specific component or assembly.

Metric drill tap sizes are in **Table 4**.

Tables 1-4 are located at the end of the chapter.

MANUAL ORGANIZATION

This chapter provides general information useful to engine owners and mechanics. In addition, this chapter discusses the tools and techniques for preventive maintenance, troubleshooting and repair.

Chapter Two provides methods and suggestions for quick and accurate problem diagnosis and repair. Troubleshooting procedures discuss typical symptoms and logical methods to pinpoint the trouble.

Chapter Three explains all periodic lubrication and routine maintenance necessary to keep the engine operating well. Chapter Three also includes recommended tune-up procedures, eliminating the need to constantly consult other chapters on the various assemblies.

Subsequent chapters describe specific systems, providing disassembly, repair, assembly and adjustment procedures in simple step-by-step form. If a repair is impractical for a home mechanic, it is so indicated. It is usually faster and less expensive to take such repairs to a dealer or repair shop. Specifications concerning a specific system are included at the end of the appropriate chapter.

NOTES, CAUTIONS AND WARNINGS

The terms NOTE, CAUTION and WARNING have specific meanings in this manual. A NOTE provides additional information to make a step or procedure easier or clearer. Disregarding a NOTE could cause inconvenience but would not cause damage or personal injury.

A CAUTION emphasizes areas where equipment damage could occur. Disregarding a CAUTION could cause permanent mechanical damage; however, personal injury is unlikely.

A WARNING emphasizes areas where personal injury or even death could result from negligence. Mechanical damage may also occur. WARNINGS *are to be taken seriously*. In some cases, serious injury or death has resulted from disregarding similar warnings.

SAFETY FIRST

Professional mechanics can work for years and never sustain a serious injury. By observing a few rules of common sense and safety, it is possible to enjoy many safe hours servicing the machine. Ignoring these rules can cause injury or damage to equipment.

1. Never use gasoline as a cleaning solvent.
2. Never smoke or use a torch in the vicinity of flammable liquids, such as cleaning solvent, in open containers.
3. Use proper sized wrenches to avoid damage to fasteners and personal injury.
4. When loosening a tight or stuck nut, remember what could happen if the wrench should slip. Be careful; protect yourself accordingly.

1

2

5. When replacing a fastener, make sure to use one with the same measurements and strength as the old one. Incorrect or mismatched fasteners can result in damage to the engine and possible personal injury. Beware of fastener kits that are filled with poorly made nuts, bolts, washers and cotter pins. Refer to *Fasteners* in this chapter for additional information.
6. Keep all hand and power tools in good condition. Wipe greasy and oily tools after using them. They are difficult to hold and can cause injury. Replace or repair worn or damaged tools.
7. Keep the work area clean and uncluttered.
8. Wear safety goggles (**Figure 1**) during all operations involving drilling, grinding, the use of a cold chisel or *any* time the safety of the eyes is compromised. Safety goggles should be worn when using solvent and compressed air.
9. Keep an approved fire extinguisher nearby (**Figure 2**). Make sure it is rated for gasoline (Class B) and electrical (Class C) fires.
10. When drying bearings or other rotating parts with compressed air, never allow the air jet to rotate the bearing or part. The air jet is capable of rotating them at speeds far

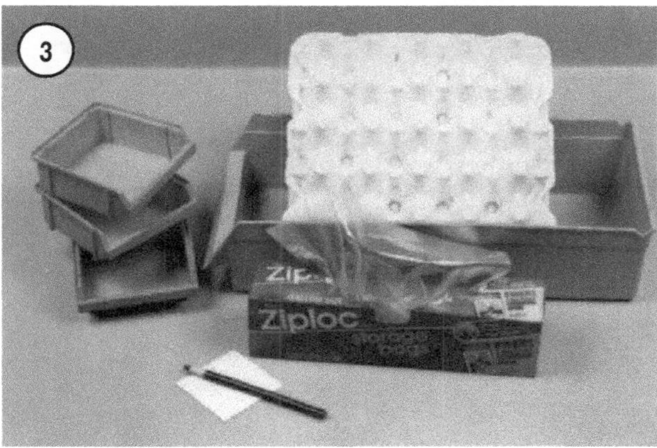

in excess of those for which they were designed. The bearing or rotating part can disintegrate and cause serious injury and damage. Hold the inner bearing race by hand to prevent bearing damage when using compressed air.

SERVICE HINTS

Most of the service procedures covered are straightforward and can be performed by anyone reasonably handy with tools. It is suggested, however, that you consider your capabilities carefully before attempting any operation involving major disassembly.

1. When disassembling engine or drive components, mark the parts for location and mark all parts that mate together. Small parts, such as bolts, can be identified by placing them in plastic sandwich bags (**Figure 3**). Seal the bags and label them. If reassembly will take place immediately, an accepted practice is to place nuts and bolts in a cupcake tin or egg carton in the order of disassembly. Because many types of ink fade if applied to tape, use a permanent ink pen.
2. Protect finished surfaces from physical damage or corrosion. Keep gasoline off painted surfaces.
3. Use penetrating oil on frozen or tight bolts, then strike the bolt head a few times with a hammer and punch (use a screwdriver on screws). Avoid the use of heat where possible, as it can warp, melt or affect the temper of parts. Heat also damages finishes, especially paint and plastics.
4. No parts removed or installed (other than bushings and bearings) in the procedures described in this manual should require unusual force during disassembly or assembly. If a part is difficult to remove or install, find out why before proceeding.
5. Cover all openings after removing parts or components to prevent contaminants and small tools from falling in.
6. Read each procedure *completely* while looking at the actual parts before starting a job. Make sure you *thoroughly* understand what is to be done and then carefully follow the procedure, step by step.

NOTE

Some of the procedures or service specifications in this manual may not be accurate if the engine has been modified or if it has been equipped with after-market equipment. If installing after-market equipment or if the engine has been modified, file all printed instructions or technical information regarding the new equipment in a folder or notebook for future reference. If the engine was purchased used, the previous owner may have modified it or installed non-stock parts. If necessary, consult with a dealer or the accessory manufacturer on service-related changes.

7. Recommendations are occasionally made to refer service or maintenance to a marine dealership or a specialist in a particular field. In these cases, the work will be done more quickly and economically than performing the work at home.
8. In procedural steps, the term *replace* means to discard a defective part and replace it with a new or exchange unit. *Overhaul* means to remove, disassemble, inspect, measure, repair or replace defective parts, reassemble and install major systems or parts.
9. Some operations require the use of a hydraulic press. It would be wiser to have these operations performed by a shop equipped for such work, rather than to try to do the job yourself with makeshift equipment that may damage the machine.
10. Repairs go much faster and easier if the machine is clean before beginning work. There are many special cleaners on the market for washing the engine and related parts. Follow the manufacturer's directions on the container for the best results. Clean all oily or greasy parts with cleaning solvent as they are removed.

WARNING

Never use gasoline as a cleaning agent. Be sure to work in a well-ventilated area when using cleaning solvent. Keep a fire extinguisher, rated for gasoline fires, on hand.

11. Much of the labor charges for repairs made by dealers are for the time involved in the removal, disassembly, assembly and reinstallation of other parts in order to reach the defective part. It is often possible to perform the preliminary operations and then take the defective unit to the dealer for repair at considerable savings.

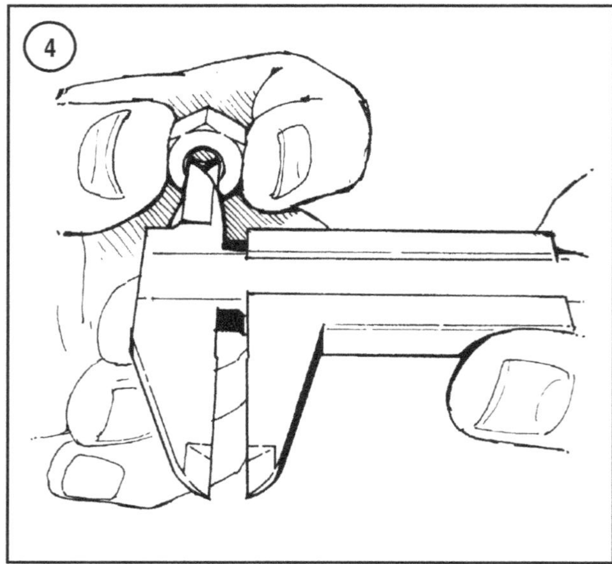

12. If special tools are required, make arrangements to get them before starting. It is frustrating and time-consuming to start a job and then be unable to complete it.

13. Make diagrams (or take a Polaroid picture) wherever similar-appearing parts are found. For instance, retaining bolts for a particular part may not be the same length. It is difficult to remember where everything came from—and mistakes are costly. It is also possible that you may be sidetracked and not return to work for days or even weeks—in which time carefully laid out parts may be disturbed.

14. When assembling parts, make sure all shims and washers are replaced exactly where they were before removal.

15. Whenever a rotating part contacts a stationary part, look for a shim or washer. Use new gaskets if there is any doubt about the condition of the old ones. A thin coat of silicone sealant on non-pressure-type gaskets may help them seal more effectively.

16. If it becomes necessary to purchase gasket material to make a gasket for the engine, measure the thickness of the old gasket (at an uncompressed point) and purchase gasket material with the same approximate thickness.

17. Use heavy grease to hold small parts in place if they tend to fall out during assembly. However, keep grease and oil away from electrical components.

18. Take time and do the job right. Do not forget that a newly rebuilt engine must be broken in just like a new one.

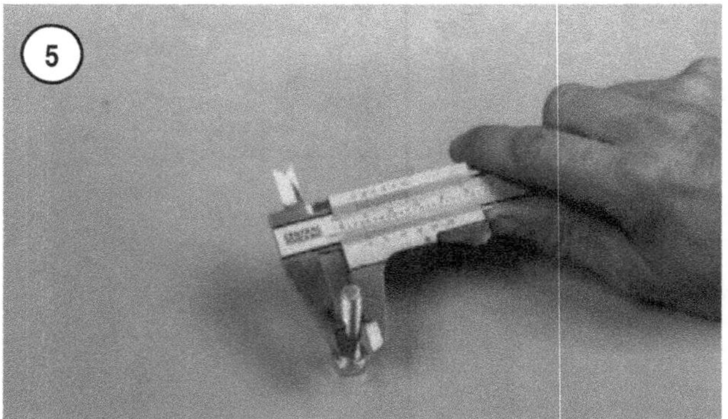

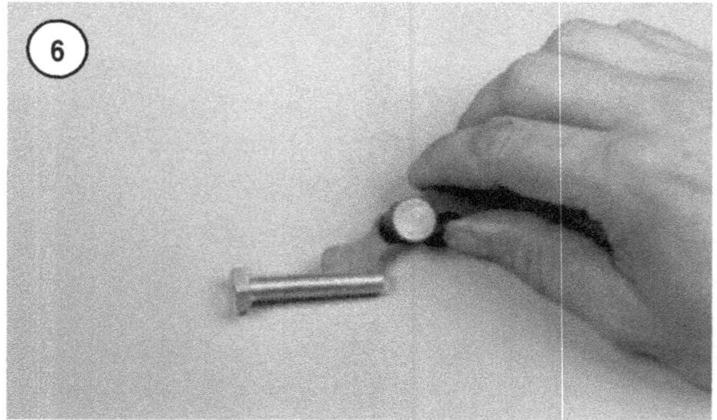

PARTS REPLACEMENT

Engine manufacturers often modify the parts of an engine during the lifetime of the engine model. When ordering parts from the dealer or other parts distributor, always order by the model and engine serial number. Refer to Chapter Six or Seven. Write the numbers down and have them available. Compare new parts to old before purchasing them. If they are not alike, have the parts manager explain the difference. **Table 1** lists model numbers.

TORQUE SPECIFICATIONS

Torque specifications throughout this manual are given in Newton-meters (N•m) and foot-pounds (ft.-lb.).

Table 3 lists general torque specifications for nuts and bolts that are not listed in the respective chapters. To use the table, first determine the size of the nut or bolt by measuring it with a vernier caliper. **Figure 4** and **Figure 5** show how to do this.

FASTENERS

The materials and designs of the various fasteners used on the engine are not arrived at by chance or accident. Fas-

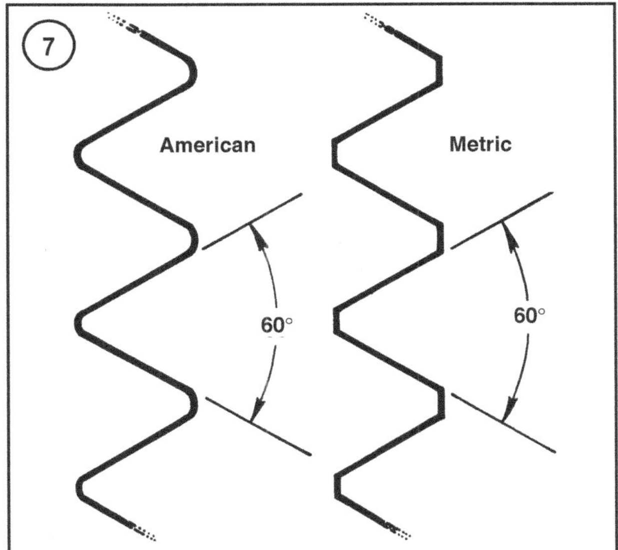

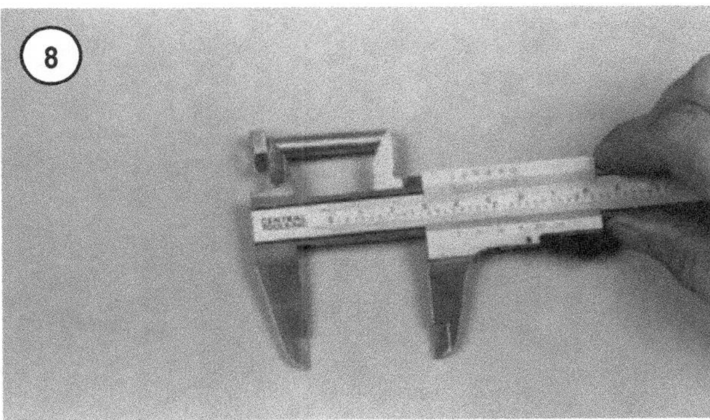

tener design determines the type of tool required to work the fastener. Fastener material is carefully selected to decrease the possibility of failure.

Nuts, bolts and screws are manufactured in a wide range of thread patterns. To join a nut and bolt, the diameter of the bolt and the diameter of the hole in the nut must be the same. It is also important that the threads on both be properly matched.

The best way to tell if the threads on two fasteners match is to turn the nut on the bolt (or the bolt into the threaded hole) by hand. Make sure both pieces are clean; remove Loctite or other sealer residue from threads if present. If excessive force is required, check the thread condition on each fastener. If the thread condition is good but the fasteners jam, the threads are not compatible. A thread pitch gauge (**Figure 6**) can also be used to determine pitch. Yanmar marine engines are manufactured with ISO (International Organization for Standardization) metric fasteners. The threads are cut differently than those of American fasteners (**Figure 7**).

Most threads are cut so that the fastener must be turned clockwise to tighten it. These are called right-hand threads. Some fasteners have left-hand threads; they must be turned counterclockwise to be tightened. Left-hand threads are used in locations where normal rotation of the equipment would tend to loosen a right-hand threaded fastener.

ISO Metric Screw Threads

ISO metric threads come in three standard thread sizes: coarse, fine and constant pitch. The ISO coarse pitch is used for most common fastener applications. The fine pitch thread is used on certain precision tools and instruments. The constant pitch thread is used mainly on machine parts and not for fasteners. The constant pitch thread, however, is used on all metric thread spark plugs.

ISO metric threads are specified by the capital letter M followed by the diameter in millimeters and the pitch (or the distance between each thread) in millimeters separated by the sign —. For example, a M8 — 1.25 bolt has a diameter of 8 millimeters with a distance of 1.25 millimeters between each thread. The measurement across two flats on the head of the bolt indicates the wrench size to be used. **Figure 5** shows how to determine bolt diameter.

NOTE
*If purchasing a bolt from a dealer or parts store, it is important to know how to specify bolt length. The correct way to measure bolt length is to measure from underneath the bolt head to the end of the bolt (**Figure 8**). Always measure bolt length in this manner to avoid purchasing or installing bolts that are too long.*

Machine Screws

There are many different types of machine screws. **Figure 9** shows a number of screw heads requiring different types of turning tools. Heads are also designed to protrude above the metal (round) or to be slightly recessed in the metal (flat). See **Figure 10**.

Bolts

Commonly called bolts, the technical name for these fasteners is *cap screw*. Metric bolts are described by the diameter and pitch (or the distance between each thread).

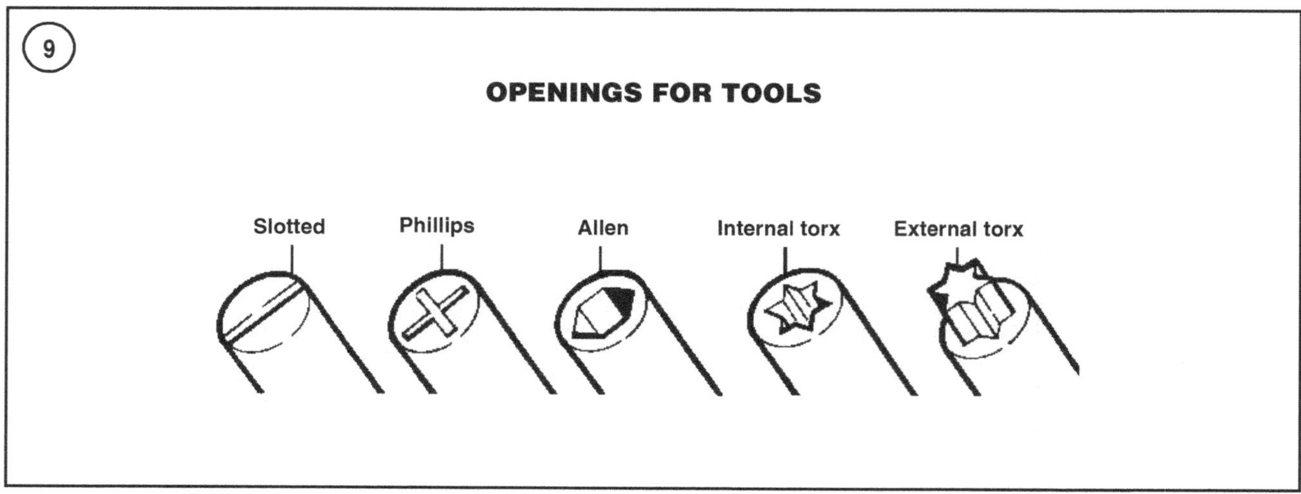

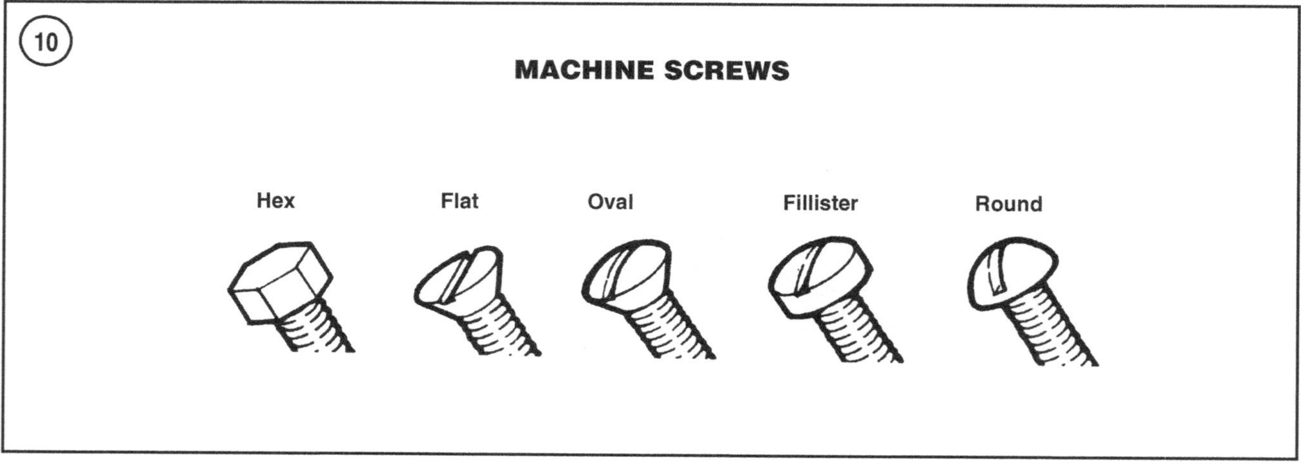

Nuts

Nuts are manufactured in a variety of types and sizes. Most are hexagonal (6-sided) and fit on bolts, screws and studs with the same diameter and pitch.

Figure 11 shows several types of nuts. The common nut is generally used with a lockwasher. Self-locking nuts have a nylon insert that prevents the nut from loosening; no lockwasher is required. Wing nuts are designed for fast removal by hand. Wing nuts are used for convenience in non-critical locations.

To indicate the size of a metric nut, manufacturers specify the diameter of the opening and the thread pitch. This is similar to bolt specifications, but without the length dimension. The measurement across two flats on the nut indicates the wrench size to be used.

Self-Locking Fasteners

Several types of bolts, screws and nuts incorporate a system that develops an interference between the bolt, screw, nut or tapped hole threads. Interference is achieved in various ways: by distorting threads, coating threads with dry adhesive or nylon, distorting the top of an all-metal nut, or using a nylon insert in the center or at the top of a nut.

Self-locking fasteners offer greater holding strength and better vibration resistance. Some self-locking fasteners can be reused if in good condition. Others, like the nylon insert nut, form an initial locking condition when the nut is first installed – the nylon forms closely to the bolt thread pattern, thus reducing any tendency for the nut to loosen. When the nut is removed, the locking efficiency is greatly reduced. It is recommended that new self-locking fasteners be installed after they are removed.

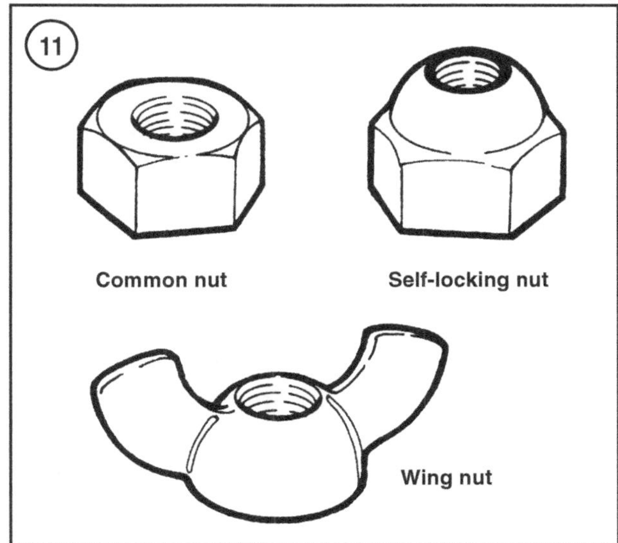

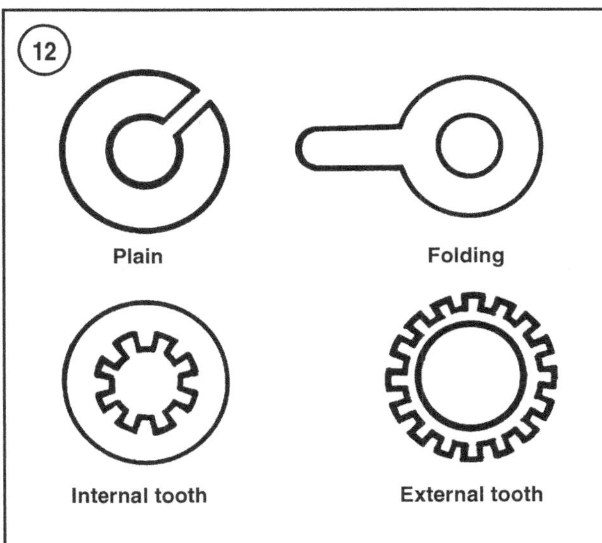

Washers

There are two basic types of washers: flat washers and lockwashers. Flat washers are simple discs with a hole to fit a screw or bolt. Lockwashers are designed to prevent a fastener from working loose due to vibration, expansion and contraction. **Figure 12** shows several types of washers. Washers are also used in the following functions:

a. As spacers.
b. To prevent galling or damage of the equipment by the fastener.
c. To help distribute fastener load during torquing.
d. As seals.

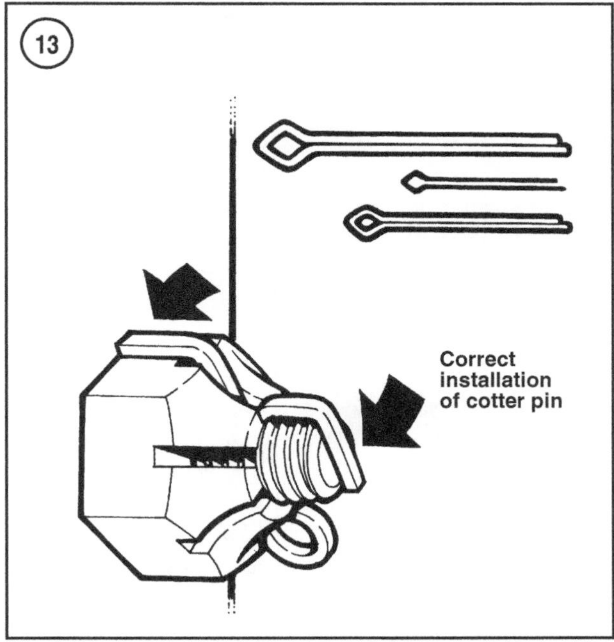

Flat washers are often used between a lockwasher and a fastener to provide a smooth bearing surface. This allows the fastener to be turned easily with a tool.

NOTE
As much care should be given to the selection and purchase of washers as that given to bolts, nuts and other fasteners. Avoid washers that are made of thin, weak materials. These will deform and crush the first time they are torqued, allowing the nut or bolt to loosen.

Cotter Pins

Cotter pins (**Figure 13**) are used to secure fasteners in a special location. The threaded stud or bolt must have a hole in it. The nut or nut lock piece will have castellations around its upper edge into which the cotter pin fits to keep it from loosening. When *properly* installed, a cotter pin is a positive locking device.

Purchase a cotter pin that will fit snugly when inserted through the nut and the mating thread part. The cotter pin should not be so tight that it has to be driven in and out, but it should not be so loose that it can move or float after it is installed.

Before installing a cotter pin, tighten the nut to the recommended torque specification. If the castellations in the nut do not line up with the hole in the bolt or stud, tighten the nut until alignment is achieved. Do not loosen the nut to make alignment. Insert a *new* cotter pin through the nut and hole, then tap the head lightly to seat it. Bend one arm over the flat on the nut and the other against the top of the stud or bolt (**Figure 13**). Cut the arms to a suitable length to prevent them from snagging on clothing or skin. When the cotter pin is bent and its arms cut to length, it should be tight. If it can be wiggled, it is improperly installed.

Do not reuse cotter pins, as their ends may break and allow the cotter pin to fall out and the fastener to loosen.

Circlips

Circlips can be internal or external design. They are used to retain items on shafts (external type) or within tubes (internal type). In some applications, circlips of varying thickness are used to control the end play of parts assemblies. These are often called selective circlips. Replace circlips during installation, as removal weakens and deforms them.

Two basic styles of circlips are available: machined and stamped circlips. Machined circlips (**Figure 14**) can be installed in either direction (shaft or housing) because both faces are machined, thus creating two sharp edges. Stamped circlips (**Figure 15**) are manufactured with one sharp edge and one rounded edge. When installing stamped circlips in a thrust situation, the sharp edge must face away from the part producing the thrust. When installing circlips, observe the following:

a. Remove and install circlips with circlip pliers. See *Circlip Pliers* in this chapter.
b. Compress or expand circlips only enough to install them.
c. After the circlip is installed, make sure it is completely seated in its groove.

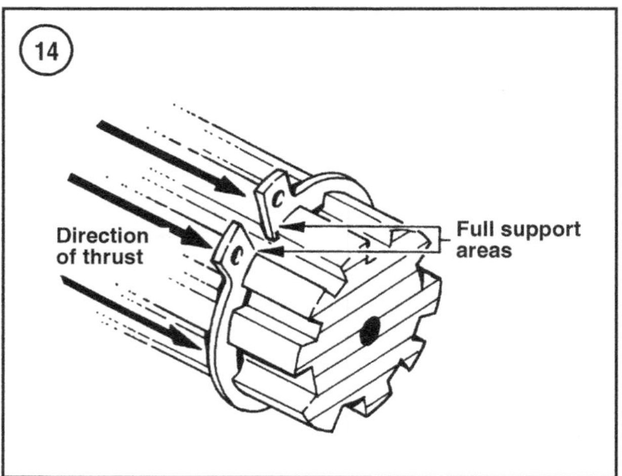

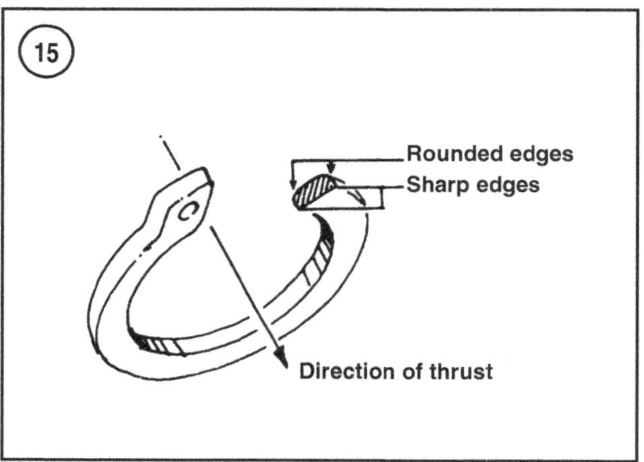

LUBRICANTS

Periodic lubrication ensures long life for any type of equipment. The *type* of lubricant used is as important as the lubrication service itself, although in an emergency the wrong type of lubricant is better than none at all. The following paragraphs describe the types of lubricants most often required. Be sure to follow the manufacturer's recommendations for lubricant types.

Generally, all liquid lubricants are called oil. They may be mineral-based (including petroleum bases), natural-based (vegetable and animal bases), synthetic-based or emulsions (mixtures). Grease is an oil to which a thickening base has been added so that the end product is semi-solid. Grease is often classified by the type of thickener added; lithium soap is commonly used.

Engine Oil

Oil for marine and automotive four-stroke engines is classified by the American Petroleum Institute (API) and the Society of Automotive Engineers (SAE) in several categories. Oil containers display these classifications on the top or label. API oil classification is indicated by letters; oils for gasoline engines are identified by an "S" and oils for diesel engines are identified by a "C".

Viscosity is an indication of the oil's thickness. The SAE uses numbers to indicate viscosity; thin oils have low numbers while thick oils have high numbers. A "W" after the number indicates that the viscosity testing was done at low temperature to simulate cold-weather operation. Engine oils fall into the 5W-30 and 20W-50 range.

Multi-grade oils (for example 10W-40) are less viscous (thinner) at low temperatures and more viscous (thicker) at high temperatures. This allows the oil to perform efficiently across a wide range of engine operating condi-

tions. The lower the number, the easier the engine will turn over in cold climates. Higher numbers are usually recommended for engine running in hot weather conditions.

Additional information is provided in Chapter Four.

Grease

Greases are graded by the National Lubricating Grease Institute (NLGI). Greases are graded by number according to the consistency of the grease; these range from No. 000 to No. 6, with No. 6 being the most solid. A typical multipurpose grease is NLGI No. 2. For specific applications, equipment manufacturers may require grease with an additive such as molybdenum disulfide (MoS_2).

RTV GASKET SEALANT

Room temperature vulcanizing (RTV) sealant is used on some pre-formed gaskets and to seal some components. RTV is a silicone gel supplied in tubes and can be purchased in a number of different colors.

Moisture in the air causes RTV to cure. Always place the cap on the tube as soon as possible when using RTV. RTV has a shelf life of one year and will not cure properly if the shelf life has expired. Check the expiration date on RTV tubes before use, and keep partially used tubes tightly sealed.

Applying RTV Sealant

Clean all gasket residue and contaminants from mating surfaces. Remove all RTV gasket material from blind attaching holes, as it will affect bolt torque.

Apply RTV sealant in a continuous bead 2-3 mm (0.08-0.12 in.) thick. Circle all mounting holes unless otherwise specified. Torque mating parts within 10 minutes after application.

THREADLOCK

Because of the marine engine's operating conditions, a threadlock (**Figure 16**) is required to help secure many of the fasteners. A threadlock will lock fasteners against vibration loosening and seal against leaks. Loctite 242 (blue) and 271 (red) are recommended for many threadlock requirements described in this manual.

Loctite 242 (blue) is a medium-strength threadlock, and component disassembly can be performed with normal hand tools. Loctite 271 (red) is a high-strength threadlock, and heat or special tools, such as a press or puller, are required for component disassembly.

Applying Threadlock

Surfaces should be clean. If a threadlock was previously applied to the component, this residue should also be removed.

Shake the Loctite container thoroughly and apply to both parts. Assemble parts and/or tighten fasteners.

BASIC HAND TOOLS

Many of the procedures in this manual can accomplished with simple hand tools and test equipment familiar to the average home mechanic. Keep tools clean and organized in a toolbox. After using a tool, wipe off dirt and grease and return the tool to its correct place. Wiping tools off is especially important if servicing the craft in areas where they can come in contact with sand. Sand is very abrasive and will cause premature wear to engine parts.

High-quality tools are essential; they are also more economical in the long run. Stay away from the advertised specials featured at some stores. These are usually a poor grade tool that can be sold cheaply. They are usually made of inferior material and are thick, heavy and clumsy. Their rough finish makes them difficult to clean, and they usually don't last very long.

Quality tools are made of alloy steel and are heat treated for greater strength. They are lighter and better balanced than poorly made ones. Their surface is smooth, making them a pleasure to work with and easy to clean. The initial cost of quality tools may be more, but they are less expensive in the long run.

The following tools are required to perform virtually any repair job. Each tool is described and the recommended sizes given. Metric size tools are required to service Yanmar diesels.

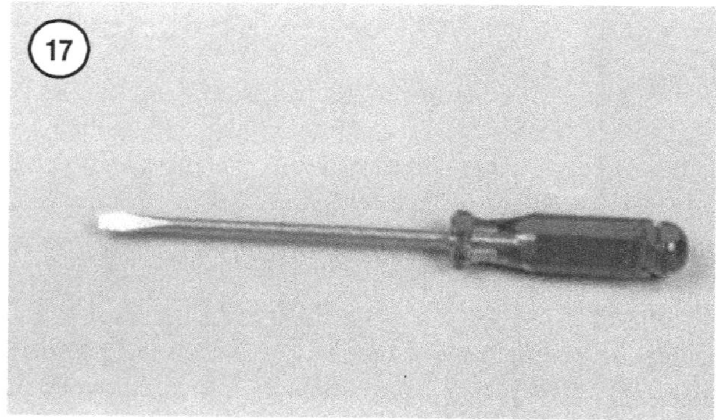

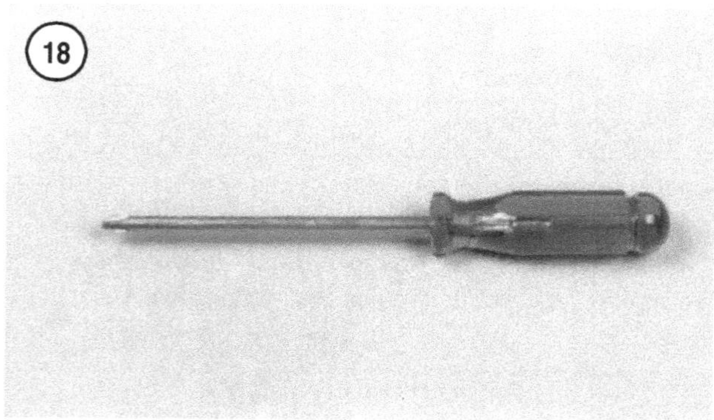

Screwdrivers

The screwdriver is a very basic tool, but if used improperly it will do more damage than good. The slot on a screw has a definite dimension and shape. Through improper use or selection, a screwdriver can damage the screw head, making removal of the screw difficult. A screwdriver must be selected to conform to the shape of the screw head used. Two basic types of screwdrivers are required: standard (flat- or slot-blade) screwdrivers (**Figure 17**) and Phillips screwdrivers (**Figure 18**).

Note the following when selecting and using screwdrivers:

1. The screwdriver must always fit the screw head. If the screwdriver blade is too small for the screw slot, damage may occur to the screw slot and screwdriver. If the blade is too large, it cannot engage the slot properly and will result in damage to the screw head.
2. Standard screwdrivers are identified by the length of their blade. A 6-inch screwdriver has a blade six inches long. The width of the screwdriver blade will vary, so make sure that the blade engages the screw slot completely.
3. Phillips screwdrivers are sized according to their point size. They are numbered one, two, three and four. The degree of taper determines the point size; the No. 1 Phillips screwdriver will be the most pointed. The points become more blunt as their number increases.

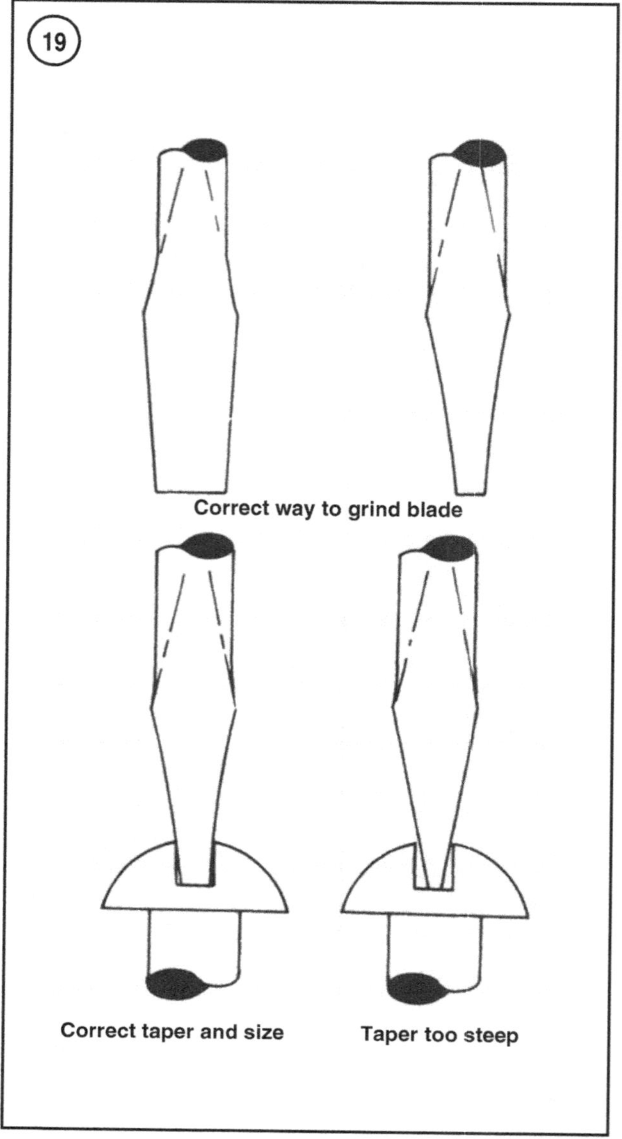

NOTE

There is another screwdriver similar to the Phillips, and that is the Reed and Prince tip. Like the Phillips, the Reed and Prince screwdriver tip forms an "X", but the Reed and Prince tip has a much more pointed tip. The Reed and Prince screwdriver should never be used on Phillips screws and vise versa. Intermixing these screwdrivers will cause damage to the screw and screwdriver.

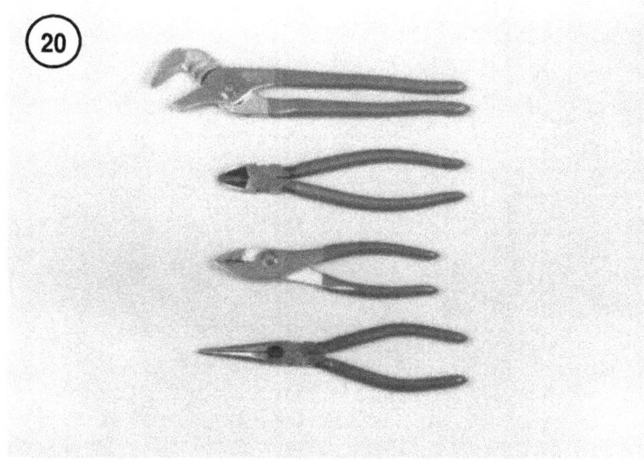

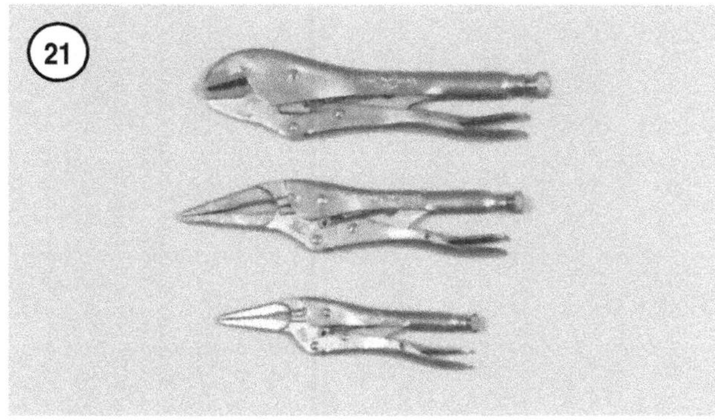

Identify them by painting the screwdriver shank underneath the handle.

4. When selecting screwdrivers, note that more power can be applied with less effort with a longer screwdriver than with a short one. Of course, there will be situations where only a short handle screwdriver can be used. Keep this in mind though, when trying to remove tight screws.
5. Because the working end of a screwdriver receives quite a bit of abuse, you should purchase screwdrivers with hardened tips. The extra money will be well spent.
6. Screwdrivers are available in sets, which often include an assortment of common and Phillips blades. If purchasing them individually, buy at least the following:
   a. Common screwdriver—5/16 × 6 in. blade.
   b. Common screwdriver—3/8 × 12 in. blade.
   c. Phillips screwdriver—size 2 tip, 6 in. blade.
   d. Phillips screwdriver—size 3 tip, 6 and 8 in. blade.
7. Use screwdrivers only for driving screws. Never use a screwdriver for prying or chiseling metal. Do not try to remove a Phillips, Torx or Allen head screw with a standard screwdriver (unless the screw has a combination head that

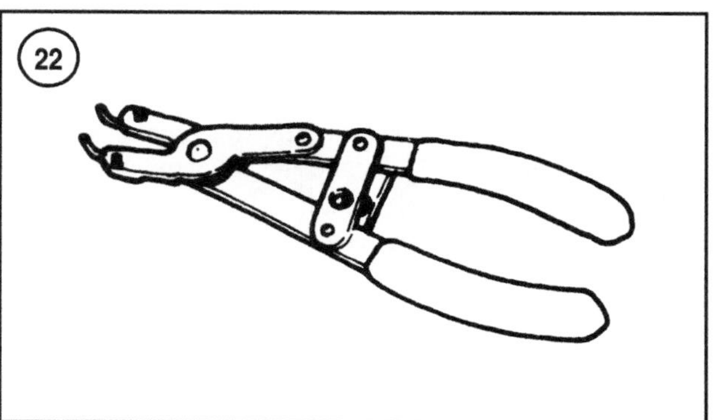

will accept either type); this can damage the head so that the proper tool will be unable to remove it.
8. Keep screwdrivers in the proper condition, and they will last longer and perform better. Always keep the tip of a standard screwdriver in good condition. **Figure 19** shows how to grind the tip to the proper shape if it becomes damaged. Note the symmetrical sides of the tip.

Pliers

Pliers come in a wide range of types and sizes. Pliers are useful for cutting, bending and crimping. They should never be used to cut hardened objects or to turn bolts or nuts. **Figure 20** shows several types of pliers.

Each type of pliers has a specialized function. Combination pliers are general-purpose pliers and are used mainly for holding and for bending. Needlenose pliers are used to hold or bend small objects. Adjustable pliers (commonly referred to as channel locks) can be adjusted to hold various sizes of objects; the jaws remain parallel to grip around objects such as pipe or tubing.

Locking Pliers

Locking pliers (**Figure 21**) are used to hold objects very tightly while another task is performed on the object. Locking pliers are available in many types for more specific tasks.

Snap Ring Pliers

Snap ring pliers (**Figure 22**) are used to remove snap rings from shafts or within engine or suspension housings. When purchasing snap ring pliers, there are two types. External pliers (spreading) are used to remove snap rings that fit on the outside of a shaft. Internal pliers (squeezing) are used to remove snap ring that fit inside a housing.

Box-end, Open-end and Combination Wrenches

Box-end and open-end wrenches are available in sets or separately in a variety of sizes. The size number stamped near the end refers to the distance between the two parallel flats on the hex head bolt or nut.

Box-end wrenches are usually superior to open-end wrenches. Open-end wrenches grip the nut on only two flats. Unless a wrench fits well, it may slip and round off the points on the nut. The box-end wrench grips on all six flats. Both 6-point and 12-point openings on box-end wrenches are available. The 6-point gives superior holding power; the 12-point allows a shorter swing radius.

Combination wrenches (**Figure 23**) are open on one side and boxed on the other. Both ends are the same size.

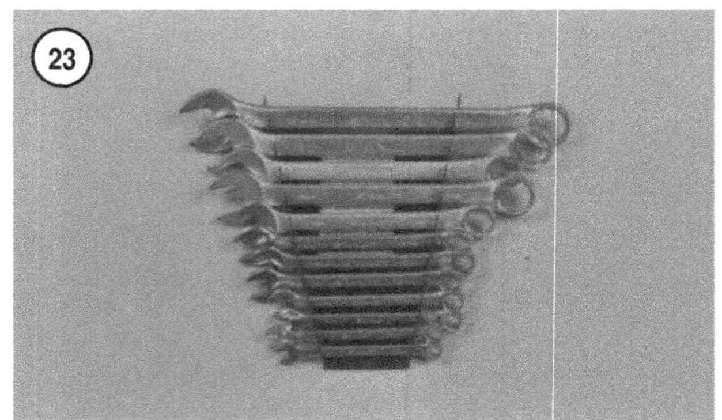

23

Adjustable Wrenches

An adjustable wrench fits a variety of nuts or bolt heads (**Figure 24**). However, it can loosen and slip, causing damage to the nut and possibly causing injury. Use an adjustable wrench only when other wrenches are not available.

Adjustable wrenches come in various sizes.

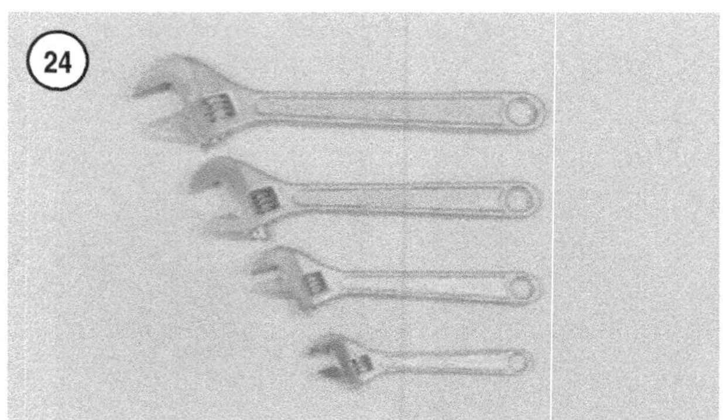

24

Socket Wrenches

This type is undoubtedly the fastest, safest and most convenient to use. Sockets that attach to a ratchet handle (**Figure 25**) are available with 6-point or 12-point openings and 1/4, 3/8, 1/2 and 3/4 in. drives (**Figure 26**). The drive size indicates the size of the square hole that mates with the ratchet handle.

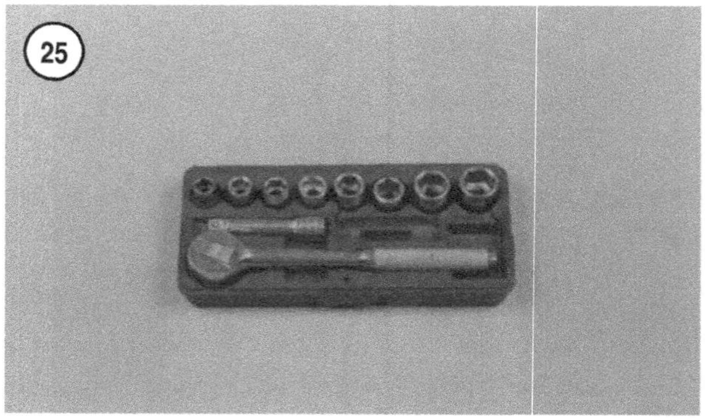

25

Torque Wrench

A torque wrench (**Figure 27**) is used with a socket to measure how tightly a nut or bolt is installed. Torque wrenches come in a wide price range and in different drive sizes. The drive size is the size of the square drive that mates with the socket.

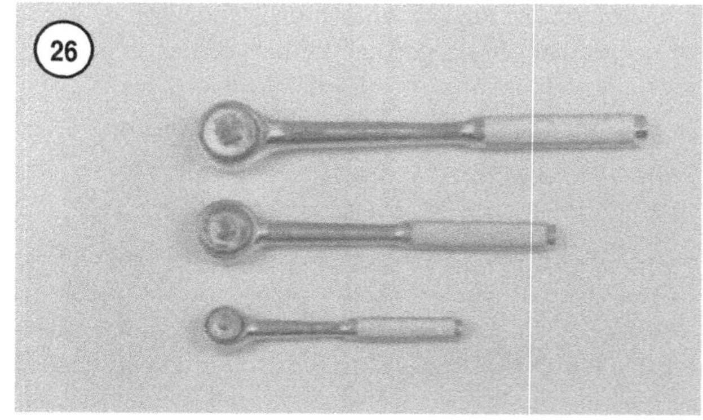

26

Impact Driver

This tool makes removal of tight fasteners easy and eliminates damage to bolts and screw slots. Impact drivers and interchangeable bits (**Figure 28**) are available at most large hardware stores, tool suppliers and motorcycle dealers. Sockets can also be used with a hand-impact driver. However, make sure the socket is designed for impact use. Do not use regular hand sockets, as they may shatter.

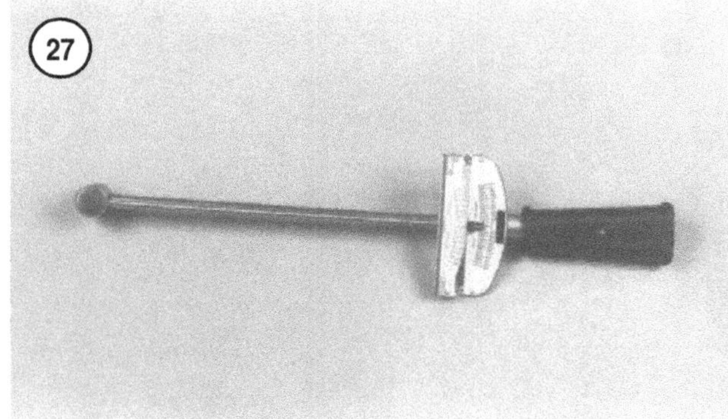

27

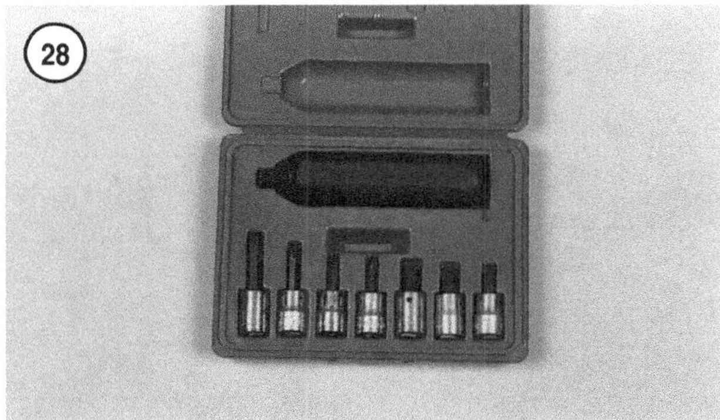

28

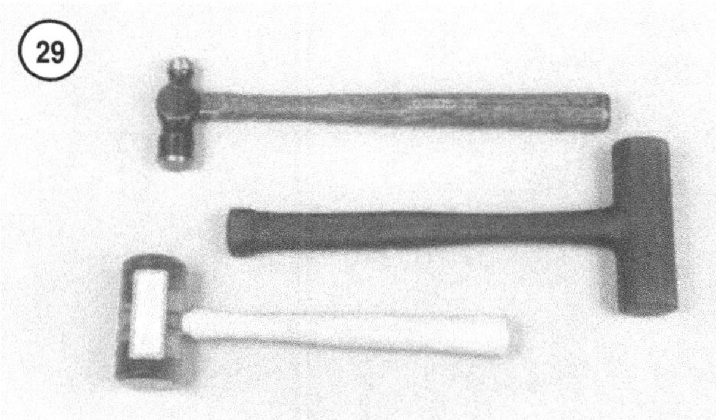

29

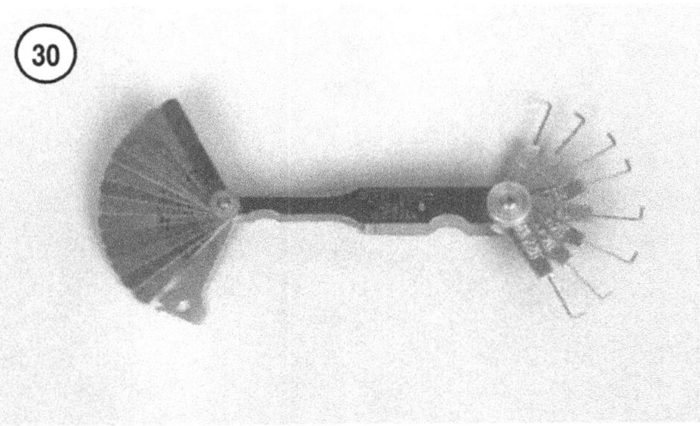

30

Hammers

The correct hammer (**Figure 29**) is necessary for many types of repairs. Use only a hammer with a face (or head) made of rubber or plastic or the soft-faced type filled with leadshot. *Never* use a metal-faced hammer on engine or jet pump parts, as severe damage will result. Ball-peen or machinist's hammers are required if striking another tool, such as a punch or impact driver. When striking a hammer against a punch, cold chisel or similar tool, the face of the hammer should be at least 1/2 in. larger than the head of the tool. If it is necessary to strike hard against a steel part without damaging it, use a brass hammer. A brass hammer can be used because brass will give when striking a harder object.

When using hammers, note the following:

1. *Always* wear safety glasses.

2. Inspect hammers for damaged or broken parts. Repair or replace the hammer as required. Do *not* use a hammer with a taped handle.

3. Always wipe oil or grease off the hammer *before* using it.

4. The head of the hammer should always strike the object squarely. Do not use the side of the hammer or the handle to strike an object.

5. Always use the correct hammer for the job.

PRECISION MEASURING TOOLS

Measurement is an important part of service. When performing many of the service procedures in this manual, a number of measurements will be required. These include basic checks, such as engine compression and spark plug gap. Measurements will be required to determine the condition of the piston and cylinder bore, crankshaft runout and so on. When making these measurements, the degree of accuracy will dictate which tool is required. Precision measuring tools are expensive. If these tools are not available, it may be more worthwhile to have the checks made at a dealer. The following is a description of the measuring tools required during engine and transmission overhaul.

Feeler Gauge

A feeler gauge (**Figure 30**) is made of a piece of a flat or round hardened steel of a specified thickness. Wire gauges are used to measure spark plug gap. Flat gauges are used for all other measurements.

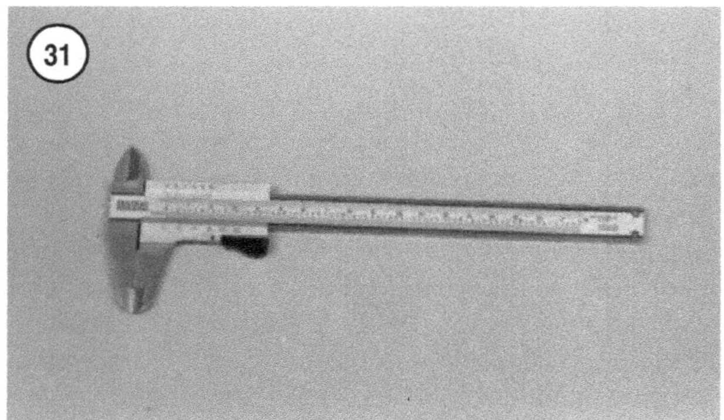

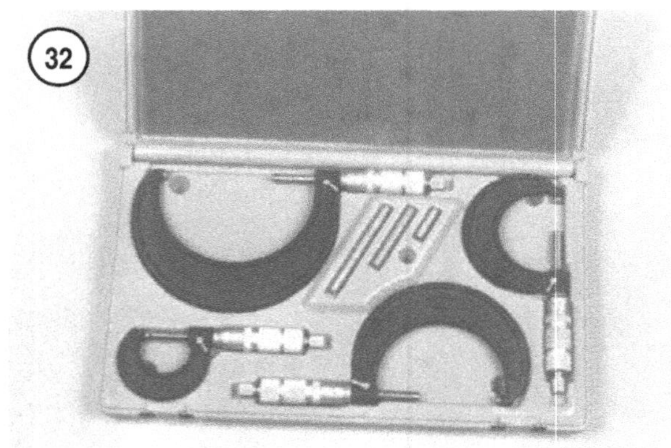

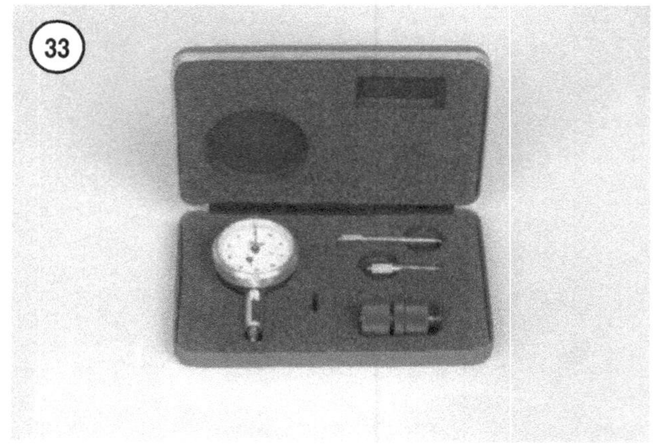

Vernier Caliper

This tool is used to obtain inside, outside and depth measurements. See **Figure 31**.

Outside Micrometers

One of the most accurate tools used for precision measurement is the outside micrometer. Outside micrometers are required to measure shim and bearing thickness and piston diameter. Outside micrometers are also used with a telescoping gauge to measure cylinder bore. Micrometers can be purchased individually or as a set (**Figure 32**).

Dial Indicator

Dial indicators (**Figure 33**) are used to check crankshaft and drive shaft runout limits. Select a dial indicator with a continuous dial (**Figure 34**).

Cylinder Bore Gauge

The cylinder bore gauge is a very specialized precision tool. The gauge set shown in **Figure 35** is comprised of a dial indicator, handle and various length adapters to adapt the gauge to different bore sizes. The bore gauge can be used to make cylinder bore measurements such as bore size, taper and out-of-round. An outside micrometer must be used to calibrate the bore gauge.

Telescoping Gauges

Telescoping gauges (**Figure 36**) can be used to measure hole diameters from approximately 8 mm (5/16 in.) to 150 mm (6 in.). The telescoping gauge does not have a scale gauge for direct readings. An outside micrometer is required to determine bore dimensions.

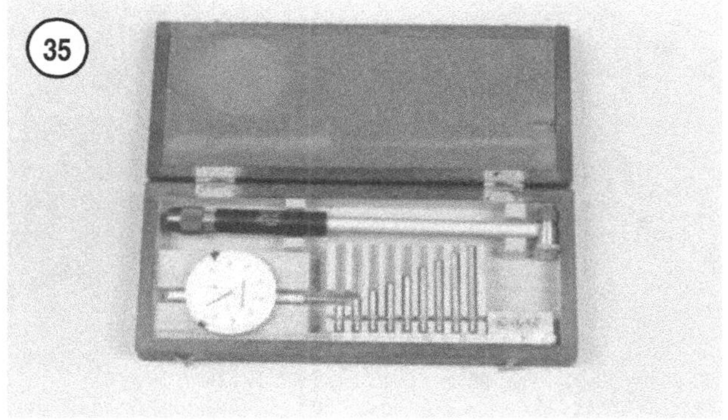

35

36

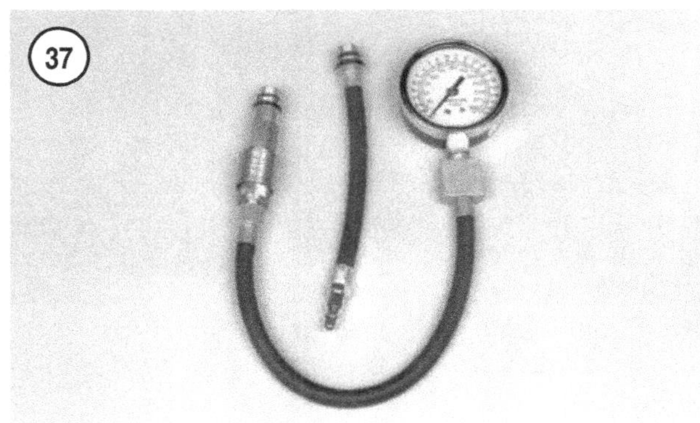

37

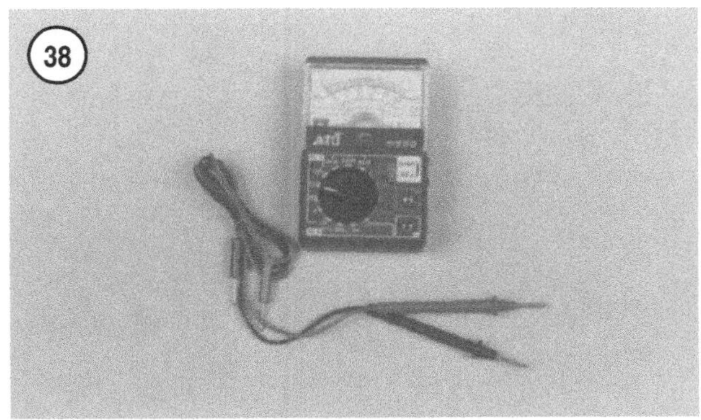

38

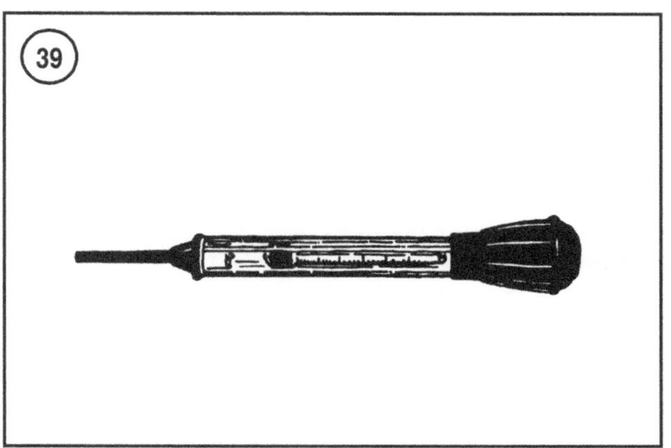

39

Compression Gauge

An engine with low compression cannot be properly tuned and will not develop full power. A compression gauge (**Figure 37**) and adapter specifically designed for diesel applications is required to measure the high cylinder compression pressure (390-470psi [2700-3300kPa]). If these specialized tools are not available, refer compression testing to a qualified technician. See Chapter Three.

Multimeter or VOM

This instrument (**Figure 38**) is required for electrical system troubleshooting.

Battery Hydrometer

A hydrometer (**Figure 39**) is the used to check a battery's state of charge. A hydrometer measures the weight or density of the sulfuric acid in the battery's electrolyte in specific gravity.

Screw Pitch Gauge

A screw pitch gauge (**Figure 40**) determines the thread pitch of bolts, screws, studs, etc. The gauge is made up of a number of thin plates. Each plate has a thread shape cut on one edge to match one thread pitch. When using a screw pitch gauge to determine a thread pitch size, fit different blade sizes onto the bolt thread until both threads match.

Magnetic Stand

A magnetic stand (**Figure 41**) is used to hold a dial indicator securely when checking the runout of a round object or when checking the end play of a shaft.

V-blocks

V-blocks (**Figure 42**) are precision-ground blocks used to hold a round object when checking its runout or condition.

Surface Plate

A surface plate can be used to check the flatness of parts or to provide a perfectly flat surface for minor resurfacing of cylinder head or other critical gasket surfaces. While industrial quality surface plates are quite expensive, the home mechanic can improvise. A thick metal plate can be used as a surface plate. The surface plate shown in **Figure 43** has a piece of sandpaper glued to its surface that is used for cleaning and smoothing machined surfaces, such as the cylinder head.

NOTE
A local machine shop can fabricate a surface plate.

Expendable Supplies

Certain expendable supplies are also required. These include grease, oil, gasket cement, shop rags and cleaning solvent. Ask the dealer for the special locking compounds, silicone lubricants and lubricants that make vehicle maintenance simpler and easier.

WARNING
Having a stack of clean shop rags on hand is important when performing engine work. However, to prevent the possibility of fire, store solvent-soaked rags in a sealed metal container until they can be washed or discarded.

NOTE
To avoid absorbing solvent and other chemicals into the skin while cleaning parts, wear a pair of petroleum-resistant rubber gloves. These can be purchased through industrial supply houses or well-equipped hardware stores.

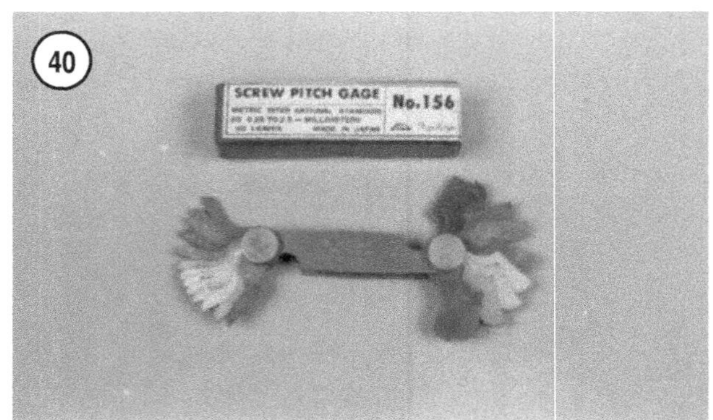

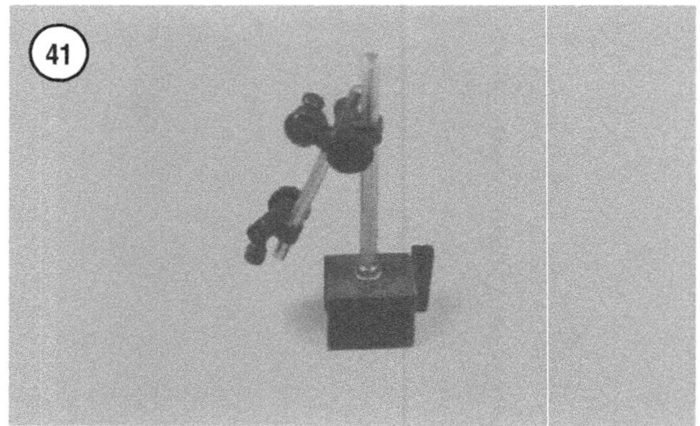

MECHANIC'S TIPS

Removing Frozen Nuts and Screws

When a fastener rusts and cannot be removed, several methods may be used to loosen it. First, apply penetrating oil such as Liquid Wrench or WD-40. Apply it liberally and let it penetrate for 10-15 minutes. Rap the fastener several times with a small hammer; do not hit it hard enough to cause damage. Reapply the penetrating oil if necessary.

For frozen screws, apply penetrating oil as described, then insert a screwdriver in the slot and rap the top of the screwdriver with a hammer. This loosens the rust so the screw can be removed in the normal way. If the screw head is too damaged to use this method, grip the head with locking pliers and twist the screw out.

Avoid applying heat unless specifically instructed, as it may melt, warp or remove the temper from parts.

Removing Broken Screws or Bolts

If the head breaks off a screw or bolt, several methods are available for removing the remaining portion.

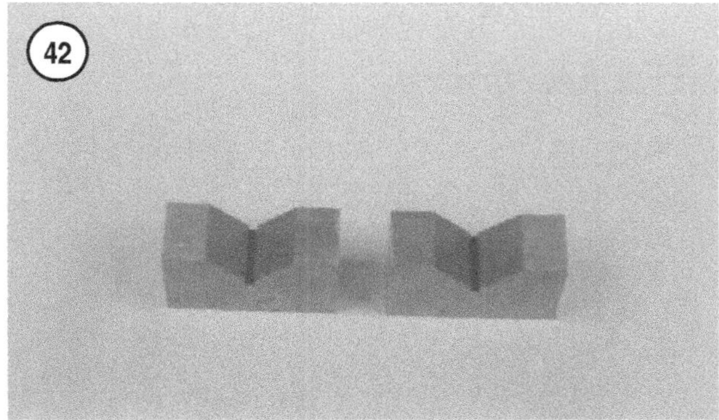

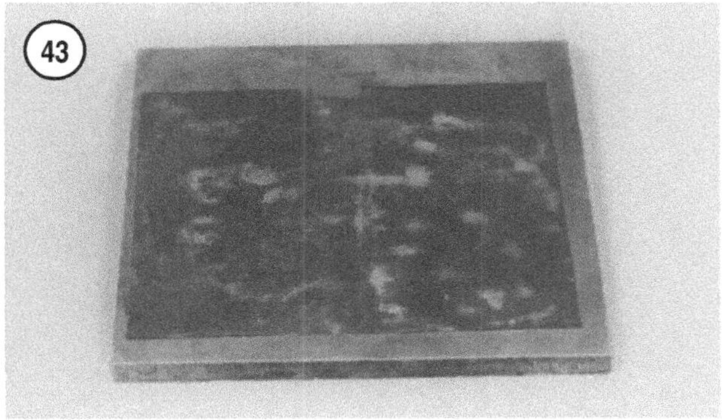

If a large portion of the remainder projects out, try gripping it with locking pliers. If the projecting portion is too small, file it to fit a wrench or cut a slot in it to fit a screwdriver. See **Figure 44**.

If the head breaks off flush, use a screw extractor. To do this, centerpunch the remaining portion of the screw or bolt. Drill a small hole in the screw and tap the extractor into the hole. Back the screw out with a wrench on the extractor. See **Figure 45**.

Remedying Stripped Threads

Occasionally, threads are stripped through carelessness or impact damage. Often the threads can be repaired by running a tap (for internal threads on nuts) or die (for external threads on bolts) through the threads. See **Figure 46**. To clean or repair spark plug threads, a spark plug tap can be used.

NOTE
*Tap and dies can be purchased individually or in a set as shown in **Figure 47**.*

If an internal thread is damaged, it may be necessary to install a Helicoil (**Figure 48**) or some other type of thread

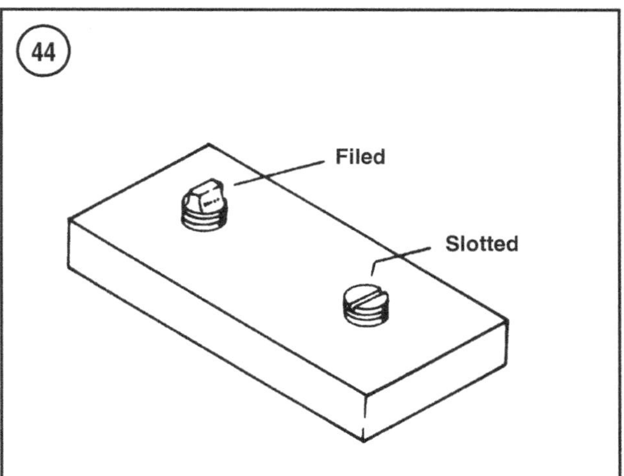

insert. Follow the manufacturer's instructions when installing their insert.

If it is necessary to drill and tap a hole, refer to **Table 4** for metric tap and drill sizes.

Removing Broken or Damaged Studs

If a stud is broken or the threads severely damaged, perform the following. A tube of Loctite 271 (red), two nuts, two wrenches and a new stud will be required during this procedure.

1. Thread two nuts onto the damaged stud. Then tighten the two nuts against each other so that they are locked.

NOTE
If the threads on the damaged stud do not allow installation of the two nuts, remove the stud with a stud remover or a pair of locking pliers.

2. Turn the bottom nut counterclockwise and unscrew the stud.
3. Clean the threads with solvent or electrical contact cleaner and allow them to dry thoroughly.
4. Install two nuts on the top half of the new stud as in Step 1. Make sure they are locked securely.
5. Coat the bottom half of a new stud with Loctite 271 (red).
6. Turn the top nut clockwise and thread the new stud securely.
7. Remove the nuts and repeat for each stud as required.
8. Follow Loctite's directions on cure time before assembling the component.

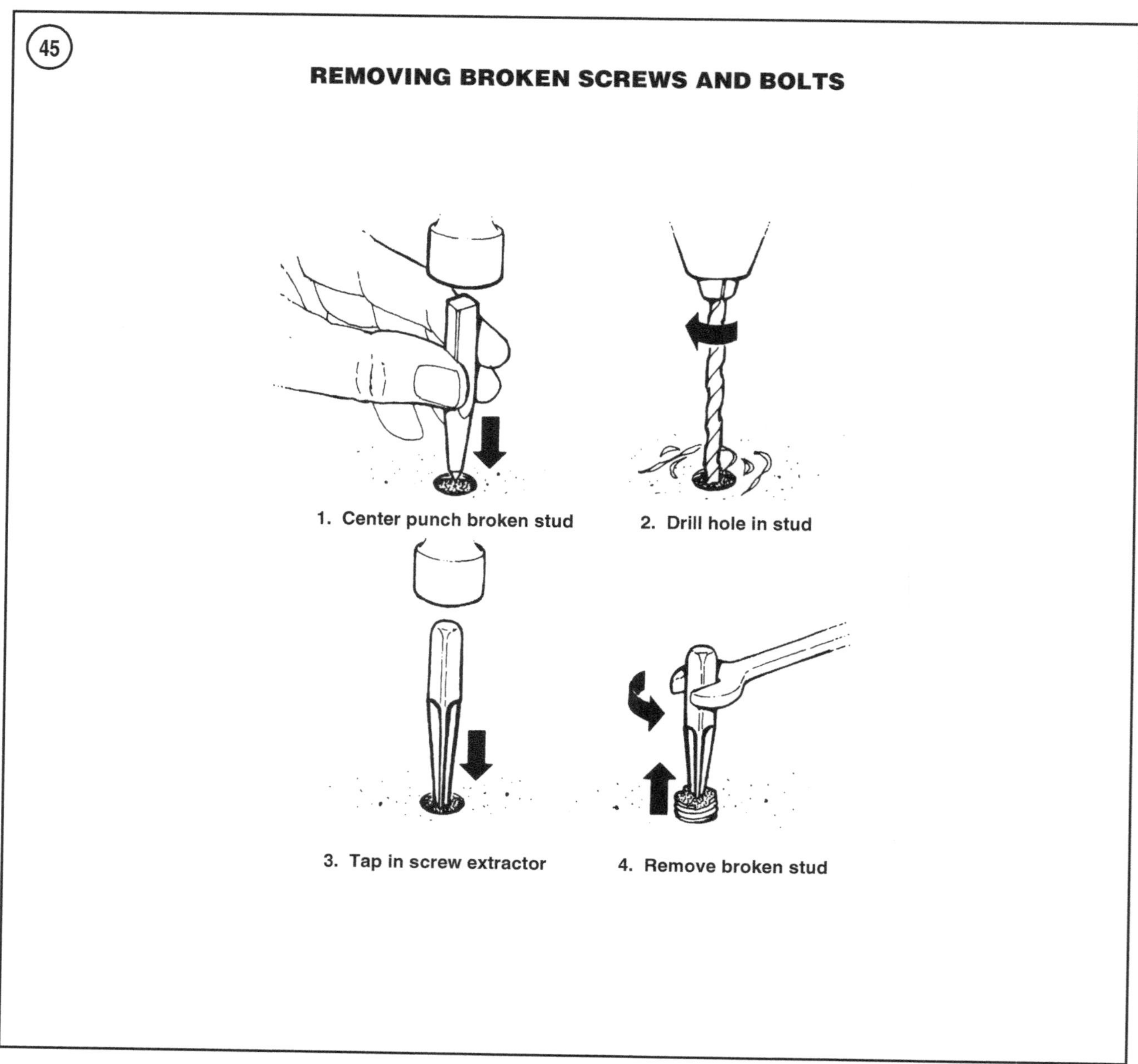

BEARING REPLACEMENT

Bearings (**Figure 49**) are used throughout the engine to reduce power loss, heat and noise resulting from friction. Because bearings are precision-made parts, they must be maintained by proper lubrication and maintenance. If a bearing is damaged, it should be replaced immediately. However, if installing a new bearing, care should be taken to prevent damage to the new bearing. While bearing replacement is described in the individual chapters where applicable, the following should be used as a guideline.

NOTE

Unless otherwise specified, install bearings with the manufacturer's mark or number facing outward.

Bearing Removal

While bearings are normally removed only when damaged, there may be times when it is necessary to remove a bearing that is in good condition. Improper bearing removal will damage the bearing and possibly the shaft or case half. Note the following when removing bearings.

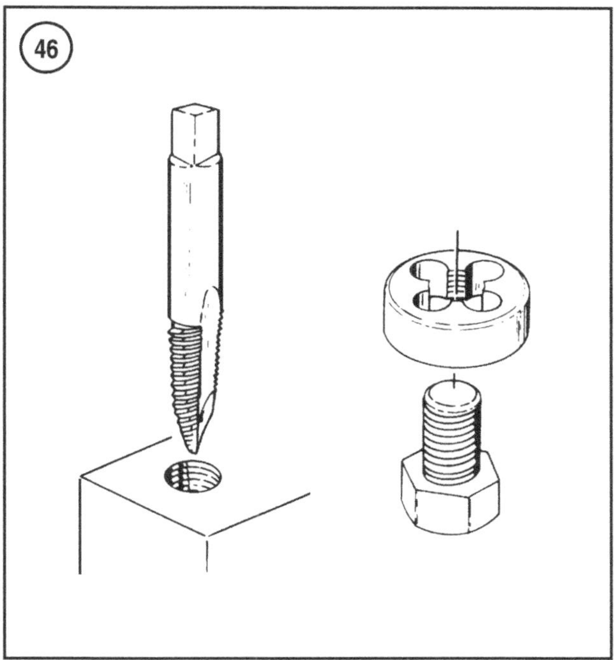

46

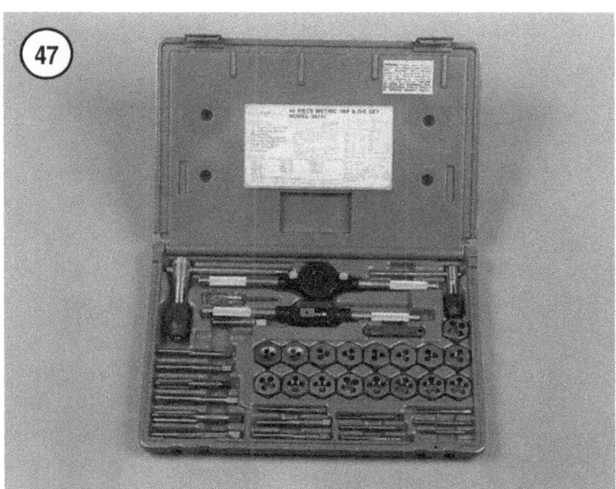

47

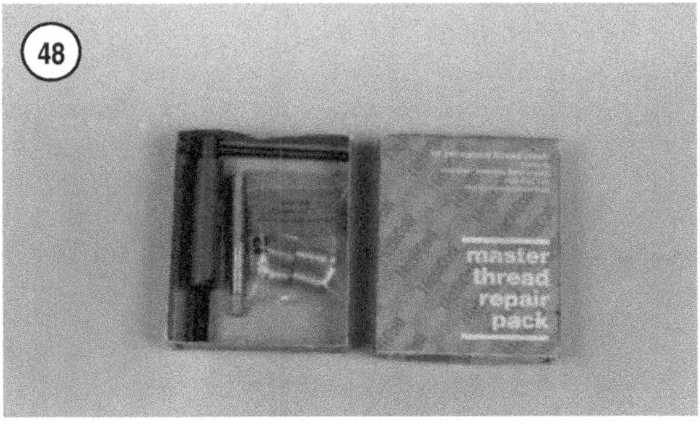

48

49

1. If using a puller to remove a bearing on a shaft, care must be taken so that shaft damage does not occur. Always place a piece of metal between the end of the shaft and the puller screw. In addition, place the puller arms next to the inner bearing race. See **Figure 50**.
2. If using a hammer to remove a bearing on a shaft, do not strike the hammer directly against the shaft. Instead, use a brass or aluminum rod between the hammer and shaft (**Figure 51**). In addition, support both bearing races with wooden blocks as shown in **Figure 51**.
3. The most ideal method of bearing removal is with a hydraulic press. However, certain procedures must be followed or damage may occur to the bearing, shaft or bearing housing. Note the following if using a press:
   a. Always support the inner and outer bearing races with a suitable size wood or aluminum ring (**Figure 52**). If only the outer race is supported, pressure applied against the bearings and/or the inner race will damage them.
   b. Always make sure the press ram (**Figure 52**) aligns with the center of the shaft. If the ram is not centered, it may damage the bearing and/or shaft.
   c. The moment the shaft is free of the bearing, it will drop to the floor. Secure the shaft to prevent it from falling.

Bearing Installation

1. When installing a bearing in a housing, pressure must be applied to the *outer* bearing race (**Figure 53**). When installing a bearing on a shaft, pressure must be applied to the *inner* bearing race (**Figure 54**).
2. When installing a bearing as described in Step 1, some type of driver will be required. Never strike the bearing directly with a hammer or the bearing will be damaged. A piece of pipe or a socket with an outer diameter that matches the bearing race will be required. **Figure 55** shows the correct way to use a socket and hammer when installing a bearing.

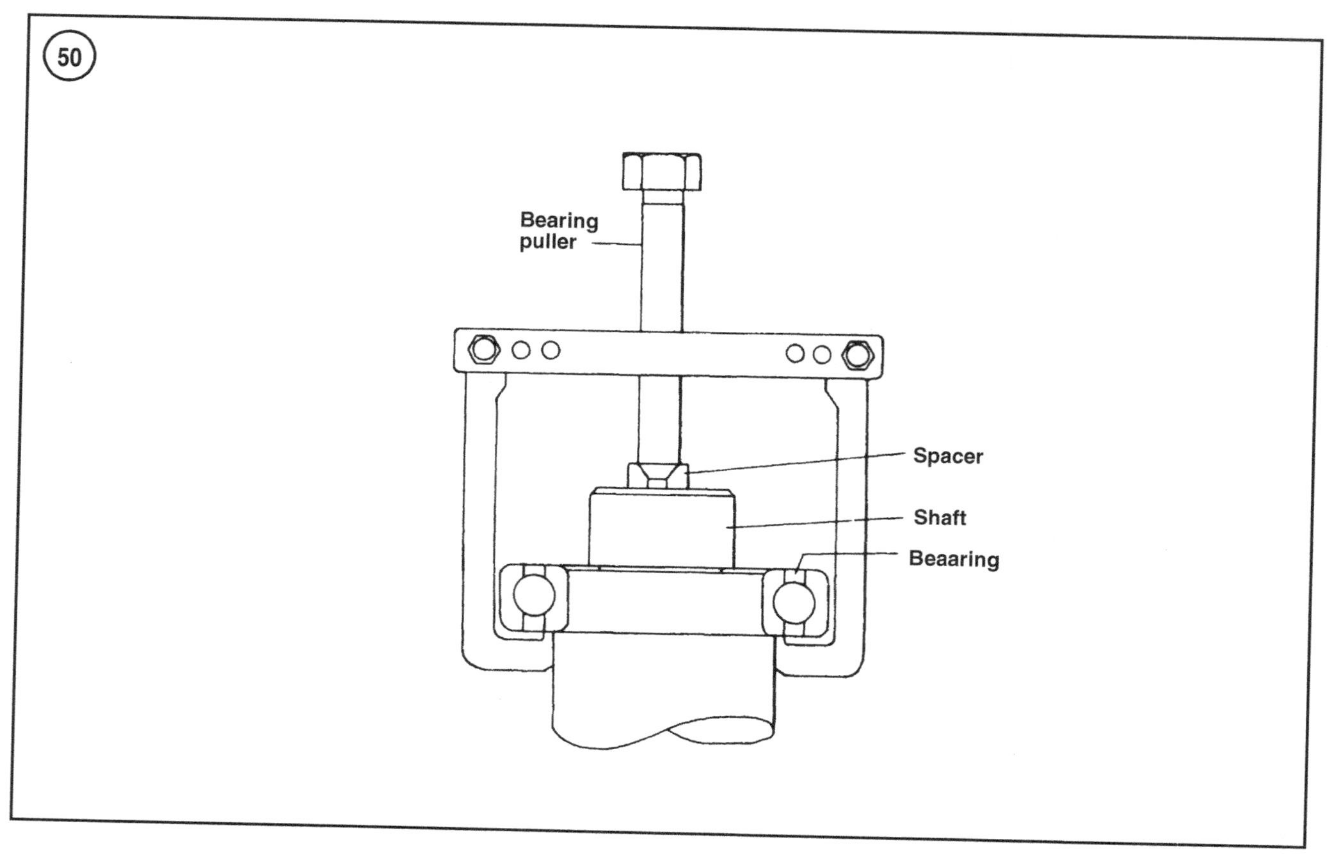

3. Step 1 describes how to install a bearing in a case half and over a shaft. However, when installing a bearing over a shaft and into a housing at the same time, a snug fit will be required for both outer and inner bearing races. In this situation, a spacer must be installed underneath the driver tool so that pressure is applied evenly across *both* races. See **Figure 56**. If the outer race is not supported as shown in **Figure 56**, the balls will push against the outer bearing track and damage it.

Shrink Fit

1. *Installing a bearing over a shaft*—If a tight fit is required, the bearing inside diameter will be smaller than the shaft. In this case, driving the bearing on the shaft using normal methods may cause bearing damage. Instead, the bearing should be heated before installation. Note the following:
   a. Secure the shaft so that it can be ready for bearing installation.
   b. Clean the bearing surface on the shaft of all residue. Remove burrs with a file or sandpaper.
   c. Fill a suitable pot or beaker with clean mineral oil. Place a thermometer (rated higher than 120° C [248° F]) in the oil. Support the thermometer so it does not rest on the bottom or side of the pot.
   d. Remove the bearing from its wrapper and secure it with a piece of heavy wire bent to hold it in the pot. Hang the bearing in the pot so that it does not touch the bottom or sides of the pot.
   e. Turn the heat on and monitor the thermometer. When the oil temperature rises to approximately 120° C (248° F), remove the bearing from the pot and quickly install it. If necessary, place a socket on the inner bearing race and tap the bearing into place. As the bearing cools, it will tighten on the shaft so work quickly when installing it. Make sure the bearing is installed all the way.

2. *Installing a bearing in a housing*—Bearings are generally installed in a housing with a slight interference fit. Driving the bearing into the housing using normal methods may damage the housing or cause bearing damage. Instead, the housing should be heated before the bearing is installed. Note the following:

CAUTION
Before heating the housing in this procedure to remove the bearings, wash the housing thoroughly with detergent and water. Rinse

51

Spacer
Shaft
Bearing
Blocks

52

Press arm
Shaft
Bearing
Spacer
Press
bed

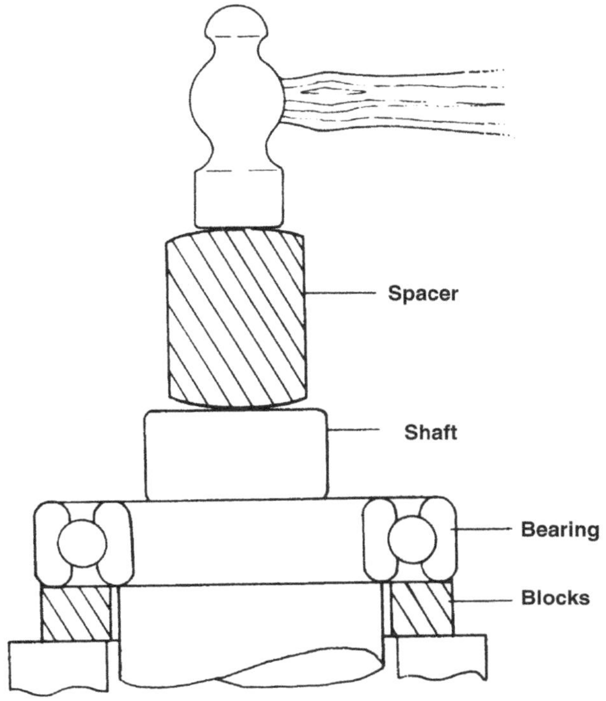

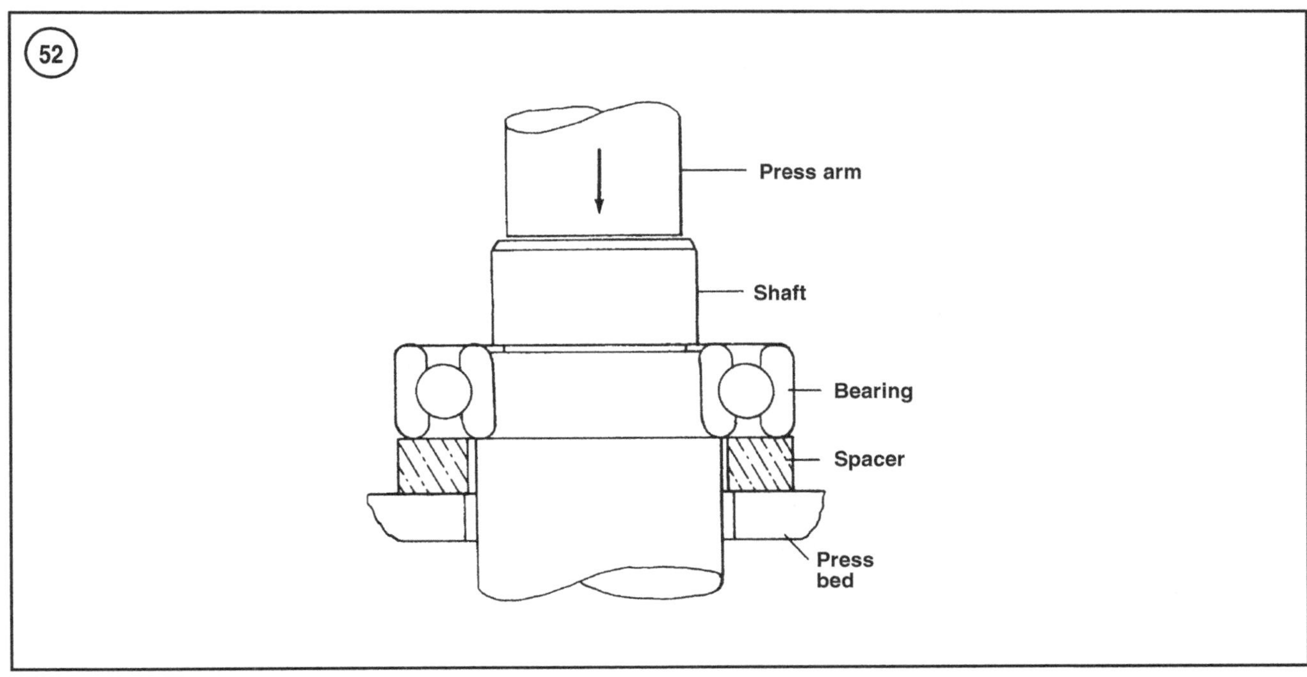

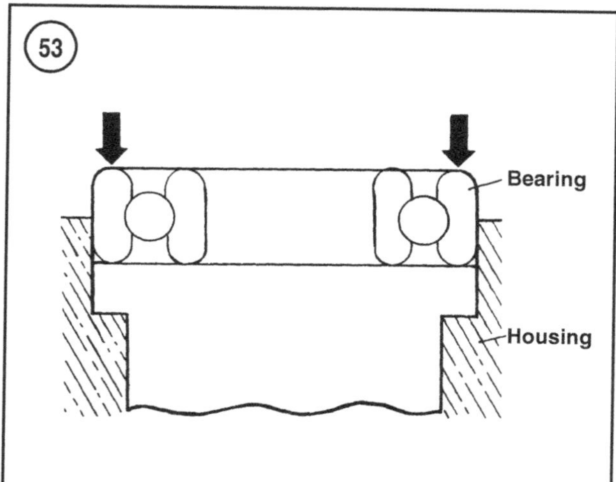

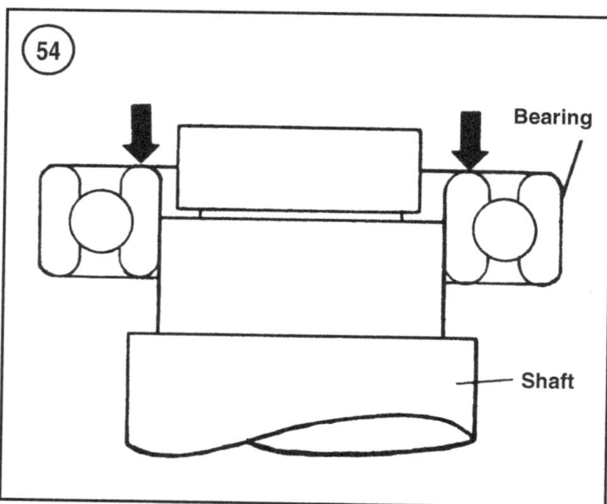

and rewash the housing as required to remove all traces of oil and other chemical deposits.

a. The housing must be heated to a temperature of approximately 212° F (100° C) in an oven or on a hot plate. Check to see that it is at the proper temperature by dropping tiny drops of water on the case; if they sizzle and evaporate immediately, the temperature is correct. Heat only one housing at a time.

CAUTION

Do not heat the housing with a torch (propane or acetylene)—never bring a flame into contact with the bearing or housing. The direct heat will destroy the case hardening of the bearing and will likely warp the housing.

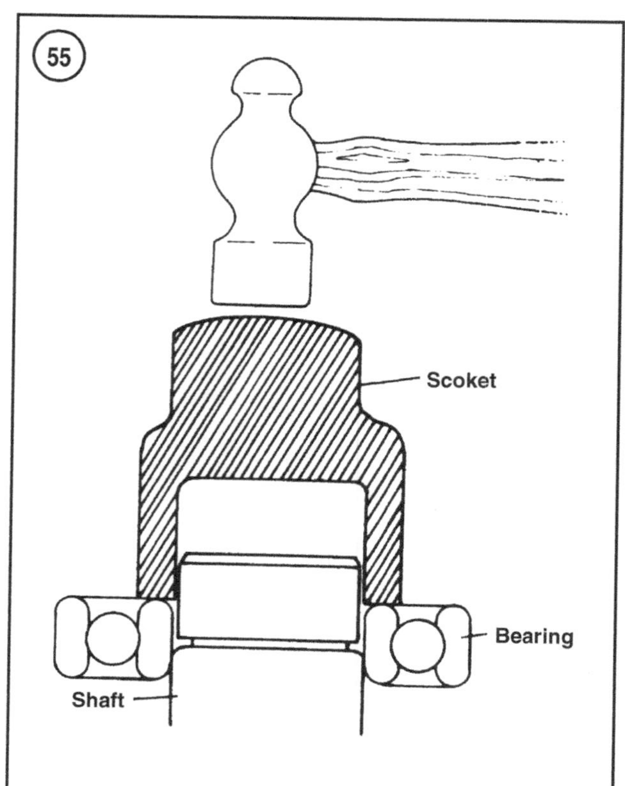

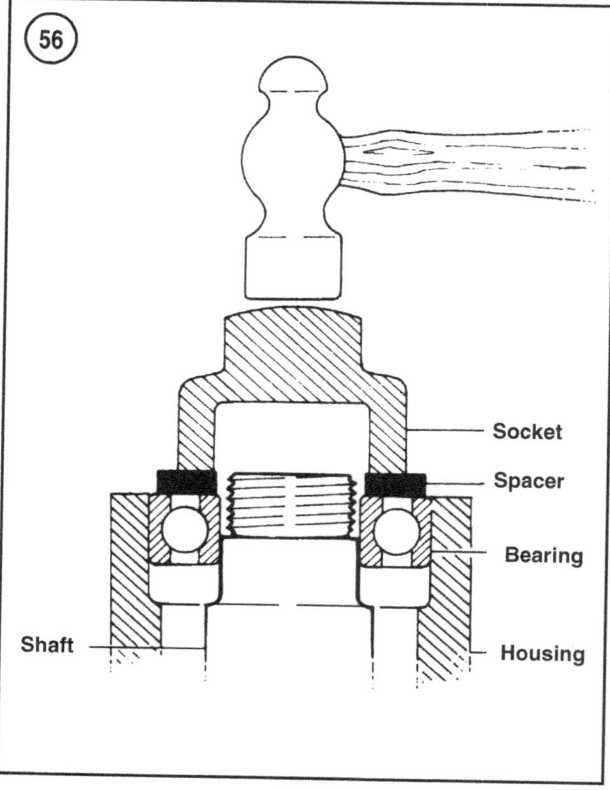

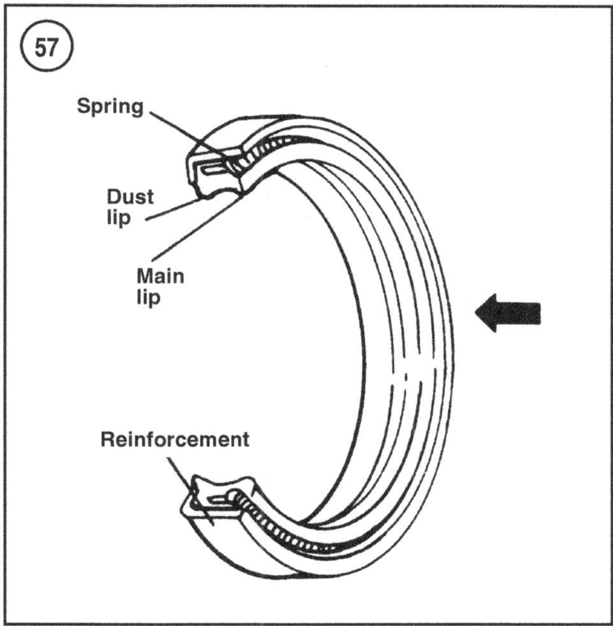

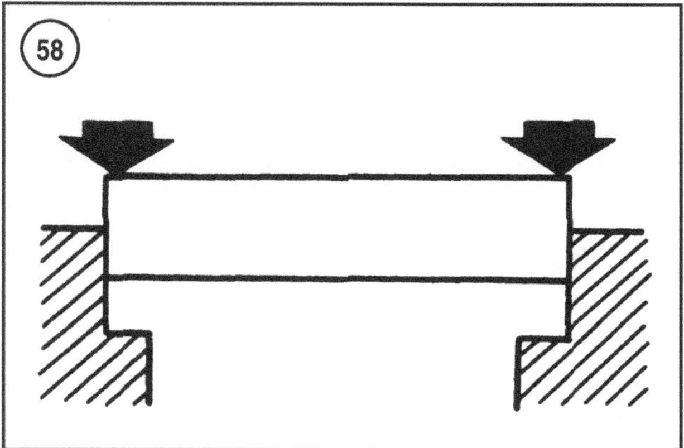

b. Remove the housing from the oven or hot plate and hold onto the housing with a kitchen potholder, heavy gloves or heavy shop cloths—*it is hot.*

NOTE
A suitable size socket and extension works well for removing and installing bearings.

c. Hold the housing with the bearing side down and tap the bearing out. Repeat for all bearings in the housing.

d. Prior to heating the bearing housing, place the new bearing in a freezer, if possible. Chilling a bearing will slightly reduce its outside diameter, while the heated bearing housing assembly will be slightly larger due to heat expansion. This will make bearing installation much easier.

NOTE
Always install bearings with the manufacturer's mark or number facing outward.

e. While the housing is still hot, install the new bearing(s) into the housing. Install the bearings by hand, if possible. If necessary, lightly tap the bearing(s) into the housing with a socket placed on the outer bearing race. *Do not* install new bearings by driving on the inner bearing race. Install the bearing until it seats completely.

SEALS

Seals (**Figure 57**) are used to contain oil, water, grease or combustion gasses in a housing or shaft. Improper removal of a seal can damage the housing or shaft. Improper installation of the seal can damage the seal. Note the following:

1. Prying is generally the easiest and most effective method of removing a seal from a housing. However, always place a rag underneath the pry tool to prevent damage to the housing.
2. Pack grease in the seal lips before the seal is installed.
3. Always install seals so that the manufacturer's numbers or marks face out.
4. Install seals with a socket placed on the outside of the seal as shown in **Figure 58**. Make sure the seal is driven squarely into the housing. Never install a seal by hitting against the top of the seal with a hammer.

Tables 1-4 are on the following pages.

Table 1 YANMAR MODELS

Model	Number of cylinders	Displacement	Horsepower /rpm	Transmission	Transmission ratio (forward gear)
1GM	1	293 cc (17.9 cu. in.)	6.5 hp/3400 rpm	KM2A	2.21, 2.62 or 3.22
1GM10	1	318 cc (19.4 cu. in.)	8 hp/3400 rpm	KM2C or KM2P	2.21, 2.62 or 3.22
2GM	2	586 cc (35.7 cu. in.)	13 hp/3400 rpm	KM2A	2.21, 2.62 or 3.22
2GMF	2	586 cc (35.7 cu. in.)	13 hp/3400 rpm	KM2A	2.21, 2.62 or 3.22
2GM20	2	636 cc (38.8 cu. in.)	16 hp/3400 rpm	KM2C or KM2P	2.21, 2.62 or 3.22
2GM20F	2	636 cc (38.8 cu. in.)	16 hp/3400 rpm	KM2C or KM2P	2.21, 2.62 or 3.22
3GM	3	879 cc (53.6 cu. in.)	20 hp/3400 rpm	KBW10D	2.14, 2.63 or 2.83
3GMF	3	879 cc (53.6 cu. in.)	20 hp/3400 rpm	KBW10D	2.14, 2.63 or 2.83
3GMD	3	879 cc (53.6 cu. in.)	20 hp/3400 rpm	KM3A	2.36, 2.61 or 3.20
3GM30	3	954 cc (58.2 cu. in.)	24 hp/3400 rpm	KM3A or KM3P	2.36, 2.61 or 3.20
3GM30F	3	954 cc (58.2 cu. in.)	24 hp/3400 rpm	KM3A or KM3P	2.36, 2.61 or 3.20
3HM	3	1126 cc (68.7 cu. in.)	27 hp/3200 rpm	KBW10E	2.14 or 2.83
3HMF	3	1126 cc (68.7 cu. in.)	27 hp/3200 rpm	KBW10E	2.14 or 2.83
3HM35	3	1282 cc (78.2 cu. in.)	30 hp/3200 rpm	KBW10E	2.14 or 2.83
3HM35F	3	1282 cc (78.2 cu. In.)	30 hp/3200 rpm	KBW10E	2.14 or 2.83

Table 2 DECIMAL AND METRIC EQUIVALENTS

Fractions	Decimal in.	Metric mm	Fractions	Decimal in.	Metric mm
1/64	0.015625	0.39688	33/64	0.515625	13.09687
1/32	0.03125	0.79375	17/32	0.53125	13.49375
3/64	0.046875	1.19062	35/64	0.546875	13.89062
1/16	0.0625	1.58750	9/16	0.5625	14.28750
5/64	0.078125	1.98437	37/64	0.578125	14.68437
3/32	0.09375	2.38125	19/32	0.59375	15.08125
7/64	0.109375	2.77812	39/64	0.609375	15.47812
1/8	0.125	3.1750	5/8	0.625	15.87500
9/64	0.140625	3.57187	41/64	0.640625	16.27187
5/32	0.15625	3.96875	21/32	0.65625	16.66875
11/64	0.171875	4.36562	43/64	0.671875	17.06562
3/16	0.1875	4.76250	11/16	0.6875	17.46250
13/64	0.203125	5.15937	45/64	0.703125	17.85937
7/32	0.21875	5.55625	23/32	0.71875	18.25625
15/64	0.234375	5.95312	47/64	0.734375	18.65312
1/4	0.250	6.35000	3/4	0.750	19.05000
17/64	0.265625	6.74687	49/64	0.765625	19.44687
9/32	0.28125	7.14375	25/32	0.78125	19.84375
19/64	0.296875	7.54062	51/64	0.796875	20.24062
5/16	0.3125	7.93750	13/16	0.8125	20.63750
21/64	0.328125	8.33437	53/64	0.828125	21.03437
11/32	0.34375	8.73125	27/32	0.84375	21.43125
23/64	0.359375	9.12812	55/64	0.859375	22.82812
3/8	0.375	9.52500	7/8	0.875	22.22500
25/64	0.390625	9.92187	57/64	0.890625	22.62187
13/32	0.40625	10.31875	29/32	0.90625	23.01875
27/64	0.421875	10.71562	59/64	0.921875	23.41562
7/16	0.4375	11.11250	15/16	0.9375	23.81250
29/64	0.453125	11.50937	61/64	0.953125	24.20937
15/32	0.46875	11.90625	31/32	0.96875	24.60625
31/64	0.484375	12.30312	63/64	0.984375	25.00312
1/2	0.500	12.70000	1	1.00	25.40000

Table 3 GENERAL TORQUE SPECIFICATIONS

Thread diameter	N•m	ft.-lb.	in.-lb.
M6	8-10	–	71-88
M8	23-27	17-20	204-239
M10	44-50	32-37	–
M12	75-85	55-63	–
M14	125-135	92-100	–
M16	200-210	147-155	–

Table 4 METRIC TAP AND DRILL SIZES

Metric tap (mm)	Drill size	Decimal equivalent	Nearest fraction
3 × 0.50	No. 39	0.0995	3/32
3 × 0.60	3/32	0.0937	3/32
4 × 0.70	No. 30	0.1285	1/8
4 × 0.75	1/8	0.125	1/8
5 × 0.80	No. 19	0.166	11/64
5 × 0.90	No. 20	0.161	5/32
6 × 1.00	No. 9	0.196	13/64
7 × 1.00	16/64	0.234	15/64
8 × 1.00	J	0.277	9/32
8 × 1.25	17/64	0.265	17/64
9 × 1.00	5/16	0.3125	5/16
9 × 1.25	5/16	0.3125	5/16
10 × 1.25	11/32	0.3437	11/32
10 × 1.50	R	0.339	11/32
11 × 1.50	3/8	0.375	3/8
12 × 1.50	13/32	0.406	13/32
12 × 1.75	13/32	0.406	13/32

Chapter Two

Troubleshooting

Every internal combustion engine requires an uninterrupted supply of fuel, air, ignition and adequate compression. If any of these are lacking, the engine will not run.

Troubleshooting is a relatively simple matter if it is done logically. The first step in any troubleshooting procedure is to define the symptoms as fully as possible and then localize the problem. Subsequent steps involve testing and analyzing those areas that could cause the symptoms. A haphazard approach may eventually solve the problem, but it can be costly in terms of wasted time and unnecessary parts replacement.

When all else fails, go back to basics—simple solutions often solve complex-appearing problems.

Never assume anything. Do not overlook the obvious. If the engine suddenly quits when running or refuses to start, check the easiest and most accessible areas first. Make sure there is fuel in the tank and that the wiring is properly connected.

Be familiar with the engine compartment and engine components so a quick visual check is possible. Learning to recognize and describe symptoms accurately will make repairs easier. If a technician is required, saying that it will not run is not the same as saying that it quit at full throttle and would not restart.

Identify as many symptoms as possible to aid in diagnosis. Note whether the engine lost power gradually or all at once, what color smoke (if any) came from the exhaust, etc.

After defining the symptoms, test and analyze those areas that could cause the problem(s). Many problems can be analyzed without expensive test equipment. A few simple checks can keep a small problem from turning into a large one. They can also avoid a large repair bill and time lost while the boat sits in a shop's service department.

On the other hand, be realistic and do not attempt repairs beyond your abilities or with makeshift tools. Marine service departments also tend to charge heavily for putting together a disassembled engine or other components that may have been abused. Some shops will not even accept such a job. Use common sense and do not get in over your head or attempt a job without the proper tools.

Proper lubrication, maintenance and periodic tune-ups as described in Chapter Three will reduce the necessity for troubleshooting. Even with the best care, however, every marine engine is prone to problems that will eventually require troubleshooting.

If installing replacement parts, do not use automotive parts. While marine components, such as starters and alternators, may appear to be the same as automotive components, they are not. Marine components have been designed to withstand the unique requirements of marine

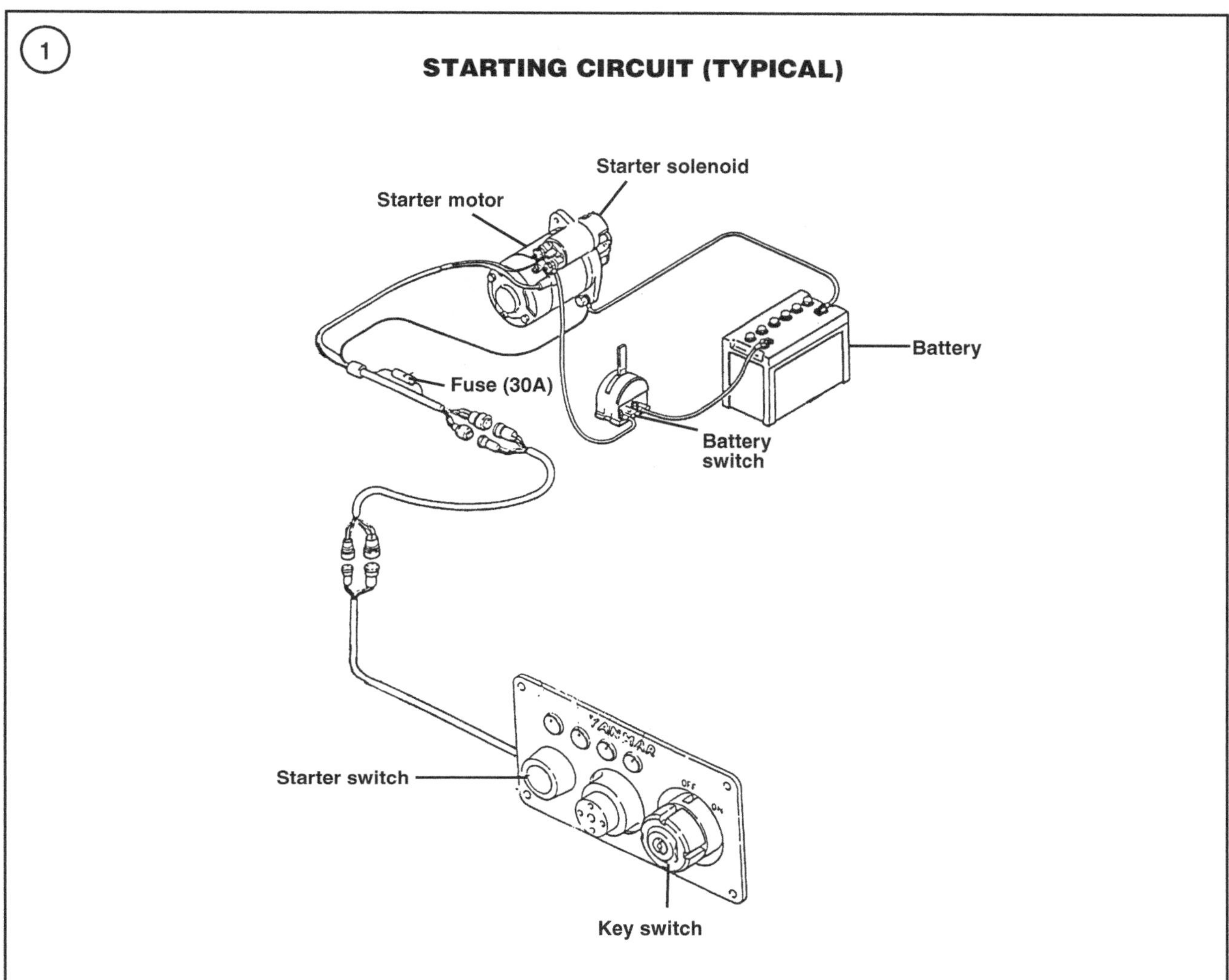

service, as well as to provide a measure of safety that is not required of automotive service. For example, a marine starter is flashproofed to prevent possible ignition of fuel vapor in the bilge. The use of an automotive starter as a replacement can result in an explosion or fire, which may cause death, serious injury or boat damage.

This chapter contains brief descriptions of each major operating system and troubleshooting procedures to be used. The troubleshooting procedures analyze common symptoms and provide logical methods of isolation. These are not the only methods. There may be several approaches to a problem, but all methods used must have one thing in common to be successful—a logical, systematic approach.

Troubleshooting diagrams for individual systems are provided within this chapter. A master troubleshooting chart (**Table 1**) is provided at the end of this chapter.

STARTING SYSTEM

The starting system consists of the battery, starter motor, starter solenoid, starter switch, key switch, fuse and connecting wiring. See **Figure 1**, typical.

Starting system problems are relatively easy to find. In many cases, the trouble is a loose or dirty connection.

Starting System Operation

The battery switch, if used, and the key switch must be in the ON positions so battery current is available to the starter circuit. When the start switch on the instrument panel is pushed, battery current flows to the starter solenoid, which mechanically engages the starter with the engine flywheel. The solenoid also directs current to the starter motor, which rotates the engine flywheel to start

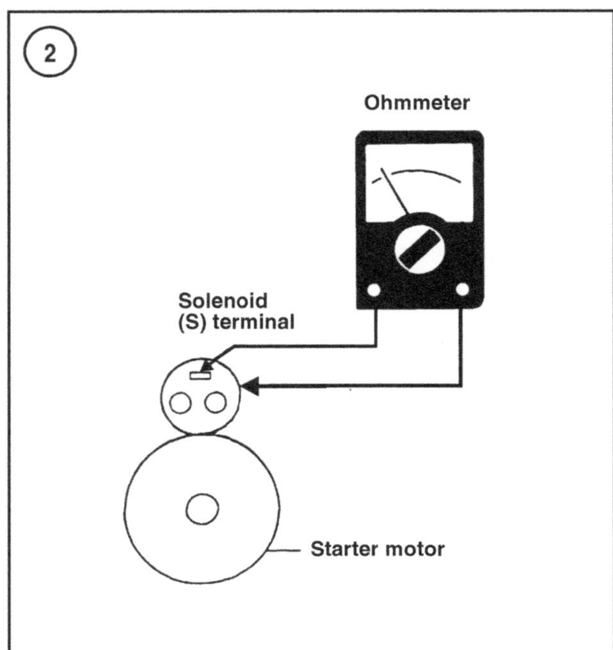

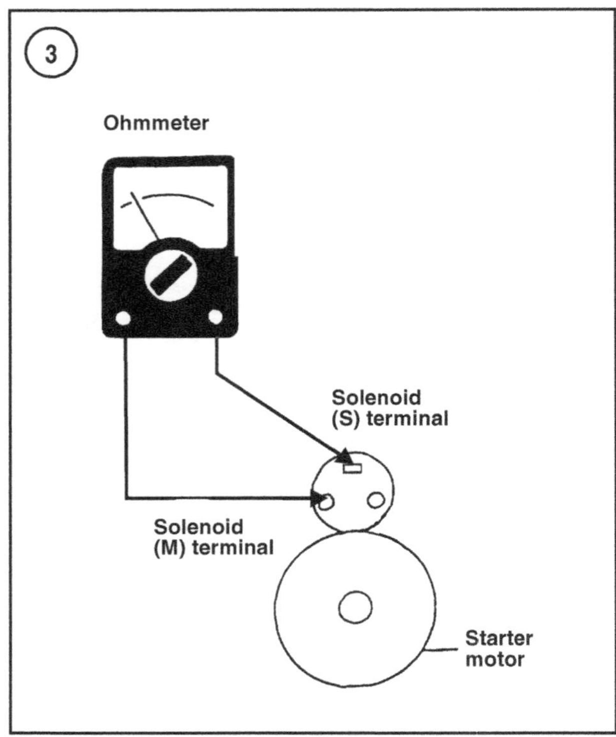

the engine. Once the engine has started and the start switch is released, the slave solenoid is de-energized. Without current to hold the solenoid in position, the starter motor overrunning clutch disengages the starter pinion from the flywheel.

On-Boat Testing

Two of these procedures require a fully charged 12-volt battery, to be used as a booster, and a pair of jumper cables. Use the jumper cables as outlined in *Jump Starting*, Chapter Nine, following all of the precautions noted. Disconnect the wiring harness and leads at the rear of the alternator before connecting a booster battery for these tests. This will protect the alternator from possible damage.

Slow running starter

1. Connect the 12-volt booster battery to the engine's battery with jumper cables. Listen to the starter running speed as the engine is cranking. If the starter running speed sounds normal, check the battery for loose or corroded connections or a low charge. Clean and tighten the connections as required. Recharge the battery if necessary.
2. If starter running speed does not sound normal, clean and tighten all starter solenoid connections and the battery ground on the engine.
3. Repeat Step 1. If the starter running speed is still too slow, replace the starter.

Starter solenoid clicks, starter does not run

1. Clean and tighten all starter and solenoid connections. Make sure the terminal eyelets are securely fastened to the wire strands and are not corroded.
2. Remove the battery terminal clamps. Clean the clamps and battery posts. Reinstall the clamps and tighten them securely.
3. If the starter still does not run, connect the 12-volt booster battery to the engine's battery with the jumper cables. If the starter still does not run, replace it.

Starter solenoid chatters (no click), starter does not run

1. Check the S terminal wire connection at the starter solenoid. Clean and tighten if necessary.
2. Disconnect the S terminal wire at the starter solenoid. Connect a jumper wire between this terminal and the positive battery post.
3. Try starting the engine. If the engine starts, check the key switch, starter switch and the system wiring for an

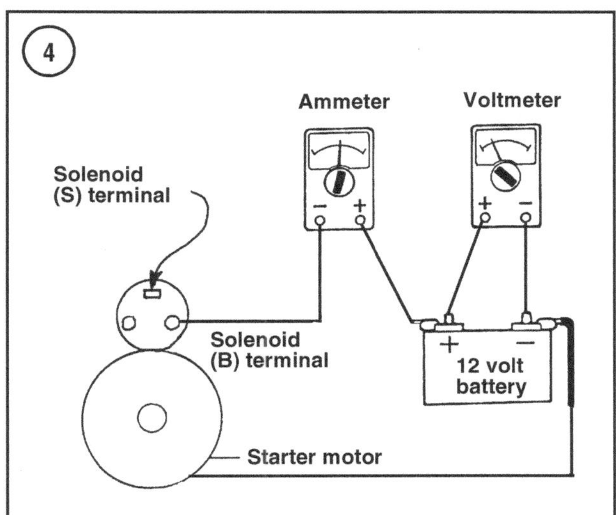

open circuit or a loose connection. If the engine does not start, replace the starter solenoid.

Starter spins but does not rotate flywheel

1. Remove the starter. See Chapter Nine.
2. Check the starter pinion gear. If the teeth are chipped or worn, inspect the flywheel ring gear for the same problem. Replace the starter and/or ring gear as required.
3. If the pinion gear is in good condition, disassemble the starter and check the armature shaft for corrosion. See *Brush Replacement*, Chapter Nine, for the disassembly procedure. If no corrosion is found, the starter drive mechanism is slipping. Replace the starter with a new or rebuilt marine unit.

Starter will not disengage when start switch is released

This problem is usually caused by a sticking solenoid or defective start switch, but the pinion may jam on the flywheel ring gear on an engine with many hours of operation.

NOTE
A low battery or loose or corroded battery connections can also cause the starter to remain engaged with the flywheel ring gear. Low voltage at the starter can cause the contacts inside the solenoid to chatter and weld together, resulting in the solenoid sticking in the ON position.

Loud grinding noises when starter runs

This can be caused by improper meshing of the starter pinion and flywheel ring gear or by a broken overrunning clutch mechanism.

1. Remove the starter. See Chapter Nine.
2. Check the starter pinion gear. If the teeth are chipped or worn, inspect the flywheel ring gear for the same problem. Replace the starter and/or ring gear as required.
3. If the pinion gear is in good condition, the overrunning clutch mechanism in the starter may be defective. Replace the starter with a new or rebuilt marine unit.

Starter Solenoid Resistance Tests

Check the starter solenoid using the following resistance tests:

CAUTION
Disconnect the negative battery cable before performing resistance tests.

1. Refer to **Figure 2** and connect an ohmmeter lead to the S terminal of the solenoid. Connect the remaining ohmmeter lead to the metal body of the solenoid. The ohmmeter should indicate approximately one ohm or less. Replace the solenoid if the ohmmeter indicates infinite resistance (no continuity).
2. Refer to **Figure 3** and connect an ohmmeter lead to the S terminal of the solenoid. Connect the remaining ohmmeter lead to the M terminal of the solenoid. The ohmmeter should indicate approximately one ohm or less. Replace the solenoid if the ohmmeter indicates infinite resistance (no continuity).

Starter Motor No-Load Current Draw Test

If troubleshooting indicates that the starter motor may be defective, use the following starter motor no-load current draw test to determine if the starter motor is in acceptable operating condition.

To perform the test, the following equipment is needed: an ammeter capable of measuring 0-100 amps, a voltmeter, a vibration tachometer and a fully charged 12-volt battery. Minimum battery capacity is 70 amp-hours for one- and two-cylinder engines and 100 amp-hours for three-cylinder engines.

1. Remove the starter motor from the engine. Securely fasten the motor in a vise or other suitable holding fixture.
2. Using a heavy gauge jumper cable, connect the ammeter in series with the positive battery terminal (**Figure 4**). Connect a voltmeter to the battery.

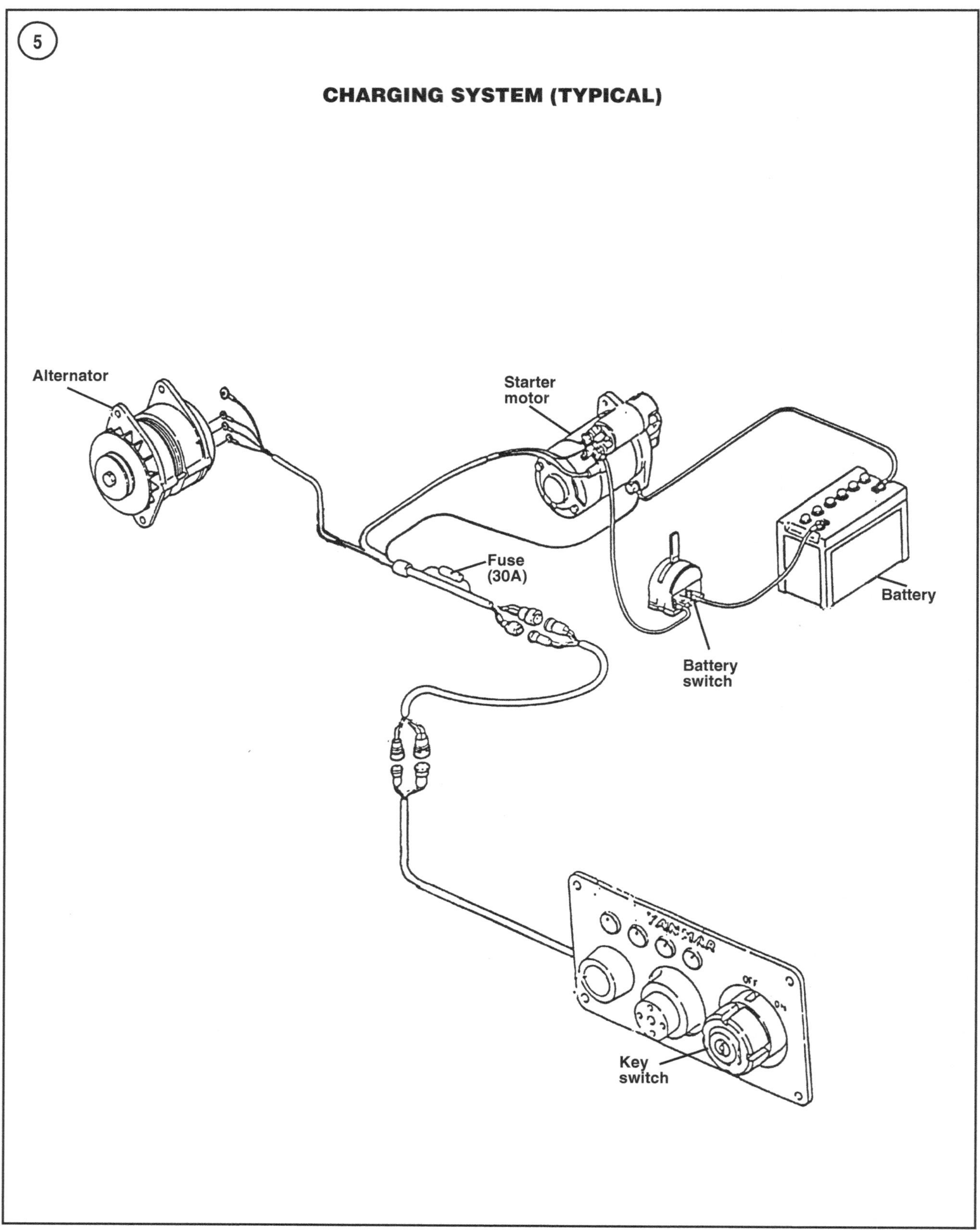
5
CHARGING SYSTEM (TYPICAL)
Alternator
Starter motor
Fuse (30A)
Battery
Battery switch
Key switch

3. Hold a vibration-type tachometer against the starter frame.
4. To operate the starter motor, connect a wire between the positive battery terminal and the S terminal on the starter solenoid.
5. Note the starter rpm, current draw and battery voltage while the motor is running, then disconnect the wire to the S terminal on the solenoid.
6. If the starter motor does not perform within the specifications listed in **Table 3**, repair or replace the motor as described in Chapter Nine.

CHARGING SYSTEM

The charging system consists of the alternator, voltage regulator, battery, key switch, instrument panel warning light, connecting wiring and fuse.

A belt driven by the engine crankshaft pulley turns the alternator, which produces electrical energy to charge the battery. As engine speed varies, the voltage output of the alternator varies. The regulator maintains the voltage to the electrical system within safe limits. The warning light on the instrument panel signals if charging is not taking place.

All models use a Hitachi alternator with an internal transistorized voltage regulator attached to the rear alternator housing. Alternator output is 35 amps (model LR135-05) or 55 amps (model LR155-20). **Figure 5** shows components of the charging circuit.

Charging system troubles are generally caused by a defective alternator, voltage regulator, battery or an inoperative charge lamp. They may also be caused by something as simple as incorrect drive belt tension.

The following are symptoms of problems that may be encountered.

1. *Battery discharges frequently*—This can be caused by a drive belt that is slightly loose. Grasp the alternator pulley with both hands and try to turn it. If the pulley can be turned without moving the belt, the drive belt is too loose. As a rule, keep the belt tight enough so that it can be deflected only about 1/2 in. under moderate thumb pressure applied between the pulleys. The battery may also be at fault; test the battery condition as described in Chapter Nine.
2. *Charging system warning lamp does not light when key switch is turned ON*—This may indicate a defective key switch, battery, voltage regulator or warning lamp. Try to start the engine. If it doesn't start, check the key switch and battery. If the engine starts, remove and test the warning lamp bulb. If the problem persists, the alternator brushes may not be making contact. Perform the System Circuitry Test in this chapter.
3. *Charging system warning lamp flashes on and off*—This usually indicates that the charging system is working intermittently. Check drive belt tension first, then check all electrical connections in the charging circuit. As a last resort, check the alternator.
4. *Charging system warning lamp comes on and stays on*—This usually indicates that no charging is taking place. First check drive belt tension, then the battery condition. Check all wiring connections in the charging system. If this does not locate the problem, check the alternator and voltage regulator as described in this chapter.
5. *Battery requires frequent addition of water or lamp requires frequent replacement*—The alternator is probably overcharging the battery. The voltage regulator is most likely at fault.
6. *Excessive noise from the alternator*—Check for loose mounting brackets and bolts. The problem may also be worn bearings or, in some cases, lack of lubrication. If an alternator whines, a shorted diode may be the problem.

CHARGING SYSTEM TESTS

The alternator is equipped with an internal transistorized regulator. The transistorized regulator contains excitation and sensing circuits. The regulator controls output voltage by switching the alternator rotor current on and off. A rectifier consisting of a set of diodes converts alternating current to direct current.

Alternator Regulated Voltage Test

This test checks the regulated voltage output of the alternator. All wires connected to the alternator for normal operation must be connected.

1. Check the alternator drive belt tension. See Chapter Three.
2. Check the battery terminals and cables for corrosion and/or loose connections. Disconnect the negative battery cable, then the positive battery cable. Clean the cable clamps and battery terminals, if necessary, then reconnect the cables.
3. Check all wiring connections between the alternator and engine to make sure they are clean and tight.
4. Connect the positive lead of a voltmeter to the BAT terminal of the alternator. Connect the negative voltmeter lead to the E terminal of the alternator. See **Figure 6.**
5. Move the engine wire harness back and forth while observing the voltmeter scale. The meter should indicate a steady battery voltage reading (approximately 12 volts).

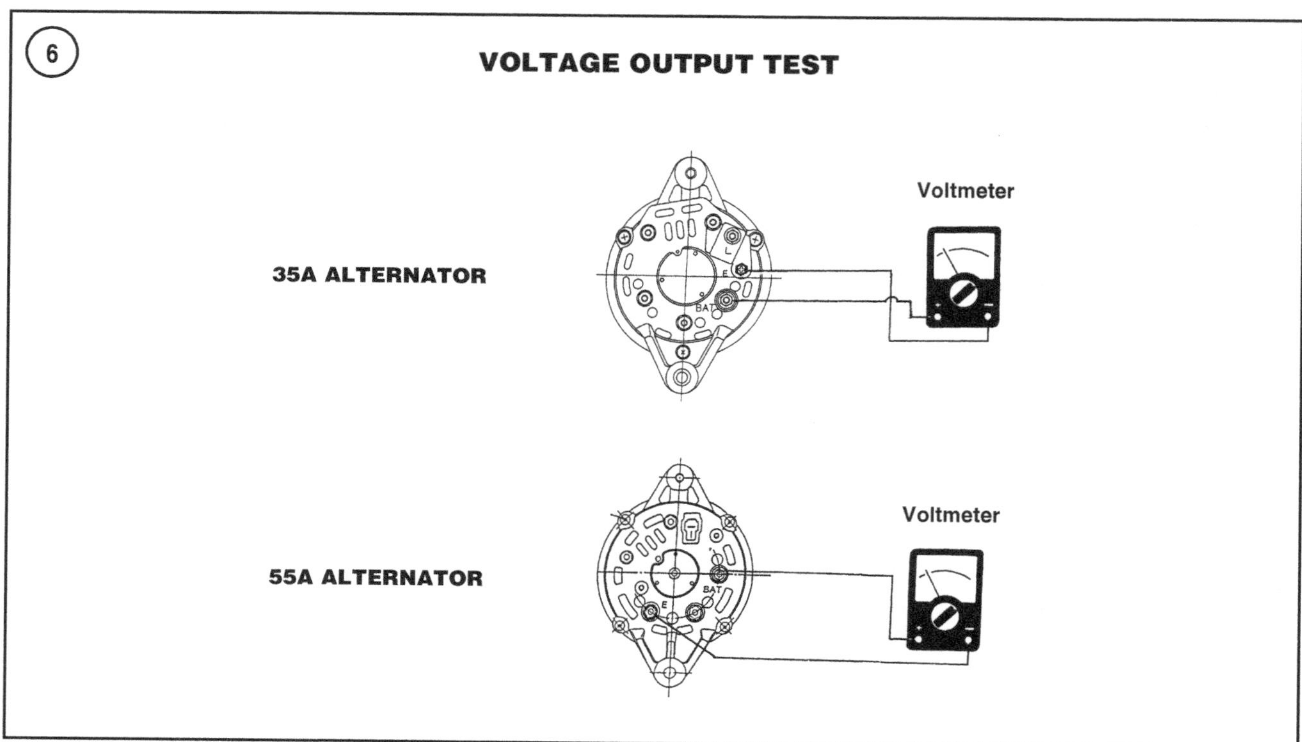

If the reading varies or if no reading is obtained, check for poor connections or damaged wiring.

6. Turn the key switch ON. Run the engine from idle up to 2,500 rpm and note the voltmeter reading. If the voltmeter does not indicate 14.2-14.8 volts, remove the alternator and have it bench tested by a dealership or qualified specialist.

Alternator Current Output Test

This test checks the current output of the alternator. All wires connected to the alternator for normal operation must be connected. Refer to **Figure 7** for this procedure.

1. Check the alternator drive belt tension. See Chapter Three.
2. Disconnect the negative battery cable.
3. Disconnect the wire from the BAT terminal on the alternator.
4. Connect the positive lead of a 0-100 amp DC ammeter to the BAT terminal and the negative lead to the disconnected wire.
5. Reconnect the negative battery cable.
6. Make sure the engine control is in the stop position.
7. Turn on all accessories and crank the engine for 15-20 seconds to remove any surface charge from the battery.
8. Turn off all accessories.
9. Connect a tachometer to the engine. Connect a carbon pile load device to the battery terminals.
10. Start the engine and run at 2,500 rpm. Adjust the carbon pile to obtain maximum alternator output. The ammeter should read the rated amperage according to the alternator model identified on the data plate on the alternator (**Figure 8**). Model LR135 alternators should produce 35 amps, and model LR155 alternators should produce 55 amps.

FUEL SYSTEM

Refer to Chapter Seven for a description of fuel system operation. A diagram of a typical fuel system is shown in **Figure 9**.

Be aware that diesel fuel injection systems require clean fuel that meets the fuel requirements specified by the engine manufacturer. Many fuel problems are a result of contaminated fuel or fuel not approved by the engine manufacturer. Refer to Chapter Three.

NOTE

Engine components outside the fuel system can also cause some of the following engine symptoms. Be sure to check other engine components that can also cause the symptoms.

7

CURRENT OUTPUT TEST

35A ALTERNATOR

Ammeter

Battery cable

55A ALTERNATOR

Ammeter

Battery cable

8

NOTE
If the fuel injection pump or a fuel injector is suspected, have it checked by a diesel engine service shop before purchasing replacement parts.

When troubleshooting the fuel system, refer to the following symptoms and possible causes:

1. *Engine will not start*—Check for an empty fuel tank, incorrect fuel or water in the fuel. Bleed the fuel system as described in Chapter Seven to be sure that fuel is routed to the fuel injection pump and to locate any restrictions, such as the fuel filter, or defective components, such as the fuel transfer pump. Check for proper operation and adjustment of the speed control mechanism, including the stop lever. Refer to Chapter Seven. Check the fuel injection timing as directed in Chapter Seven.
2. *Engine stops suddenly*—Check for an empty fuel tank, incorrect fuel or water in the fuel. Bleed the fuel system as directed in Chapter Seven to be sure that fuel is routed to the fuel injection pump and to locate any restrictions, such as the fuel filter, or defective components, such as the fuel transfer pump. Check for the proper operation and adjustment of the speed control mechanism, including the stop lever.
3. *Engine speed decreases unexpectedly*—Check for water in the fuel. Check for a clogged fuel filter element. Bleed the fuel system as described in Chapter Seven to remove air in the fuel. Check for clogged or defective fuel injection pump or fuel injector.
4. *Engine will not run under full load*—Check for a clogged fuel filter element. Check for a defective fuel transfer pump. Check for a clogged or defective fuel injection pump. Check the speed control mechanism.
5. *Engine misfires*—Check for water in the fuel. Check for a clogged fuel filter element. Bleed the fuel system as

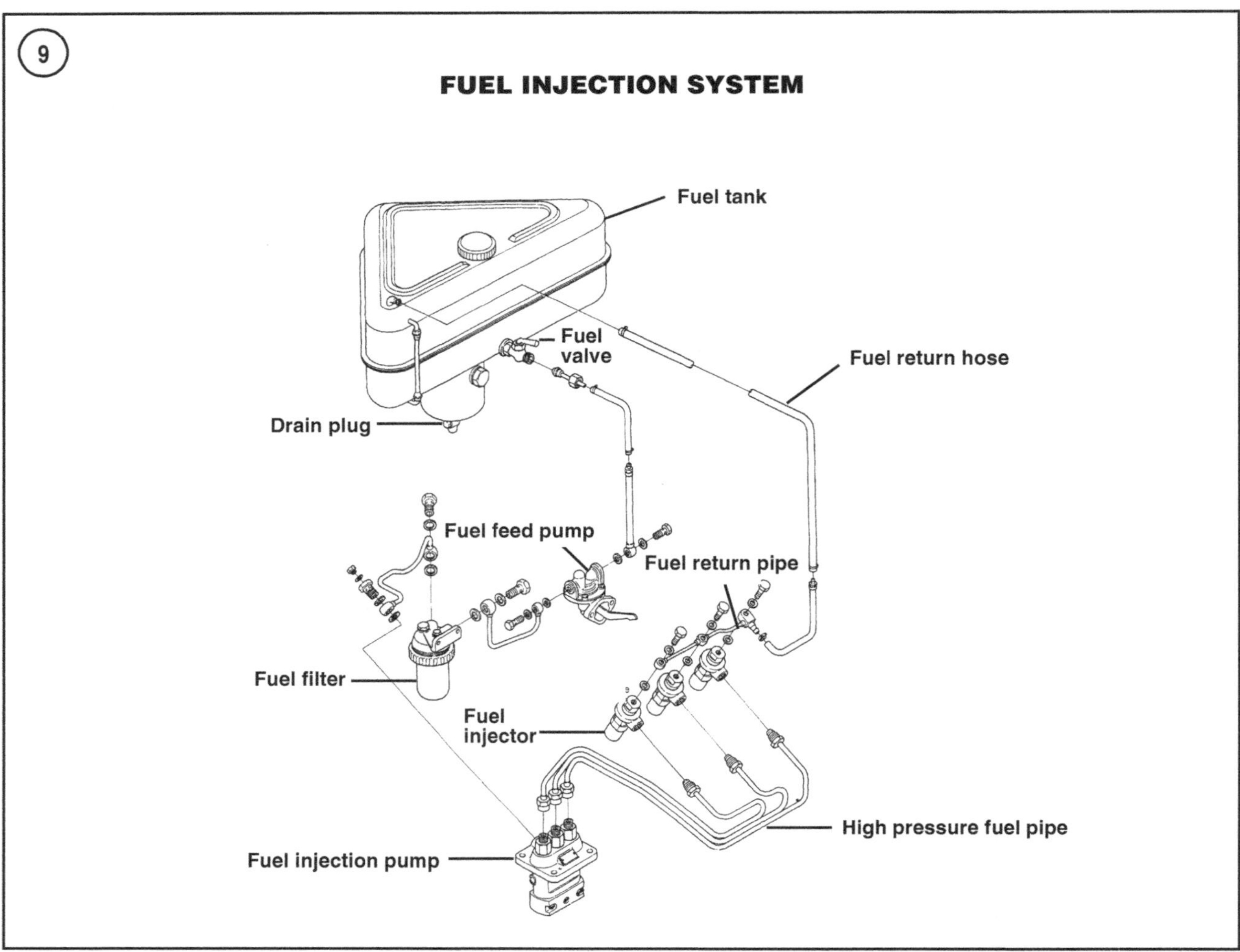

described in Chapter Seven to remove air in fuel. Check for a clogged or defective fuel injection pump or fuel injector.

WARNING
Wear goggles and protective clothing when performing the next procedure. Diesel injectors can spray with sufficient force to penetrate the skin. Have a fire extinguisher rated for fuel and electrical fires on hand.

To identify a faulty fuel injector on multicylinder engines, loosen the fuel injector fuel line nut with the engine running to reduce fuel pressure (only slight loosening is required). If the engine runs worse, the injector is operating satisfactorily. If the engine runs the same, the injector or the fuel injection pump is not operating properly. If no fuel appears at the fuel line, the fuel injection pump is defective.

6. *Engine knocks*—Check the fuel injection pump timing as described in Chapter Seven. Check for a defective fuel injection pump.

COOLING SYSTEM

The engine may be equipped with a seawater cooling system or freshwater cooling system. Refer to Chapter Eight for identification and description of the cooling system.

Engine Overheating

A problem in the cooling system generally causes engine overheating; however, other engine problems can also cause overheating. Note the possible causes in the following list:

1. *Loose pump drive belt (except 1GM models)*—A loose drive belt prevents the circulating pump from operating at the proper speed.

2. *Loose hose or pipe connections*—Air may be drawn into the suction side of the system.

3. *Worn or defective water pump*—A worn or defective pump may not provide sufficient cooling water.

4. *Dirty cooling system*—Debris in the cooling system prevents adequate heat transfer to the cooling water.

5. *Defective or incorrect thermostat*—A defective thermostat may stay closed or not open sufficiently to allow hot water to leave the engine. An incorrect thermostat may open at a temperature higher than specified, thereby raising the temperature of the cooling water in the engine. Conversely, a thermostat that stays open and doesn't close or opens at a low temperature will cause the engine to run at less than optimum temperature.

ENGINE EXHAUST SMOKE

The engine should emit colorless exhaust smoke or smoke that appears no more than a light haze. If the exhaust smoke is black, white or blue, an engine problem exists.

Blue Smoke

Blue exhaust smoke indicates that oil is burning during the combustion process. Look for a condition that allows oil to enter the combustion chamber, such as a broken piston, broken or stuck piston rings, a damaged cylinder wall, worn valves or guides, a defective crankcase vent, or an overfilled oil sump.

White Smoke

Unburned fuel causes white exhaust smoke. The unburned fuel may be due to retarded fuel injection timing or insufficient compression pressure. Low compression pressure may be caused by a damaged cylinder gasket, broken piston rings, leaking valves or incorrectly adjusted valves. Raw, unburned fuel may be due to incorrect fuel (low cetane rating) or a defective injector.

NOTE
White smoke may also be due to coolant leaking into the combustion chamber.

Black Smoke

Black exhaust smoke results from excess fuel (rich) that forms soot when burned. Either excess fuel or insufficient air can cause black smoke. Some possible causes are a defective fuel injection pump, poor injector spray pattern, low injection opening pressure, clogged air intake, restricted exhaust system or low compression pressure.

ENGINE NOISES

Often the first evidence of an internal engine problem is a strange noise. That knocking, clicking or tapping sound never heard before may be warning of impending trouble.

While engine noises can indicate problems, they are difficult to interpret correctly; inexperienced mechanics can be seriously misled by them.

Remember that diesels are much noisier than gasoline engines and have a normal clatter at idle, especially when cold. It is necessary to become accustomed to these normal noises in order to detect possible problem-associated noises.

Professional mechanics often use a special stethoscope for isolating engine noises. The home mechanic can do nearly as well with a sounding stick, which can be an ordinary piece of dowel, a length of broom handle or a section of small hose. Place one end in contact with the area in question and the other end near the ear to hear sounds emanating from that area. There are many strange sounds coming from even a normal engine. If possible, have an experienced mechanic help sort out the noises.

Clicking or Tapping Noises

Clicking or tapping noises usually come from the valve train and indicate excessive valve clearance. A sticking valve may also sound like a valve with excessive clearance. In addition, excessive wear in valve train components can cause similar engine noises.

Knocking Noises

A heavy, dull knocking is usually caused by a worn main bearing. The noise is loudest when the engine is working hard, such as accelerating at low speed. It is possible to isolate the trouble to a single bearing by disabling the fuel injectors on multicylinder engines one at a time. By disabling the fuel injector nearest the bearing, the knock will be reduced or disappear.

Worn connecting rod bearings may also produced a knock, but the sound is usually more metallic. As with a main bearing, the noise is worse during acceleration. It may increase in transition from acceleration to coasting. Disabling the fuel injectors will help isolate this knock as well.

A double knock or clicking usually indicates a worn piston pin. Disabling fuel injectors on multicylinderengines will isolate this to a particular piston; however, the noise will increase when the affected piston is reached.

A loose flywheel and excessive crankshaft end play also produce knocking noises. While similar to main bearing noises, they are usually intermittent, not constant, and they do not change when fuel injectors are disabled. If caused by a loose flywheel or coupling, the noise is generally heard at idle or during rapid deceleration. It is a good idea to recheck flywheel/coupler bolt torque whenever accessible.

Some mechanics confuse piston pin noise with piston slap (excessive piston clearance). The double knock will distinguish piston pin noise. Piston slap will always be louder when the engine is cold.

ENGINE TROUBLESHOOTING

These procedures assume the starter cranks the engine over normally. If not, refer to the *Starting System* section of this chapter.

Engine Will Not Start

This can be caused by the fuel system or by insufficient compression pressure. Refer to troubleshooting in the *Fuel System* section of this chapter. Refer to Chapter Three and check valve adjustment. Check for low compression pressure by performing a compression pressure check as described in Chapter Three. Repair the engine as required to obtain the correct compression pressure.

Engine Misses

This can be caused by the fuel system. Refer to troubleshooting in the *Fuel System* section of this chapter. Sticking intake or exhaust valves can also cause the engine to misfire.

Engine Stops Suddenly

This can be caused by engine seizure, a governor malfunction or a problem in the fuel system. Attempt to start the engine to determine if the engine rotates freely. Refer to Chapter Three to check governor adjustment or to Chapter Seven to repair the governor. If a fuel system problem is suspected, refer to troubleshooting in the *Fuel System* section of this chapter.

Engine Will Not Run Under Load

Refer to troubleshooting in the *Fuel System* section in this chapter.

Low Oil Pressure

Low engine oil pressure may be caused by leakage in the oil circuit, excessive bearing clearance, a clogged oil filter, a loose oil regulator valve or incorrect oil viscosity. Low oil pressure may also be caused by engine overheating or oil dilution by fuel in the crankcase.

Verify low oil pressure by performing the oil pressure test described in this chapter.

If the engine is overheating, refer to troubleshooting in the *Cooling System* section in this chapter.

COOLING SYSTEM

The temperature warning lamp should signal cooling system problems before there is any damage. If the engine is stopped at the first indication of trouble, serious damage is unlikely.

With standard cooling systems in which seawater is drawn into the engine, circulated and then expelled, cooling system problems are generally mechanical—a defective pump or thermostat, a loose or broken drive belt or passages plugged with contamination.

Closed cooling systems are more complex in that they use a heat exchanger, which transfers heat from the engine coolant to seawater without the two coming in contact. The closed portion of the cooling system is pressurized (like an automotive cooling system) and uses a 50/50 mixture of ethylene glycol antifreeze and pure soft water. Check this system periodically to make sure it can hold pressure up to 13 psi.

Heat exchangers used in closed cooling systems collect salt, lime and other contaminants in their passages, leading to a gradual decrease in cooling efficiency. For this reason, they should be removed every two years and the seawater passages cleaned with a wire brush and compressed air.

LUBRICATION SYSTEM

Refer to **Figure 10, Figure 11** and **Figure 12** for lubrication system diagrams. A rotor type oil pump receives oil

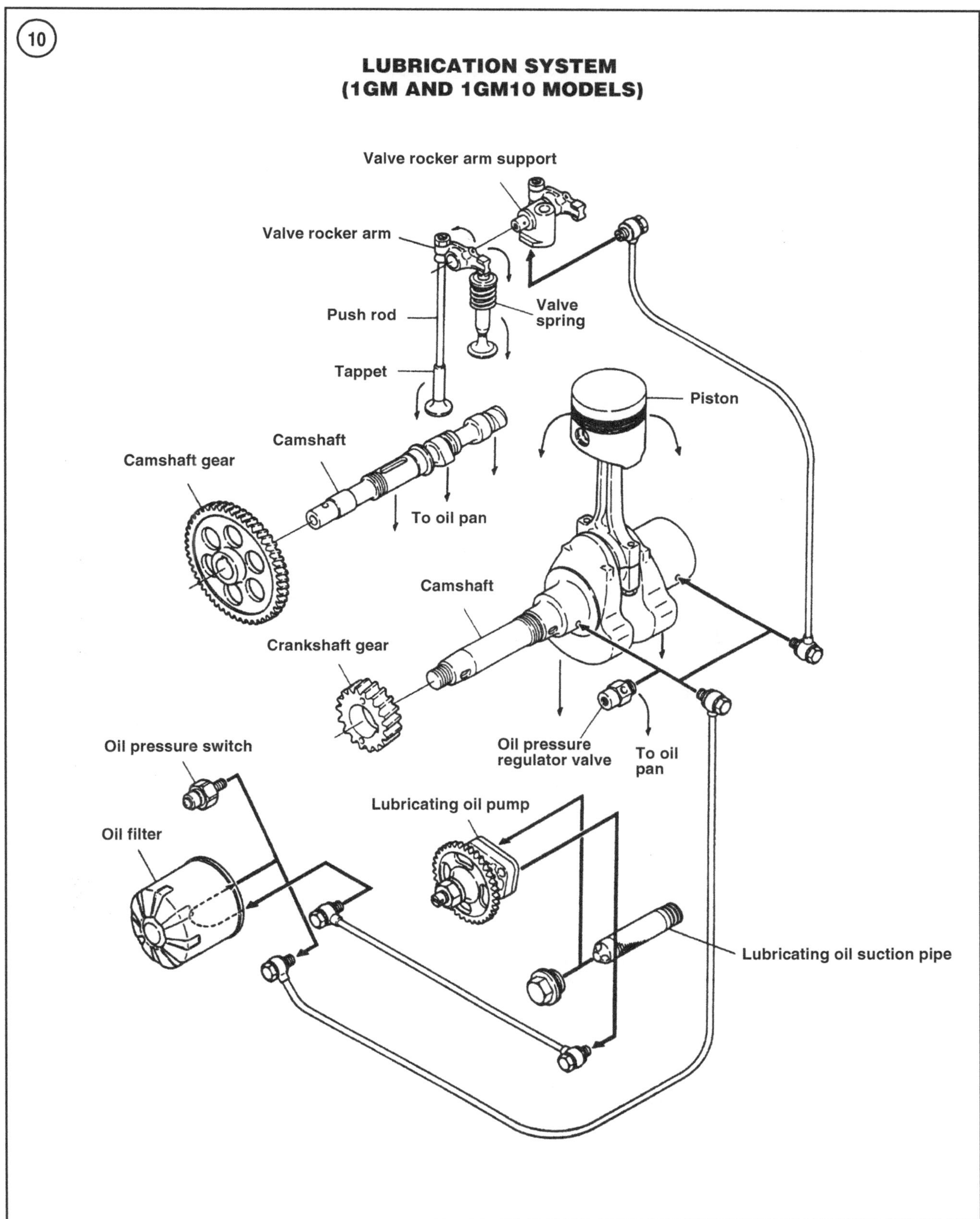
10
LUBRICATION SYSTEM
(1GM AND 1GM10 MODELS)
Valve rocker arm support
Valve rocker arm
Push rod
Valve spring
Tappet
Piston
Camshaft
Camshaft gear
To oil pan
Camshaft
Crankshaft gear
Oil pressure switch
Oil pressure regulator valve
To oil pan
Lubricating oil pump
Oil filter
Lubricating oil suction pipe

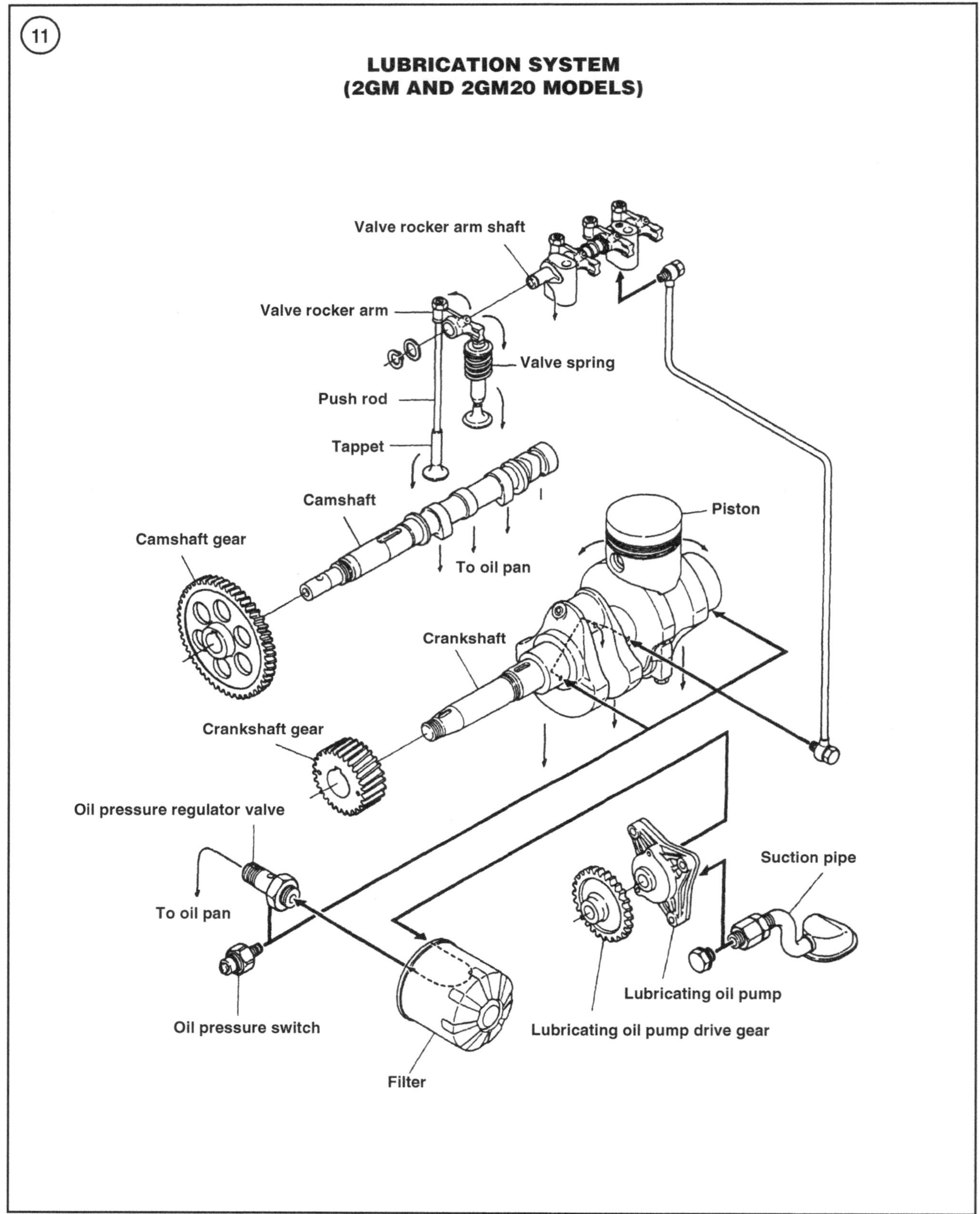
11
LUBRICATION SYSTEM
(2GM AND 2GM20 MODELS)
Valve rocker arm shaft
Valve rocker arm
Valve spring
Push rod
Tappet
Camshaft
Piston
Camshaft gear
To oil pan
Crankshaft
Crankshaft gear
Oil pressure regulator valve
Suction pipe
To oil pan
Lubricating oil pump
Oil pressure switch
Lubricating oil pump drive gear
Filter

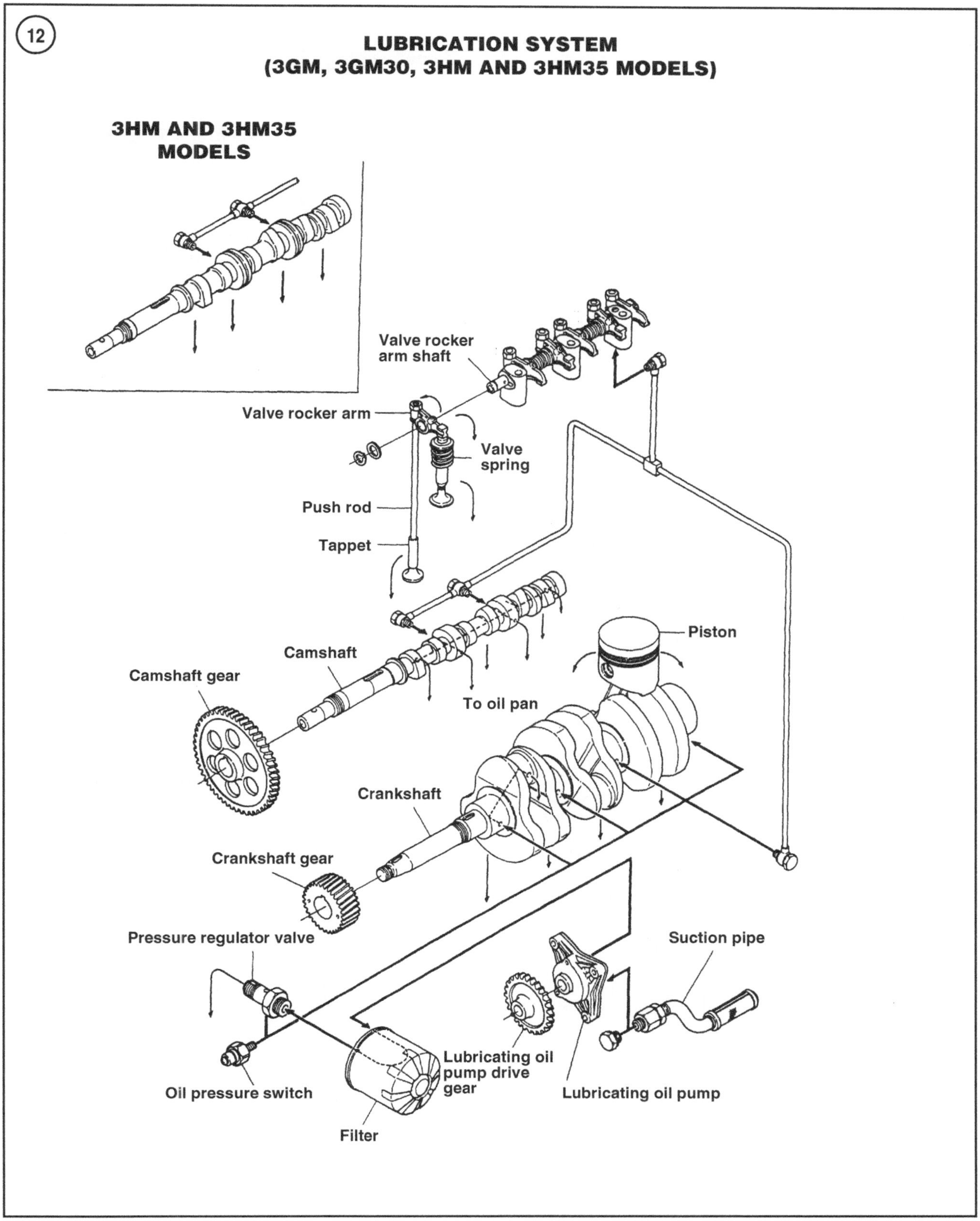

(12)

LUBRICATION SYSTEM (3GM, 3GM30, 3HM AND 3HM35 MODELS)

from a pickup located in the oil pan, then forces oil to the necessary engine components. The oil pump is driven by the crankshaft gear.

An oil pressure relief valve regulates oil pressure at 300-400 kPa (43-57 psi). When oil pressure exceeds the desired pressure, the relief valve opens and expels oil into the timing gearcase. A low oil pressure warning light on the instrument panel and a warning alarm buzzer activate if oil pressure is below 9.8 kPa (1.4 psi).

Refer to Chapters Five, Six and Nine for service procedures.

Oil Pressure Test

The engine is equipped with an oil pressure warning light and alarm that are activated if low oil pressure occurs. To verify low oil pressure, perform the following oil pressure test.

1. Disconnect the wire lead from the oil pressure sender (**Figure 13**, typical).

2. Remove the oil pressure sender.
3. Connect a suitable oil pressure gauge.
4. Start the engine and note the oil pressure reading at idle and wide open throttle.
5. Compare the gauge readings with the specifications in **Table 3**.

Table 1 ENGINE TROUBLESHOOTING

Trouble	Probable cause	Correction
Engine cranks slowly	Battery faulty or low charge	Charge or replace battery
	Faulty starter motor	Repair or replace starter motor
	Incorrect engine oil viscosity	Replace with proper engine oil
Engine will not crank	Discharged battery	Charge or replace battery
	Corroded battery terminals	Clean terminals
	Loose connection in starting circuit	Clean and tighten all connections
	Defective starting switch	Replace switch
	Starting motor brushes dirty	Clean or replace brushes
	Jammed starter drive gear	Loosen starter motor to free gear
	Faulty starter motor	Replace motor
	Seized engine	Inspect and repair
Engine will not start	Empty fuel tank	Fill tank with proper fuel
	Dirty or plugged fuel filter	Clean fuel filters
	Air in injection lines	Bleed air in injection lines
	Faulty fuel feed pump	Repair fuel feed pump
	Faulty fuel injection pump	Repair fuel injection pump
	Faulty governor	Repair governor
	Misadjusted controls	Adjust speed and stop controls
	Improper fuel injection timing	Adjust fuel injection timing
	Poor valve seating	Check for broken or weak valve springs, warped stems, carbon and gum deposits and insufficient tappet clearance
	Damaged cylinder head gasket	Check for leaks around gasket when engine is cranked; if a leak is found, replace gasket
	Worn or broken piston rings	Replace worn or broken rings; check cylinders for out-of-round and taper
Engine stops suddenly	Empty fuel tank	Fill fuel tank
	Air in fuel lines	Bleed fuel lines

(continued)

Table 1 ENGINE TROUBLESHOOTING (continued)

Trouble	Probable cause	Correction
Engine stops suddenly (continued)	Governor malfunction	Repair governor
	Engine seized	Inspect and repair
Engine slows unexpectedly	Overload	Locate cause for overload and rectify
	Fuel filter or fuel lines clogged	Inspect and unclog or replace
	Air in fuel system	Bleed air in fuel system
	Water in fuel	Remove water
	Misadjusted governor	Adjust governor
	Piston or bearing seizure	Repair damaged components; determine cause
Engine will not run under full load	Clogged fuel filter	Clean fuel filter
	Faulty fuel feed pump	Repair fuel feed pump
	Worn fuel injection pump	Repair or replace fuel injection pump
Engine knocks	Excessive bearing clearance	Inspect and repair
	Loose rod bolt	Inspect and repair
	Loose flywheel or coupling bolt	Tighten bolt
	Incorrect injection timing	Adjust timing
	Excessive fuel injected into cylinder	Inspect fuel injection pump and injectors
Low oil pressure	Oil leaks	Inspect and repair
	Excessive bearing clearance	Inspect and repair
	Clogged oil filter element	Clean or replace filter element
	Faulty oil pressure regulator valve	Repair oil pressure regulator valve
	Low oil viscosity	Replace oil; check for dilution due to fuel leaking into crankcase
Overheating	Dirty cooling system	Flush cooling system
	Faulty thermostat	Replace thermostat
	Insufficient coolant flow	Check water pump; check for blockage in system
	Insufficent coolant in closed system	Fill with proper coolant
	Air entering system	Check for loose clamps and damaged hoses

Table 2 STARTER MOTOR NO-LOAD SPECIFICATIONS

Model	Volts	Max. amperage	Speed (rpm)
3HM, 3HMF, 3HM35	12	90	4000 or higher
All other models	12	60	7000 or higher

Table 3 OIL PRESSURE

At 850 rpm	
all models	50 kPa (7 psi)
At 3400 rpm	
3HM and 3HM35	300-400 kPa (43-58 psi)
At 3600 rpm	
all models	
except 3HM and 3HM35	300-400 kPa (43-58 psi)

Chapter Three

Operation, Lubrication, Maintenance and Tune-up

A diesel engine *must have* clean air, fuel, and oil. Regular preventive maintenance and proper lubrication will pay dividends in longer engine and transmission life, as well as safer boat operation.

The lubrication and maintenance intervals provided in **Table 1** are those recommended for normal operation. If the boat is used under continuous heavy duty or other severe operating conditions, including infrequent use, perform maintenance and lubrication more frequently.

Keep the engine and accessory units clean and free of dirt, grime and grease buildup. It is much easier and safer to perform service on a clean engine. It is also much easier to pinpoint any leaks.

Tables 1-6 are located at the end of this chapter.

NOTE
Except where specified, F and D series engines are included when a basic model number is specified. For example, if model 3GM is called out in a procedure, the procedure also applies to 3GMD and 3GMF.

FUEL REQUIREMENTS

The recommended fuel is number 2 (2-D) diesel fuel. Be sure the fuel is clean and free of water.

NOTE
Poor fuel is one of the leading causes of rough engine operation or failure to start.

Dirty fuel or water in the fuel can cause expensive damage to the fuel injection pump and fuel injectors. Refer to Chapter Seven.

PREOPERATIONAL CHECKS

Before starting the engine for the first time each day, perform the following checks:

1. Remove the engine compartment cover or hatch and check for the presence of fuel fumes. If the boat is equipped with a bilge blower, turn it on for a few minutes. If the smell of strong fumes is present, determine the source and correct the problem before proceeding.

WARNING
Always have a Coast Guard-approved fire extinguisher close when working around the engine.

2. Check the engine oil level as described in this chapter. Add oil if the level is low.
3. Check the electrolyte level in each battery cell as described in this chapter. Add distilled water if necessary.

4. Check the condition of all drive belts. If a belt is in doubtful condition, replace it.
5. Check all water hoses for leaks, loose connections and general condition. Repair or replace as required.
6. Check the oil level in the transmission as described in this chapter. Add lubricant if necessary.
7. Check the bilge for excessive water; if present, drain or pump dry.
8. Check the propeller for damage. Repair or replace the propeller if damaged.
9. Remove any water or dirt in the fuel tank by opening the fuel tank drain valve.
10. Check the fuel level in the fuel tank and add fuel as needed.
11. Open the seacock and close any water drain valves.
12. Operate controls and check for free operation.
13. Connect the battery cables to the battery (if disconnected).
14. Open the fuel tank valve.
15. Reinstall the engine compartment cover or hatch.

STARTING CHECKLIST

After performing the preoperational checks, observe the following starting procedure:

Engines Without Remote Control

1. If equipped with a bilge blower, operate it for at least five minutes before starting the engine.
2. Move the clutch control lever to the NEUTRAL position.
3. Move the speed control lever to the MEDIUM SPEED position.
4. Hold the decompression lever in the OPERATION position.
5. Rotate the key switch to the ON position. The alarm buzzer will come on.

WARNING
Always have a fully charged fire extinguisher on hand before attempting to start the engine.

CAUTION
Do not operate the starter for more than 15 seconds, or the starter motor may be damaged due to overheating.

6. Start the engine by pushing the start button. The alarm lights and buzzer should go off.

CAUTION
If the alarm buzzer or lamps remain on after the engine starts, stop the engine and determine the cause.

3

Engines Equipped With Remote Control

Warm engine

1. If equipped with a bilge blower, operate it for at least five minutes before starting the engine.
2. Move the speed control lever to the MEDIUM SPEED position.
3. Rotate the key switch to the ON position. The alarm buzzer will come on.

WARNING
Always have a fully charged fire extinguisher on hand before attempting to start the engine.

CAUTION
Do not push the starter for more than 15 seconds, or the starter motor may be damaged due to overheating.

4. Start the engine by pushing the start button. The alarm lights and buzzer should go off.

CAUTION
If the alarm buzzer or lamps remain on after the engine starts, stop the engine and determine the cause.

Cold engine

1. If equipped with a bilge blower, operate it for at least five minutes before starting the engine.
2. Move the speed control lever to the HIGH SPEED position. Injection timing is retarded when starting with the lever in the HIGH SPEED position.
3. Move the decompression lever to the DECOMPRESSION position.
4. Rotate the key switch to the ON position. The alarm buzzer will come on.

WARNING
Always have a fully charged fire extinguisher on hand before attempting to start the engine.

CAUTION
Do not operated the starter for more than 15 seconds, or the starter motor may be damaged due to overheating.

5. Start the engine by pushing the start button. While engaging the starter, move the decompression lever to the COMPRESSION position. The alarm lights and buzzer should go off.

CAUTION

If the alarm buzzer or lamps remain on after the engine starts, stop the engine and determine the cause.

6. Move the speed control lever to the MEDIUM SPEED position.
7. Allow the engine to warm for approximately five minutes before applying full load to the engine.

STOPPING THE ENGINE

Note the following items when stopping the engine.
1. Place the transmission in neutral, then allow the engine to idle for five minutes before stopping the engine.
2. Momentarily raise engine speed to blow out any residue in the cylinders, then pull the engine stop knob or lever.

CAUTION

Do not stop the engine using the decompression lever. Doing so may leave sufficient fuel in the cylinders to damage the engine when started.

3. Close the seacock. If ambient temperature is below freezing while the engine is not running, drain water in cooling system after engine has cooled.

EMERGENCY ENGINE STOPPING

To safely stop a diesel engine when the normal stopping controls are inoperative or ineffective, block the engine's air intake. A flat plate is desirable if it will adequately cover the opening. A rag may also be used, but do not allow the rag to enter the engine.

POST-OPERATIONAL CHECKS

Perform the following maintenance after each use.
1. If the boat was used in salt or polluted water, flush the cooling system with freshwater as described in this chapter. This will minimize corrosion and buildup of deposits in the cooling system.
2. Disconnect the battery cables from the battery, negative cable first. Remove the battery from the boat to prevent theft, if necessary.
3. Shut off the fuel tank valve(s).

4. Top off the fuel tank(s), if possible. This will minimize the possibility of moisture condensation in the tank(s).
5. If water is present in the bilge, either drain it or pump it dry.
6. Wash the interior and exterior surfaces of the boat with freshwater.

ENGINE MAINTENANCE AND LUBRICATION

The maintenance tasks discussed in this section should be performed at the intervals indicated in **Table 1**. These intervals are only guidelines, however. Consider the frequency and extent of boat use when establishing the actual intervals. Perform the tasks more frequently if the boat is used under severe service conditions.

Engine Oil

Engine oil designed for use in diesel engines must meet specifications particular to diesel engine operation. The Society for Automotive Engineers (SAE) specifies the

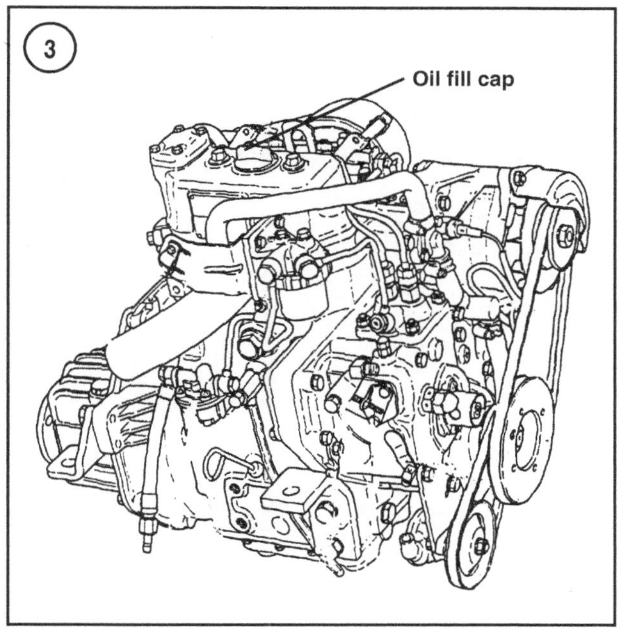

criteria that engine oils must meet to attain a diesel engine oil classification of CA, CB, CC or CD. The classification system ranges from CA for light diesel engine service to CD for severe diesel engine service. Yanmar specifies engine oils with classification CB or CC for use in the Yanmar diesel engines covered in this manual.

Do not mix oil brands. For instance, do not add a different oil brand than what is in the crankcase when topping off the oil level, except if necessary. Use only a high-quality oil. Yanmar recommends Shell Rotella, Caltex RPM Delo, Mobil Delvac, Esso Standard and BP Energol.

Refer to **Table 2** for the recommended oil viscosity.

Engine Oil Level Check

All engines will consume a certain amount of oil as a lubricating and cooling agent. The amount depends on engine use and engine condition. During the engine break-in period, the engine consumes more oil while the piston rings seat in the cylinder bore. Engines with high hours of use may burn more oil due to worn engine components. Engines generally consume more oil at higher engine speeds.

When to check engine oil is generally determined by the engine's oil consumption rate. If the engine has a high oil consumption rate, then check the oil level before each use or daily. If engine oil consumption is low, check the oil level weekly. The best procedure is to check the oil level before operating the engine.

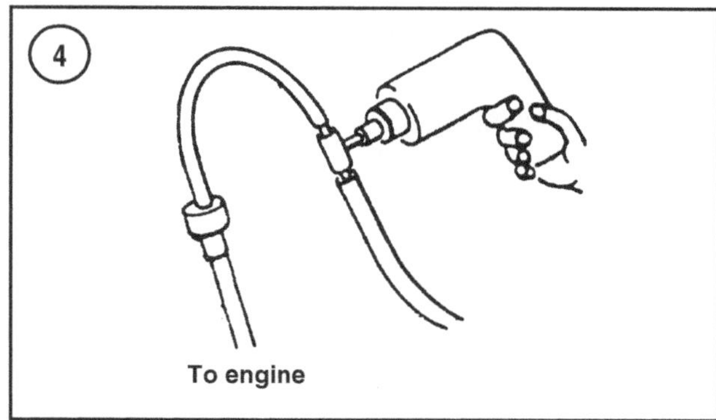

Whenever checking the oil level, always allow approximately five minutes for the oil in the upper end to drain back into the crankcase oil pan.

1. With the boat at rest in the water and the engine off, pull out the dipstick. See **Figure 1** for the typical location. Wipe it with a clean rag or paper towel, reinsert it and pull it out again. Note the oil level on the dipstick.
2. Add oil, if necessary, so the oil level reaches the full mark on the dipstick. Remove the oil fill plug (**Figure 2**) or oil filler cap (**Figure 3**) and add oil through the hole in the rocker arm cover.

Engine Oil and Filter Change

During normal engine operation, change the engine oil after every 100 hours of operation. Replace the engine oil filter after every 300 hours of operation. During break-in of a new or overhauled engine, change the engine oil after the first 20 hours of use, then after the next 30 hours of use. Change the engine oil at normal intervals thereafter.

Refer to the *Engine Oil* section in this chapter for the recommended oil type. Refer to **Table 2** for viscosity and **Table 3** for crankcase oil capacity.

Most installations do not leave enough space to permit the use of the oil pan drain plug. For this reason, an oil drain suction pump is the most common device used to drain the crankcase oil. The pump has a long, flexible hose, which is inserted into the oil dipstick tube and fed into the crankcase. Several makes of pumps are available from marine supply dealers. Some are hand-operated, some are motorized and others are designed to be operated with an electric drill (**Figure 4**).

Direct the used oil into a sealable container and properly dispose of it.

NOTE

Never dispose of motor oil in the trash, on the ground, down a storm drain or overboard. Many service stations accept used motor oil and waste haulers provide curbside used motor oil collection. Do not combine other fluids with motor oil to be recycled. To locate a recycler, contact the American Petroleum Institute (API) at ***www.recycleoil.org****.*

The oil filter is a disposable spin-on type. An oil filter wrench can be used to remove the filter, but do not use it to install the new filter. Overtightening the filter may cause it to leak.

The installed angle of the engine affects oil level in the crankcase. To assure that the oil is drained and replaced properly, perform the following procedure with the boat at rest in the water.

1. Start the engine and warm it to normal operating temperature under load, then shut it off.
2. Remove the dipstick and wipe it clean with a lint-free cloth or paper towel.
3. Insert the oil drain pump hose into the dipstick tube as far as it will go.
4. Insert the other pump hose into a sealable container large enough to hold the oil from the crankcase. Refer to **Table 3** to determine the capacity of the engine crankcase.
5. Operate the pump until it has removed all of the oil possible from the crankcase. Remove the pump hose from the dipstick tube.
6. Place a drain pan or other suitable container under the filter (**Figure 5**) to catch any oil spillage when the filter is removed.
7. Unscrew the filter counterclockwise. Use the filter wrench if the filter is tight.
8. Wipe the gasket surface on the engine block clean with a paper towel.
9. Coat the neoprene gasket on the new filter with a thin coat of clean engine oil.
10. Screw the new filter onto the engine by hand until the gasket just touches the engine block. At this point, there will be a very slight resistance when turning the filter.
11. Tighten the filter another 2/3 turn by hand. Using a filter wrench can lead to overtightening the filter. This can damage the filter or cause an oil leak.
12. Remove the oil filler cap or plug from the rocker arm cover. See **Figure 2** (single cylinder models) or **Figure 3** (multicylinder models).
13. Reinstall the dipstick in the dipstick tube.
14. Refer to **Table 3** to determine the crankcase capacity of the engine. Pour the specified amount of oil into the rocker am cover opening and install the oil filler cap or plug. Wipe up any spills on the cover.

NOTE

Check the area under and around the oil filter for leaks while the engine is running in Step 15.

15. Start the engine and let it idle for five minutes, then shut off the engine.
16. Wait approximately five minutes, then remove the dipstick. Wipe the dipstick clean with a lint-free cloth or paper towel and reinsert it in the dipstick tube. Remove the dipstick a second time and check the oil level. Add oil, if necessary, to bring the level up to the full mark, but do not overfill.

Fuel System Service

Diesel fuel injection systems require clean fuel that meets the fuel requirements specified by the engine manufacturer. Due to the close tolerances required in the fuel injection system, diesel engines are particularly susceptible to dirt or other contaminants in the fuel. Use only clean

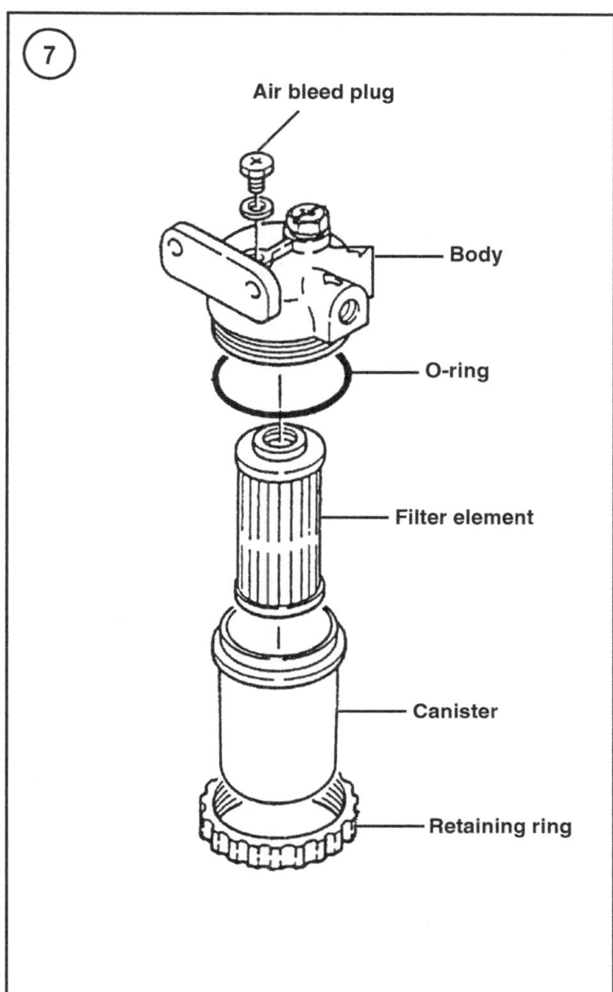

fuel and maintain the fuel filter and fuel system components to prevent a fuel system malfunction.

WARNING
Serious fire hazards always exist around diesel fuel. Do not allow any smoking in areas where fuel is present. Always have a fire extinguisher, rated for fuel and electrical fires, on hand when refueling or servicing any part of the fuel system.

Fuel lines

Periodically inspect all fuel lines for leakage and damage. Replace or tighten them as required. Do not overtighten a fitting to try to stop a leak; overtightening may damage the fitting threads or the fuel line sealing surfaces.

Air that enters the fuel system due to a damaged fuel line or loose connection may cause the engine to missfire. Bleed the fuel system as described in this chapter.

Fuel filter

Using clean fuel and maintaining the fuel system are extremely important when operating a diesel engine. Diesel fuel, in addition to its obvious function as fuel, provides lubrication for various components of the injection system. Due to close operating tolerances, dirty fuel can cause major damage to the fuel injection pump and injectors. The engine is equipped with a fuel filter (**Figure 6**, typical) to remove dirt from the fuel before it enters the fuel injection pump.

After every 50 hours of operation, or more frequently if necessary, remove and disassemble the fuel filter and clean the inside of the fuel bowl and filter element. The filter body contains a replaceable element. Replace the element after every 250 hours of operation or more frequently if dirt clogs the element after fewer hours of operation. It is a good practice to replace the fuel filter every season or if the engine has not been operated for an extended period.

NOTE
The boat may be equipped with additional fuel filters. Be sure to clean and maintain those filters according to the manufacturer's instructions.

NOTE
If the fuel filtering system is inadequate to properly protect the engine, consult with a marine dealership that has experience with diesel engines for fuel filter recommendations.

Refer to **Figure 7** when using the following procedure to clean the filter or replace the filter element:

1. Position a receptacle under the filter to catch spilled fuel.
2. Unscrew the retaining ring and remove the canister and filter element. Note that the O-ring may remain on the filter body or on the canister.
3. Remove the element from the canister. If dirty or damaged, discard the element.
4. Clean the canister in clean diesel fuel.
5. Install the filter element in the canister.
6. Install a new O-ring on the canister.
7. Install the canister on the filter body, then install the retainer ring and tighten it hand-tight.

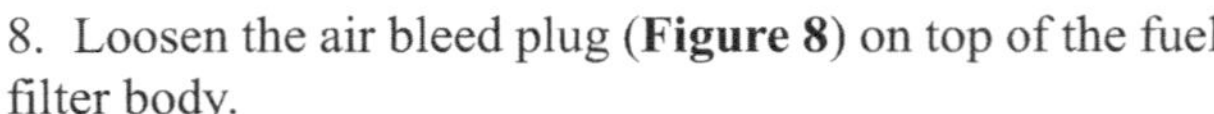

8. Loosen the air bleed plug (**Figure 8**) on top of the fuel filter body.

9. Make sure the fuel tank valve is open, then operate the primer lever on the fuel transfer pump (**Figure 9**).

10. Operate the lever while observing the fuel emitted around the bleed plug. Air will be emitted along with the fuel. Stop operating the lever when the fuel is free of air, then tighten the air bleed plug.

Bleeding air from the fuel system

Whenever air enters the fuel injection system, such as when the fuel tank runs dry, components are replaced, or a fuel line is damaged or disconnected, bleed the air from the fuel system to prevent engine misfire. Refer to Chapter Seven for the air bleeding procedure.

Air Filter

An air filter (A, **Figure 10**, typical) removes airborne dirt and debris. Within the air filter canister is a reuseable polyurethane filter element. Clean the filter element after every 250 hours of operation or more frequently if the engine operates in a dirty environment. Inspect the filter element before each operating season to be sure it is clean and undamaged.

Use the following procedure to remove and clean the filter element:

1. Unsnap the filter canister retaining clip (B, **Figure 10**) and remove the canister and filter element.

2. Separate the filter element from the canister (**Figure 11**). Note the mesh cone inside the foam filter.

3. Inspect the foam for holes, tears or other damage. Discard the foam if damaged.

4. Clean the foam filter and mesh cone in soapy water. If the foam filter cannot be cleaned, discard it and install a new filter. Let the foam filter dry.

5. Reassemble and reinstall the filter by reversing the removal procedure.

NOTE

*Be sure the intake tube (C, **Figure 10**) of the canister points slightly downward and not upward; otherwise, water can enter the tube and run into the filter.*

Drive Belts

Inspect all drive belts at regular intervals to make sure they are in good condition and are properly tensioned. Replace worn, frayed, cracked or glazed belts. The components to which they direct power are essential to the safe and reliable operation of the boat. If correct adjustment is maintained on each belt, all will usually give the same service life. For this reason and because of the cost involved in replacing an inner belt (requiring the removal of the

outer belt), it is a good idea to replace all belts as a set. The added expense is small compared to the cost of replacing the belts individually, and replacing each belt reduces the possibility of a breakdown on the water, which could cost far more in time and money.

Make sure the drive belts are properly tensioned at all times. If loose, the belts will not drive the driven components at maximum efficiency. The belts will also wear rapidly because of the increased friction caused by slippage. Belts that are too tight will be overstressed and prone to premature failure. An excessively tight belt will also overstress the water pump or alternator bearings, resulting in premature failure.

Alternator drive belt adjustment (models equipped with seawater cooling)

1. Check alternator drive belt tension by depressing the drive belt at the midway point on the belt (A, **Figure 12**). The belt should deflect approximately 0.4 inch (10 mm) with moderate finger pressure.

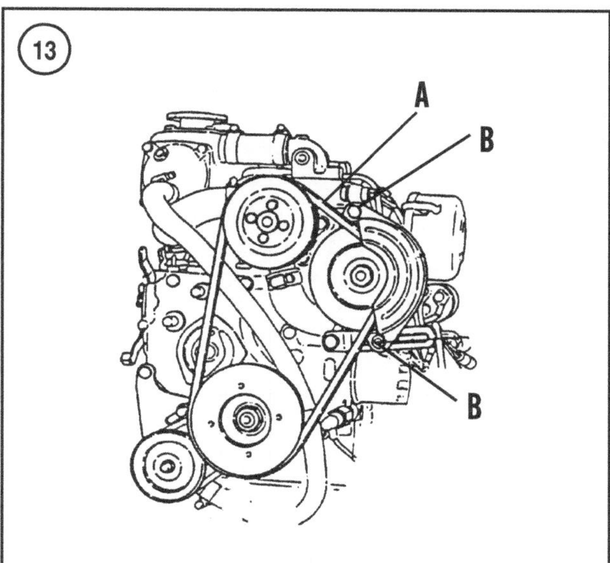

2. To adjust alternator drive belt tension, loosen the alternator retaining nuts (B, **Figure 12**), then reposition the alternator. Retighten the retaining bolts and recheck belt tension.

Alternator drive belt adjustment (models equipped with freshwater cooling)

The alternator drive belt also drives the freshwater cooling pump on engines so equipped.

1. Check alternator drive belt tension by depressing the drive belt at the midway point on the belt (A, **Figure 13**). The belt should deflect approximately 0.4 in (10 mm) with moderate finger pressure.

2. To adjust alternator drive belt tension, loosen the alternator retaining bolts (B, **Figure 12**), then reposition the alternator. Retighten the retaining bolts and recheck belt tension.

Seawater pump drive belt adjustment (2GM, 2GM20, 3GM, 3GM30, 3HM And 3HM35 models)

1. Check seawater pump drive belt tension by depressing the drive belt at the midway point on the belt (A, **Figure 14**). The belt should deflect approximately 0.24 in (6 mm) with moderate finger pressure.

2. To adjust seawater pump drive belt tension, loosen the screws (B, **Figure 14**) that retain the water pump mounting plate. Reposition the plate to obtain the correct belt tension, then retighten the bolt and nut. Recheck belt tension.

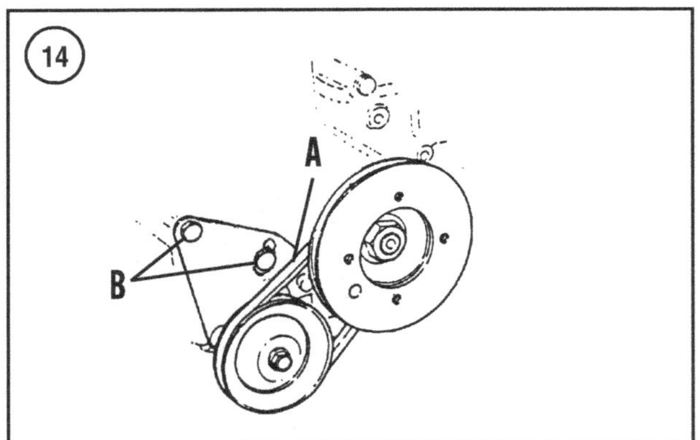

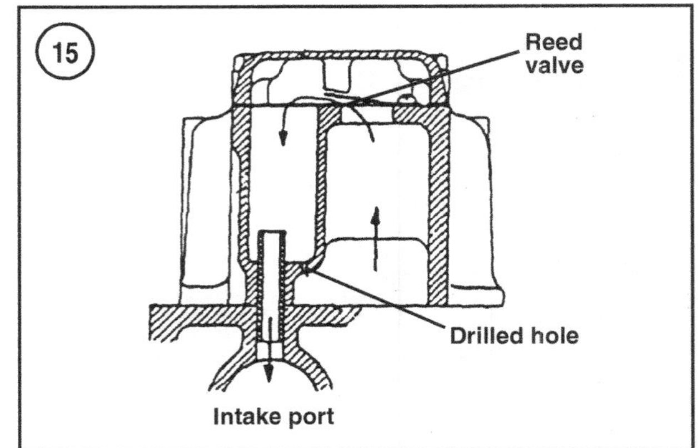

Alternator drive belt replacement (all models)

1. Loosen the alternator retaining nuts (B, **Figure 12**).
2. Move the alternator inward sufficiently to allow removal of the belt from the pulleys and remove the belt.
3. Clean the pulley grooves so they are dry and free of rust or other corrosion.
4. Place the new belt in the pulley grooves.
5. Adjust belt tension as previously described.

Seawater pump drive belt replacement (2GM, 2GM20, 3GM, 3GM30, 3HM and 3HM35 models)

1. Remove the alternator drive belt as described in the previous section.
2. Loosen the screws that secure the seawater pump mounting plate (B, **Figure 14**).
3. Move the alternator inward sufficiently to allow removal of the belt from the pulleys and remove the belt.
4. Clean the pulley grooves so they are dry and free of rust or other corrosion.
5. Place the new belt in the pulley grooves.
6. Adjust belt tension as previously described.

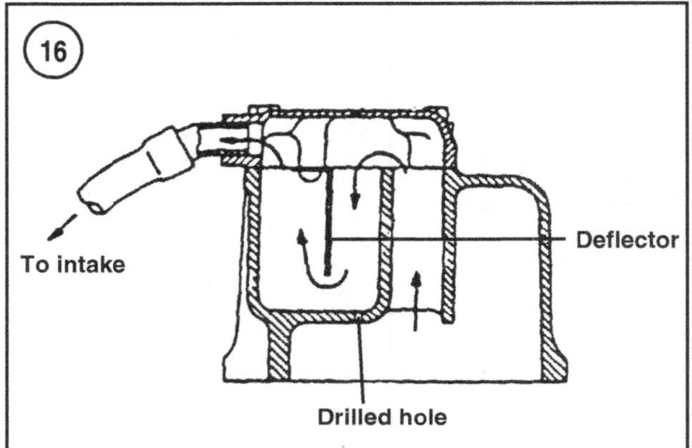

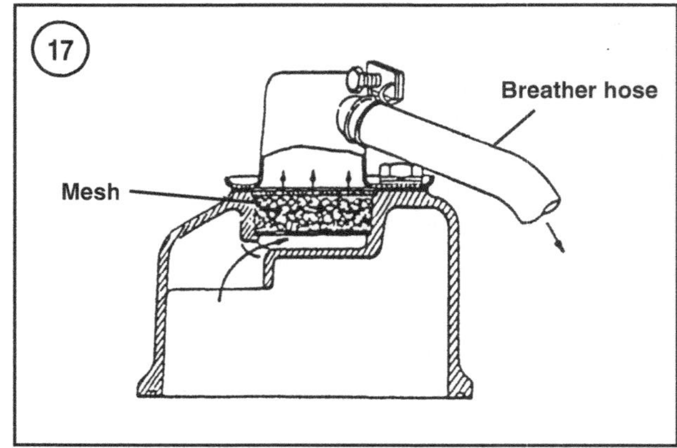

Crankcase Breather

The crankcase breather assembly vents crankcase pressure into the intake port or manifold. This produces a negative pressure in the crankcase. If the breather malfunctions, oil may be forced past the piston rings, oil seals and gaskets.

Periodic maintenance is not normally required unless excessive oil gasses clog the crankcase breather. This is usually indicated by blue exhaust smoke or oil in the intake port or manifold. If the breather must be cleaned frequently, determine the cause, such as broken or stuck piston rings.

Refer to Chapter Five or Six for service procedures for the crankcase breather. Refer to the following paragraphs for a description of the breather on specific models.

On 1GM and 1GM10 models, a reed valve system located on the rocker arm cover controls crankcase gas movement. See **Figure 15**. The reed valve opens when the downward moving piston increases crankcase gas pres-

18

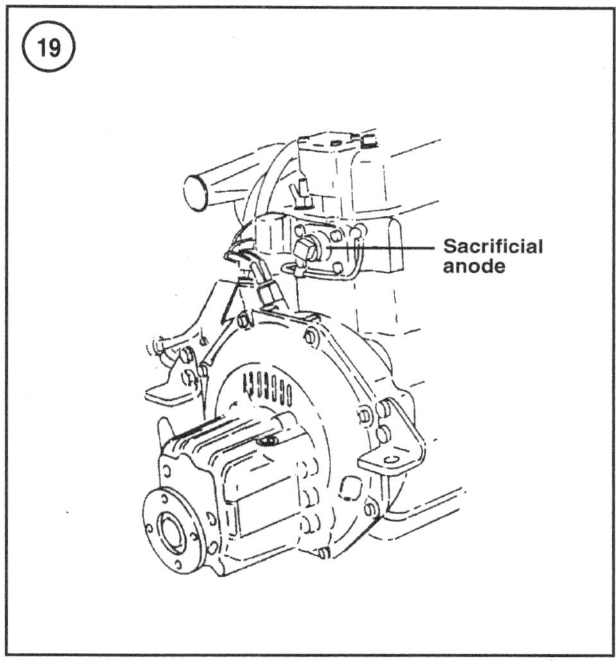

19

sure. The reed valve closes when the piston moves up in the cylinder. This creates a negative pressure in the crankcase, which helps the piston rings seal against the cylinder bore. A hole in the breather chamber routes oil back to the crankcase; however, excessive oil will pass through the connecting tube into the intake port.

On 2GM, 2GM20, 3GM and 3GM30 models, the crankcase breather is located on the rocker arm cover. A labyrinth system separates oil from the crankcase gas. See **Figure 16**. A hole in the breather chamber routes oil back into the engine, however, excessive oil will pass into the breather tube to the intake port or intake manifold.

On 3HM and 3HM35 models, a mesh assembly on top of the rocker arm cover separates oil from the crankcase

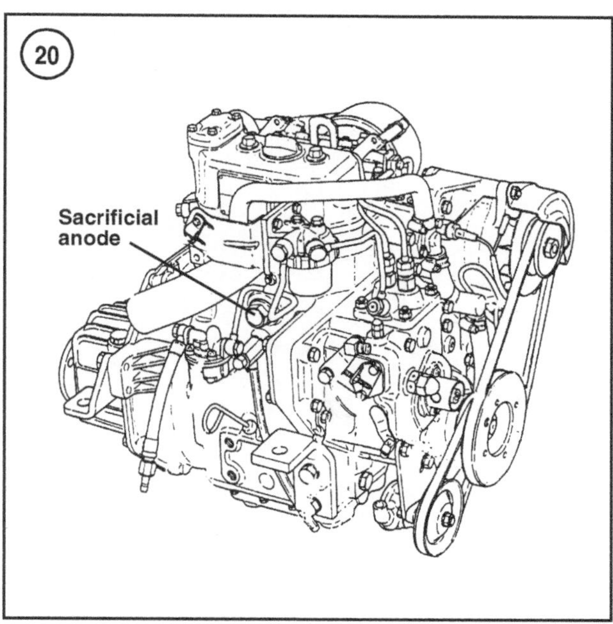

20

gases. See **Figure 17**. A breather tube routes the crankcase gases to the intake manifold.

Anticorrosion Maintenance

The engines are equipped with sacrificial anodes that provide protection against galvanic corrosion. Sacrificial anodes are relatively inexpensive and easily replaceable components that provide adequate corrosion protection in most situations where light-to-moderate corrosion conditions exist. Anodes are made of a highly active zinc alloy.

Check the condition of the anodes periodically and frequently. Replace any anode that is corroded to 50 percent of its original size.

Engine models 1GM and 1GM10 are equipped with a single sacrificial anode that is attached to a plate located on the cylinder block (**Figure 18**). A threaded type sacrificial anode is used on 2GM, 2GM20, 3GM, 3GM30, 3HM and 3HM35 model engines. One anode is located in the cylinder head (**Figure 19**), and one anode is located in the cylinder block on 2GM and 2GM20 model engines (**Figure 20**), while two anodes are located in the cylinder block on 3GM, 3GM30, 3HM and 3HM35 model engines.

Proceed as follows to service the sacrificial anodes:

1GM and 1GM10 models

1. Drain the cooling system.

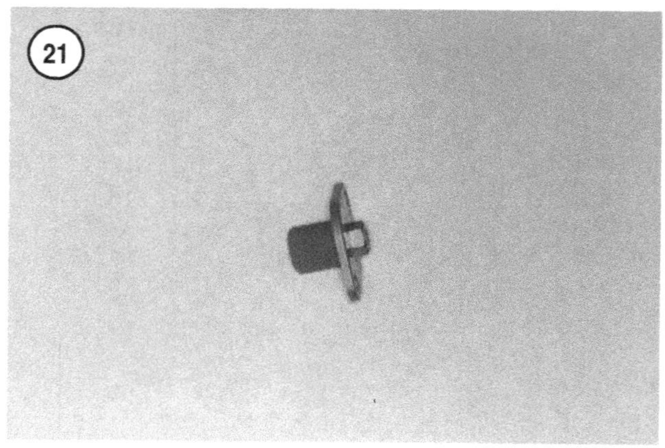
21

2. Unscrew the mounting plate (**Figure 18**) and remove the sacrificial anode (**Figure 21**).
3. Use a wire brush and remove corrosion on the anode. Clean the mounting plate and mounting surface on the engine block.
4. Inspect the anode and compare it with the dimensions of a new anode shown in **Figure 22**. Replace the anode if dimensions are less than 50 percent of original size.
5. Install a new gasket on the anode (**Figure 23**).

NOTE

Do not apply any sealer to the anode mounting plate or to the engine block. Sealer or corroded mating surfaces will prevent good electrical contact, which is necessary for optimum anode protection.

6. Reassemble and reinstall the sacrificial anode in the engine.

2GM, 2GM20, 3GM, 3GM30, 3HM and 3HM35 models

1. Drain the cooling system.
2. Unscrew the sacrificial anodes in the cylinder head (**Figure 19**) and cylinder block (**Figure 20**).
3. Use a wire brush to remove corrosion from the anode. Clean the threads on the anode and in the engine.
4. Inspect the anode and compare it with the dimensions of a new anode shown in **Figure 22**. Replace the anode if dimensions are less than 50 percent of original size.
5. Install a new gasket on the anode (**Figure 23**).

NOTE

Do not apply any sealer to threads on the anode or in the engine. Sealer or corroded threads will prevent good electrical contact, which is necessary for optimum anode protection.

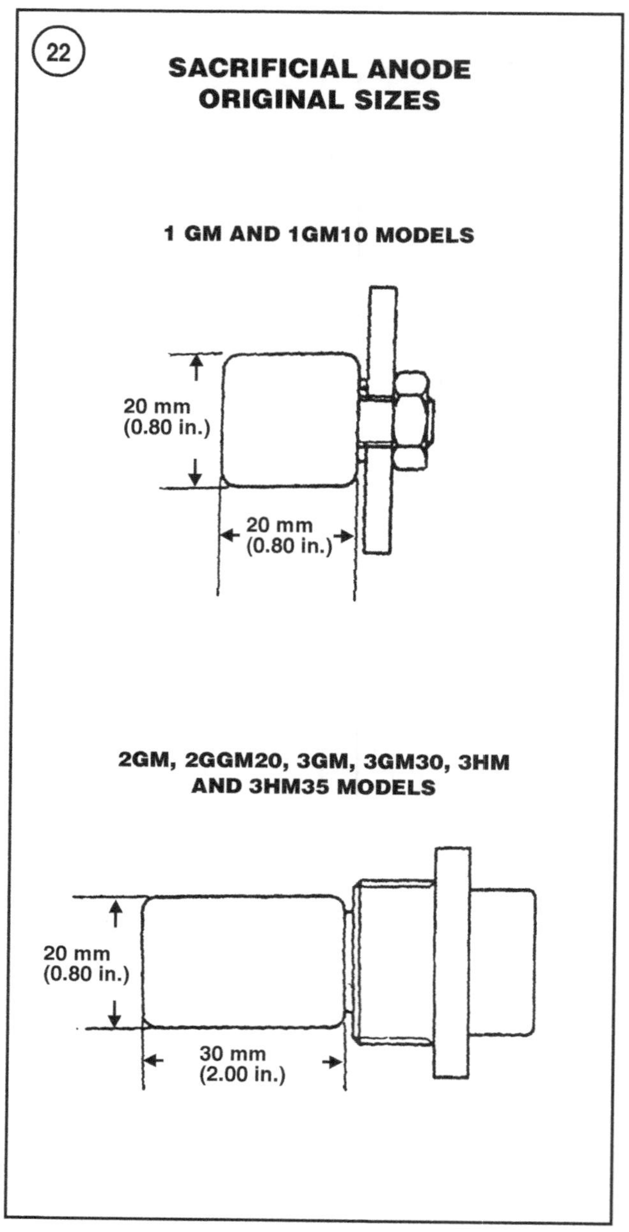

6. Reassemble and reinstall the sacrificial anode in the engine.

COOLING SYSTEM

Refer to Chapter Eight for a description of the two types of cooling systems that are used on the Yanmar marine diesel engines covered in this manual. A freshwater

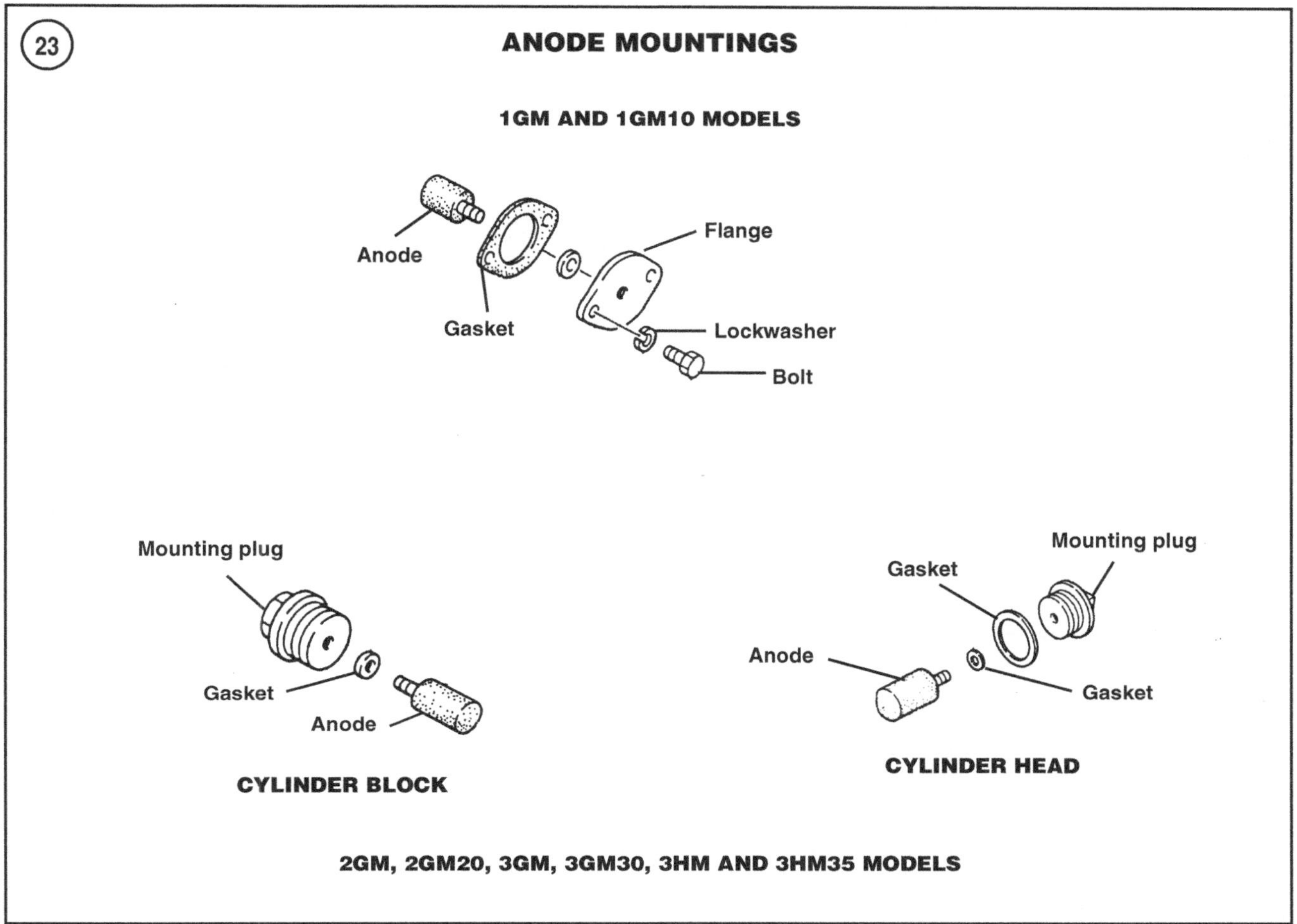

(closed) cooling system requires additional maintenance due to the freshwater portion of the system, which includes a freshwater pump and may include an antifreeze mixture.

Seawater (Standard) Cooling Systems

Flushing the system

Flushing procedures may differ depending upon engine installation and the location of the water pump. Regardless of pump location, cooling water must always circulate through the water pump whenever the engine is running to prevent damage to the pump impeller. On models equipped with a closed cooling system, both pumps must be supplied with cooling water.

The following procedure provides steps to flush the cooling system of engines equipped with a seawater cooling system as well as the seawater portion on engines equipped with a closed cooling system. This procedure may be used for most engines, but modification of the procedure may be necessary for some installations.

1. Detach the inlet hose from the water pump.

2. Connect a hose from a water tap to the inlet of the water pump.

3. Open the water tap.

4. With the transmission in neutral, start the engine and run at normal idle until the engine reaches normal operating temperature.

5. Observe the water being flushed from the cooling system. When the flow is clear, shut the engine off, then shut off the water tap.

6. Reconnect the inlet hose to the water pump.

NOTE

Refer to Chapter Eight to flush and refill the freshwater portion of a closed cooling system or to service the heat exchanger.

Freshwater (Closed) Cooling Systems

Inspection

WARNING
*When performing any service work on the engine or cooling system, never remove the pressure fill cap on the exhaust manifold (**Figure 24**), drain coolant or disconnect any hose while the engine is hot. Scalding fluid and steam may be blown out under pressure and cause serious injury.*

Once a year, or whenever troubleshooting the cooling system, check the following items. If the proper equipment is not available, have the tests performed by a radiator shop.

1. Loosen and remove the pressure fill cap (**Figure 24**).
2. Check the cap seals for tears or cracks. Check for a bent or distorted cap. Rinse the cap under warm tap water to flush away any loose rust or dirt particles.
3. Inspect the cap neck seat for dents, distortion or contamination. Wipe the sealing surface with a clean cloth to remove any rust or dirt.
4. Check the fluid level and fill the system if necessary as described in the *Check/Fill Coolant* section in this chapter.
5. Check all cooling system hoses for damage or deterioration. Replace any hose that is questionable. Make sure all hose clamps are tight.
6. Check the heat exchanger (**Figure 25**) for cracks or damage. Service, if necessary, as described in Chapter Eight.

Check/fill coolant (not equipped with remote reservoir)

WARNING
*Do not remove the fill pressure cap (**Figure 24**) from the pressurized cooling system when the engine is hot.*

1. Loosen and remove the pressure fill cap (**Figure 24**).
2. Check the level of fluid in the system. It should be level with the iron plate at the bottom of the filler neck.

NOTE
Excess coolant (above proper level) will be expelled when coolant reaches operating temperature.

3. If the exhaust manifold is not properly filled, add coolant. Refer to the *Coolant* section in this chapter for proper coolant.

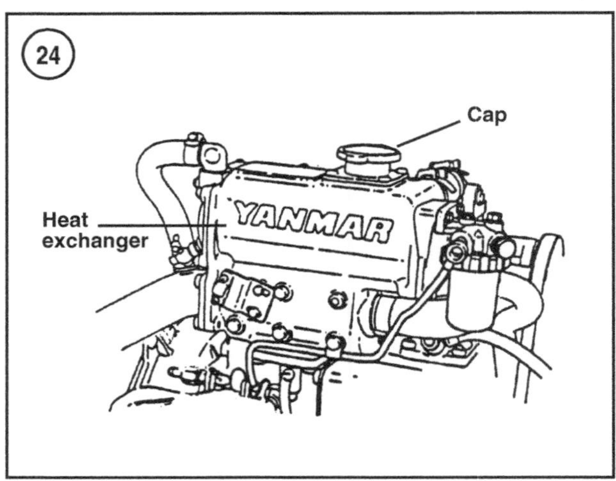

Check/Fill Coolant (Equipped With a Remote Reservoir)

Refer to **Figure 26**.

1. Check the level of the coolant in the remote reservoir tank (**Figure 26**) when the engine is cold. The coolant level should be between the marks on the tank.
2. If the coolant level is low, but the tank is not dry, add coolant to the tank. Refer to the following section for the proper coolant mixture.

WARNING
*Do not remove the pressure fill cap (**Figure 24**) from the pressurized cooling system when the engine is hot.*

3. If the coolant level is low, but the tank is dry, remove the pressure fill cap on the exhaust manifold (**Figure 24**). Add coolant to the exhaust manifold so it is full, replace the cap, then add coolant to the remote reservoir tank to the proper level.
4. Run the engine until it reaches normal operating temperature, then let the engine cool. Recheck the coolant level in the remote tank and, if necessary, refill the remote reservoir tank.

Coolant

Only use a high-quality ethylene glycol-based antifreeze designed for aluminum engines. Mix the antifreeze with water in a 50/50 ratio. Coolant capacity is listed in **Table 4**. When mixing antifreeze with water, use only soft or distilled water. Distilled water can be purchased at supermarkets in gallon containers. Do not use tap or salt water because it will damage engine parts.

25

FRESHWATER HEAT EXCHANGER (TYPICAL)

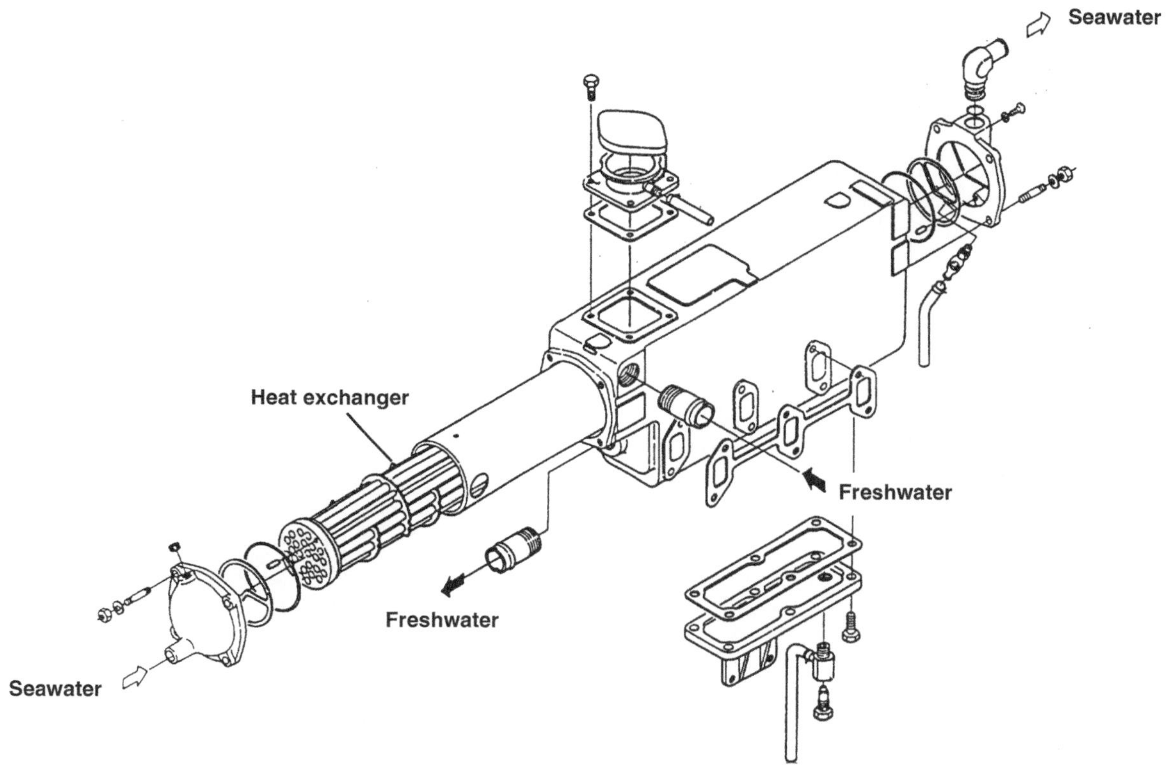

Seawater

Heat exchanger

Freshwater

Freshwater

Seawater

26

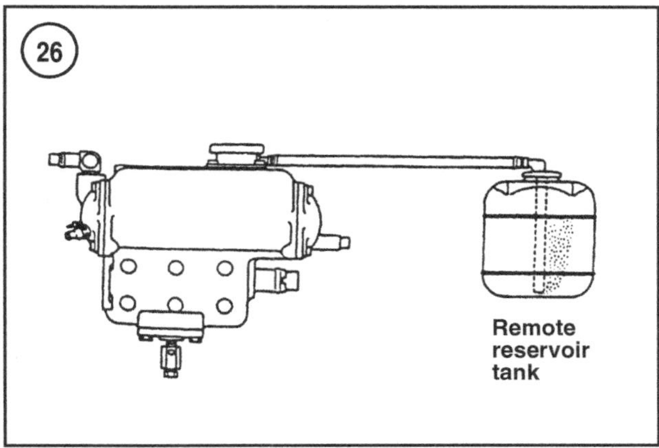

WARNING

Do not siphon coolant by mouth with a hose. The coolant mixture is poisonous and ingesting even a very small amount may cause illness. Observe warning labels on antifreeze containers. Make sure to discard used antifreeze in a safe and suitable manner and wipe up any spills. Do not store antifreeze in open containers. Keep antifreeze out of the reach of children and animals.

WARNING

The EPA has classified ethylene glycol as an environmental toxic waste. It is illegal to flush it down a drain or pour it on the ground. Put it in suitable containers and dispose of it according to local regulations.

CAUTION

Be careful not to spill antifreeze on painted surfaces, as it may damage the surface. Wash any spilled antifreeze immediately with soapy water, then rinse the area thoroughly with clean water.

Flushing and refilling freshwater coolant system

Use the following procedure to flush and refill the freshwater coolant system. Refer to the preceding section to flush the seawater portion of a freshwater coolant system.

Replace the coolant in the freshwater coolant system after every 500 hours of operation or annually, whichever occurs first.

CAUTION

Perform the following procedure when the engine is cold.

1. Remove the pressure fill cap (**Figure 24**).

NOTE

Position the drain hoses in suitable containers to catch coolant when draining the coolant from the exhaust manifold and engine.

2. Open the drain valve at the end of the heat exchanger (A, **Figure 27**) and the drain plug on the underside of the exhaust manifold (B).
3. Unscrew the drain plug on the side of the engine block (**Figure 28**, typical).
4. If an excessive accumulation of scale is apparent on the interior of the cooling system, use an automotive cooling system cleaner. Be sure to thoroughly flush out the cooling system with freshwater afterward.
5. Close the drain plug on the exhaust manifold and the drain plug on the engine block.

6A. Engines without a remote reservoir—Fill the exhaust manifold with coolant. The coolant should be level with the iron plate at the bottom of the filler neck.

6B. Engines with a remote reservoir—Pour coolant into the exhaust manifold so it is full. Install the pressure fill cap, then add coolant to the remote reservoir tank to the proper level.

7. Run the engine until it reaches normal operating temperature, then let the engine cool. Recheck the coolant level and, if necessary, add coolant.

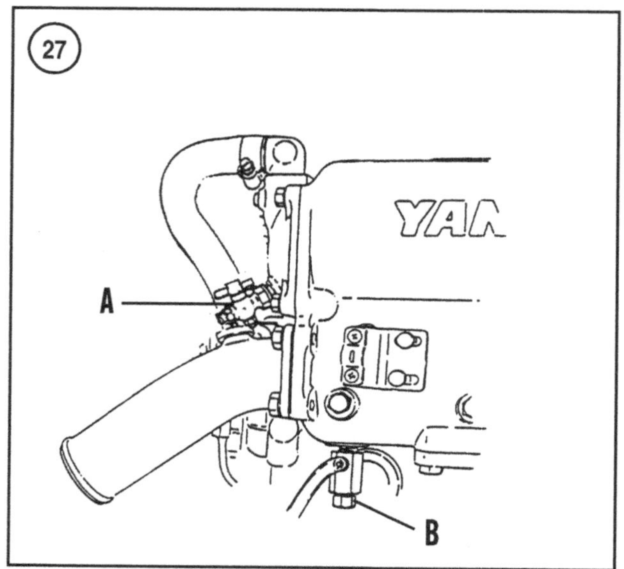

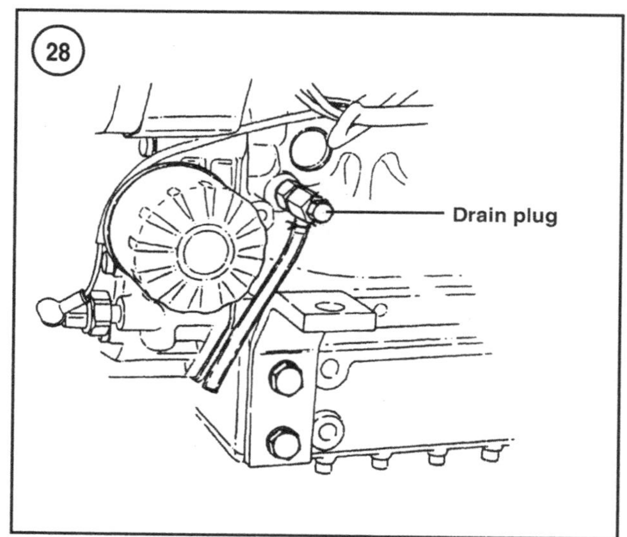

BATTERY

Inspect the electrical connections and make sure they are secure and corrosion-free. If corrosion is present at the terminal ends, detach the wires, clean the corrosion and reattach. Make sure that wires are correctly routed and will not contact moving parts or touch hot (especially exhaust) parts.

Remove the battery vent caps and check battery electrolyte level. It should be about 3/16 in. above the plates or even with the bottom of the filler wells. See **Figure 29**. Test the battery condition with a hydrometer (**Figure 30**). See Chapter Nine.

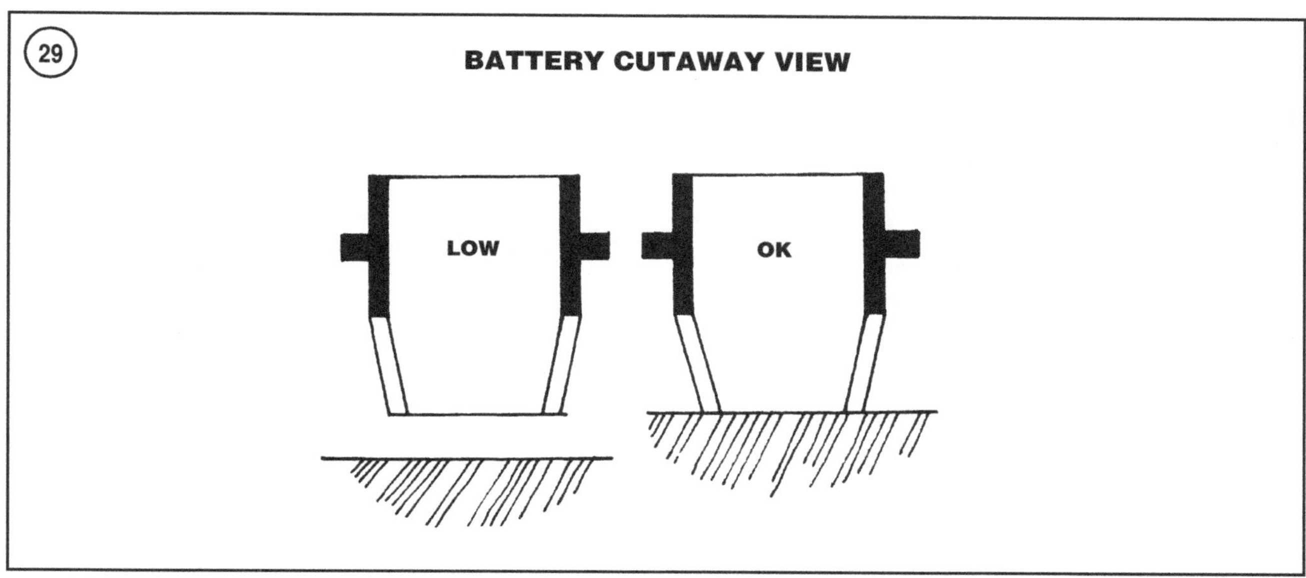

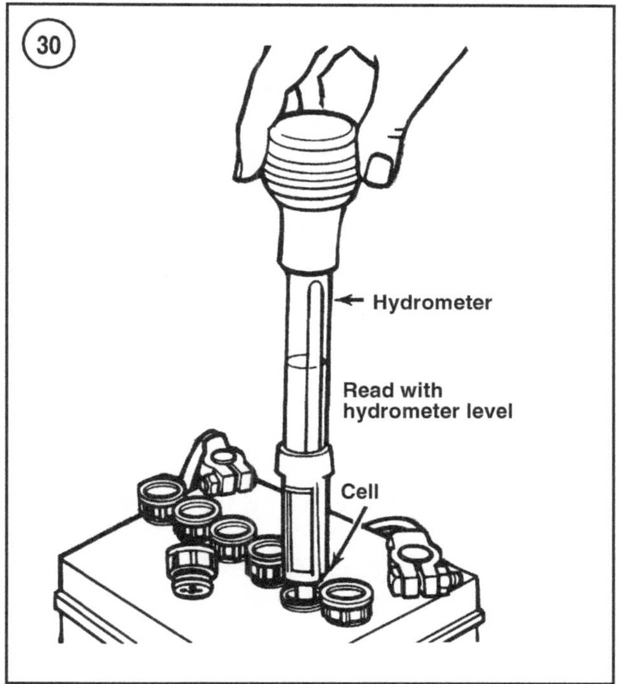

ENGINE TUNE-UP

A smooth-running, dependable marine engine is more than a convenience. At sea, it can be the difference between life and death. To keep the engine running right, follow a regular program of preventive maintenance.

Part of any preventive maintenance program is a thorough engine tune-up. A tune-up is a series of adjustments necessary to restore and maintain maximum power and performance.

Perform an engine tune-up as needed at periodic intervals to maintain maximum engine performance. If the engine is used infrequently, perform a tune-up at least once a season.

A tune-up consists of the following:

1. Compression test.
2. Valve adjustment.
3. Idle speed adjustment.

Careful and accurate adjustment is crucial to a successful engine tune-up. Each procedure in this section must be performed exactly as described and in the order presented.

NOTE

Some engine settings, such as maximum engine speed and torque level, are controlled by adjusting screws in the governor assembly. These adjusting screws are set by the manufacturer and secured by a lockwire to prevent unauthorized adjustment. Adjustment of these screws should be performed only by trained personnel. Detaching a lockwire may void the engine warranty. Improper adjustment can cause engine damage.

Compression Test

Check the compression of each cylinder as the first step in a tune-up. A compression test measures the compression pressure at the end of the compression stroke. Its results can be used to assess general cylinder and valve

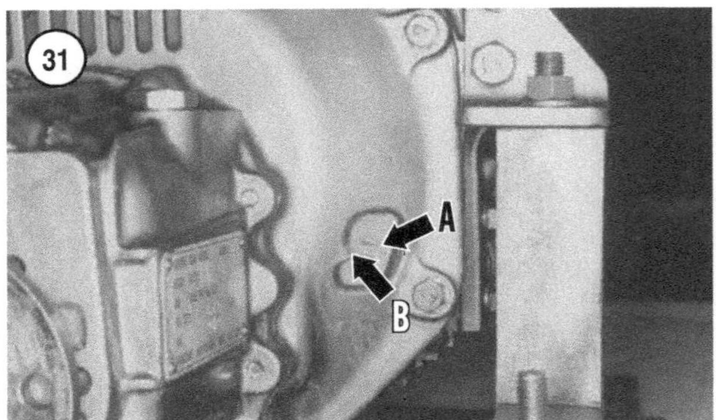

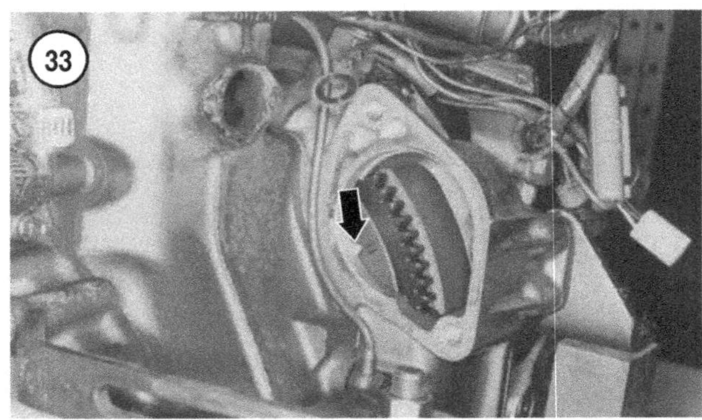

condition. In addition, it can warn of developing problems inside the engine. If more than a 43 psi. (300 kPa) difference exists between the highest and lowest reading cylinders on multicylinderengines, the engine cannot be tuned to develop its maximum power. Specified cylinder pressure is 390-470 psi (2700-3300 kPa).

A compression reading that is below the desired compression pressure indicates that engine repair is required because of worn or broken rings, leaky or sticking valves or a combination of all.

If the compression test readings are lower than desired, isolate the cause by performing a wet compression test. Remove the precombustion chamber (refer to Chapter Seven). Perform the wet compression test in the same way as the dry test, except pour approximately one tablespoon of heavy engine oil (at least SAE 30) into the injector hole before performing Steps 7-9. If the wet compression readings are significantly higher than the dry compression readings, the cause for the low dry compression reading is probably worn or broken rings. If there is little difference between the readings, the problem may be due to leaky or sticking valves or a faulty cylinder head gasket. If two adjacent cylinders on a multicylinderengine read low on both tests, the head gasket may be leaking between the cylinders.

Excessively high compression readings indicate carbon buildup in the cylinder.

NOTE
A special type compression gauge and adapter is required to measure the compression pressure in the cylinder. If the necessary compression test gauge is not available, have a diesel technician perform the test.

1. Be sure cooling water is connected to the engine.
2. Run the engine until it reaches normal operating temperature, then shut it off.

CAUTION
Be sure to remove all the injectors on a multicylinderengine to prevent inadvertent starting.

3. Remove the fuel injector(s) as described in Chapter Seven.
4. Clean the injector hole.
5. Rotate the engine to blow out any carbon.
6. Install the compression gauge and, if necessary, the adapter.
7. Crank the engine at least five turns or until there is no further increase in compression shown on the tester gauge.
8. Record the reading. Relieve the tester pressure valve and remove the compression tester.
9. Repeat Steps 4-8 for each remaining cylinder on multicylinderengines.

Valve Clearance Adjustment

Valve clearance is the gap between the end of the valve stem and the underside of the rocker arm. A specified valve clearance must be maintained for the valves to operate as designed. Insufficient valve clearance will cause

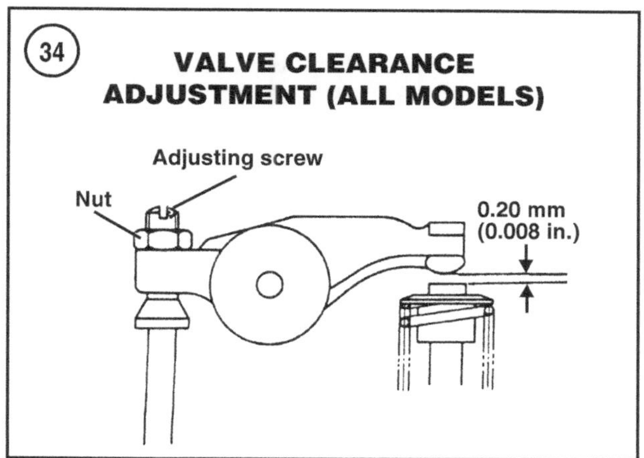

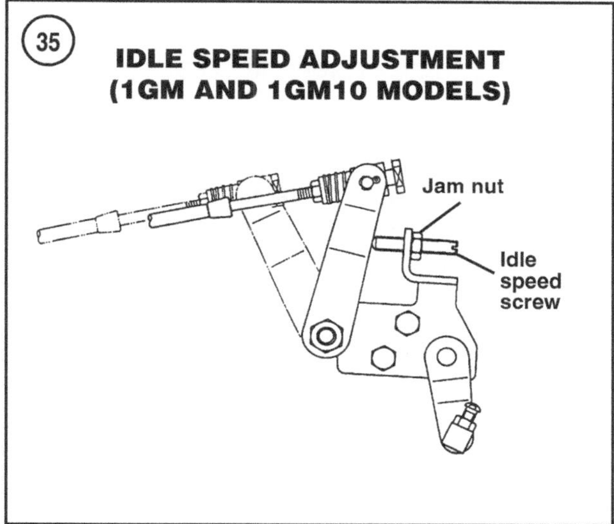

rough engine operation and possible engine damage, such as burnt valves. Excessive valve clearance will reduce engine performance. The recommended interval for valve adjustment is after every 300 hours of operation. However, it is a good practice to check the valve clearances during each tune-up.

The engine must be cold when adjusting valve clearance. On multicylinderengines, the cylinder nearest the flywheel is the number one cylinder.

1. Remove the rocker arm cover as described in Chapter Five or Six.
2. Observe the flywheel (A, **Figure 31**) through the opening in the clutch cover. A cylinder is at top dead center if the mark on the flywheel is aligned with the reference pointer (B) on the clutch cover.
3. Rotate the crankshaft with a wrench on the crankshaft pulley retaining nut (**Figure 32**).

CAUTION

Always rotate the crankshaft in the normal running direction (clockwise at crankshaft pulley); otherwise the water pump impeller will be damaged.

4. Rotate the crankshaft nut clockwise so the 1T mark on the flywheel aligns with the reference pointer (B, **Figure 31**) on the clutch cover. The piston must be on its compression stroke.

NOTE

*Some transmissions do not have an opening in the clutch cover. Remove the starter to view the timing marks on the flywheel (**Figure 33**).*

NOTE

When the piston is on its compression stroke and at top dead center, both valves will be closed. This can be determined by the position of the intake and exhaust rocker arms. Both should have free play, which indicates that the valves are closed.

5. Measure the clearance between the rocker arm and valve stem (**Figure 34**). Correct valve clearance is 0.2 mm (0.008 in.).
6. If the clearance is incorrect, loosen the locknut, then rotate the adjusting screw on the rocker arm (**Figure 34**). Hold the adjusting screw, then tighten the locknut. Recheck the valve clearance.

7A. 2GM and 2GM20 engines—Rotate the crankshaft 360° so the 2T mark on the flywheel aligns with the reference pointer (B, **Figure 31**) on the clutch cover. The piston for number 2 cylinder must be on its compression stroke (see preceding NOTE). Perform Steps 5 and 6.

7B. 3GM, 3GM30, 3HM and 3HM35 engines—Rotate the crankshaft 240° so the 3T mark on the flywheel aligns with the reference pointer (B, **Figure 31**) on the clutch cover. The piston for number 3 cylinder must be on its compression stroke (see preceding NOTE). Perform Steps 5 and 6.

8. Reinstall the rocker arm cover.

Idle Speed Adjustment

The correct idle speed is 825-875 rpm. Refer to the following procedure to adjust the idle speed.

1. Run the engine until it reaches normal operating temperature.
2. Place the transmission in neutral.
3. Loosen the jam nut on the idle speed screw (**Figure 35** or **Figure 36**).

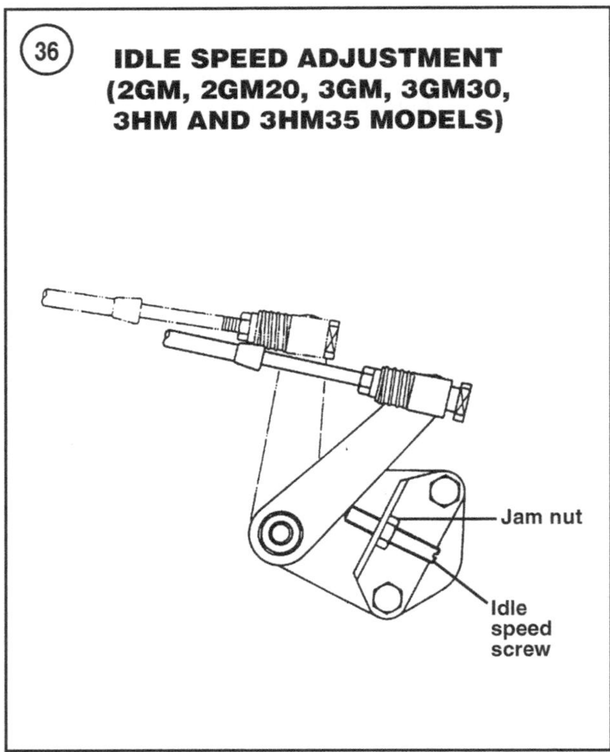

4. Adjust the idle speed screw until the engine idles at 825-875 rpm, then retighten the locknut.

5. On engines equipped with remote control, measure the gap between the cable end fitting (A, **Figure 37** or **Figure 38**) and lever fitting (B). The specified gap is 1-3 mm (0.04-0.12 in.). To adjust the gap, rotate the nut (C) on the cable.

TRANSMISSION

Transmission Oil

Transmission models KM2A, KM2C, KM2P, KM3A and KM3P

The recommended transmission oil is an engine oil that meets API classification CC. The recommended viscosity is SAE 10W-30. Change the transmission oil after every 250 hours of operation.

Transmission models KBW10D and KBW10E

The recommended transmission oil is automatic transmission oil (ATF). The oil must be classified a Dexron oil. Change the transmission oil after every 250 hours of operation.

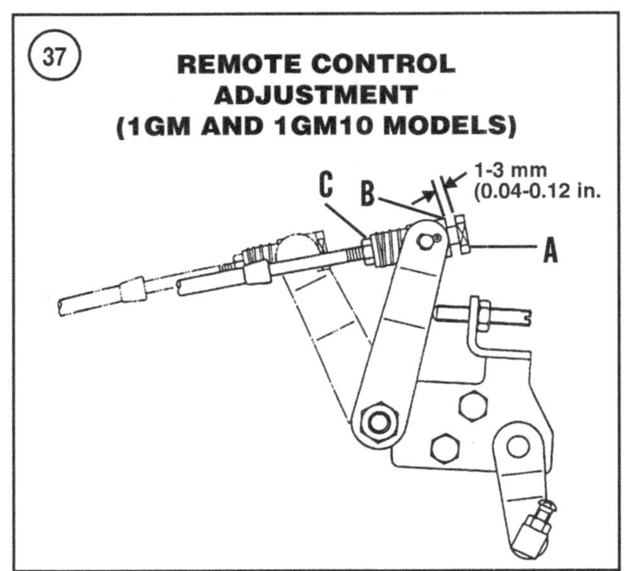

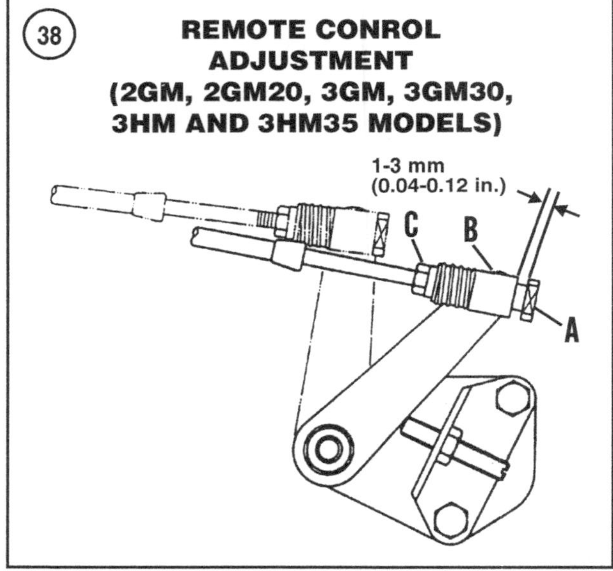

Transmission Oil Level Check

Check the transmission oil level on a weekly basis.

1. With the boat at rest in the water and the engine off, unscrew the dipstick (**Figure 39**, typical). Wipe it with a clean rag or paper towel. Reinsert the dipstick, but do not screw it in. Pull out the dipstick and read the oil level on the dipstick.

2. Add oil, if necessary, through the dipstick hole so the oil level reaches the full mark on the dipstick. Use the oil recommended in the preceding section.

Table 1 MAINTENANCE SCHEDULE

Daily	Check fuel level
	Check engine oil level
Weekly	Check battery
	Check air filter
	Check transmission oil level
	Check drive belt tension
	Check electrical wiring
Every 50 hours	Clean fuel filter
Every 100 hours	Change engine oil
	Drain fuel tank
Every 250 hours	Replace air filter element
	Replace fuel filter element
	Change transmission oil
Every 300 hours	Replace engine oil filter
	Adjust engine valves
Every 500 hours	Inspect thermostat
Every 1500 hours	Inspect seawater pump
Every 2000 hours	Replace thermostat
Annually	Replace freshwater (closed system) antifreeze

Table 2 ENGINE OIL VISCOSITY

Ambient Temperature	Oil viscosity
Below 50° F (10° C)	10W, 20W or 20/20W
50° - 68° F (1° - 20° C)	20 or 20/20W
68° - 95° F (20° - 35° C)	30 or 40
Above 95° F (35° C)	50

Table 3 ENGINE OIL CRANKCASE CAPACITY

Model	Oil capacity
1GM, 1GM10	1.4 qt. (1.3 L)
2GM, 2GM20	2.1 qt. (2.0 L)
3GM, 3GM30	2.8 qt. (2.6 L)
3HM, 3HM35	5.7 qt. (5.4 L)

Table 4 FRESHWATER (CLOSED) COOLING SYSTEM CAPACITY

Model	Capacity
2GM20F	2.9 L (0.77 gal.)
3GM30F	3.4 L (0.9 gal.)
3HM35F	4.9 L (1.3 gal.)

Table 5 TUNE-UP SPECIFICATIONS

Model	Idle rpm (no-load)	Full throttle rpm (no-load)	Fuel injection timing	Valve clearance
1GM	850	3750	15° BTDC	0.2 m (0.008 in.)
1GM10	850	3825	15° BTDC	0.2 m (0.008 in.)
2GM	850	3750	15° BTDC	0.2 m (0.008 in.)
2GMF	850	3750	15° BTDC	0.2 m (0.008 in.)
2GM20	850	3825	15° BTDC	0.2 m (0.008 in.)
2GM20F	850	3825	15° BTDC	0.2 m (0.008 in.)
3GM	850	3750	18° BTDC	0.2 m (0.008 in.)
3GMF	850	3750	18° BTDC	0.2 m (0.008 in.)
3GMD	850	3750	18° BTDC	0.2 m (0.008 in.)
3GM30	850	3825	18° BTDC	0.2 m (0.008 in.)
3GM30F	850	3825	18° BTDC	0.2 m (0.008 in.)
3HM	850	3600	21° BTDC	0.2 m (0.008 in.)
3HMF	850	3600	21° BTDC	0.2 m (0.008 in.)
3HM35	850	3625	21° BTDC	0.2 m (0.008 in.)
3HM35F	850	3625	21° BTDC	0.2 m (0.008 in.)

Table 6 COMPRESSION SPECIFICATIONS

Pressure (all models)	Maximum difference between cylinders
390-470 psi (2700-3800 kPa)	43 psi (300 kPa)

Chapter Four

Lay-up and Fitting Out

LAY-UP

Boats that are stored for more than a month require careful preparation for the lay-up. This is necessary to prevent the engine from freezing. A thorough service will also minimize damage from corrosion or fuel system contamination. Begin the service, if possible, while the boat is still in the water.

If the boat has been removed from the water, a supply of cooling water must be made available to the engine. This can be accomplished using a water hose attached to the water pump inlet. Always start the water flow before starting the engine.

CAUTION
Some of the following steps require water for the cooling system. The boat must be in the water, or a source of water must be connected to the seawater cooling pump.

NOTE
Except where specified, F and D series engines are included when a basic model number is specified. For example, if model 3GM is called out in a procedure, the procedure also applies to 3GMD and 3GMF.

1. Run the engine until it reaches normal operating temperature.
2. Change the engine oil and filter as described in Chapter Three.
3. Use a suitable engine fogging oil as instructed by the oil manufacturer.
4. Thoroughly inspect the engine, including the cooling and fuel systems. Perform service work that will protect against damage during extended storage, such as replacing hoses and gaskets. Make a list of problems that should be corrected before the boat is returned to service.
5. If the engine is equipped with freshwater cooling, flush and change the freshwater coolant as described in Chapter Three.
6. Drain the seawater cooling system as described in this chapter. Be sure to drain or blow out all portions of the system.

NOTE
In some instances, such as to prevent rust formation, it may be desirable to fill the seawater cooling system with an antifreeze solution. Refer to the following section in this chapter.

7. If the seawater cooling system was drained, remove the seawater pump impeller as described in Chapter Eight. Lubricate the impeller with dishwashing soap, then install the impeller in the pump housing. Assemble the pump, but do not tighten the cover retaining screws.

NOTE
Make a highly visible sign as a reminder that the seawater pump is inoperable. Attach the sign to the controls.

8. Apply lubricant to the control cables and all linkage pivot points.
9. Loosen belt tension for the pump and alternator drive belts.
10. Seal or cover all engine openings to prevent the entrance of water, dirt or debris. Make a list of all the sealed locations to be sure they are all uncovered when returning the engine to service.
11. Wipe any dirt or corrosion off the engine and transmission, then use a rag to apply oil or a rust inhibitor to all engine surfaces.
12. Fill the fuel tank so less condensation will form. Add a good-quality antibacterial additive (biocide) and fuel stabilizer to the fuel tank.
13. Remove the battery from the boat. Tape the vent holes closed and clean the battery case with a baking soda solution to remove any traces of corrosion and acid, then rinse with cold water. Check the electrolyte level in each cell and top off with distilled water as required. Cover the terminals with a light coat of petroleum jelly. Store the battery in a cool, dry place.

NOTE
Remove the battery from storage every 30-45 days. Check electrolyte level and slow-charge for five or six hours at 6 amperes.

COOLING SYSTEM DRAINING

The engine seawater cooling system must be properly drained for storage during the winter months in areas where temperatures fall below 32° F (0° C). If it is not, the engine block or cooling system may be cracked by the expansion of frozen water.

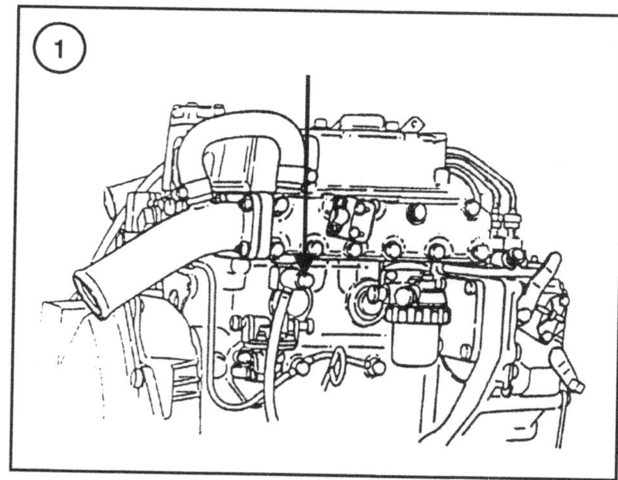

The following procedures are designed to help prevent unnecessary engine damage during winter storage.

To ensure that the cooling system is completely drained, it may be necessary to readjust the position of the engine to drain all water.

It is possible that some water will remain in the system. Filling it with an antifreeze solution will protect the seawater cooling system.

Seawater Cooling System

1. Place a suitable container under each drain, if space permits. This will prevent water from draining into the bilge.

NOTE
If no water flows from a drain, check the drain to make sure it is not obstructed or plugged.

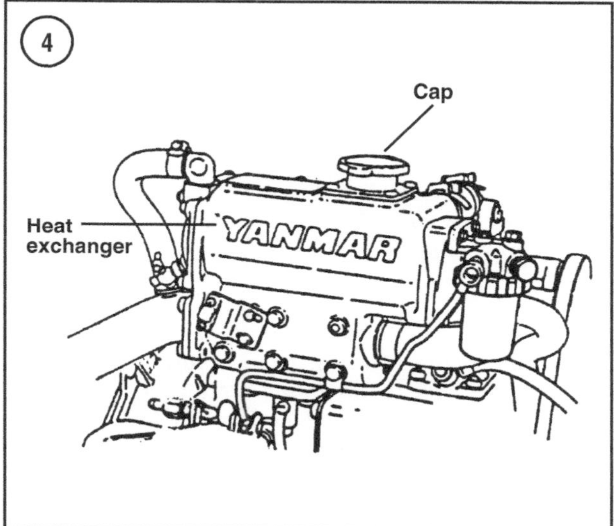

2. On 3GM, 3GM30, 3HM and 3HM35 engines, open the drain on the underside of the exhaust manifold (**Figure 1**, typical).

3. Open the drain on the cylinder block (**Figure 2**, typical).

4. Remove the lower end of all cooling system hoses from the engine, pump and exhaust manifold. Lower the hoses and allow them to completely drain. Reconnect the hoses and clamp securely.

NOTE
On 1GM and 1GM10 engines, access is restricted to the upper water pump cover screw. If a suitable tool is not available, it may be necessary to remove the crankshaft pulley for access to all of the water pump cover screws.

5. Loosen the cover screws on the seawater pump (**Figure 3**, typical) and drain any water in the pump. If the gasket is damaged, remove the cover and install a new gasket and the cover.
6. Allow the cooling system to drain completely, then close all drains.

Adding antifreeze

The following procedure pertains to seawater cooling systems and is designed to provide additional protection against damage due to freezing temperatures while the boat is in storage.

CAUTION
Do not run the engine after performing the storage service procedure that follows. Before returning the boat to service, drain the seawater cooling system as described in this chapter.

1. Refer to Chapter Eight to remove the thermostat and gasket. Discard the gasket.
2. Make sure the seacock or water inlet to the seawater pump is closed.
3. Pour a 50/50 solution of pure soft water and ethylene glycol antifreeze through the thermostat hole into the engine until the cylinder head, block and manifold are full.
4. Reinstall the thermostat with a new gasket.

Freshwater (Closed) Cooling System

The freshwater section of a cooling system need not be drained during winter months, provided it is filled with a 50/50 solution of pure soft water and ethylene glycol antifreeze. However, if draining the freshwater cooling system is necessary, use the following procedure.

Note that the following procedures address the freshwater and seawater sections of the cooling system separately. If the freshwater portion is not being drained, follow the draining procedure for the seawater section.

Freshwater (closed) cooling section

1. Place containers under the drains, if space permits. This will prevent coolant from draining into the bilge.
2. Remove the pressure fill cap from the heat exchanger (**Figure 4**).

WARNING
Ethylene glycol is an environmental toxic waste that cannot be legally flushed down a drain or poured on the ground. Put it in suit-

able containers and dispose of it according to local regulations. Make sure to wipe up any spills and cover any containers of antifreeze. Keep antifreeze out of the reach of children and animals.

3. Open the drain on the underside of the exhaust manifold (**Figure 1**).
4. Open the drain on the engine block (**Figure 2**, typical).
5. Allow the freshwater section to drain completely.
6. On models equipped with a remote reservoir, disconnect the hose to the engine and drain the coolant from the reservoir. Reconnect the hose.
7. Close the drain plugs.
8. If refilling the freshwater section, refer to Chapter Three for the filling procedure.

Seawater cooling section

Refer to the following procedure to drain the seawater section.

1. Place a suitable container under the drain, if space permits. This will prevent water from draining into the bilge.

NOTE

If no water flows from the drain, check the drain to make sure it is not obstructed or plugged.

2. Open the drain on the underside of the exhaust manifold end cap (**Figure 2**).
3. Allow the water to drain completely, then close the drain.
4. Loosen the cover screws on the seawater pump (**Figure 3**) and drain any water in the pump. If the gasket is damaged, remove the cover and install a new gasket and the cover.
5. Remove the lower end of the cooling system hoses from the pump and exhaust manifold. Lower the hoses and allow them to completely drain. Then reconnect the hoses and clamp securely.

NOTE

It is possible that undrained water may remain. Protect the seawater cooling section by filling it with an antifreeze solution.

FITTING OUT

Preparing the boat for use after storage is easier if the engine was properly prepared before storage. Refer to the list of needed work that was to be performed before returning the engine to service. If there is other work to be done, determine if the work is easier, and possibly more economical, if performed before returning the engine to service.

1. Remove all covers placed over engine openings during lay-up.
2. If the seawater cooling system is filled with an antifreeze solution, drain the antifreeze from the system using the draining procedure described for the seawater cooling system or the procedure for the seawater section if equipped with a freshwater (closed) cooling system.
3. If left loose during lay-up, tighten the seawater pump cover screws (**Figure 3**).
4. Adjust belt tension for the water pump and alternator drive belts as described in Chapter Three.
5. Replace all fuel filters.
6. If equipped with a fuel tank drain valve, open the drain valve and remove any water that may have accumulated in the tank.

WARNING

Be sure to have a Coast Guard-approved fire extinguisher on hand whenever working around fuel.

NOTE

If the fuel in the fuel tank is dirty, old or contaminated with water, drain or pump out the fuel. Clean the tank and refill with fresh, clean fuel. Although fuel filters will remove most contaminants, excessively dirty fuel may clog the filters or enter the engine, causing damage.

7. Bleed the fuel system as described in Chapter Seven.
8. Check the battery electrolyte level and fill if necessary. Make certain the battery has a full charge; recharge if necessary. Clean the battery terminals and install the battery, making sure the cables are connected properly. Cover the battery terminals with a light coat of petroleum jelly.
9. Check the crankcase oil level. Add oil, if necessary. If the oil was not changed at time of lay-up or if the engine has been in storage for an extended period of time, change the oil and oil filter.
10. Move the engine control to the STOP position. Position the decompression lever in the ON position. Engage the starter and crank the engine for 30 seconds. This procedure will pump engine oil to the engine bearings and other engine parts.
11. On engines equipped with a freshwater cooling system, check the coolant. If the coolant is contaminated or has reached its scheduled replacement time, drain, flush and refill the freshwater cooling system.

12. Thoroughly inspect the engine. Check for leakage, rust or corrosion that will affect engine operation. Check all hoses for deterioration and clamps for tightness.
13. Check all through-hull fittings.
14. Make sure water is available to the cooling system.
15. Operate all engine controls to be sure they operate properly and smoothly.
16. Start and run engine. Check for oil and water leaks. Check engine operation.
17. Tune-up engine as described in Chapter Three.

Chapter Five

Single-Cylinder Engines

This chapter covers the Yanmar 1GM and 1GM10 single-cylinder, diesel engines.

The engine consists of a cast-iron cylinder block, containing a full-length water jacket around the cylinder.

The crankshaft rotates counterclockwise as viewed from the flywheel. Two main bearings support the crankshaft, with the front bearing providing the thrust surfaces. The crankshaft gear drives the rotor-type oil pump located in the lower front of the engine block.

The camshaft is gear driven and located in the engine block above the crankshaft. One end of the camshaft is supported by a ball bearing (front), and the other rides directly in the block (rear). In addition to operating the valves, the camshaft operates the fuel transfer pump and has an actuating lobe for the injection pump attached at the front.

Valve actuation is via mechanical lifters and pushrods acting on the rocker arms mounted in the cylinder head.

Engine specifications (**Table 1**) and tightening torques (**Table 2**) are located at the end of this chapter.

DIESEL ENGINE FUNDAMENTALS

Diesel engines are compression ignition engines, as opposed to gasoline engines, which are identified as spark ignition engines. The intake, compression, ignition, expansion and exhaust cycle occur in the same sequence for compression ignition engines as for spark ignition engines. The major differences are how the fuel is introduced into the combustion chamber and how the ignition is accomplished.

The principle of operation for compression ignition engines is to compress air in the cylinder without fuel; as the pressure increases, so does the temperature. The temperature of the compressed air is sufficient to ignite the diesel fuel injected into the cylinder. To achieve the required high-compression pressure/temperature, diesel engines have compression ratios between 16:1 and 22:1. These high compression ratios raise the cylinder air temperature to approximately 1000° F. Diesel fuel will ignite at approximately 750° F. Therefore, diesel fuel injected into the cylinder will immediately begin to burn.

A high-pressure fuel delivery system is necessary to inject fuel into the cylinder. The injector pressure must be higher than air pressure in the cylinder, and the fuel must be forced through the small openings in the fuel injector to properly atomize the fuel. Refer to Chapter Seven for fuel and governor system operation.

Refer to **Figure 1**. During the intake stroke, air is drawn into the cylinder.

During the compression stroke, the air is compressed to raise its temperature. The seal between the piston and the

①

4-STROKE DIESEL ENGINE PRINCIPLES

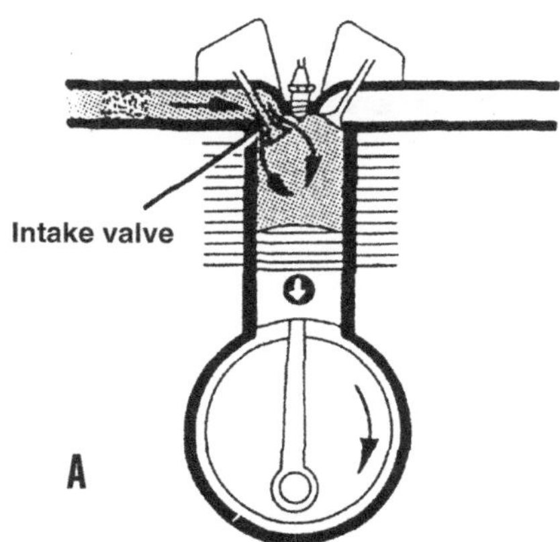

As the piston travels downward, the exhaust valve closes and the intake valve opens, allowing air to be drawn into the cylinder. When the piston reaches the bottom of its travel (BDC), the intake valve closes and remains closed for the next 1 1/2 revolutions of the crankshaft.

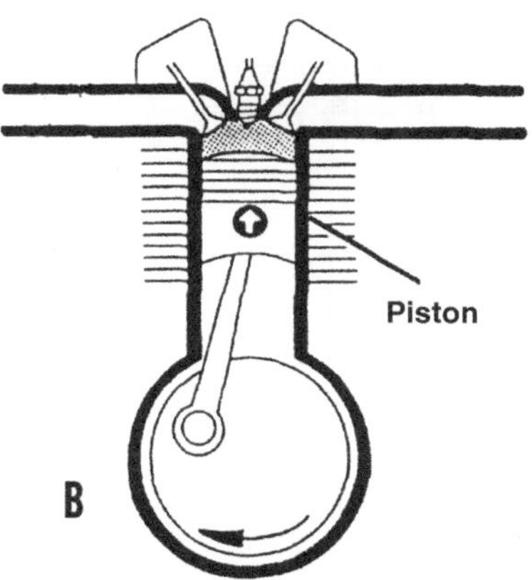

When the crankshaft continues to rotate, the piston moves upward, compressing the air.

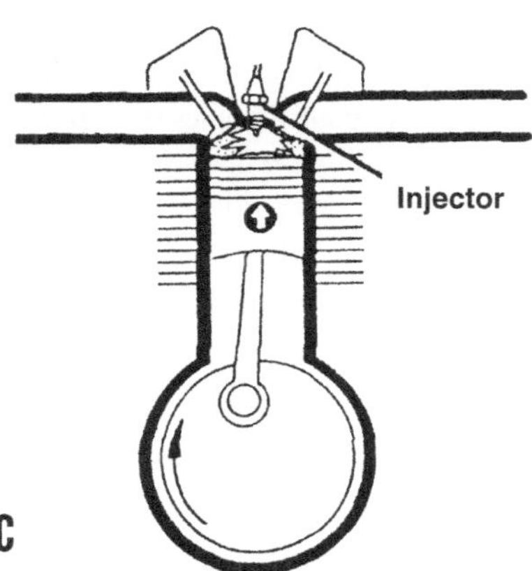

As the piston almost reaches the top of its travel, the injector sprays fuel into the combustion chamber. The fuel is ignited by the heat of compression. The piston continues to top dead center (TDC) and is pushed downward by the expanding gases.

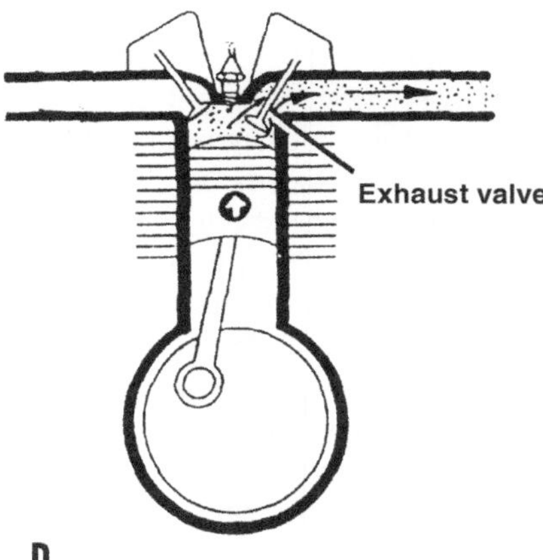

When the piston almost reaches BDC, the exhaust valve opens and remains open until the piston is near TDC. The upward travel of the piston forces the exhaust gases out of the cylinder. After the piston has reached TDC, the exhaust valve closes and the cycle repeats.

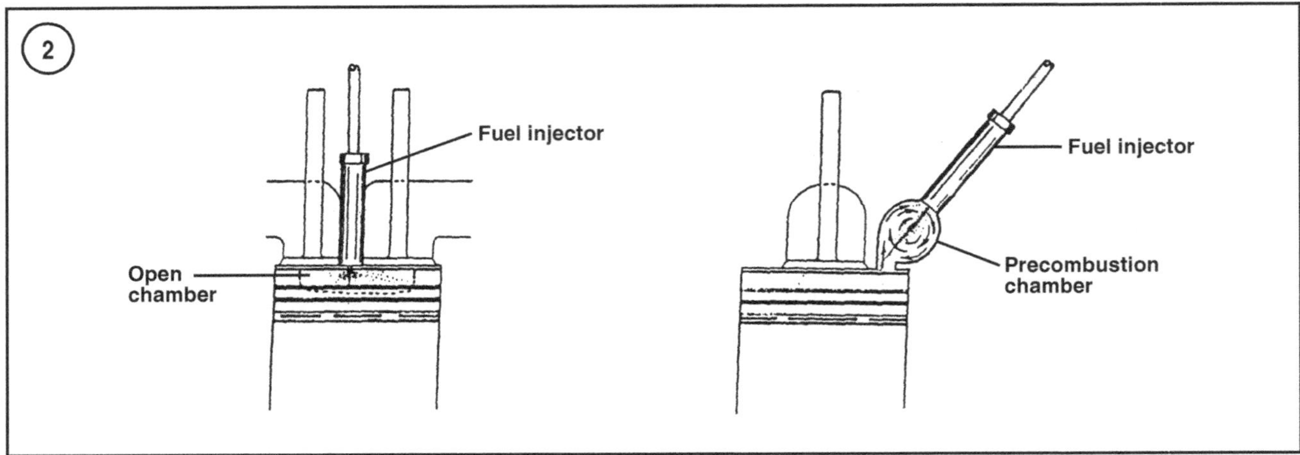

cylinder must not permit compression leakage, which could lower the temperature of the compressed air. Also, the cylinder must not contain fuel that could ignite prematurely during compression.

Near the end of the compression stroke, fuel is injected into the cylinder and ignited by compressed air. Fuel injection continues during several degrees of crankshaft rotation, depending upon desired speed and load. Expansion of the air caused by the burning fuel pushes the piston down on the expansion (power) stroke.

The exhaust valve opens just before the piston reaches the bottom of travel. The exhaust valve remains open as the piston moves upward pushing burned (exhausted) gasses from the cylinder.

Different combustion chamber designs may be used on diesel engines to accomodate specific engine operating criteria. An open combustion chamber (direct injection) design is illustrated in **Figure 2**. The fuel and air are confined to one area. Usually the piston crown is concave to form the combustion chamber and provide turbulence required for mixing the fuel with the compressed air. The shape of the combustion chamber and the shape of the injection spray pattern are matched so that fuel will be distributed evenly throughout the chamber.

The Yanmar engines covered in this manual are equipped with a precombustion chamber for each cylinder (**Figure 2**). The precombustion chamber increases combustion efficiency, which produces greater power with reduced emmissions. Combustion first occurs in the precombustion chamber when hot, compressed air enters the precombustion chamber just as fuel is injected. Combustion continues as the fuel and air are mixed and forced from the precombustion chamber into the engine cylinder. Additional mixing and ignition are completed in the cylinder.

ENGINE SERIAL NUMBER AND CODE

The engine serial number and model designation are located on a plate attached to the rocker cover (**Figure 3**). The engine serial number is also stamped on the side of the cylinder block (**Figure 4**).

Have the engine model number and serial number available when ordering parts. Record the engine model and serial numbers and store them for future reference in case the identification plate on the engine is defaced or lost.

REPLACEMENT PARTS

When installing new parts on the engine, make sure the part is designed for use on a marine engine. Automotive and marine engine parts may look similar; however, automotive parts may not be capable of operating in a harsh marine environment.

Use only Yanmar parts or parts approved for use on marine engines.

ENGINE REMOVAL PRECAUTIONS

Some service procedures can be performed with the engine in the boat; others require removal. The boat design and service procedure to be performed determines whether the engine must be removed.

WARNING
The engine is heavy, awkward to handle and has sharp edges. It may shift or drop suddenly during removal. To prevent serious injury, always observe the following precautions.

1. Never place any part of your body where a moving or falling engine may trap, cut or crush you.
2. If you must push the engine during removal, use a board or similar tool to keep your hands out of danger.
3. Make sure the hoist is designed to lift engines and has enough load capacity for your engine.
4. Make sure the hoist is securely attached to safe lifting points on the engine.
5. The engine should not be difficult to lift with a proper hoist. If it is, stop lifting, lower the engine back onto its mounts and make sure the engine has been completely separated from the vessel.

Removal/Installation

While specific procedures cannot address all engine installations, refer to the following general instructions when removing the engine.

1. Disconnect the negative battery cable.
2. Close the seacock and drain the cooling system as described in Chapter Four.
3. Disconnect the intake water hose from the seawater cooling pump.
4. Close the fuel shutoff valve and disconnect the fuel line and the fuel return line.
5. Disconnect the remote control cables.
6. Disconnect the electrical wiring harness connectors.
7. Disconnect the electrical wires from the electric starter motor and solenoid that will interfere with engine removal.
8. Detach the exhaust system.
9. Detach the driveshaft from the transmission output flange. 5
10. Remove the engine retaining bolts.
11. Remove the engine and transmission.
12. Remove the transmission from the engine as described in Chapter Ten.
13. Engine installation is the reverse of removal, plus the following:
    a. Tighten the engine mounting bolts securely.
    b. Securely tighten the output flange-to-driveshaft bolts.
    c. Bleed the fuel system at the fuel filter as described under Fuel Filter in Chapter Three.

VALVE COVER

Refer to **Figure 5**.

To remove the valve cover, proceed as follows:

1. Make sure the decompression lever is in the OFF position.
2. Unscrew the retaining nut (**Figure 6**).
3. Remove the valve cover.
4. Remove the gasket.
5. Clean the gasket surfaces on the valve cover and cylinder head.
6. Reverse the removal steps to install the valve cover. Be sure to install the breather pipe (19, **Figure 5**).

BREATHER ASSEMBLY

A reed-type breather is located in the valve cover. Refer to Chapter Three for a description of breather operation.

To service the reed portion of the breather, remove the breather cover (**Figure 7**). The reed (**Figure 8**) should lie flat. Replace the reed if it is split, cracked or otherwise damaged.

Check the oil return hole (**Figure 9**) inside the breather chamber in the valve cover. If the hole is obstructed, remove the valve cover and clean out the hole.

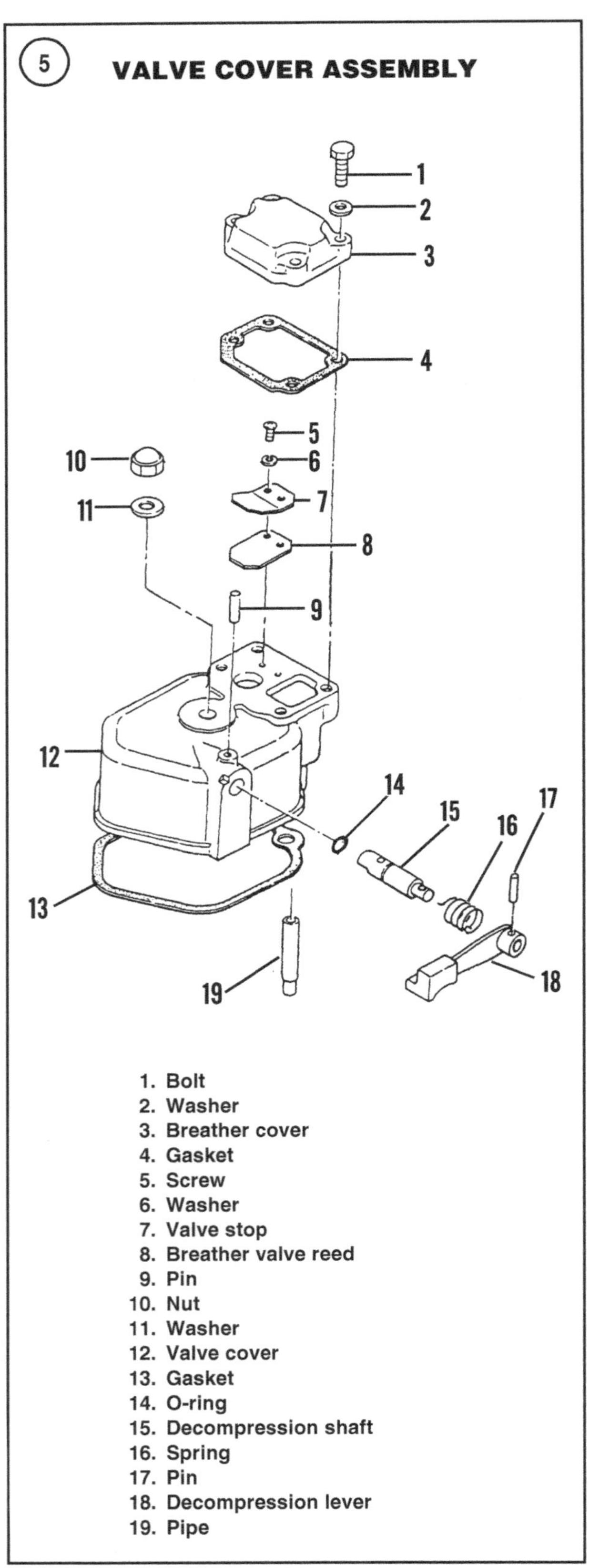
5
VALVE COVER ASSEMBLY
1
2
3
4
5
6
7
8
9
10
11
12
13
14
15
16
17
18
19
1. Bolt
2. Washer
3. Breather cover
4. Gasket
5. Screw
6. Washer
7. Valve stop
8. Breather valve reed
9. Pin
10. Nut
11. Washer
12. Valve cover
13. Gasket
14. O-ring
15. Decompression shaft
16. Spring
17. Pin
18. Decompression lever
19. Pipe

6

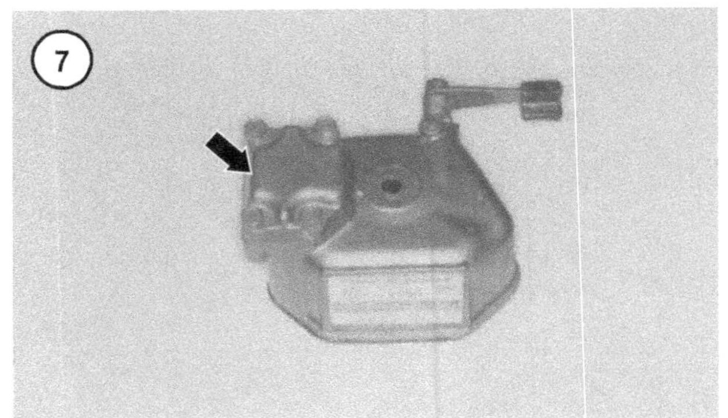
7

8

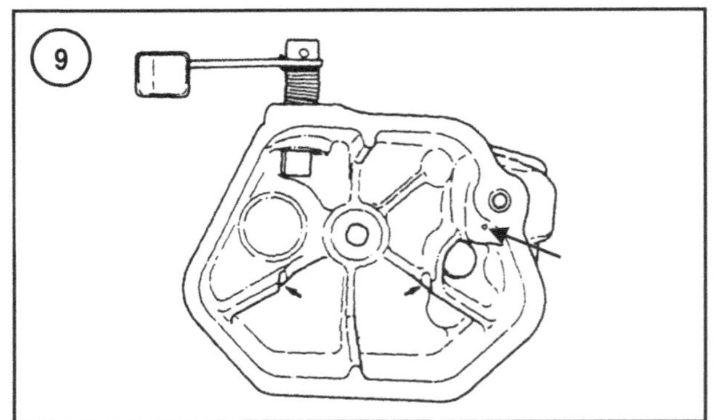
9

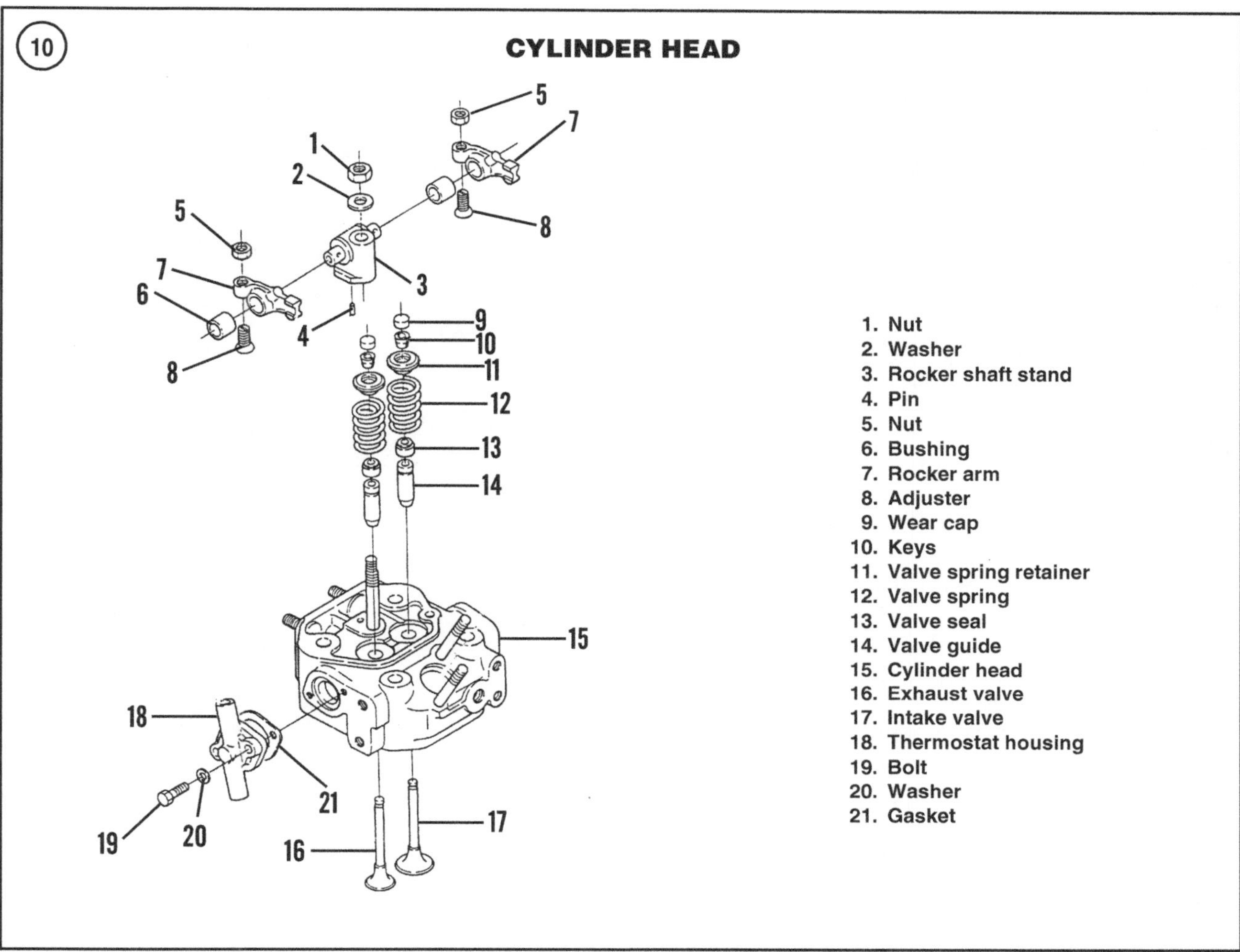

DECOMPRESSION MECHANISM

The decompression mechanism on the valve cover forces the exhaust valve open to reduce compression pressure in the cylinder. Reducing compression pressure enables the starter to rotate the crankshaft faster during starting.

If the mechanism must be repaired, proceed as follows:

1. Remove the valve cover as previously described.

NOTE
*The lever retaining pin (17, **Figure 5**) is tapered. Drive the pin out toward top of lever.*

2. Using a suitable punch, drive out the retaining pin.
3. Remove the shaft assembly from the valve cover.
4. Inspect the mechanism and replace any damaged parts.
5. Reverse the removal procedure to reassemble the decompression mechanism. Note the following:
   a. The straight end of the spring must sit behind the lug on the valve cover. Position the hooked spring end on top of the lever.
   b. The shaft and lever must be properly assembled or the taper pin and tapered holes in the shaft and lever will not align. The cutout portion of the shaft must be down when the lever points toward the pulley end of the engine.

CYLINDER HEAD

Removal

In some instances, it may be possible to remove the cylinder head for service without removing the engine. If engine removal is necessary, refer to the previous engine removal procedure. Refer to **Figure 10** for an exploded view of the cylinder head assembly.

To remove the cylinder head, proceed as follows:

1. Disconnect the negative battery cable.
2. If not previously performed, drain the cooling system as described in Chapter Four.
3. Remove the alternator as described in Chapter Nine.
4. If not previously disconnected, detach the exhaust hose from the exhaust elbow.
5. Loosen the hose clamps and remove the water hose (A, **Figure 11**) from the exhaust elbow and thermostat housing.
6. Remove the exhaust elbow.
7. Disconnect the lower water hose (B, **Figure 11**) from the thermostat housing.
8. Disconnect the wire lead from the water temperature sender (**Figure 12**).
9. Remove the air cleaner and the air cleaner base (**Figure 13**).
10. Remove the fuel injector and precombustion chamber as described in Chapter Seven.
11. Remove the valve cover as previously described.
12. Remove the rocker arm stand retaining nut (A, **Figure 14**), then remove the rocker assembly (B).
13. Remove the push rods (**Figure 15**) and mark them so they can be reinstalled in their original positions.
14. Detach the oil line fitting (**Figure 16**) from the cylinder head.
15. Unscrew the cylinder head retaining nuts (**Figure 17**) in a crossing pattern.
16. Remove the cylinder head and head gasket.

Inspection

1. If service to the valves or rocker arm assembly is required, refer to the *Valves* and *Rocker Shaft Assembly* sections.

16

17

18

2. Check the cylinder head for signs of oil or water leakage before cleaning. Look for corrosion or foreign material in the oil and water passages.

3. Without removing the valves, remove all deposits from the combustion chamber. Use a fine wire brush dipped in solvent or make a scraper from hardwood. Be careful not to scratch or gouge the combustion chamber.

4. After all carbon is removed from the combustion chamber and ports, clean the entire head in solvent. Look for cracks or other visible signs of damage. Clean the passages with a stiff spiral brush, then blow the particles out with compressed air.

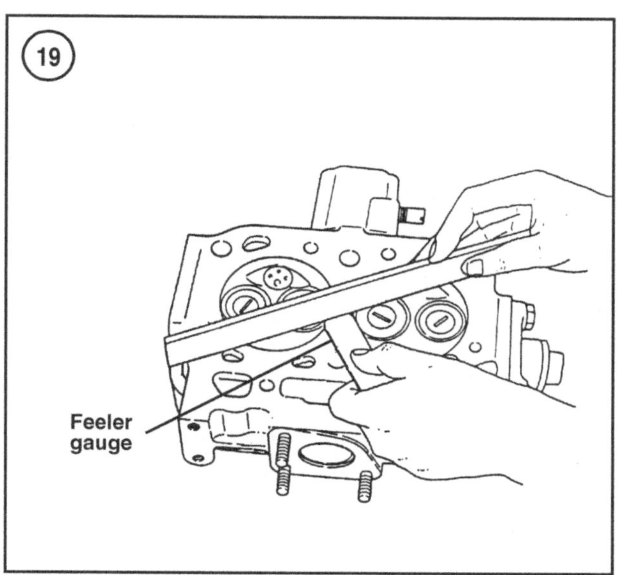

19

NOTE
If deposits are found in the intake or exhaust port, remove the valves and clean the ports.

5. Clean all carbon off the piston top.

6. Check the cylinder head studs for damage and replace them if necessary. If a stud is loose, tighten it using the following procedure:

   a. Install two nuts on the stud as shown in **Figure 18**.
   b. Rotate the nuts so they contact each other, then hold one nut and tighten the other nut against the first nut.
   c. Tighten the stud in the cylinder block by turning the top nut until reaching a torque of 60 N•m (44 ft.-lb.).
   d. Hold the bottom nut, loosen the top nut, and remove both nuts.

7. Check the threaded rocker arm support stud for damaged threads. Replace it if necessary.

8. Check for warpage of the cylinder head-to-block gasket surface with a straightedge and feeler gauge (**Figure 19**). Measure diagonally, as well as end to end. If the gap exceeds 0.07 mm (0.003 in.), have the head resurfaced by a machine shop.

Installation

1. Make sure the cylinder head and block gasket surfaces are clean.

5

2. Recheck all oil and water passages for cleanliness.
3. Apply Three Bond 50 gasket sealer to both sides of a new cylinder head gasket.
4. Place the new head gasket over the cylinder head studs on the block. Make sure the TOP mark (**Figure 20**) on the gasket is up.
5. Carefully lower the head onto the cylinder block.
6. Apply engine oil to the threads on the cylinder head studs.
7. Install and tighten the cylinder head retaining nuts finger-tight.
8. Tighten the nuts following the sequence shown in **Figure 21** to a torque of 75 N•m (55 ft.-lb.). Tighten the nuts in three equal steps until reaching the final torque setting.
9. Attach the oil line fitting (**Figure 16**) to the cylinder head.
10. Install the push rods (**Figure 15**) in their original positions.
11. Install the rocker assembly (B, **Figure 14**) and the rocker arm stand retaining nut (A). Tighten the nut to 37 N•m (27 ft.-lb.).
12. Install the fuel injector and precombustion chamber as described in Chapter Seven.
13. Install the air cleaner base (**Figure 13**) and the air cleaner.
14. Connect the wire lead to the water temperature sender (**Figure 12**).
15. Connect the lower water hose (B, **Figure 11**) to the thermostat housing.
16. Install the exhaust elbow.
17. Install the alternator.
18. If the engine is installed in the boat, proceed as follows:
    a. Attach the water hose (A, **Figure 11**) to the exhaust elbow and thermostat housing, then tighten the hose clamps.
    b. Attach the exhaust hose to the exhaust elbow.
    c. Connect the negative battery cable to the negative battery terminal.
19. Adjust the valve clearance as described in Chapter Three.
20. Reinstall the valve cover.

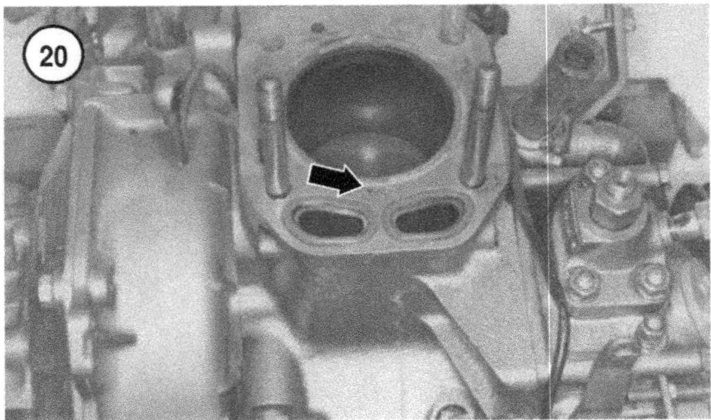

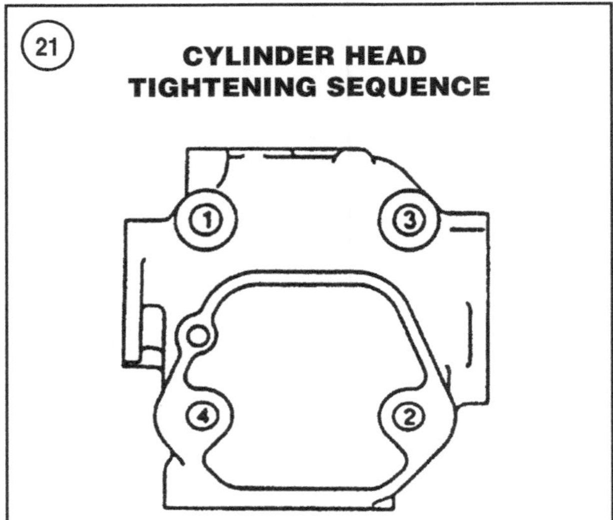

ROCKER SHAFT ASSEMBLY

Each valve is actuated by a rocker arm that rides on a shaft (**Figure 22**). Each rocker arm is equipped with a bushing in the rocker arm bore. Ribs in the valve cover retain the rocker arms on the rocker shafts.

1. Remove the valve cover as previously described.
2. Remove the rocker arm stand retaining nut (A, **Figure 14**), then remove the rocker assembly (B).
3. Inspect the rocker arm. The pad on the rocker arm that contacts the valve stem must be smooth. Replace the rocker arm if the pad is damaged or excessively worn. Check the adjusting screw push rod seat for galling. Replace the adjusting screw if it is damaged or excessively worn.
4. Inspect and measure the inside diameter of the rocker arm bushing and the outside diameter of the rocker arm shaft. Replace the rocker arm or rocker arm shaft stand if the measurements exceed the specifications in **Table 1**.

NOTE
The rocker arm and bushing are available only as a unit assembly.

5. Reassemble and reinstall the rocker arm assembly by reversing the removal procedure. Adjust valve clearance as described in Chapter Three.

22

VALVE COMPONENTS

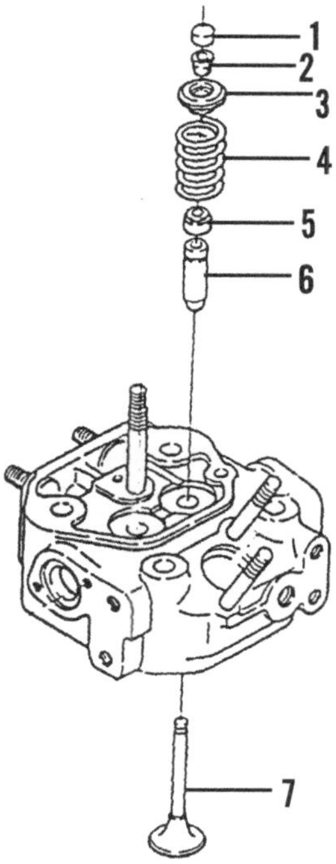

1 2 3 4 5 6 7

1. Wear cap
2. Keys
3. Valve spring retainer
4. Valve spring
5. Valve seal
6. Valve guide
7. Valve

23

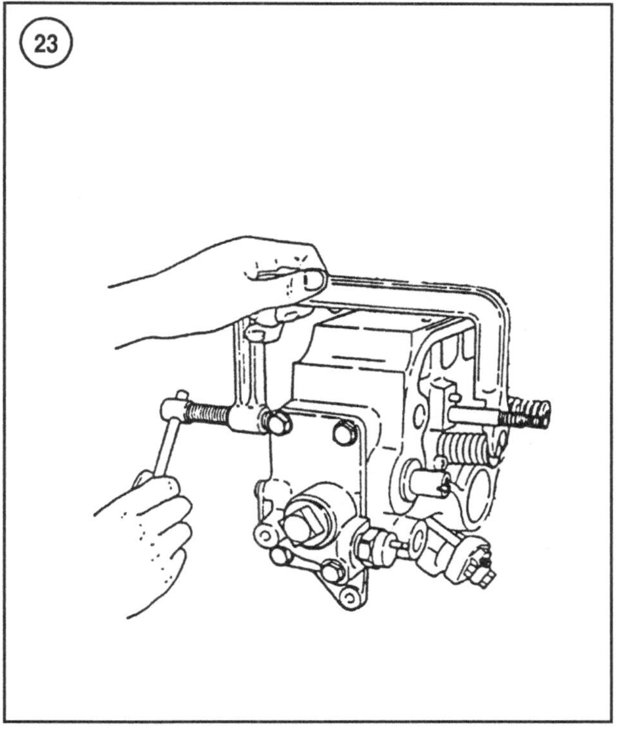

VALVES AND VALVE SEATS

Servicing the valves, guides and valve seats must be done by a dealer or machine shop, as special knowledge and expensive machine tools are required.

A general practice among those who do their own service is to remove the cylinder head, perform all disassembly except valve removal and take the head to a dealer or machine shop for inspection and service. Since the cost is low relative to the required effort and equipment, this is usually the best approach, even for experienced mechanics. The following procedures are provided to acquaint the home mechanic with the procedure.

Valve Removal

Refer to **Figure 22**.

1. Remove the cylinder head as described in this chapter.
2. Remove the rocker shaft assembly as described in this chapter.
3. Remove the wear cap (1, **Figure 22**) on the valve stem.
4. Compress the valve spring with a compressor like the one shown in **Figure 23**.

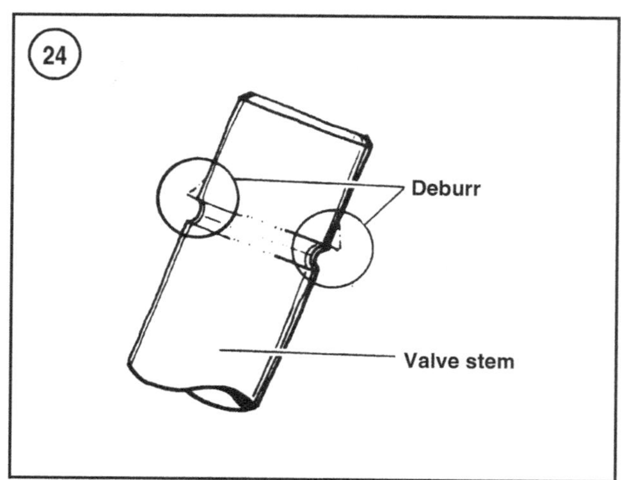

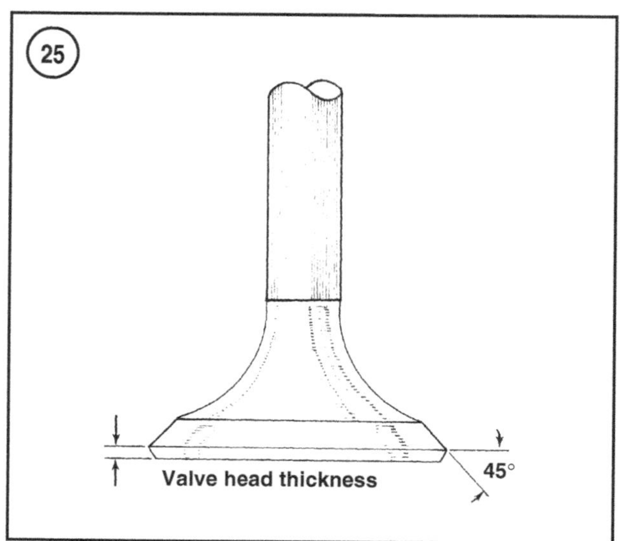

5. Remove the valve keys (2, **Figure 22**) and release the spring tension.
6. Remove the valve spring retainer and valve spring.

CAUTION
*Remove any burrs from the valve stem lock grooves (**Figure 24**) before removing the valve to prevent damage to the valve guide.*

7. Remove the valve.
8. Remove and discard the valve stem seal (5, **Figure 22**).
9. Repeat Steps 3-8 for the remaining valve.

Inspection

1. Clean the valves with a fine wire brush or buffing wheel. Discard any cracked, warped or burned valves.
2. Measure the valve stems at the top, center and bottom for wear. A machine shop can do this when the valves are ground.

NOTE
*Check the thickness of the valve edge or margin after the valves have been ground. See **Figure 25**. Any valve with a margin less than 0.75 mm (0.030 in.) should be discarded.*

3. Remove all carbon and varnish from the valve guides with a stiff spiral wire brush.

NOTE
The next step assumes that all valve stems have been measured and are within specifications. Replace valves with worn stems before performing this step.

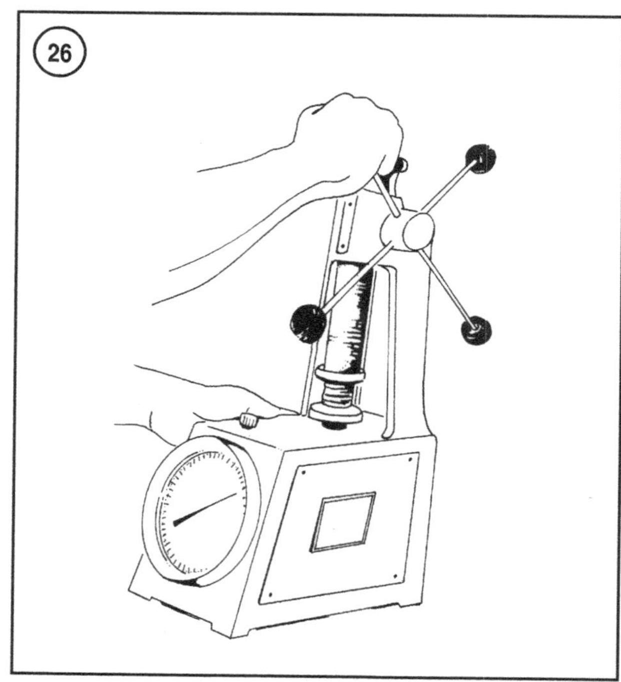

4. Insert each valve into the guide from which it was removed. Holding the valve just slightly off its seat, rock it back and forth in a direction parallel with the rocker arms. This is the direction in which the greatest wear normally occurs. If the valve stem rocks more than slightly, the valve guide is probably worn.
5. If there is any doubt about valve guide condition after performing Step 4, measure the valve guide. Compare the results with specifications in **Table 1**. Worn guides must be replaced.

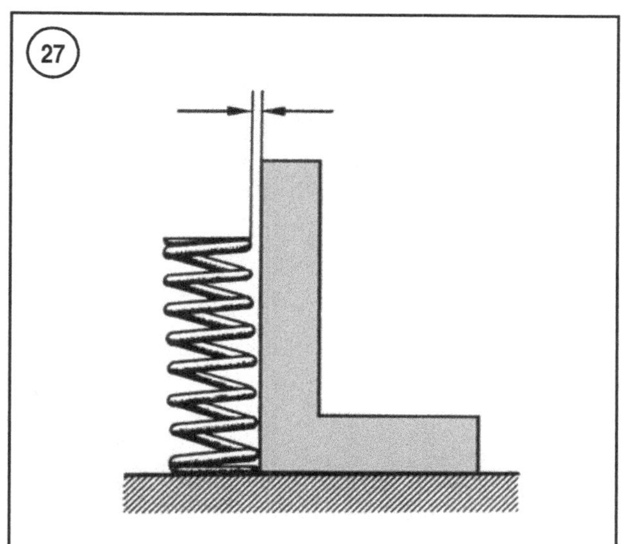

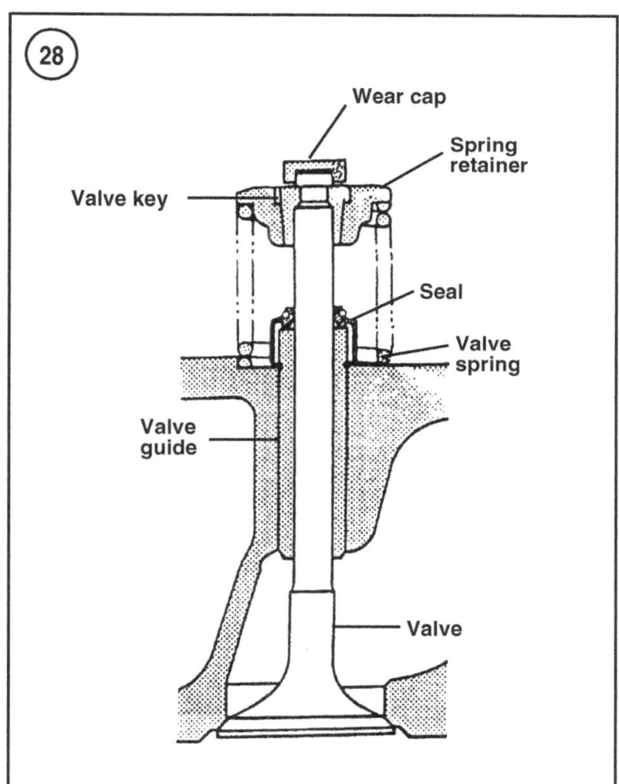

6. Test the valve springs under load on a spring tester (**Figure 26**). Replace any spring that does not meet the specification in **Table 1**.

7. Inspect the valve seats. If worn or burned, they must be reconditioned. This is a job for a dealer or machine shop, although the procedure is described in this chapter.

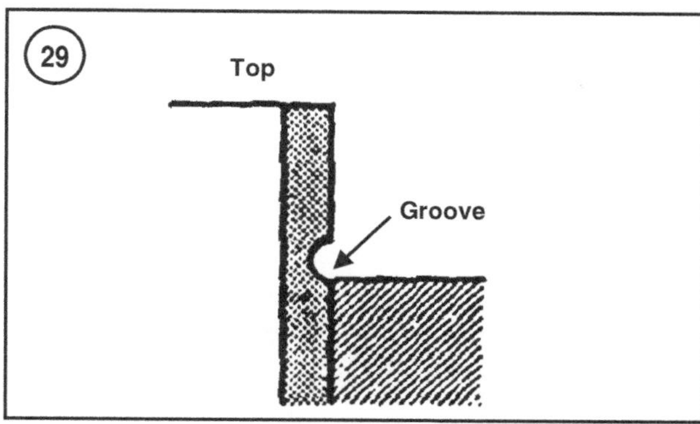

8. Check each spring on a flat surface with a steel square. See **Figure 27**. Slowly revolve the spring 360° and note the space between the top of the coil and the square. If it exceeds 1.4 mm (0.055 in.) at any point, replace the spring.
9. Check the valve guides (**Figure 28**) for wear and looseness. Refer to **Table 1** for valve guide specifications. A loose valve guide must be replaced.

Valve Guide Replacement

The cylinder head is equipped with replaceable valve guides (6, **Figure 22**). The intake and exhaust valve guides are identical. Take the cylinder head to a dealership or machine shop if valve guide replacement is required.

When installing the valve guides, the grooved end must be toward the top of the cylinder head. The groove must be flush with the head surface as shown in **Figure 29**.

PUSH RODS

1. Remove the rocker arms as previously described.
2. Remove the push rods and mark them so they can be reinstalled in their original positions.
3. Inspect push rod ends for damage. Maximum allowable runout is 0.03 mm (0.0012 in.).
4. Reinstall the push rods by reversing removal procedure. Adjust valve clearance as described in Chapter Three.

PISTON/CONNECTING ROD ASSEMBLY

Piston/Connecting Rod Removal

1. Remove the engine as described in this chapter.
2. Place a suitable container under the oil pan and remove the drain plug. Let the crankcase oil drain, then reinstall the drain plug.

5

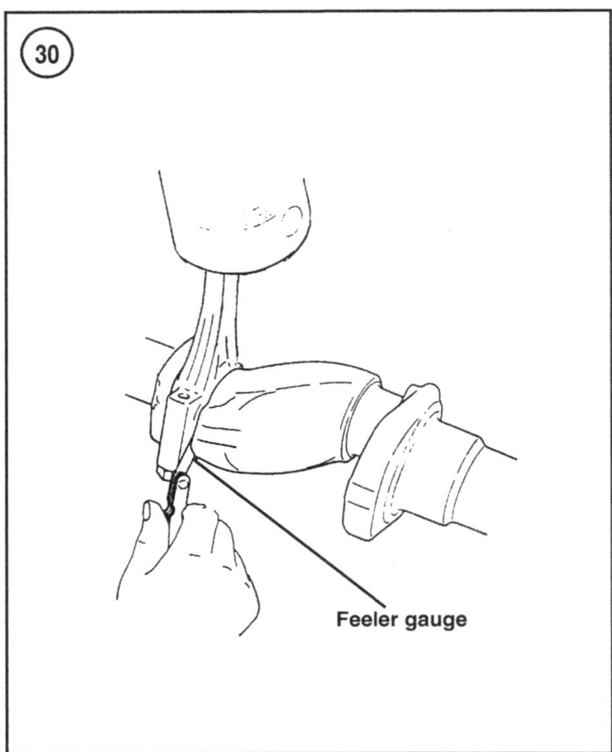

3. Remove the cylinder head as described in this chapter.

NOTE
Note the location of the long screw when removing the oil pan retaining screws.

4. Remove the oil pan.

5. Rotate the crankshaft until the piston is at bottom dead center. Pack the cylinder bore with clean shop rags. Remove the carbon ridge at the top of the cylinder bore with a ridge reamer. These can be rented for use. Vacuum out the shavings, then remove the shop rags.

6. Rotate the crankshaft until the connecting rod is centered in the bore. Measure the connecting rod side clearance with a flat feeler gauge (**Figure 30**). If the clearance exceeds specifications (**Table 1**), replace the connecting rod during reassembly.

7. Remove the connecting rod bolts. Lift off the cap, along with the lower bearing insert.

8. Use a wooden hammer handle to push the piston and connecting rod from the bore.

9. Remove the piston rings with a ring remover (**Figure 31**).

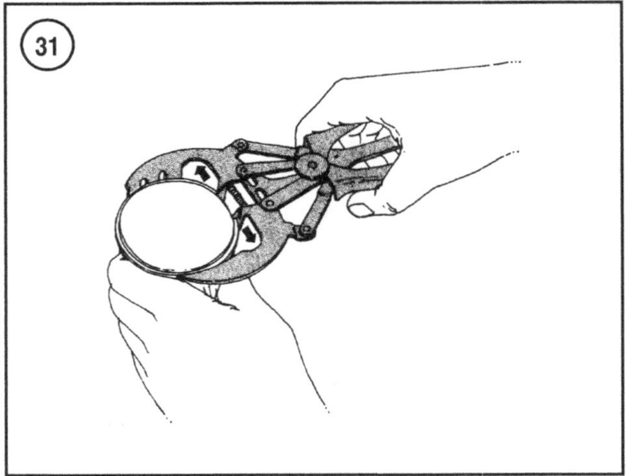

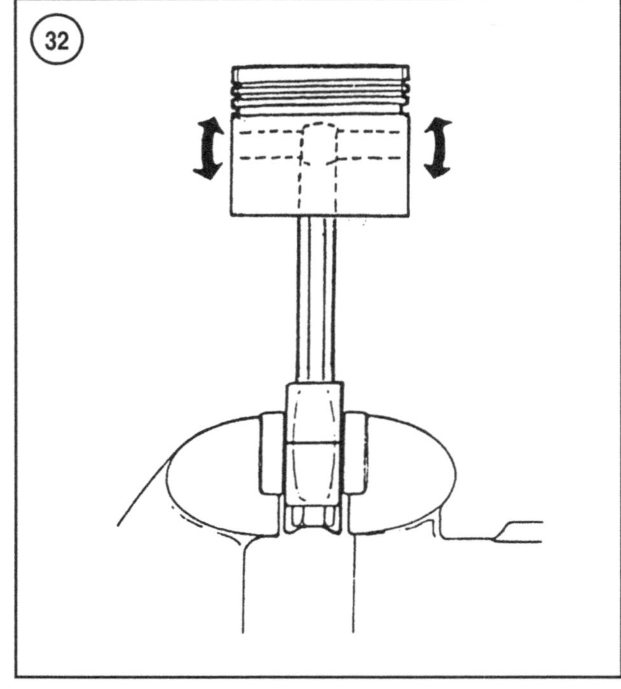

Piston Pin Removal/Installation

The steel piston pin rides directly in the piston and the connecting rod bushing. Circlips at each end retain the piston pin in the piston.

1. Before removing the piston, place the crankshaft end of the connecting rod in a vise with soft jaws. Rock the piston as shown in **Figure 32**. Any rocking motion (do not confuse with the normal sliding motion) indicates wear on the piston pin, piston pin bore or connecting rod small end bore (or a combination of these).

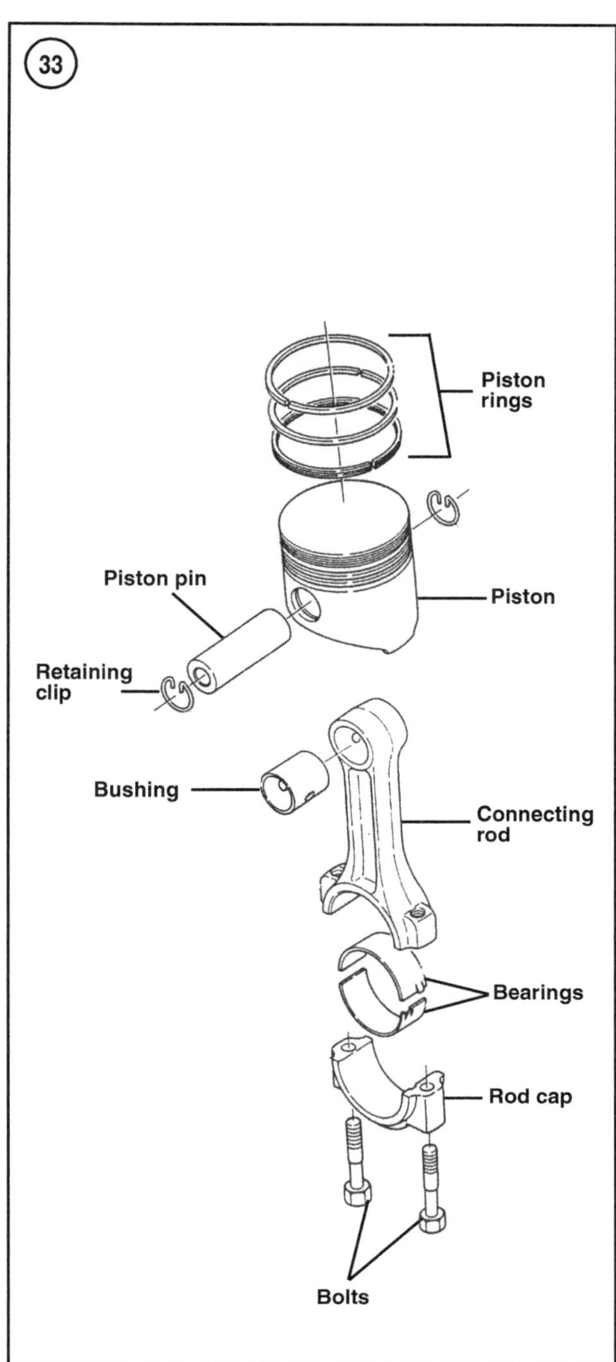

2. Remove the clip from each side of the piston pin bore (**Figure 33**) with a small screwdriver or scribe. Hold a thumb over one edge of the clip when removing it to prevent the clip from springing out.

3. Use a wooden dowel or suitable tool and push out the piston pin. If the pin is difficult to remove, heat the piston with a hair dryer. Separate the piston from the connecting rod.

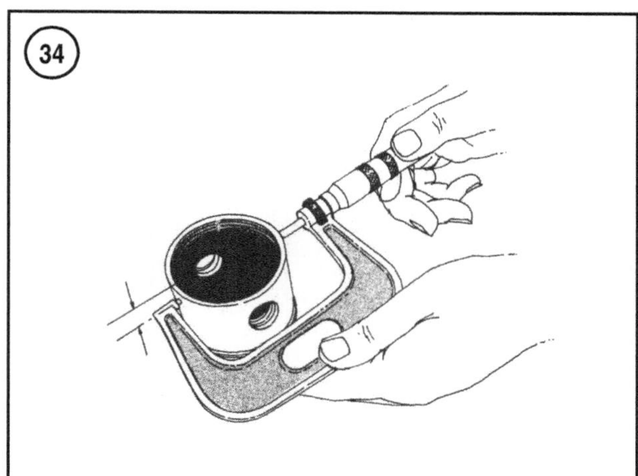

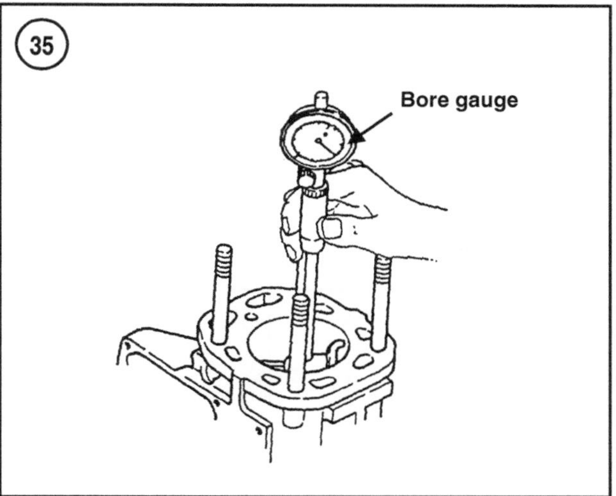

Piston/Cylinder Bore Check

Unless precision measuring equipment is available, have this procedure done by a machine shop.

1. Measure the piston diameter with a micrometer (**Figure 34**) at a right angle to the piston pin bore 9 mm (0.35 in.) from the bottom of the piston skirt.
2. Measure the cylinder bore diameter at several points with a bore gauge (**Figure 35**). **Figure 36** shows the points of normal cylinder wear. Measure the cylinder parallel to the crankshaft and at a right angle to the crankshaft. Record all measurements and refer to **Table 1** for cylinder specifications. If necessary, rebore the cylinder and install a new piston and ring assembly.

5

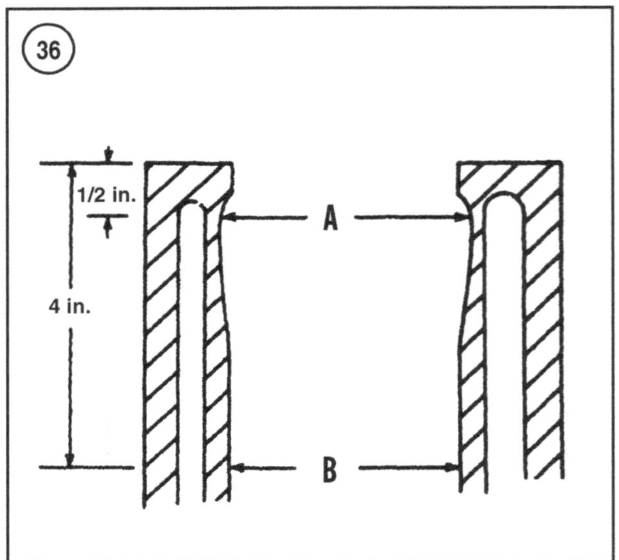

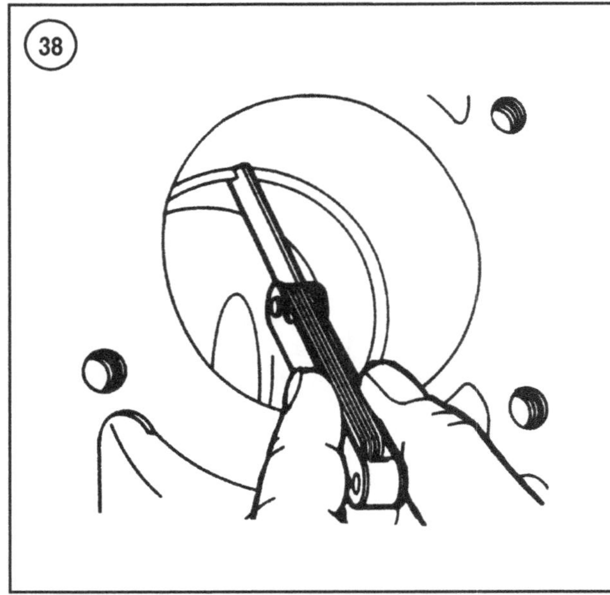

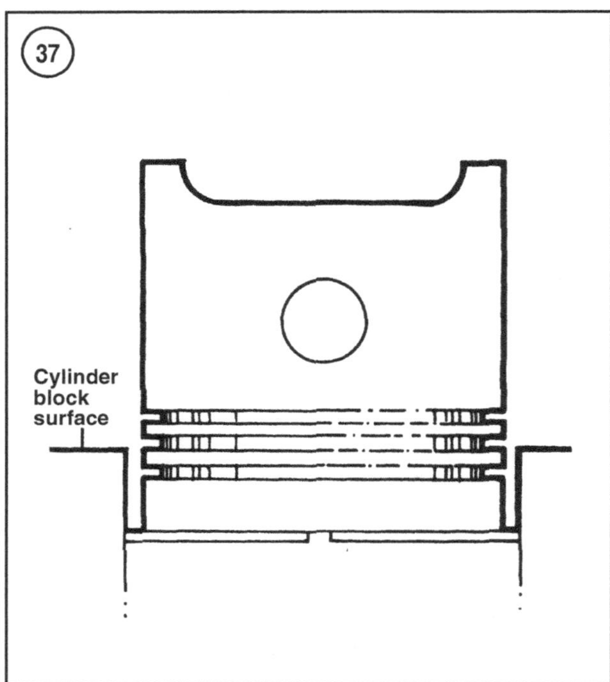

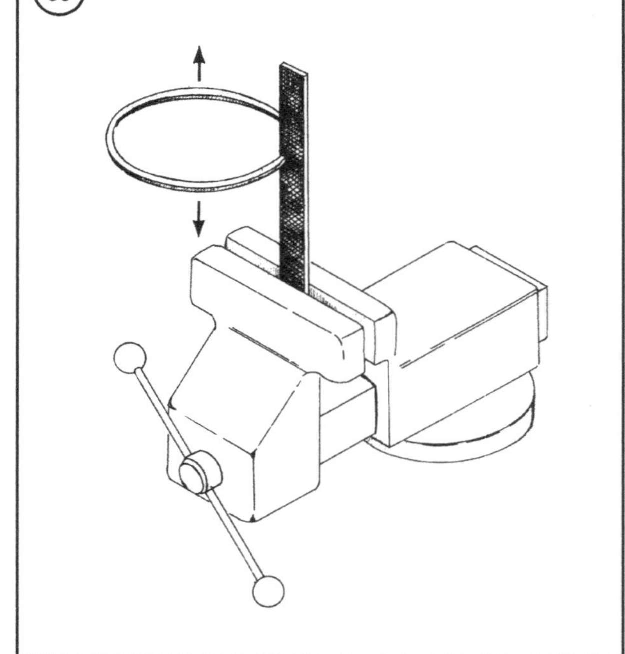

3. If the cylinder bore is damaged or excessively worn, rebore the cylinder bore and install a new piston. If the piston is worn, but the cylinder bore is acceptable, install a new piston.

NOTE

Provide the machine shop with the new piston so the cylinder can be bored to the correct dimension.

Piston Ring Fit/Installation

1. Check the ring gap of each piston ring. To do this, position the ring at the bottom of the ring travel area and square it by tapping gently with an inverted piston. See **Figure 37**.

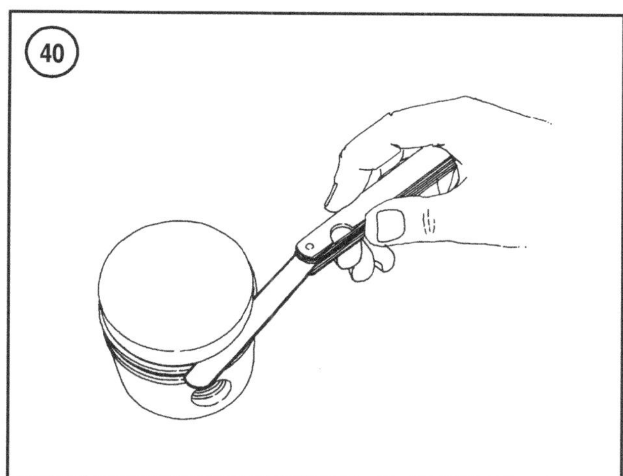

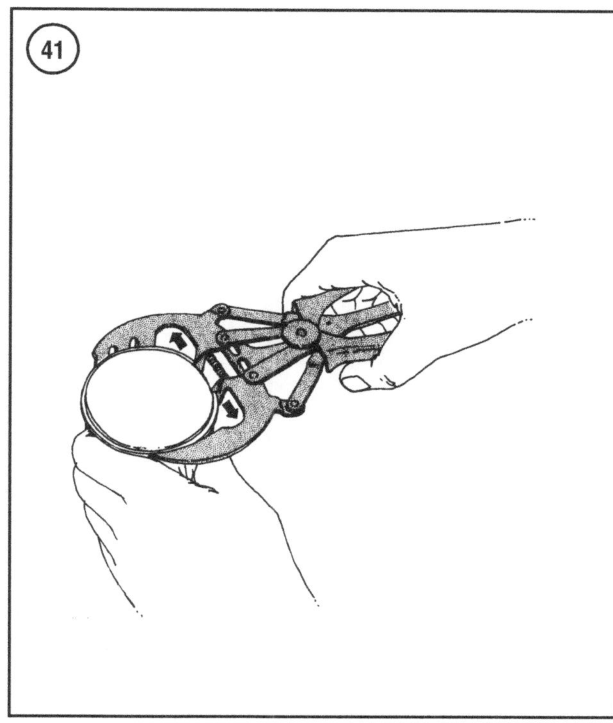

NOTE
If the cylinder has not been rebored, check the gap at the bottom of the ring travel, where the cylinder is the least worn.

2. Measure the ring gap with a feeler gauge as shown in **Figure 38**. Compare the measurement with specifications in **Table 1**. If the measurement is not within specification, the rings must be replaced as a set. Check the gap of new rings as well. If the gap is too small, file the ends of the ring to correct it (**Figure 39**).

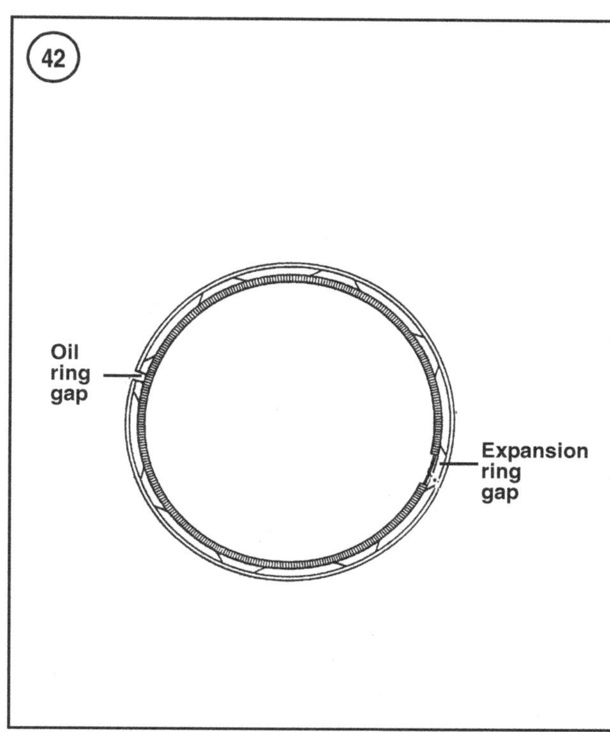

3. Check the side clearance of the rings as shown in **Figure 40**. Place the feeler gauge alongside the ring all the way into the groove. If the measurement is not within specifications (**Table 1**), either the rings or the ring grooves are worn. Inspect and replace them as required.

4. Use a ring expander tool (**Figure 41**) to carefully install the oil control ring, then the compression rings. The oil ring consists of two pieces, the outer ring and the inner expansion spring. Assemble the oil ring on the piston so the expansion spring gap is on the opposite side of the piston from the ring end gap. See **Figure 42**. The second compression ring is tapered while the top compression ring has a barrel face. The top of each compression ring is marked and must face toward the piston crown.

Connecting Rod Inspection

Have the connecting rod checked for straightness by a dealer or machine shop.

The piston pin end of the connecting rod is equipped with a bushing. Refer to **Table 1** for bushing specifications. If bushing replacement is required, a press is necessary to remove the old bushing and install a new bushing. The oil holes in the bushing and connecting rod must align. Ream the bushing to obtain the desired clearance in **Table 1**.

5

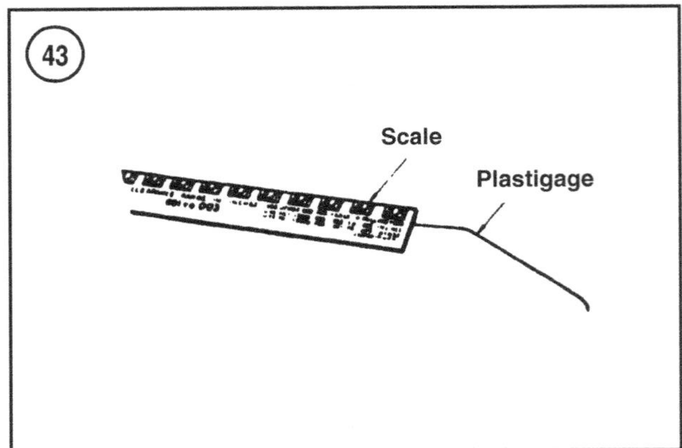

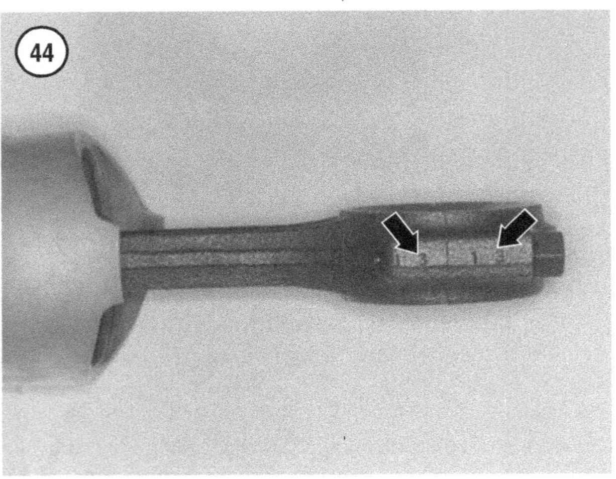

Connecting Rod Bearing Clearance Measurement

1. Place the connecting rod and upper bearing half on the connecting rod journal.
2. Cut a piece of Plastigage the width of the bearing (**Figure 43**). Place the Plastigage on the journal, then install the rod cap and bearing. Be sure to install the cap so the marks on the cap and rod are on the same side (**Figure 44**).

NOTE
Do not place Plastigage over the journal oil hole.

3. Tighten the connecting rod cap to the specification in **Table 2**. Do not rotate the crankshaft while the Plastigage is in place.
4. Remove the connecting rod cap. To determine bearing clearance, compare the width of the flattened Plastigage to the markings on the envelope (**Figure 45**). If the clearance is excessive, have the crankshaft reground and install undersize bearings.

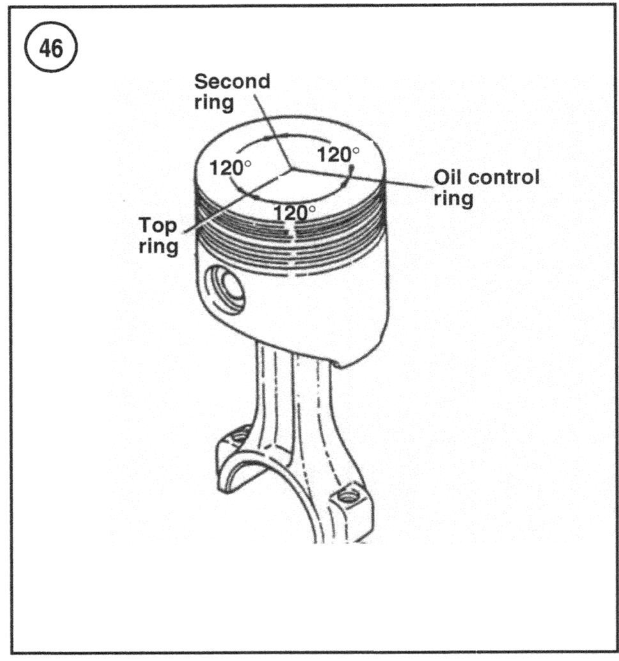

Piston/Connecting Rod Installation

1. Rotate the crankshaft so the crankpin is at bottom dead center.
2. Make sure the ring gaps are positioned as shown in **Figure 46**.
3. Immerse the entire piston in clean engine oil. Coat the cylinder wall with oil.
4. Install a piston ring compressor around the piston rings.

CAUTION
Use extreme care in Step 5 to prevent the connecting rod from nicking the crankshaft journal.

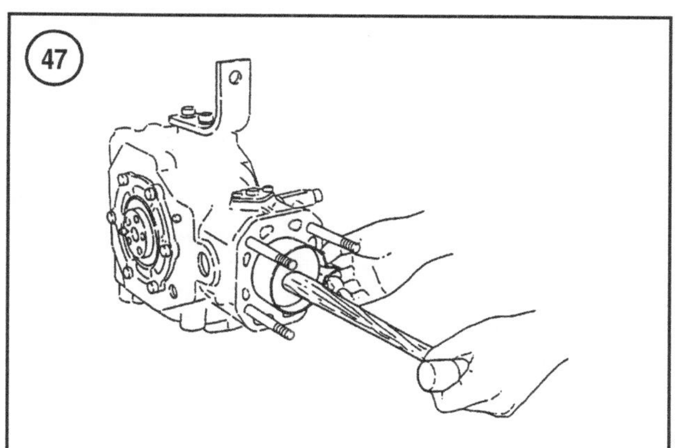

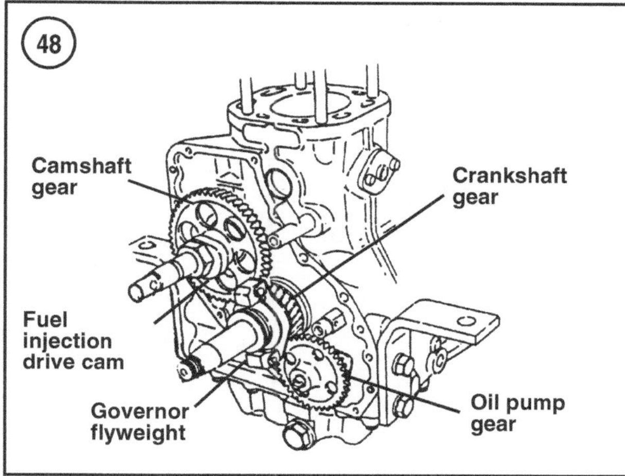

5. Position the piston so the numbered side of the rod (**Figure 44**) faces toward the camshaft side of the engine. Insert the piston/connecting rod assembly into the cylinder (**Figure 47**). Lightly tap on the piston crown with a wooden hammer handle to insert the piston. Make sure the rod does not bang against the crankshaft.

6. Clean the connecting rod bearings carefully, including the back sides. Coat the crankpin journal and bearings with clean engine oil. Place the bearings in the connecting rod and cap.

7. Pull the connecting rod and bearing into position against the crankpin. Lightly lubricate the connecting rod bolt threads with engine oil.

8. Install the connecting rod cap. Make sure the rod and cap are properly aligned. Install the bolts finger-tight.

9. Tighten the cap retaining bolts to the specifications in **Table 2**.

10. Check the connecting rod side play as described under *Piston/Connecting Rod Removal* in this chapter.

11. Reassemble the engine by reversing the disassembly procedures.

TIMING GEARCASE

The timing gearcase covers the camshaft and crankshaft gears and the oil pump (**Figure 48**). The timing gearcase also contains the governor mechanism and serves as the mounting location for the fuel injection pump. A ball bearing in the timing gearcase supports the outer end of the crankshaft.

To remove and reinstall the timing gearcase, proceed as follows:

1. Disconnect the negative battery cable.
2. Remove the alternator as described in Chapter Eight.
3. Remove the oil filter.
4. Detach the control cables from the speed control lever and the stop lever (**Figure 49**).
5. Remove the fuel injection pump as described in Chapter Seven.

NOTE

If a suitable tool is not available to hold the crankshaft pulley when unscrewing the retaining nut, remove the starter and prevent flywheel rotation by inserting a screwdriver into the ring gear teeth.

6. Remove the crankshaft pulley retaining nut. Use a suitable puller to remove the crankshaft pulley (**Figure 50**). Remove the drive key from the crankshaft.
7. Remove the water pump as described in Chapter Eight.
8. Remove the manual starter cover (**Figure 51**).
9. Remove the setscrew in the end of the camshaft (A, **Figure 52**), then remove the manual starter drive pin (B).
10. Remove the timing gearcase (**Figure 53**).
11. Remove the gasket and any residue from the gearcase and crankcase surfaces.
12. If crankshaft or starter seal replacement is necessary, proceed as follows:

50

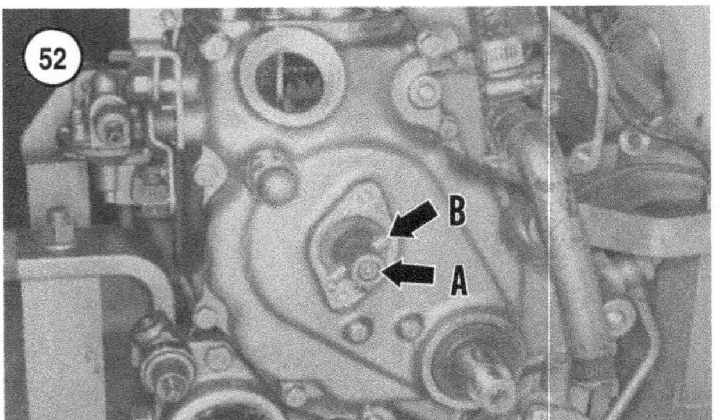

52

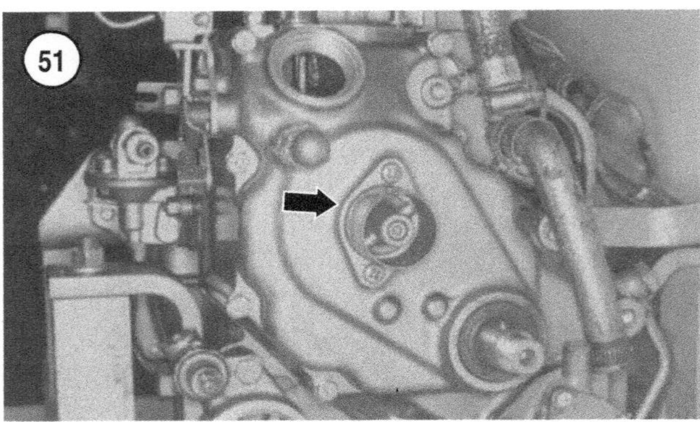
51

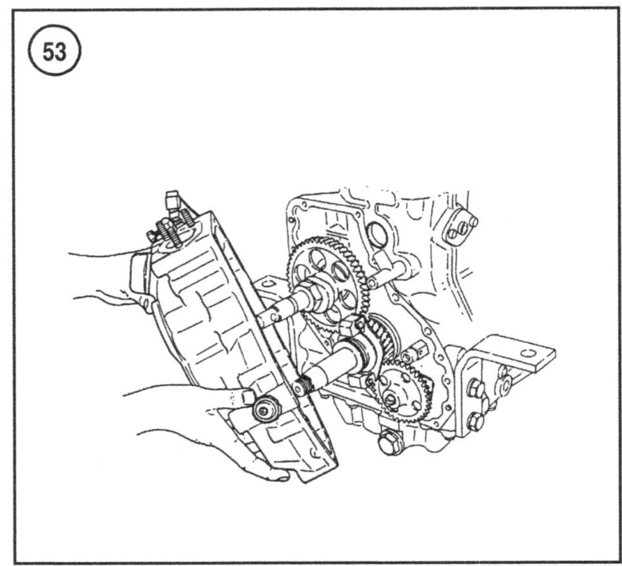
53

a. Pry the old seal from the gearcase with a large screwdriver. Work carefully to prevent damage to the gearcase seal surface.
b. Clean the seal recess in the cover with solvent and blow it dry with compressed air.
c. Apply gasket sealer to the periphery of the seal.
d. Position a new seal in the cover recess with its open end facing the inside of the gearcase. Drive the seal into place with a suitably sized seal driver or socket.

13. If crankshaft bearing replacement is necessary, proceed as follows:

a. Refer to Chapter Seven to remove the governor shaft from timing gearcase.
b. Pry the seal from the gearcase with a large screwdriver. Work carefully to prevent damage to the gearcase seal surface.
c. Drive or press out the bearing (**Figure 54**). Force the bearing toward the inside of the gearcase.
d. Clean the seal and bearing recesses in the cover with solvent and blow them dry with compressed air.
e. Drive or press in a new bearing until the bearing seats in the recess in the gearcase.
f. Apply gasket sealer to the periphery of the seal.
g. Position a new seal in the cover recess with its open end facing the inside of the gearcase. Drive the seal into place with a suitably sized seal driver or socket.
h. Refer to Chapter Seven to reinstall the governor shaft.

14. Reverse the removal procedure to reinstall the timing gearcase. Tighten the gearcase retaining screws to the specification in **Table 2**.

LUBRICATION SYSTEM

Refer to Chapter Two for lubrication system operation, diagrams and oil pressure test.

Oil Pump

The engine oil pump is mounted on the front (timing gear) side of the cylinder block (**Figure 48**).

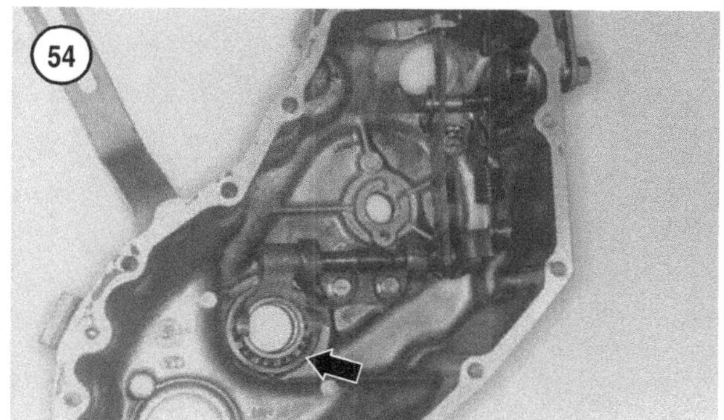

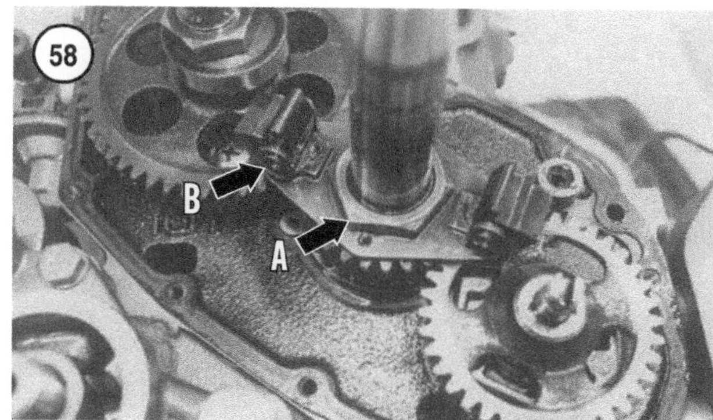

Removal and installation

1. Remove the timing gearcase as previously described.
2. Remove the governor thrust washer (**Figure 55**), thrust bearing (**Figure 56**) and thrust sleeve (**Figure 57**) from the crankshaft.
3. Using a suitable tool (if available, Yanmar special tool 124085-92700), unscrew the crankshaft nut (A, **Figure 58**).
4. Remove the governor flyweight assembly (B, **Figure 58**).

NOTE
Early model engines may be equipped with a nut on the oil pump shaft.

5. *Early models*—Unscrew the oil pump nut. To prevent the pump gear from rotating, insert an Allen wrench into a pump mounting screw through a hole in the oil pump drive gear.
6. Reach through the holes in the oil pump gear and unscrew the pump retaining screws (**Figure 59**).
7. Remove the oil pump and gasket.
8. Clean any gasket residue from the oil pump and engine.

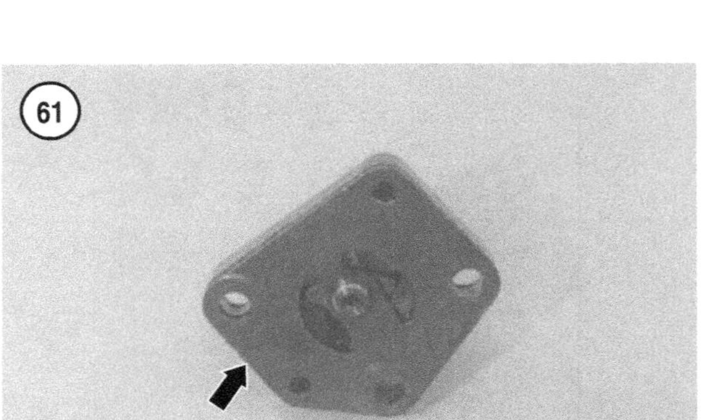

9. Installation is the reverse of removal. Tighten the oil pump retaining screws to the tightening torque specified in **Table 2**. Make sure the governor flyweight assembly is positioned on the locating pins (**Figure 60**). Tighten the crankshaft nut to the torque specified in **Table 2**.

Disassembly, inspection and reassembly

1. Remove the oil pump cover (**Figure 61**).
2. Lift out the inner and outer pump rotors (**Figure 62**).
3. Thoroughly clean all parts in solvent and dry with compressed air.
4. Check the drive spindle and pump rotors for signs of wear, scoring or damage. Replace damaged parts.

NOTE
Replace the oil pump as a unit if any parts are damaged.

5. Reinstall the inner rotor in the pump body. Reinstall the outer rotor in the pump body.
6. Measure the clearance between the inner rotor tip and outer rotor tip (**Figure 63**). Compare the measurement with the specification in **Table 1**.

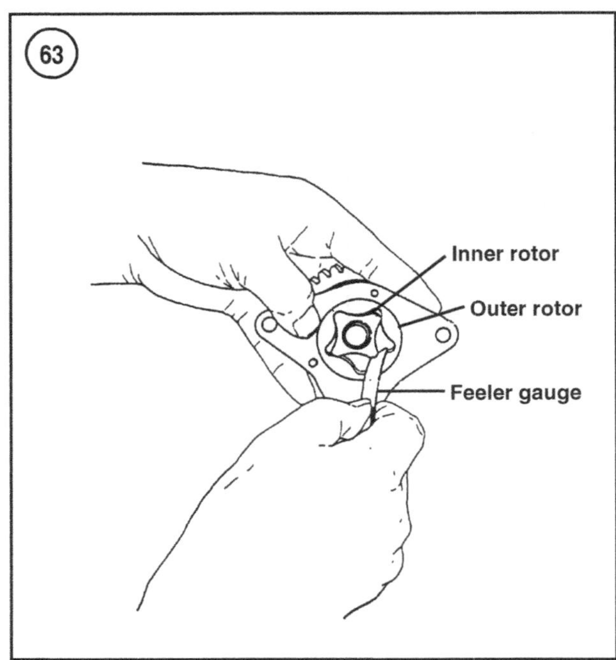

7. Measure the clearance between the outer rotor and the pump body (**Figure 64**). Compare the measurement with specifications in **Table 1**.
8. Place a straightedge across the pump body. Measure the side clearance between the rotors and straightedge with a flat feeler gauge (**Figure 65**). Compare with specifications in **Table 1**.
9. Measure the diameter of the inner rotor shaft. Measure the shaft bore of the pump body. Calculate shaft clearance and compare it with specifications in **Table 1**.
10. If any clearance measured in Steps 6-9 is not within specification, replace the pump. Individual components are not available. The pump must be replaced as a unit.
11. When reassembling the oil pump, make sure to lubricate the rotors, body and shaft with engine oil.

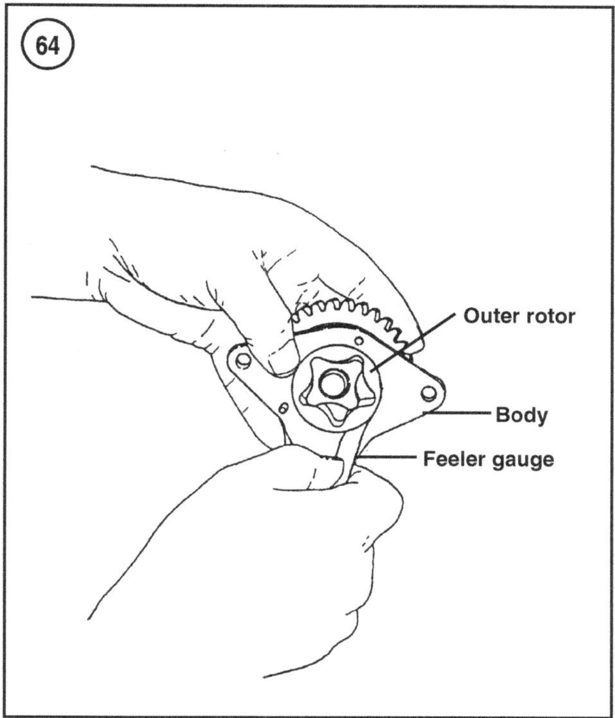

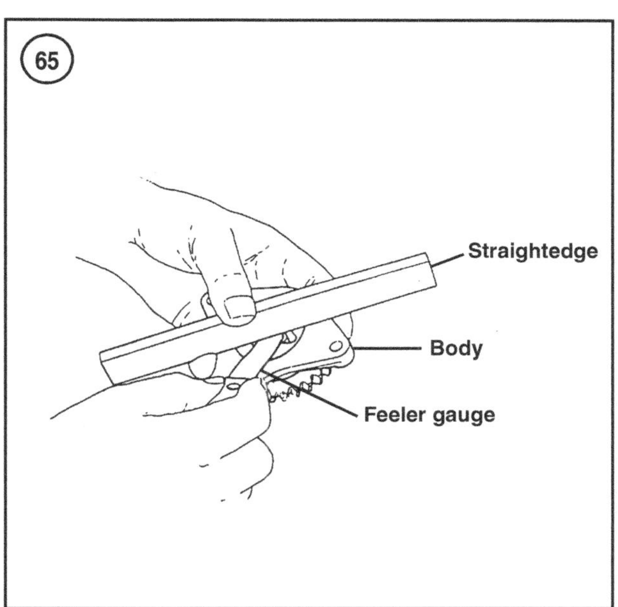

Pressure relief valve

An oil pressure relief valve is threaded into the front (timing gear) of the engine (**Figure 66**). When oil pressure exceeds 300-400 kPa (43-57 psi), the relief valve opens and expels oil into the timing gear area.

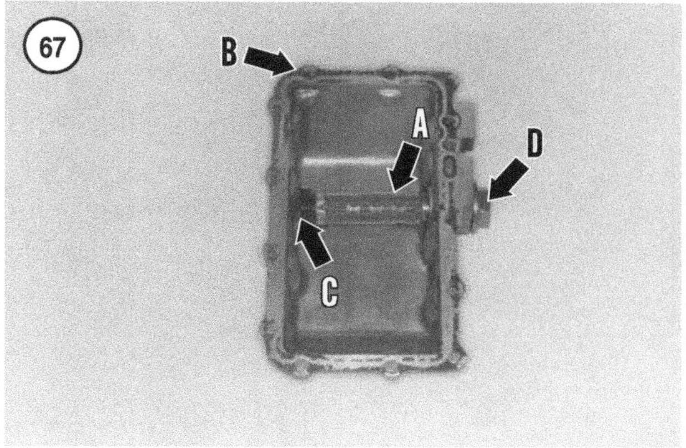

Do not attempt to disassemble the oil pressure relief valve. The valve is sealed and it must be replaced as a unit assembly.

Oil pickup

The oil pickup (A, **Figure 67**) is located in the oil pan (B). The pickup includes a strainer to prevent foreign matter from entering the lubrication system. A spring (C) keeps the pickup in position in the oil pan.

NOTE

When removing the drain plug in the oil pan, be aware that the spring will force the plug out when the threads disengage.

Remove the drain plug (D) for access to the oil pickup.

FLYWHEEL

Removal/Installation

1. Remove the engine from the boat.
2. Remove the transmission.

68

69

70

CRANKSHAFT ASSEMBLY

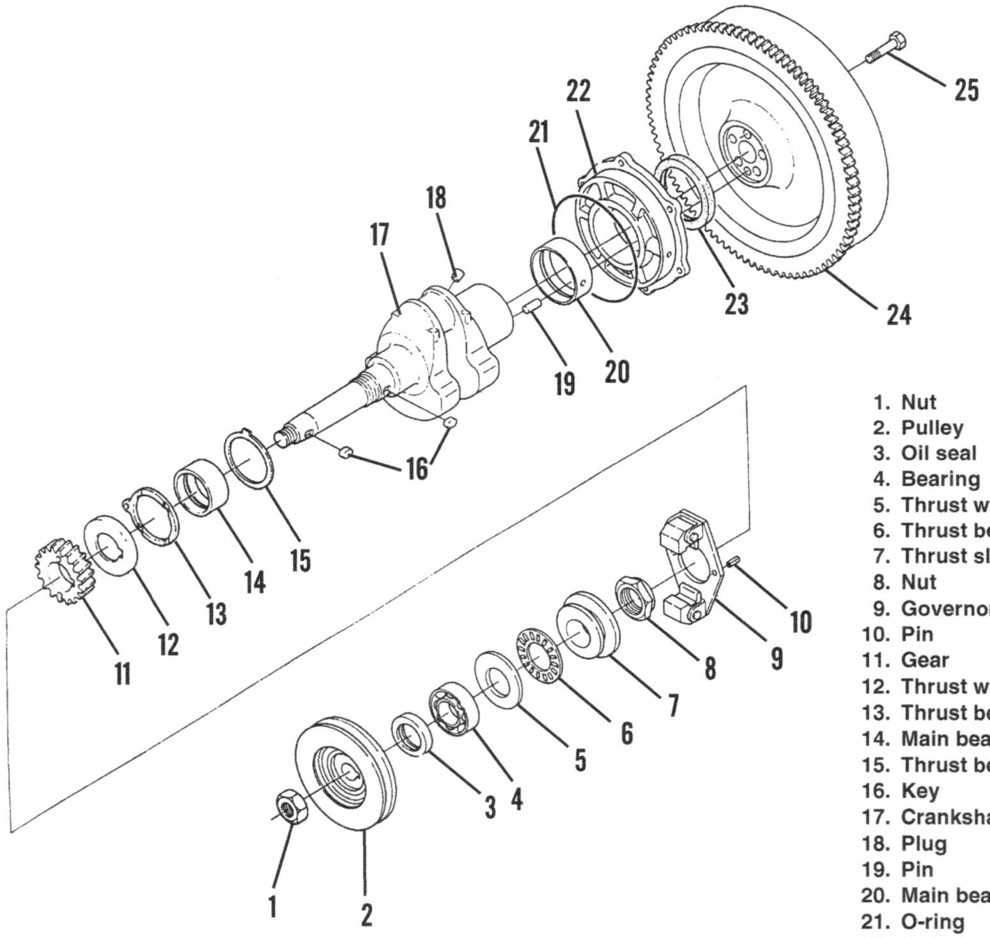

1. Nut
2. Pulley
3. Oil seal
4. Bearing
5. Thrust washer
6. Thrust bearing
7. Thrust sleeve
8. Nut
9. Governor flyweight assy
10. Pin
11. Gear
12. Thrust washer
13. Thrust bearing
14. Main bearing
15. Thrust bearing
16. Key
17. Crankshaft
18. Plug
19. Pin
20. Main bearing
21. O-ring
22. Main bearing holder
23. Oil seal
24. Flywheel
25. Bolt

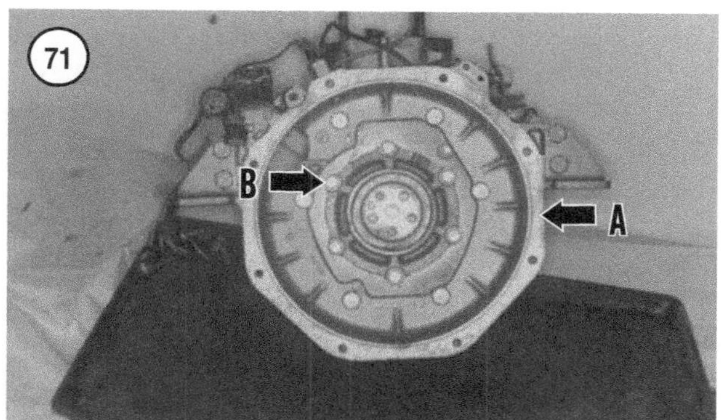

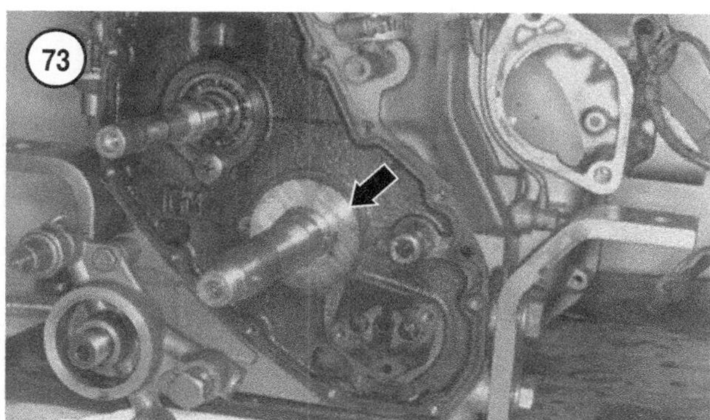

3. Remove the drive disc (**Figure 68**).
4. Gradually loosen and remove the flywheel bolts, working in a diagonal pattern. Install two drive disc bolts into two outer holes in the flywheel (**Figure 69**), then use the screws to pull and remove the flywheel.
5. Inspect the ring gear. If the ring gear is excessively worn or damaged, use the following procedure to remove the ring gear:
   a. Heat the ring gear evenly, then drive the ring gear off the flywheel.
   b. Heat the ring gear prior to installation. Drive the ring gear onto the flywheel, being careful not to damage the gear teeth.
6. Reverse the removal procedure to install the flywheel. Tighten the flywheel retaining bolts to the torque specified in **Table 2**. Refer to Chapter Ten to install the drive disc and transmission.

DRIVE DISC

Refer to Chapter Ten for drive disc procedures (**Figure 68**).

CRANKSHAFT

Removal and Installation

Refer to **Figure 70**.
1. Remove the flywheel as previously described.
2. Remove the bellhousing (A, **Figure 71**).
3. Remove the piston and connecting rod as previously described.
4. Remove the oil pump as previously described.
5. Remove the crankshaft gear (**Figure 72**).
6. Refer to *Camshaft* to remove the camshaft gear.
7. Remove the thrust washer (**Figure 73**) and thrust bearing (**Figure 74**).

NOTE
Support the crankshaft while removing the main bearing housing in the next step.

8. Remove the main bearing housing (B, **Figure 71**).
9. Remove the crankshaft.
10. Proceed as follows to replace the crankshaft seal in the main bearing housing:
   a. Pry the old seal from the main bearing housing with a large screwdriver. Work carefully to prevent damage to the main bearing housing seal surface.
   b. Clean the seal recess in the housing with solvent and dry with compressed air.
   c. Apply gasket sealer to the periphery of the seal.

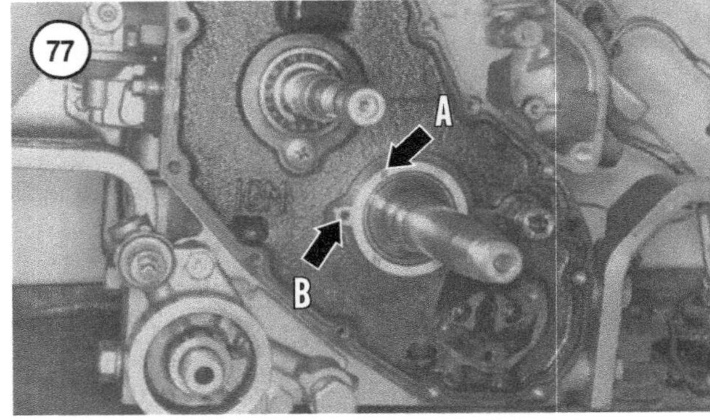

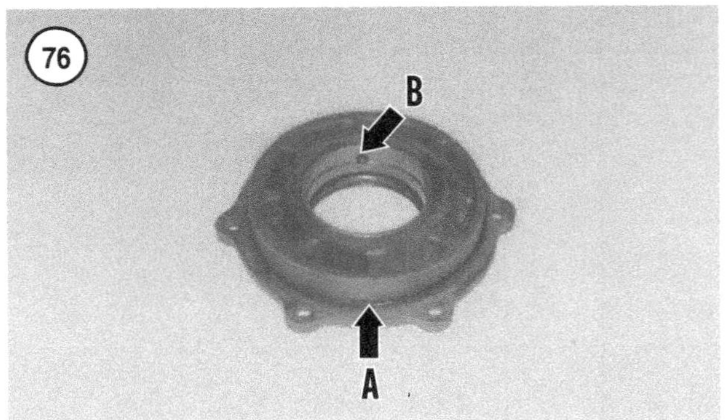

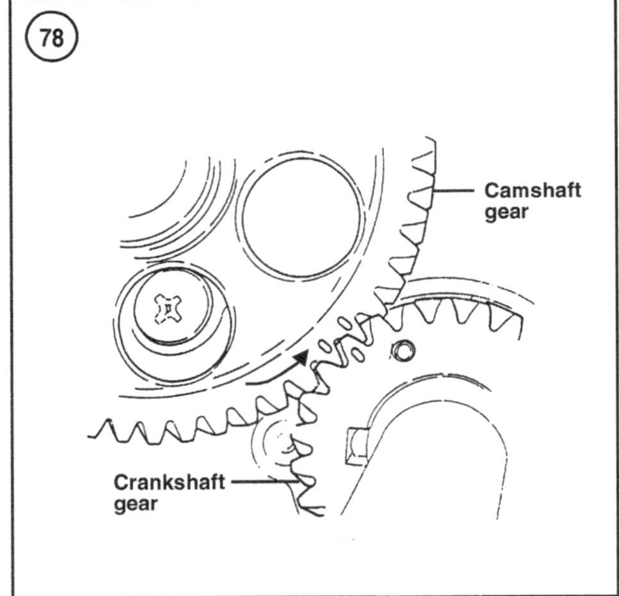

d. Position the new seal in the housing recess with its open end facing the inside of the bearing housing. Drive the seal into place with a suitably sized seal driver.

11. Refer to *Main Bearings* for information concerning inspection of the main bearings and thrust bearings.

12. Reinstall the crankshaft by reversing the removal procedure while noting the following:

a. Thoroughly lubricate the main bearings and thrust bearings.

b. Install the inner, front thrust bearing so the oil grooves are toward the inside of the crankcase and the tab fits into the recess (**Figure 75**) in the crankcase. Apply a light coating of grease to hold the thrust bearing in place.

c. Install a new O-ring (A, **Figure 76**) on the main bearing housing.

d. Tighten the main bearing housing bolts to the torque specified in **Table 2**.

e. Install the outer front thrust bearing so the oil grooves (A, **Figure 77**) are toward the outside of the crankcase and the tab (B) fits onto the pin in the crankcase.

f. Install the thrust washer (**Figure 73**) so the beveled side of the inner hole is toward the crankcase.

g. Measure crankshaft end play by inserting a feeler gauge between the crankshaft main journal and the inner thrust bearing, or by installing a dial gauge that measures fore and aft movement of the flywheel or crankshaft. Using a large screwdriver, force the crankshaft back and forth. Measure crankshaft end play and compare the measurement with the specification in **Table 1**. Replace the inner thrust bearing to obtain the desired end play.

h. Align the timing marks (**Figure 78**) on the camshaft and crankshaft gears when installing the crankshaft gear.

i. Check gear backlash by installing a dial indicator as shown in **Figure 79** or by rotating the gear teeth with soft solder between the gear teeth. Compare the measurement with the specification in **Table 1**.

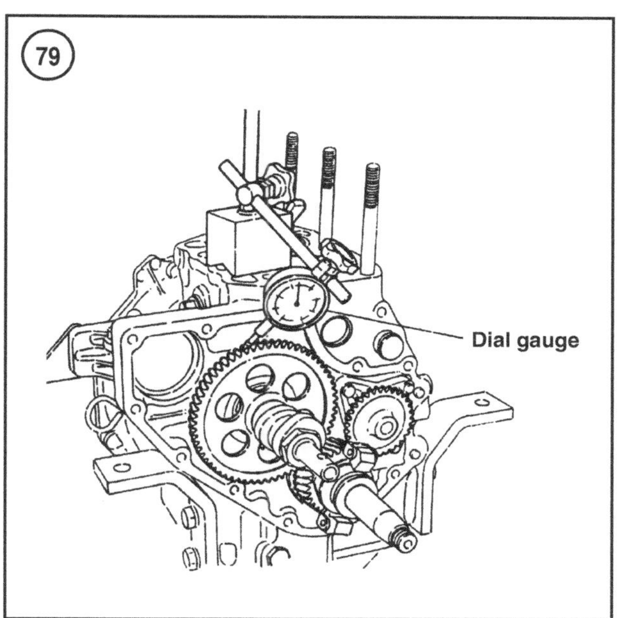

If gear backlash is incorrect, replace the camshaft and crankshaft gears.

Inspection

1. Clean the crankshaft thoroughly with solvent. Blow out the oil passages with compressed air.
2. Check the main and connecting rod journals for wear, scratches, grooves, scoring or cracks. Check the oil seal contact surface for burrs, nicks or other sharp edges that might damage a seal during installation.

NOTE
Unless precision measuring equipment is available, have a machine shop perform Step 3.

3. Check all journals against specifications (**Table 1**) for out-of-roundness and taper. Have the crankshaft reground, if necessary, and install new undersize bearings.

MAIN BEARINGS

The crankshaft is supported at each end by bushing-type main bearings. The front main bearing is located in the crankcase and the rear main bearing is located in the removable main bearing carrier. Thrust bearings located at the front of the crankshaft control crankshaft end play. Refer to **Figure 70**.

Remove the crankshaft as described in the previous section for access to the main bearings and thrust washers. Unless precision measuring equipment is available, have a dealership or machine shop measure main bearing dimensions. Refer to specifications in **Table 1**.

If bearing replacement is necessary, have the main bearings replaced by a dealership or machine shop. Make sure the oil holes (B, **Figure 76**) in the main bearings align with the oil passages in the crankcase and main bearing carrier.

CAMSHAFT

Removal and Installation

1. Remove the fuel transfer pump (**Figure 80**).
2. Remove the crankshaft as previously described.
3. Prevent rotation of the camshaft gear by holding a screwdriver or other tool against the camshaft bearing retaining screw (**Figure 81**).
4. Remove the camshaft gear nut (A, **Figure 82**), fuel injection pump cam (B) and camshaft gear (C).
5. Position the engine so the valve lifters will not fall out when the camshaft is withdrawn/removed.

5

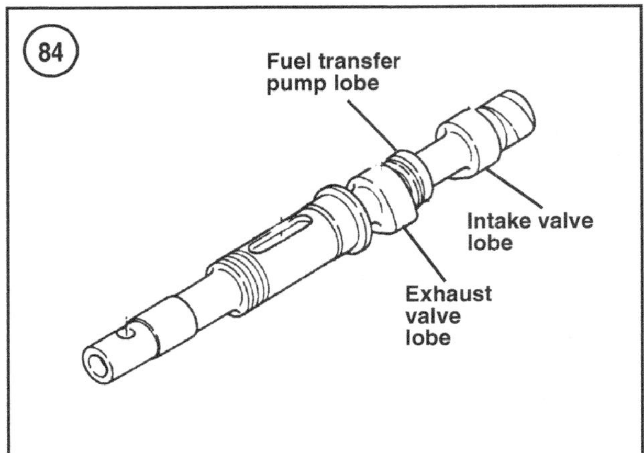

6. Remove the bearing retaining screw (**Figure 83**), then withdraw the camshaft.
7. Remove the valve lifters and mark them so they may be reinstalled in their original locations.
8. Check the rear bearing journal and lobes for signs of wear or scoring.

NOTE

If precision measuring equipment is not available, have a dealership or machine shop perform Step 9.

9. Measure the rear camshaft journal diameter and lobes (**Figure 84**) and compare the measurement to the specification in **Table 1**. Replace the camshaft if the journal or lobes do not meet specifications.
10. Measure the stem diameter of the valve lifters and compare the measurement to the specification in **Table 1**. Measure the lifter bores in the cylinder block. Calculate the lifter clearance and compare it with the specification in **Table 1**. Replace the valve lifters if they do not meet specifications. Replace the valve lifter if the lifter face is scored, galled, excessively worn or otherwise damaged.
11. Replace the ball bearing if it is damaged or feels rough during rotation.
12. Installation is the reverse of removal. Note the following:
   a. If installing a new camshaft, coat the camshaft lobes with camshaft break-in lubricant. If reinstalling the original camshaft, apply heavy oil to the camshaft lobes.
   b. Lubricate the camshaft bearing journal with heavy engine oil before reinstallation.
   c. Lightly tap the end of the camshaft to seat the ball bearing in the engine. Rotate the camshaft to be sure it rotates freely.
   d. Align the timing marks (**Figure 78**) on the camshaft and crankshaft gears when installing the camshaft gear.
   e. Install the fuel injection cam so the side marked with a zero is out (**Figure 85**).
   f. Check gear backlash by installing a dial indicator as shown in **Figure 79** or by rotating the gear teeth with soft solder between the gear teeth. Compare

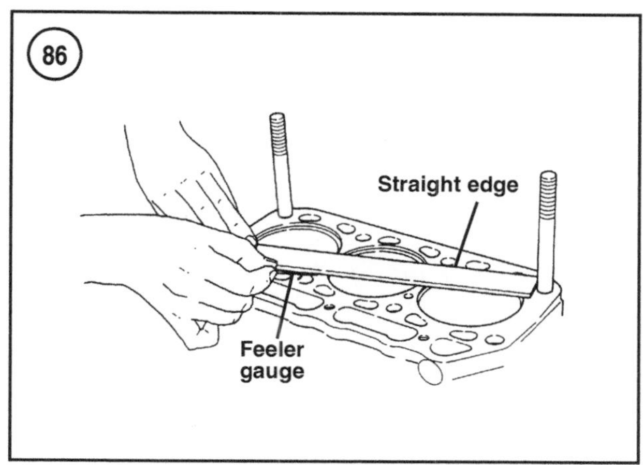

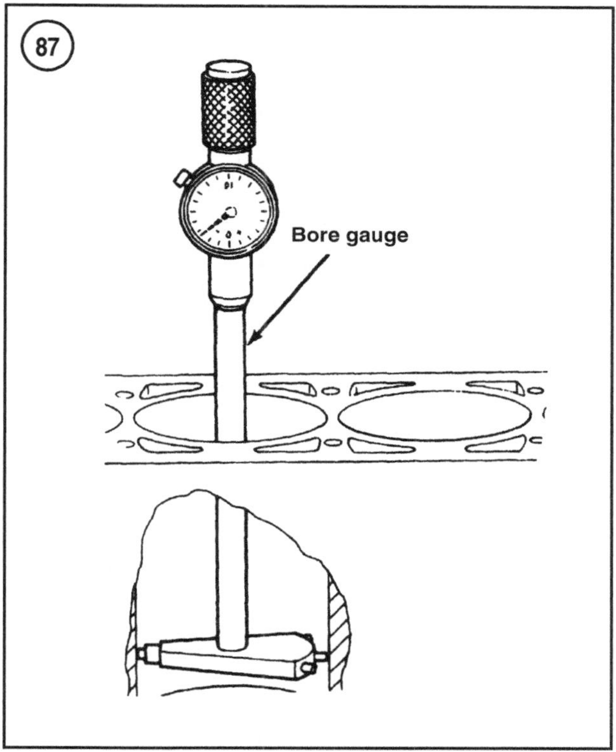

the measurement with the specification in **Table 1**. If gear backlash is incorrect, replace the camshaft and crankshaft gears.

CYLINDER BLOCK

Cleaning and Inspection

1. Clean the block thoroughly with solvent. Remove any gasket or RTV sealant residue from the machined surfaces. Check all core plugs for leaks and replace any that are suspect. See *Core Plug Replacement* in this chapter. Check oil and coolant passages for sludge, dirt and corrosion while cleaning. If the passages are very dirty, have the block boiled out by a machine shop. Blow out all passages with compressed air. Check the threads in the head bolt holes to make sure they are clean. If dirty, use a tap to restore the threads and remove any deposits.

2. Examine the block for cracks. To confirm suspicions about possible leakage areas, use a mixture of one part kerosene and two parts engine oil. Coat the suspected area with this solution, then wipe dry and immediately apply a solution of zinc oxide dissolved in wood alcohol. If any discoloration appears in the treated area, the block is cracked and should be replaced.

3. Check the flatness of the cylinder block deck or top surface. Place an accurate straightedge on the block. If there is any gap between the block and straightedge, measure it with a flat feeler gauge (**Figure 86**). Measure from end to end and from corner to corner. Have the block resurfaced if it is warped more than 0.07 mm (0.0028 in.).

4. Measure the cylinder bore with a bore gauge (**Figure 87**) for out-of-roundness or excessive wear as described in *Piston/Cylinder Bore Check* in this chapter. If the cylinder exceeds maximum tolerances, rebore the cylinder. Rebore the cylinder if the cylinder walls are badly scuffed, scored or otherwise damage.

Core Plug Replacement

Check the condition of the front (**Figure 88**) and rear (**Figure 89**) core plugs in the block whenever the engine is out of the boat for service. If any signs of leakage or corrosion are found around one core plug, replace both of them. Core plugs in the cylinder block prevent damage to the block should the coolant freeze.

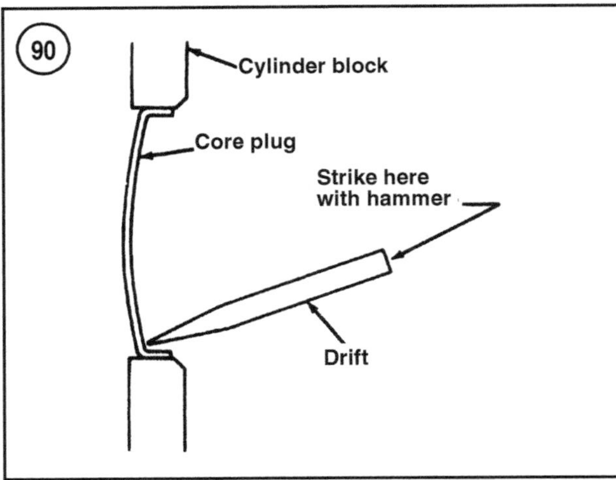

NOTE

Core plugs can be replaced inexpensively by a machine shop. If machine work is being performed on the engine, have the core plugs replaced at the same time.

Removal/Installation

CAUTION

Do not drive core plugs into the engine casting. It will be impossible to retrieve them and they can restrict coolant circulation, resulting in serious engine damage.

1. Tap the bottom edge of the core plug with a hammer and drift. Use several sharp blows to push the bottom of the plug inward, tilting the top out (**Figure 90**).
2. Grip the top of the plug firmly with pliers. Pull the plug from its bore (**Figure 91**) and discard it.

NOTE

The core plugs can also be removed by drilling a hole in the center of the plug and prying it out with an appropriate size drift or pin punch. When removing a large core plug, the use of a universal impact slide hammer is recommended.

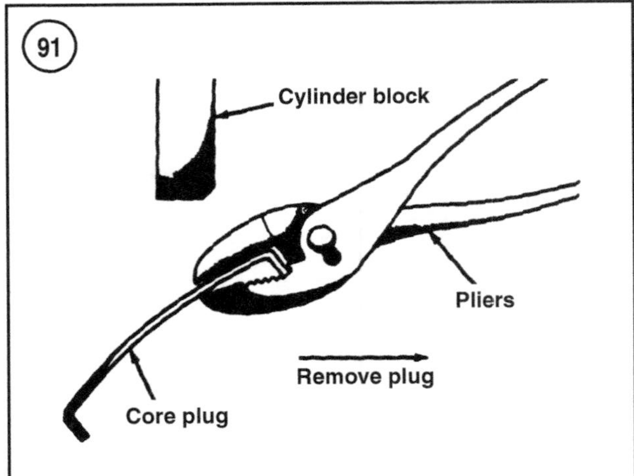

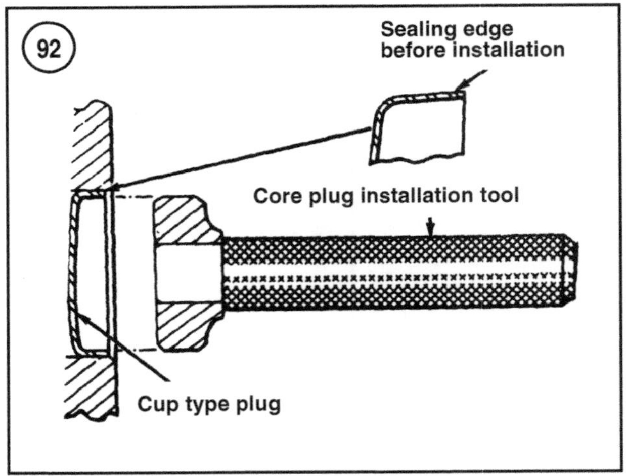

3. Clean the plug bore thoroughly to remove all traces of the old sealer. Inspect the bore for any damage that might interfere with proper sealing of the new plug.
4. Coat the inside diameter of the plug bore and the outer diameter of the new plug with sealer. Use an oil-resistant sealer if the plug is to be installed in an oil gallery or a water-resistant sealer for plugs installed in the water jacket.
5. Install the new core plug with an appropriate size core plug installation tool (**Figure 92**), driver or socket. The outside edge of the plug should be 2-3 mm (0.08-0.12 in.) inside the block.
6. Repeat Steps 1-5 to replace each remaining core plug.

Table 1 ENGINE SPECIFICATIONS (1GM, 1GM10)

Bore	
1GM	72 mm (2.83 in.)
1GM10	75 mm (2.95 in.)
Stroke	72 mm (2.83 in.)
Displacement	
1GM	293 cc (17.9 cu. in.)
1GM10	318 cc (19.4 cu. in.)
Number of cylinders	1
Cylinder bore diameter	
1GM	72.000-72.030 mm (2.8346-2.8358 in.)
1GM10	75.000-75.030 mm (2.9528-2.9540 in.)
Cylinder bore out-of-round limit	
1GM	0.1 mm (0.004 in.)
1GM10	0.02 mm (0.0008 in.)
Cylinder block warpage limit	
1GM	0.05 mm (0.002 in.)
1GM10	0.07 mm (0.0028 in.)
Piston diameter	
1GM	
Standard	71.913-71.943 mm (2.8312-2.8324 in.)
Wear limit	71.850 mm (2.8287 in.)
1GM10	
Standard	74.910-74.940 mm (2.9492-2.9504 in.)
Wear limit	74.850 mm (2.9468 in.)
Piston top clearance	0.68-0.88 mm (0.027-0.035 in.)
Piston ring side clearance	
Top ring	0.065-0.100 mm (0.0026-0.0039 in.)
Second ring	0.035-0.070 mm (0.0014-0.0028 in.)
Oil ring	0.020-0.055 mm (0.0008-0.0022 in.)
Ring end gap (all rings)	0.20-0.40 mm (0.008-0.016 in.)
Piston pin diameter	19.991-20.000 mm (0.7870-0.7874 in.)
Piston pin hole diameter	
In piston	19.995-20.008 mm (0.7872-0.7877 in.)
In rod	20.000 mm (0.7874 in.)
Piston pin clearance	
In rod	0.025-0.047 mm (0.0010-0.0019 in.)
In piston	0.005 mm tight-0.017 mm loose (0.0002 in. tight-0.0007 in. loose)
Piston ring width	
Top & second ring	1.97-1.99 mm (0.0776-0.0783 in.)
Oil control ring	3.97-3.99 mm (0.1563-0.1571 in.)
Crankshaft main journal diameter	
Timing gear end	43.950-43.964 mm (1.7303-1.7309 in.)
Flywheel end	59.950-59.964 mm (2.3602-2.3608 in.)
Journal out-of-round—max.	0.01 mm (0.0004 in.)
Crankshaft end play	0.06-0.19 mm (0.0024-0.0075 in.)
Crankshaft runout—max.	0.15 mm (0.006 in.)
Main bearing clearance	
Timing gear end	0.036-0.092 mm (0.0014-0.0036 in.)
Flywheel end	0.036-0.095 mm (0.0014-0.0037 in.)
Crankshaft thrust bearing—min.	
Front	2.75 mm (0.108 in.)
Inner	2.25 mm (0.089 in.)
Crankpin diameter	39.950-39.964 mm (1.5728-1.5734 in.)
Journal out-of-round—max.	0.01 mm (0.0004 in.)
Crankpin bearing clearance	0.028-0.086 mm (0.0011-0.0034 in.)
Connecting rod side clearance	0.2-0.4 mm (0.008-0.016 in.)
Cylinder head warpage—max.	0.07 mm (0.003 in.)
Camshaft	
Valve lobe lift	29.000 mm (1.1417 in.)
Fuel pump lobe lift	22.000 mm (0.8661 in.)

(continued)

5

Table 1 ENGINE SPECIFICATIONS (1GM, 1GM10) (continued)

Camshaft (continued)	
Journal diameter	20.000 mm (0.7874 in.)
Runout	0.02 mm max. (0.0008 in. max.)
Timing gear backlash	0.05-0.13 mm (0.002-0.005 in.)
Maximum allowable	0.3 mm (0.012 in.)
Push rod runout—max.	0.03 mm (0.0012 in.)
Valve lifter	
Type	Mechanical
Outside diameter	10.000 mm (0.3937 in.)
Outside diameter—min.	9.95 mm (0.3917 in.)
Clearance in block	0.025-0.060 mm (0.0010-0.0024 in.)
Max. clearance	0.10 mm (0.004 in.)
Valve face angle	45°
Valve seat angle	45°
Valve head margin	0.75-1.15 mm (0.030-0.045 in.)
Seat width (int. and exh.)	1.77 mm (0.070 in.)
Valve depth—max.	1.25 mm (0.049 in.)
Valve stem clearance (int. and exh.)	0.045-0.070 mm (0.0018-0.0028 in.)
Max. stem clearance	0.15 mm (0.006 in.)
Valve stem diameter	7.000 mm (0.2756 mm)
Valve stem wear limit	6.900 mm (0.2717 in.)
Valve stem runout—max.	0.03 mm (0.0012 in.)
Valve guide diameter	7.000 mm (0.2756 mm)
Valve guide wear limit	7.080 mm (0.2878 in.)
Valve guide protrusion	7.0 mm (0.276 in.)
Valve spring	
Standard free length	38.5 mm (1.52 in.)
Min. free length	37 mm (1.46 in.)
Installed height	29.2 mm (1.15 in.)
Pressure at installed height	16.16 kg at 29.2 mm (35.63 lb. at 1.15 in.)
Rocker arm shaft clearance	0.016-0.052 mm (0.0006-0.0020 in.)
Rocker arm shaft clearance—max.	0.15 mm (0.006 in.)
Rocker arm bore wear limit	12.10 mm (0.476 in.)
Rocker arm shaft wear limit	11.90 mm (0.468 in.)
Oil pump	
Inner rotor tip-to-outer rotor tip	0.050-0.105 mm (0.0020-0.0041 in.)
Max.	0.15 mm (0.006 in.)
Outer rotor-to-pump body	0.050-0.105 mm (0.0020-0.0041 in.)
Max.	0.15 mm (0.006 in.)
Rotor side clearance	0.030-0.080 mm
Max.	0.13 mm (0.005 in.)
Shaft clearance	0.015-0.050 mm (0.0006-0.0020 in.)
Max.	0.20 mm (0.0079 in.)

Table 2 TIGHTENING TORQUES

Fastener	N•m	ft.-lb.	in.-lb.
Camshaft gear	70-80	52-59	–
Connecting rod bolts	25	18	–
Crankshaft nut	80-100	59-74	–
Cylinder head nut	75	55	–
Exhaust elbow	45	33	–
Flywheel	65-70	48-52	–
Main bearing housing	25	18	–
Oil pump	9	–	80
Rocker shaft support	37	27	–
Timing gearcase	9	–	80

Chapter Six

Multicylinder Engines

This chapter covers the Yanmar 2GM, 2GM20, 3GM, 3GM30, 3HM and 3HM35 multicylinder, marine diesel engines.

The engine consists of a cast iron cylinder block with full-length water jackets around each cylinder. 2GM, 3GM, 3HM (including F and D series) engines have replaceable cast iron cylinder liners.

Crankshaft rotation is counterclockwise as viewed from the flywheel. On two cylinder engines, the crankshaft operates in three main bearings, with the center bearing providing the thrust surfaces. On three cylinder engines, the crankshaft operates in four main bearings, with the third bearing providing the thrust surfaces. The crankshaft gear drives the rotor-type oil pump located in the lower front of the engine block.

The camshaft is gear driven and located in the block above the crankshaft. One end of the camshaft is supported by a ball bearing (front) and the other rides directly in the block (rear).

On three cylinder engines, the camshaft is equipped with two additional bearings. In addition to operating the valves, the camshaft operates the fuel transfer pump and has an actuating lobe for the injection pump attached at the front.

Valve actuation is via mechanical lifters and pushrods acting on the rocker arms mounted in the cylinder head.

The cylinders on 2GM and 2GM20 engines are numbered from rear (flywheel) to front (timing gearcase): 1-2.

The cylinders on 3GM, 3GM30, 3HM and 3HM35 engines are numbered from rear (flywheel) to front (timing gearcase): 1-2-3. The firing order is 1-2-3.

Engine specifications (**Tables 1-3**) and tightening torques (**Table 4**) are located at the end of this chapter.

Refer to Chapter Five for diesel engine fundamentals.

NOTE

Except where specified, F and D series engines are included when a basic model number is specified. For example, if model 3GM is called out in a procedure, the procedure also applies to 3GMD and 3GMF.

ENGINE SERIAL NUMBER AND CODE

The engine serial number and model designation plate is attached to the timing gearcase (**Figure 1**). The engine serial number is also stamped on the side of the cylinder block (**Figure 2**).

Have the engine model number and serial number available when ordering parts. Record the engine model and serial numbers and store them for future reference in case the identification plate on the engine is defaced or lost.

REPLACEMENT PARTS

When installing new parts on the engine, make sure the part is designed for use on a marine engine. Automotive and marine engine parts may look similar; however, automotive parts may not be capable of operating in a harsh marine environment.

Use only Yanmar parts or parts approved for use on marine engines.

ENGINE

Precautions

Some service procedures can be performed with the engine in the boat; others require removal. The boat design and service procedure to be performed determines whether the engine must be removed.

WARNING
The engine is heavy, awkward to handle and has sharp edges. It may shift or drop suddenly during removal. To prevent serious injury, always observe the following precautions.

1. Never place any part of your body where a moving or falling engine may trap, cut or crush you.
2. If you must push the engine during removal, use a board or similar tool to keep your hands out of danger.
3. Be sure the hoist is designed to lift engines and has enough load capacity for the engine.
4. Be sure the hoist is securely attached to safe lifting points on the engine.
5. The engine should not be difficult to lift with a proper hoist. If it is, stop lifting, lower the engine back onto its mounts and make sure the engine has been completely separated from the vessel.

Removal/Installation

While specific procedures cannot address all engine installations, refer to the following general instructions when removing the engine.

1. Detach the negative battery cable from the negative battery terminal.
2. Close the seacock. Drain the cooling system, including

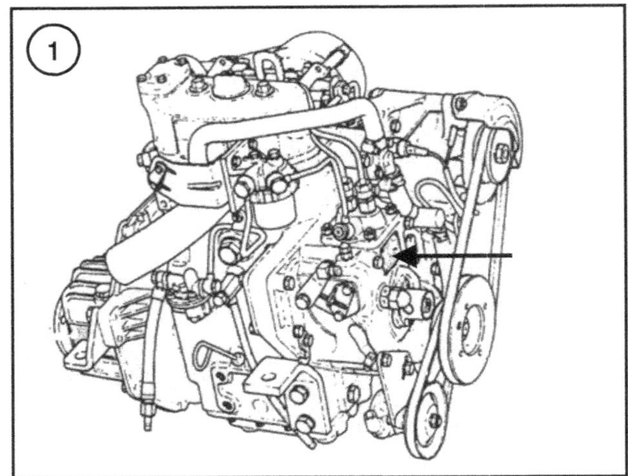

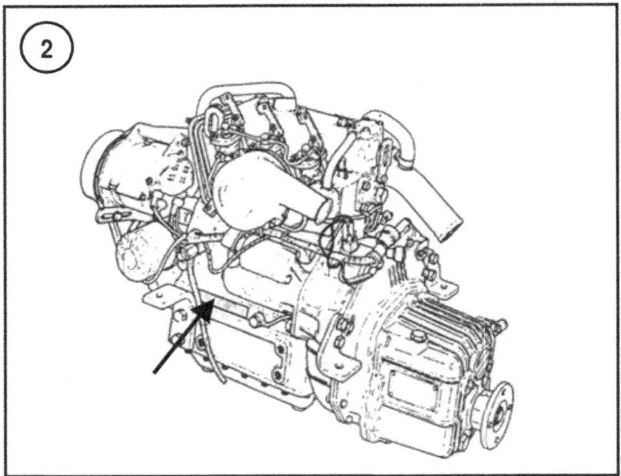

the freshwater system, if so equipped, as described in Chapter Four.
3. Disconnect the intake water hose from the seawater cooling pump.
4. Close the fuel shutoff valve and disconnect the fuel line and the fuel return line.
5. Disconnect the remote control cables.
6. Disconnect the electrical wiring harness connectors.
7. Disconnect the electrical wires from the electric starter motor and solenoid that will interfere with engine removal.
8. Detach the exhaust system.
9. Detach the driveshaft from the transmission output flange.
10. Remove the engine retaining bolts.
11. Remove the engine and transmission.
12. Remove the transmission from the engine as described in Chapter Ten or Eleven.

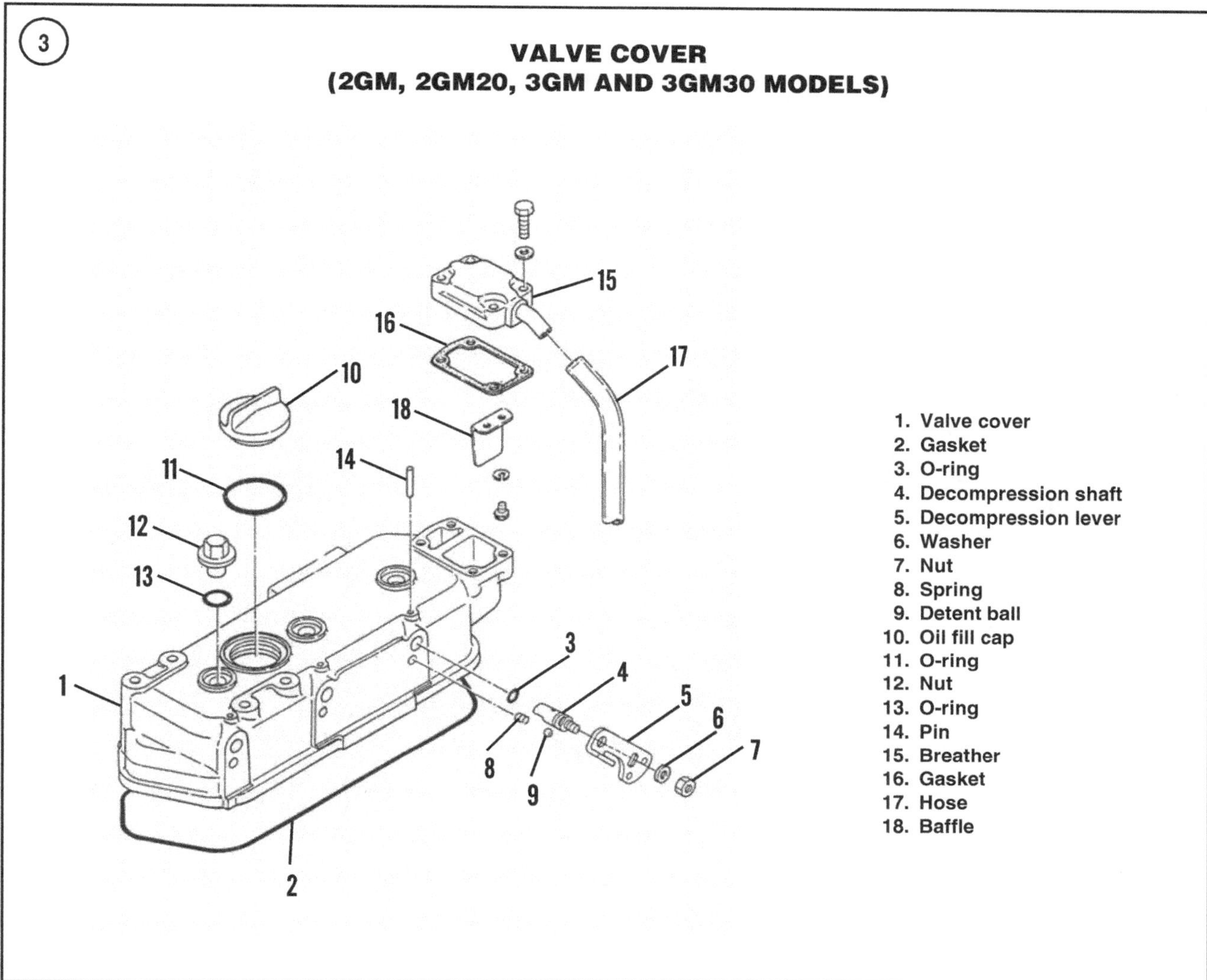

13. Engine installation is the reverse of removal, plus the following:
    a. Tighten the engine mounting bolts securely.
    b. Securely tighten the output flange-to-driveshaft bolts.
    c. Bleed the fuel system at the fuel filter as described under *Fuel Filter* in Chapter Three.
    d. Refill the freshwater cooling system, if so equipped, as described in Chapter Eight.

VALVE COVER

Refer to **Figure 3** and **Figure 4** for an exploded view of the valve cover assembly.

To remove the valve cover, proceed as follows:

1. Be sure the decompression lever is in the OFF position.
2. Disconnect the breather hose.
3. Unscrew the retaining nuts.
4. Remove the valve cover.
5. Remove the gasket.
6. Clean the gasket surfaces on the valve cover and cylinder head.
7. Reverse the removal steps to install the valve cover.

BREATHER ASSEMBLY

The crankcase breather is located in the valve cover. Refer to Chapter Three for a description of breather operation.

To service the breather, proceed as follows:

1. Remove the valve cover.
2. Remove the breather cover.

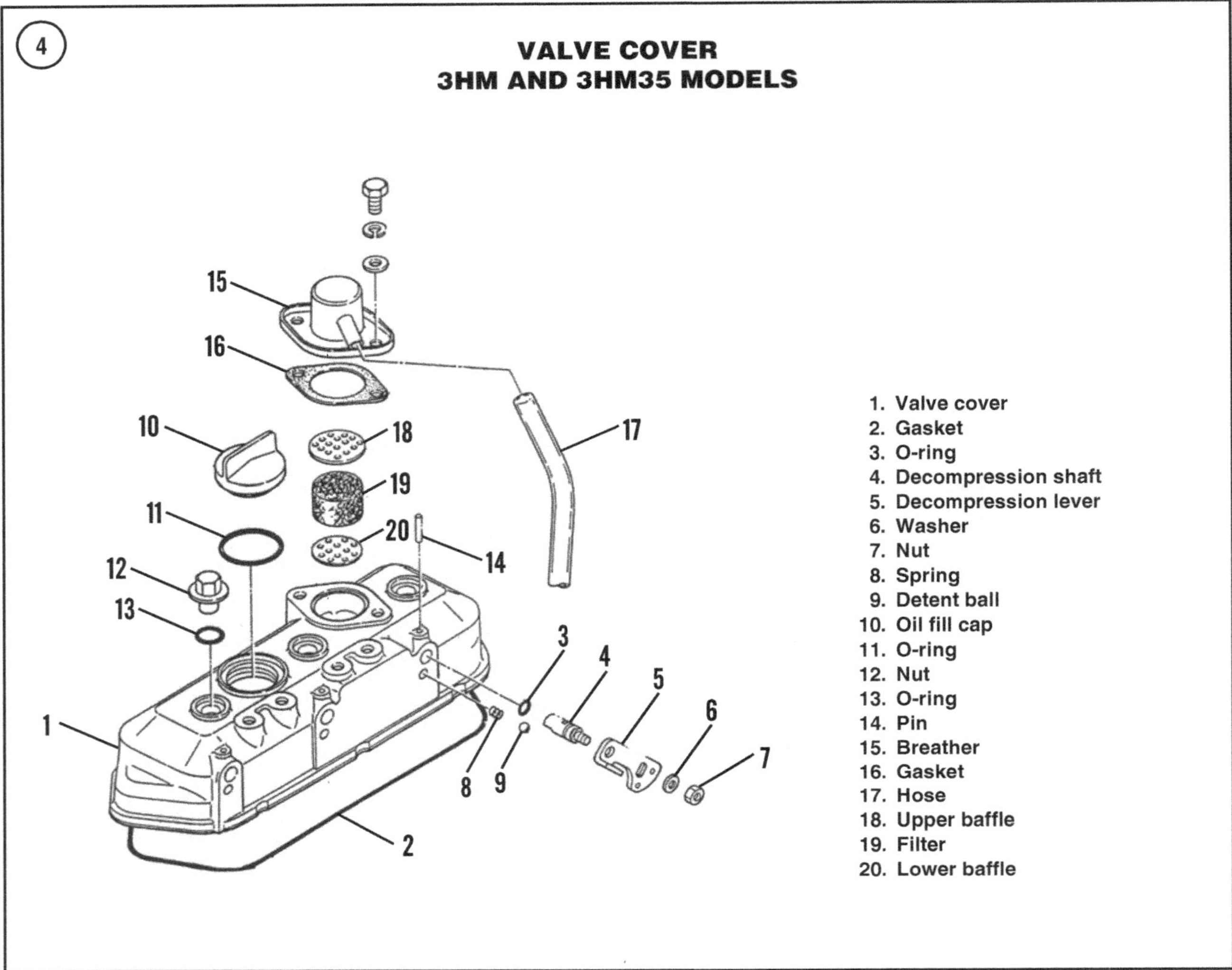

3. Clean the breather components and valve cover using solvent. Be sure the drain hole in the valve cover is open.
4. *3HM and 3HM35 models*—Replace the mesh breather element if it cannot be cleaned or if it is damaged.
5. Reassemble the breather by reversing the disassembly procedure. Note that the lower baffle (20, **Figure 4**) on 3HM and 3HM35 engines is smaller than the upper plate (18).

DECOMPRESSION MECHANISM

The decompression mechanism on the valve cover forces the exhaust valves open to reduce compression pressure in the cylinders. Reducing compression pressure enables the starter to rotate the crankshaft faster during starting. Refer to **Figure 3** and **Figure 4**.

If the mechanism must be repaired, proceed as follows:

1. Remove the valve cover as previously described.
2. Using a suitable punch, drive out the retaining pin.

NOTE
The detent ball and spring will be loose when you remove the shaft assembly in Step 3.

3. Remove the shaft assembly from the valve cover.
4. Inspect the mechanism and replace the damaged parts.
5. Reverse the removal procedure to reassemble the decompression mechanism. Note the following:
   a. Assemble the shaft and lever so the lever points up while the flat on the valve end of the shaft is down.

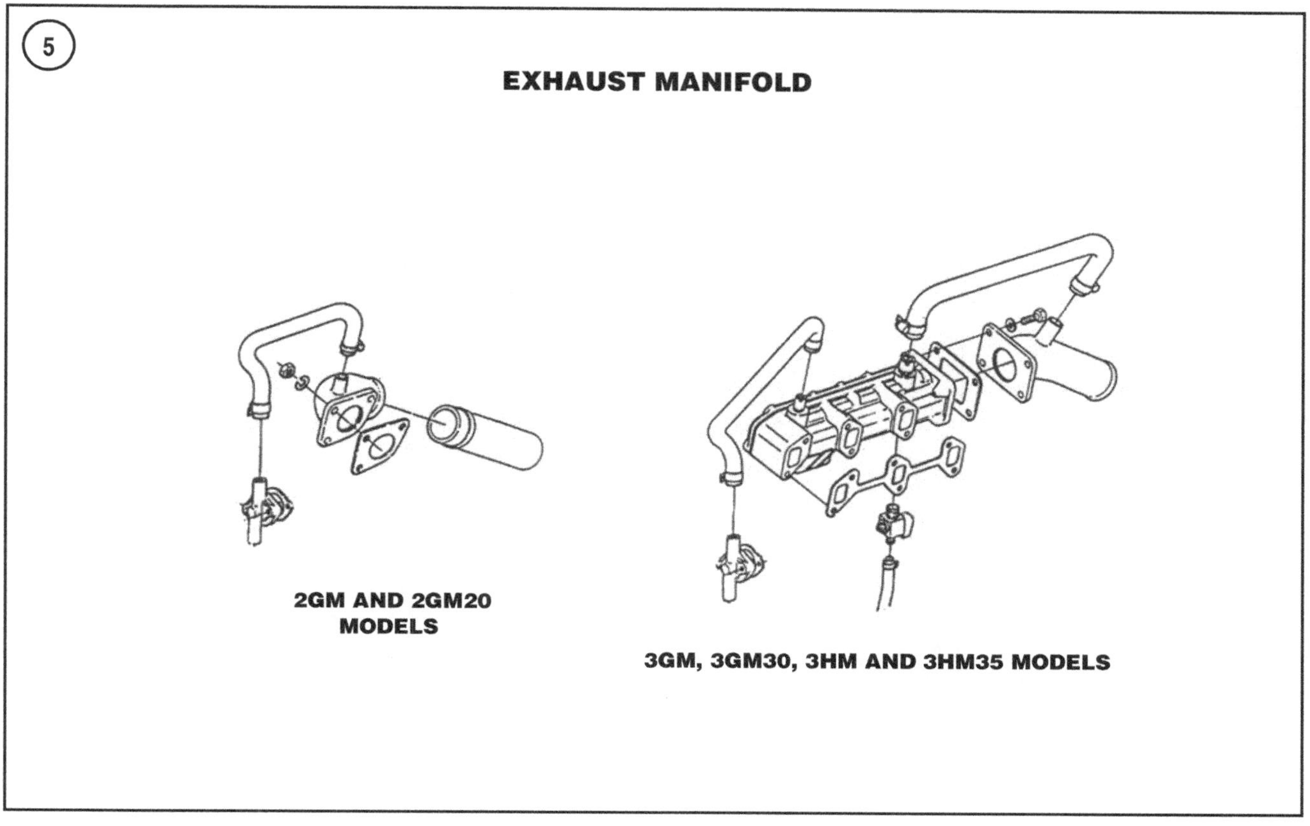

EXHAUST MANIFOLD

On 2GM models, the exhaust manifold is an elbow that is attached to the cylinder head (**Figure 5**). A hose from the thermostat cover directs cooling water into the exhaust elbow.

On 3GM models, the exhaust manifold contains water passages that allow water to cool the manifold. A hose from the thermostat cover directs cooling water into the exhaust manifold (**Figure 5**). A hose from the exhaust manifold directs water from the exhaust manifold into the exhaust elbow.

The exhaust manifold on 2GMF, 2GM20F, 3GMF, 3GM30F, 3HMF and 3HM35F models is combined with the coolant reservoir for the freshwater (closed) cooling system (**Figure 6**). Refer to Chapter Eight for a description of the freshwater (closed) cooling system.

Removal and Installation

2GM models

Refer to **Figure 5**.

1. Detach the exhaust hose from the exhaust elbow.
2. Loosen the hose clamps and remove the water hose from the exhaust elbow and thermostat housing.
3. Remove the exhaust elbow from the cylinder head.
4. Clean any gasket residue from the exhaust elbow and cylinder head.
5. Check the exhaust elbow for warpage, carbon buildup and corrosion.
6. Reinstall the exhaust elbow by reversing the removal procedure. Tighten the retaining nuts to the torque specified in **Table 2**.

3GM, 3GM30, 3HM and 3HM35 models with seawater cooling

Refer to **Figure 5**.

1. Detach the exhaust hose from the exhaust elbow.
2. Loosen the hose clamps and remove the water hose from the exhaust manifold and thermostat housing.
3. Open the drain valve on the underside of the exhaust manifold.
4. Remove the exhaust manifold from the cylinder head.
5. If necessary, remove the water hose and exhaust elbow from the exhaust manifold.

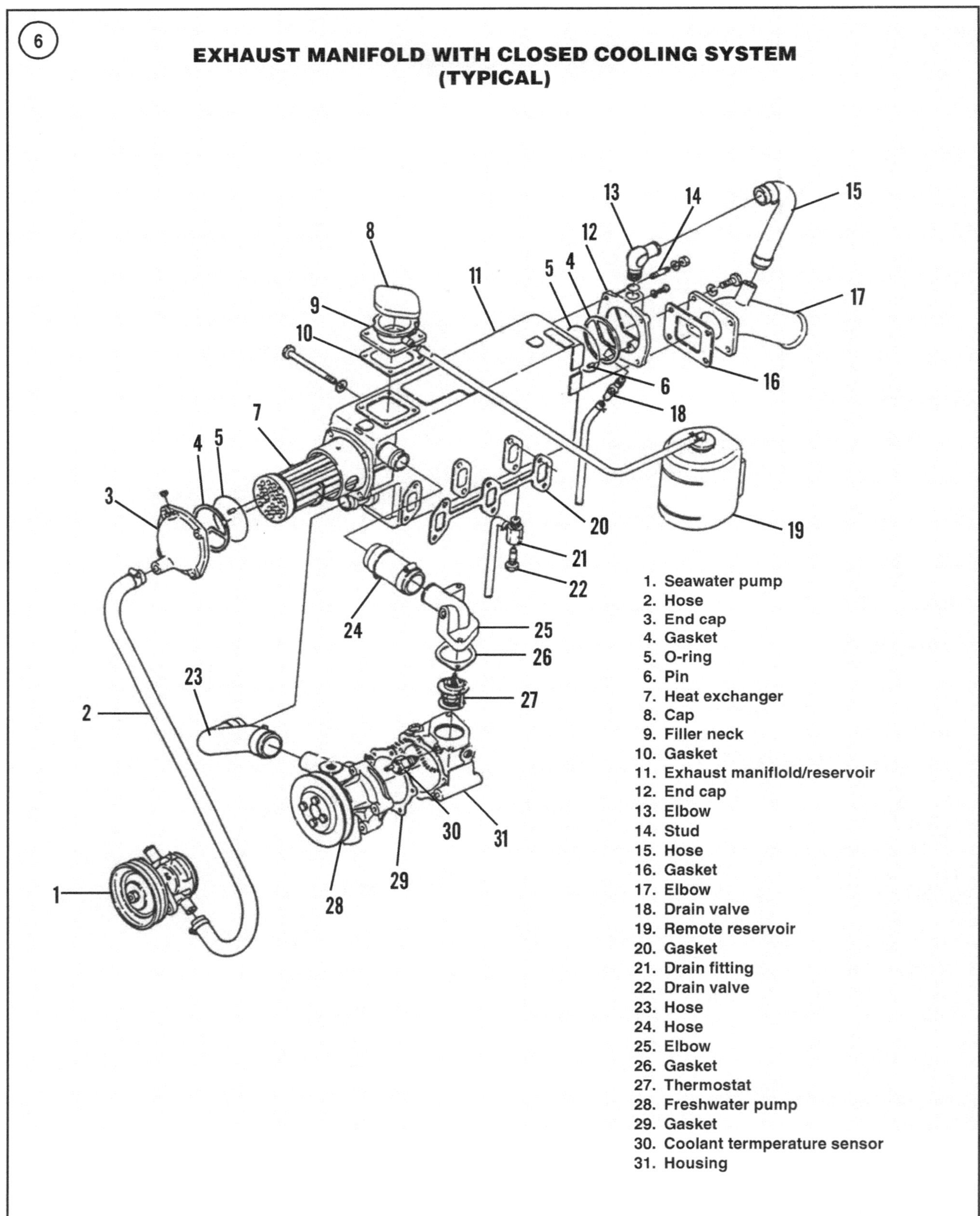
6
EXHAUST MANIFOLD WITH CLOSED COOLING SYSTEM
(TYPICAL)
1
2
3
4
5
7
8
9
10
11
5
4
12
13
14
15
17
16
6
18
19
20
21
22
23
24
25
26
27
28
29
30
31
1. Seawater pump
2. Hose
3. End cap
4. Gasket
5. O-ring
6. Pin
7. Heat exchanger
8. Cap
9. Filler neck
10. Gasket
11. Exhaust maniflold/reservoir
12. End cap
13. Elbow
14. Stud
15. Hose
16. Gasket
17. Elbow
18. Drain valve
19. Remote reservoir
20. Gasket
21. Drain fitting
22. Drain valve
23. Hose
24. Hose
25. Elbow
26. Gasket
27. Thermostat
28. Freshwater pump
29. Gasket
30. Coolant termperature sensor
31. Housing

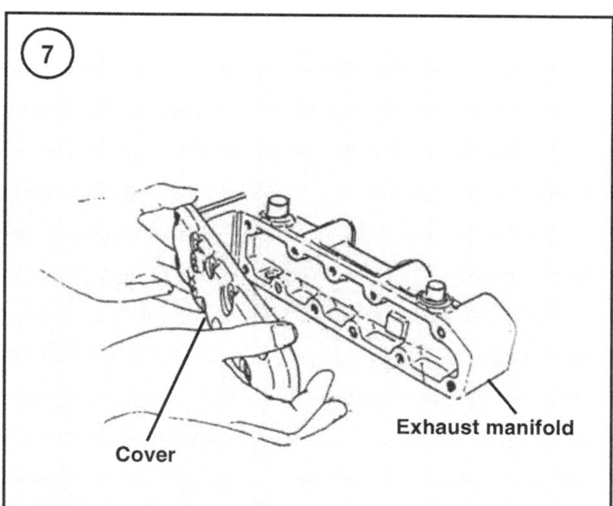

6. Clean any gasket residue from the exhaust manifold and cylinder head.
7. Remove the exhaust manifold cover retaining screws and remove the manifold cover (**Figure 7**).
8. Inspect the exhaust manifold and cover for warpage, carbon buildup and corrosion.
9. Reinstall the exhaust manifold and cover by reversing the removal procedure. Tighten the retaining nuts to the torque specified in **Table 2**.

2GMF, 2GM20F, 3GMF, 3GM30F, 3HMF and 3HM35F models with freshwater (closed) cooling system

Refer to **Figure 6**.
1. Refer to Chapter Four and drain the cooling system.
2. Detach the exhaust hose from the exhaust elbow.
3. Remove the water hose from the exhaust manifold and thermostat housing.
4. Remove the water hose from the exhaust manifold and freshwater pump.
5. Disconnect the water hoses from the manifold end caps.
6. Disconnect the water hose to the overflow tank.
7. Remove the exhaust manifold from the cylinder head.
8. Clean any gasket residue from the exhaust manifold and cylinder head.
9. Check the exhaust manifold for warpage, carbon buildup and corrosion.
10. If necessary, refer to Chapter Eight to service the heat exhanger inside the exhaust manifold.
11. Reverse the removal procedure to install the exhaust manifold. Tighten the manifold bolts to the torque specified in **Table 2**. Fill the freshwater section of the closed cooling system with coolant as described in Chapter Three.

CYLINDER HEAD

Removal

In some instances, the cylinder head may be removed for service without removing the engine. If engine removal is necessary, refer to the engine removal procedure. Refer to **Figure 8** for an exploded view of the cylinder head assembly.

To remove the cylinder head, proceed as follows:
1. Disconnect the negative battery cable from the negative battery terminal.
2. If not previously performed, drain the cooling system as described in Chapter Four.
3. Remove the alternator as described in Chapter Eight.
4. Remove the exhaust manifold as previously described.
5. Disconnect the wire lead from the water temperature sender (**Figure 9**).
6A. *Engines with standard cooling*—Disconnect the lower water hose (**Figure 9**) from the thermostat housing.
6B. *Engines with freshwater (closed) cooling system*—Remove the freshwater pump as described in Chapter Eight.
7. Remove the air cleaner and the air cleaner base.
8. Remove the fuel injector and precombustion chamber as described in Chapter Seven.
9. Remove the valve cover as previously described.
10. Remove the nuts that retain the rocker arm stands (**Figure 10**), then remove the rocker shaft assembly.
11. Remove the push rods and mark them so they can be reinstalled in their original positions.
12. Detach the oil line fitting from the cylinder head.
13. Unscrew the smaller cylinder head retaining bolts first, then unscrew the larger bolts and nuts in a crossing pattern.
14. Remove the cylinder head and head gasket.

Inspection

1. Refer to the *Anticorrosion Maintenance* section in Chapter Three. Remove and inspect the sacrificial anode. Install the anode in the cylinder head after completing cylinder head service.
2. If service to the valves or rocker assembly is required, refer to the *Valves* and *Rocker Assembly* sections.
3. Check the cylinder head for signs of oil or water leakage before cleaning. Look for corrosion or foreign material in the oil and water passages.

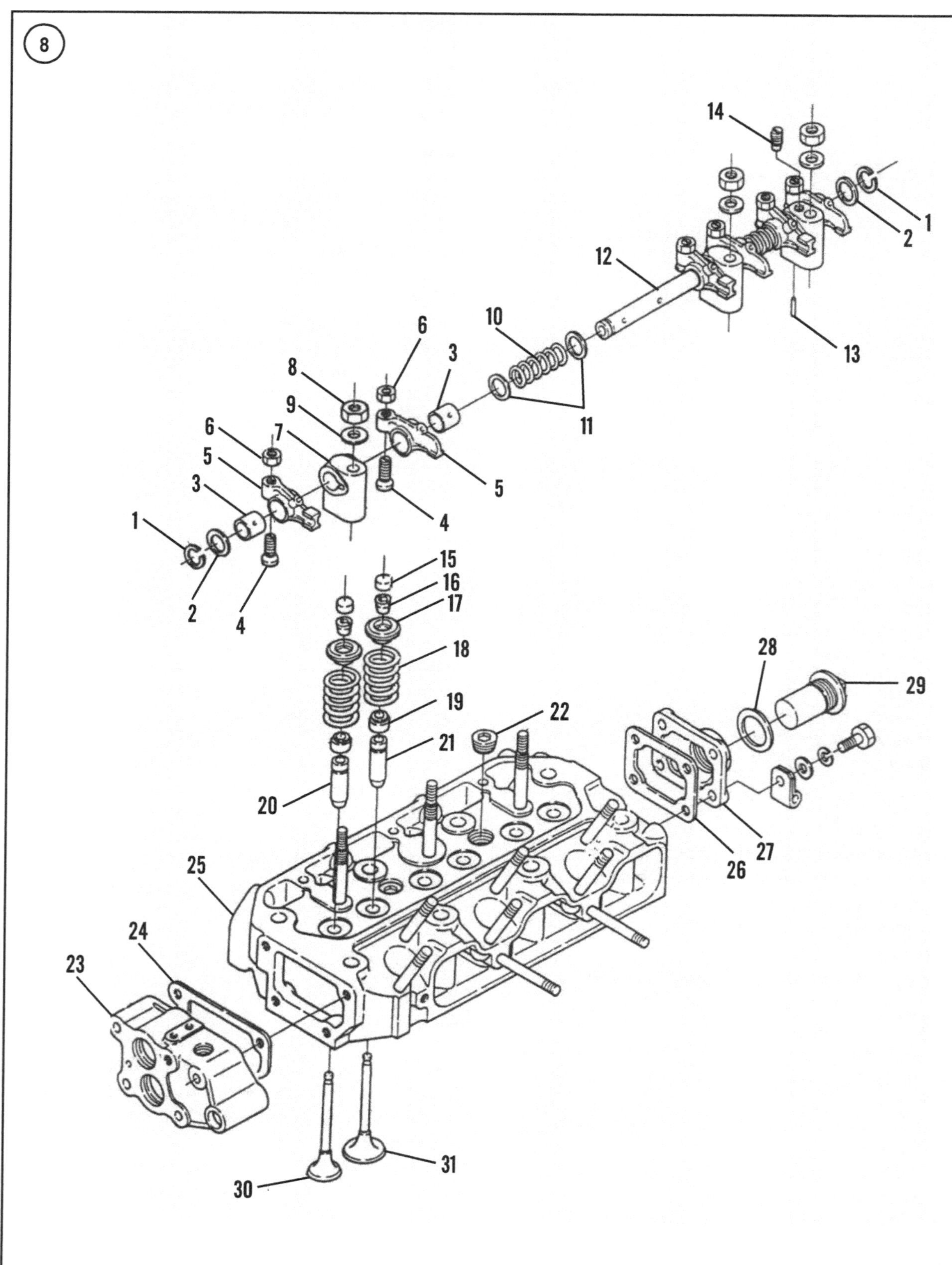
8
14
1
2
12
10
13
6
3
8
11
9
6
7
5
5
3
4
1
2
4
15
16
17
18
28
29
19
22
21
20
25
26
27
24
23
30
31

CYLINDER HEAD

1. Snap ring
2. Washer
3. Bushing
4. Adjuster
5. Rocker arm
6. Nut
7. Rocker shaft stand
8. Nut
9. Washer
10. Spring
11. Washer
12. Rocker arm shaft
13. Pin
14. Locating screw
15. Wear cap
16. Keys
17. Valve spring retainer
18. Vavle spring
19. Valve seal
20. Exhaust valve guide
21. Intake valve guide
22. Plug
23. Thermostat housing
24. Gasket
25. Cylinder head
26. Gasket
27. End cap
28. Washer
29. Sacrificial anode
30. Exhaust valve
31. Intake valve

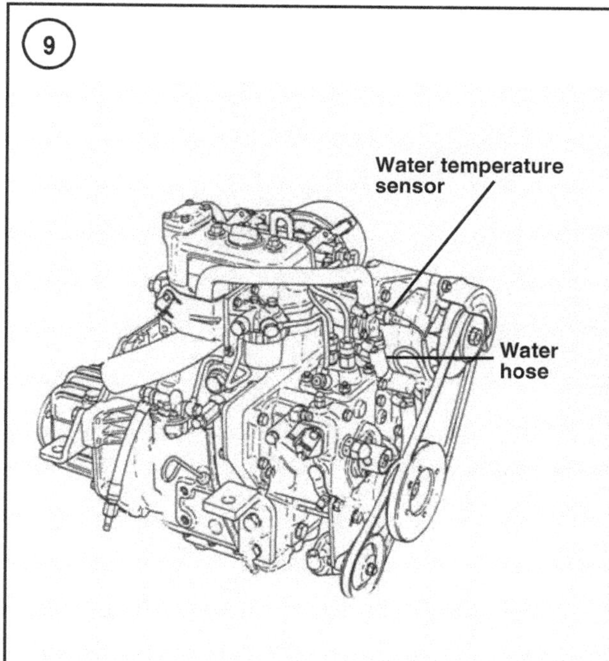

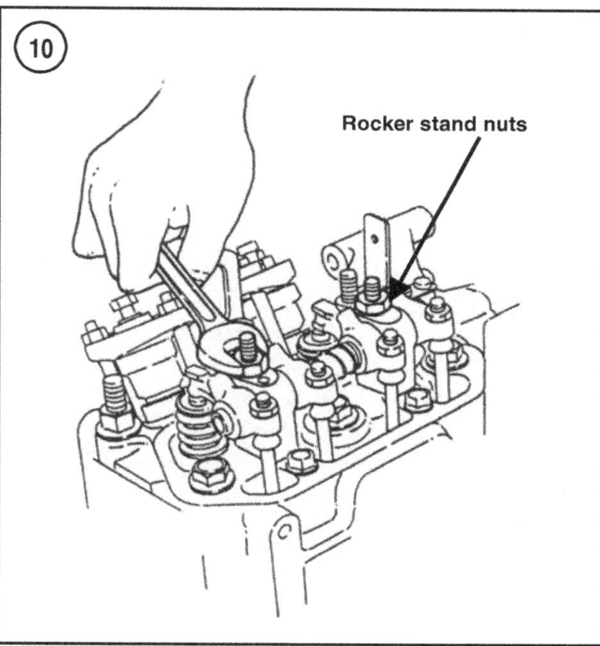

4. Without removing the valves, remove all deposits from the combustion chamber. Use a fine wire brush dipped in solvent or make a scraper from hardwood. Be careful not to scratch or gouge the combustion chamber.

5. After all carbon is removed from the combustion chamber and ports, clean the entire head in solvent. While

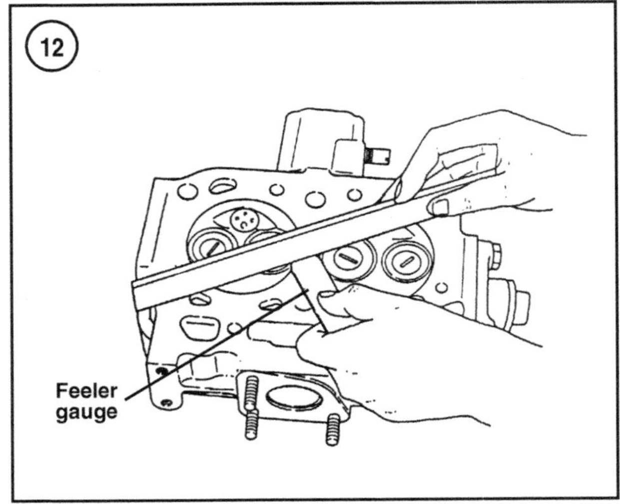

cleaning, look for cracks or other visible signs of damage. Clean the passages with a stiff spiral brush, then blow them out with compressed air.

NOTE
If deposits are found in the intake or exhaust ports, remove the valves and clean the ports.

6. Clean away all carbon on the piston top.
7. Check the cylinder head studs for damage and replace them if necessary. If a stud is loose, tighten it using the following procedure:
   a. Install two nuts on the stud as shown in **Figure 11**, typical.
   b. Rotate the nuts so they contact each other, then hold one nut and tighten the other nut against the first nut.
   c. Tighten the stud in the cylinder block by turning the top nut until reaching a torque of 80 N•m (59 ft.-lb.).
   d. Hold the bottom nut, loosen the top nut, and remove both nuts.
8. Check the threaded rocker arm support stud for damaged threads. Replace if necessary.
9. Check for warpage of the cylinder head-to-block gasket surface with a straightedge and feeler gauge (**Figure 12**). Measure diagonally, as well as end to end. If the gap exceeds 0.07 mm (0.003 in.), have the head resurfaced by a machine shop.

Installation

1. Make sure the cylinder head and block gasket surfaces are clean.
2. Recheck all visible oil and water passages for cleanliness.
3. Apply Three Bond 50 gasket sealer to both sides of a new cylinder head gasket.

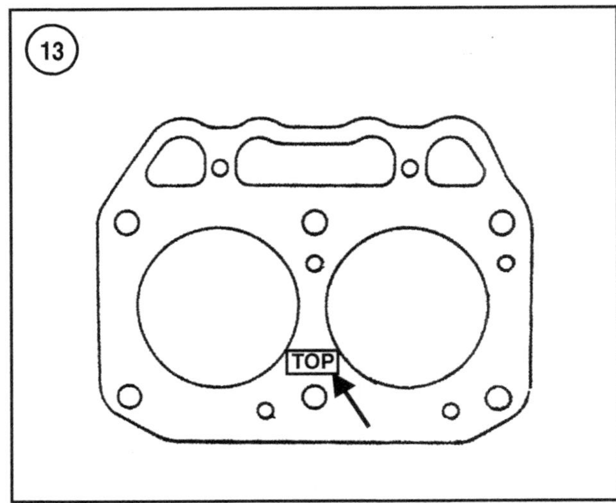

4. Place the new head gasket over the cylinder head studs on the block. Be sure the TOP mark (**Figure 13**) on the gasket is up.
5. Carefully lower the head onto the cylinder block.
6. Apply engine oil to the threads on the cylinder head studs.
7. Install and tighten the cylinder head retaining nuts finger-tight.
8. Tighten the nuts and bolts following the sequence shown in **Figure 14** to the torque specified in **Table 2**. Tighten the nuts and bolts in three equal steps until reaching the final torque setting.
9. If removed, install the sacrificial anode into the cylinder head.
10. Attach the oil line fitting to the cylinder head.
11. Install the push rods in their original position.

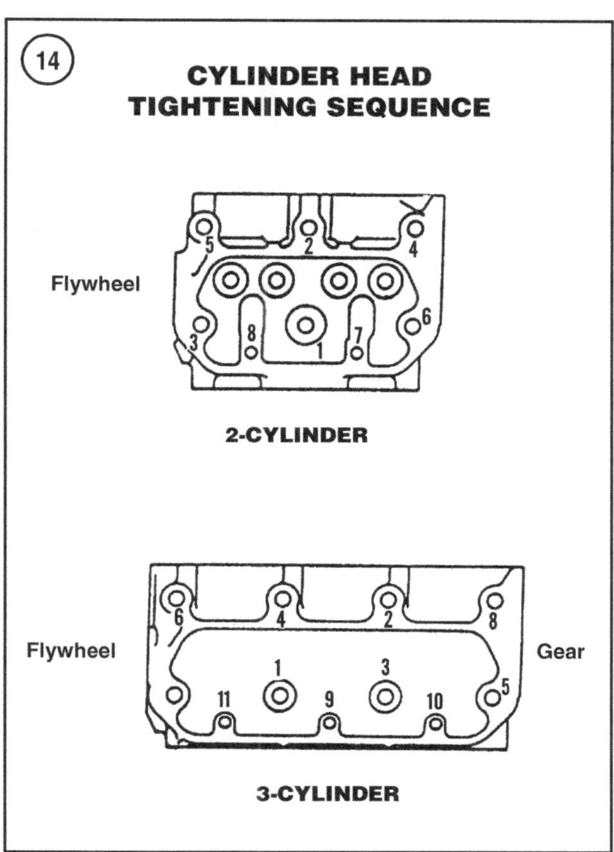

12. Install the rocker assembly and the rocker arm stand retaining nuts (**Figure 10**). Tighten the nuts to 37 N•m (27 ft.-lb.).

13. Install the fuel injector and precombustion chamber as described in Chapter Seven.

14. Install the exhaust manifold.

15. Install the air cleaner base and the air cleaner.

16. Connect the wire lead to the water temperature sender (**Figure 9**).

17A. Engines with standard cooling—Connect the lower water hose (**Figure 9**).

17B. Engines with freshwater (closed) cooling system—Install the freshwater pump as described in Chapter Eight.

18. Install the alternator.

19. If the engine is installed in the boat, proceed as follows:

   a. Attach the exhaust hose to the exhaust elbow.
   b. On engines equipped with a closed cooling system, fill the cooling system as described in Chapter Four.
   c. Connect the negative battery cable to the negative battery terminal.

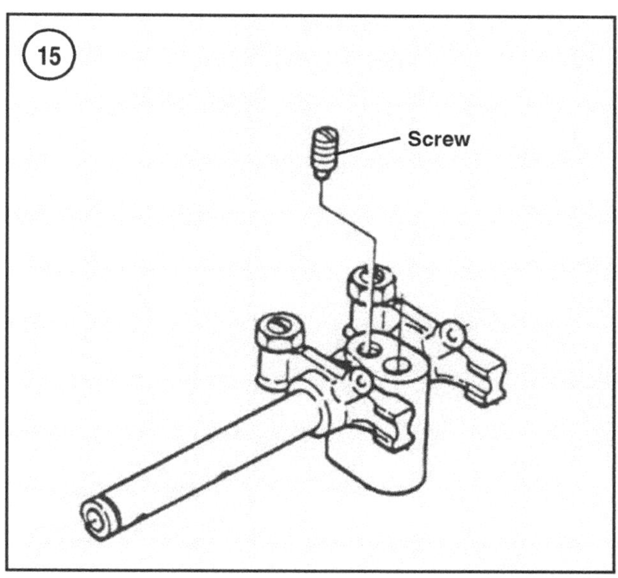

20. Adjust the valve clearance as described in Chapter Three.

21. Reinstall the valve cover.

ROCKER SHAFT ASSEMBLY

Each valve is actuated by a rocker arm that rides on a shaft (**Figure 8**). Each rocker arm is equipped with a bushing in the rocker arm bore. A snap ring at each end of the rocker arm shaft retains the rocker arms on the rocker shafts.

1. Remove the valve cover as previously described.
2. Remove the rocker arm stand retaining nuts (**Figure 10**), then remove the rocker shaft assembly.

NOTE
The rocker arms on 2GM and 2GM20 engines are identical, but rocker arms on 3GM, 3GM30, 3HM and 3HM35 engines are designed for use with the intake or exhaust valves.

3. Remove the snap rings at both ends of the rocker shaft and remove the rocker shaft components.
4. If necessary, unscrew the locating screw in the end support stand (**Figure 15**) and separate the rocker shaft from the stand.
5. Inspect each rocker arm. The pad on the rocker arm that contacts the valve stem must be smooth. Replace the rocker arm if the pad is damaged or excessively worn. Check the adjusting screw push rod seat for galling. Replace the adjusting screw if it is damaged or excessively worn.

6

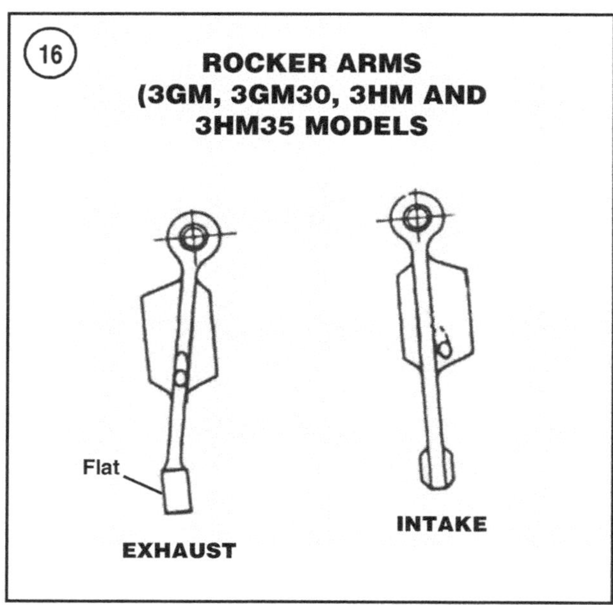

6. Inspect and measure the inside diameter of the rocker arm bushing and the outside diameter of the rocker arm shaft. Replace the rocker arm or rocker arm shaft if the measurements exceed the specifications listed in **Tables 1-3**.

NOTE
The rocker arm and bushing are available only as a unit.

7. Reassemble and reinstall the rocker arm assembly by reversing the removal procedure. On 3GM, 3GM30, 3HM and 3HM35 engines, identify the intake and exhaust valves as shown in **Figure 16**, then position them on the shaft in the order shown in **Figure 17**.
8. Adjust the valve clearance as described in Chapter Three.

VALVES AND VALVE SEATS

Servicing the valves, guides and valve seats must be done by a dealer or machine shop, as special knowledge and expensive machine tools are required.

A general practice among those who do their own service is to remove the cylinder head, perform all disassembly except valve removal and take the head to a dealer or machine shop for inspection and service. Since the cost is low relative to the required effort and equipment, this is usually the best approach, even for experienced mechanics. The following procedures are provided to acquaint the home mechanic with the procedure.

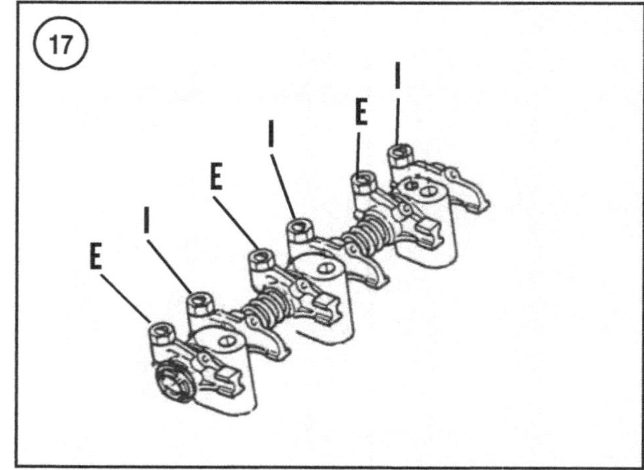

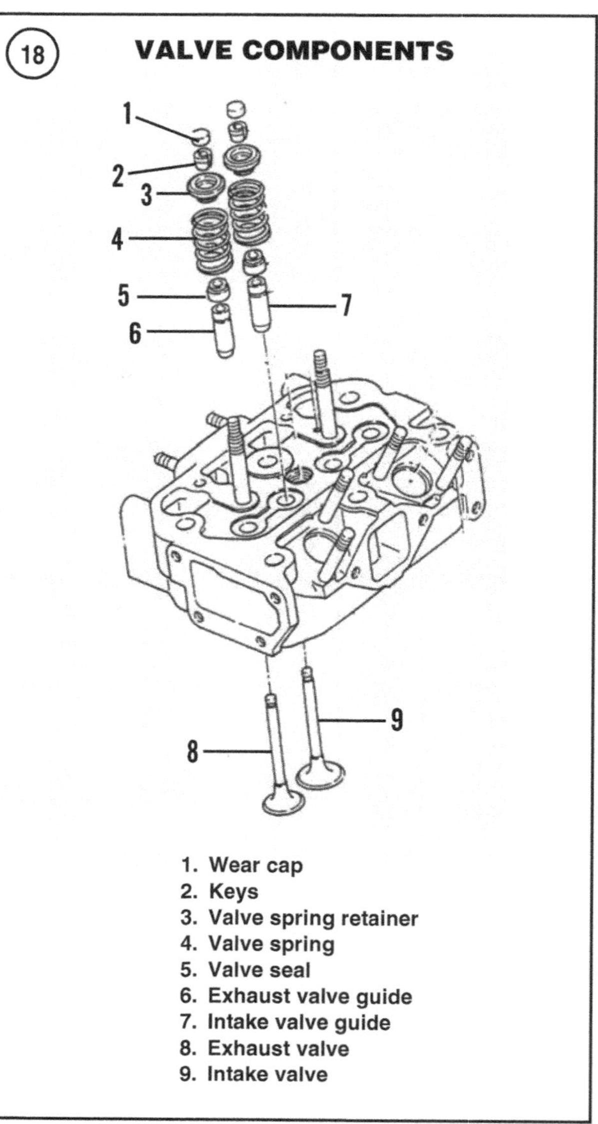

1. Wear cap
2. Keys
3. Valve spring retainer
4. Valve spring
5. Valve seal
6. Exhaust valve guide
7. Intake valve guide
8. Exhaust valve
9. Intake valve

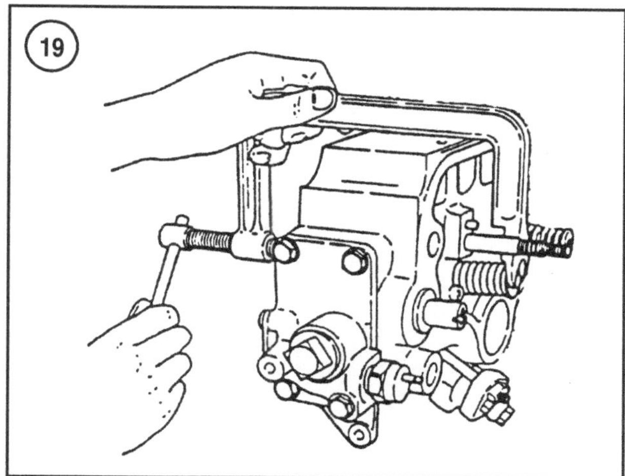

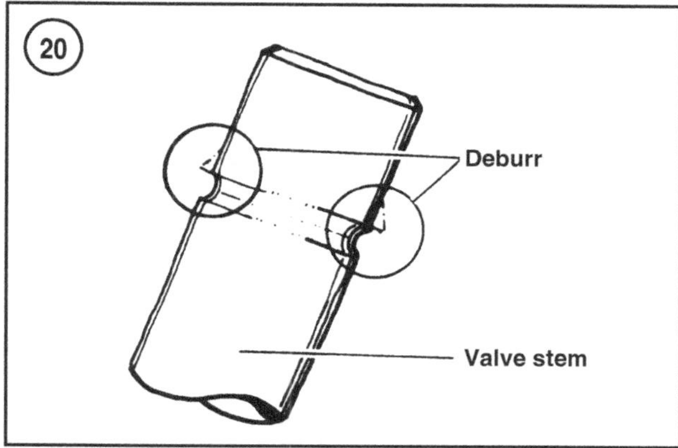

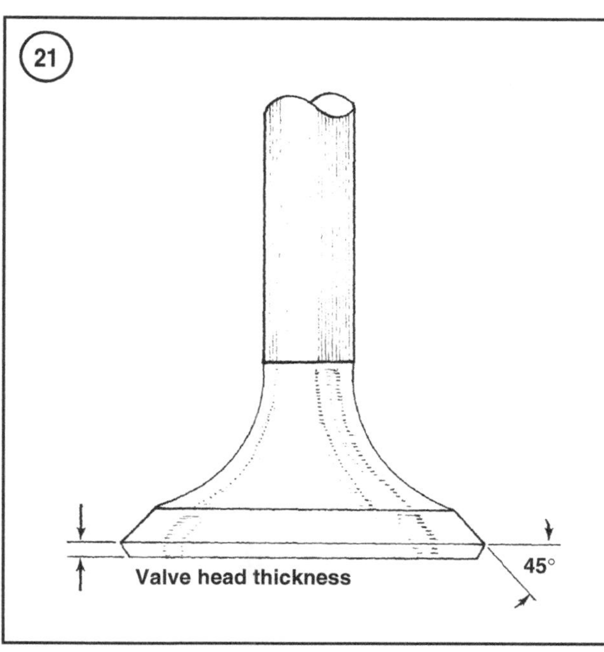

Valve Removal

Refer to **Figure 18** for this procedure.

1. Remove the cylinder head as described in this chapter.
2. Remove the rocker shaft assembly as described in this chapter.
3. Remove the wear cap (1, **Figure 18**) on the valve stem.
4. Compress the valve spring with a compressor like the one shown in **Figure 19**.
5. Remove the valve keys (2, **Figure 18**) and release the spring tension.
6. Remove the valve spring retainer and valve spring.

6

CAUTION

*Remove any burrs from the valve stem lock grooves (**Figure 20**) before removing the valve to prevent damage to the valve guide.*

7. Remove the valve.
8. Remove and discard the valve stem seal (5, **Figure 18**).
9. Repeat Steps 3-8 for the remaining valves.

Inspection

1. Clean the valves with a fine wire brush or buffing wheel. Discard any cracked, warped or burned valves.
2. Measure the valve stems at the top, center and bottom for wear. A machine shop can do this when the valves are ground.

NOTE

*Check the thickness of the valve edge or margin after the valves have been ground. See **Figure 21**. Any valve with a margin less than 0.75 mm (0.030 in.) should be discarded.*

3. Remove all carbon and varnish from the valve guides with a stiff spiral wire brush.

NOTE

The next step assumes that all valve stems have been measured and are within specifications. Replace valves with worn stems before performing this step.

4. Insert each valve into the guide from which it was removed. Holding the valve just slightly off its seat, rock it back and forth in a direction parallel with the rocker arms. This is the direction in which the greatest wear normally occurs. If the valve stem rocks more than slightly, the valve guide is probably worn.
5. If there is any doubt about valve guide condition after performing Step 4, measure the valve guide. Compare the

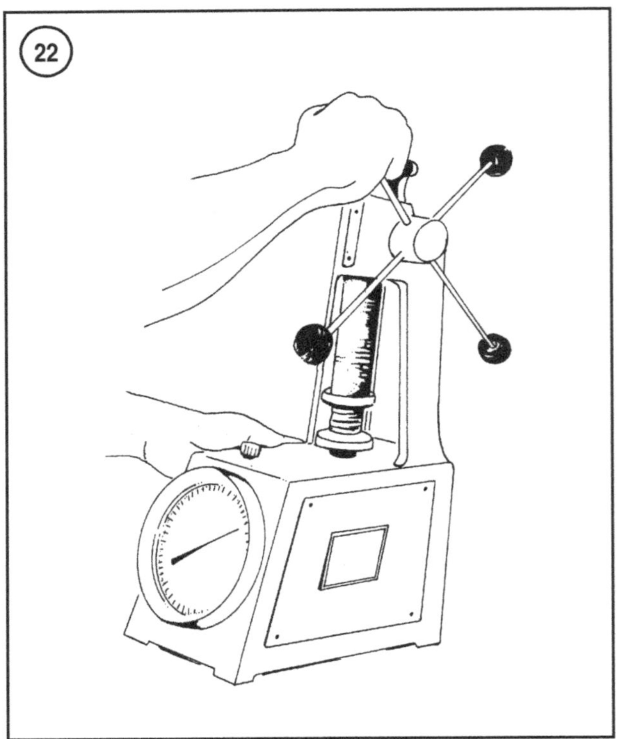

22

results with specifications in **Tables 1-3**. Worn guides must be replaced.

6. Test the valve springs under load on a spring tester (**Figure 22**). Replace any spring that does not meet the specification listed in **Tables 1-3**.

7. Inspect the valve seats. If worn or burned, they must be reconditioned.This is a job for a dealer or machine shop, although the procedure is described in this chapter.

8. Check each spring on a flat surface with a steel square. See **Figure 23**. Slowly revolve the spring 360° and note the space between the top of the coil and the square. If it exceeds 1.4 mm (0.055 in.) at any point, replace the spring.

9. Check the valve guides for wear and looseness. Refer to **Tables 1-3** for valve guide specifications. A loose valve guide must be replaced.

Valve Guide Replacement

The cylinder head is equipped with replaceable valve guides. The intake and exhaust valve guides are different in shape. Refer to **Figure 24**. The intake valve guide has a straight inside bore, while the exhaust valve guide has a stepped opening at the lower end of the guide.

Take the cylinder head to a dealership or machine shop if valve guide replacement is required.

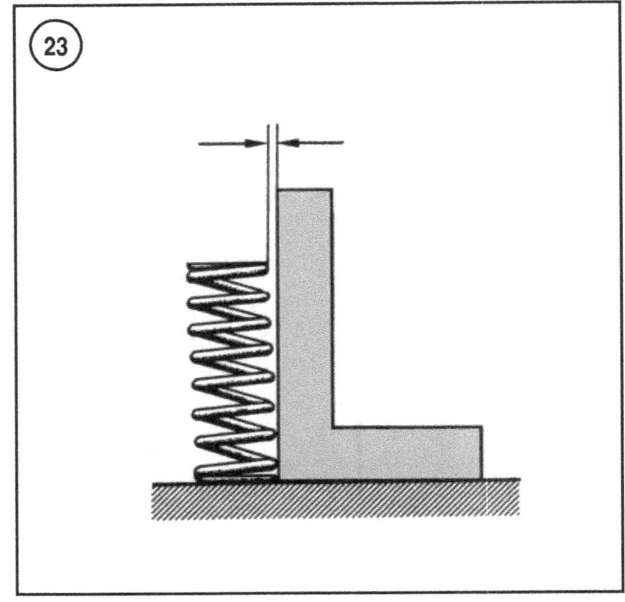

23

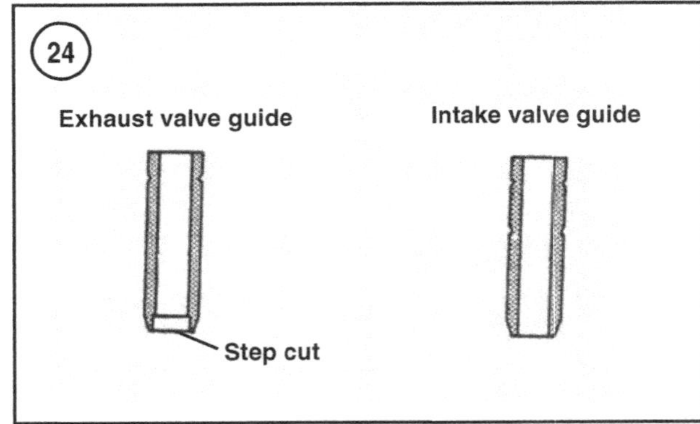

24

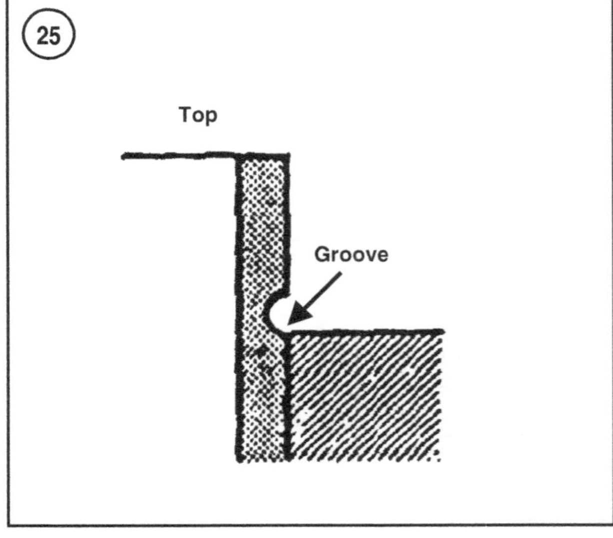

25

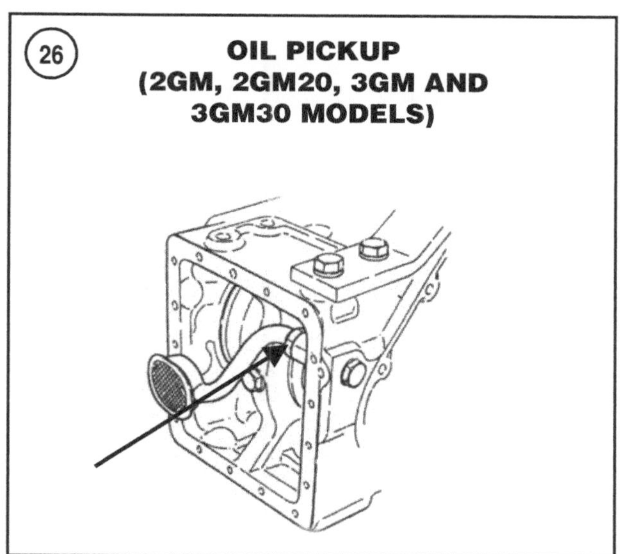

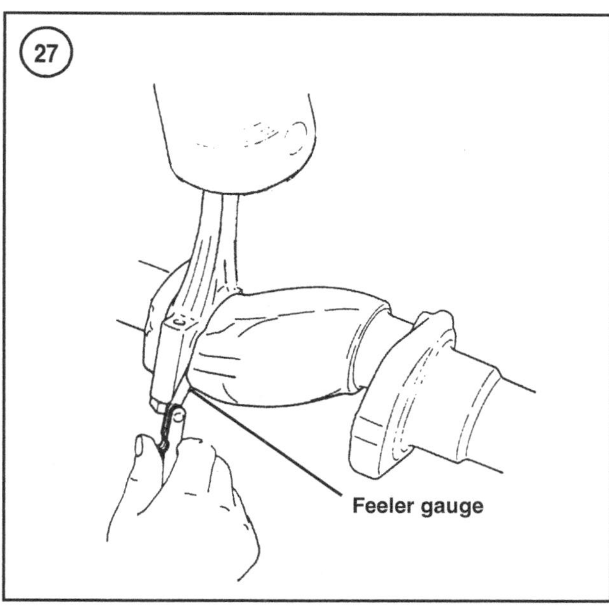

When installing the valve guides, the grooved end must be toward the top of the cylinder head. The groove must be flush with the head surface as shown in **Figure 25**.

PUSH RODS

1. Remove the rocker arms as previously described.
2. Remove the push rods and mark them so they can be reinstalled in their original positions.
3. Inspect the push rod ends for damage. Maximum allowable runout is 0.03 mm (0.0012 in.).

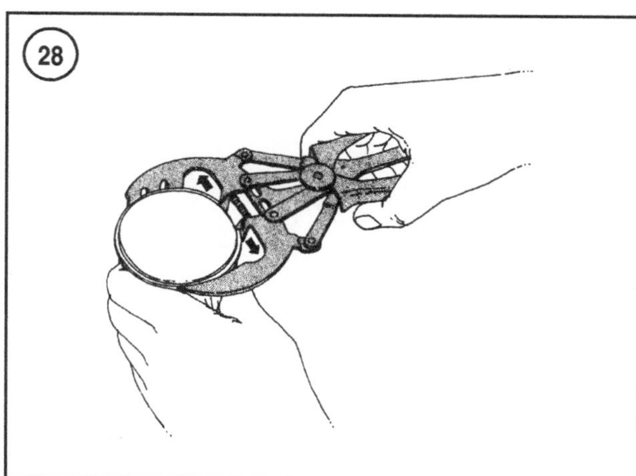

4. Reinstall the push rods by reversing the removal procedure. Adjust valve clearance as described in Chapter Three.

PISTON/CONNECTING ROD ASSEMBLY

Piston/Connecting Rod Removal

1. Remove the engine as described in this chapter.
2. Place a suitable container under the oil pan and remove the drain plug. Let the crankcase oil drain, then reinstall the drain plug.
3. Remove the cylinder head as described in this chapter.
4. Remove the oil pan.
5. *On 2GM, 2GM20, 3GM and 3GM30 models*—Loosen the oil pickup jam nut (**Figure 26**) and remove the oil pickup.
6. Rotate the crankshaft until the piston is at bottom dead center. Pack the cylinder bore with clean shop rags. Remove the carbon ridge at the top of the cylinder bore with a ridge reamer. These can be rented for use. Vacuum out the shavings, then remove the shop rags.
7. Rotate the crankshaft until the connecting rod is centered in the bore. Measure the clearance between the connecting rod and the crankshaft journal flange with a flat feeler gauge (**Figure 27**). If the clearance exceeds specifications (**Tables 1-3**), replace the connecting rod during reassembly.
8. Remove the connecting rod bolts. Lift off the cap, together with the lower bearing insert.
9. Use a wooden hammer handle to push the piston and connecting rod from the bore.
10. Remove the piston rings with a ring remover (**Figure 28**).

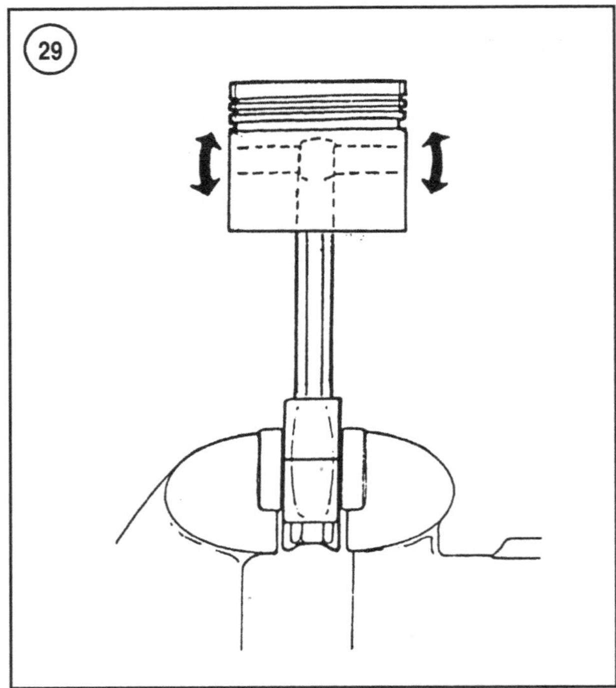
29

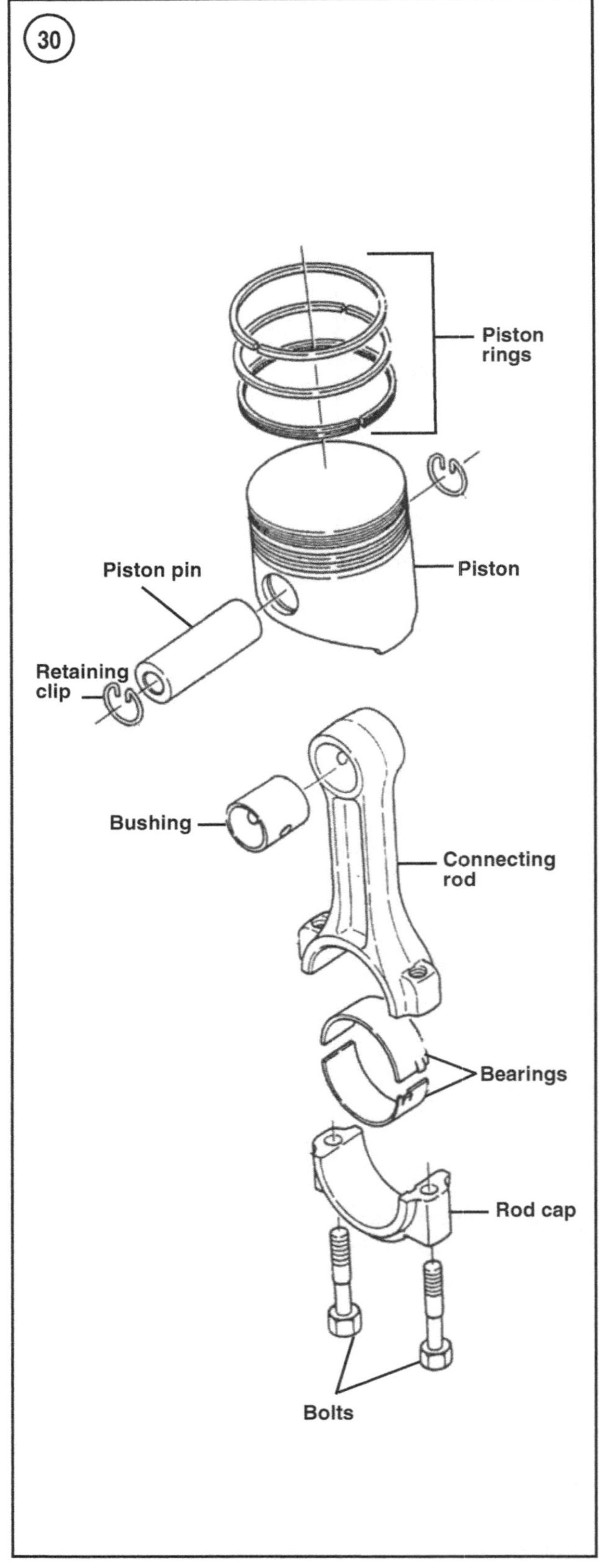

30

Piston Pin Removal/Installation

The steel piston pin rides directly in the piston and in a bushing in the connecting rod. Circlips at each end retain the piston pin in the piston.

1. Before removing the piston, place the crankshaft end of the connecting rod in a vise with soft jaws. Rock the piston as shown in **Figure 29**. Any rocking motion (do not confuse with the normal sliding motion) indicates wear on the piston pin, piston pin bore or connecting rod small end bore (or combination of these).
2. Remove the clip from each side of the piston pin bore (**Figure 30**) with a small screwdriver or scribe. Hold a thumb over one edge of the clip when removing it to prevent the clip from springing out.
3. Use a wooden dowel or suitable tool and push out the piston pin. If the pin is difficult to remove, heat the piston with a hair dryer. Separate the piston from the connecting rod.

Piston/Cylinder Bore Check

Unless precision measuring equipment is available, have this procedure done by a machine shop.

1. Measure the piston diameter with a micrometer (**Figure 31**) at a right angle to the piston pin bore 9 mm (0.35 in.) from the bottom of the piston skirt.

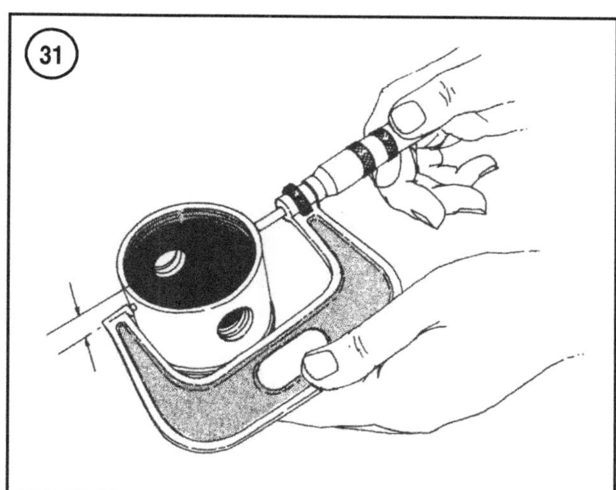

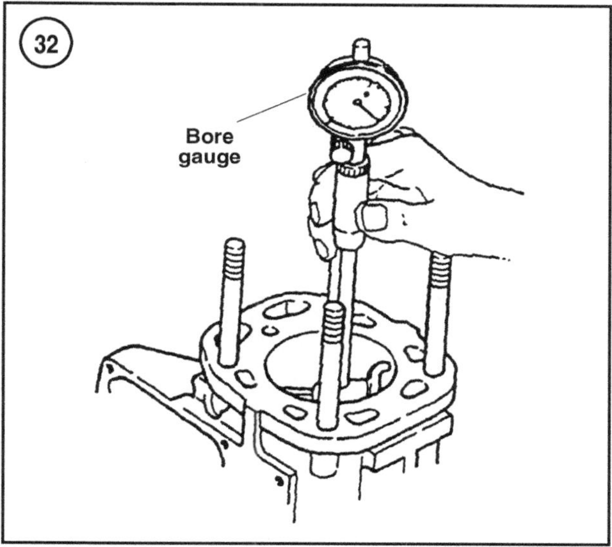

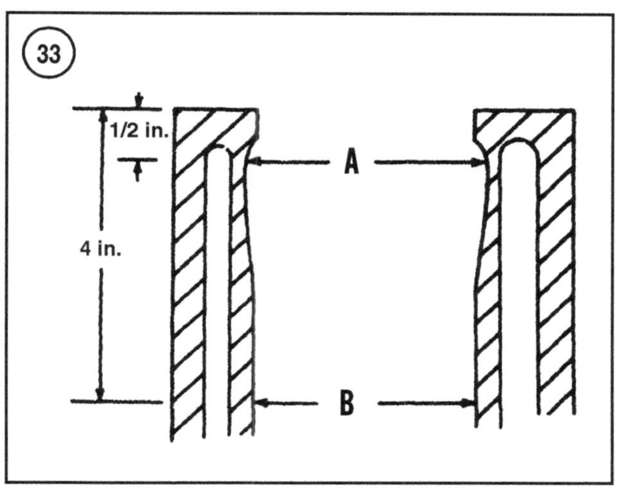

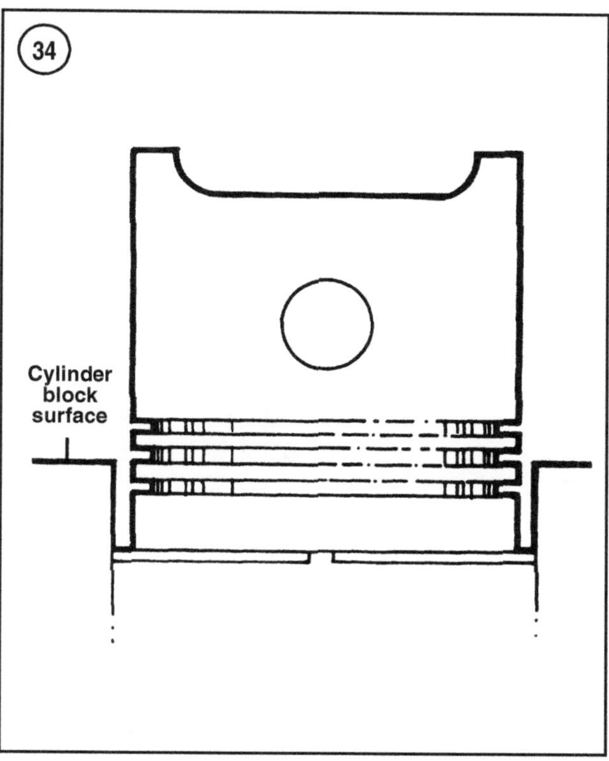

2. Measure the cylinder bore diameter at several points with a bore gauge (**Figure 32**). **Figure 33** shows the points of normal cylinder wear. Measure the cylinder parallel to the crankshaft and at a right angle to the crankshaft. Record all measurements and refer to **Table 1** for cylinder specifications. If necessary, rebore the cylinder and install a new piston and ring assembly.

3. If the cylinder bore is damaged or excessively worn, rebore the cylinder bore and install a new piston. If the piston is worn, but the cylinder bore is good, install a new piston.

NOTE
Obtain the new piston and take it to the machine shop so the cylinder can be bored to the correct oversize dimension.

Piston Ring Fit/Installation

1. Check the ring gap of each piston ring. To do this, position the ring at the bottom of the ring travel area and square it by tapping gently with an inverted piston. See **Figure 34**.

NOTE
If the cylinder has not been rebored, check the gap at the bottom of the ring travel, where the cylinder is least worn.

6

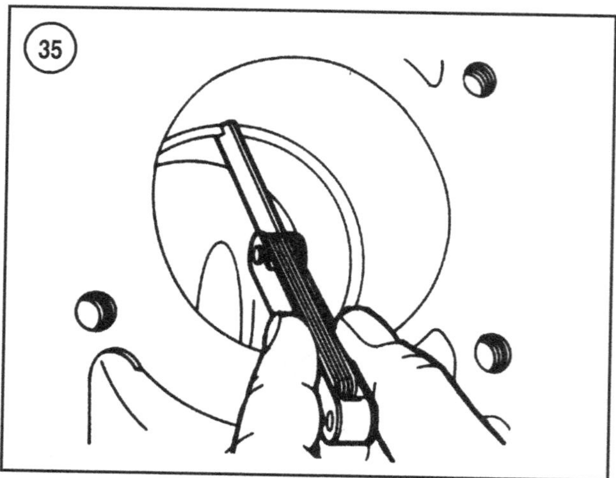

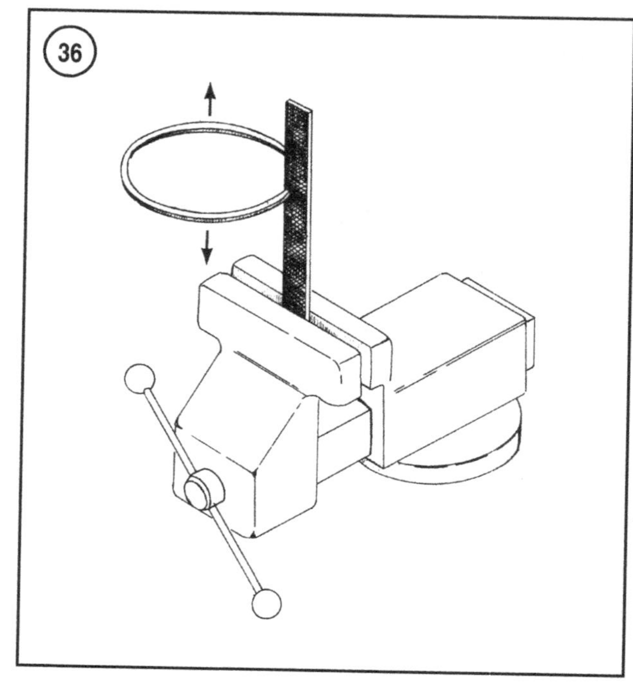

2. Measure the ring gap with a feeler gauge as shown in **Figure 35**. Compare the measurement with specifications in **Tables 1-3**. If the measurement is not within specification, the rings must be replaced as a set. Check the gap of new rings as well. If the gap is too small, file the ends of the ring to correct it (**Figure 36**).

3. Check the side clearance of the rings as shown in **Figure 37**. Place the feeler gauge alongside the ring all the way into the groove. If the measurement is not within specifications (**Tables 1-3**), either the rings or the ring grooves are worn. Inspect and replace them as required.

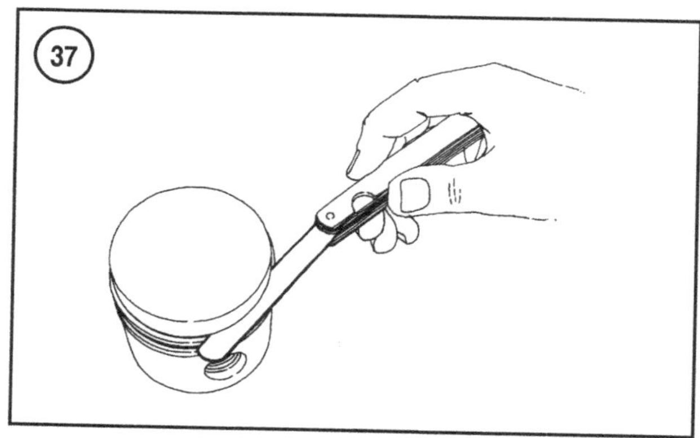

4. Using a ring expander tool (**Figure 38**), carefully install the oil control ring, then the compression rings. The oil ring consists of two pieces, the outer ring and the inner expansion spring. Assemble the oil ring on the piston so the expansion spring gap is on the opposite side of the piston from the ring end gap. See **Figure 39**. The second compression ring is tapered while the top compression ring has a barrel face. The top of each compression ring is marked and must face toward the piston crown.

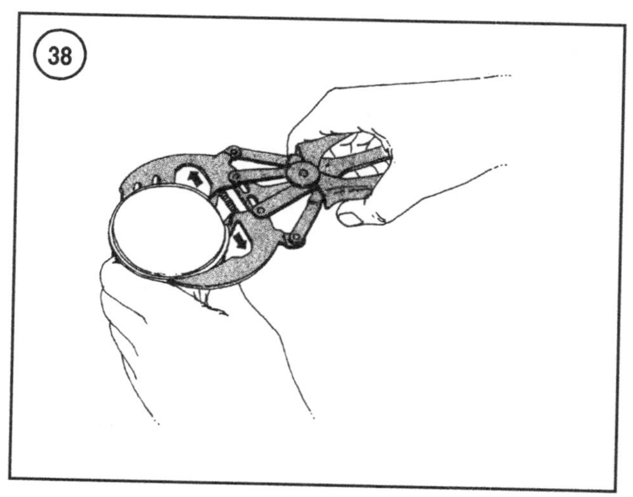

Connecting Rod Inspection

Have the connecting rod checked for straightness by a dealer or machine shop.

The piston pin end of the connecting rod is equipped with a bushing. Refer to **Tables 1-3** for bushing specifications. If bushing replacement is required, a press is necessary to remove the old bushing and install a new bushing. The oil holes in the bushing and connecting rod must align. Ream the bushing to obtain the desired clearance in **Tables 1-3**.

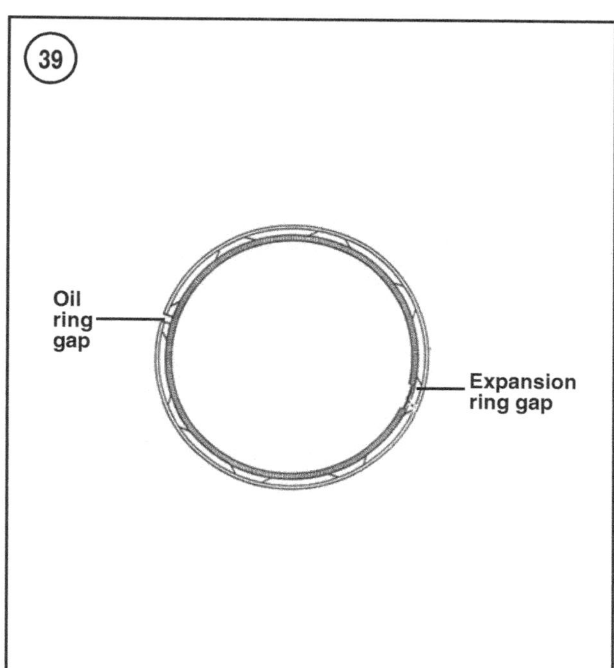

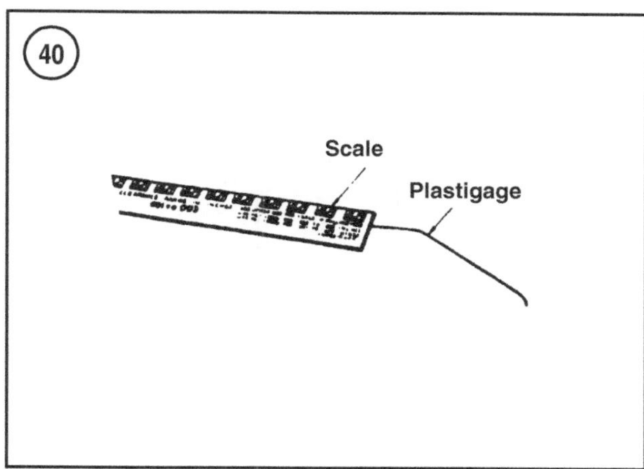

Connecting Rod Bearing Clearance Measurement

1. Place the connecting rod and upper bearing half on the connecting rod journal.

2. Cut a piece of Plastigage the width of the bearing (**Figure 40**). Place the Plastigage on the journal, then install the rod cap and bearing. Be sure to install the cap so the marks on the cap and rod are on the same side (**Figure 41**).

NOTE
Do not place Plastigage over the journal oil hole.

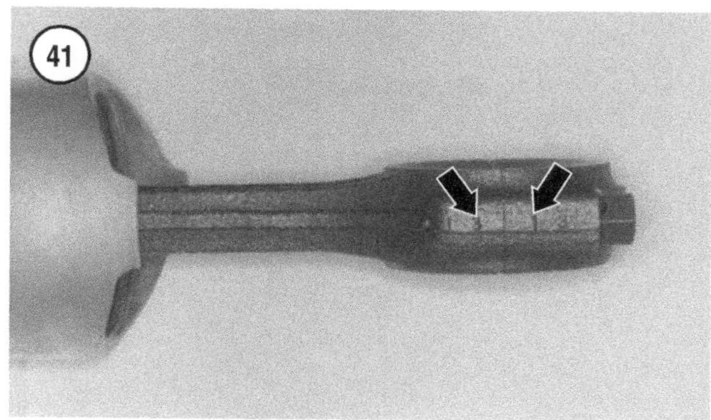

3. Tighten the connecting rod cap to specification (**Table 4**). Do not rotate the crankshaft while the Plastigage is in place.
4. Remove the connecting rod cap. To determine bearing clearance, compare the width of the flattened Plastigage to the markings on the envelope (**Figure 42**). If the clearance is excessive, have the crankshaft reground and install undersize bearings.

Piston/Connecting Rod Installation

1. Rotate the crankshaft so the crankpin is at bottom dead center.
2. Make sure the ring gaps are positioned as shown in **Figure 43**.
3. Immerse the entire piston in clean engine oil. Coat the cylinder wall with oil.
4. Install a piston ring compressor on the piston around the piston rings.

CAUTION
Use extreme care in Step 5 to prevent the connecting rod from nicking the crankshaft journal.

6

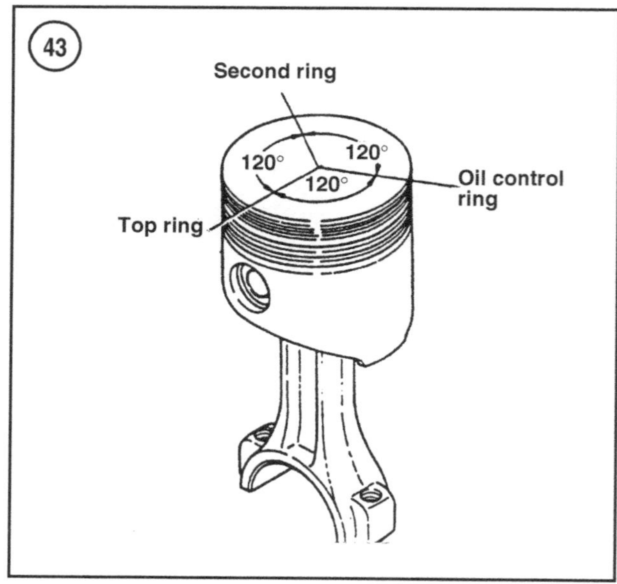

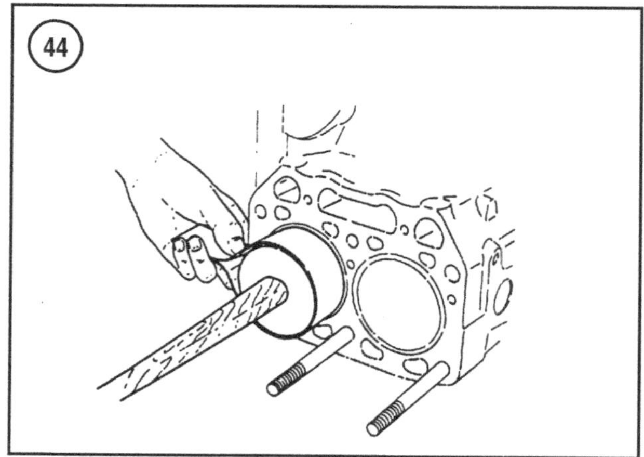

5. Position the piston so the numbered side of the rod (**Figure 41**) is toward the camshaft side of the engine. Insert the piston/connecting rod assembly into the cylinder (**Figure 44**). Lightly tap on the piston crown with a wooden hammer handle to insert the piston. Make sure the rod does not bang against the crankshaft.

6. Clean the connecting rod bearings carefully, including the back sides. Coat the crankpin journal and bearings with clean engine oil. Place the bearings in the connecting rod and cap.

7. Pull the connecting rod and bearing into position against the crankpin. Lightly lubricate the connecting rod bolt threads with engine oil.

8. Install the connecting rod cap. Make sure the rod and cap are properly aligned. Install the cap bolts finger-tight.

9. Tighten the cap retaining bolts to specification (**Table 4**).

10. Check the connecting rod side clearance as described under *Piston/Connecting Rod Removal* in this chapter.

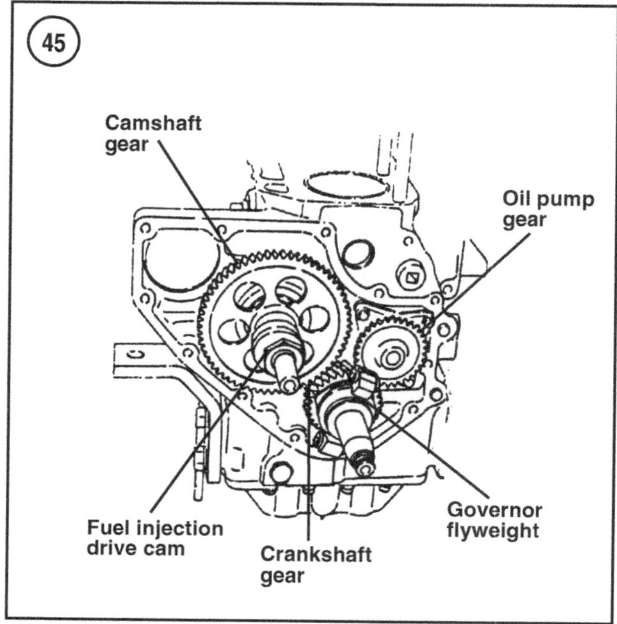

TIMING GEARCASE

The timing gearcase covers the camshaft and crankshaft gears and the oil pump (**Figure 45**). The timing gearcase also contains the governor mechanism and serves as the mounting location for the fuel injection pump. A ball bearing in the timing gearcase supports the outer end of the crankshaft.

To remove and reinstall the timing gearcase, proceed as follows:

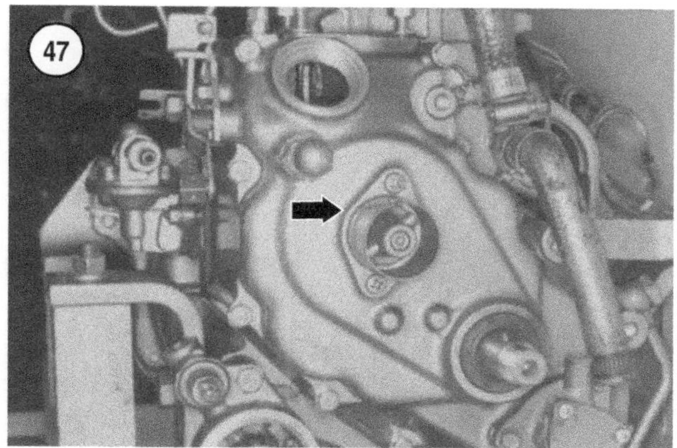

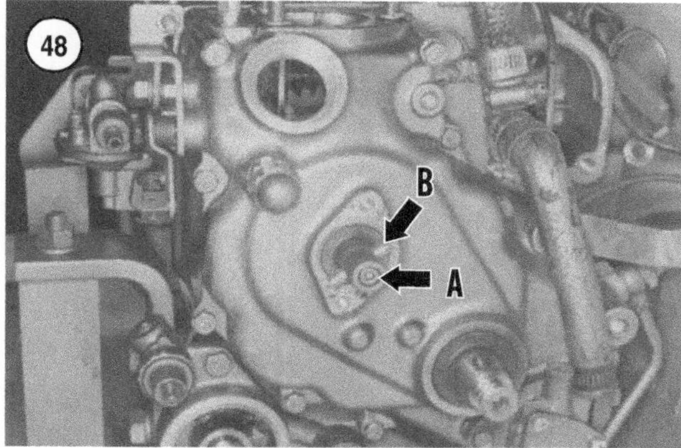

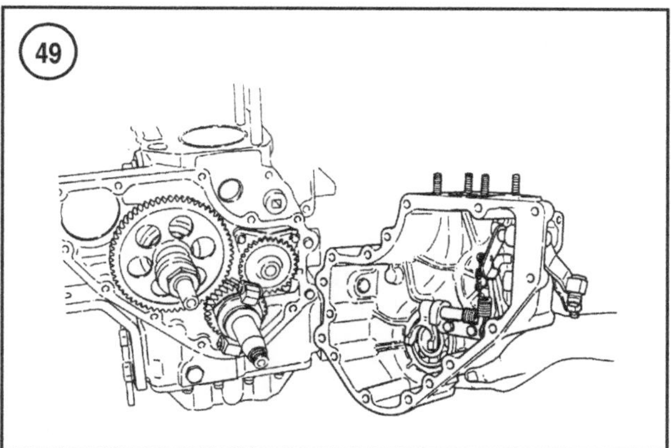

1. Disconnect the negative battery cable from the negative battery terminal.

2. Remove the alternator as described in Chapter Nine.

3. Remove the oil filter.

4. Detach the control cables from the speed control lever and the stop lever.

5. Remove the fuel injection pump as described in Chapter Seven.

6. Remove the seawater pump as described in Chapter Eight.

7. Remove the crankshaft pulley retaining nut. Using a suitable puller, remove the crankshaft pulley (**Figure 46**, typical). Remove the drive key from the crankshaft.

8. Remove the manual starter cover (**Figure 47**, typical).

9. Remove the setscrew in the end of the camshaft (A, **Figure 48**, typical), then remove the manual starter drive pin (B).

10. Remove the timing gearcase (**Figure 49**).

11. Remove the gasket and any residue from the gearcase and crankcase surfaces.

12. If crankshaft or starter seal replacement is necessary, proceed as follows:

   a. Pry the old seal from the gearcase with a large screwdriver. Work carefully to prevent damage to the gearcase seal surface.
   b. Clean the seal recess in the cover with solvent and blow it dry with compressed air.
   c. Apply gasket sealer to the periphery of the seal.
   d. Position a new seal in the cover recess with its open end facing the inside of the gearcase. Drive the seal into place with a suitably sized seal driver or socket.

13. If crankshaft bearing replacement is necessary, proceed as follows:

   a. Refer to Chapter Seven and remove governor shaft from timing gearcase.
   b. Pry the seal from the gearcase with a large screwdriver. Work carefully to prevent damage to the gearcase seal surface.
   c. Drive or press out the bearing. Force the bearing toward the inside of the gearcase.
   d. Clean the seal and bearing recesses in the cover with solvent and blow them dry with compressed air.
   e. Drive or press in a new bearing until the bearing seats in the recess in the gearcase.
   f. Apply gasket sealer to the periphery of the seal.
   g. Position a new seal in the cover recess with its open end facing the inside of the gearcase. Drive the seal into place with a suitably sized seal driver or socket.
   h. Refer to Chapter Seven and reinstall the governor shaft.

14. Reverse the removal procedure to reinstall the timing gearcase. Refer to **Table 4** for the tightening torque of the gearcase retaining screws.

6

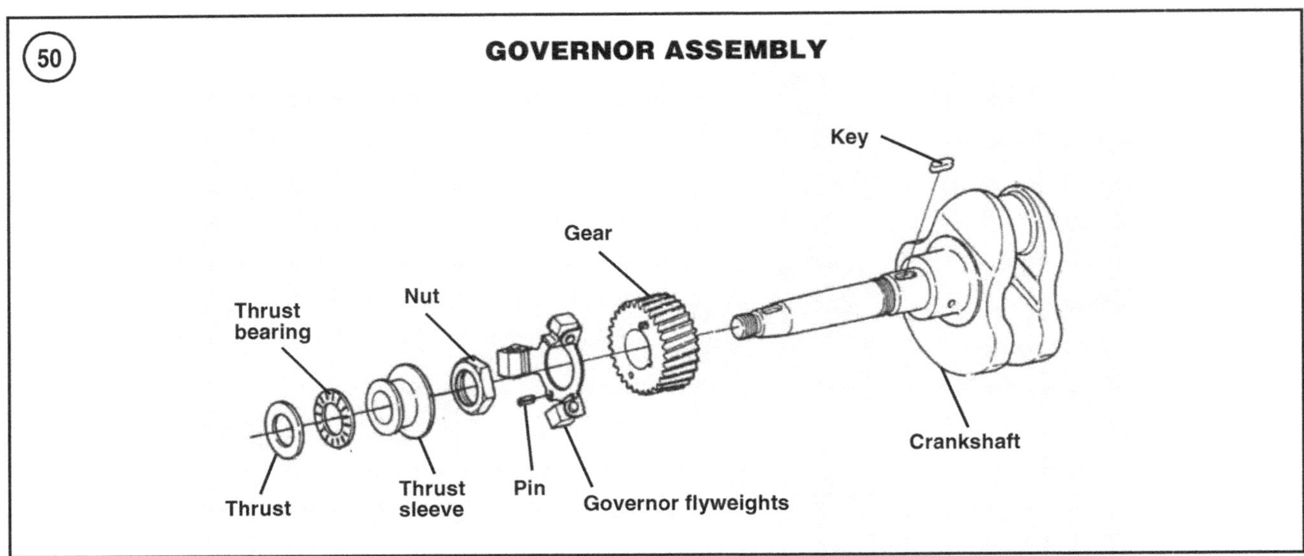

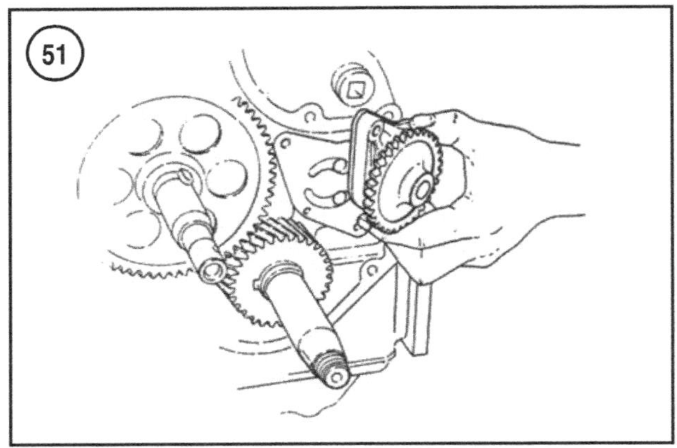

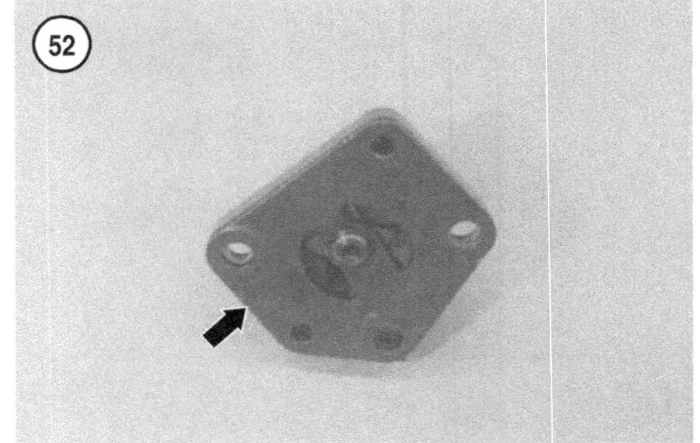

LUBRICATION SYSTEM

Refer to Chapter Two for lubrication system operation, diagrams and oil pressure test.

Oil Pump

The oil pump is mounted on the front (timing gear) side of the cylinder block (**Figure 45**).

Removal and installation

1. Remove the timing gearcase as previously described.
2. Remove the governor thrust washer (**Figure 50**), thrust bearing and thrust sleeve from the crankshaft.
3. Using a suitable tool (if available, Yanmar special tool 124085-92700), unscrew the crankshaft nut.
4. Remove the governor flyweight assembly.
5. Remove the oil pump (**Figure 51**) and gasket.
6. Clean any gasket residue from the oil pump and engine.

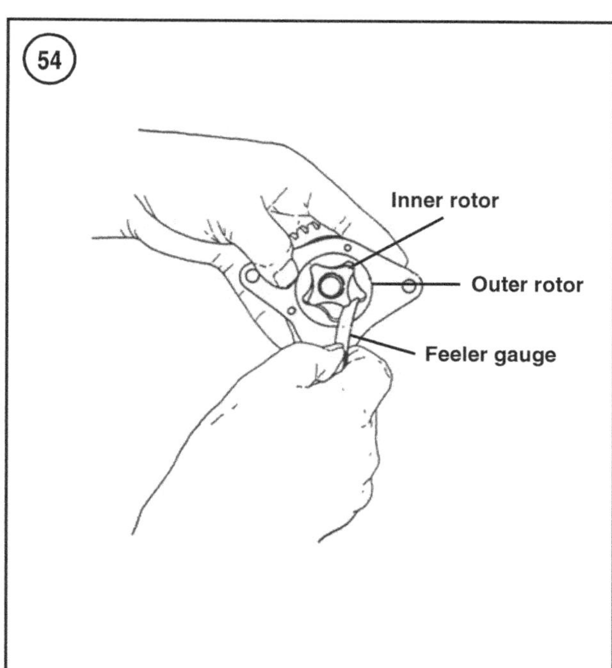

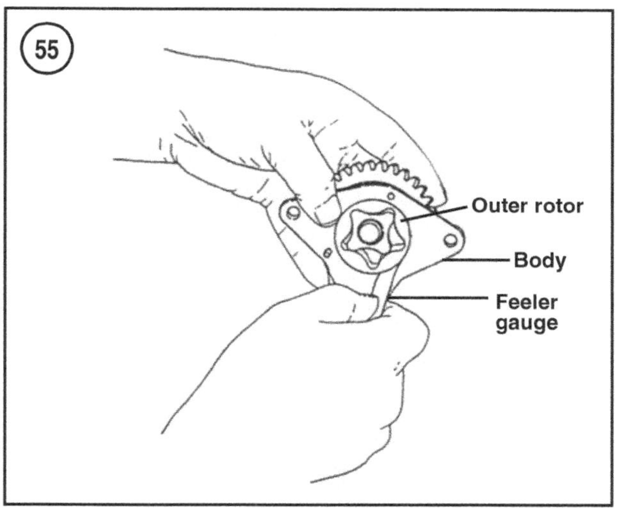

7. Installation is the reverse of removal. Tighten the oil pump retaining screws to the tightening torque specified in **Table 2**. Be sure the governor flyweight assembly is positioned on the locating pin (**Figure 50**).Tighten the crankshaft nut to the tightening torque specified in **Table 4**.

Disassembly, inspection and reassembly

1. Remove the oil pump cover (**Figure 52**).
2. Lift out the inner and outer pump rotors (**Figure 53**).

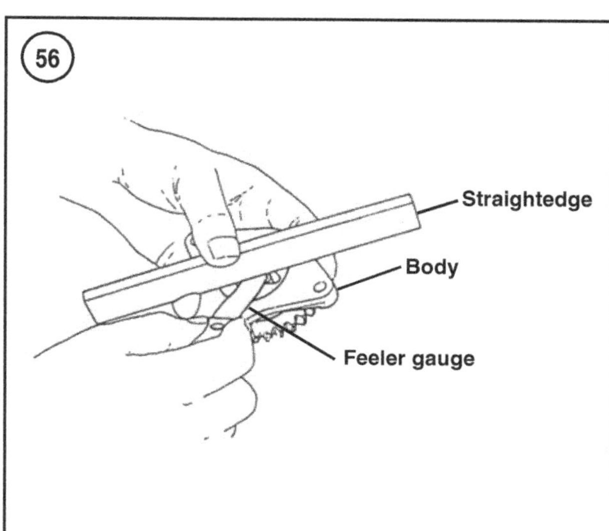

3. Thoroughly clean all parts in solvent and blow them dry with compressed air.
4. Check the drive spindle and pump rotors for signs of wear, scoring or damage. Replace damaged parts.

NOTE
The oil pump shaft and gear are pressed together; do not attempt to disassemble them. The oil pump must be replaced as a unit assembly if any parts are damaged.

5. Reinstall the inner rotor in the pump body. Reinstall the outer rotor in the pump body.
6. Measure the clearance between the inner rotor tip and outer rotor tip (**Figure 54**). Compare the results with specifications in **Table 1**.
7. Measure the clearance between the outer rotor and the pump body (**Figure 55**). Compare the results with specifications in **Table 1**.
8. Place a straightedge across the pump body. Measure the side clearance between the rotors and straightedge with a flat feeler gauge (**Figure 56**). Compare the measurement with specifications in **Tables 1-3**.
9. Measure the diameter of the inner rotor shaft. Measure the shaft bore of the pump body. Calculate shaft clearance and compare it with specifications in **Tables 1-3**.
10. If any clearance measured in Steps 6-9 is not with specifications, replace the pump. Individual components are not available. The pump must be replaced as a unit.
11. When reassembling the oil pump, be sure to lubricate the rotors, body and shaft with engine oil.

6

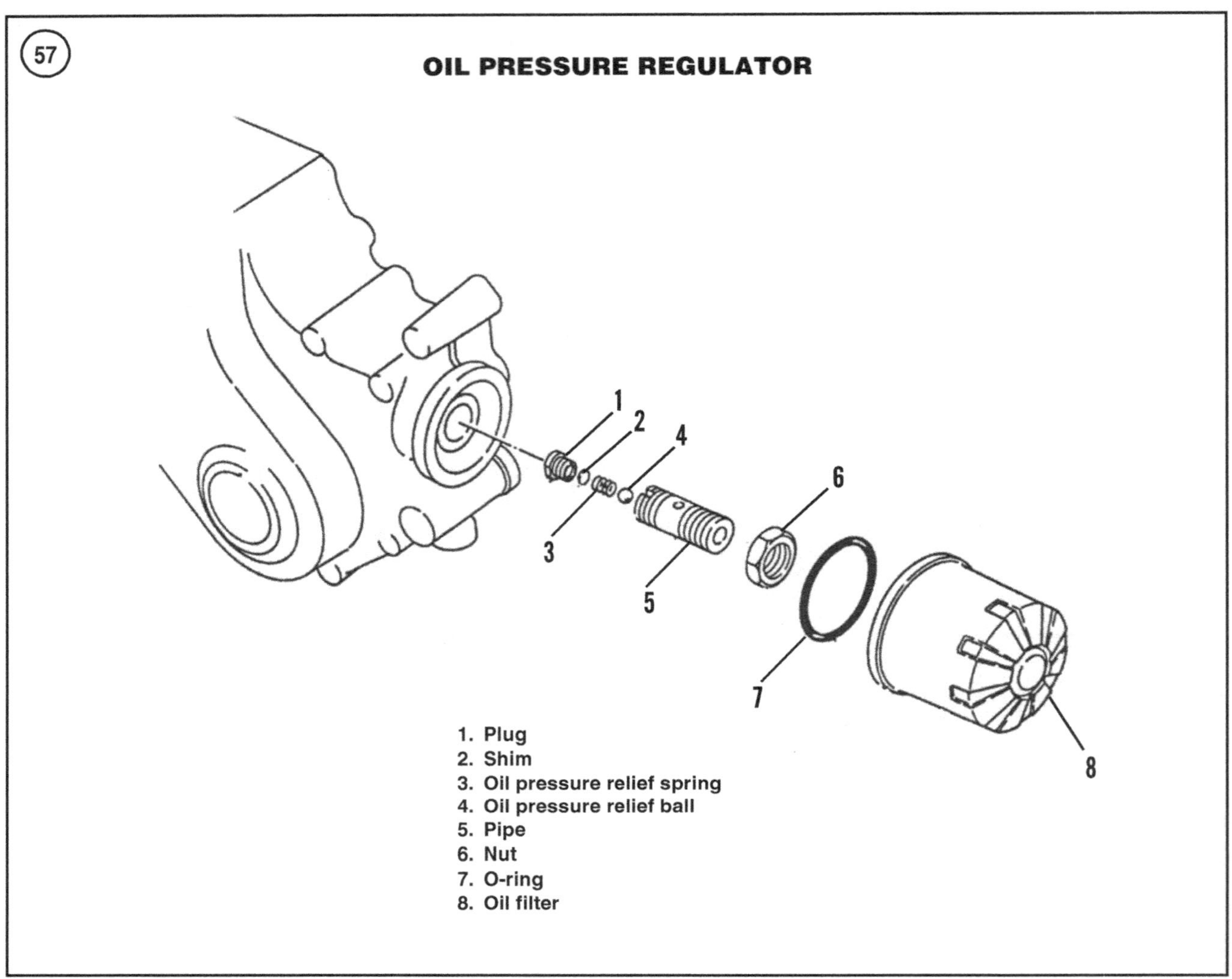

Pressure relief valve

An oil pressure relief valve is located in the oil filter mounting pipe (**Figure 57**). If oil pressure exceeds 300-400 kPa (43-57 psi), the relief valve opens and expels oil into the timing gearcase.

Do not attempt to disassemble the oil pressure relief valve. The valve is sealed and it must be replaced as a unit assembly.

Oil pickup

The oil pickup is located in the oil pan. The pickup includes a strainer to prevent foreign matter from entering the lubrication system.

To remove the oil pickup, remove the oil pan and unscrew the jam nut (**Figure 58**).

FLYWHEEL

Removal/Installation

1. Remove the engine from the boat.
2. Remove the transmission.
3. Remove the drive disc (**Figure 59**, typical).
4. Gradually loosen and remove the flywheel bolts, working in a diagonal pattern. Install two drive disc screws into two outer holes in the flywheel (**Figure 60**, typical), then use the screws to pull and remove the flywheel.
5. Inspect the ring gear. If the ring gear is excessively worn or damaged, use the following procedure to remove the ring gear:
   a. Heat the ring gear evenly, then drive the ring gear off the flywheel.

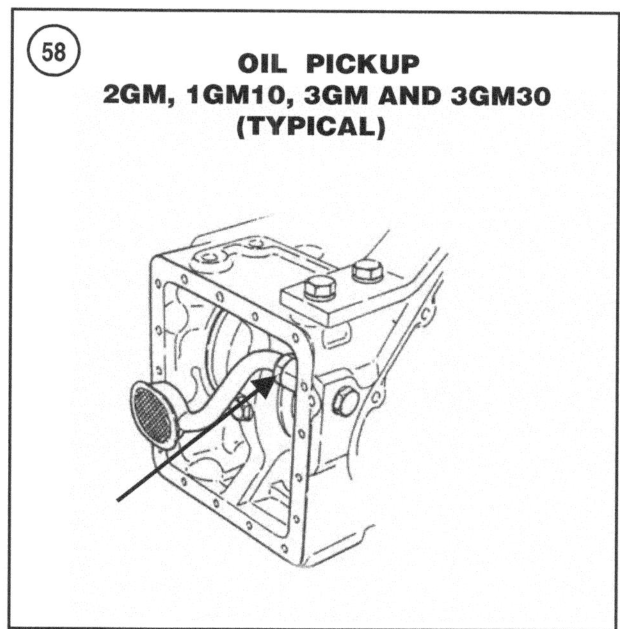

b. Heat the ring gear prior to installation. Drive the ring gear onto the flywheel while being careful not to damage the gear teeth.

6. Reverse the removal procedure to install the flywheel. Tighten the flywheel retaining bolts to the tightening torque specified in **Table 4**. Refer to Chapters Ten and Eleven to install the drive disc and transmission.

DRIVE DISC

Refer to Chapters Ten and Eleven for information concerning the drive disc (**Figure 59**).

CRANKSHAFT

Removal and Installation

Refer to **Figure 61** for an exploded view of the crankshaft assembly.

1. Remove the flywheel as previously described.
2. Remove the bellhousing (A, **Figure 62**, typical).
3. Remove the piston and connecting rod as previously described.
4. Remove the oil pump as previously described.
5. Remove the crankshaft gear.
6. Install a dial indicator as shown in **Figure 63** and measure crankshaft end play. Compare the measurement with the specification in **Tables 1-3**. If end play is excessive, inspect the main bearing as described in *Main Bearings*.
7. Remove the main bearing housing (B, **Figure 62**, typical).
8. Position the engine so the crankshaft is vertical with the flywheel end up.
9. Attach a hoist to the flywheel end of the crankshaft.

NOTE
Two-cylinder engines are equipped with one intermediate bearing carrier. Three-cylinder engines are equipped with two intemediate bearing carriers.

10. Remove the retaining bolt(s) for the intermediate main bearing carrier(s). See **Figure 64**.

NOTE
Adjusting the lifting tension on the crankshaft may ease or increase the force necessary to unscrew the retaining bolt(s) for the intermediate main bearing carrier(s).

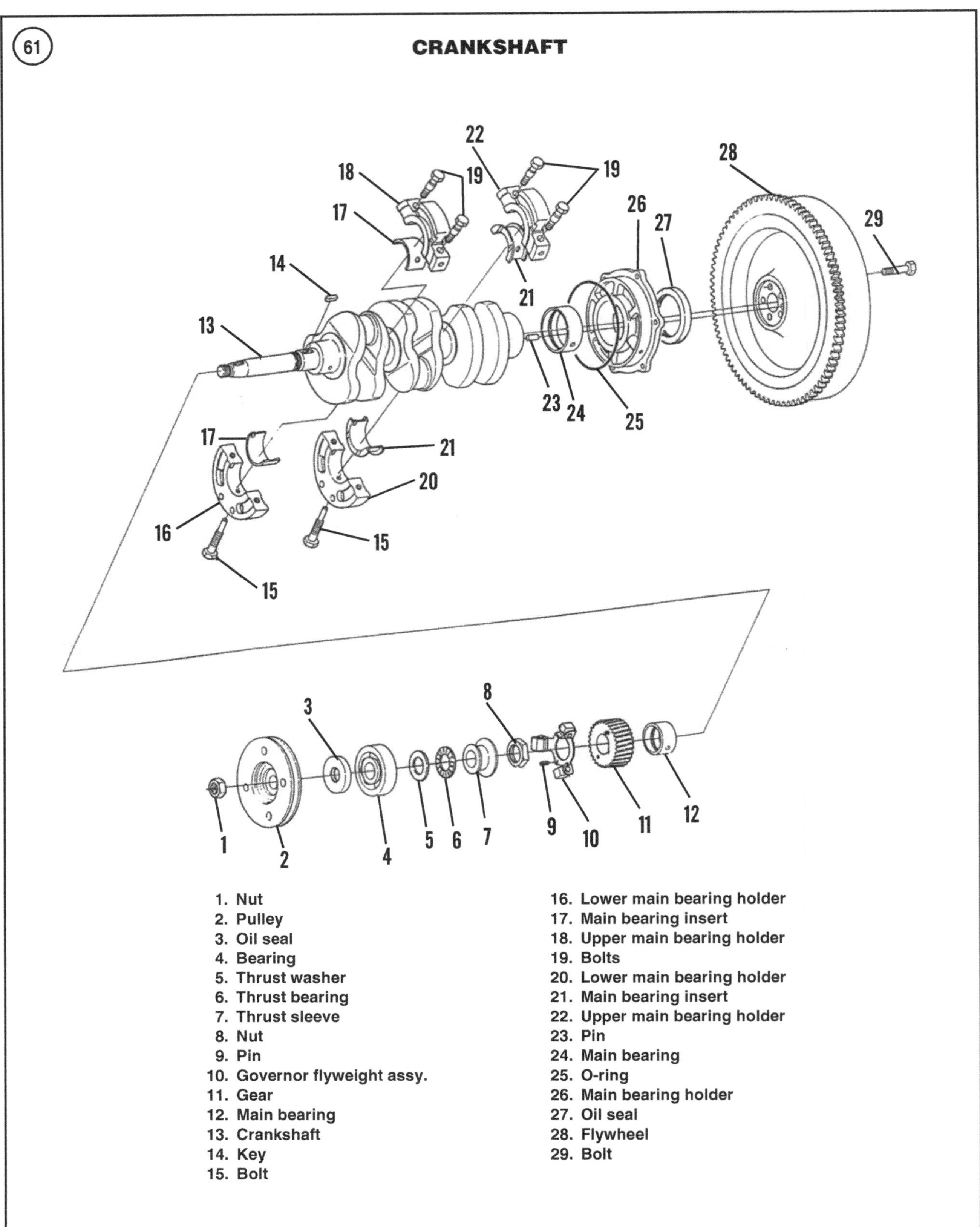
61
CRANKSHAFT
1. Nut
2. Pulley
3. Oil seal
4. Bearing
5. Thrust washer
6. Thrust bearing
7. Thrust sleeve
8. Nut
9. Pin
10. Governor flyweight assy.
11. Gear
12. Main bearing
13. Crankshaft
14. Key
15. Bolt
16. Lower main bearing holder
17. Main bearing insert
18. Upper main bearing holder
19. Bolts
20. Lower main bearing holder
21. Main bearing insert
22. Upper main bearing holder
23. Pin
24. Main bearing
25. O-ring
26. Main bearing holder
27. Oil seal
28. Flywheel
29. Bolt

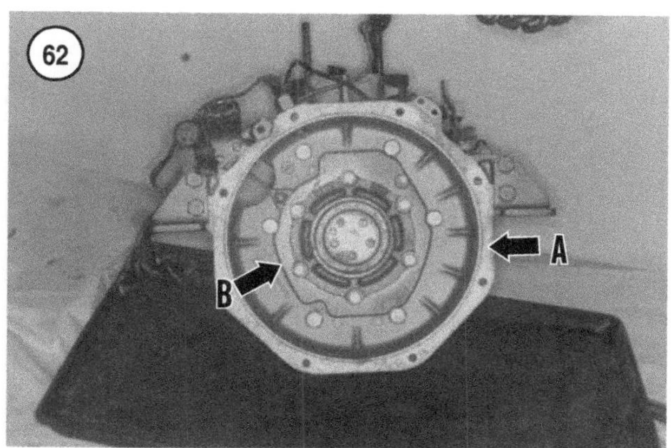

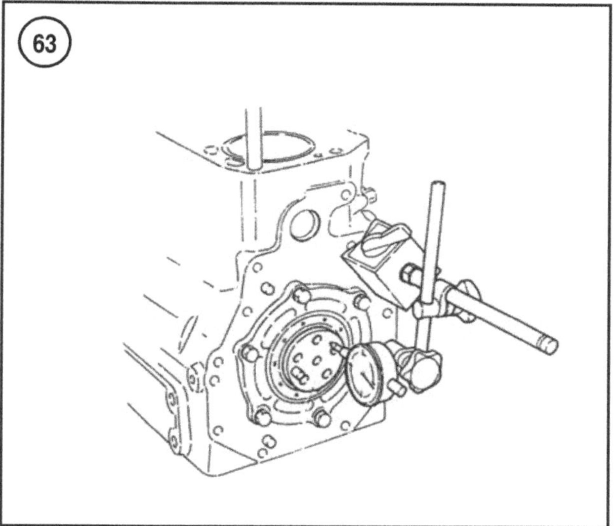

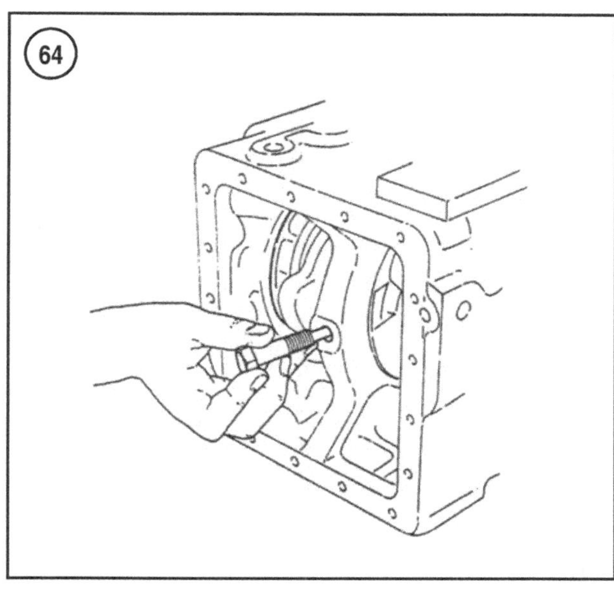

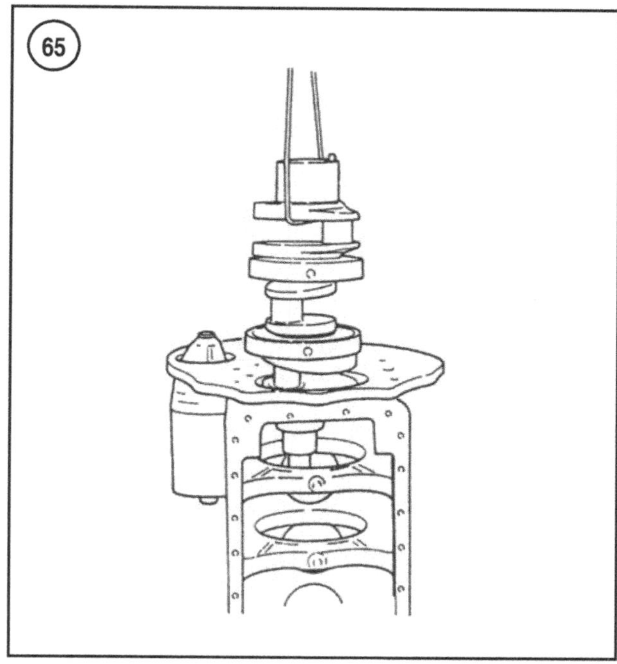

11. Carefully lift the crankshaft out of the engine (**Figure 65**).

12. Proceed as follows to replace the crankshaft seal in the main bearing housing:

   a. Pry the old seal from the main bearing housing with a large screwdriver. Work carefully to prevent damage to the main bearing housing seal surface.
   b. Clean the seal recess in the housing with solvent and blow it dry with compressed air.
   c. Apply gasket sealer to the periphery of the seal.
   d. Position the new seal in the housing recess with its open end facing the inside of the bearing housing. Drive the seal into place with a suitably sized seal driver.

13. Refer to the *Main Bearings* section for information concerning service to the main bearings and thrust bearings.

14. Reinstall the crankshaft by reversing the removal procedure while noting the following:

   a. Thoroughly lubricate the main bearings and thrust bearings.
   b. Be sure to install a new O-ring on the main bearing housing.
   c. Tighten the main bearing and intermediate housing bolts to the tightening torque specified in **Table 4**. After tightening, rotate the crankshaft to be sure it rotates freely. If not, loosen, then retighten the intermediate main bearing housing bolts.

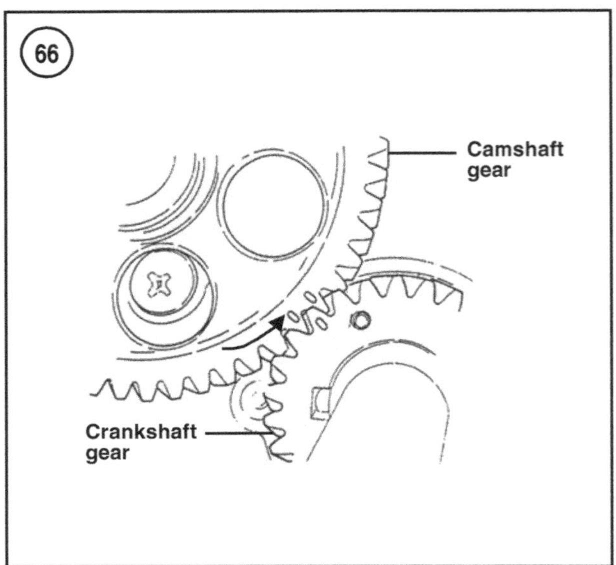

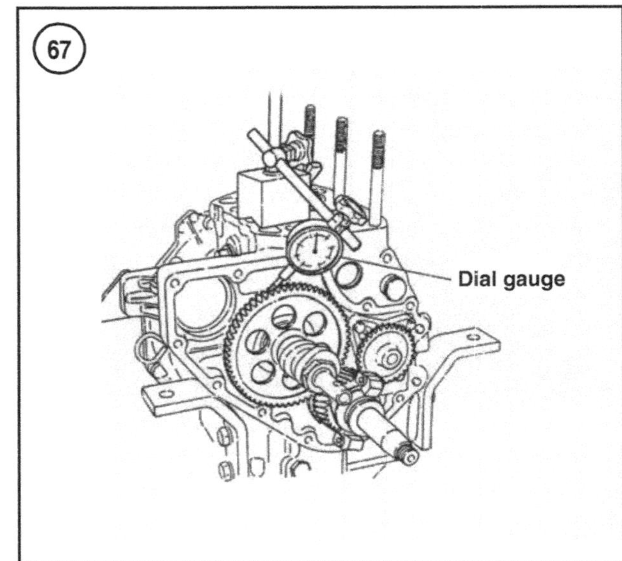

d. Install a dial indicator as shown in **Figure 63** and measure crankshaft end play. Compare the measurement with the specification in **Tables 1-3**. If end play is incorrect, refer to the *Main Bearings* section to determine the cause.
e. Align the timing marks (**Figure 66**) on the camshaft and crankshaft gears when installing the crankshaft gear.
f. Check timing gear backlash by installing a dial indicator as shown in **Figure 67** or by rotating the gear teeth with soft solder between the gear teeth. Compare the measurement with the specification in **Tables 1-3**. If gear backlash is incorrect, replace the camshaft and crankshaft gears.

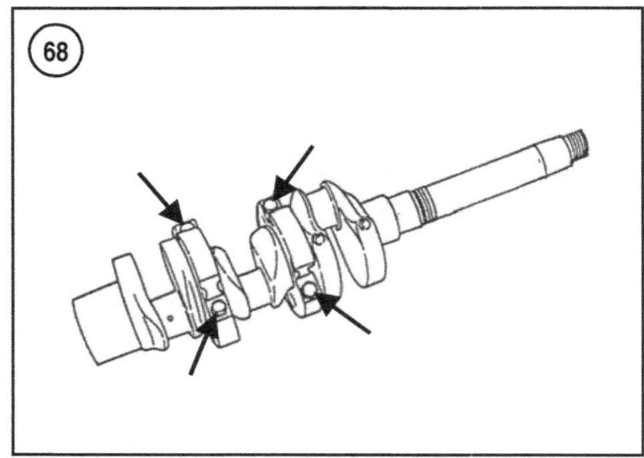

Inspection

1. Clean the crankshaft thoroughly with solvent. Blow out the oil passages with compressed air.
2. Check the main and connecting rod journals for wear, scratches, grooves, scoring or cracks. Check oil seal surface for burrs, nicks or other sharp edges that might damage a seal during installation.

NOTE
Unless precision measuring equipment is available, have a machine shop perform Step 3.

3. Check all journals against specifications (**Tables 1-3**) for out-of-roundness and taper. Have the crankshaft reground, if necessary, and install new undersize bearings.

MAIN BEARINGS

The crankshaft is supported at each end by insert-type main bearings. The front main bearing is located in the crankcase and the rear main bearing is located in the removable main bearing carrier. The intermediate, insert-type bearing is held in a removable bearing housing. See **Figure 61**. Two intermediate bearings are used on three-cylinder engines, while one intermediate bearing is used on two-cylinder engines.

Crankshaft thrust (end play) is controlled by the intermediate bearing on two-cylinder engines. On three-cylinder engines, the intermediate bearing nearest the flywheel controls crankshaft thrust.

Remove the crankshaft as described in the previous section for access to the main bearings. Unless precision

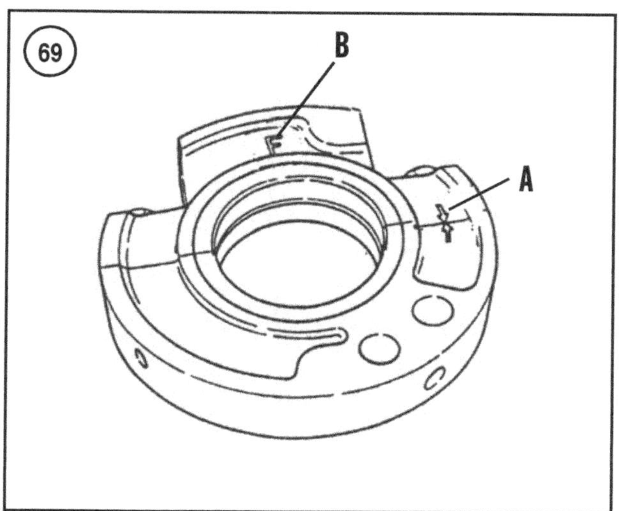

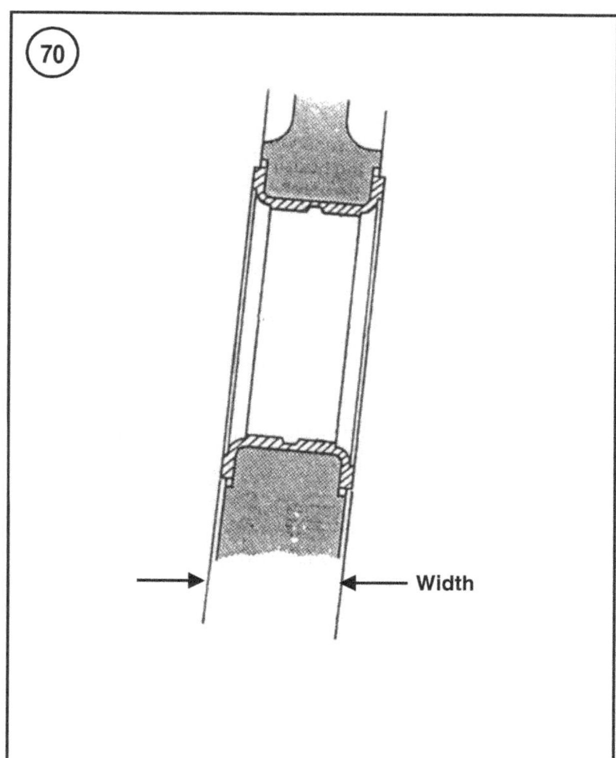

measuring equipment is available, have a dealership or machine shop measure main bearing dimensions. Refer to specifications in **Tables 1-3**.

If front or rear bearing replacement is necessary, have the main bearings replaced by a dealership or machine shop. Be sure the oil holes in the main bearings align with the oil passages in the crankcase and main bearing carrier.

Intermediate Main Bearing

1. Remove the intermediate bearing housing bolts (**Figure 68**).
2. Separate the intermediate bearing housing halves from the crankshaft.
3. Inspect the bearings for excessive wear and damage.
4. Reassemble the intermediate bearing housing including the bearing inserts. Assemble the bearing housing so the arrows (A, **Figure 69**) at the parting surfaces are on the same side. Tighten the bolts to the torque specified in **Table 2**.
5. Measure the crankshaft and bearing diameters and compare them with the specifications in **Tables 1-3**.
6. Measure the width of the intermediate thrust bearing (**Figure 70**) and compare it with the specification in **Table 1**.
7. Be sure to lubricate the bearing inserts with oil before installing the intermediate main bearing housing on the crankshaft. Install the bearing housing on the crankshaft so the F mark (B, **Figure 69**) on the housing faces toward the flywheel end of the crankshaft.
8. Tighten the bearing housing bolts to the torque specified in **Table 4**.

CAMSHAFT

Removal and Installation

1. Remove the fuel transfer pump (**Figure 71**, typical).
2. Remove the crankshaft as previously described.
3. Prevent rotation of the camshaft gear by holding a screwdriver or other tool against the camshaft bearing retaining screw (**Figure 72**, typical).
4. Remove the camshaft gear nut (**Figure 73**), fuel injection pump cam and camshaft gear.

5. Position the engine so the valve lifters will not fall out when the camshaft is withdrawn.

6. Remove the bearing retaining screw (**Figure 74**), then withdraw the camshaft.

7. Remove the valve lifters and mark them so they may be reinstalled in their original locations.

NOTE
If precision measuring equipment is not available, have Step 8 performed by a dealership or machine shop.

8. Check the bearing journal(s) and lobes for signs of wear or scoring.

9. Measure the bearing journal(s) and lobes (**Figure 75**) and compare the results to the specifications in **Tables 1-3**. Replace the camshaft if the journal or lobes do not meet specifications.

10. Measure the stem diameter of the valve lifters and compare it to the specification in **Tables 1-3**. Measure the lifter bores in the cylinder block. Calculate the lifter clearance and compare it with the specification in **Tables 1-3**. Replace the valve lifters if they do not meet specifications. Replace the valve lifter if the lifter face is scored, galled, excessively worn or otherwise damaged.

11. Replace the ball bearing if it is damaged or feels rough during rotation.

12. Installation is the reverse of removal. Note the following:

   a. If installing a new camshaft, coat the camshaft lobes with camshaft break-in lubricant. If reinstalling the original camshaft, apply heavy oil to the camshaft lobes.
   b. Lubricate the camshaft bearing journal(s) with heavy engine oil before reinstallation.
   c. Lightly tap the end of the camshaft to seat the ball bearing in the engine. Rotate the camshaft to be sure it rotates freely.
   d. Align the timing marks (**Figure 76**) on the camshaft and crankshaft gears when installing the camshaft gear.
   e. Install the fuel injection cam so the side marked with a zero is out (**Figure 77**, typical).
   f. Check gear backlash by installing a dial indicator as shown in **Figure 67** or by rotating the gear teeth with soft solder between the gear teeth. Compare the measurement with the specification in **Tables 1-3**. If gear backlash is incorrect, replace the camshaft and crankshaft gears.

72

CYLINDER BLOCK

Cleaning and Inspection

1. Clean the block thoroughly with solvent. Remove any gasket or RTV sealant residue from the machined surfaces. Check all core plugs for leaks and replace any that are suspect. See *Core Plug Replacement* in this chapter. Check oil and coolant passages for sludge, dirt and corrosion while cleaning. If the passages are very dirty, have the block boiled out by a machine shop. Blow out all passages with compressed air. Check the threads in the head bolt holes to be sure they are clean. If dirty, use a tap to restore the threads and remove any deposits.

2. Examine the block for cracks. To confirm suspicions about possible leakage areas, use a mixture of one part kerosene and two parts engine oil. Coat the suspected area with this solution, then wipe dry and immediately apply a solution of zinc oxide dissolved in wood alcohol. If any discoloration appears in the treated area, the block is cracked and should be replaced.

NOTE
On 2GM, 3GM and 3HM engines, remove the cylinder liners to check the cylinder block deck for warpage in Step 3.

3. Check the flatness of the cylinder block deck or top surface. Place an accurate straightedge on the block. If there is any gap between the block and straightedge, measure it with a flat feeler gauge (**Figure 78**). Measure from end to end and from corner to corner. Have the block resurfaced if it is warped more than 0.07 mm (0.0028 in.).

4. *On 2GM20, 3GM30 and 3HM35 models*—Measure the cylinder bores with a bore gauge (**Figure 79**) for out-of-roundness or excessive wear as described in *Piston/Clylinder Bore Check* in this chapter. If the cylinders exceed maximum tolerances, they must be rebored.

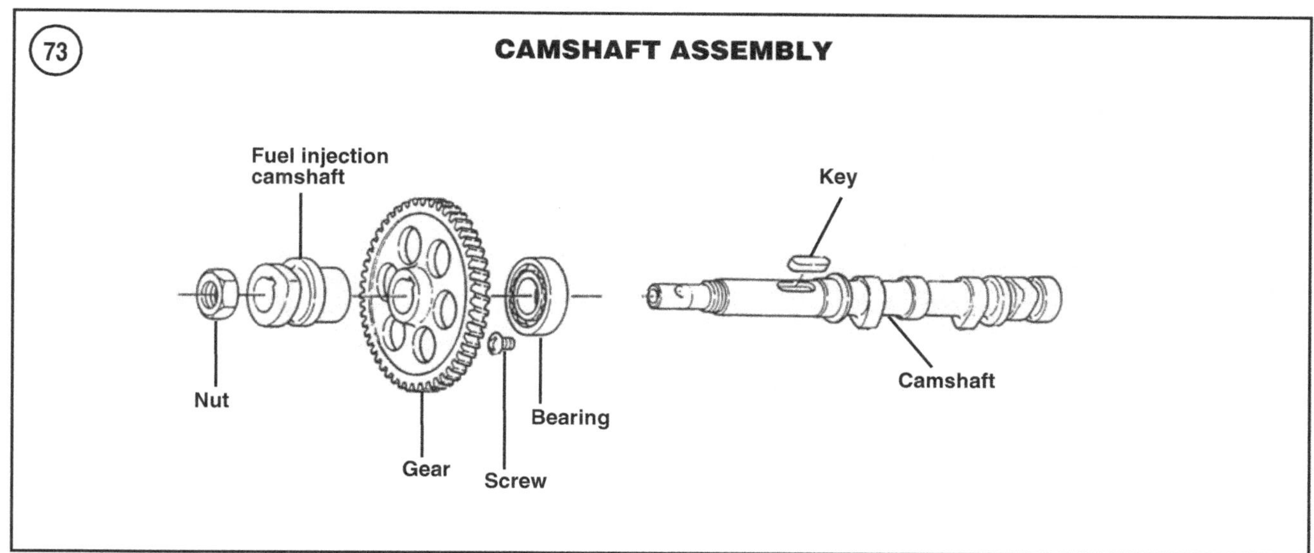

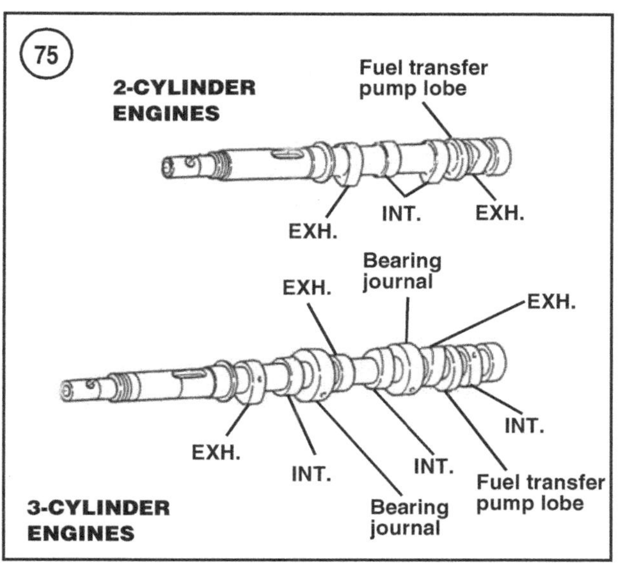

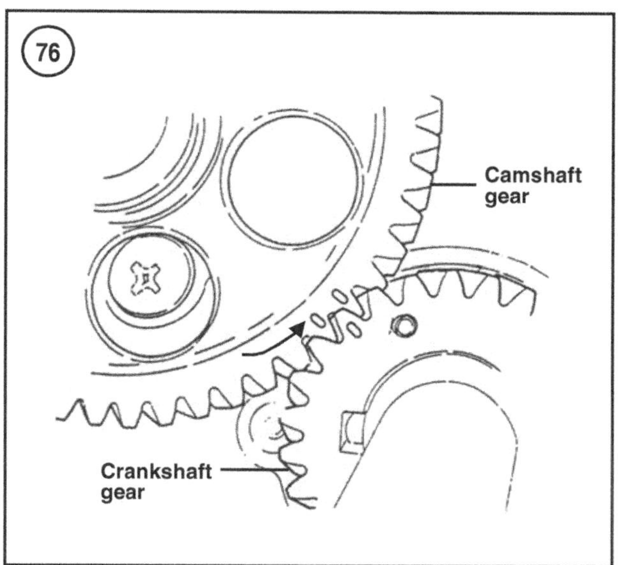

6

Reboring is also necessary if the cylinder walls are badly scuffed or scored.

Cylinder Liners 2GM, 3GM and 3HM (Including F and D Series) Models

Have cylinder liners replacement performed by a dealership or diesel engine shop. The liner is available in different outside diameters so a precise fit between the liner and cylinder block may be obtained. The upper flanged end of the liner fits in a step at the upper end of the cylinder bore. Each liner must protrude above the cylinder

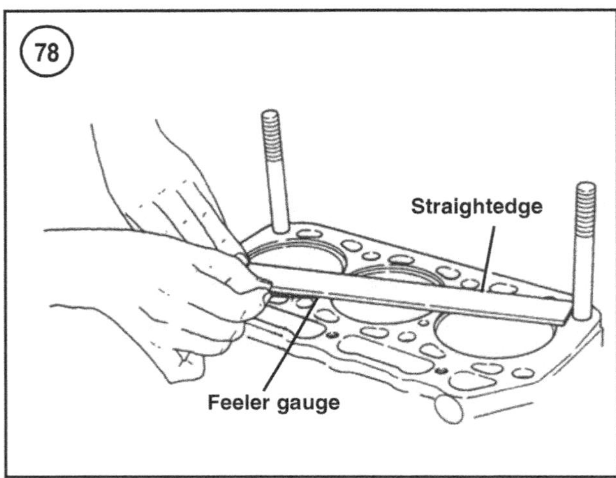

block surface. When the cylinder head is installed, the clamping force of the head against the liner protrusion secures the liner in place. The protrusion also establishes a gas-tight seal between the liner and the head gasket. Inspect the liners as follows:

NOTE
The liner is a close fit in the block, but it may be movable. Distortion or corrosion may freeze the liner in the block, which will necessitate a puller to remove the liner.

1. Measure liner protrusion above the cylinder block (**Figure 80**) and compare the result with the specification in **Tables 1-3**.
   a. Excess protrusion may damage the head gasket. Excess protrusion may be caused by improper seating of the liner flange in the block, possibly due to corrosion.
   b. Insufficient protrusion may allow compression leaks and liner movement in the block. Insufficient protrusion may be due to a worn liner or cylinder block.

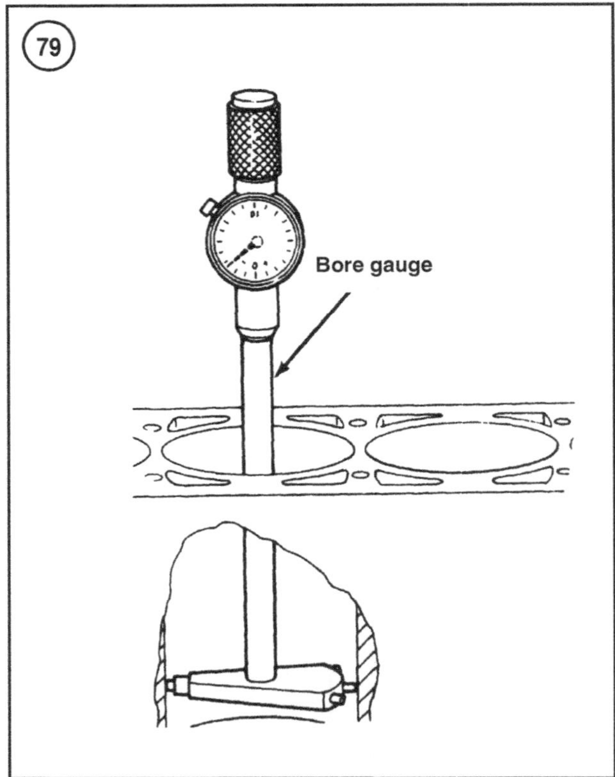

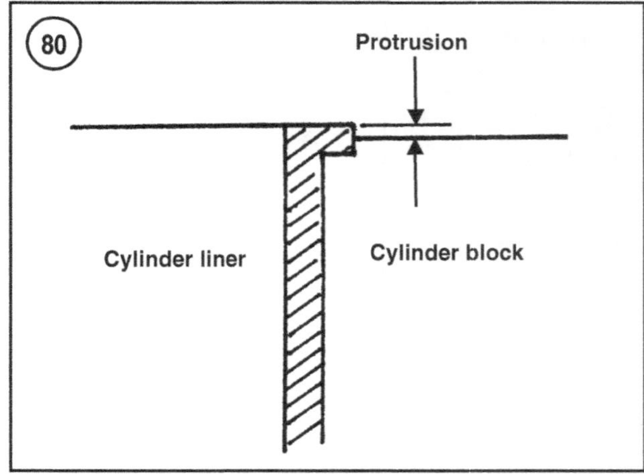

2. Measure the cylinder liner bore at several locations to determine if the liner is out-of-round or distorted. Compare measurements with the specification in **Tables 1-3**. Replace the liner if the measurements exceed the specification.
3. Inspect the liner bore. Replace the liner if it is rusty, corroded or otherwise damaged.

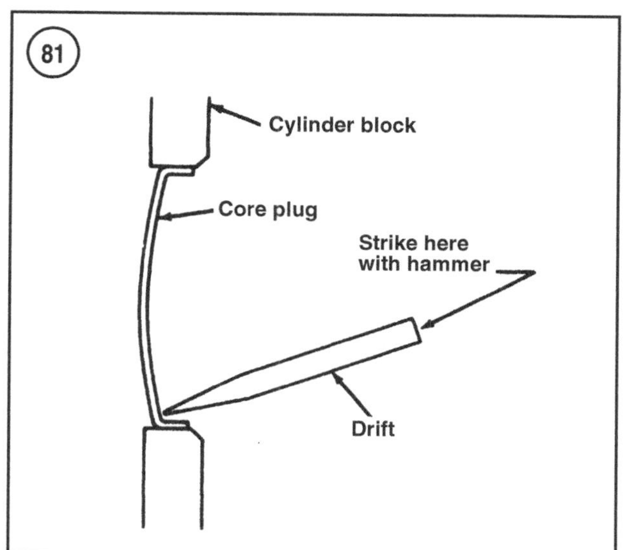

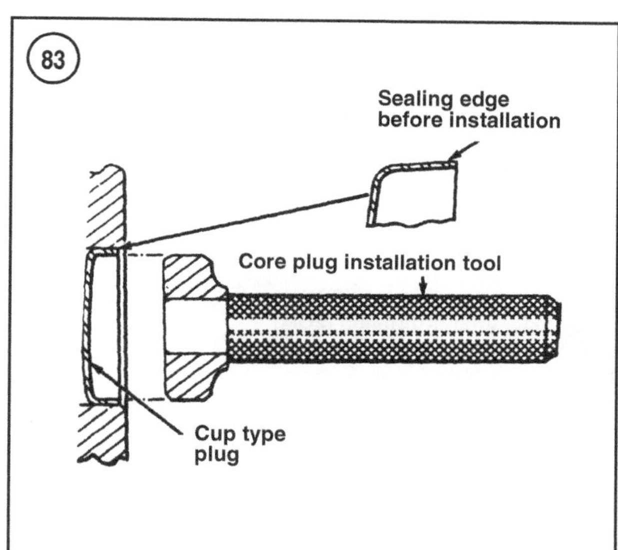

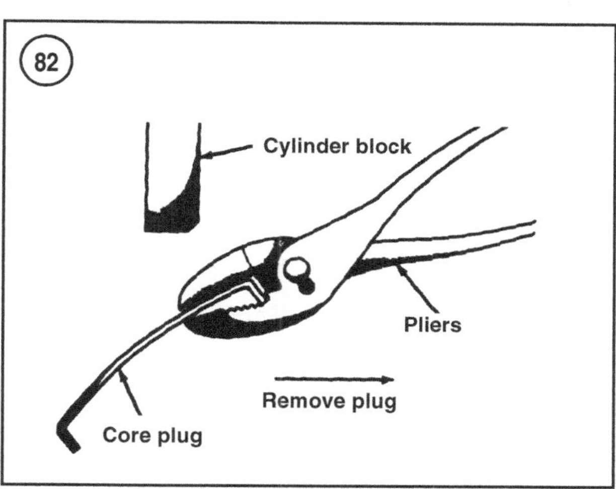

Core Plug Replacement

Check the condition of all core plugs in the block whenever the engine is out of the boat for service. If any signs of leakage or corrosion are found around one core plug, replace them all. Core plugs in the cylinder block prevent damage to the block should the coolant freeze. The cylinder block of 2GM, 3GM and 3HM engines is equipped with cast iron, removable cylinder liners. See *Cylinder Liners* in this chapter.

NOTE
A machine shop can replace core plugs inexpensively. If machine work on the engine is necessary, have the core plugs replaced at the same time.

Removal and Installation

CAUTION
Do not drive core plugs into the engine casting. It will be impossible to retrieve them and they can restrict coolant circulation, resulting in serious engine damage.

1. Tap the bottom edge of the core plug with a hammer and drift. Use several sharp blows to push the bottom of the plug inward, tilting the top out (**Figure 81**).
2. Grip the top of the plug firmly with pliers. Pull the plug from its bore (**Figure 82**) and discard.

NOTE
It is also possible to remove core plugs by drilling a hole in the center of the plug and prying it out with an appropriate size drift or pin punch. When removing a large core plug, the use of a universal impact slide hammer is recommended.

3. Clean the plug bore thoroughly to remove all traces of the old sealer. Inspect the bore for any damage that might interfere with proper sealing of the new plug.
4. Coat the inside diameter of the plug bore and the outer diameter of the new plug with sealer. Use an oil-resistant sealer if the plug is to be installed in an oil gallery or a water-resistant sealer for plugs installed in the water jacket.
5. Install the new core plug with an appropriate size core plug installation tool (**Figure 83**), driver or socket. Position the outside edge of the plug 2-3 mm (0.08-0.12 in.) inside the block.
6. Repeat Steps 1-5 to replace each remaining core plug.

Table 1 ENGINE SPECIFICATIONS (2GM AND 2GM20)

Bore	
2GM	72 mm (2.83 in.)
2GM20	75 mm (2.95 in.)
Stroke	72 mm (2.83 in.)
Displacement	
2GM	586 cc (35.7 cu. in.)
2GM20	636 cc (38.8 cu. in.)
Number of cylinders	2
Firing order	1-2
Cylinder liner diameter (2GM)	72.000 mm (2.8346 in.)
Cylinder liner protrusion (2GM)	0.005-0.075 mm (0.0002-0.0030 in.)
Cylinder bore diameter (2GM20)	75.000-75.030 mm (2.9528-2.9540 in.)
Bore/liner out-of-round—max.	0.02 mm (0.0008 in.)
Cylinder block warpage—max.	0.05 mm (0.002 in.)
Piston diameter	
2GM	
Standard	71.913-71.943 mm (2.8312-2.8324 in.)
Wear limit	71.850 mm (2.8287 in.)
2GM20	
Standard	74.910-74.940 mm (2.9492-2.9504 in.)
Wear limit	74.850 mm max. (2.9468 in.)
Piston top clearance	0.68-0.88 mm (0.027-0.035 in.)
Piston ring side clearance	
Top ring	0.065-0.100 mm (0.0026-0.0039 in.)
Second ring	0.035-0.070 mm (0.0014-0.0028 in.)
Oil ring	0.020-0.055 mm (0.0008-0.0022 in.)
Ring end gap (all rings)	0.20-0.40 mm (0.008-0.016 in.)
Piston pin diameter	19.991-20.000 mm (0.7870-0.7874 in.)
Piston pin hole diameter	
In piston	19.995-20.008 mm (0.7872-0.7877 in.)
In rod	20.000 mm (0.7874 in.)
Piston pin clearance	
In rod	0.025-0.047 mm (0.0010-0.0019 in.)
In piston	0.005 mm tight-0.017 mm loose (0.0002 in. tight-0.0007 in. loose)
Piston ring width	
Top and second ring	1.97-1.99 mm (0.0776-0.0783 in.)
Oil control ring	3.97-3.99 mm (0.1563-0.1571 in.)
Crankshaft main journal diameter	
Timing gear end	43.950-43.964 mm (1.7303-1.7309 in.)
Center	43.950-43.964 mm (1.7303-1.7309 in.)
Flywheel end	59.950-59.964 mm (2.3602-2.3608 in.)
Journal out-of-round—max.	0.01 mm (0.0004 in.)
Crankshaft end play	0.09-0.19 mm (0.0035-0.0075 in.)
Crankshaft runout—max.	0.15 mm (0.006 in.)
Main bearing clearance	
Timing gear end	0.036-0.092 mm (0.0014-0.0036 in.)
Center	0.036-0.092 mm (0.0014-0.0036 in.)
Flywheel end	0.036-0.095 mm (0.0014-0.0037 in.)
Intermediate thrust bearing width—min.	24.63 mm (0.970 in.)
Crankpin diameter	39.950-39.964 mm (1.5728-1.5734 in.)
Journal out-of-round—max.	0.01 mm (0.0004 in.)
Crankpin bearing clearance	0.028-0.086 mm (0.0011-0.0034 in.)
Connecting rod side clearance	0.2-0.4 mm (0.008-0.016 in.)
Cylinder head warpage—max.	0.07 mm (0.003 in.)
Camshaft	
Valve lobe lift	35.000 mm (1.3780 in.)
Fuel pump lobe lift	33.000 mm (1.2992 in.)
Journal diameter	30.000 mm (1.1811 in.)
Runout	0.02 mm max. (0.0008 in. max.)

(continued)

Table 1 ENGINE SPECIFICATIONS (2GM AND 2GM20) (continued)

Timing gear backlash	0.05-0.13 mm (0.002-0.005 in.)
Maximum allowable	0.3 mm (0.012 in.)
Push rod runout—max.	0.03 mm (0.0012 in.)
Valve lifter	
Type	Mechanical
Outside diameter	10.000 mm (0.3937 in.)
Outside diameter—min.	9.95 mm (0.3917 in.)
Clearance in block	0.010-0.040 mm (0.0004-0.0016 in.)
Max. clearance	0.10 mm (0.004 in.)
Valve face angle	45°
Valve seat angle	45°
Valve head margin	0.75-1.15 mm (0.030-0.045 in.)
Seat width (int. and exh.)	1.77 mm (0.070 in.)
Valve depth—max.	1.25 mm (0.049 in.)
Valve stem clearance	
Intake	0.040-0.065 mm (0.0016-0.0026 in.)
Exhaust	0.045-0.070 mm (0.0018-0.0028 in.)
Max. stem clearance	0.15 mm (0.006 in.)
Valve stem diameter	7.000 mm (0.2756 in.)
Valve stem wear limit	6.900 mm (0.2717 in.)
Valve stem runout—max.	0.03 mm (0.0012 in.)
Valve guide diameter	7.000 mm (0.2756 in.)
Valve guide wear limit	7.080 mm (0.2878 in.)
Valve guide protrusion	7.0 mm (0.276 in.)
Valve spring	
Standard free length	38.5 mm (1.52 in.)
Min. free length	37 mm (1.46 in.)
Installed height	29.2 mm (1.15 in.)
Pressure at installed height	16.16 kg at 29.2 mm (35.63 lb. at 1.15 in.)
Rocker arm shaft clearance	0.016-0.052 mm (0.0006-0.0020 in.)
Rocker arm shaft clearance—max.	0.15 mm (0.006 in.)
Rocker arm bore wear limit	14.10 mm (0.555 in.)
Rocker arm shaft wear limit	13.90 mm (0.547 in.)
Oil pump	
Inner rotor tip-to-outer rotor tip	0.050-0.105 mm (0.0020-0.0041 in.)
Max.	0.15 mm (0.006 in.)
Outer rotor-to-pump body	0.050-0.105 mm (0.0020-0.0041 in.)
Max.	0.15 mm (0.006 in.)
Rotor side clearance	0.030-0.080 mm
Max.	0.13 mm (0.005 in.)
Shaft clearance	0.015-0.050 mm (0.0006-0.0020 in.)
Max.	0.20 mm (0.0079 in.)

Table 2 ENGINE SPECIFICATIONS (3GM AND 3GM30)

Bore	
3GM	72 mm (2.83 in.)
3GM30	75 mm (2.95 in.)
Stroke	72 mm (2.83 in.)
Displacement	
3GM	879 cc (53.6 cu. in.)
3GM30	954 cc (58.2 cu. in.)
Number of cylinders	3
Firing order	1-2-3
Cylinder liner diameter (3GM)	72.000 mm (2.8346 in.)
Cylinder liner protrusion (3GM)	0.005-0.075 mm (0.0002-0.0030 in.)
Cylinder bore diameter (3GM30)	75.000-75.030 mm (2.9528-2.9540 in.)
Bore/liner out-of-round—max.	0.02 mm (0.0008 in.)

(continued)

6

Table 2 ENGINE SPECIFICATIONS (3GM AND 3GM30) (continued)

Cylinder block warpage—max.	0.05 mm (0.002 in.)
Piston diameter	
3GM	
Standard	71.913-71.943 mm (2.8312-2.8324 in.)
Wear limit	71.850 mm (2.8287 in.)
3GM30	
Standard	74.910-74.940 mm (2.9492-2.9504 in.)
Wear limit	74.850 mm (2.9468 in.)
Piston top clearance	0.68-0.88 mm (0.027-0.035 in.)
Piston ring side clearance	
Top ring	0.065-0.100 mm (0.0026-0.0039 in.)
Second ring	0.035-0.070 mm (0.0014-0.0028 in.)
Piston ring side clearance (continued)	
Oil ring	0.020-0.055 mm (0.0008-0.0022 in.)
Ring end gap (all rings)	0.20-0.40 mm (0.008-0.016 in.)
Piston pin diameter	19.991-20.000 mm (0.7870-0.7874 in.)
Piston pin hole diameter	
In piston	19.995-20.008 mm (0.7872-0.7877 in.)
In rod	20.000 mm (0.7874 in.)
Piston pin clearance	
In rod	0.025-0.047 mm (0.0010-0.0019 in.)
In piston	0.005 mm tight-0.017 mm loose (0.0002 in. tight-0.0007 in. loose)
Piston ring width	
Top and second ring	1.97-1.99 mm (0.0776-0.0783 in.)
Oil control ring	3.97-3.99 mm (0.1563-0.1571 in.)
Crankshaft main journal diameter	
Timing gear end	43.950-43.964 mm (1.7303-1.7309 in.)
Center	43.950-43.964 mm (1.7303-1.7309 in.)
Flywheel end	59.950-59.964 mm (2.3602-2.3608 in.)
Journal out-of-round—max.	0.01 mm (0.0004 in.)
Crankshaft end play	0.09-0.19 mm (0.0035-0.0075 in.)
Crankshaft runout—max.	0.15 mm (0.006 in.)
Main bearing clearance	
Timing gear end	0.036-0.092 mm (0.0014-0.0036 in.)
Center	0.036-0.092 mm (0.0014-0.0036 in.)
Flywheel end	0.036-0.095 mm (0.0014-0.0037 in.)
Crankpin diameter	39.950-39.964 mm (1.5728-1.5734 in.)
Journal out-of-round—max.	0.01 mm (0.0004 in.)
Intermediate thrust bearing width—min.	24.63 mm (0.970 in.)
Crankpin bearing clearance	0.028-0.086 mm (0.0011-0.0034 in.)
Connecting rod side clearance	0.2-0.4 mm (0.008-0.016 in.)
Cylinder head warpage—max.	0.07 mm (0.003 in.)
Camshaft	
Valve lobe lift	35.000 mm (1.3780 in.)
Fuel pump lobe lift	33.000 mm (1.2992 in.)
Journal diameter	
End journal	30.000 mm (1.1811 in.)
Center journal	41.500 mm (1.6339 in.)
Runout	0.02 mm max. (0.0008 in. max.)
Timing gear backlash	0.05-0.13 mm (0.002-0.005 in.)
Maximum allowable	0.3 mm (0.012 in.)
Push rod runout—max.	0.03 mm (0.0012 in.)
Valve lifter	
Type	Mechanical
Outside diameter	10.000 mm (0.3937 in.)
Outside diameter—min.	9.95 mm (0.3917 in.)
Clearance in block	0.010-0.040 mm (0.0004-0.0016 in.)
Max. clearance	0.10 mm (0.004 in.)
Valve face angle	45°
Valve seat angle	45°

(continued)

Table 2 ENGINE SPECIFICATIONS (3GM AND 3GM30) (continued)

Valve head margin	0.75-1.15 mm (0.030-0.045 in.)
Seat width (int. and exh.)	1.77 mm (0.070 in.)
Valve depth—max.	1.25 mm (0.049 in.)
Valve stem clearance	
Intake	0.040-0.065 mm (0.0016-0.0026 in.)
Exhaust	0.045-0.070 mm (0.0018-0.0028 in.)
Max. stem clearance	0.15 mm (0.006 in.)
Valve stem diameter	7.000 mm (0.2756 in.)
Valve stem wear limit	6.900 mm (0.2717 in.)
Valve stem runout—max.	0.03 mm (0.0012 in.)
Valve guide diameter	7.000 mm (0.2756 in.)
Valve guide wear limit	7.080 mm (0.2878 in.)
Valve guide protrusion	7.0 mm (0.276 in.)
Valve spring	
Standard free length	38.5 mm (1.52 in.)
Min. free length	37 mm (1.46 in.)
Installed height	29.2 mm (1.15 in.)
Pressure at installed height	16.16 kg at 29.2 mm (35.63 lb. at 1.15 in.)
Rocker arm shaft clearance	0.016-0.052 mm (0.0006-0.0020 in.)
Rocker arm shaft clearance—max.	0.15 mm (0.006 in.)
Rocker arm bore wear limit	14.10 mm (0.555 in.)
Rocker arm shaft wear limit	13.90 mm (0.547 in.)
Oil pump	
Inner rotor tip-to-outer rotor tip	0.050-0.105 mm (0.0020-0.0041 in.)
Max.	0.15 mm (0.006 in.)
Outer rotor-to-pump body	0.050-0.105 mm (0.0020-0.0041 in.)
Max.	0.15 mm (0.006 in.)
Rotor side clearance	0.030-0.080 mm
Max.	0.13 mm (0.005 in.)
Shaft clearance	0.015-0.050 mm (0.0006-0.0020 in.)
Max.	0.20 mm (0.0079 in.)

Table 3 ENGINE SPECICATIONS (3HM AND 3HM35)

Bore	
3HM	75 mm (2.95 in.)
3HM35	80 mm (3.15 in.)
Stroke	85 mm (3.35 in.)
Displacement	
3HM	1126 cc (68.7 cu. in.)
3HM35	1282 cc (78.2 cu. in.)
Number of cylinders	3
Firing order	1-2-3
Cylinder bore diameter (3HM35)	80.000-80.030 mm (3.1496-3.1508 in.)
Cylinder liner diameter (3HM)	75.00 mm (2.9528 in.)
Max.	75.10 mm (2.9567 in.)
Cylinder liner protrusion (3HM)	0.005-0.075 mm (0.0002-0.0030 in.)
Bore/liner out-of-round—max.	0.02 mm (0.0008 in.)
Cylinder block warpage—max.	0.05 mm (0.002 in.)
Piston diameter	
3HM	
Standard	74.907-74.937 mm (2.9491-2.9503 in.)
Wear limit	74.850 mm max. (2.9468 in.)
3HM35	
Standard	79.902-79.932 mm (3.1457-3.1470 in.)
Wear limit	79.840 mm max. (3.1433 in.)
Piston top clearance	0.66-0.86 mm (0.026-0.034 in.)
Piston ring side clearance	
Top ring	0.065-0.100 mm (0.0026-0.0039 in.)
Second ring	0.035-0.070 mm (0.0014-0.0028 in.)

(continued)

6

Table 3 ENGINE SPECICATIONS (3HM AND 3HM35) (continued)

Piston ring side clearance (continued)	
Oil ring	0.020-0.055 mm (0.0008-0.0022 in.)
Ring end gap (3HM)	
Top ring	0.20-0.40 mm (0.008-0.016 in.)
Second ring	0.20-0.40 mm (0.008-0.016 in.)
Oil ring	0.20-0.40 mm (0.008-0.016 in.)
Ring end gap (3HM35)	
Top ring	0.25-0.45 mm (0.010-0.018 in.)
Second ring	0.20-0.40 mm (0.008-0.016 in.)
Oil ring	0.25-0.45 mm (0.010-0.018 in.)
Piston pin diameter	22.991-23.000 mm (0.9052-0.9055 in.)
Piston pin hole diameter	
In piston	22.995-23.008 mm (0.9053-0.9058 in.)
In rod	23.000 mm (0.9055 in.)
Piston pin clearance	
In rod	0.025-0.047 mm (0.0010-0.0019 in.)
In piston	0.005 mm tight-0.017 mm loose (0.0002 in. tight-0.0007 in. loose)
Piston ring width	
Top and second ring	1.97-1.99 mm (0.0776-0.0783 in.)
Oil control ring	3.97-3.99 mm (0.1563-0.1571 in.)
Crankshaft main journal diameter	
Timing gear end	46.950-46.964 mm (1.8484-1.8490 in.)
Intermediate	46.950-46.964 mm (1.8484-1.8490 in.)
Flywheel end	64.950-64.964 mm (2.5571-2.5576 in.)
Journal out-of-round—max.	0.01 mm (0.0004 in.)
Crankshaft end play	0.09-0.18 mm (0.0035-0.007 in.)
Crankshaft runout—max.	0.15 mm (0.006 in.)
Main bearing clearance	
Timing gear end	0.036-0.095 mm (0.0014-0.0037 in.)
Intermediate	0.036-0.095 mm (0.0014-0.0037 in.)
Flywheel end	0.036-0.099 mm (0.0014-0.0039 in.)
Intermediate thrust bearing width—min.	29.63 mm (1.166 in.)
Crankpin diameter	43.950-43.964 mm (1.7303-1.7309 in.)
Journal out-of-round—max.	0.01 mm (0.0004 in.)
Crankpin bearing clearance	0.036-0.092 mm (0.0014-0.0036 in.)
Connecting rod side clearance	0.2-0.4 mm (0.008-0.016 in.)
Cylinder head warpage—max.	0.07 mm (0.003 in.)
Camshaft	
Valve lobe lift	35.000 mm (1.3780 in.)
Fuel pump lobe lift	33.500 mm (1.3189 in.)
Journal diameter	
End journal	30.000 mm (1.1811 in.)
Center journal	41.500 mm (1.6339 in.)
Runout	0.02 mm max. (0.0008 in. max.)
Timing gear backlash	0.05-0.13 mm (0.002-0.005 in.)
Maximum allowable	0.3 mm (0.012 in.)
Push rod runout—max.	0.03 mm (0.0012 in.)
Valve lifter	
Type	Mechanical
Outside diameter	10.000 mm (0.3937 in.)
Outside diameter—min.	9.95 mm (0.3917 in.)
Clearance in block	0.010-0.040 mm (0.0004-0.0016 in.)
Max. clearance	0.10 mm (0.004 in.)
Valve face angle	45°
Valve seat angle	45°
Valve head margin	0.85-1.15 mm (0.034-0.045 in.)
Seat width (int. and exh.)	1.77 mm (0.070 in.)
Valve depth—max.	1.55 mm (0.061 in.)

(continued)

Table 3 ENGINE SPECICATIONS (3HM AND 3HM35) (continued)

Valve stem clearance	
Intake	0.040-0.065 mm (0.0016-0.0026 in.)
Exhaust	0.045-0.070 mm (0.0018-0.0028 in.)
Max. stem clearance	0.15 mm (0.006 in.)
Valve stem diameter	7.000 mm (0.2756 in.)
Valve stem wear limit	6.900 mm (0.2717 in.)
Valve stem runout—max.	0.03 mm (0.0012 in.)
Valve guide diameter	7.000 mm (0.2756 in.)
Valve guide wear limit	7.080 mm (0.2878 in.)
Valve guide protrusion	7.0 mm (0.276 in.)
Valve spring	
Standard free length	38.5 mm (1.52 in.)
Min. free length	37 mm (1.46 in.)
Installed height	30.2 mm (1.19 in.)
Pressure and installed height	14.43 kg at 30.2 mm (31.81 lb. at 1.19 in.)
Rocker arm shaft clearance	0.016-0.052 mm (0.0006-0.0020 in.)
Rocker arm shaft clearance—max.	0.15 mm (0.006 in.)
Rocker arm bore wear limit	14.10 mm (0.555 in.)
Rocker arm shaft wear limit	13.90 mm (0.547 in.)
Oil pump	
Inner rotor tip-to-outer rotor tip	0.050-0.105 mm (0.0020-0.0041 in.)
Max.	0.15 mm (0.006 in.)
Outer rotor-to-pump body	0.050-0.105 mm (0.0020-0.0041 in.)
Max.	0.15 mm (0.006 in.)
Rotor side clearance	0.030-0.080 mm
Max.	0.13 mm (0.005 in.)
Shaft clearance	0.015-0.050 mm (0.0006-0.0020 in.)
Max.	0.20 mm (0.0079 in.)

Table 4 TIGHTENING TORQUES

Fastener	N•m	ft.-lb.	in.-lb.
Connecting rod	25	18	216
Cylinder head			–
M8	30	22	–
M12	120	88	–
3HM, 3HM35			
M8	30	22	–
M12	130	95	–
Exhaust elbow (2GM, 2GM20)	45	33	–
Exhaust manifold (3-cylinder)	45	33	–
Flywheel	65-70	48-51	–
Intermediate bearing housing			
2GM, 2GM20, 3GM, 3GM30	30-35	22-25	–
3HM, 3HM35	45-50	33-36	–
Retaining (set) bolt	45-50	33-36	–
Rear main bearing housing	25	18	–
Timing gearcase	15	11	–
Oil pump	8	–	17

6

Chapter Seven

Fuel Injection and Governor Systems

This chapter describes operation of the fuel injection and governor systems and service procedures. Refer to Chapter Two for troubleshooting procedures. Refer to Chapter Three for maintenance procedures. Refer to Chapter Five for a description of diesel engine operation.

Tables 1-3 are located at the end of this chapter.

WARNING
Serious fire hazards always exist around diesel fuel. Do not allow any smoking in areas where fuel is present. Always have a fire extinguisher, rated for fuel and electrical fires, on hand when refueling or servicing any part of the fuel system.

WARNING
Fuel emerges from the injector and high-pressure fuel fittings with sufficient force to penetrate the skin, which may cause blood poisoning. Wear goggles and cover exposed skin when working on high-pressure components.

FUEL INJECTION FUNDAMENTALS

Engine operation is described under *Diesel Engine Fundamentals* in Chapter Five.

The major components of the diesel fuel system are the fuel tank, fuel filters, injection pump and injection nozzle(s) (**Figure 1**). A feed (transfer) pump moves fuel from the fuel tank through the filters to the fuel injection pump. Governor operation is described in *Governor System* in this chapter.

Fuel Injection Pump

The fuel injection pump forces fuel into the fuel injector(s), which direct fuel into the engine combustion chamber. The pump raises fuel pressure to approximately 17000 kPa (2540 psi), while also controlling the time and amount of fuel injected.

The diesel injection pumps used on the engines covered in this manual operate on the plunger and cam principle. Refer to **Figure 2** and **Figure 3**. A rotating cam in the engine causes a plunger in the fuel injection pump to move in a cylinder and pump fuel to the injector nozzle. A delivery valve and spring establish the beginning and ending of injection while also maintaining residual pressure in the injection line. The plunger is designed to alter fuel flow when it is rotated. Fuel control is achieved by moving the fuel control rack, which rotates the fuel plunger pinion and plunger.

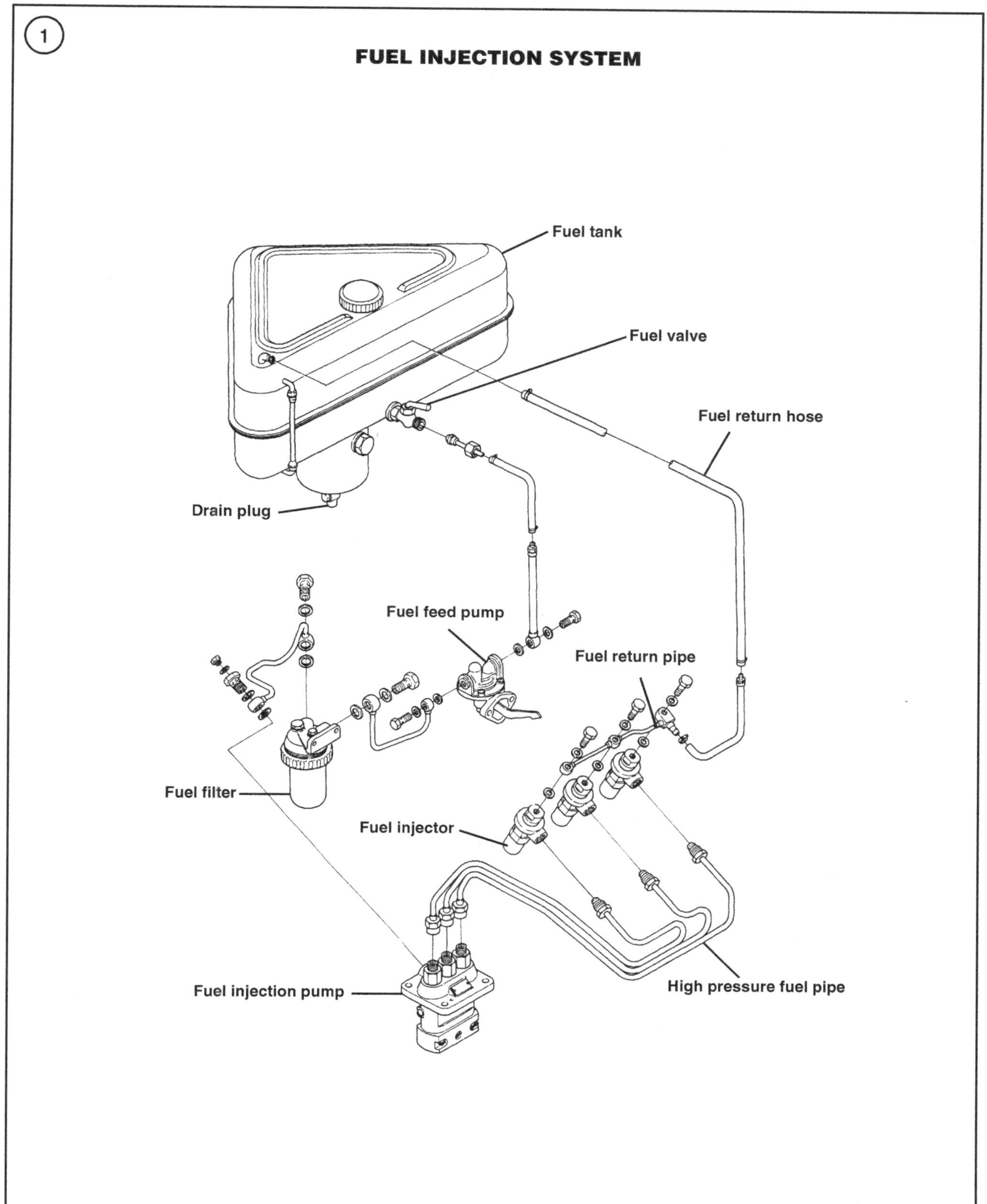
1
FUEL INJECTION SYSTEM
Fuel tank
Fuel valve
Fuel return hose
Drain plug
Fuel feed pump
Fuel return pipe
Fuel filter
Fuel injector
Fuel injection pump
High pressure fuel pipe

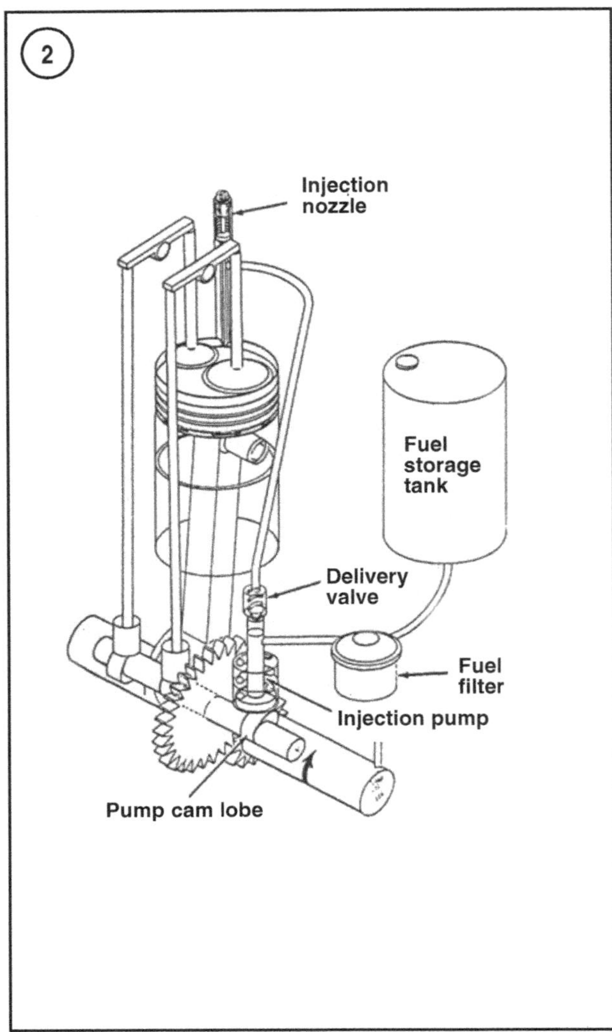

Individual pumping elements are used on single-cylinder engines as shown in **Figure 4**. Multiple-cylinder engines are equipped with pumping elements combined in a single unit as shown in **Figure 5**.

Fuel injection pumps are precision-built units that require clean fuel to operate properly. The extremely close tolerances and high injection pressure dictate that specialized equipment and experienced technicians are needed to service fuel injection pumps. If properly operated and maintained, a fuel injection pump will provide long-lasting, trouble-free service.

Fuel Injector

A fuel injector (A, **Figure 6**) is required for each cylinder to inject fuel into the combustion chamber. A high-pressure fuel line (B, **Figure 6**) directs fuel from the fuel injection pump to the fuel injector, while a fuel return line (C, **Figure 6**) carries bypass fuel back to the fuel tank. Refer to **Figure 7** for an exploded view of the fuel injector.

The engines covered in this manual are equipped with an inward opening, throttling-pintle type fuel injector (**Figure 8**). High fuel pressure from the injection pump enters the injection nozzle, surrounds the nozzle valve and forces the valve away from the seat. The pressure exerted by the spring above the nozzle holds the nozzle valve closed until the pressure of the fuel rises higher than spring pressure. The fuel delivered by the pump sprays from the nozzle tip into the combustion chamber when the valve opens. After the fuel is injected, fuel pressure decreases and the spring once again closes the valve.

The injection nozzle atomizes the fuel to help mix fuel with the compressed air in the engine's cylinder. The fuel must be broken into very small particles so that the fuel will quickly absorb heat from the compressed (hot) air, change to a vapor, then ignite. The design of the nozzle tip affects the size and shape of the fuel spray. The throttling pintle reduces the amount of fuel injected for a given orifice and causes a delay in the injection of the principal amount of fuel.

Excess fuel is routed from the injectors back to the fuel tank through a fuel return line.

Fuel and Fuel Filters

Clean, moisture-free fuel is very important to a diesel fuel system. As well as acting as the fuel for combustion, diesel fuel is also a lubricant for many of the internal moving parts in the fuel system. The close tolerances of the injection pump and nozzles are easily damaged by solid particles in the fuel as well as by water in the fuel.

All diesel fuel contains some sulfur, which forms sulfuric acid if water mixes with the sulfur. The sulfuric acid will quickly erode the precision parts of the pump and nozzles. Extra care must be exercised in the storage and handling of diesel fuel to prevent contamination.

Diesel fuel is graded according to the composition of the fuel after passing through the refining process. Common diesel fuel grades are 1D and 2D, with 1D the lighter fuel. The recommended fuel for the Yanmar engines covered by this manual is 2-D diesel fuel.

Filters are included within the system to remove solid particles and absorb moisture. In many cases, at least two filtering stages plus a water trap are incorporated to help ensure only clean fuel reaches the fuel injection pump. The primary filter (nearest the fuel tank) removes sediment and water from the fuel. The secondary filter removes very fine particles from the fuel. Both filters must

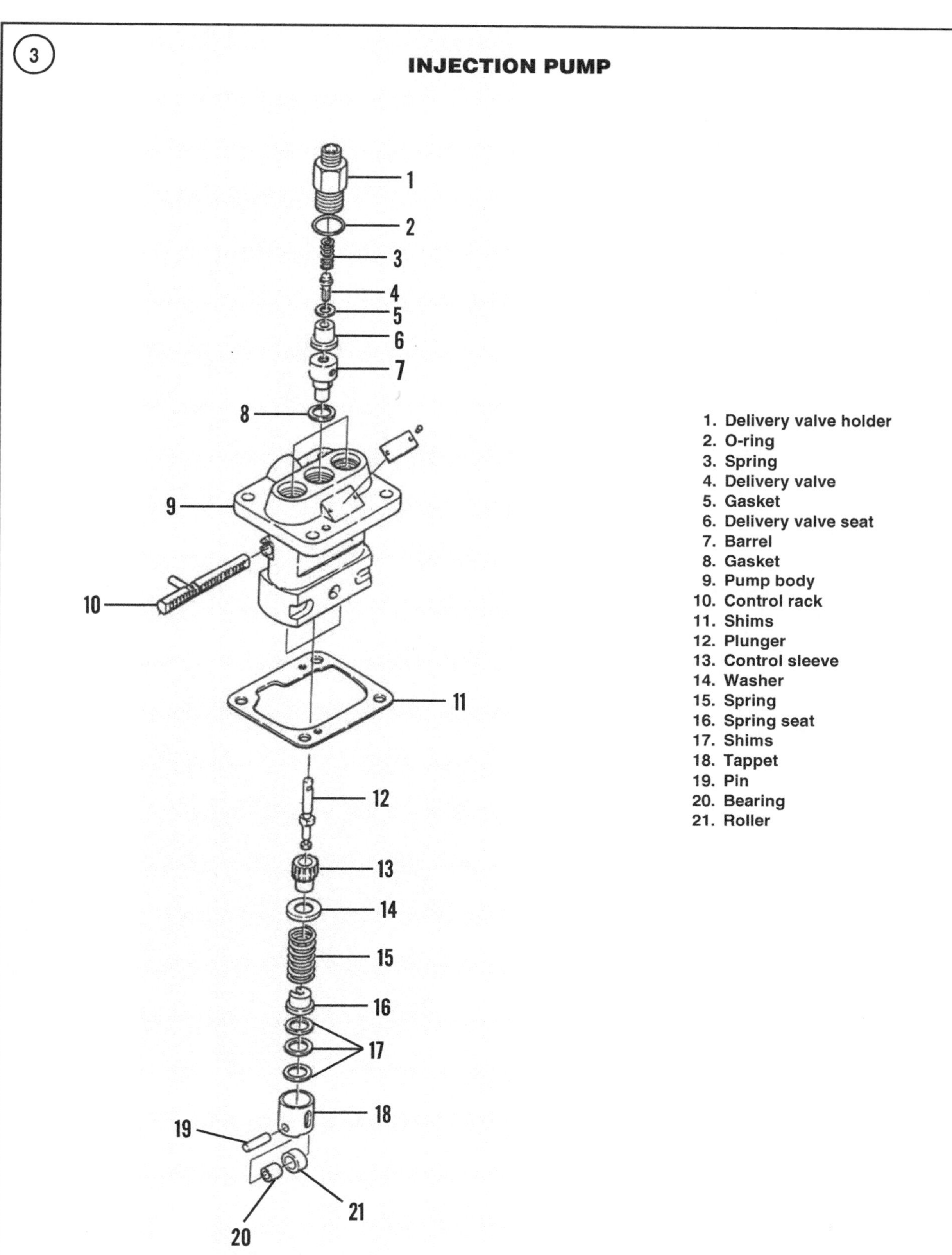
3
INJECTION PUMP
1
2
3
4
5
6
7
8
9
10
11
12
13
14
15
16
17
18
19
20
21
1. Delivery valve holder
2. O-ring
3. Spring
4. Delivery valve
5. Gasket
6. Delivery valve seat
7. Barrel
8. Gasket
9. Pump body
10. Control rack
11. Shims
12. Plunger
13. Control sleeve
14. Washer
15. Spring
16. Spring seat
17. Shims
18. Tappet
19. Pin
20. Bearing
21. Roller

be operating properly to adequately protect the fuel injection system. Failure to maintain fuel filters and use clean fuel can result in engine stoppage and expensive replacement or repair of the injection pump or injectors.

Fuel Transfer Pump

The fuel transfer pump (A, **Figure 9**) moves fuel from the fuel tank to the fuel injection pump. The pump is necessary when the fuel tank is lower than the fuel injection pump. A primer lever on the side of the transfer pump permits manual operation of the fuel pump diaphragm. Priming or bleeding the fuel system requires operation of the primer lever so fuel flows to the injection system with the engine stopped.

FUEL INJECTION SYSTEM BLEEDING

Air in the fuel system can cause rough engine operation or stoppage. Bleeding purges air from the system. Bleed the system anytime fuel line connections are disconnected or fuel components are removed. To ensure all air is removed, perform the complete bleeding procedure described in the following steps:

1. Open the bleed screw on the fuel filter (**Figure 10**). Make sure the fuel valve on the fuel tank is open.

NOTE
Be prepared to contain and wipe up expelled fuel.

2. Operate the priming lever (B, **Figure 9**) on the fuel transfer pump while observing the fuel expelled from the bleed screw hole. Continue to operate the priming lever until air-free fuel is expelled, then close the air bleed screw.

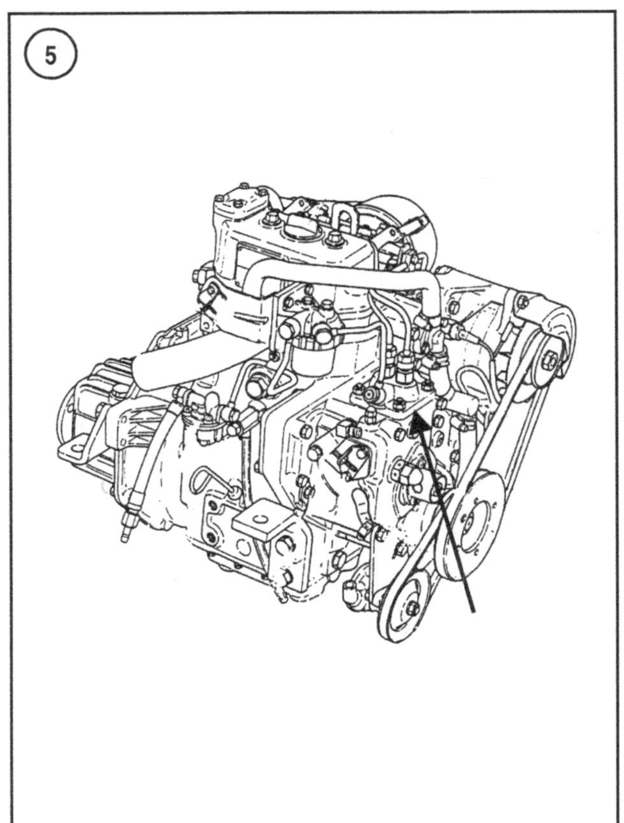

3. Open the air bleed screw (**Figure 11**) on the fuel injection pump.

4. Operate the priming lever (B, **Figure 9**) on the fuel transfer pump while observing the fuel expelled from the bleed screw hole. Continue to operate the priming lever until air-free fuel is expelled, then close the air bleed screw.

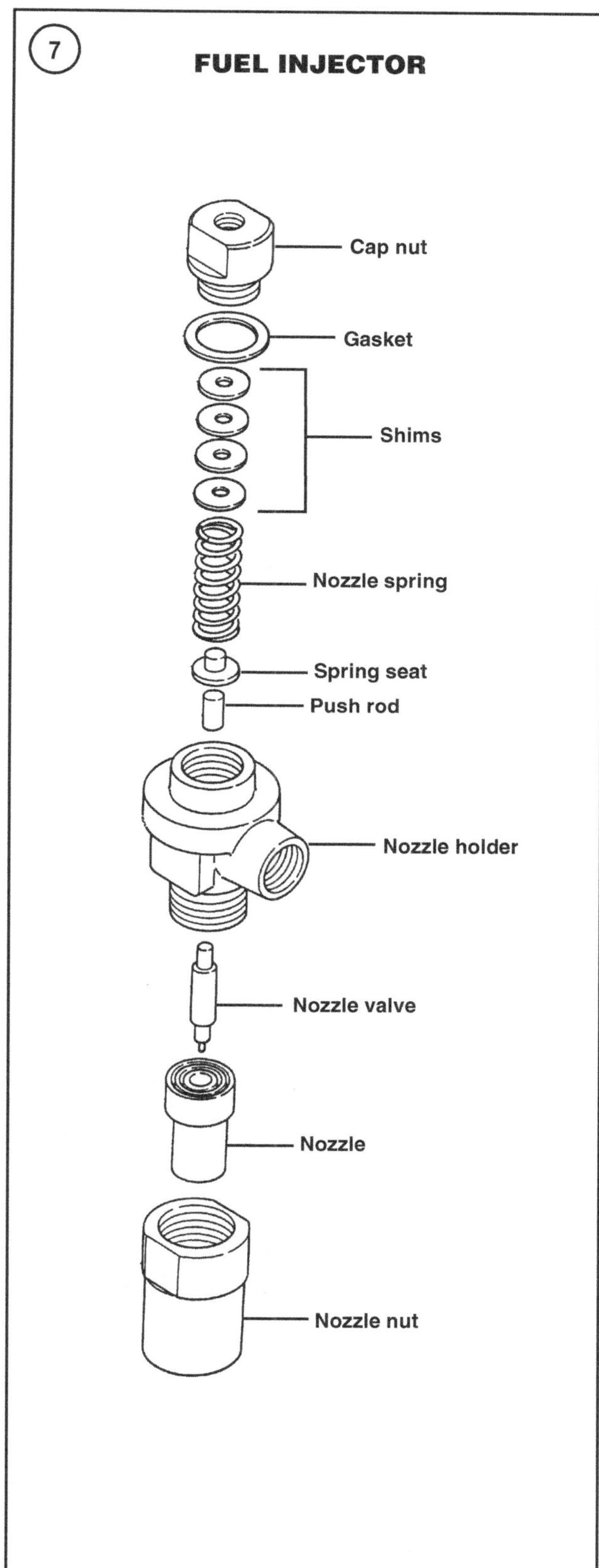
7
FUEL INJECTOR
Cap nut
Gasket
Shims
Nozzle spring
Spring seat
Push rod
Nozzle holder
Nozzle valve
Nozzle
Nozzle nut

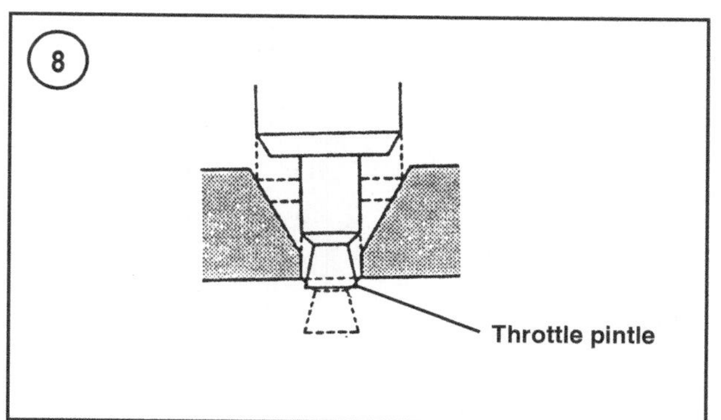
8
Throttle pintle

9
B
A

10

11

5. Loosen the fitting nut (**Figure 12**) on the injector(s) just enough to expel fuel.
6. Move the engine speed control to the full throttle position.
7. Move the decompression lever to the ON position.

NOTE
Do not operate the starter for more than 30 seconds; otherwise the starter may be damaged due to overheating.

8. Operate the starter until air-free fuel flows from the injector(s).
9. Tighten the injector fuel line fitting nut(s) to 20 N•m (15 ft.-lb.).
10. Operate the starter and listen for the distinctive noise that indicates the injector is operating.

FUEL INJECTION TIMING

Similar to ignition timing on a gasoline engine, the fuel must be injected at the proper time to obtain optimum combustion.

Injection timing is determined by the relationship between the injection pump plunger and the injection camshaft in the engine. The rotating cam acts against the roller on the pump plunger in the fuel injection pump (**Figure 13**) to force up the plunger and pump fuel to the injector nozzle. Moving the fuel injection pump up or down on its mounting surface changes the point on the cam that the plunger begins vertical movement, thereby changing when injection occurs.

Shims between the injection pump and its mounting surface on the engine are used to adjust fuel injection timing (**Figure 13**). Increasing shim thickness retards injection timing, while decreasing shim thickness advances injection timing.

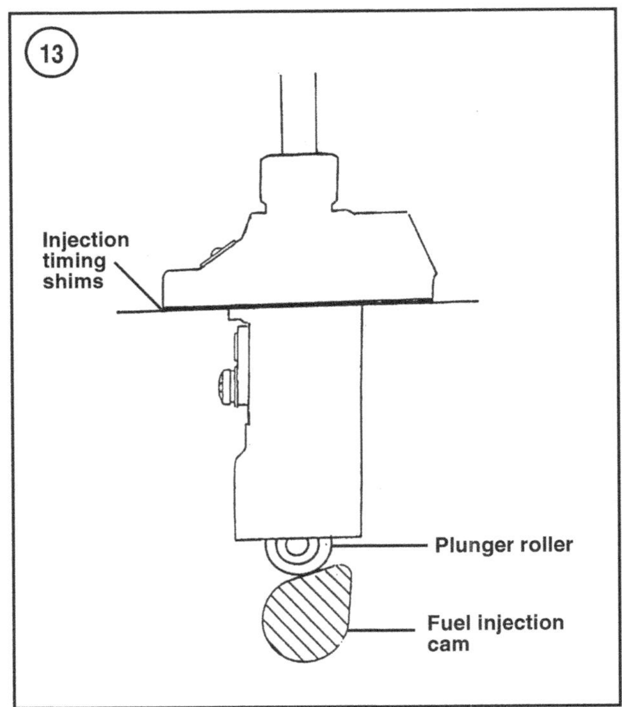

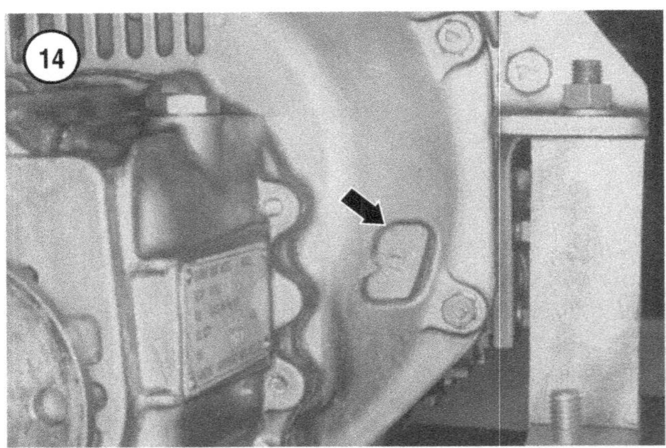

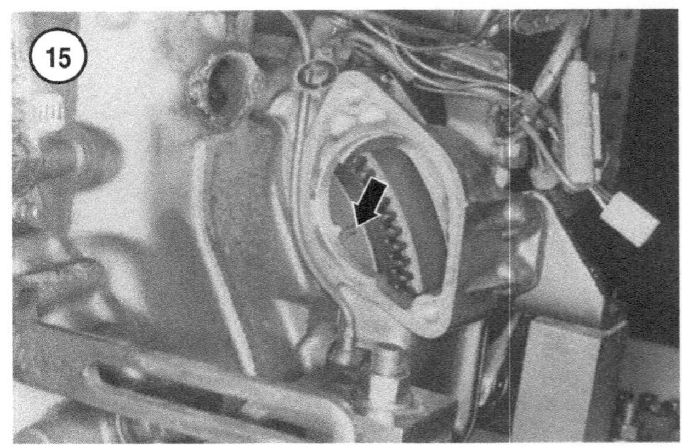

16

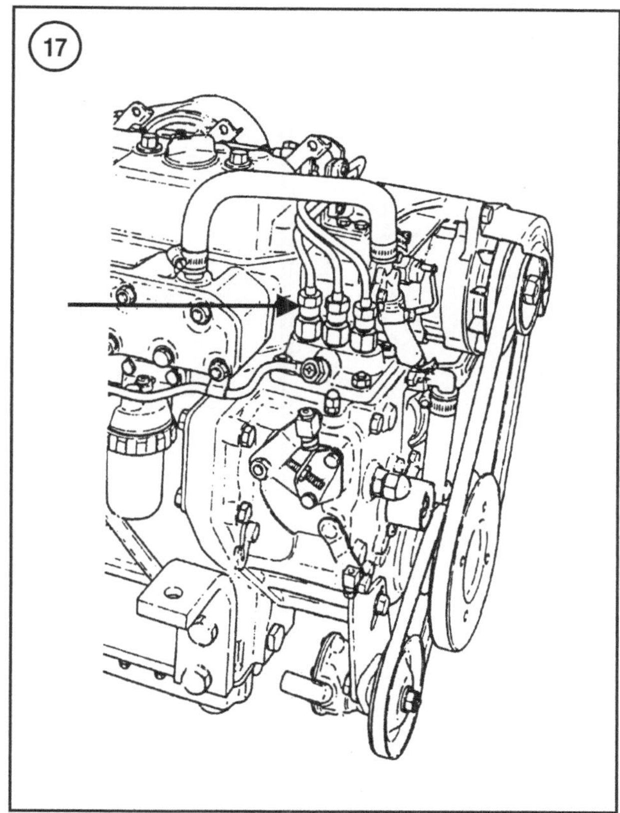
17

Adjust Fuel Injection Timing

1. Make sure there is no air in the fuel system. If necessary, bleed the fuel system as described in the previous section.

2. If there is no flywheel observation hole in the clutch cover (**Figure 14**), remove the starter motor so the timing marks on the flywheel (**Figure 15**) are visible.

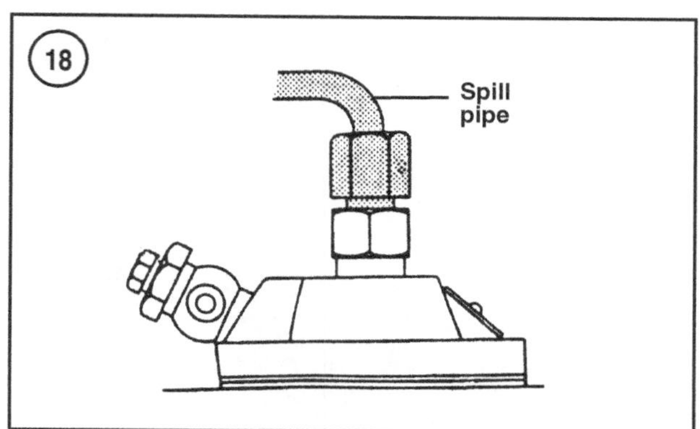

18

3A. On 1GM and 1GM10 models—Unscrew the fuel injection line retaining nut (**Figure 16**) and disconnect the fuel line from the pump.

NOTE
On 2GM, 2GM20, 3GM, 3GM30, 3HM and 3HM35 engines, the cylinder nearest the flywheel is the number one cylinder.

3B. On 2GM, 2GM20, 3GM, 3GM30, 3HM and 3HM35 models—Unscrew the fuel injection line retaining nut (**Figure 17**) for the number one cylinder fuel injection line, then disconnect the fuel line from the pump.

4. Install a spill pipe on the pump in place of the high-pressure fuel line (**Figure 18**).

NOTE
If a spill pipe is not available or cannot be fabricated, observe fuel flow in the open nipple.

5. Place the speed control lever at the mid-throttle position.

NOTE
Do not use the starter motor when rotating the crankshaft.

NOTE
Always rotate the crankshaft in the normal running direction (clockwise at the crankshaft pulley); otherwise the water pump impeller may be damaged.

6. Rotate the crankshaft with the crankshaft pulley retaining nut until the 1T mark on the flywheel appears.

NOTE
The piston must be on its compression stroke. If fuel does not appear in the spill pipe, the piston may not be on the compres-

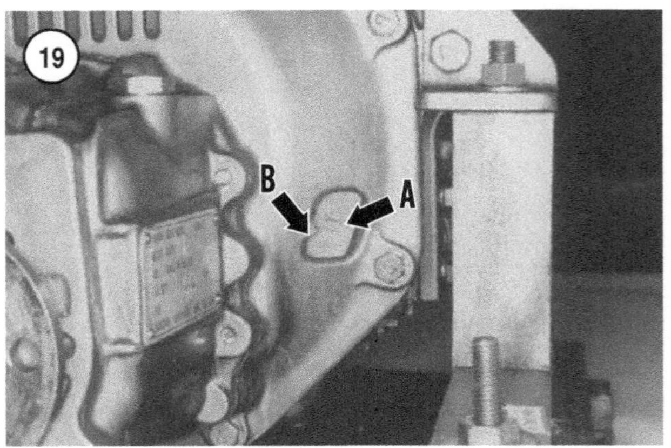

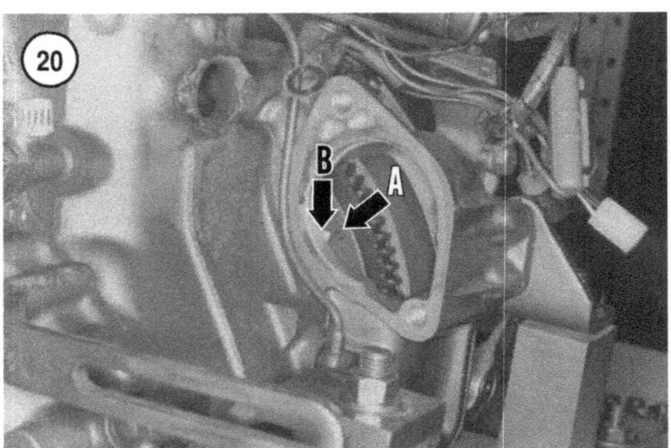

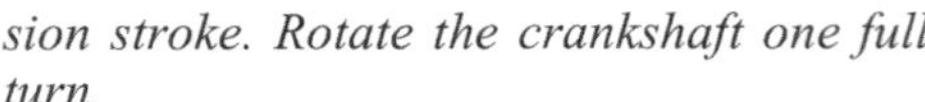
sion stroke. Rotate the crankshaft one full turn.

7. Slowly rotate the crankshaft while observing the fuel in the fuel nipple on the injection pump and the timing marks on the flywheel.
8. When fuel appears in the spill pipe, the injection timing mark on the flywheel (A, **Figure 19**) should align with the reference pointer (B) on the clutch cover. If viewing marks through the starter hole, the injection timing mark on the flywheel (A, **Figure 20**) should align with the reference mark (B) on the clutch cover.

NOTE
There are two timing marks for each cylinder on the flywheel: a mark for top dead center (TDC) and the injection timing mark. The TDC mark is identified by a T next to the mark. Near the TDC mark is another mark, the injection timing mark, which has no identifying letters or numbers. The injection timing mark is to the right of the TDC mark when viewing the mark through the starter hole, or to the left of the TDC mark when viewing the mark through the clutch cover hole.

9. If the injection timing is not correct, remove the fuel injection pump as described in this chapter.
10. Measure the shim pack located between the pump and engine mounting surface (**Figure 21**).
11A. *Injection timing retarded*—If injection timing is retarded, decrease the shim thickness to advance injection timing. Decreasing shim thickness 0.1 mm will advance injection timing one degree.
11B. *Injection timing advanced*—If injection timing is advanced, increase the shim thickness to retard injection timing. Increasing shim thickness 0.1 mm will retard injection timing one degree.

12. Install the shims and injection pump, then recheck injection timing.
13. On 2GM, 2GM20, 3GM, 3GM30, 3HM and 3HM35 models—Check fuel injection timing for the remaining cylinders. Use the injection timing mark adjacent to the 2T or 3T marks for the cylinder being checked. If injection timing is incorrect for the number two or three cylinders, have a Yanmar dealership or diesel fuel injection shop inspect the injection pump.

FUEL INJECTOR

Each cylinder is equipped with a fuel injector (**Figure 22**). Refer to *Fuel Injector* in the *Fuel Injection Fundamentals* section of this chapter for information regarding fuel injector operation.

Maintaining optimum fuel injector performance is primarily dependent on using clean fuel. Dirt or debris in the fuel is the predominant cause of poor injector performance. The injector is also subject to the heat and byproducts of combustion. The fuel injector nozzle is protected from combustion heat by a heat shield. However, heat and

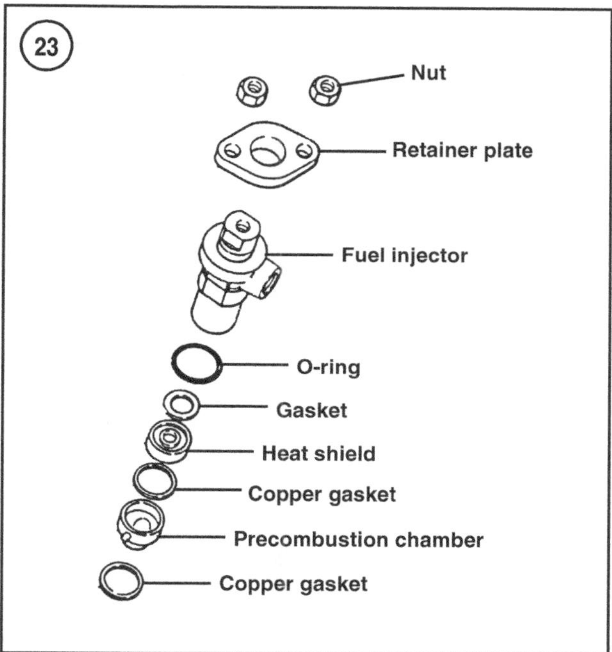

combustion byproducts eventually affect injector operation. Clogging may affect the spray pattern, which may cause misfiring and decreased engine performance. Yanmar does not specify when a fuel injector should be removed for cleaning. A periodic maintenance schedule can be formulated based on when engine performance declines due to the injector becoming clogged. An injector should perform properly for several hundred hours before requiring service; otherwise, operating procedures, fuel type or condition, or another engine problem are responsible for unsatisfactory injector operation.

Injector service should be limited to removal for external cleaning. Have a Yanmar dealership or diesel fuel injection shop perform internal cleaning or overhaul.

Removal and Installation

Refer to **Figure 23** for an exploded view of the fuel injector and precombustion chamber assembly.

1. Thoroughly clean the fuel injector and the area around the injector to make sure debris will not fall into the engine.

NOTE
Plug or cap all fuel openings to prevent the entrance of dirt or debris.

NOTE
Note the location of all washers so they can be returned to their original positions.

2. Detach the fuel return line from the nipple on the fuel injector. On multicylinder engines, the fuel return line must be removed from all injectors. Hold the injector and remove the fuel return line nut (A, **Figure 24**) and return line fitting.
3. If necessary, unscrew the fuel line retaining brackets. Detach the high-pressure fuel line (B, **Figure 24**) from the fuel injector.
4. Unscrew the retainer plate nuts (A, **Figure 25**), then remove the retainer plate (B).
5. Remove the fuel injector (**Figure 26**).
6. Extract the heat shield and gasket (**Figure 27**). The gasket resides in a groove in the top of the heat shield.

NOTE
Do not damage the precombustion chamber when removing it in Step 7 if it is tight in the cylinder head. If necessary, remove the cylinder head to dislodge the precombustion chamber.

7. Extract the precombustion chamber and copper gaskets (**Figure 28**). Note that there is a copper gasket (**Figure 29**) above and below the chamber; make sure to remove the bottom gasket after removing the chamber.

8. On models so equipped, remove and discard the O-ring on the fuel injector (**Figure 23**).

9. Plug the opening in the cylinder head to prevent the entry of dirt or debris.

10. Refer to the following section for injector testing and cleaning information.

11. Inspect the precombustion chamber. If damaged, discard the chamber. Clean the heat shield.

12. Discard the gaskets and install new gaskets. Thoroughly remove any gasket residue in the top of the heat shield.

13. Install the bottom copper gasket in the injector bore in the cylinder head.

14. Install the precombustion chamber with the holes toward the cylinder head. Align the pin on the side of the precombustion chamber (**Figure 30**) with the groove in the injector bore (**Figure 31**).

15. Install the upper copper gasket onto the precombustion chamber.

16. Install the heat shield and gasket. The open side of the heat shield must be down.

17. Install the O-ring onto the fuel injector (**Figure 29**).

18. Install the fuel injector into the injector bore in the cylinder head (**Figure 26**).

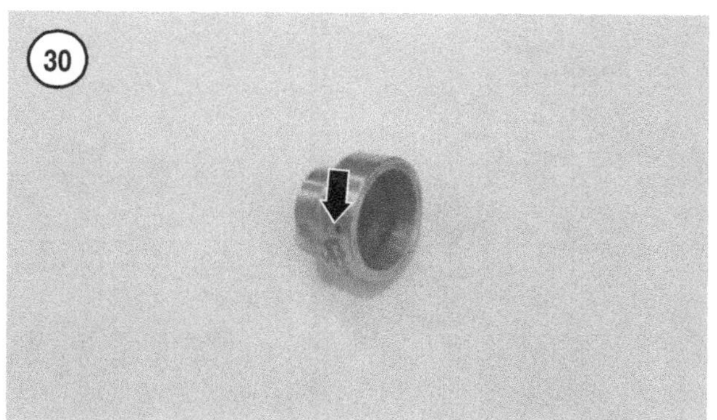

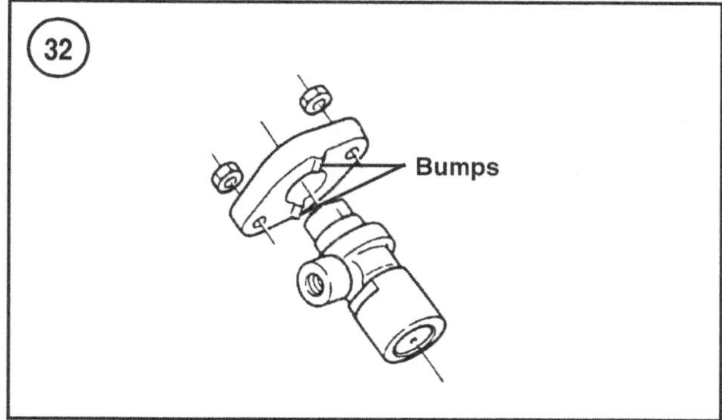

19. Connect the high-pressure fuel line to the injector.

20. Install the retainer plate so the side with bumps (**Figure 32**) is down and contacts the injector.

21. Install the retaining nuts. Tighten the nuts evenly to 20 N•m (14.5 ft.-lb.).

22. Connect the fuel return line.

23. Reattach fuel line retaining brackets.

24. Bleed the fuel injection system as described in this chapter. Run the engine and check for leaks.

FUEL INJECTION PUMP

The fuel injection pump is built to precise specifications and is easily damaged by contamination from dirt or debris. Due to the close tolerances in the pump and the special tools and equipment required for overhaul and testing, have a Yanmar dealership or diesel fuel injection shop perform any unnecessary service.

Removal and Installation

WARNING
Serious fire hazards always exist around diesel fuel. Do not allow any smoking in areas where fuel is present. Always have a fire extinguisher, rated for fuel and electrical fires, on hand when servicing any part of the fuel system.

1. Close the fuel shutoff valve.
2. Thoroughly clean the fuel injection pump and the area around the pump of all debris.

NOTE
Plug or cap all fuel openings to prevent the entrance of debris.

3. Detach the fuel supply line from the fuel injection pump (A, **Figure 33**).
4. Unscrew the fuel line retaining brackets. Remove the fuel injection line(s) between the fuel injection pump and fuel injector(s) (B, **Figure 33**).
5. Remove the injection pump retaining nuts (C, **Figure 33**).

NOTE
Removing the oil fill cap on 1GM and 1GM10 models provides access to the gov-

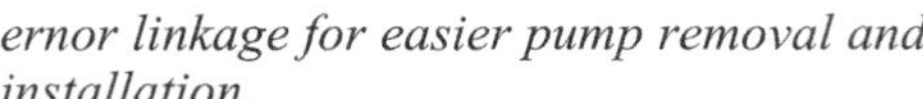
ernor linkage for easier pump removal and installation.

6. Lift the injection pump out of the engine while carefully disengaging the governor linkage from the pump.
7. Remove the timing shims (**Figure 34**) and set them aside for reinstallation.
8. To reinstall the injection pump, reverse the removal procedure. Make sure to reinstall the timing shims and engage the control rack pin (**Figure 35**) with the governor lever fork. Tighten the pump retaining nuts to 25 N•m (18 ft.-lb.). Bleed the fuel injection system as previously described. Run the engine and check for leaks.

FUEL TRANSFER PUMP

The engine is equipped with a fuel transfer pump (A, **Figure 36**) to move fuel from the fuel tank to the fuel filter and fuel injection pump. A cam lobe on the engine camshaft operates the pump lever (**Figure 37**), which moves the fuel pump diaphragm to pump the fuel. Fuel pump pressure is approximately 9.7 kPa (1.4 psi).

The transfer pump output port on 1GM and 1GM10 engines is on the left side with the pump mounted on the engine. On all other engines, the output port is on the right side.

Fuel Pump Testing

WARNING
Always have a fire extinguisher, rated for fuel and electrical fires, on hand when servicing any part of the fuel system. Clean up any spilled fuel as soon as possible.

1. Loosen the air bleed screw (**Figure 38**) on the fuel filter.

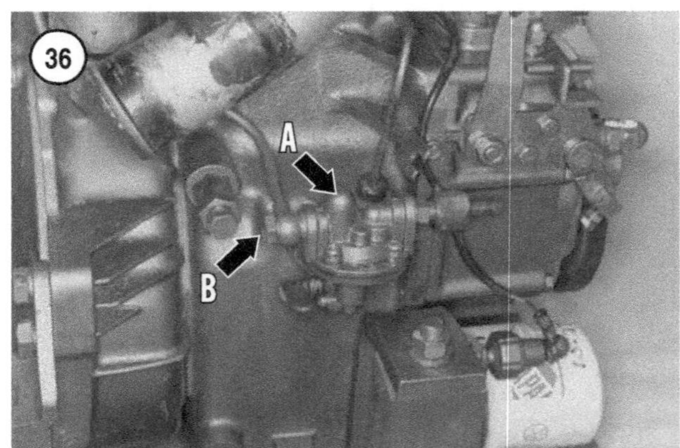

2. Operate the engine starter. If the fuel transfer pump is operating properly, fuel will flow from the air bleed screw hole.
3. If fuel does not flow from the air bleed screw hole, disconnect the output fuel line (B, **Figure 36**) from the fuel pump.

NOTE
Be prepared to catch fuel expelled from the pump.

4. Operate the engine starter. If fuel does not flow from the fuel pump, replace the pump.

Removal and Installation

1. Close the fuel tank valve.

NOTE
Account for the sealing washers on the fuel hose ends.

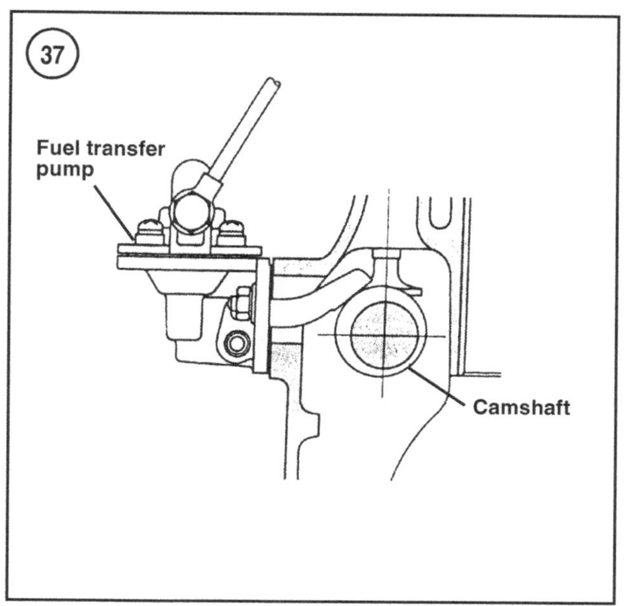

2. Disconnect the fuel lines (A, **Figure 39**) from the fuel transfer pump.
3. Remove the fuel pump retaining bolts (B, **Figure 39**), and then remove the pump.
4. Clean any gasket material from the engine and the fuel pump.
5. Reverse the removal procedure to install the fuel transfer pump. Bleed the fuel injection system as described in this chapter.

NOTE
The transfer pump output port on 1GM and 1GM10 engines is on the left side with the pump mounted on the engine. On all other engines, the output port is on the right side.

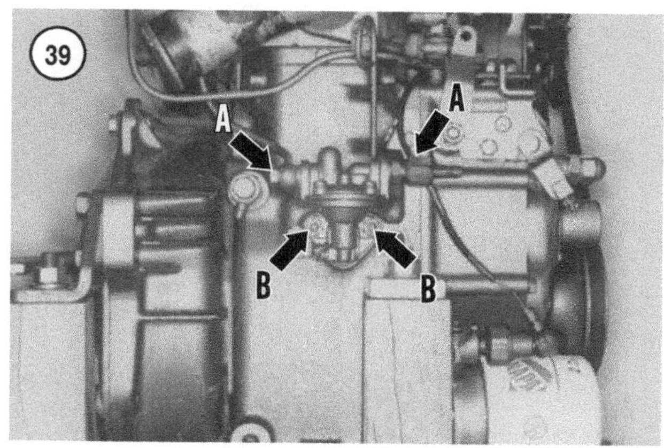

Overhaul

7

Internal parts for the fuel transfer pump are not available. Replace a defective pump; do not attempt to overhaul it.

FUEL LINES

The fuel system utilizes both rubber and steel lines. When replacing fuel lines, use only lines recommended by the manufacturer or a diesel engine shop. Purchase the formed steel fuel lines from a Yanmar dealership. If necessary, a diesel fuel injection shop can fabricate fuel lines. All lines must be secured by brackets to prevent fractures or splitting due to vibration.

Inspection

Periodically inspect the fuel lines for leaks and damage, such as dented or bent steel lines, or cut or abraded rubber lines. Leaks may be due to loose fittings or damage. Tighten loose fittings and recheck the leak after operating the engine. Do not overtighten a fitting to try to stop a leak; overtightening may damage the fitting threads or the fuel line sealing surfaces. If tightening does not stop the leak, disassemble the fuel line and inspect the line and seat to determine the cause of the leak. If sealing surfaces are damaged, replace the fuel line and, if necessary, the fuel fitting or component.

NOTE
Always operate the engine and check for leaks after reconnecting the fuel lines.

Fuel lines with banjo fittings (A, **Figure 40**) are equipped with copper sealing washers (B) on *both* sides of the fitting. Copper washers harden with age and will not

seal properly if reused. Always install *new* washers when reconnecting a fitting.

The fuel lines are secured with brackets to prevent leaks due to engine vibration. Periodically check that fuel lines are properly secured with brackets. The high-pressure fuel injection lines are held by a rubber pad in the bracket (**Figure 41**). Replace any rubber pads that are missing or no longer holding the line securely.

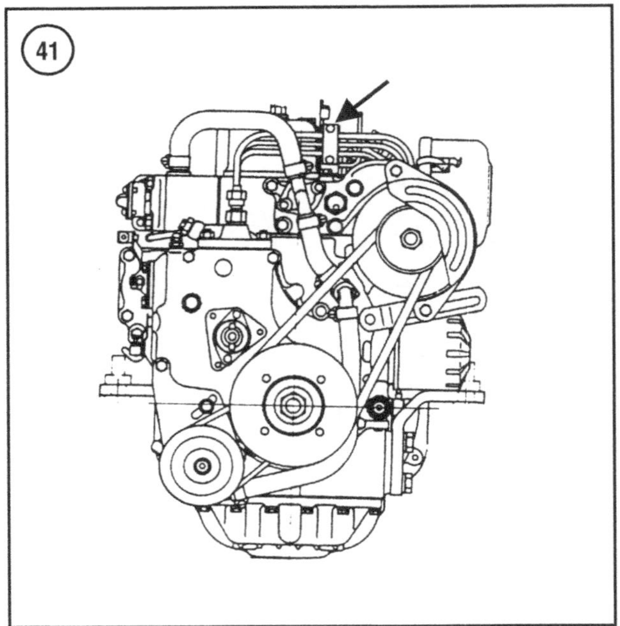

GOVERNOR SYSTEM

Operation

The governor components are in the timing gearcase (**Figure 42**, typical). The purpose of the governor system is to maintain engine speed regardless of the load imposed.

The mechanical governor system utilizes centrifugal force to monitor and adjust engine speed. Refer to **Figure 43, Figure 44** and **Figure 45**. A set of flyweights are mounted on the crankshaft. When engine speed increases, the flyweights are thrown out. When engine speed decreases, the flyweights recede. Trapped between the flyweights is a flanged sleeve that moves in and out with the flyweights, pushing against a forked governor arm. The forked governor arm transfers motion to the governor lever, which is connected to the fuel injection pump fuel control rack. The governor spring tension forces the speed control lever against the governor lever, which forces the injection pump speed control rack to the full open throttle position. When load on the engine increases and engine speed decreases, the governor sleeve is withdrawn, which through the linkage moves the speed control rack to increase fuel injection. When load on the engine decreases and engine speed increases, the governor sleeve extends, which moves the linkage to overcome governor spring tension. The linkage moves the speed control rack and decreases fuel injection.

The governor controls engine speed in an operating range between idle speed and maximum governed speed. Maximum governed speed is critical as it sets the upper limit of engine operation. Exceeding the maximum governed speed can cause overspeeding, which may result in engine failure.

A fuel limiter screw sets maximum injection pump fuel delivery. When the governor senses a decrease in engine speed, the fuel control rack moves to the full fuel position. The factory-adjusted fuel limiter screw stops the governor linkage at a point that provides maximum, but not excessive, fuel delivery to the engine.

43

GOVERNOR SYSTEM OPERATION

Speed control handle
Speed control lever
Fuel control rack
Fuel injection pump
Pivot point
Decrease
Increase
Idle adjuster
No-load maximum speed limiter
Governor lever 2
Crankshaft gear
Governor spring
Pivot point
Fuel control lever
Governor weight
Governor sleeve
Pivot point
Governor lever 1
Fuel injection limiter

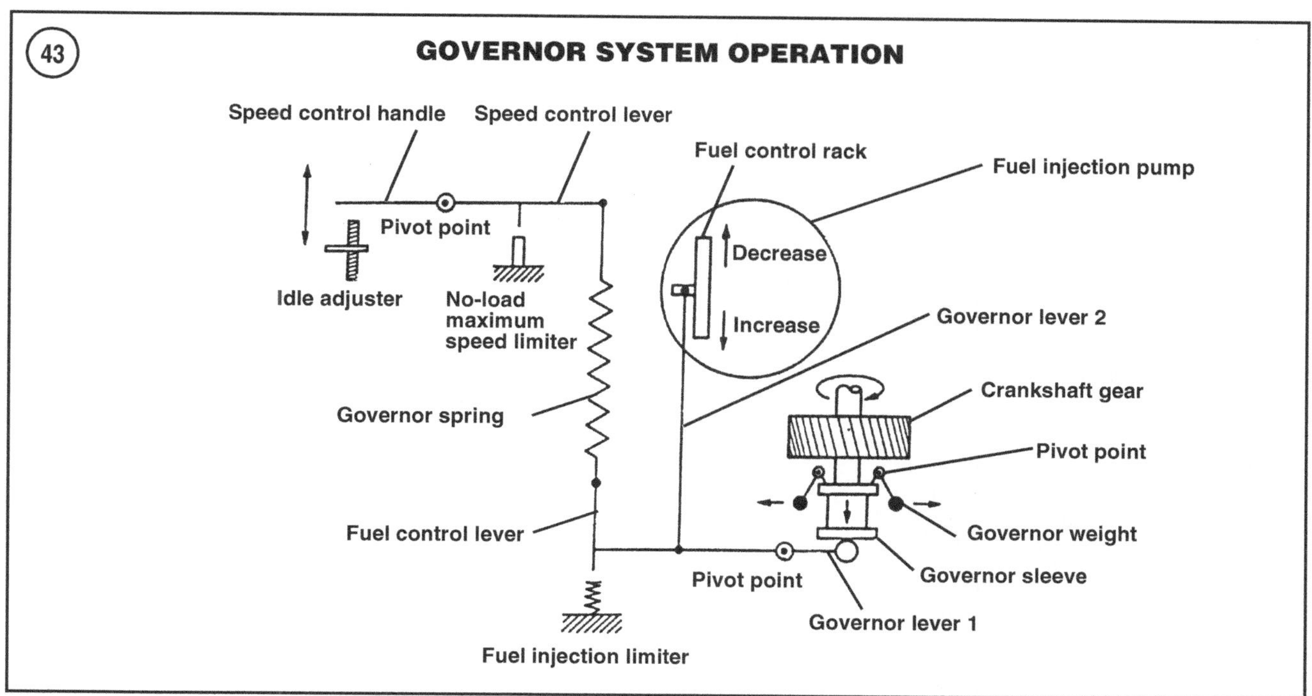

44

GOVERNOR SYSTEM

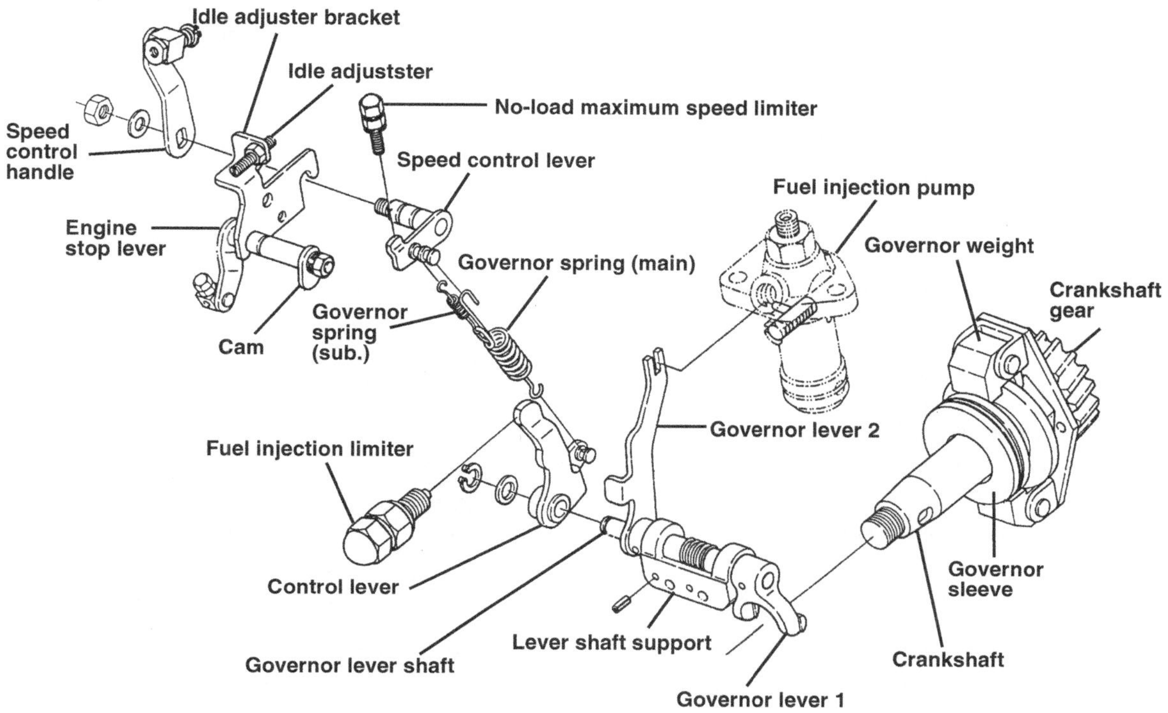

Idle adjuster bracket
Idle adjustster
No-load maximum speed limiter
Speed control handle
Speed control lever
Fuel injection pump
Engine stop lever
Governor weight
Governor spring (main)
Crankshaft gear
Cam
Governor spring (sub.)
Governor lever 2
Fuel injection limiter
Governor sleeve
Control lever
Lever shaft support
Crankshaft
Governor lever shaft
Governor lever 1

7

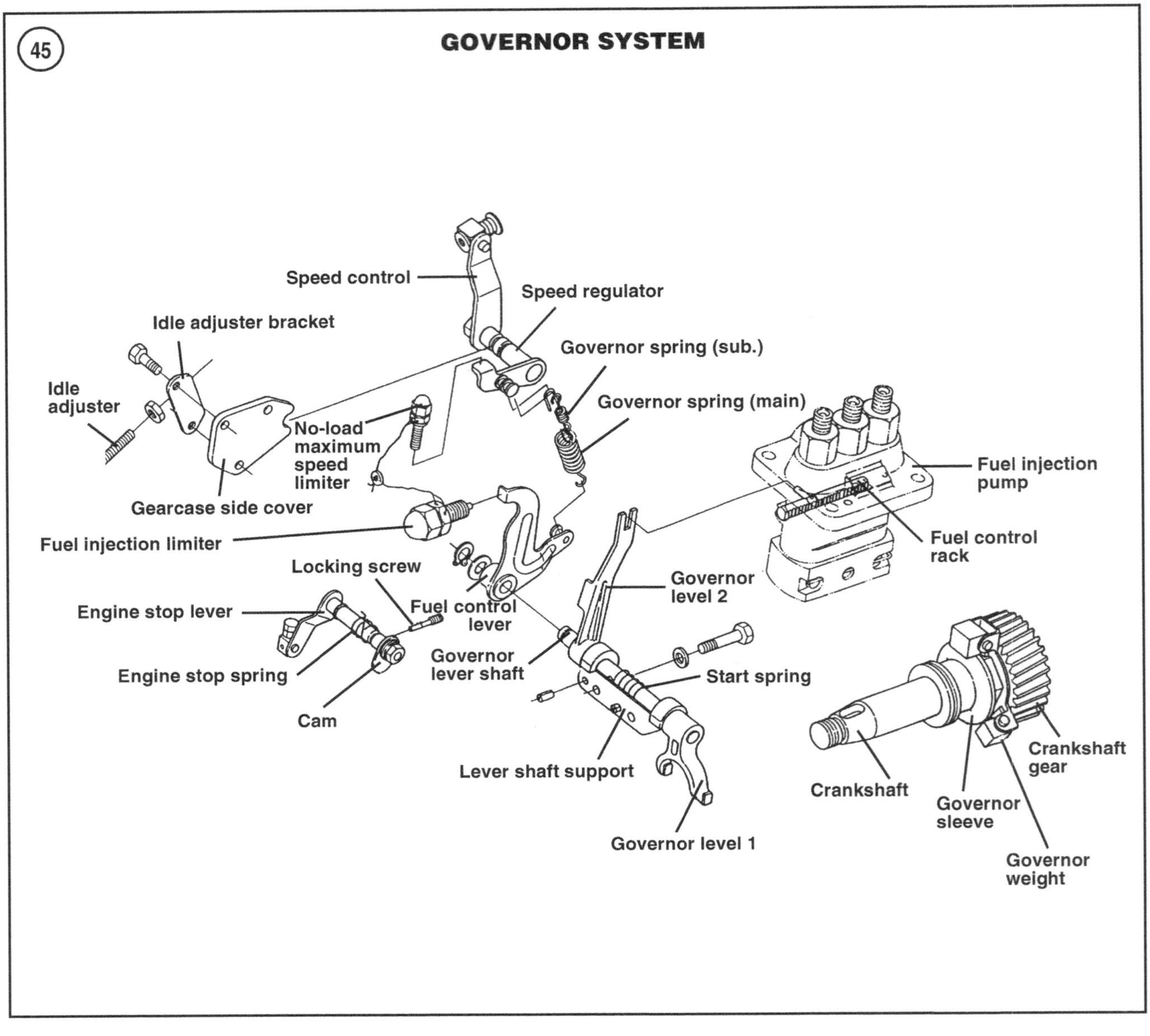

45

GOVERNOR SYSTEM

Speed control
Speed regulator
Idle adjuster bracket
Governor spring (sub.)
Idle adjuster
Governor spring (main)
No-load maximum speed limiter
Fuel injection pump
Gearcase side cover
Fuel control rack
Fuel injection limiter
Locking screw
Governor level 2
Engine stop lever
Fuel control lever
Governor lever shaft
Start spring
Engine stop spring
Cam
Crankshaft gear
Lever shaft support
Crankshaft
Governor sleeve
Governor level 1
Governor weight

Adjustments

Yanmar recommends that only idle speed adjustment should be performed by non-authorized service technicians. Refer to Chapter Three for the idle speed procedure.

Other adjustments, such as no-load maximum governed speed and fuel limiter screw setting, are set by the manufacturer. Incorrect adjustment can damage the engine. To prevent tampering, a safety wire is attached to each screw and a lead seal is affixed to the wire or the screw assembly is marked (**Figure 46**). Removing or cutting the wire or seal or altering the marked screw position will void the engine warranty.

46

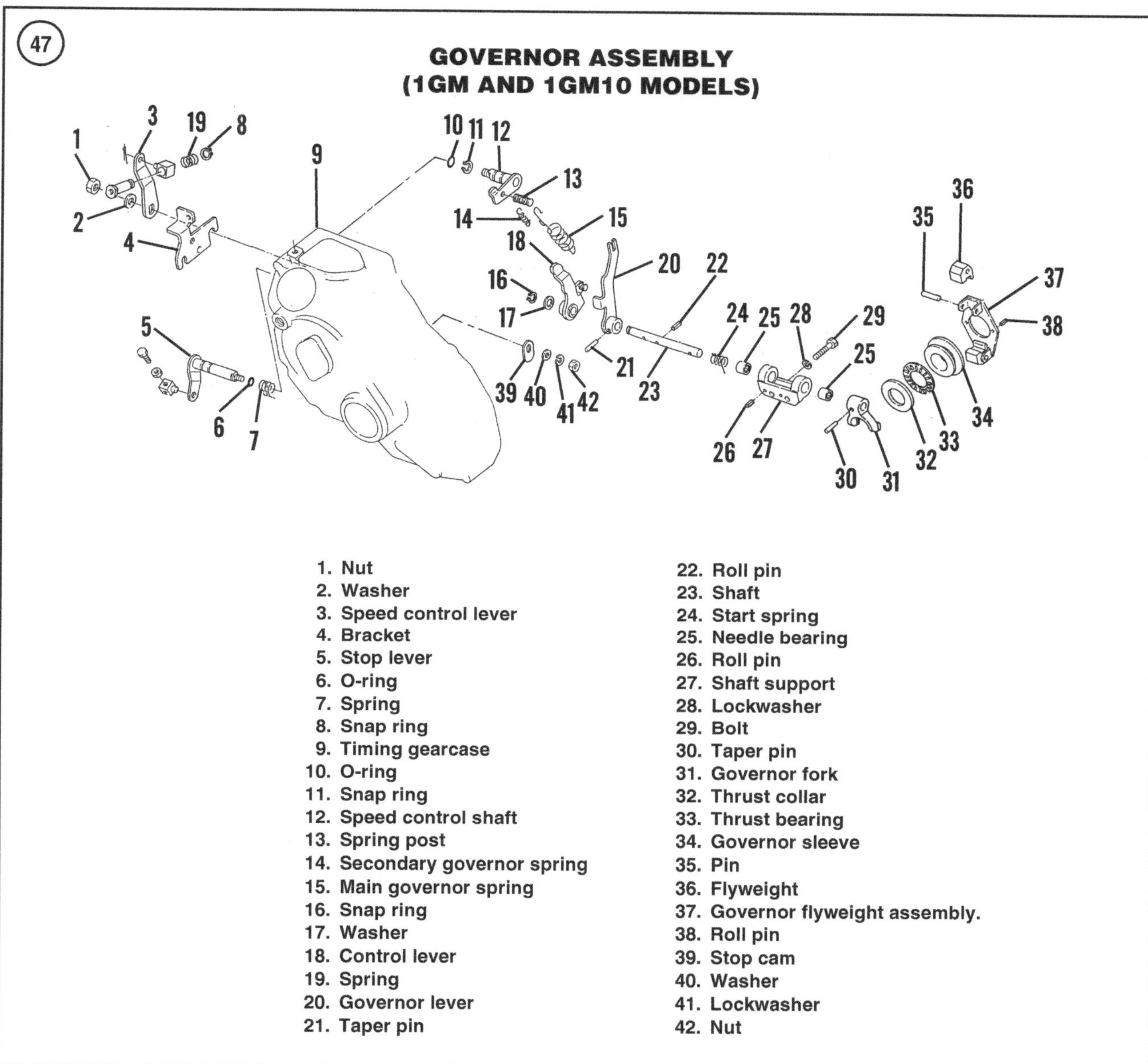

Removal/Inspection/Installation

The governor components are contained in the timing gearcase (**Figure 42**, typical). Refer to **Figure 47** or **Figure 48** for an exploded view of the governor mechanism.

1. Remove the timing gearcase as described in Chapter Five or Six.

NOTE
Do not distort or damage the governor spring.

2. Carefully disconnect the governor spring (15, **Figure 47** or **Figure 48**).

3. Check the governor shaft assembly for damage or looseness. Excessive play can cause improper governor operation. The shaft rides in bearings and should rotate smoothly without binding. The pinned levers should be tight on the shaft.

NOTE
Tapered pins secure the levers to the shaft. Remove a pin by driving against the small end of the pin.

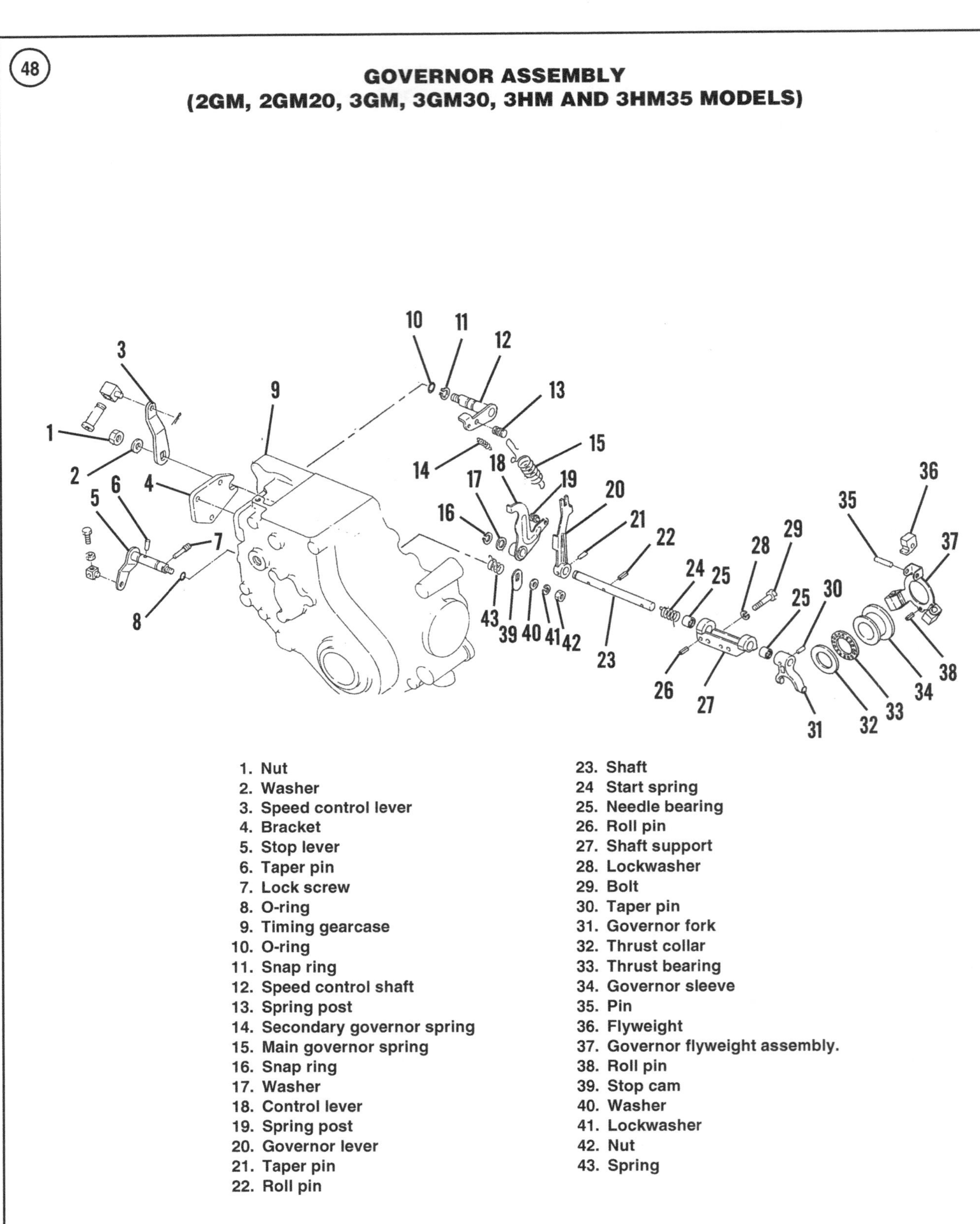

GOVERNOR ASSEMBLY (2GM, 2GM20, 3GM, 3GM30, 3HM AND 3HM35 MODELS)

1. Nut
2. Washer
3. Speed control lever
4. Bracket
5. Stop lever
6. Taper pin
7. Lock screw
8. O-ring
9. Timing gearcase
10. O-ring
11. Snap ring
12. Speed control shaft
13. Spring post
14. Secondary governor spring
15. Main governor spring
16. Snap ring
17. Washer
18. Control lever
19. Spring post
20. Governor lever
21. Taper pin
22. Roll pin
23. Shaft
24 Start spring
25. Needle bearing
26. Roll pin
27. Shaft support
28. Lockwasher
29. Bolt
30. Taper pin
31. Governor fork
32. Thrust collar
33. Thrust bearing
34. Governor sleeve
35. Pin
36. Flyweight
37. Governor flyweight assembly.
38. Roll pin
39. Stop cam
40. Washer
41. Lockwasher
42. Nut
43. Spring

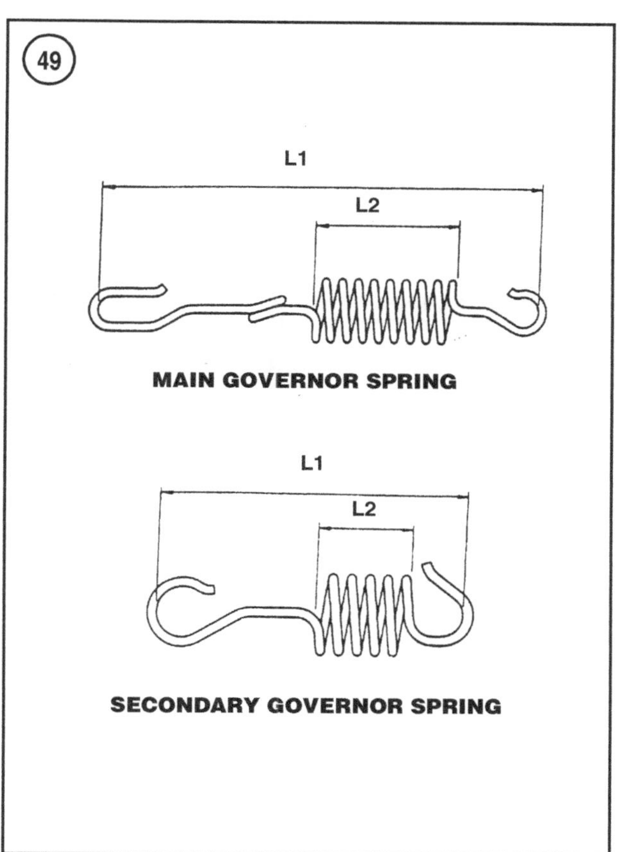

4. If disassembly of the governor shaft assembly is required, remove the retaining bolts (29, **Figure 47** or **Figure 48**) and remove the shaft assembly. To disassemble the components, detach the snap ring (16), then drive out the tapered pins that retain the levers. Replace the worn parts.

5. Remove the idle adjuster bracket and side cover (4, **Figure 47** or **Figure 48**).

6. Check the speed control lever and shaft (12, **Figure 47** or **Figure 48**) for excessive play between the shaft and the timing gearcase and between the lever and the shaft.

   a. If the shaft is loose in the timing gearcase, remove the nut (1, **Figure 47** or **Figure 48**), then remove the speed control lever (3). Remove the shaft (12) and determine if the shaft, the timing gearcase or both are worn. Replace or repair the worn part.
   b. If the lever is loose on the shaft, remove the nut (1, **Figure 47** or **Figure 48**), then remove the speed control lever (3). Determine if the lever, the shaft or both are worn. Replace any worn parts.

7A. *On 1GM and 1GM10 models*—Check the stop shaft (5, **Figure 47**) for excessive play between the shaft and the timing gearcase. If excessive play is evident, remove the nut (42), then withdraw the shaft. Determine if the shaft, the timing gearcase or both are worn. Replace or repair any worn parts.

7B. *On 2GM, 2GM20, 3GM, 3GM30, 3HM and 3HM35 models*—Check the stop shaft (5, **Figure 48**) for excessive play between the shaft and the timing gearcase. If excessive play is evident, drive out the taper pin (6) by driving against the small end of the pin. Remove the locking screw (7). Remove the nut (42), then remove the shaft. Determine if the shaft, the timing gearcase or both are worn. Replace or repair any worn parts.

8. Inspect the governor springs for damage and distortion. Measure the length of the main and secondary governor springs as shown in **Figure 49**. Replace either spring if its free length dimension is not as specified in **Table 2**. If either spring is questionable, take it to a Yanmar dealership for testing.

9. Remove and inspect the thrust collar (32, **Figure 47** or **Figure 48**). Replace the thrust collar if damaged or if the thickness is less than 2.9 mm (0.114 in.).

10. Remove the thrust bearing (33, **Figure 47** or **Figure 48**). Replace the bearing if damaged.

11. Remove the governor sleeve (34, **Figure 47** or **Figure 48**). Inspect the governor sleeve and crankshaft for damage. Refer to the specifications in **Table 3**.

12. Check the operation of the flyweight assembly (37, **Figure 47** or **Figure 48**). The flyweights should move smoothly without excessive looseness. The contact surface in the flyweight groove should not be excessively worn. The flyweight assembly must be replaced as a complete assembly. Remove the crankshaft nut as described in Chapter Five or Six to remove the flyweight assembly.

13. Reassemble the governor assembly by reversing the disassembly procedure while noting the following:

   a. Do not distort the governor springs during installation.
   b. Install the governor springs so the long hook end engages the speed control lever (12, **Figure 47** or **Figure 48**).
   c. Install the secondary governor spring (14, **Figure 47** or **Figure 48**) so the lower end of the spring fits in the loop on the main governor spring.
   d. Note that the pins securing the levers on the shafts are tapered. The lever should fit tightly on the shaft after the pin is installed. If not, replace the worn part.
   e. Check the movement of all the parts after assembly. Motion should be smooth without binding.

14. Reinstall the timing gearcase as described in Chapter Five for single cylinder engines or Chapter Six for multicylinder engines.

Table 1 TIGHTENING TORQUES

Fastener	N•m	ft.-lb.	in.-lb.
Injector fuel nut	20	15	–
Injection pump retaining nuts	25	18	–

Table 2 GOVERNOR SPRING FREE LENGTH

	1GM, 1GM10	2GM, 2GM20	3GM, 3GM30, 3HM, 3HM35
Main governor spring			
L1	76 mm (2.99 in.)	78 mm (3.07 in.)	78 mm (3.07 in.)
L2	18 mm (0.71 in.)	20 mm (0.79 in.)	20 mm (0.79 in.)
Secondary governor spring			
L1	26 mm (1.02 in.)	23 mm (0.90 in.)	23 mm (0.90 in.)
L2	5 mm (0.20 in.)	10 mm (0.39 in.)	10 mm (0.39 in.)

Table 3 GOVERNOR SLEEVE AND CRANKSHAFT SPECIFICATIONS

Governor sleeve inside diameter	25.053-25.083 mm (0.9863-0.9875 in.)
Governor sleeve length—wear limit	14.8 mm (0.583 in.)
Crankshaft diameter	24.972-24.993 mm (0.9831-0.9840 in.)
Governor sleeve clearance on crankshaft	0.060-0.111 mm (0.0024-0.0044 in.)
Maximum allowable clearance	0.20 mm (0.008 in.)

Chapter Eight

Cooling System

This chapter covers service procedures for the thermostat, engine water pump, seawater pumps, drive belts and connecting hoses in both standard and closed cooling systems.

Cooling system flushing procedures are provided in Chapter Three. Drain and refill procedures are described in Chapter Four.

Table 1 and **Table 2** are located at the end of this chapter.

NOTE
Except where specified, F and D series engines are included when a basic model number is specified. For example, if model 3GM is called out in a procedure, the procedure also applies to 3GMD and 3GMF.

COOLING SYSTEMS

Seawater (Standard) Cooling System

All engines are equipped with a seawater cooling system. The water in which the boat is being operated is used as a coolant to absorb engine heat. Water from outside the boat passes through the water intake to the impeller-type seawater pump located on the engine (**Figure 1**, typical). The seawater pump sends the water to the engine for circulation through the engine block, head and manifold.

A thermostat controls water circulation to provide quick engine warm-up and maintain a constant operating temperature.

Refer to typical cooling system diagrams in **Figure 2**, **Figure 3** and **Figure 4**.

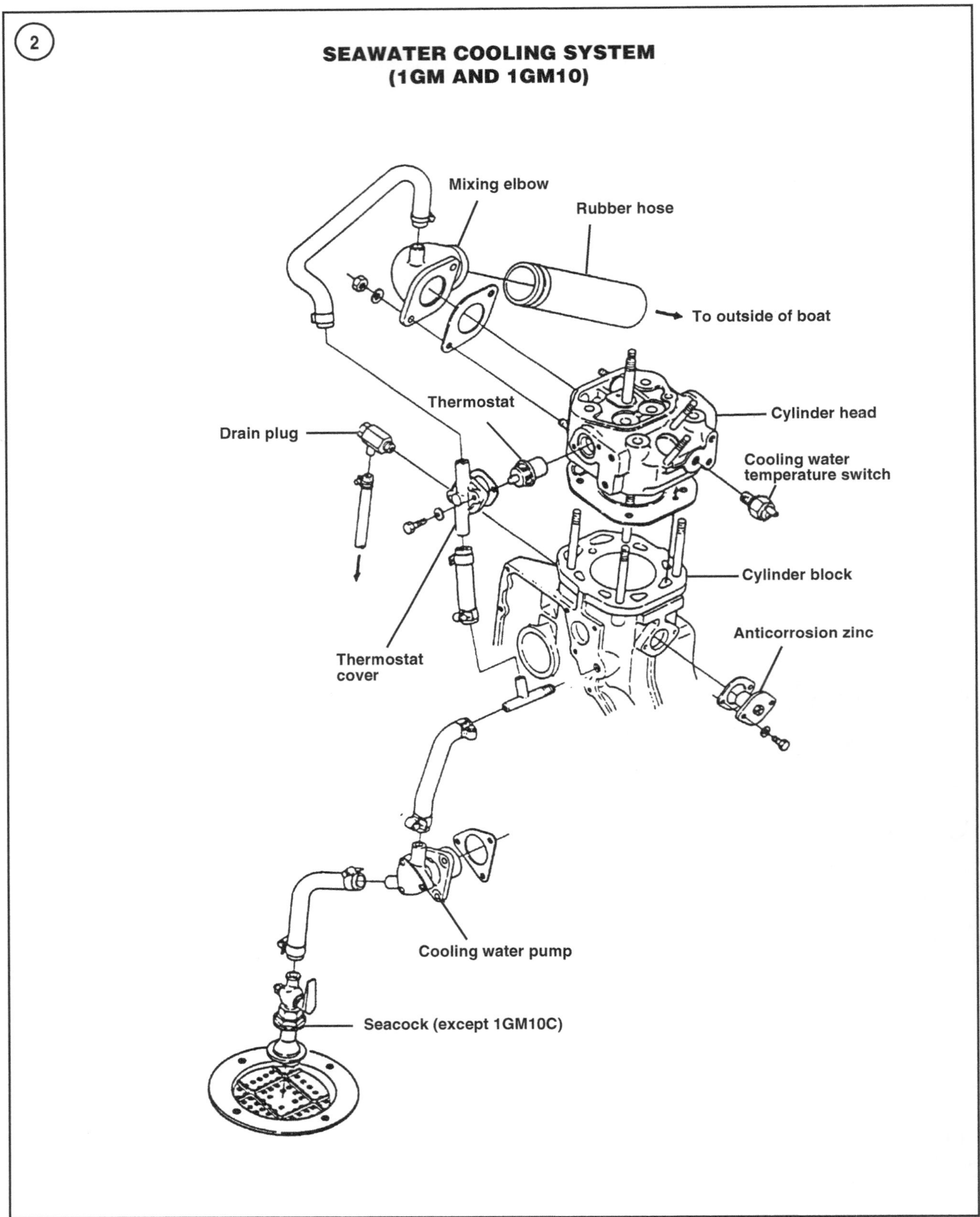
2
SEAWATER COOLING SYSTEM
(1GM AND 1GM10)
Mixing elbow
Rubber hose
To outside of boat
Thermostat
Cylinder head
Drain plug
Cooling water
temperature switch
Cylinder block
Anticorrosion zinc
Thermostat
cover
Cooling water pump
Seacock (except 1GM10C)

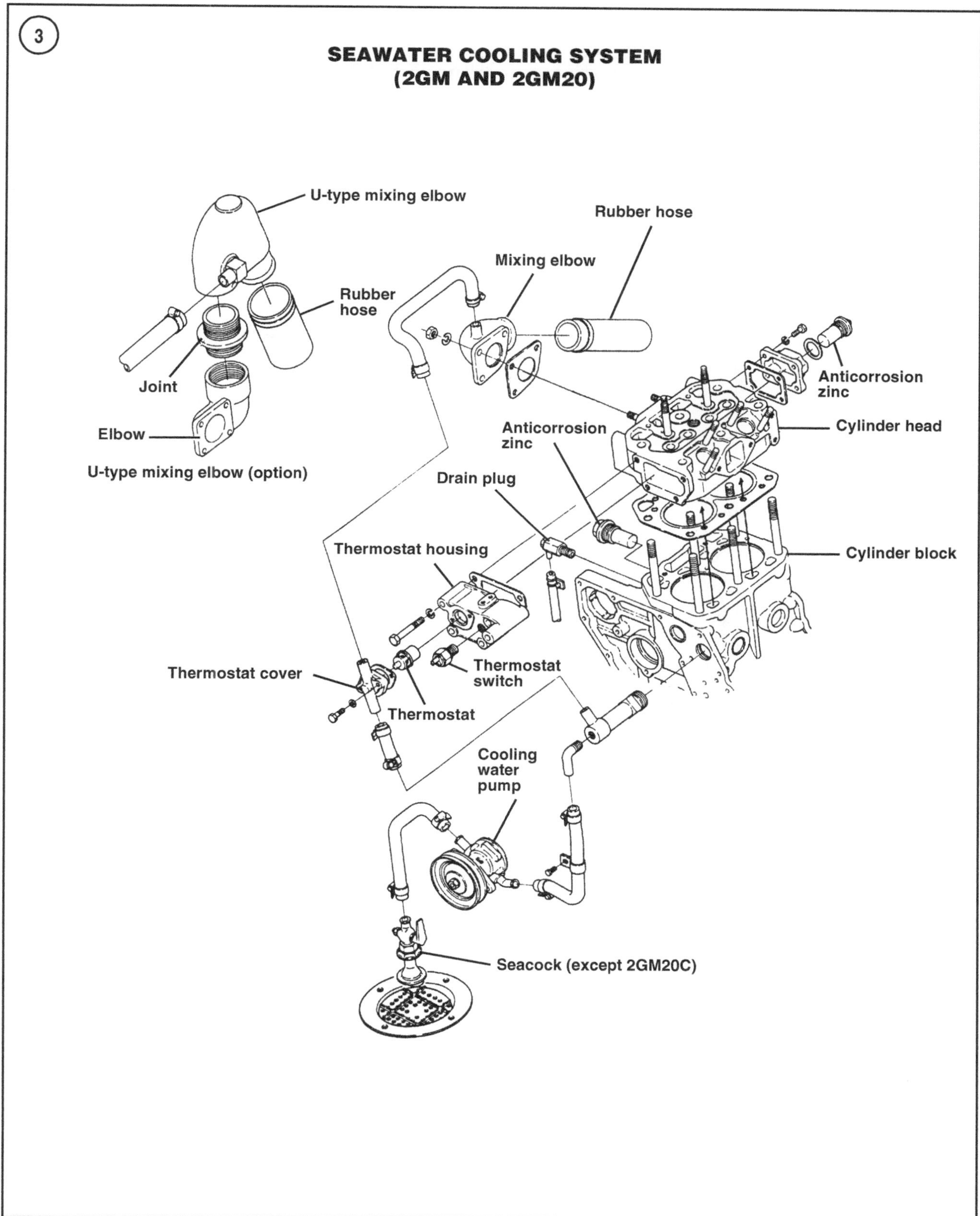
3
SEAWATER COOLING SYSTEM
(2GM AND 2GM20)
U-type mixing elbow
Rubber hose
Mixing elbow
Rubber hose
Joint
Elbow
U-type mixing elbow (option)
Anticorrosion zinc
Cylinder head
Anticorrosion zinc
Drain plug
Thermostat housing
Cylinder block
Thermostat cover
Thermostat switch
Thermostat
Cooling water pump
Seacock (except 2GM20C)

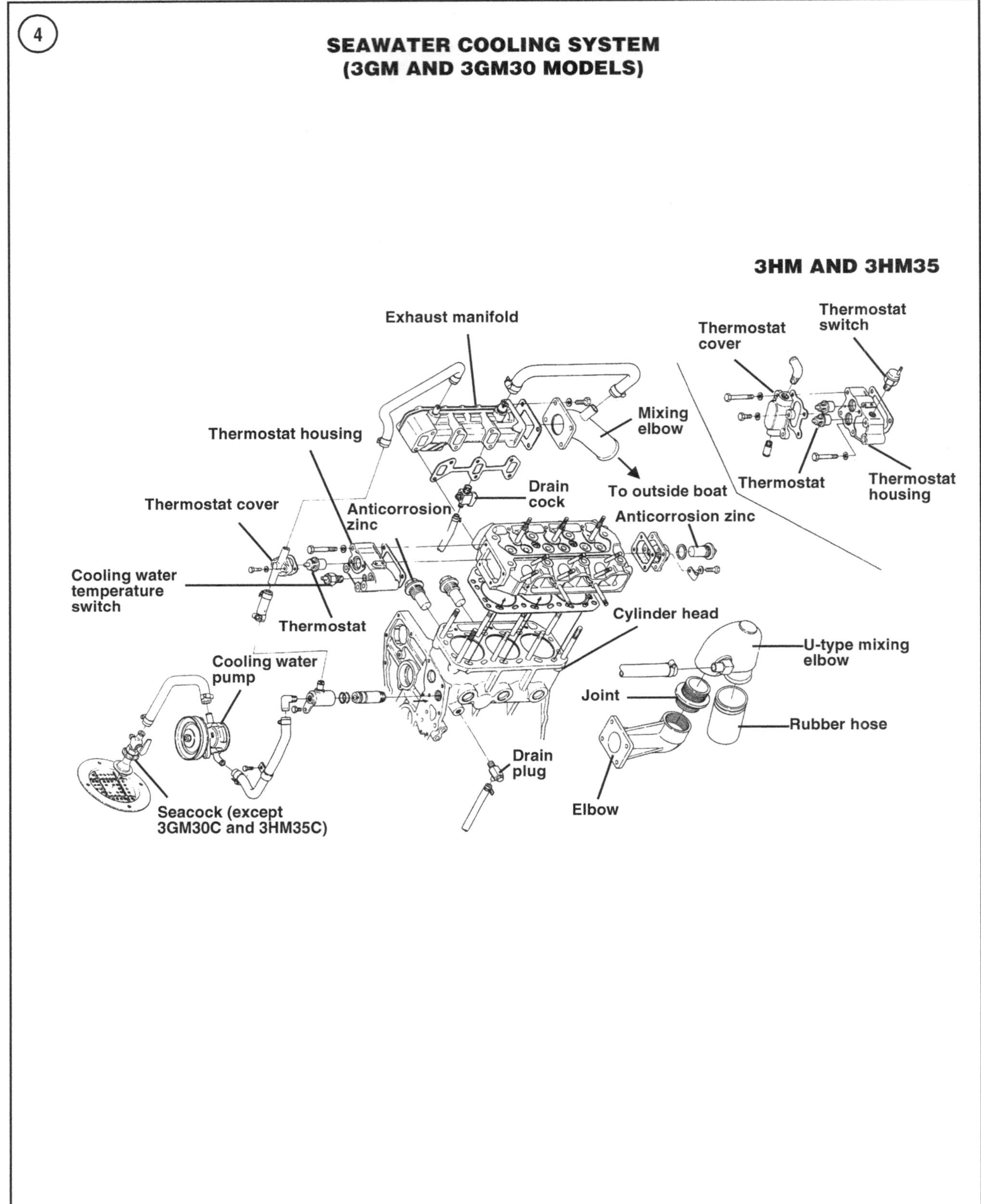
4
SEAWATER COOLING SYSTEM
(3GM AND 3GM30 MODELS)
3HM AND 3HM35
Exhaust manifold
Thermostat cover
Thermostat switch
Thermostat housing
Mixing elbow
Drain cock
To outside boat
Thermostat
Thermostat housing
Thermostat cover
Anticorrosion zinc
Anticorrosion zinc
Cooling water temperature switch
Thermostat
Cylinder head
Cooling water pump
U-type mixing elbow
Joint
Rubber hose
Drain plug
Elbow
Seacock (except 3GM30C and 3HM35C)

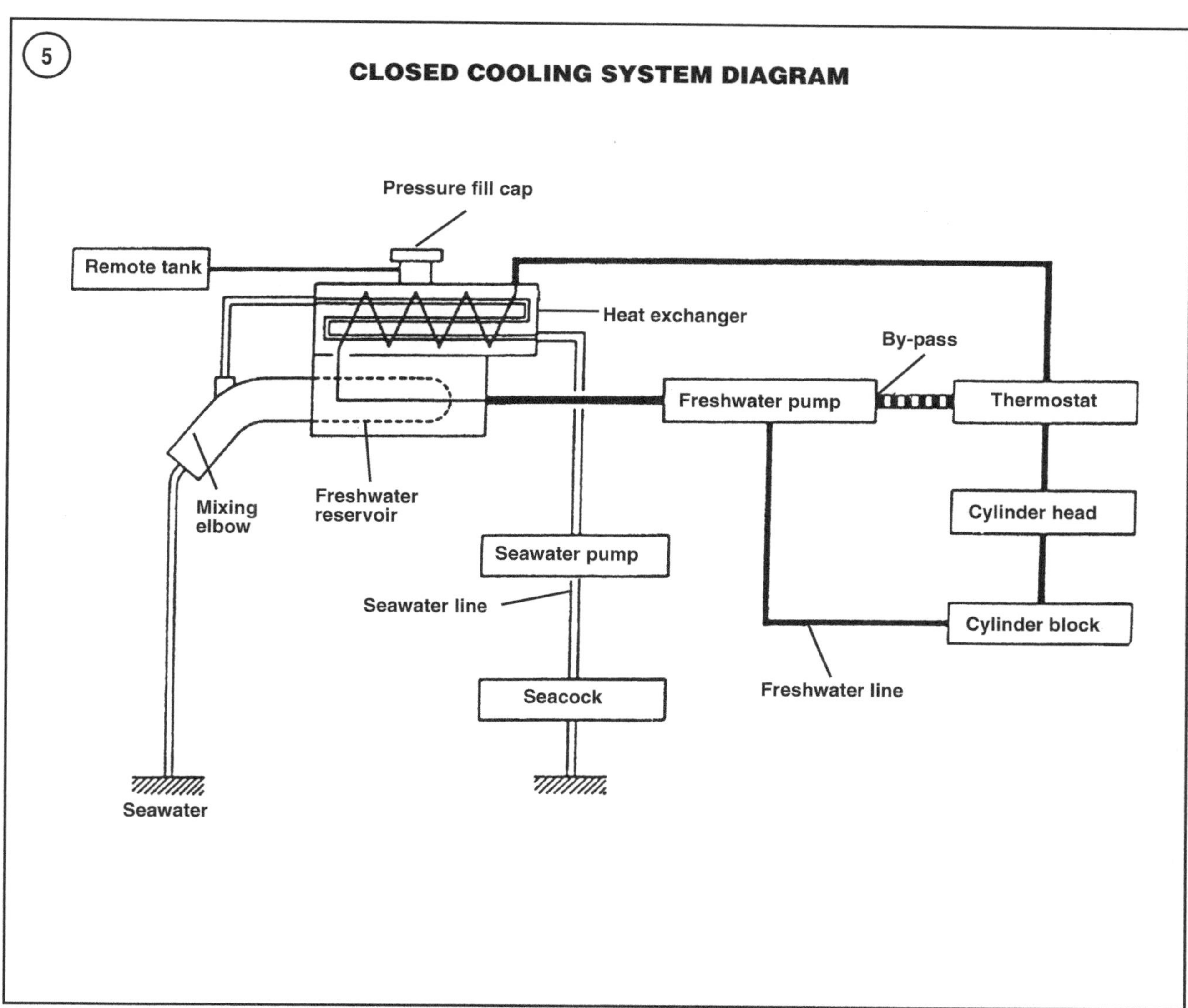

Freshwater (Closed) Cooling System

Two- and three-cylinder engines with a model number ending in F are equipped with seawater and freshwater (closed) cooling systems

The closed cooling system is divided into two separate subsystems: one uses seawater and the other uses a coolant mixture of distilled water and ethylene glycol antifreeze. The subsystem containing the coolant is referred to as the freshwater system. Refer to the typical freshwater cooling system diagram in **Figure 5**. Typical components are shown in **Figure 6**.

Various configurations of the closed cooling system are used, but all function essentially the same. The seawater system operation is similar to the standard cooling system previously described, except as follows:

a. Coolant in the closed cooling system cools the engine block, cylinder head and exhaust manifold.
b. A belt-driven seawater pump (**Figure 1**), located at the front of the engine, delivers seawater to the heat exchanger, instead of passing seawater directly into the engine.

After passing through the seawater pump, the seawater travels through a series of parallel copper tubes in the heat exchanger, where it absorbs engine heat before returning to the exhaust elbow for discharge from the boat. **Figure 7** shows a typical heat exchanger.

The freshwater system pump circulates the coolant mixture inside the engine to absorb engine heat. This

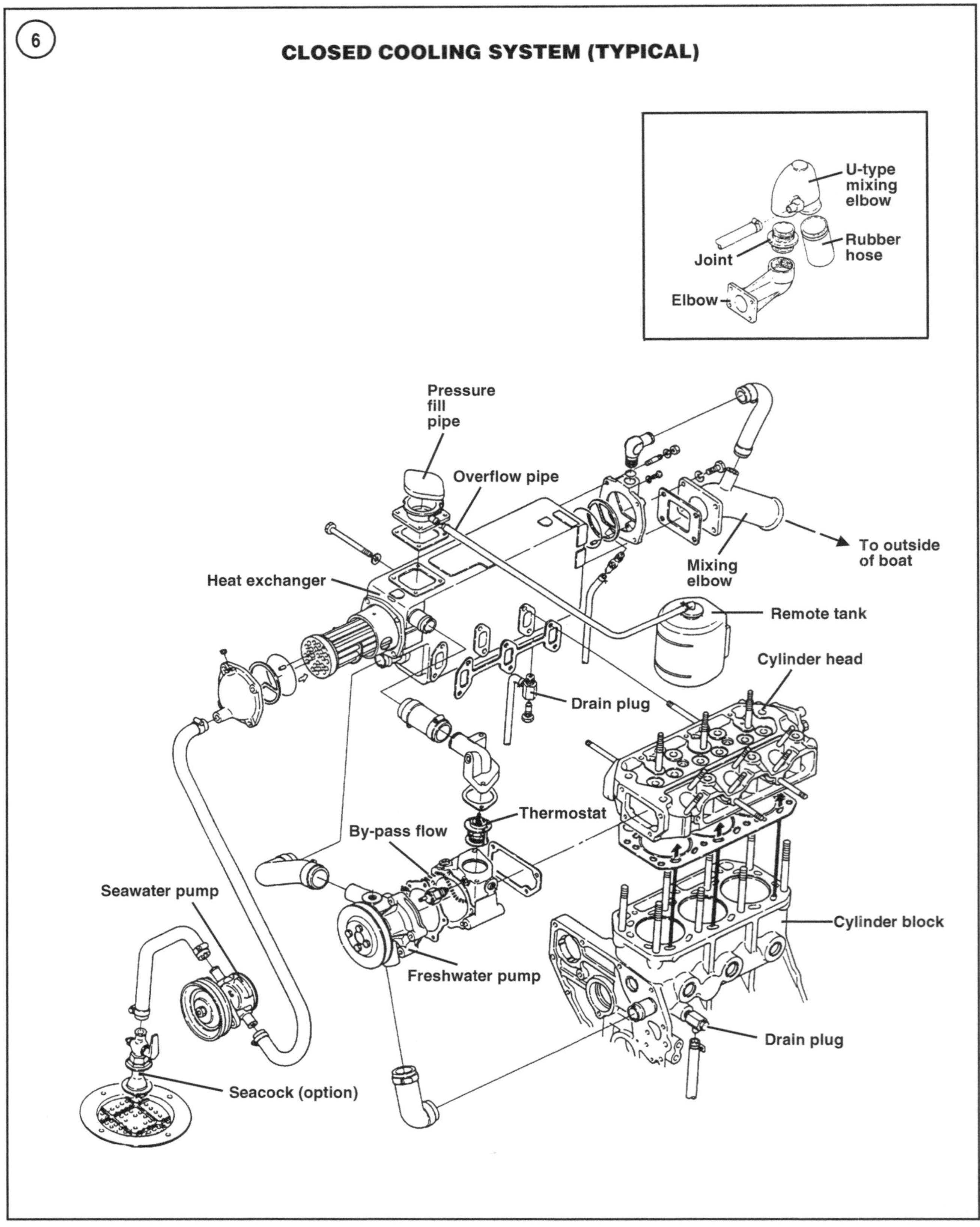
6
CLOSED COOLING SYSTEM (TYPICAL)
U-type mixing elbow
Rubber hose
Joint
Elbow
Pressure fill pipe
Overflow pipe
To outside of boat
Mixing elbow
Heat exchanger
Remote tank
Cylinder head
Drain plug
Thermostat
By-pass flow
Seawater pump
Cylinder block
Freshwater pump
Drain plug
Seacock (option)

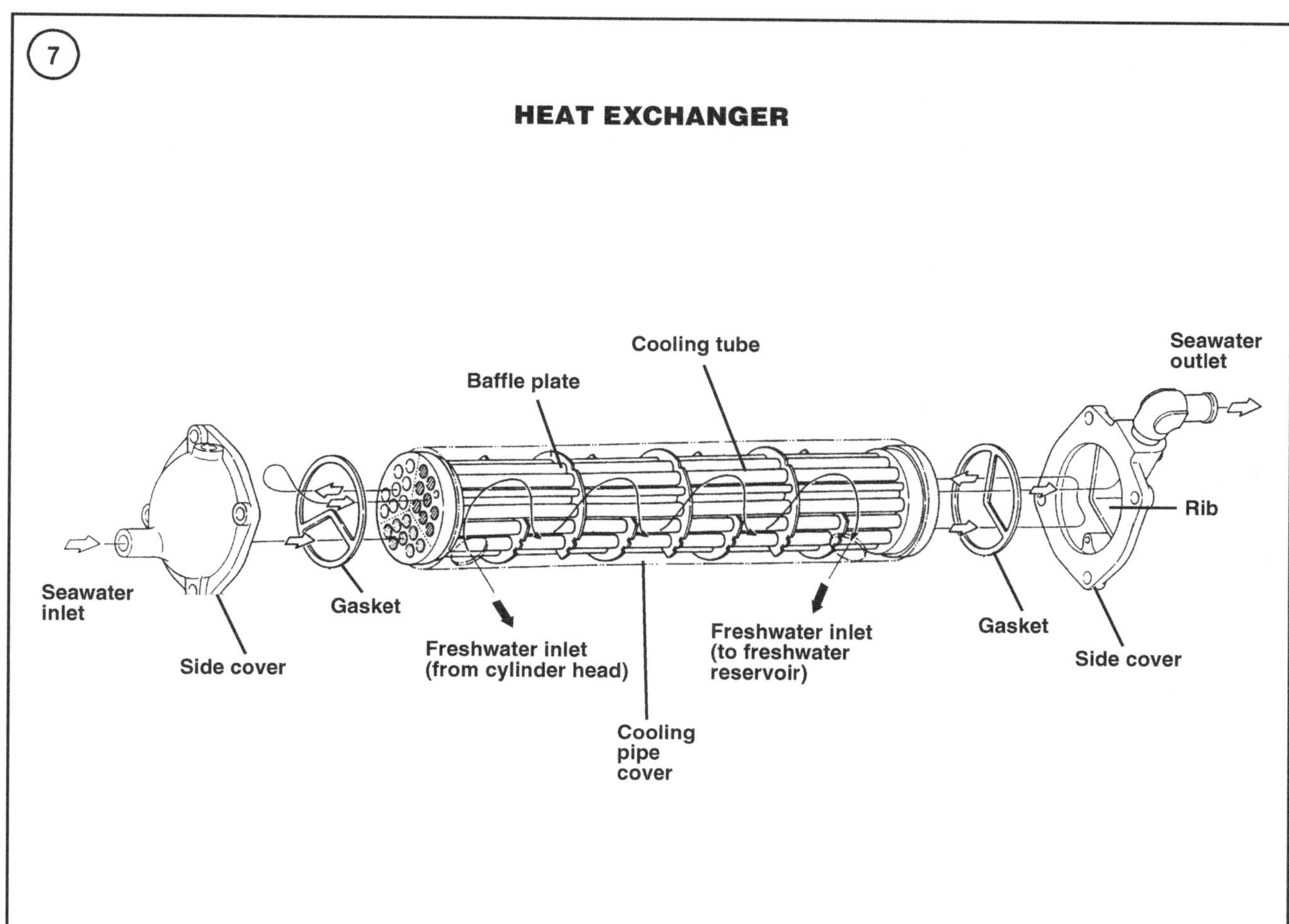

coolant travels to the heat exchanger, where the heat absorbed from engine operation passes through the parallel copper tubes to the water in the seawater system.

Engine cooling is thus accomplished without seawater entering the engine. This eliminates the corrosion, deposit buildup and debris accumulation that occurs in a standard cooling system, resulting in longer engine life—especially if the boat is used in saltwater.

Like an automotive cooling system, the freshwater section is pressurized at 13 psi. This raises the boiling point of the coolant to permit higher operating temperatures for increased engine efficiency.

A thermostat controls coolant circulation. When the thermostat closes, it prevents coolant from entering the heat exchanger, rerouting it back to the engine circulating pump. Once the thermostat opens, it closes off the passage to the circulating pump and sends the coolant through the heat exchanger before returning it to the engine pump. This provides quick engine warm-up and maintains a constant operating temperature.

THERMOSTAT

The thermostat blocks coolant flow to the exhaust manifold (standard cooling) or heat exchanger (closed cooling) when the engine is cold. As the engine warms, the thermostat gradually opens, allowing coolant to circulate through the system.

CAUTION

Do not operate the engine without a thermostat. This can lead to serious engine damage.

Thermostats are rated according to their opening temperature. The opening temperature value is stamped on the thermostat. The thermostat should start to open at the temperature stamped on the thermostat and should be fully open at 25° F (14° C) above that temperature. Check the thermostat rating after removing the thermostat and compare it to the specifications in **Table 2**.

Removal/Installation

Seawater cooling systems

The thermostat on 1GM and 1GM10 engines is located in the cylinder head (**Figure 2**). The thermostat on two- and three-cylinder engines is located in the thermostat housing (**Figure 3** and **Figure 4**). 3HM and 3HM35 engines are equipped with two thermostats (**Figure 4**).

1. Drain the seawater from the engine as described in Chapter Four.
2. Loosen the hose clamps and disconnect the hoses from the thermostat cover (**Figure 8**).
3. Remove the thermostat cover retaining bolts and washers. Remove the cover and the gasket. Discard the gasket.
4. Remove the thermostat (**Figure 9**). On 3HM and 3HM35 engines, remove both.
5. Test the thermostats as described in this chapter.
6. Clean the thermostats cover and housing or cylinder head mating surfaces of all gasket residue.
7. Install the thermostat in the housing or cylinder head with its thermostatic element facing the engine. The thermostat flange must fit into the housing recess.
8. Coat both sides of a new gasket with sealant and install the gasket onto the thermostat cover.
9. Install the cover. Note that the inlet and outlet nipples are stepped. Install the cover so the outermost nipple faces down, as shown in **Figure 10**. Tighten the bolts securely.
10. Reconnect the hoses to the thermostat cover and tighten the clamps securely.
11. Operate the engine and check for leaks. Operate the engine until it reaches normal operating temperature. Immediately shut down the engine if overheating occurs and correct the problem.

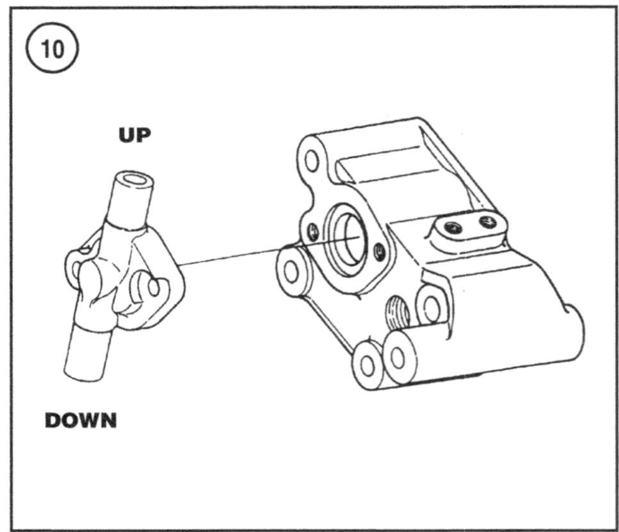

Freshwater cooling systems

1. Drain the coolant from the engine as described in Chapter Four.
2. Loosen the hose clamp (**Figure 11**) securing the coolant hose to the thermostat cover.
3. Remove the thermostat cover retaining bolts and washers (**Figure 11**). Remove the cover and the hose. Discard the gasket.
4. Remove the thermostat (**Figure 12**).
5. Test the thermostat as described in this chapter.
6. Clean the thermostat cover and housing mating surfaces of all gasket residue.
7. Install the thermostat in the housing with its thermostatic element facing the housing. The thermostat flange must fit into the housing recess.
8. Coat both sides of a new gasket with sealant and install the gasket onto the thermostat cover.

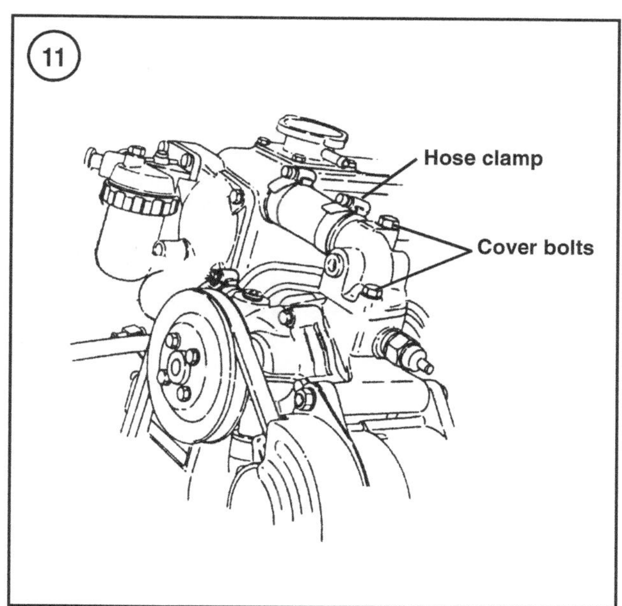

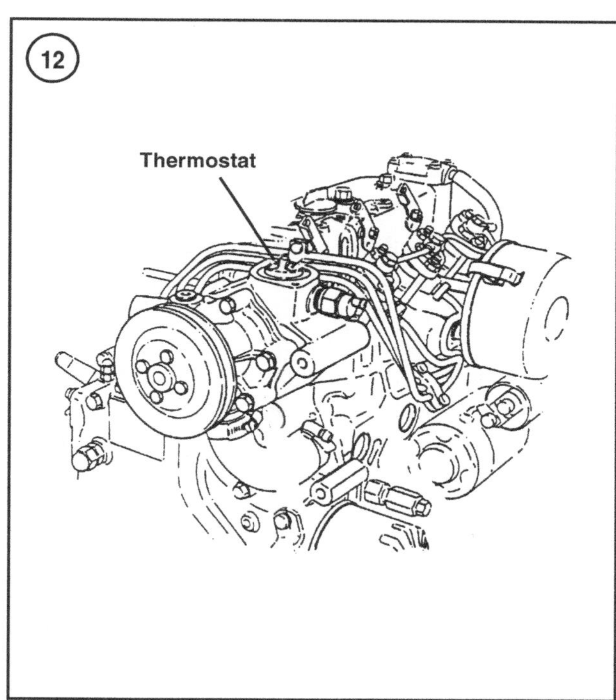

9. Install the cover while connecting it to the coolant hose. Tighten the bolts securely.

10. Tighten the hose clamp securely.

11. Operate the engine and check for leaks. Operate the engine until it reaches normal operating temperature. Immediately shut down the engine if overheating occurs and correct the problem.

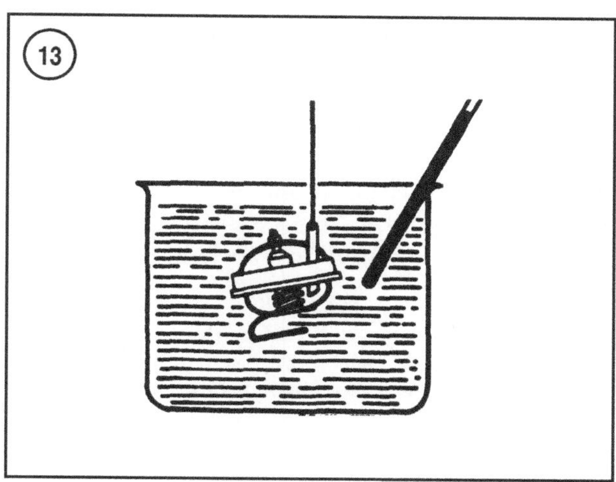

Testing (Out of Engine)

1. Pour some tap water (not distilled water or coolant) into a container that can be heated. Submerge the thermostat in the water and suspend a thermometer as shown in **Figure 13**.

NOTE
Suspend the thermostat with wire so it does not contact the pan.

2. Heat the water until the thermostat starts to open. Check the water temperature on the thermometer. It should be approximately the same as the temperature value stamped on the thermostat. If the thermostat has not started to open at this temperature, replace it.
3. Heat the water another 25° F (14° C) above the temperature value stamped on thermostat. The thermostat should now be fully open. If it is not, replace it.
4. Allow the water to cool to 10° F (6° C) under the thermostat's rated opening temperature. If the thermostat valve is not fully closed at this temperature, replace it.
5. Remove the thermostat from the water and let it cool to room temperature. Make sure the valve seals tightly by holding the thermostat up to a light. If light is visible around the edge of the valve, replace the thermostat.

Testing (In Engine)

Thermostat operation can be tested without removing it from the engine or reservoir. This procedure requires the use of two thermomelt sticks (**Figure 14**) available from marine supply or automotive parts stores. A thermomelt stick looks like a carpenter's pencil and is made of a chemically impregnated wax material that melts at a specific temperature.

This technique can be used to check thermostat opening by marking the thermostat housing with two thermomelt sticks: one with a temperature lower than the thermostat opening temperature, and one with a temperature higher than the full open position. When the coolant or water reaches the first temperature, the mark made by that stick will melt. The mark made by the second stick will not melt until the coolant or water increases to that temperature.

WARNING
Do not remove the pressure fill cap from a freshwater (closed) cooling system while the engine is warm. Coolant may blow out of the heat exchanger and cause serious personal injury.

Overheated Engine

1. Relieve the freshwater cooling system pressure by carefully removing the pressure fill cap from the heat exchanger. See **Figure 15**, typical.
2. Rub a 180° F (82° C) thermomelt stick on the thermostat cover.
3. Start the engine and run at a fast idle.
4. If no coolant flows into the heat exchanger by the time the mark starts to melt, either the thermostat is stuck closed or the water pump is failing. Remove the thermostat and test it as described in this chapter. If the results are satisfactory, replace the water pump.

Slow Engine Warm-Up

1. Relieve the freshwater cooling system pressure by carefully removing the pressure fill cap from the heat exchanger. See **Figure 15**, typical.
2. Rub the 160° F (71° C) thermomelt stick on the thermostat cover.
3. Start the engine and run at a fast idle.
4. If coolant or water flows into the heat exchanger before the mark starts to melt, the thermostat is stuck open and should be replaced.

HOSE REPLACEMENT

Replace any hoses that are cracked, brittle, or very soft and spongy. If a hose is in doubtful condition, replace it to be on the safe side. Hoses in some installations are extremely difficult to change; attention to hose condition can prevent a failure while off-shore.

Hose manufacturers generally rate cooling system hose life at two years. How long the hoses will last depends a great deal on how much the boat is used and how well the system is maintained; however, it is a good idea to change all hoses every two years. Always replace a cooling system hose with the same type as removed. Pleated rubber hoses do not have the same strength as reinforced molded hoses. Check the hose clamp condition and install new marine-grade clamps with a new hose, if necessary.

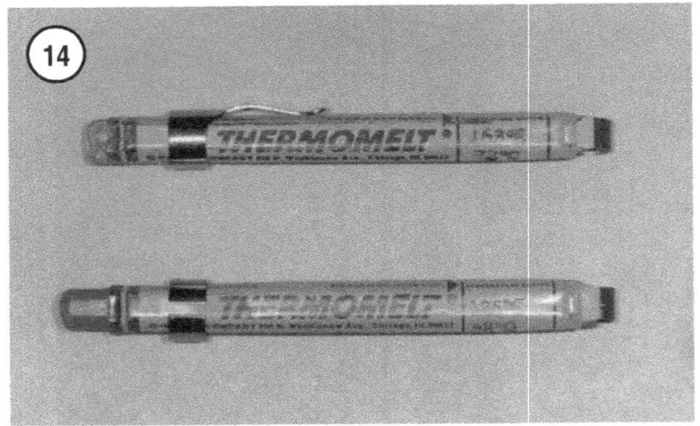

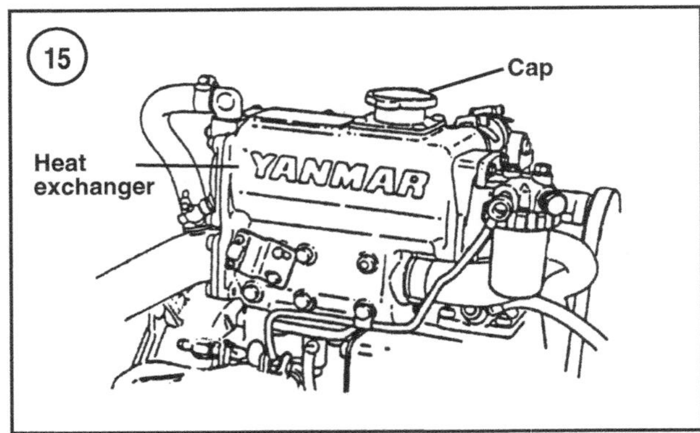

Partially drain the cooling system when replacing upper hoses. Completely drain it when replacing lower hoses.

1. Loosen the clamp at each end of the hose to be removed. Grasp the hose and twist it off the fitting with a pulling motion.
2. If the hose is corroded to the fitting and will not twist free, remove the clamp and insert a small screwdriver or pick tool between the hose and the fitting. Work the tool around the fitting, then remove the hose.
3. Clean any rust or corrosion from the fitting with a wire brush.
4. Wipe the inside diameter of the new hose with liquid detergent and install the hose ends on the fittings with a twisting motion.
5. Position the new clamps at least 1/4 in. (6.4 mm) from the end of the hose. Make sure to position the clamp screw for easy access with a screwdriver or nut driver. Tighten each clamp snugly.

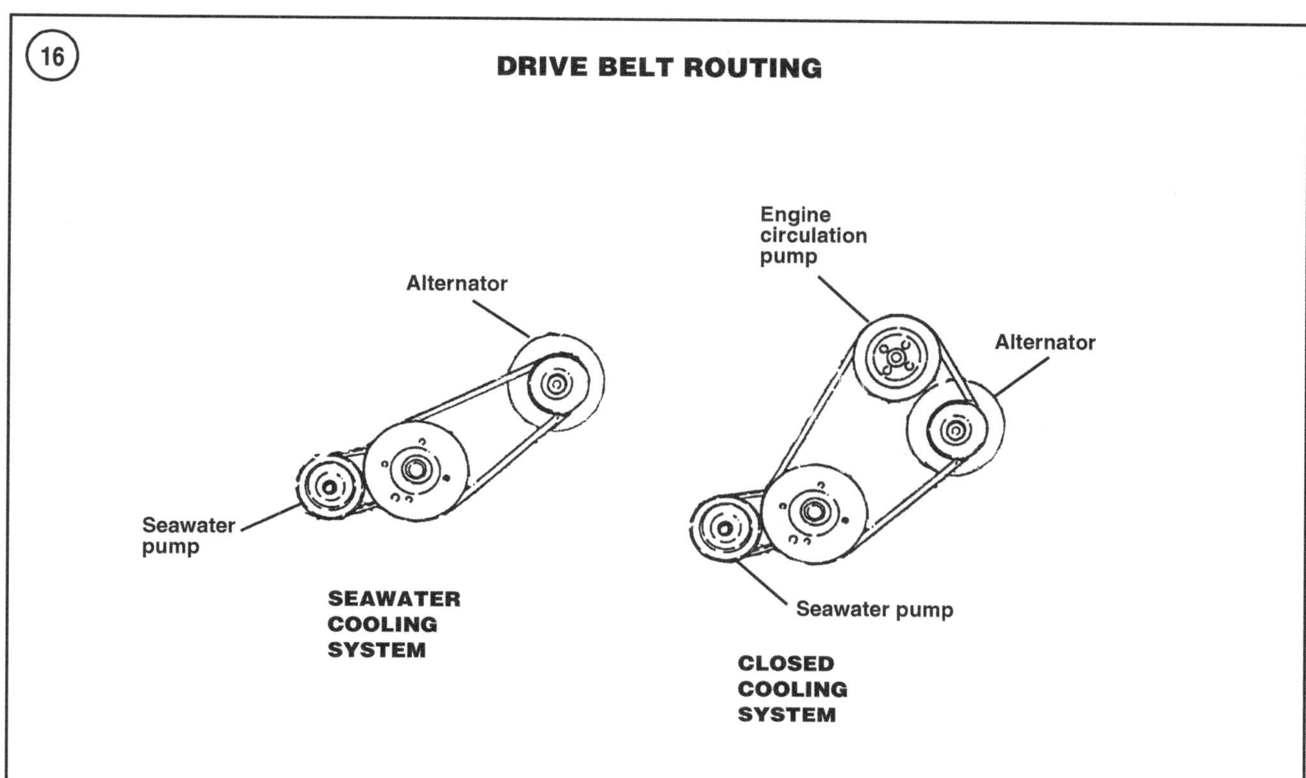

6. Refill the cooling system. Start the engine and check for leaks. Recheck the clamps for tightness after operating the engine for a few hours.

DRIVE BELTS

Inspect all drive belts at regular intervals to make sure they are in good condition and are properly tensioned. Replace worn, frayed, cracked or glazed belts immediately. The components to which they direct power are essential to the safe and reliable operation of the boat. If correct adjustment is maintained on each belt, all will usually give the same service life. For this reason, and because of the cost involved in replacing an inner belt (requiring the removal of the outer belt), it is a good idea to replace all belts as a set. The added expense is small compared to the cost of replacing the belts individually and eliminates the possibility of a breakdown on the water, which could cost far more in time and money.

Drive belts should be properly tensioned at all times. If loose, the belts will not permit the driven components to operate at maximum efficiency. The belts will also wear rapidly because of the increased friction caused by slippage. Belts that are too tight will be overstressed and prone to premature failure. An excessively tight belt will also overstress the bearings, resulting in premature failure.

Only install heavy-duty belts. Do not install light-duty belts, such as those designed for automobile use.

Refer to **Figure 16** for drive belt routing diagrams.

Belt Adjustment

Refer to Chapter Three for belt adjustment procedures.

Belt Replacement

Alternator drive belt replacement

Replace the alternator drive belt as follows:

1. Loosen the alternator bracket and pivot bolts (**Figure 17**, typical).
2. Move the alternator toward the engine and slip the belt off the crankshaft and alternator pulleys, and if equipped with freshwater cooling, the circulating water pump pulley.
3. Install a new belt over the pulleys.
4. Move the alternator away from the engine and adjust the belt tension as described in Chapter Three.

8

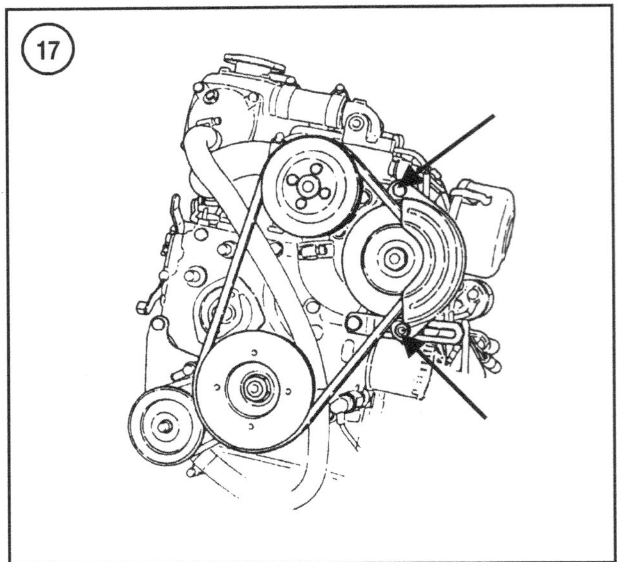
17

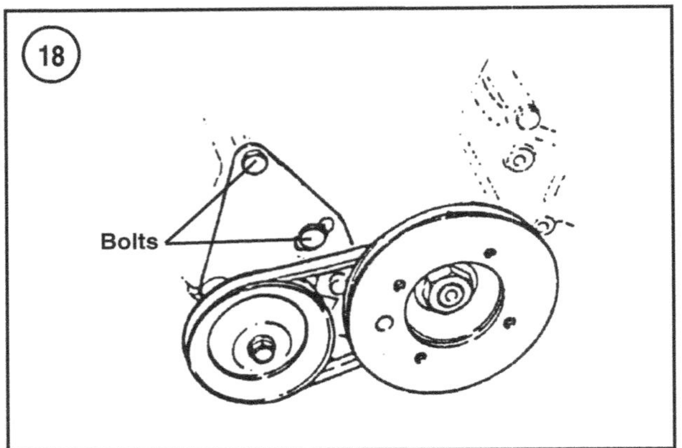

18

19

Seawater pump drive belt replacement (except 1GM and 1GM10 engines)

Replace the seawater drive belt as follows:

1. Loosen the alternator bracket and pivot bolts (**Figure 17**, typical).
2. Move the alternator toward the engine and slip the belt off the crankshaft and alternator pulleys, and if equipped with freshwater cooling, the circulating water pump pulley.
3. Loosen the seawater pump bracket and pivot bolts (**Figure 18**, typical).
4. Move the seawater pump toward the engine and slip the belt off the crankshaft and pump pulleys.
5. Install a new belt over the pulleys.
6. Move the seawater pump away from the engine and adjust the belt tension as described in Chapter Three.
7. Install the alternator drive belt onto the crankshaft and alternator pulleys, and if equipped with freshwater cooling, the circulating water pump pulley.
8. Move the alternator away from the engine and adjust the belt tension as described in Chapter Three.

SEAWATER PUMP

All engines covered in this manual use a seawater pump (**Figure 19**, typical). The seawater pump on 1GM and 1GM10 engines is driven by the end of the oil pump driveshaft. All other engines use a belt-driven seawater pump. A rubber impeller inside the pump moves water through the pump. The pump draws water into the intake port as the impeller vanes flex outward, and it pumps water out of the discharge port as the impeller vanes flex inward, as shown in **Figure 20**.

The impeller only operates in a counterclockwise rotation (viewed from cover side of pump) and remains in a flexed (compressed) position at all times. Over time, this causes the impeller to take a set in one direction. Turning an impeller over and attempting to turn it against its natural set will cause premature impeller failure and engine damage from overheating.

Replace the impeller every time the water pump is disassembled. The impeller must only be reused if there is no other option. If the impeller must be reused, reinstall the impeller in its original position.

Overheating and extensive engine damage can result from a faulty water pump. Therefore, it is highly recommended that the water pump impeller, seals and gaskets be inspected after every 1,500 hours of operation as a preventive maintenance measure. Individual operating conditions may dictate that the pump will require service more often.

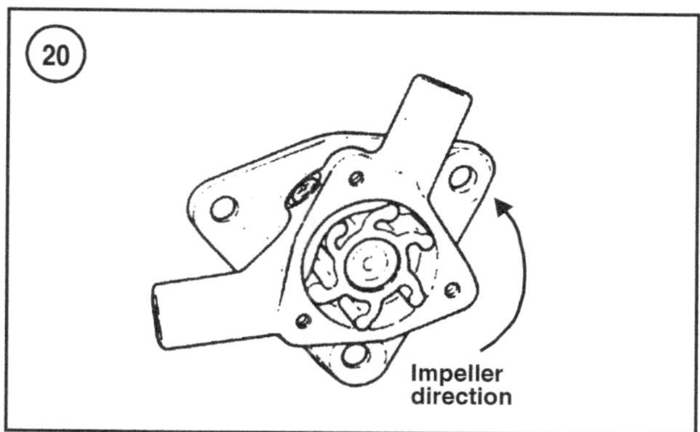

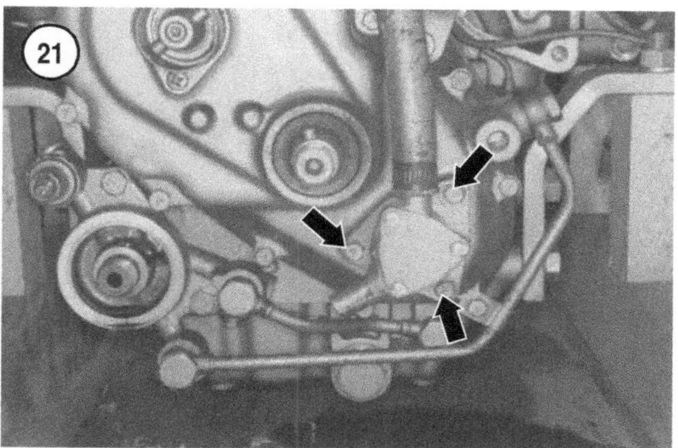

Seawater Pump Precautions

The seawater pump suffers from many misconceptions about its ability to withstand operation without water being supplied to it. All impellers are made of some variation of rubber. The water pump housing is made of metal. If a piece of rubber is rubbed across a piece of metal, there is severe friction and considerable heat buildup. However, if the metal is flooded with water while the rubber is moved across it; the friction would be greatly reduced and the heat buildup non-existent.

Basically, the water pump works the same way. The water passing through the pump lubricates and cools the impeller and pump housing. Without the water, the pump will overheat and the impeller will begin to melt almost instantaneously. Of course, this can be secondary to the potential damage to the engine from overheating.

Once the impeller sustains *any* damage, its pumping ability is greatly diminished because the impeller can no longer seal adequately. The impeller must seal on its edges, as well as the blade tips.

If the engine was run without an adequate supply of water to the pump, disassemble the pump and replace the impeller and any other damaged parts.

Water Pump Operating Mistakes

Do not run an engine immediately after pulling a boat out of water. This is an extremely risky operation, but here is why some people often seem to get away with it. If an engine has just been pulled out of the water, there is residual water in the cooling system and engine that drains back down to the water pump. This water will lubricate the water pump for a short period of time (perhaps a couple of minutes), but the pump will be damaged as soon as the heat from operation evaporates all water in the system. Do not operate the pump without an adequate water supply.

Do not start an engine with the boat out of the water, but without a water supply, to make sure the motor will run when the boat is launched. This is an unacceptable and very dangerous procedure. If an engine has been sitting for any length of time, the water pump is completely dry and the impeller will sustain immediate damage if the engine is operated without an adequate water supply. Water must be supplied to the pump through the boat's water intake or supplied under pressure from a flushing device.

CAUTION
Supply the pump with an adequate water supply anytime the engine is running.

Do not crank the engine for an extended period, such as during troubleshooting. This is detrimental to a water pump that is completely dry. Consider attaching a flushing device before initially cranking an engine with a dry water pump. This will ensure the pump is wet and will not be damaged. It will not be necessary to keep the water supply flowing during all cranking periods; it is just important to keep the pump wet during extended cranking.

Removal/Installation

1GM and 1GM10

1. If the boat is in water, make sure the seacock is closed.
2. Drain the seawater from the engine as described in Chapter Four.
3. Loosen the hose clamps, then detach the water hoses from the seawater pump.
4. Remove the pump retaining screws (**Figure 21**) and remove the pump. Remove and discard the gasket, if so

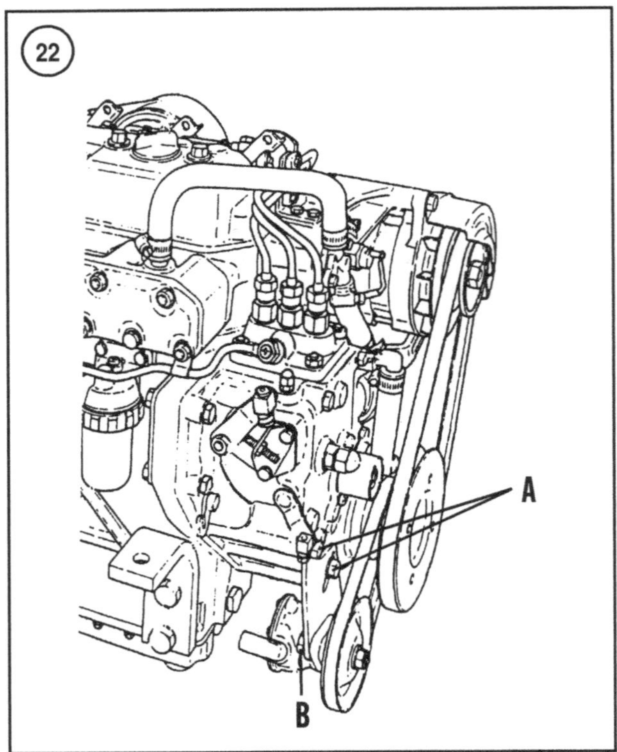

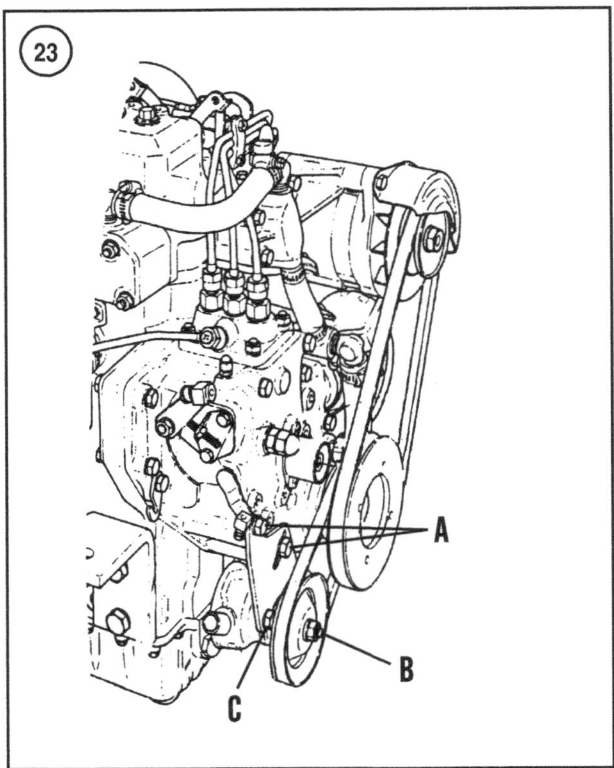

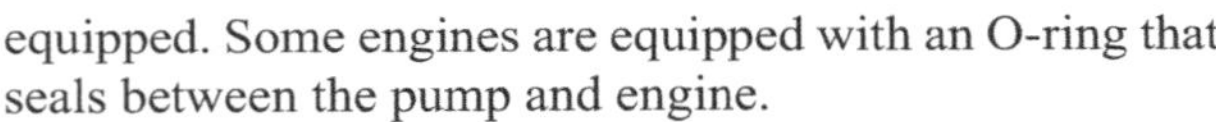
equipped. Some engines are equipped with an O-ring that seals between the pump and engine.

5. Reverse the removal steps to install the pump. Refer to **Table 1** for the tightening torque of the pump retaining screws.

2GM, 2GM20, 3GM and 3GM30

1. If the boat is in water, make sure the seacock is closed.

2. Drain the seawater from the engine as described in Chapter Four.

3. Loosen the hose clamps, then detach the water hoses from the seawater pump.

4. Loosen the seawater pump bracket and pivot bolts (A, **Figure 22**).

5. Move the seawater pump toward the engine and slip the drive belt off the pump pulley.

6. Remove the pump mounting bolts (B, **Figure 22**), then separate the pump from the mounting bracket.

7. Reverse the removal steps to install the pump. Refer to **Table 1** for the tightening torque of the pump mounting bolts. Adjust the belt tension as described in Chapter Three.

3HM and 3HM35

1. If the boat is in water, make sure the seacock is closed.

2. Drain the seawater from the engine as described in Chapter Four.

3. Loosen the hose clamps, then detach the water hoses from the seawater pump.

4. Loosen the seawater pump bracket and pivot bolts.

5. Move the seawater pump toward the engine and slip the drive belt off the pump pulley.

6. Unscrew the pulley retaining nut (B, **Figure 23**), then remove the pulley for access to the pump mounting bolts.

7. Remove the mounting bolts (C, **Figure 23**), then separate the pump from the mounting bracket.

8. Reverse the removal steps to install the pump. Refer to **Table 1** for the tightening torque of the pump mounting bolts. Adjust the belt tension as described in Chapter Three.

Disassembly/Reassembly

1GM and 1GM10

1. Remove the three screws securing the pump cover to the body (1, **Figure 24**).

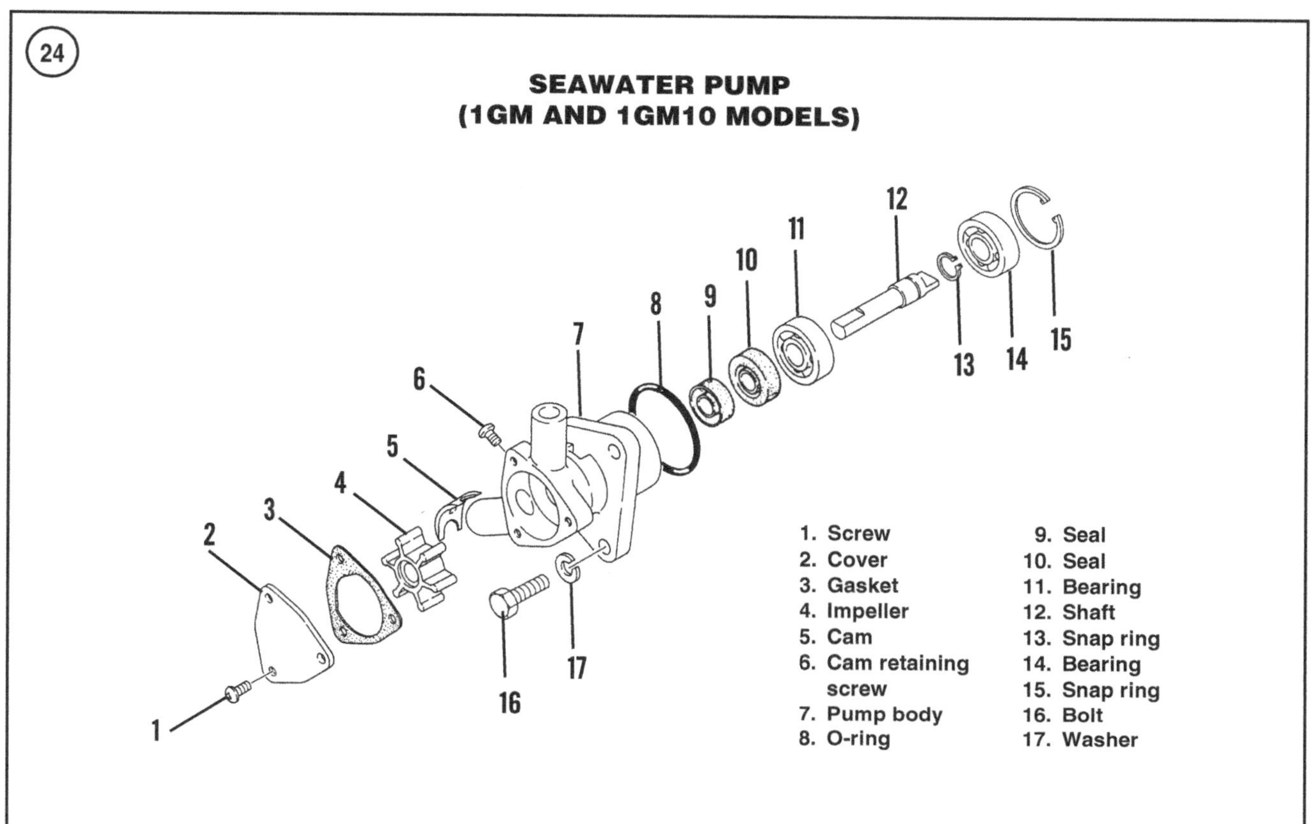

8

2. Remove the cover (2, **Figure 24**) and gasket (3). Discard the gasket.

3. Extract the impeller (4, **Figure 24**) from the pump body.

4. Rotate the pump shaft to check the bearings for roughness, excessive wear or other damage. Do not remove the shaft assembly unless replacement is necessary.

5. Unscrew the cam retaining screw (6, **Figure 24**), then remove the cam (5).

6. Remove the snap ring (15, **Figure 24**) at the rear of the pump body.

7. Lightly tap the impeller shaft toward the rear of the pump to remove the impeller shaft and bearing assembly.

NOTE

When removing bearings, note the snap ring located between the bearings.

8. Press the bearings (11 and 14, **Figure 24**) from the pump shaft (12) using a universal press plate and arbor press. Force each bearing away from the locating snap ring (13, **Figure 24**).

9. Extract or push out the seals (9 and 10, **Figure 24**).

10. Clean all metal components with solvent, then dry them with compressed air.

11. Thoroughly clean all gasket material from all mating surfaces.

12. Inspect the pump shaft (12, **Figure 24**) for grooves in the seal contact area.

13. Inspect the impeller (4, **Figure 24**) for cracked blades or excessive wear at the tips of the blades. Replace the impeller if any defects are observed.

14. Inspect the pump body and cover for grooves or other damage. A damaged or excessively worn body or cover will reduce pump efficiency and may damage a new impeller.

15. Install the shaft seal (9, **Figure 24**) so the lip is toward the impeller side of the pump body.

16. Install the oil seal (10, **Figure 24**) so the lip is toward the bearing side of the pump body.

17. If removed, install the snap ring (13, **Figure 24**) into the groove in the impeller shaft.

18. Press the shaft bearings onto the pump shaft until they seat fully against the snap ring. Press only on the bearing inner races.

19. Install the shaft and bearing assembly into the body. Install the snap ring (15, **Figure 24**).

20. Install the cam (5, **Figure 24**) and the cam retaining screw (6).

NOTE
Replace the pump impeller anytime it is removed from the pump. If the original impeller must be reused, make sure to install it in the same rotational direction as originally installed.

21. Lightly lubricate the tips and sides of the impeller. Install the impeller into the pump body by rotating the impeller counterclockwise. Be certain all impeller blades bend in the same direction (**Figure 25**).
22. Install the cover and gasket.
23. Install the three screws securing the pump cover to the body.

2GM, 2GM20, 3GM and 3GM30

1. Remove the six screws securing the pump cover (19, **Figure 26**) to the body (12).
2. Remove the cover and gasket. Discard the gasket.
3. Extract the impeller (17, **Figure 26**) from the pump body.
4. Rotate the pump shaft to check the bearings for roughness, excessive wear or other damage. Do not remove the shaft assembly unless replacement is necessary.
5. Unscrew the pulley retaining nut, then remove the pulley (3, **Figure 26**) and spacer (4).
6. Remove the snap ring (5, **Figure 26**) at the rear of the pump body.
7. Lightly tap the impeller shaft (9, **Figure 26**) toward the front of the pump to remove the impeller shaft and bearing assembly.
8. Unscrew the cam retaining screw (13, **Figure 26**), then remove the cam (16).
9. Remove the seal ring (10, **Figure 26**) and bearing cover (8) from the shaft.
10. Press the bearings from the pump shaft using a universal press plate and arbor press. Force each bearing toward the threaded end of the shaft. Note the spacer (7, **Figure 26**) between the bearings.
11. Extract or push out the seal.
12. Clean all metal components in solvent, then dry them with compressed air.
13. Thoroughly clean all gasket material from all mating surfaces.
14. Inspect the pump shaft for grooves in the seal contact area.
15. Inspect the impeller for cracked blades or excessive wear at the tips of the blades. Replace the impeller if any defects are observed.

25

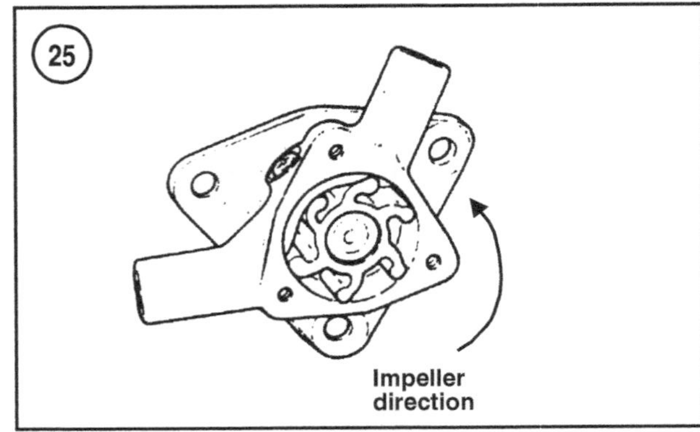

16. Inspect the pump body and cover for grooves or other damage. A damaged or excessively worn body or cover will reduce pump efficiency and may damage a new impeller.
17. Press the bearings onto the shaft with the spacer (7, **Figure 26**) between the bearings. Seat the bearings against the shoulder on the shaft. Press only on the bearing inner races.
18. Install the seal (11, **Figure 26**) into the pump body so the lip is toward the impeller side of the body.
19. Install the cam (16, **Figure 26**), then install the cam retaining screw (13).
20. Install the bearing cover (8, **Figure 26**) with the concave side toward the bearing.
21. Install the seal ring (10, **Figure 26**) onto the shaft.
22. Install the shaft assembly into the pump body.
23. Install the snap ring (5, **Figure 26**).
24. Install the spacer (4, **Figure 26**), pulley (3), washer (2) and nut (1), then tighten the nut.

NOTE
Replace the pump impeller anytime it is removed from the pump. If the original impeller must be reused, make sure to install it in the same rotational direction as originally installed.

25. Lightly lubricate the tips and sides of the impeller. Install the impeller into the pump body by rotating the impeller counterclockwise. Be certain all impeller blades bend in the same direction (**Figure 27**).
26. Install the cover (19, **Figure 26**) and gasket.
27. Install the six screws securing the pump cover to the body.

3HM and 3HM35

1. Remove the six screws (19, **Figure 28**) securing the pump cover (18) to the body (12).

(26)

SEAWATER PUMP
(2GM, 2GM20, 3GM AND 3GM30 MODELS)

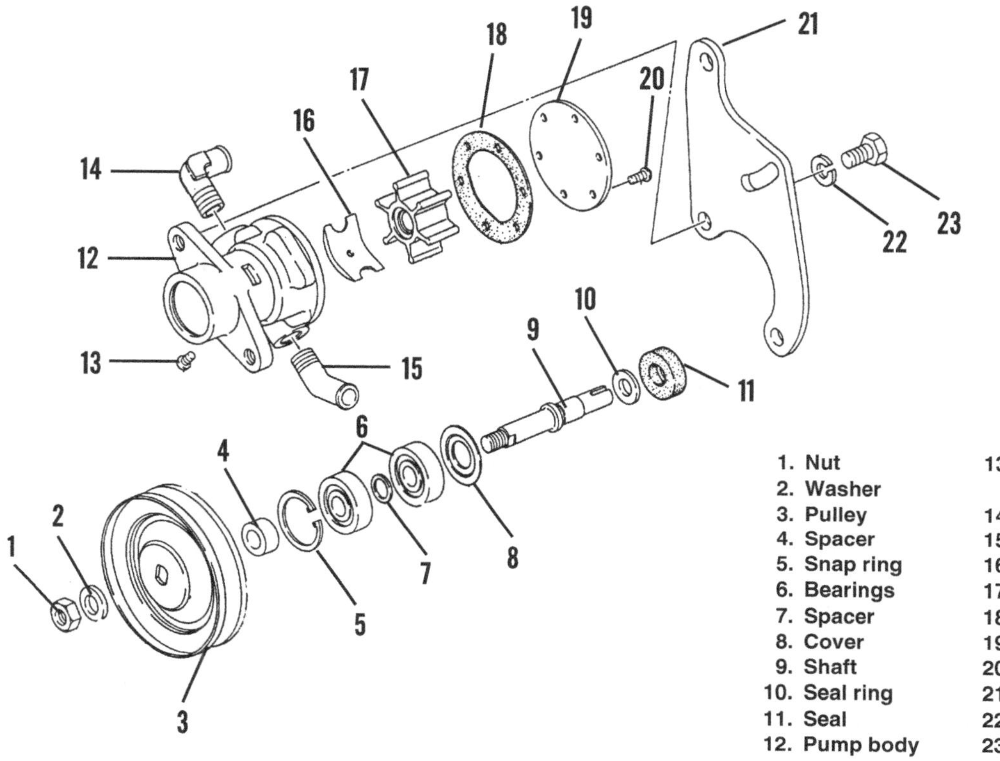

1. Nut
2. Washer
3. Pulley
4. Spacer
5. Snap ring
6. Bearings
7. Spacer
8. Cover
9. Shaft
10. Seal ring
11. Seal
12. Pump body
13. Cam retaining screw
14. Elbow
15. Elbow
16. Cam
17. Impeller
18. Gasket
19. Cover
20. Screw
21. Bracket
22. Lockwasher
23. Bolt

(27)

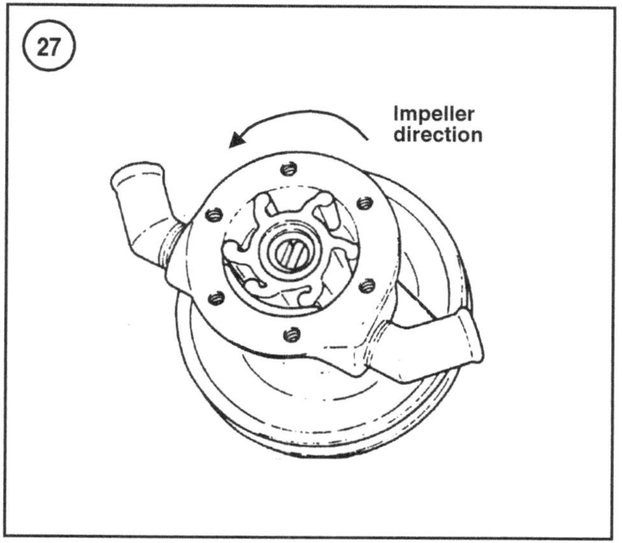

2. Remove the cover (18, **Figure 28**) and gasket (17). Discard the gasket.

3. Extract the impeller (16, **Figure 28**) from the pump body and remove the drive key (8).

4. Rotate the pump shaft to check the bearings for roughness, excessive wear or other damage. Do not remove the shaft assembly unless replacement is necessary.

5. Remove the snap ring (4, **Figure 28**).

6. Lightly tap the impeller shaft (7, **Figure 28**) toward the front of the pump to remove the impeller shaft and bearing assembly.

7. Unscrew the cam retaining screw (14, **Figure 28**), then remove the cam (15).

NOTE

When removing bearings, note the snap ring located between the bearings.

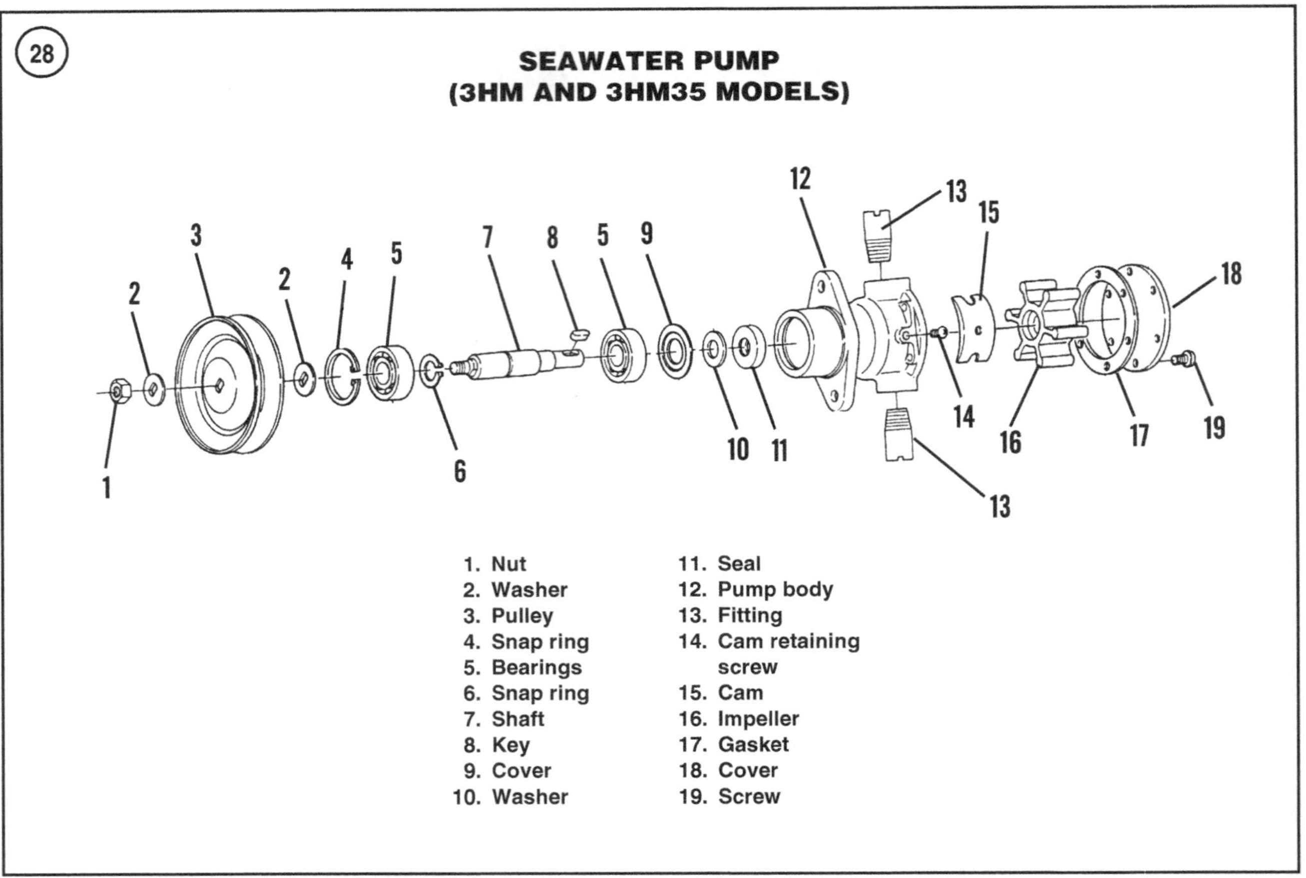

8. Press the bearings from the pump shaft using a universal press plate and arbor press. Force each bearing away from the locating snap ring (6, **Figure 28**).

9. Extract or push out the seal (11, **Figure 28**).

10. Clean all metal components solvent, then dry them with compressed air.

11. Thoroughly clean all gasket material from all mating surfaces.

12. Inspect the pump shaft for grooves in the seal contact area.

13. Inspect the impeller for cracked blades or excessive wear at the tips of the blades. Replace the impeller if any defects are observed.

14. Inspect the pump body and cover for grooves or other damage. A damaged or excessively worn body or cover will reduce pump efficiency and may damage a new impeller.

15. Install the shaft seal (11, **Figure 28**) so the lip is toward the impeller side of the pump body.

16. If removed, install the snap ring (6, **Figure 28**) into the groove in the impeller shaft.

17. Press the shaft bearings onto the pump shaft until fully seated against the snap ring. Press only on the bearing inner races.

18. Install the bearing cover (9, **Figure 28**) with the concave side toward the bearing.

19. Install the washer (10, **Figure 28**) onto the shaft.

20. Install the shaft assembly into the pump body. Install the snap ring (4, **Figure 28**).

21. Install the slotted washers (2, **Figure 28**), pulley (3) and nut (1), then tighten the nut.

22. Install the impeller drive key (8, **Figure 28**) in the slot in the impeller shaft.

NOTE

Replace the pump impeller anytime it is removed from the pump. If the original impeller must be reused, be sure to install it in the same rotational direction as originally installed.

23. Lightly lubricate the tips and sides of the impeller. Install the impeller into the pump body by rotating the im-

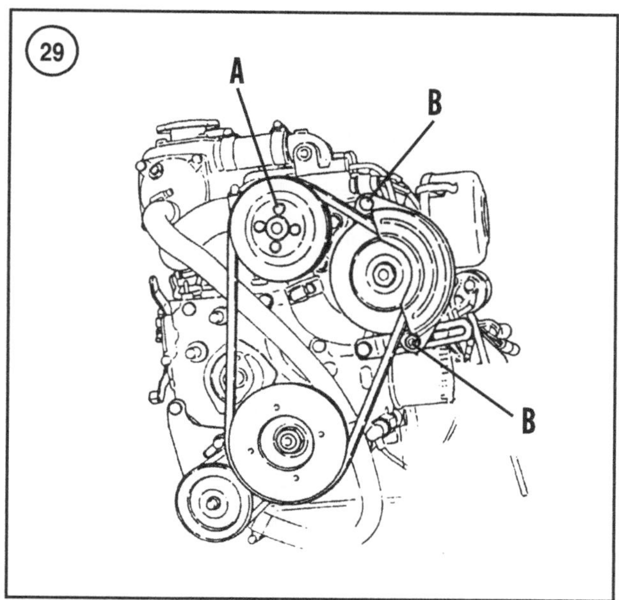

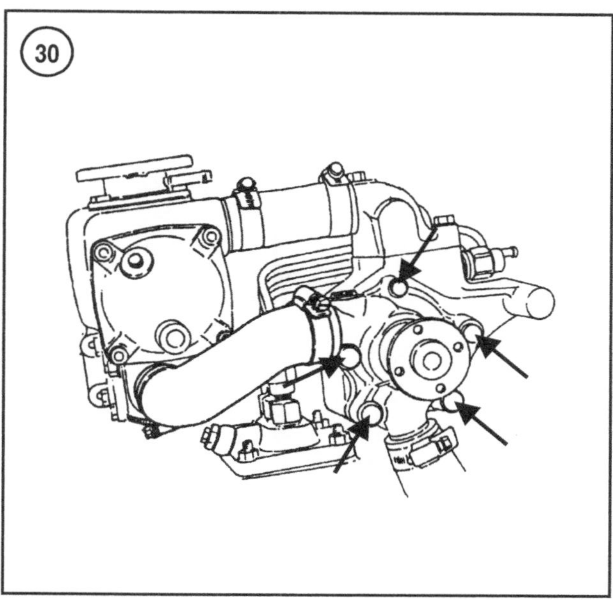

peller counterclockwise. Be certain all impeller blades are facing the same direction (**Figure 27**).

24. Install the cover (18, **Figure 28**) and gasket.
25. Install the six screws securing the pump cover to the body.

FRESHWATER PUMP

The freshwater circulating pump may warn of impending failure by making noise. If the seal is defective, coolant or water may leak from behind the pump pulley. It is recommended that the pump be replaced as an assembly. Individual replacement parts are available.

Removal/Installation

1. Drain the freshwater cooling system. Refer to Chapter Four.

NOTE
If pump pulley removal is not necessary, proceed to Step 3.

2. Loosen, but do not remove, the pump pulley retaining bolts (A, **Figure 29**).
3. Loosen the alternator adjusting and pivot bolts (B, **Figure 29**). Swivel the alternator toward the engine and remove the drive belt from the pump pulley.
4. Unscrew the pump pulley screws and remove the pulley.
5. Unclamp and disconnect the hoses from the circulating pump and detach any hose brackets that interfere with access to the water pump bolts.

NOTE
Note the length of the pump retaining bolts during removal and, if necessary, mark them according to location.

6. Remove the pump retaining bolts (**Figure 30**). Remove the pump and gasket. Discard the gasket.
7. Clean all gasket residue from the pump and engine block mounting surfaces.
8. Installation is the reverse of removal. Tighten the water pump fasteners to the tightening torque specified in **Table 1**. Adjust drive belts as described in Chapter Three. Fill the freshwater section of closed cooling systems with coolant. See Chapter Three. Start the engine and check for leaks.

FRESHWATER COOLING SYSTEM MAINTENANCE

Pressure Testing

If the freshwater (closed) cooling system requires frequent topping off, it probably has a leak. Small leaks in a cooling system are not easy to locate; the hot coolant evaporates as fast as it leaks out, preventing the formation of tell-tale rusty or grayish-white stains.

A pressure test of the freshwater section will usually help to pinpoint the source of the leak. The procedure is very similar to that used in pressure testing automotive

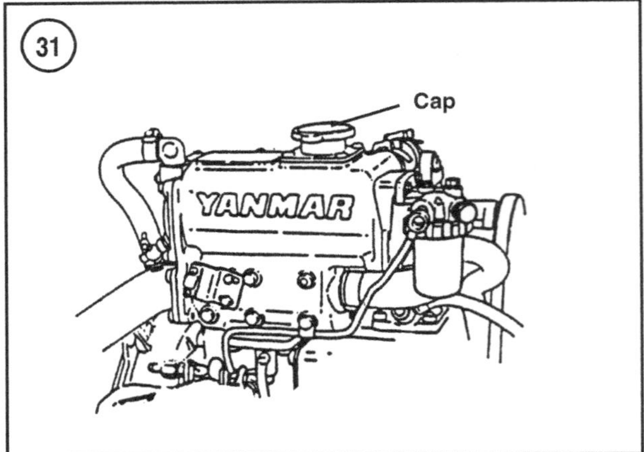

cooling systems and requires the same type of pressure tester.

1. Remove the pressure fill cap from the heat exchanger. See **Figure 31**, typical.
2. Wash the cap with clean water to remove any debris or deposits from its sealing surfaces.
3. Check the gasket, if so equipped, and rubber seal on the cap for cuts, cracks, tears or deterioration. See **Figure 32**. Replace the cap if the seal is damaged. Make sure the locking tabs on the cap are not damaged or bent.
4. Dip the cap in water and attach it to a cooling system pressure tester, using the adapters supplied with the tester. See **Figure 33**.
5. Pump the pressure to 13 psi (90 kPa). If the cap fails to hold pressure for 30 seconds without dropping under 11 psi (76 kPa), replace it.
6. Inspect the filler neck seat and sealing surface (**Figure 32**) for nicks, dents, distortion or contamination. Wipe the sealing surface with a clean cloth to remove any rust or dirt. Make sure the locking cams are not bent or damaged.
7. Check coolant level. It should be within 1 in. (25.4 mm) of the filler neck. Top off if necessary.
8. Connect the cooling system pressure tester to the filler neck and pressurize the system to 15 psi (104 kPa). If pressure does not hold constant for at least two minutes, check all hoses, gaskets, drain plugs, drain valves and other potential leak points for leakage. Listen for a hissing or bubbling sound while the system is under pressure.
9. If no leaks are found, disconnect the seawater outlet hose from the heat exchanger (**Figure 34**). Repressurize the system to 15 psi (104 kPa) and note the outlet connection on the heat exchanger. If water flows from the connection, air bubbles are visible in the water or a bubbling or hissing noise is heard, there is probably a leak between the fresh and seawater sections within the heat exchanger.

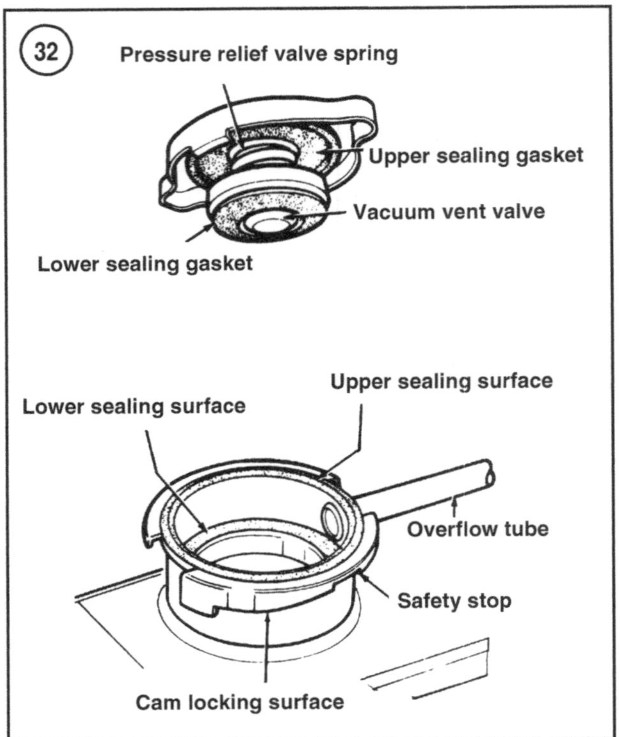

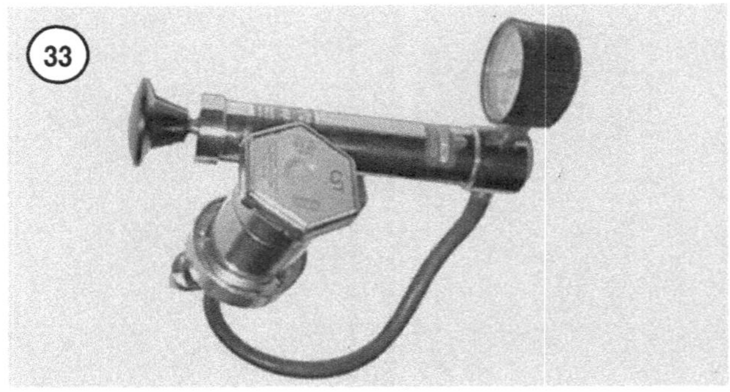

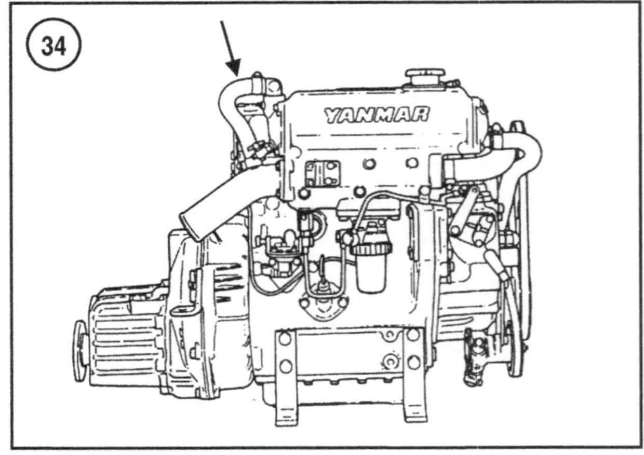

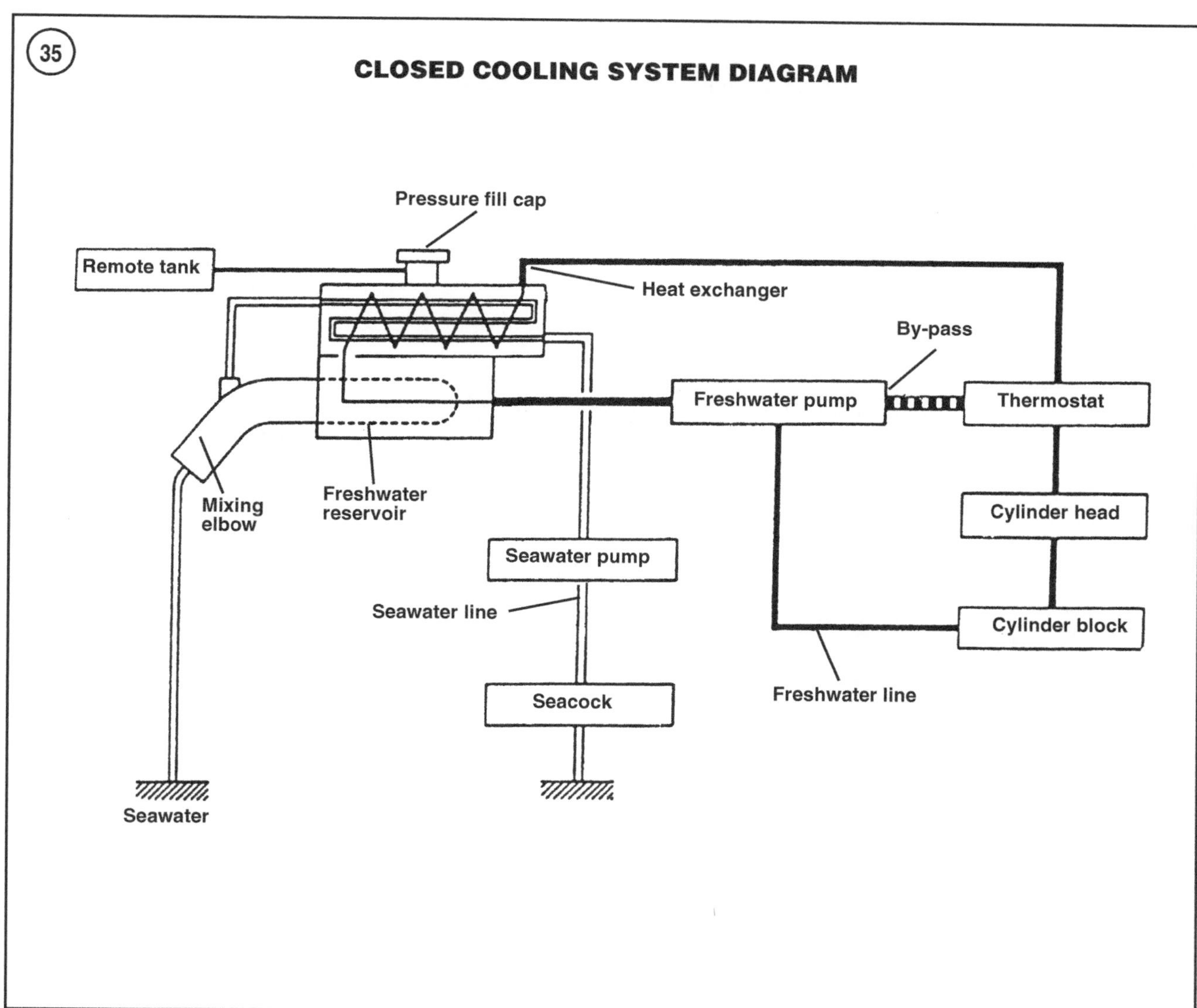

10. If no signs of leakage can be found in Step 8 or Step 9, yet the coolant level continues to require frequent topping off, there is probably an internal leak. This could be caused by a blown head gasket, loose cylinder head, or a cracked or porous head or block.

Cleaning

Flush and clean the freshwater section every other season or periodically as needed. Use any high-quality automotive cooling system cleaning solution to remove scale, rust, mineral deposits or other contamination. Use the cleaning solution according to the manufacturer's directions.

If extremely dirty or corroded, flush out the remaining deposits with a pressure flushing device. Refer to the cooling system flow diagram (**Figure 35**) and follow the manufacturer's instructions regarding the connection of the pressure flushing device and procedure to be followed.

Cleaning the Seawater Section of the Heat Exchanger

Contaminants and minerals collect inside the copper tubes in the seawater section of the heat exchanger during engine operation. Such foreign material reduces the ability of the heat exchanger to operate efficiently and, if not removed periodically, will eventually lead to engine over-

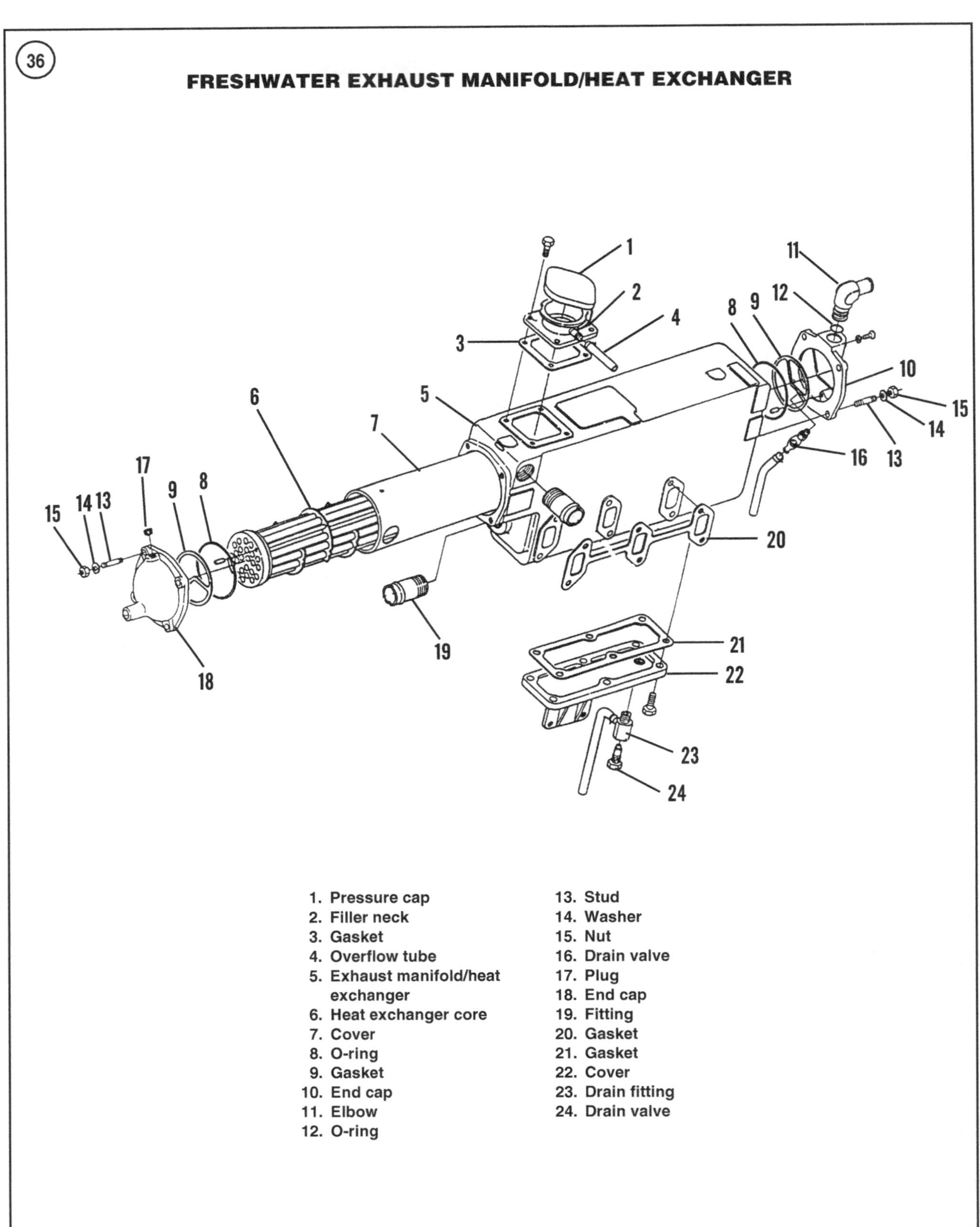
36
FRESHWATER EXHAUST MANIFOLD/HEAT EXCHANGER
1. Pressure cap
2. Filler neck
3. Gasket
4. Overflow tube
5. Exhaust manifold/heat exchanger
6. Heat exchanger core
7. Cover
8. O-ring
9. Gasket
10. End cap
11. Elbow
12. O-ring
13. Stud
14. Washer
15. Nut
16. Drain valve
17. Plug
18. End cap
19. Fitting
20. Gasket
21. Gasket
22. Cover
23. Drain fitting
24. Drain valve

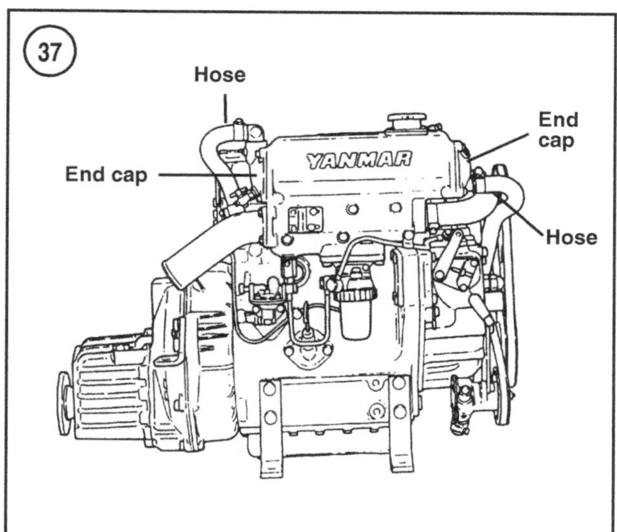

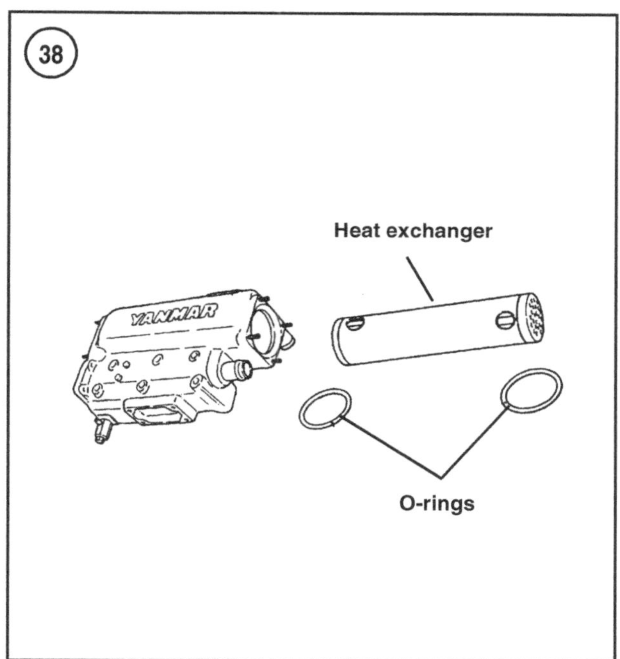

heating. It is recommended to remove and clean the heat exchanger whenever the coolant is changed. Refer to **Figure 36**.

1. Drain both sections of the cooling system. Refer to Chapter Four. Loosen the hose clamps and disconnect the seawater inlet and outlet hoses from the end caps (**Figure 37**).
2. Remove the end cap retaining bolts.
3. Remove the heat exchanger end caps. Remove and discard the gaskets.

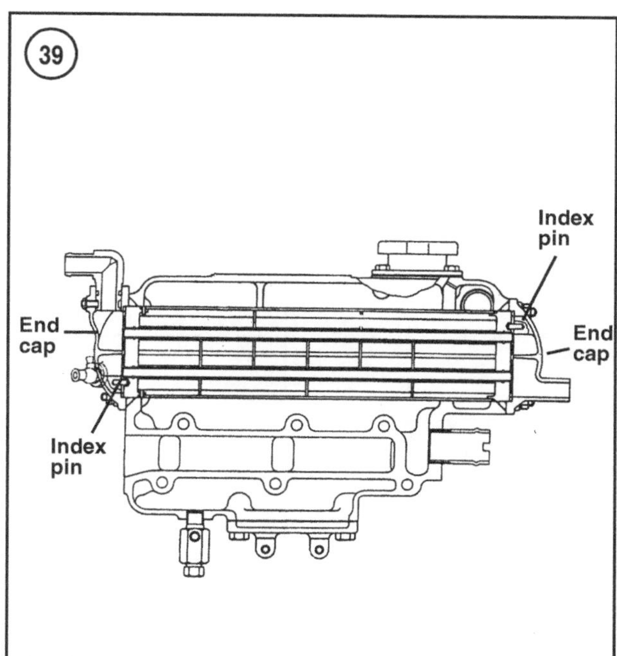

4. Remove the heat exchanger (**Figure 38**).

NOTE
If the heat exchanger is plugged or contains heavy scale deposits, take it to a marine dealership or automotive radiator repair shop for proper cleaning to avoid potential damage to the unit.

5. Clean all gasket residue from the end caps and heat exchanger sealing surfaces.
6. Insert an appropriate-size wire brush into each passage in the heat exchanger. Work the brush back and forth with a vigorous motion, but work carefully to avoid damage to the soldered joints.
7. Remove the brush, hold the heat exchanger vertically and blow loosened particles out with compressed air.
8. Repeat Step 6 and Step 7 as necessary to remove as much of the accumulated deposits as possible.
9. Reinstall the heat exchanger by reversing the removal procedure. Position the heat exchanger so the index pins (**Figure 39**) in both ends fit in the holes in the end caps.
10. Fill the freshwater section with coolant. Refer to Chapter Three. Start the engine and check for leaks.

SEAWATER COOLING SYSTEM MAINTENANCE

The only maintenance required for the seawater cooling system is periodic flushing. Refer to Chapter Three.

Table 1 TIGHTENING TORQUES

Fastener	N•m	ft.-lb.	in.-lb.
Seawater pump			
1GM, 1GM10	9	–	80
All other models	25	18	–
Freshwater pump	20-25	–	177-221

Table 2 RECOMMENDED THERMOSTAT

Model	Opening temperature	Full open temperature
All engines		
Seawater system	108° F (42° C)	126° F (52° C)
Freshwater system	160° F (71° C)	185° F (85° C)

Chapter Nine

Electrical System

All engines covered in this manual are equipped with a 12-volt, negative-ground electrical system. Many electrical problems can be traced to a simple cause such as a blown fuse, a loose or corroded connection, a loose alternator drive belt or a frayed wire. While these are easily corrected problems that may not appear to be important, they can quickly lead to serious difficulty if allowed to go uncorrected.

Complete overhaul of electrical components, such as the alternator or starter motor, may not be practical or economical. In some cases, the necessary bushings, bearings or other worn parts are not available for individual replacement.

If tests indicate a unit with problems other than those discussed in this chapter, replace it with a new or rebuilt marine unit. Make certain, however, that the new or rebuilt part is an exact replacement for the defective one removed. Also be sure to isolate and correct the cause of the failure before installing a replacement. For example, an uncorrected short in an alternator circuit will most likely burn out a new alternator as quickly as it damaged the old one. If in doubt, always consult an expert.

This chapter provides service procedures for the battery, charging system, starting system and switches. Wiring diagrams are included at the end of this book. **Table 1** and **Table 2** are located at the end of this chapter.

NOTE

Except where specified, F and D series engines are included when a basic model number is specified. For example, if model 3GM is called out in a procedure, the procedure also applies to 3GMD and 3GMF.

BATTERY

Because batteries used in marine applications endure far more rigorous treatment and are often used differently than those used in an automotive charging system, they are constructed differently. However, battery advancements developed for automotive batteries have been applied to marine batteries. This has resulted in new battery designs that provide the boater with more choices. A battery may be selected that better accommodates the electrical requirements for the engine and the boat's accessories than the typical older, wet-cell battery designs.

If buying a new battery, consult with a marine dealership that sells a full line of marine batteries. To obtain the best advice, provide the engine model and a list of electri-

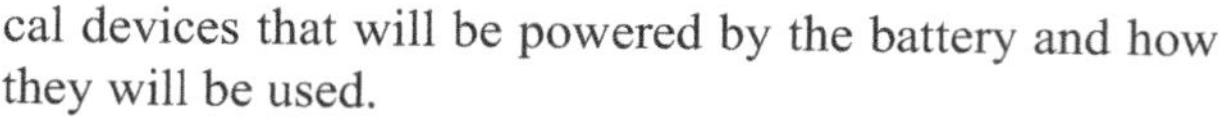

cal devices that will be powered by the battery and how they will be used.

Automotive batteries should be used *only* in an emergency situation when a suitable marine battery is not available. If used, the automotive battery should be replaced with a suitable marine battery as soon as possible.

Refer to **Table 1** for recommended battery capacity.

Safety Precautions

When working with batteries, use extreme care to avoid spilling or splashing the electrolyte. This solution contains sulfuric acid, which can ruin clothing and cause serious chemical burns. If any electrolyte is spilled or splashed on clothing or skin, immediately neutralize with a solution of baking soda and water, then flush the area with an abundance of clean water.

WARNING
Electrolyte splashed into the eyes is extremely dangerous. Always wear safety glasses while working with batteries. If electrolyte is splashed into the eyes, call a physician immediately, force the eyes open and flood with cool, clean water for approximately five minutes.

If electrolyte is spilled or splashed onto any surface, it should be immediately neutralized with baking soda and water solution and then rinsed with clean water. While batteries are being charged, highly explosive hydrogen gas forms in each cell. Some of this gas escapes through filler cap openings and may form an explosive atmosphere in and around the battery. This condition can exist for several hours. Sparks, an open flame or a lighted cigarette can ignite this gas, causing an internal battery explosion and possible serious personal injury.

Take the following precautions to prevent injury.

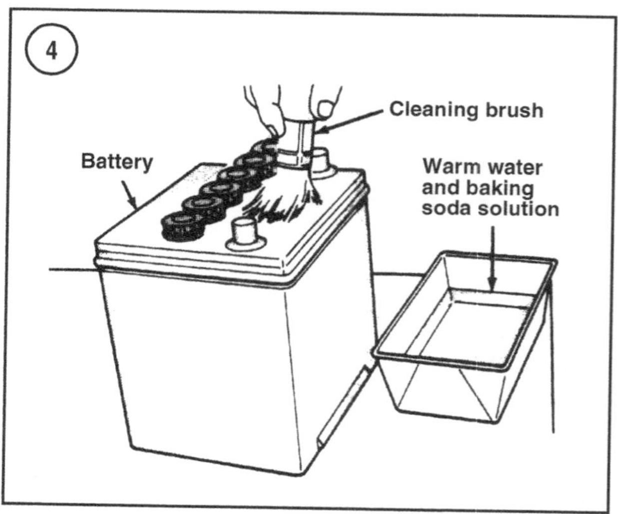

1. Do not smoke or permit any open flame near any battery being charged or that has been recently charged.

2. Do not disconnect live circuits at battery terminals, since a spark usually occurs when a live circuit is broken.

3. Take care when connecting or disconnecting any battery charger. Make sure its power switch is off before

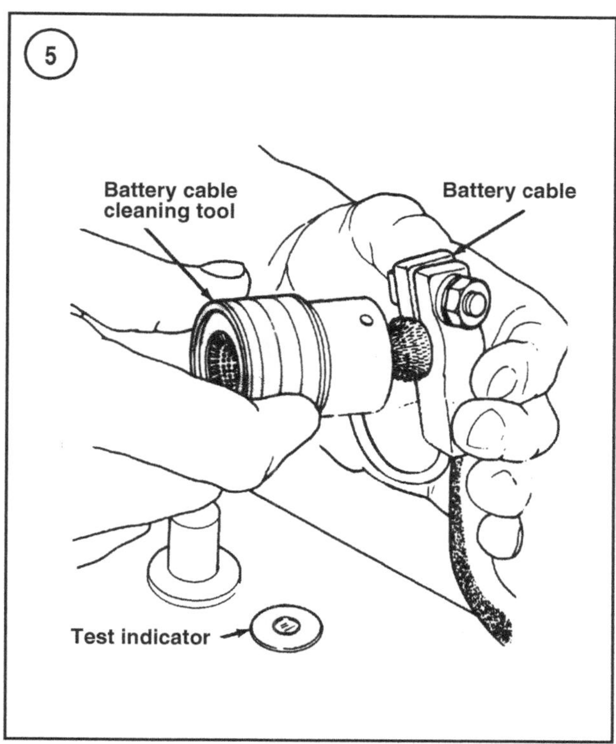

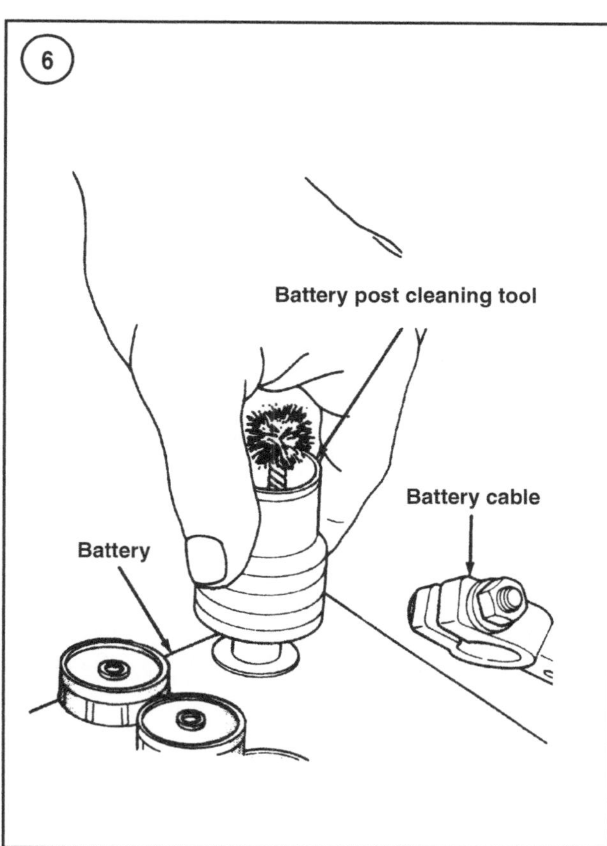

making or breaking any connection. Poor connections are a common cause of electrical arcs that cause explosions.

Care and Inspection

The following battery maintenance information applies to unsealed, wet-cell batteries. Although some of the procedures also apply to other types of batteries, consult the battery manufacturer for specific recommendations.

1. Disconnect both battery cables (negative first, then positive) and remove the battery hold-down or retainer clamp. See **Figure 1** for a typical open installation and **Figure 2** for a typical enclosed installation.

NOTE
*Some batteries have a carry strap built in for use in Step 2. See **Figure 3**.*

2. Attach a battery carrier or carrier strap to the terminal posts and lift the battery from the battery tray. Remove the battery from the engine compartment.
3. Check the entire battery case for cracks or other damage.
4. If the battery has removable vent caps, cover the vent holes in each cap with small pieces of masking tape.

NOTE
Keep cleaning solution out of the battery cells in Step 5, or the electrolyte will be seriously weakened.

5. Scrub the top of the battery with a stiff bristle brush, using a baking soda and water solution (**Figure 4**). Rinse the battery case with clear water and wipe it dry with a clean cloth or paper towels. Remove the masking tape from the filler cap vent holes, if so equipped.
6. Inspect the battery tray or container in the engine compartment for corrosion. Remove and clean it, if necessary, with the baking soda and water solution. Rinse it with clear water and wipe it dry, then reinstall.
7. Clean the battery cable clamps with a stiff wire brush or one of the many tools made for this purpose (**Figure 5**). The same tool is used for cleaning the battery posts (**Figure 6**).
8. Reposition the battery on the battery tray or container and remove the carrier or strap. Install and tighten the hold-down device.
9. Reinstall the positive battery cable, then the negative battery cable.

CAUTION
Be sure the battery cables are connected to their proper terminals. Reversing the polarity can damage the alternator.

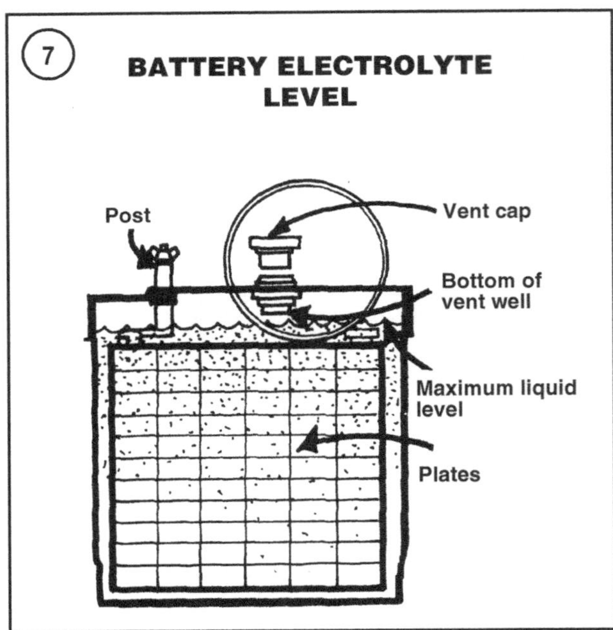

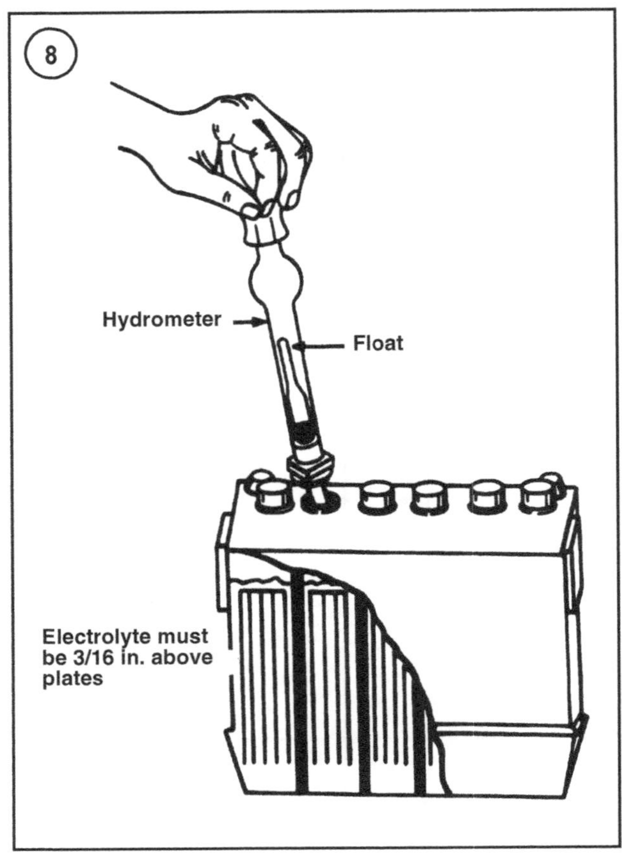

10. Tighten the battery cable connections to 9 ft.-lb. (12 N•m). Overtightening the connections can cause damage to the battery case. Coat the connections with petroleum jelly, or a light mineral grease. Aerosol anti-corrosion sprays can also be used.

NOTE
Do not overfill the battery cells in Step 11. The electrolyte expands due to heat from charging and may overflow if the level is more than 1/4 in. (6 mm) above the battery plates.

11. Remove the filler caps and check the electrolyte level. The electrolyte should cover the battery plates by at least 3/16 in. (4.8 mm). See **Figure 7**. Top off with distilled water to the bottom of the fill ring in each cell, if necessary.

Battery Testing

Hydrometer testing is the best way to check battery condition. Use a hydrometer with numbered graduations from 1.100-1.300 rather than one with color-coded bands. To use the hydrometer, squeeze the rubber ball, insert the tip in a cell and release the ball (**Figure 8**).

NOTE
Do not attempt to test a battery with a hydrometer immediately after adding water to the cells. Run the engine or charge the battery for 15-20 minutes prior to testing.

Draw enough electrolyte to float the weighted float inside the hydrometer. When using a temperature-compensated hydrometer, release the electrolyte and repeat this process several times to make sure the thermometer has adjusted to the electrolyte temperature before taking the reading.

Hold the hydrometer vertically and note the number aligned with the surface of the electrolyte (**Figure 9**). This is the specific gravity for the cell. Return the electrolyte to the cell from which it came.

The specific gravity of the electrolyte in each battery cell is an excellent indicator of that cell's condition. A fully charged cell will read 1.260 or more at 80° F (27° C). If the cells test below 1.220, the battery must be recharged. Charging is also necessary if the specific gravity varies more than 50 points from cell to cell.

NOTE
If a temperature-compensated hydrometer is not used, add 0.004 to the specific gravity reading for every 10° above 80° F (27° C).

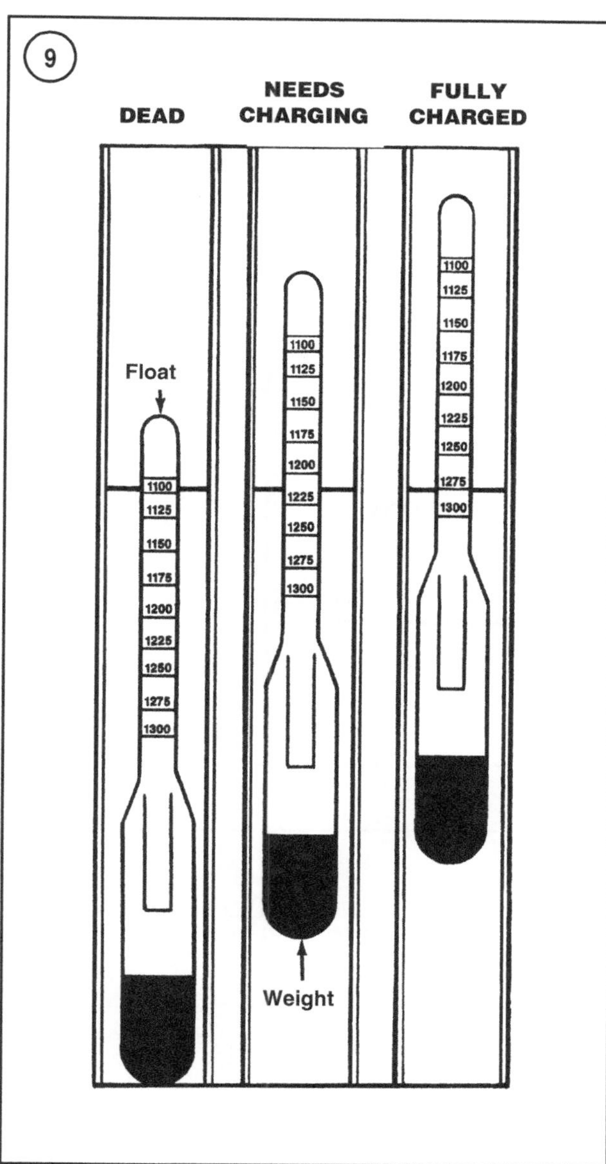

For every 10° below 80° F (27° C), subtract 0.004.

Charging

Maintain batteries used for starting in a good state of charge. Check the battery with a voltmeter as shown in **Figure 10**. Recharge any battery that cannot deliver at least 9.6 volts under a starting load. If recharging does not bring it up to strength or if it does not hold the charge, replace the battery.

A cold battery will not accept a charge readily. If the temperature is below 40° F (5° C), allow the battery to warm up to room temperature before charging. The battery does not have to be removed from the boat before charging, but it is a recommended procedure since a charging battery gives off highly explosive hydrogen gas. In many boats, the area around the battery is not well ventilated and the gas may remain in the area for several hours after the charging procedure has been completed. Sparks or flames occurring near the battery can cause it to explode, spraying battery acid over a wide area.

Disconnect the negative battery cable first, then the positive battery cable. Make sure the electrolyte is full. Remove the vent caps and place a folded paper towel over the vent openings to absorb any electrolyte that may splatter as the battery charges.

Connect the charger to the battery; negative to negative, positive to positive. If the charger output is variable, select a 10-12 amp setting. Set the voltage selector to 12 volts and plug the charger in. Once the battery starts to accept a charge, reduce the charge rate to a level that will prevent excessive gassing.

The length of time required to recharge a battery depends upon its rating, state of charge and temperature. Generally speaking, the current input time should equal the battery amp-hour rating. For example, a 45 AH battery will require a 9-amp charging rate for five hours (9 × 5 = 45) or a 15-amp charging rate for three hours (15 × 3 = 45). Check charging progress with the hydrometer.

9

Jump Starting

If the battery becomes discharged, it is possible to start and run the engine by jump starting it from another battery.

Before jump starting a battery when temperatures are 32° F (0° C) or lower, check the condition of the electrolyte. If it is not visible or if it appears to be frozen, do *not* attempt to jump start the battery, as the battery may explode or rupture.

WARNING
Use extreme caution when connecting a booster battery to one that is discharged to avoid personal injury or damage to the system.

1. Connect the jumper cables in the order and sequence shown in **Figure 11**.

WARNING
An electrical arc may occur when the final connection is made. This could cause an explosion if it occurs near the battery. For this reason, the final connection should be made

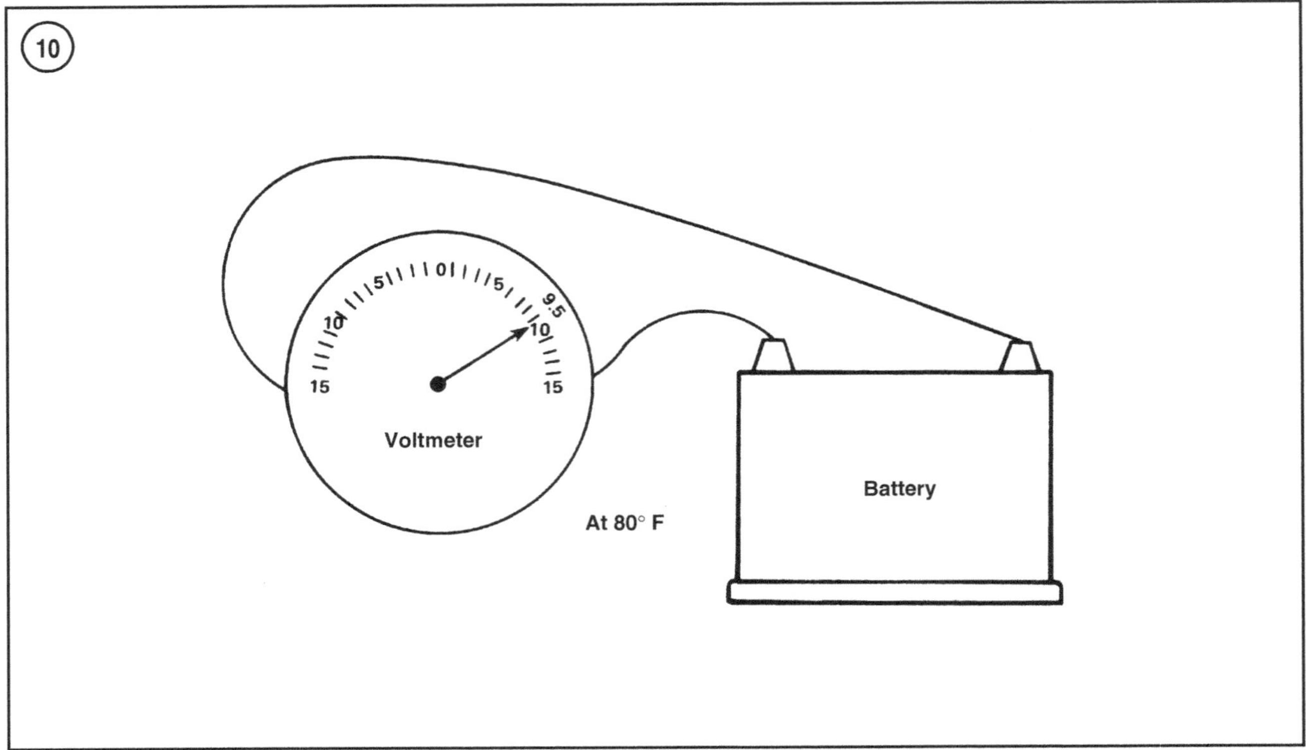

to the alternator mounting bracket or another good engine ground and not the battery itself.

2. Check that all jumper cables are out of the way of moving parts on both engines.
3. Start the engine with the good battery and run at a moderate speed.
4. Start the engine with the discharged battery. Once it starts, run it at a moderate speed.

CAUTION
Racing the engine may damage the electrical system.

5. Remove the jumper cables in the exact reverse order shown in **Figure 11**. Begin at point 4, then disconnect at points 3, 2 and 1.

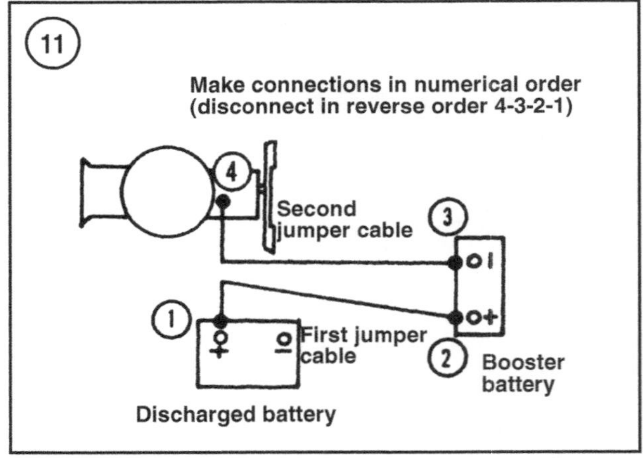

Battery Cables

Poor terminal connections will cause excessive resistance. Defective cable insulation can cause partial short circuits. Both conditions may result in an abnormal voltage drop in the starter motor cable. When this happens, the resulting hard-start condition will place further strain on the battery. Check cable condition and terminal connections periodically.

ELECTRICAL PROTECTION

Some electrical systems are equipped with a battery cutoff switch connected between the positive terminal of the battery and the starter solenoid. The switch provides a means to cut off all circuits from the battery in case of fire

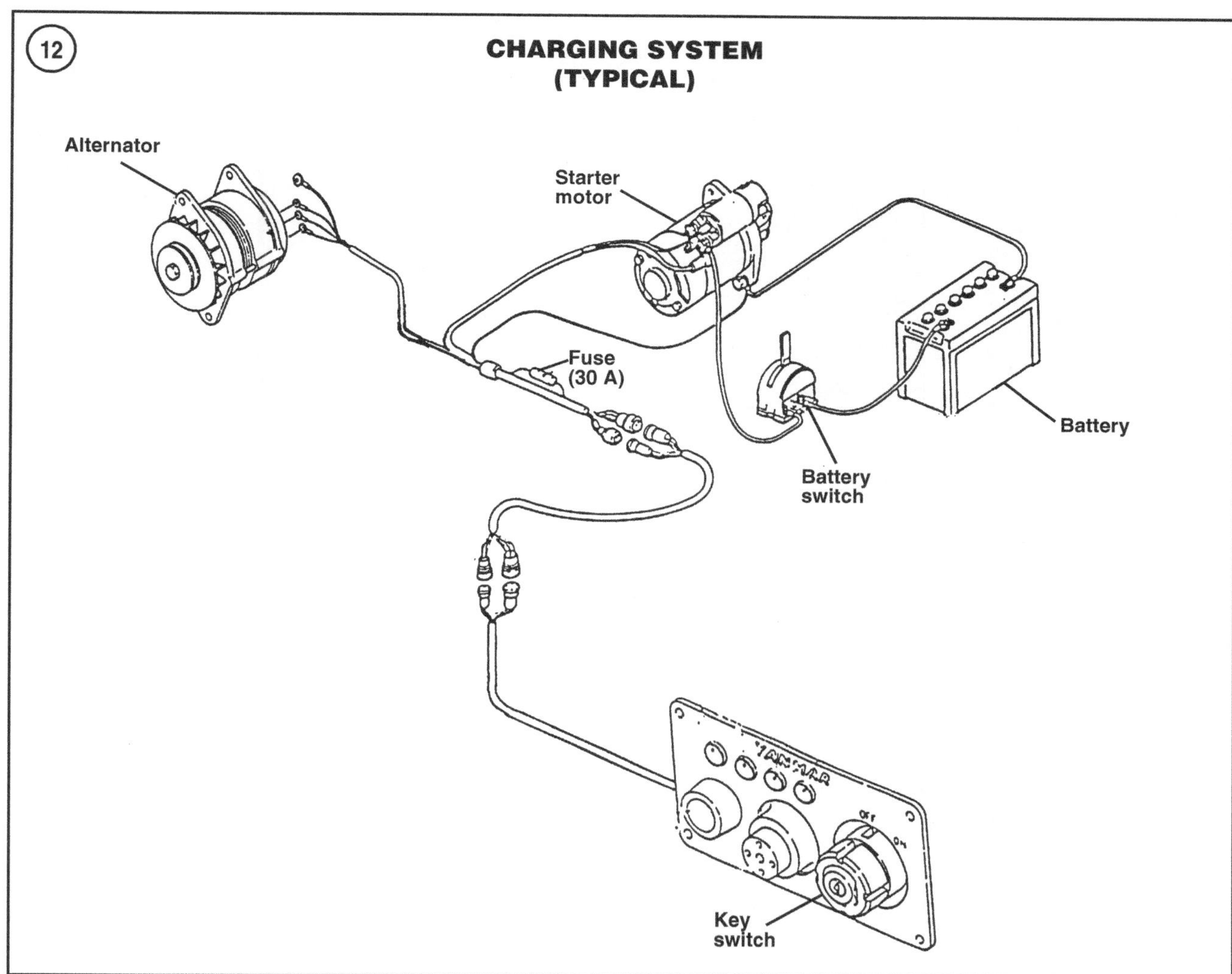

or other electrical emergencies. Using the cutoff switch also prevents any electrical drain on the battery.

All engines are equipped with a 30-amp fuse installed in the wiring harness between the ignition switch and starter motor. If a failure occurs in any part of the electrical system, always check the fuse first to see if it is blown. Usually, the trouble is a short circuit in the wiring. This may be caused by worn insulation or by a wire that has worked its way loose and shorted to ground.

Treat a blown fuse as more than a minor annoyance; it serves as a warning that something is wrong in the electrical system. Before replacing a fuse, determine what caused it to blow and correct the problem. Always carry several spare fuses of the proper amperage values onboard. Never replace a fuse with one of higher amperage rating than that specified for use. Failure to follow these basic rules could result in heat or fire damage to major parts or even the loss of the entire vessel.

CHARGING SYSTEM

The charging system consists of the battery, alternator, voltage regulator, ignition switch, charge lamp and connecting wiring. All engines are equipped with a Hitachi alternator. Refer to **Figure 12** for a typical charging system.

Preliminary Testing

The first indication of charging system trouble is usually a slow engine cranking speed or running lights that dim as engine speed decreases. This will often occur long before the ammeter or voltmeter indicates that there is a

potential problem. When charging system trouble is first suspected, perform the following:

1. Check the alternator drive belt for correct tension (Chapter Three).
2. Check the battery to make sure it is in satisfactory condition and fully charged and that all connections are clean and secure.
3. Check all connections at the alternator to make sure they are clean and secure.
4. If the charging system is not performing as it should after each of the above points has been carefully checked and any unsatisfactory conditions corrected, refer to Chapter Two and perform the *Charging System Tests*.

Alternator Removal/Installation

This section provides alternator replacement procedures. Complete alternator overhaul is not practical for the home mechanic. In some cases, replacement parts are unavailable.

This procedure is generalized to cover all applications. Access to the alternator is quite limited in some engine compartments and care should be taken to avoid personal injury.

1. Disconnect the negative battery cable.
2. Disconnect all wiring harnesses and leads at the rear of the alternator. See **Figure 13**, typical.

NOTE

When loosening the retaining nut on an alternator terminal, hold the terminal with a wrench to prevent the terminal from rotating.

3. Loosen the alternator adjusting and pivot bolts (**Figure 14**, typical).
4. Swivel the alternator toward the engine and remove the drive belt from the alternator pulley.
5. Support the alternator with one hand and remove the adjusting and pivot bolts, noting the position of any washers or spacers used. Remove the alternator.
6. Installation is the reverse of removal. Tighten fasteners securely and adjust drive belt tension (Chapter Three) before reconnecting wiring harnesses and leads to the rear of the alternator.

NOTE

Make sure the rubber boots at the end of the wires fit snugly over the terminals on the alternator, otherwise, the wire ends and terminals may corrode.

STARTING SYSTEM

The starting system consists of the battery, starter motor, starter solenoid, starter switch, key switch, fuse and connecting wiring. See **Figure 12**, typical.

Yanmar marine engines are equipped with a Hitachi starter motor. The starter solenoid is enclosed in the drive housing to protect it from exposure to dirt and adverse weather conditions.

Starter service requires experience and special tools. Refer to Chapter Two for troubleshooting procedures. The procedures described below consist of removal, installation and brush replacement. Any repairs inside the unit itself (other than brush replacement) should be performed by a dealer or certified electrical shop. Installation of a professionally rebuilt marine-type unit is generally less expensive and more practical.

Starter Removal/Installation

1. Disconnect the negative battery cable.

2. Disconnect the solenoid terminal wires. See **Figure 15**.
3. Remove the starter motor mounting bolts. Pull the starter motor away from the flywheel and remove it from the engine.
4. Installation is the reverse of removal. Tighten mounting bolts to torque specified in **Table 2**.

Solenoid Removal/Installation

To remove the solenoid it is necessary to partially disassemble the starter. Note that the starter used on series 1GM, 1GM10, 2GM, 2GM20, 3GM and 3GM30 engines are equipped with an antitorque spring that stabilizes the actuating yoke.

1. Remove the starter as previously described.
2. Disconnect the solenoid terminal wires (**Figure 15**).
3. Remove the screws securing the solenoid to the starter. The solenoid will be loose but still attached to the actuating yoke in the starter. It is necessary to partially disassemble the starter to remove the solenoid and yoke.
4. Remove the two throughbolts (29, **Figure 16** or 33, **Figure 17**).

NOTE
Do not allow the armature to move forward because the commutator may slide out of the brushes, which will require disassembly of the rear of the starter to reinstall the brushes.

5. Carefully separate the drive end cover (3, **Figure 16**) from the frame (15 or 22) so the armature shaft withdraws from the drive end housing, but stays in position in the frame.
6. Remove the solenoid with the actuating yoke (6, **Figure 16** or 7, **Figure 17**) and spring, if so equipped.
7. Remove the yoke and spring, if so equipped, from the solenoid.

8A. To install the solenoid on models equipped with an antitorque spring, reverse the disassembly procedure while noting the following:

a. Position the antitorque spring on the solenoid plunger so the spring ends fit in the holes in the solenoid (**Figure 18**).
b. Position the yoke in the solenoid plunger so the notch on the yoke fits against the closed end of the anti-torque spring as shown in **Figure 18**.
c. Make sure the open end of the yoke properly engages the ears on the overrunning clutch body (**Figure 19**).

8B. To install the solenoid on models *not* equipped with an antitorque spring, reverse the disassembly procedure while noting the following:

a. Make sure that the pads on the open end of the yoke properly fit between the flanges on the overrunning clutch body.

9

Brush Replacement

1GM, 1GM10, 2GM, 2GM20, 3GM and 3GM30 models

Brush replacement requires partial disassembly of the starter.

1. Disconnect the positive lead from the solenoid.
2. Remove the cover (26, **Figure 16**) on the end cap.
3. Detach the E-ring (25, **Figure 16**) and remove the washers from the armature shaft.
4. Remove the brush holder retaining screws (30, **Figure 16**).
5. Remove the two throughbolts (29, **Figure 16**).
6. Separate the end cover (21, **Figure 16**) from the starter.
7. Note the position of the brushes in the brush holder. Use a suitable tool to pull back and hold the brush retaining clip, then remove the brush. See **Figure 20**, typical. Repeat this step to remove the remaining brushes.
8. Remove the brush holder from the armature shaft.
9. Use an ohmmeter or self-powered test lamp to check for continuity between the insulated brush holder and the base of the brush holder assembly. See **Figure 21**. If there is continuity, replace the brush holder.
10. Inspect brush and brush spring condition. Measure brush length. Replace all brushes if any are oil-soaked or worn to 12 mm (0.47 in.) or less in length. Replace any broken or distorted brush springs.

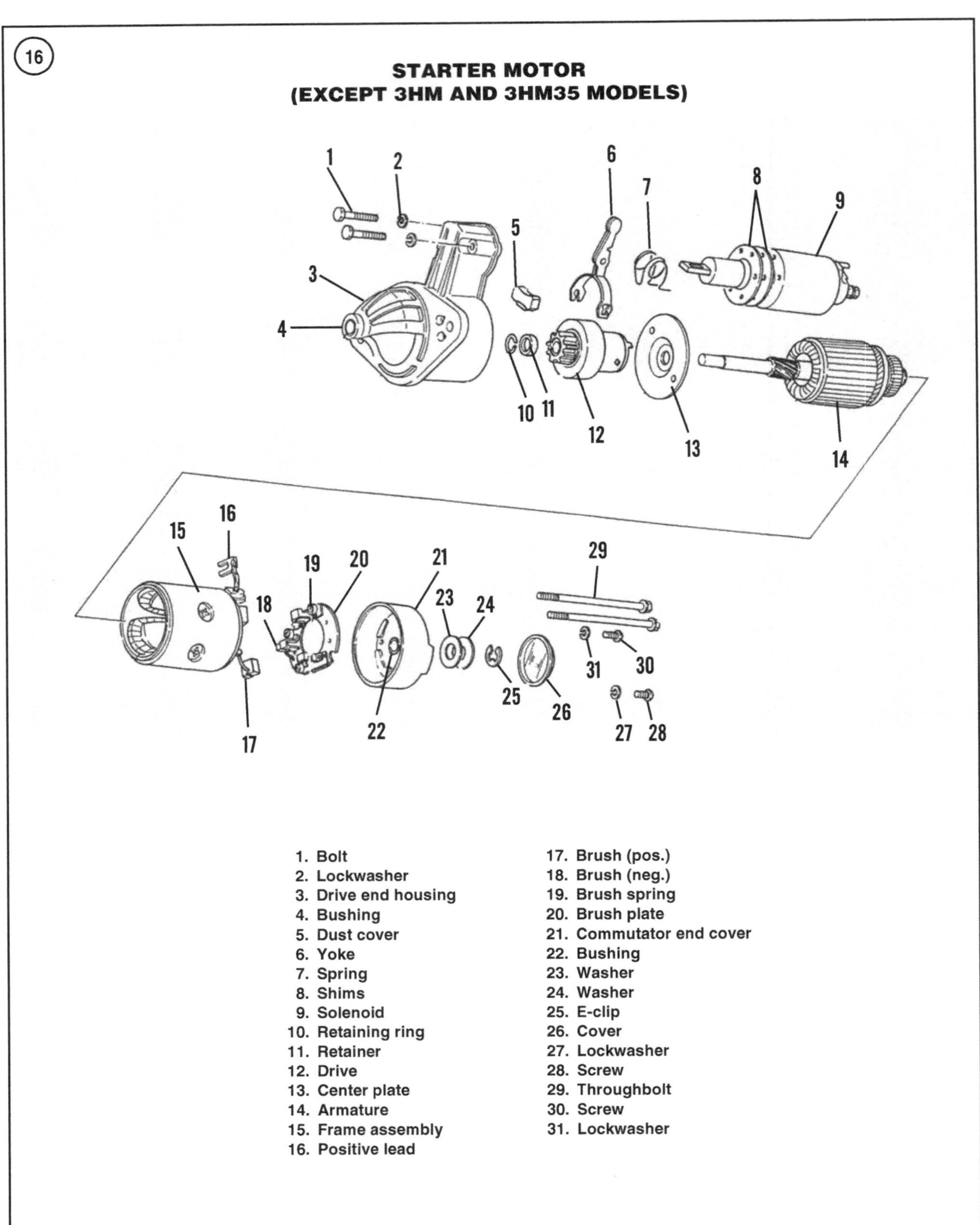

STARTER MOTOR (EXCEPT 3HM AND 3HM35 MODELS)

1. Bolt
2. Lockwasher
3. Drive end housing
4. Bushing
5. Dust cover
6. Yoke
7. Spring
8. Shims
9. Solenoid
10. Retaining ring
11. Retainer
12. Drive
13. Center plate
14. Armature
15. Frame assembly
16. Positive lead
17. Brush (pos.)
18. Brush (neg.)
19. Brush spring
20. Brush plate
21. Commutator end cover
22. Bushing
23. Washer
24. Washer
25. E-clip
26. Cover
27. Lockwasher
28. Screw
29. Throughbolt
30. Screw
31. Lockwasher

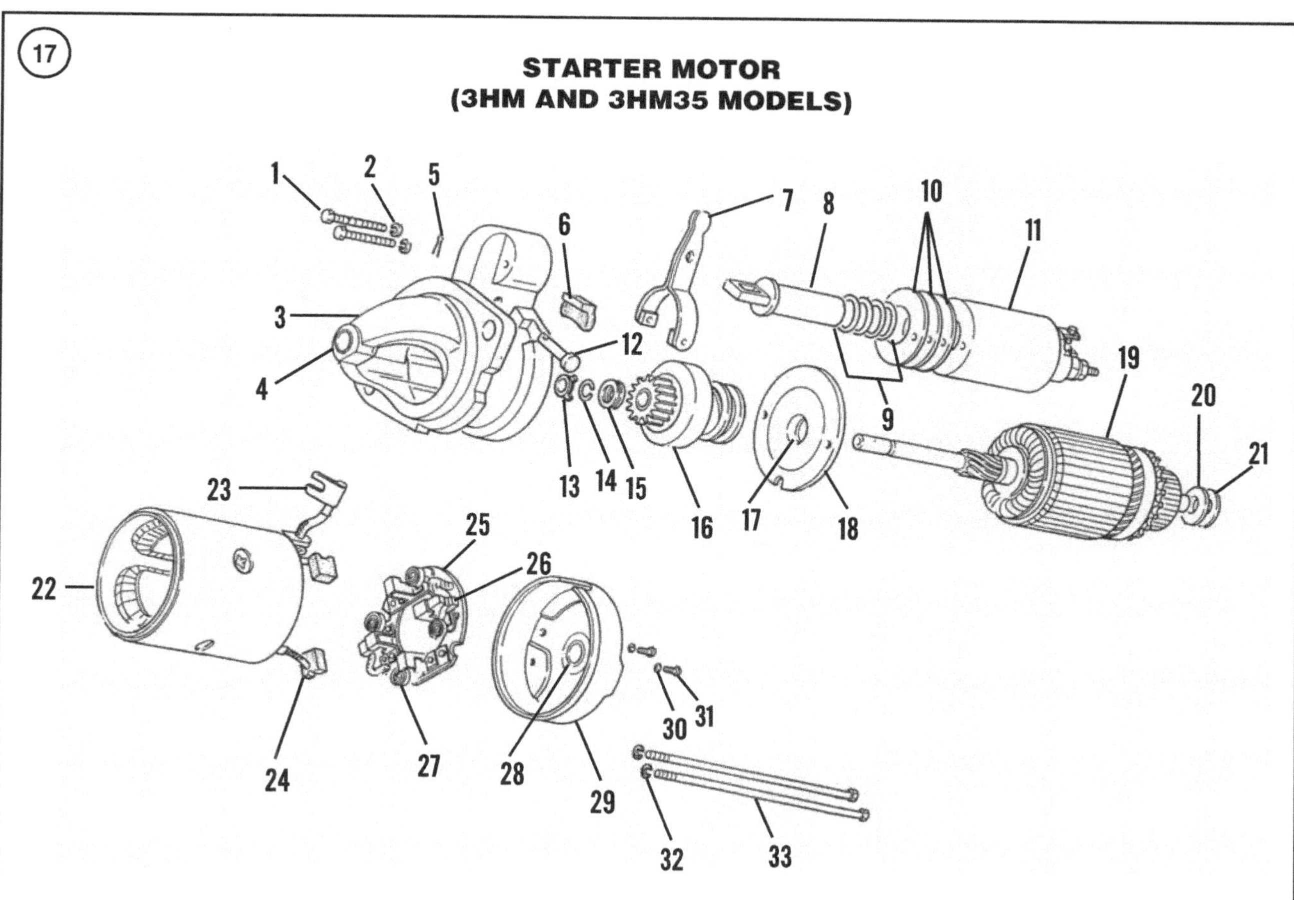

1. Bolt
2. Lockwasher
3. Drive end housing
4. Bushing
5. Clip
6. Dust cover
7. Yoke
8. Actuator
9. Washers
10. Shims
11. Solenoid
12. Pin
13. Stopper washer
14. Circlip
15. Retainer
16. Drive
17. Bushing
18. Center plate
19. Armature
20. Washer
21. Washer
22. Frame assembly
23. Positive lead
24. Positive brush
25. Brush plate
26. Negative brush
27. Brush spring
28. Bushing
29. Commutator end cap
30. Lockwasher
31. Screw
32. Lockwasher
33. Throughbolt

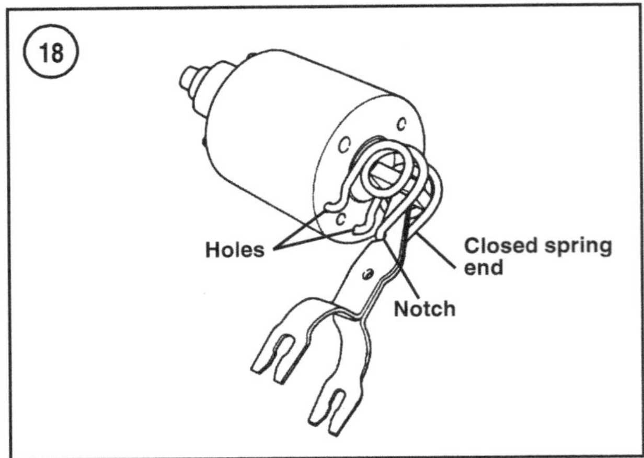

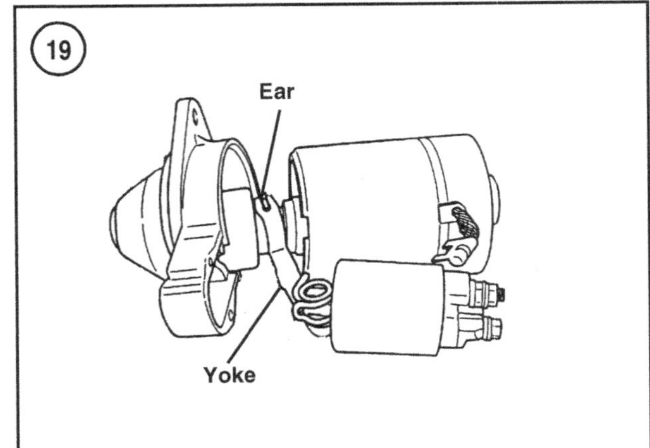

11. To replace ground (negative) brushes, remove the brush lead attaching screws from the starter frame. Remove the brushes and install new ones.
12. To replace field coil brushes, cut the insulated brush leads as close as possible to the field coils. Attach new brush leads and solder the connections together with rosin core solder and a 300-watt soldering iron.

NOTE
Always replace brushes in complete sets.

13. Install the brush end holder.
14. Pull back and hold the brush retaining clip with a wire hook, then install the brush. Repeat this step to install the remaining brushes. Make sure the brush springs rest in the small cutout on top of each brush.
15. Reassembly is the reverse of Steps 1-6.

3HM and 3HM35 models

Brush replacement requires partial disassembly of the starter.

1. Disconnect the positive lead (23) from the solenoid.
2. Remove the brush holder retaining screws (31, **Figure 17**).
3. Remove the two throughbolts (33, **Figure 17**).
4. Separate the end cap (29) from the starter.
5. Note the position of the brushes in the brush holder. Use a suitable tool to pull back and hold the brush retaining clip, then remove the brush. See **Figure 20**, typical. Repeat this step to remove the remaining brushes.
6. Remove the brush holder from the armature shaft.
7. Use an ohmmeter or self-powered test lamp to check for continuity between the insulated brush holder and the base of the brush holder assembly. See **Figure 21**. If there is continuity, replace the brush holder.

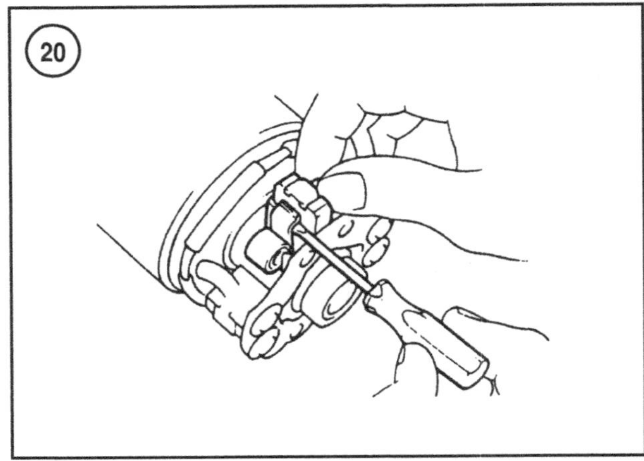

8. Inspect brush and brush spring condition. Measure brush length. Replace all brushes if any are oil-soaked or worn to 14 mm (0.55 in.) or less in length. Replace any broken or distorted brush springs.
9. To replace ground (negative) brushes, remove the brush lead attaching screws from the starter frame. Remove the brushes and install new ones.
10. To replace field coil (positive) brushes, cut the insulated brush leads as close as possible to the field coils. Attach new brush leads and solder the connections together with rosin core solder and a 300-watt soldering iron.

NOTE
Always replace brushes in complete sets.

11. Install the brush end holder.
12. Pull back and hold the brush retaining clip with a wire hook, then install the brush. Repeat this step to install the remaining brushes. Make sure the brush springs rest in the small cutout on top of each brush.
13. Reassembly is the reverse of Steps 1-4.

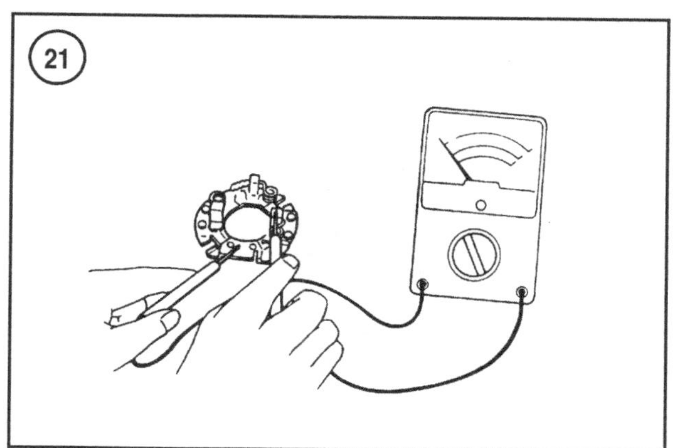

21

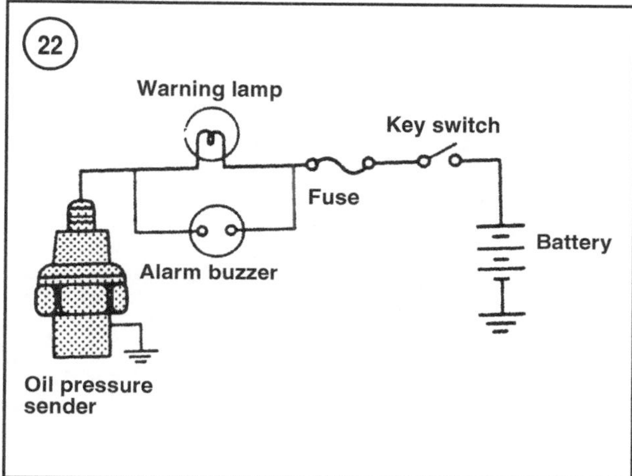

22

SWITCHES

The instrument panel is equipped with two switches: a key switch and a start switch. A lighting switch is also used on instrument panels equipped with a tachometer. Most engines are also equipped with a battery cutoff switch. Refer to the following sections to check the operation of these switches. Also refer to the wiring diagrams at the back of this manual.

Key Switch

The key switch is mounted on the instrument panel. When the key is in the ON position, the switch directs current to the circuits it controls.

Perform voltage or resistance checks to determine if the switch is operating properly.

23

Start Switch

The start switch mounted on the instrument panel is a push-button switch that closes the starter motor circuit when the button is depressed.

Perform voltage or resistance checks to determine if the switch is operating properly.

Battery Cutoff Switch

The battery cutoff switch is connected between the positive terminal of the battery and the starter solenoid. The switch provides a means to cutoff all circuits from the battery in case of fire or other electrical emergencies. Using the cutoff switch also prevents any electrical drain on the battery.

To test the switch, check for voltage at the starter solenoid terminal, or disconnect the positive battery cable and check the switch using an ohmmeter.

SENDERS

The engine is equipped with senders that trigger warning lights and the alarm buzzer if engine oil pressure or water temperature reaches a dangerous level. The senders are essentially switches that complete an electrical circuit.

Oil Pressure Sender

Refer to the oil pressure circuit in **Figure 22**. The sender is closed at zero oil pressure, which allows current to light the warning lamp and sound the alarm buzzer when the key switch is on. When oil pressure rises above 9.8-29.4 kPa (1.4-4.3 psi), the sender opens, the warning lamp goes out and the alarm buzzer quits.

The oil pressure sender on 1GM and 1GM10 is located on the oil filter adapter as shown in **Figure 23**. The oil

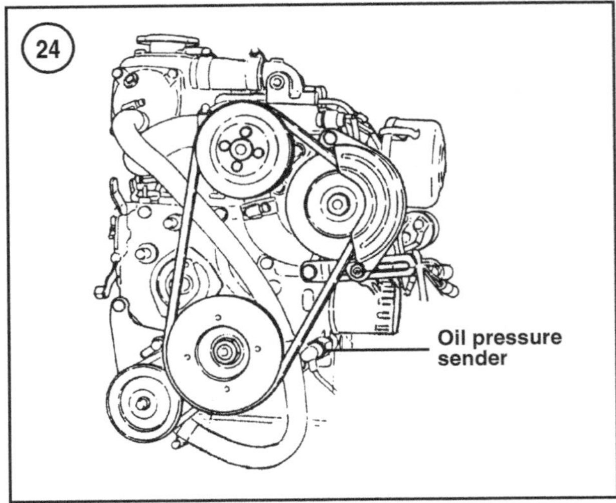

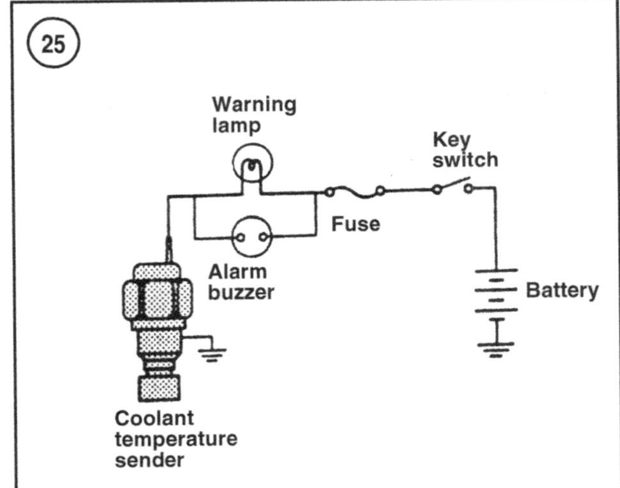

pressure sender on 2GM, 2GM20, 3GM, 3GM30, 3HM and 3HM35 engines is located below the oil filter as shown in **Figure 24**.

To check the oil pressure sender, proceed as follows:

CAUTION
Before checking the oil pressure sender, make sure the engine is filled with oil.

1. Disconnect the wire at the sender terminal.
2. Connect an ohmmeter between the sender terminal and the hex on the base of the sender.
3. With the engine off, the meter should show continuity.
4. Start the engine. As the oil pressure builds above 9.8 kPa (1.4 psi), the meter should switch from continuity to no continuity. If it does not, replace the sender unit.

Coolant Temperature Sender

Refer to the coolant temperature circuit in **Figure 25**. The sender is open at ambient temperature, which prevents current from lighting the warning lamp and activating the alarm buzzer. When coolant rises above the specification, the sender closes, the warning lamp and the alarm buzzer come on.

On 1GM and 1GM10 engines, the coolant temperature sensor is located on the cylinder head (**Figure 26**). The coolant temperature sensor on two or three cylinder engines is located on the front or side of the thermostat housing (**Figure 27**, typical).

Two different senders may be used depending on the type of cooling system. Engines equipped with seawater cooling are equipped with a sender that is color-coded white and has a closed temperature of 148-154° F (63-67° C). Engines equipped with freshwater cooling are equipped with a sender that is color-coded green and has a closed temperature of 193-202° F (89-95° C).

To check the coolant sender, proceed as follows:

1. Remove the switch from the engine.
2. Connect a digital ohmmeter to the switch.
3. Immerse the sending unit and a cooking thermometer in a container of oil.
4. Heat the container over a flameless heat source and note the ohmmeter reading. The switch should close as follows:
   a. seawater switch (white)—148-154° F (63-67° C).
   b. freshwater switch (green)—193-202° F (89-95° C).
5. Remove the container from the heat and let it cool. The switch should reopen as follows:
   a. seawater switch (white)—136° F (58° C).
   b. freshwater switch (green)—190° F (88° C).
6. Replace the switch if it does not function as specified at each temperature range.

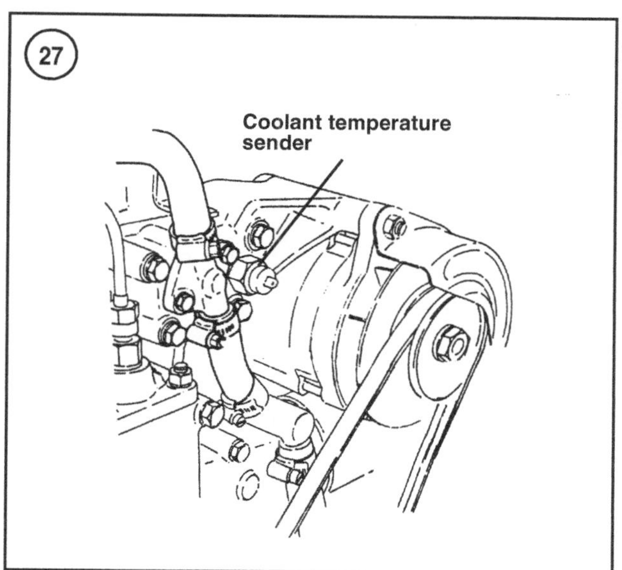

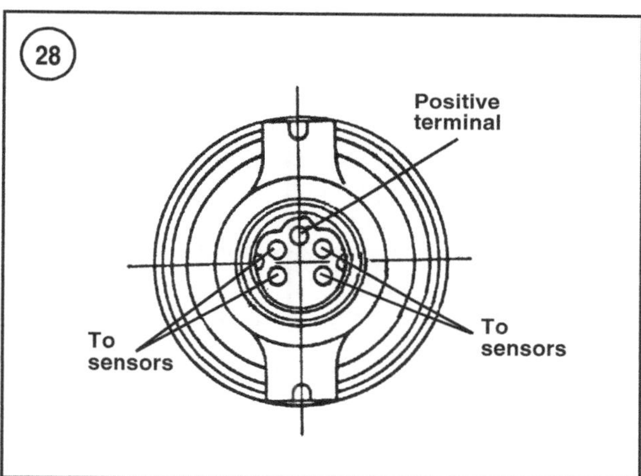

WARNING LAMPS

Engines covered by this manual are equipped with an instrument panel that has three warning lamps. The warning lamps illuminate to indicate high coolant temperature, low oil pressure or insufficient charging current.

Coolant and Oil Pressure Warning Lamps

1. To check the circuit for the coolant or oil pressure warning lamp, detach the lead from the coolant temperature or oil pressure sender.
2. With the key switch ON, ground the sender lead. The warning lamp should come on.
3. To determine if a bulb is defective, substitute a good bulb. All warning lamps use the same type of bulb.

Charging System Warning Lamp

The warning lamp for the charging circuit should illuminate when the key switch is ON and the engine is not running, or when there is a malfunction in the charging circuit.

1. To check the circuit for the charging system warning lamp, detach the lead from the L terminal on the alternator.
2. With the key switch ON, ground the detached lead. The charge system warning lamp should come on.
3. To determine if the charging system bulb is defective, substitute a good bulb. All warning lamps use the same type of bulb.
4. If a good bulb does not light, check the charging system as described in Chapter Two.

ALARM BUZZER

The alarm buzzer provides an audible warning in addition to the coolant and oil pressure warning lamps. Two types of alarm buzzers are used: a buzzer with two leads and a buzzer with multiple leads. Note the terminal locations in **Figure 28** for the buzzer equipped with multiple leads.

1. Check the alarm buzzer while it is installed.
   a. Detach the lead from the coolant temperature or oil pressure sender.
   b. With the key switch ON, ground the sender lead. The alarm buzzer should come on.
2. Check the alarm buzzer with all leads disconnected from the buzzer or with the buzzer removed from the instrument panel.
   a. On the buzzer with multiple terminals, note the terminal locations in **Figure 28**.
   b. Connect a 12-volt battery to the terminals as follows: Connect a positive battery lead to positive buzzer terminal. Connect the negative battery lead to each of the remaining buzzer terminals. The buzzer should sound; if it does not, replace the buzzer.

TACHOMETER

Some engines may be equipped with a tachometer. A sensor located on the clutch housing (**Figure 29**) provides an electrical signal that drives the tachometer. The electromagnetic sensor counts the teeth on the flywheel ring

gear as it rotates. The sensor sends the resulting electrical signal to the tachometer, which converts it into indicator needle movement.

NOTE
While the sensors for all engines are interchangeable, the tachometers are not. Due to the difference in number of ring gear teeth, the tachometer used on 3HM and 3HM35 engines is not interchangeable with other engines.

Before troubleshooting the tachometer, check for faulty connections, then recheck tachometer operation. If the problem remains, refer to the following sections.

Tachometer Sender

To check the tachometer sender, proceed as follows:

1. Disconnect the leads from the sender (**Figure 29**).
2. With the engine stopped, use an ohmmeter to check the resistance between the sender terminals. Resistance should be 1500-1700 ohms.
3. Run the engine. Measure the alternating current voltage between the sender terminals. The voltage reading should be at least one volt.
4. If the sender fails either test, replace the sender.

Tachometer Gauge

To check the tachometer gauge unit, proceed as follows:

1. Disconnect the red/black and black wire leads from the tachometer. With the key switch ON, measure the voltage between the two wires. There should be 10-16 volts (battery voltage). If not, determine the cause.
2. Disconnect the orange and blue/red wire leads from the tachometer. Run the engine. Measure the alternating current voltage between the orange and blue/red wire leads. The voltage reading should be at least one volt.
3. If the voltage reading in Step 2 is less than one volt, check the wires and connections and check the sender as described in the preceding section.
4. If the voltage readings in Steps 1 and 2 are satisfactory, replace the tachometer.

Table 1 BATTERY CAPACITY (MINIMUM)

Model	Voltage	Battery capacity
1GM, 1GM10	12 V	70 amp-hours
2GM, 2GM20	12 V	70 amp-hours
3GM, 3GM30, 3HM	12 V	70 amp-hours
3HM35	12 V	100 amp-hours

Table 2 ALTERNATOR AND STARTER MOTOR TIGHTENING TORQUES

Model	Alternator mounting bolt	Starter motor mounting bolts
1GM, 1GM10, 2GM, 2GM20, 3GM, 3GM30	22-27 N•m (16-20 ft.-lb.)	45-50 N•m (33-37 ft.-lb.)
3HM, 3HM35	22-27 N•m (16-20 ft.-lb.)	75-80 N•m (55-59 ft.-lb.)

Chapter Ten

Transmission—KM Series

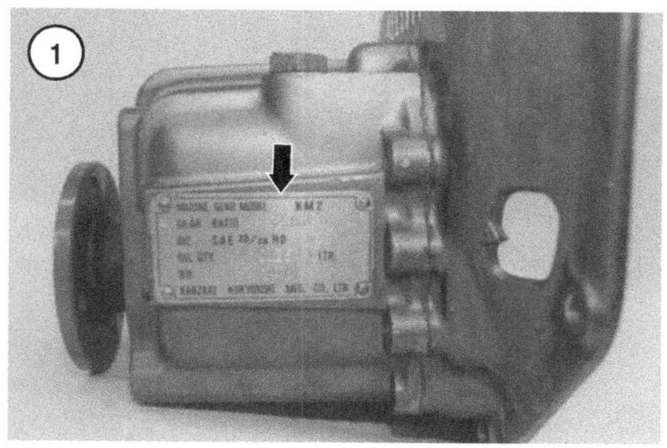

This chapter covers the Kanzaki KM2A, KM2C, KM2P, KM3A and KM3P marine transmissions that are attached to Yanmar 1GM, 1GM10, 2GM, 2GM20, 3GMD and 3GM30 engines. Refer to **Table 1** for a cross-reference of engine and transmission models. The identification plate located on the transmission case (**Figure 1**, typical) specifies the transmission model.

The KM2 and KM3 series transmissions are inline transmissions that provide forward and reverse direction. All gears are constant mesh. A cone-type clutch engages internally tapered gears to transmit power to the output shaft. Oil contained in the transmission case lubricates the internal transmission components.

Basic design is the same for all the transmissions with the exception of the shifting mechanism. Transmissions with a P suffix are equipped with a shifting device that engages detent notches in the shifter housing. All other models use spring-loaded pins and a spring-loaded actuator that engage detents and ramps on the shift shaft.

Refer to Chapter Three for maintenance information.

Tables 1-7 are located at the end of this chapter.

OPERATION

The input shaft on the transmission engages the drive disc attached to the engine flywheel. Because this is a constant-mesh transmission, engine power is transmitted to all gears. Power flows to the output shaft when the cone clutch engages either the forward gear or the reverse gear. In **Figure 2**, the cone clutch is shown engaged with the forward gear. Because power flows from the input shaft gear through the reverse idler gear to the reverse gear, the reverse gear rotates in the opposite direction of the forward gear. When the cone clutch engages the reverse gear, the output shaft rotates in reverse.

On Model KM2A, KM2C and KM3A transmissions, moving the shift lever (**Figure 3**) rotates the shift shaft. When the shift shaft rotates, the shifter slides the cone clutch into engagement with the forward or reverse gear, or into neutral. When the shifter reaches the proper position, the upper spring-loaded detent pin sits on a ramp that

(2)

CONE CLUTCH

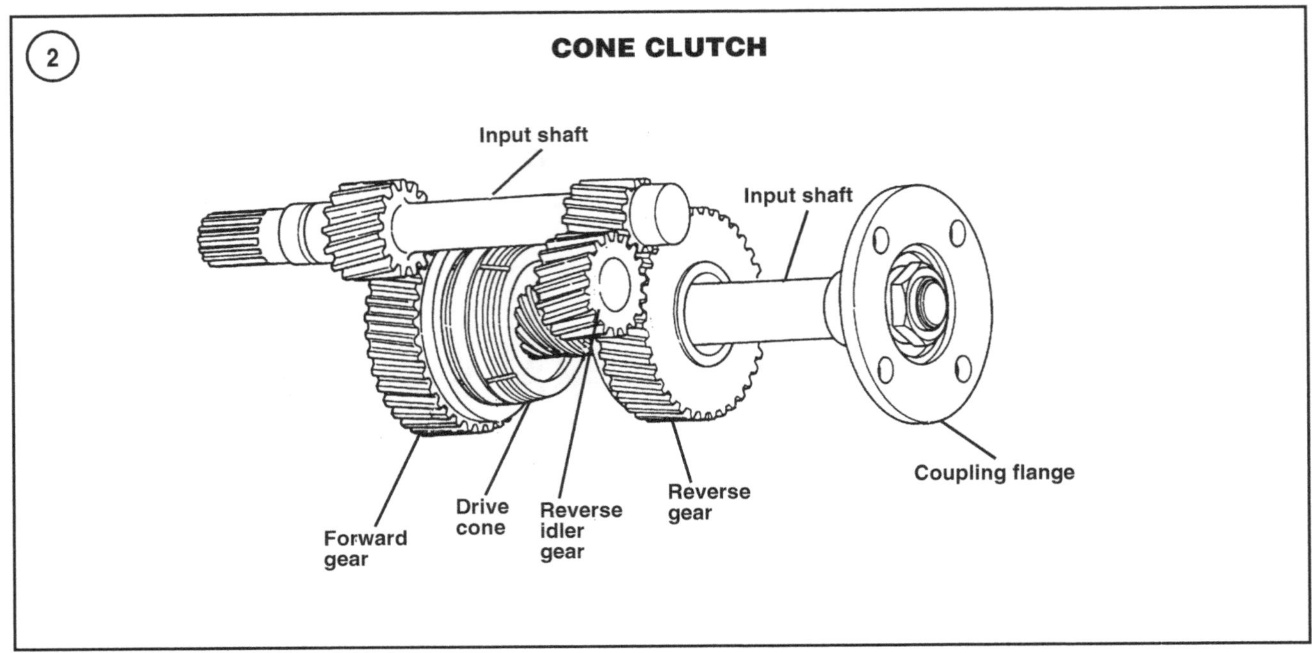

(3)

SHIFTER (KM2A, KM2C AND KM3A MODELS)

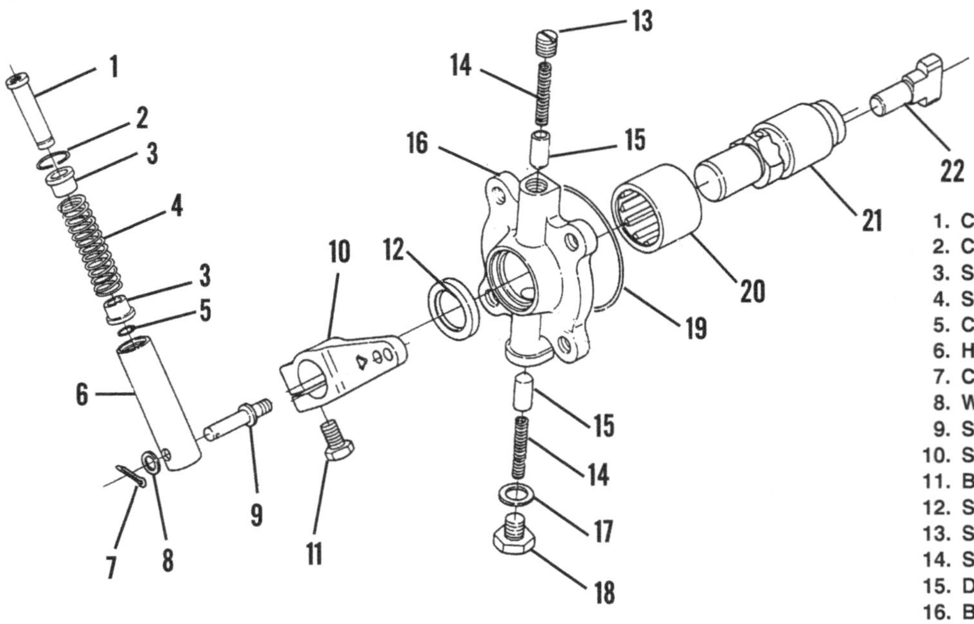

1. Connector
2. Circlip
3. Spring retainer
4. Spring
5. Circlip
6. Holder
7. Cotter pin
8. Washer
9. Stud
10. Shift lever
11. Bolt
12. Seal
13. Setscrew
14. Spring
15. Detent pin
16. Body
17. Gasket
18. Plug
19. O-ring
20. Bearing
21. Shift shaft
22. Shifter

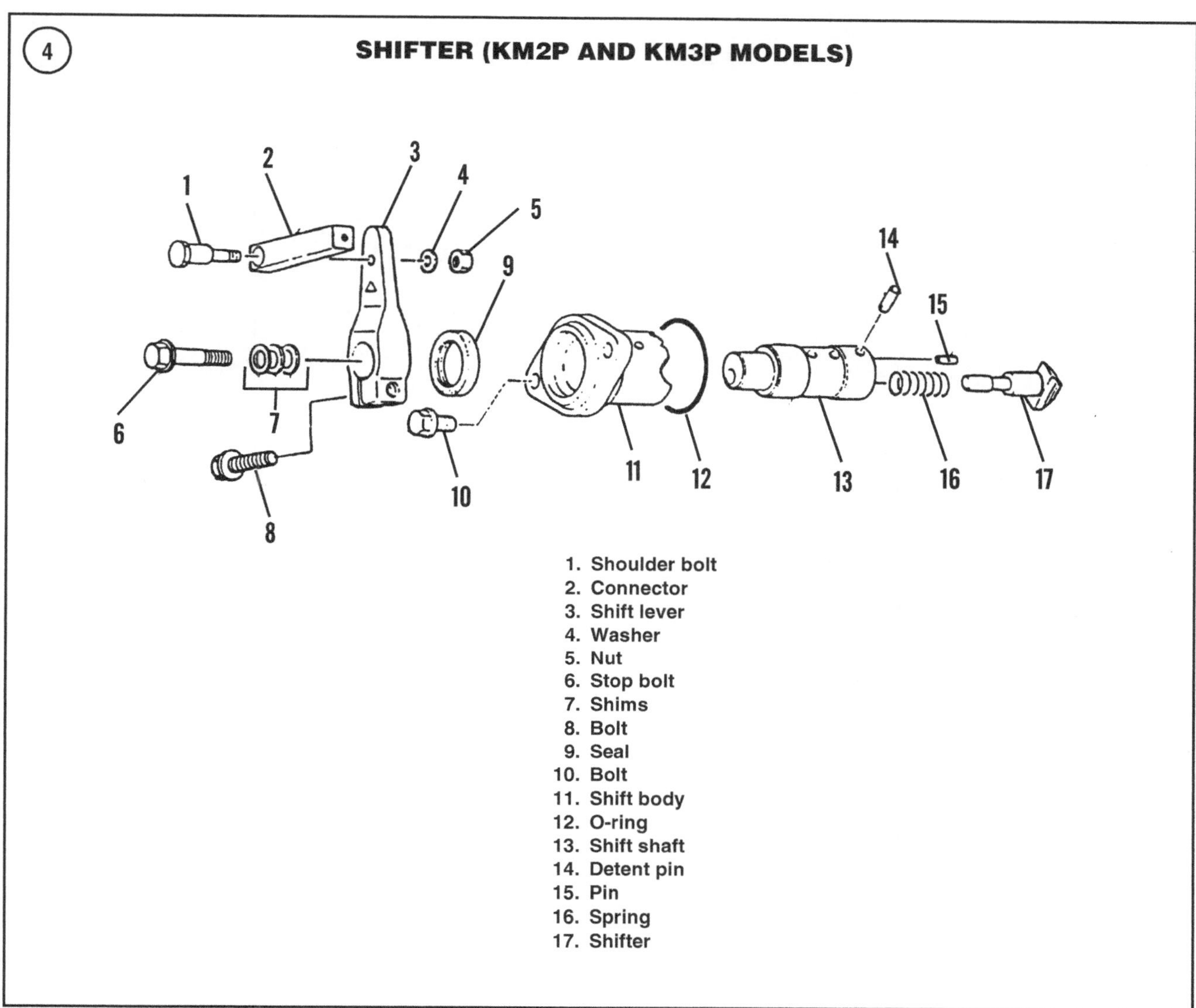

forces the shifter to push the clutch cone into the gear. The springs in the shift actuator hold the shifter in position.

The shifter mechanism on Model KM2P and KM3P transmissions includes a spring-loaded shifter (**Figure 4**). Movement of the shift lever forces the shifter to move the cone clutch against the forward or reverse gear. Detent notches in the shift housing hold the shifter pin in position.

REMOVAL/INSTALLATION

The following procedure addresses units that are accessible. In some cases, it may be necessary to remove the engine and transmission as a unit before removing the transmission from the engine. If engine removal is necessary, refer to Chapter Five for single-cylinder models and Chapter Six for multi-models.

1. If not previously disconnected, disconnect the remote control cable from the transmission shift lever.

2. If not previously disconnected, disconnect the drive coupling from the transmission drive flange.

3. Remove the bolts that secure the transmission to the engine bellhousing.

4. Remove the transmission from the engine.

5. Reinstall the transmission by reversing the removal procedure. Make sure to align the splines on the transmission input shaft and the drive disc during installation. Tighten the transmission retaining bolts to the torque specified in **Table 2**.

OVERHAUL

Disassembly

1. Remove the drain plug (A, **Figure 5**) and drain the transmission oil.

2. The output flange retaining nut is staked (**Figure 6**). Use a chisel to cut away the staked portion so the nut will rotate.

NOTE
The output flange retaining nut has left-hand threads.

3. Use a tool or other device to hold the output flange so it cannot rotate.

4. Unscrew the output flange retaining nut by rotating the nut clockwise (left-hand threads).

5. Remove the oil dipstick (**Figure 7**).

6. Remove the shifter retaining bolts (B, **Figure 5**) and remove the shifter assembly.

7. Remove the transmission flange retaining bolts.

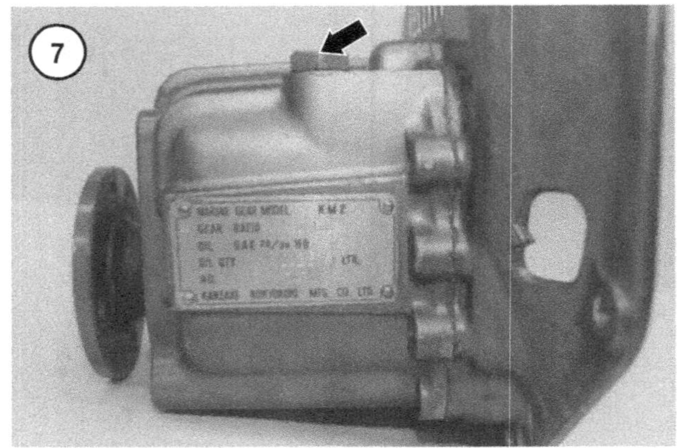

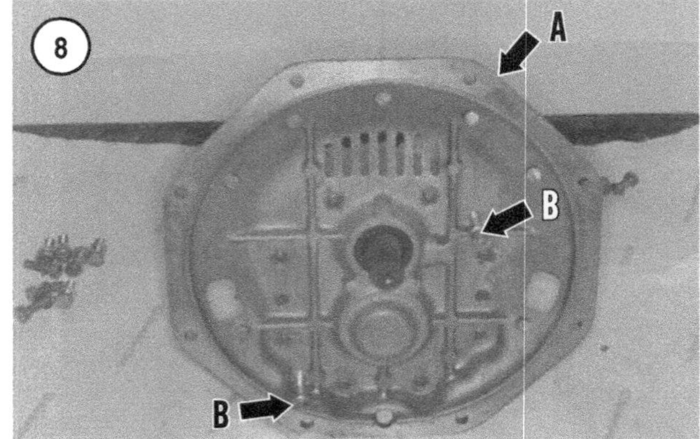

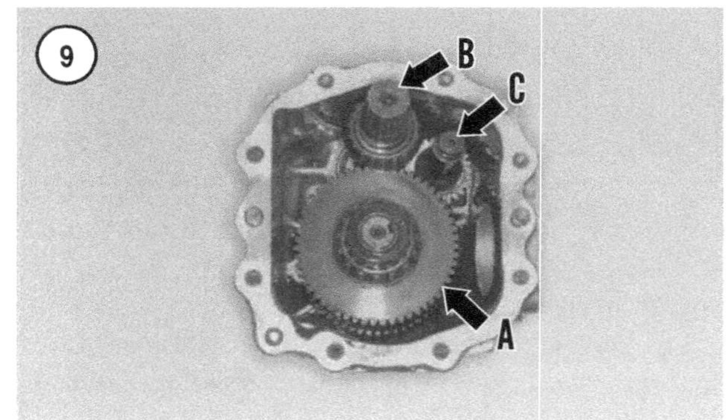

NOTE
In Step 8, position the transmission so the transmission input shaft is up when removing the transmission flange so the transmission shafts will not fall out.

8. Tap on the transmission flange (A, **Figure 8**) using a soft-faced hammer to dislodge the flange. If tapping will not dislodge the flange, install jackscrews (B) into the

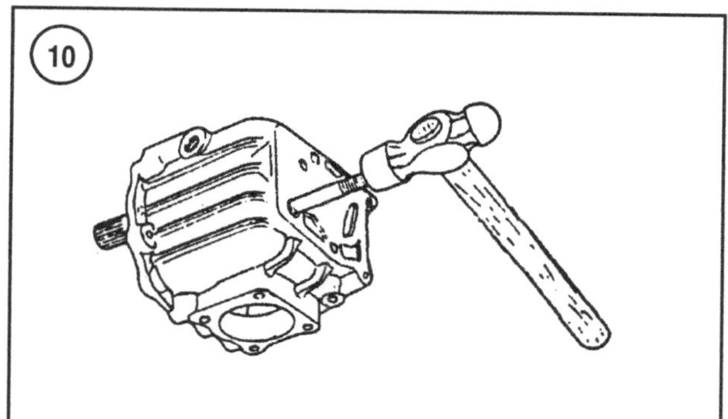

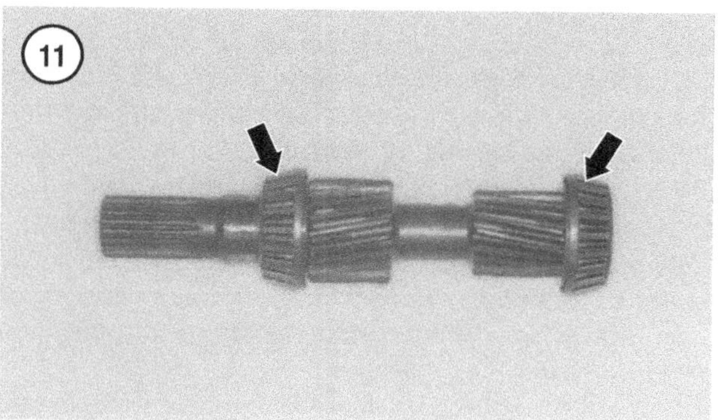

threaded holes in the flange and rotate the jackscrews to force the flange off the transmission case. Position the transmission with the input shaft up, then remove the flange from the transmission case.

9. Remove the output shaft (A, **Figure 9**) assembly from the transmission case and set aside for disassembly.

10. The input shaft (B, **Figure 9**) and intermediate shaft (C) assemblies must be removed together. Proceed as follows:

   a. Insert a suitably sized bolt or rod through the hole in the rear of the transmission that supports the intermediate shaft (**Figure 10**).

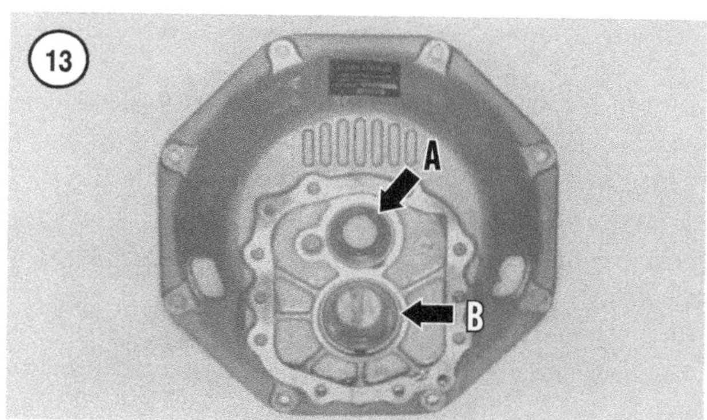

   b. Carefully drive out the intermediate shaft while removing the intermediate and input shaft assemblies from the transmission case.

11. Using a large screwdriver, pry out the oil seal in the transmission case. Be careful not to damage the case or the adjacent bearing race.

12. Using a large screwdriver, pry out the oil seal in the transmission mounting flange. Be careful not to damage the case or the adjacent bearing race.

13. If inspection indicates additional disassembly is necessary, refer to the following sections.

Inspection

Input shaft

1. Check the gear teeth for excessive wear, corrosion and mechanical damage. Check the teeth for galling, chips, cracks, missing pieces, distortion or discoloration from overheating. Replace the input shaft if the gears are damaged.

2. Inspect the input shaft bearings (**Figure 11**) and seal surfaces for excessive wear, grooves, metal transfer and discoloration from overheating. Use a press to remove damaged bearings and to install new bearings.

NOTE

Shims behind the outer bearing race in the mounting flange determine bearing preload for the input shaft bearings. Save the shims and reinstall them if reusing the original parts.

3. Inspect the input shaft bearing outer races in the transmission case (A, **Figure 12**) and mounting flange (A, **Figure 13**). If either race is damaged or excessively worn, remove it using a suitable puller.

Intermediate shaft

1. Remove and discard the O-ring (**Figure 14**) at the end of the shaft.
2. Remove the thrust washer, gear and roller bearings.
3. Inspect the bearings, shaft and reverse idler gear inside diameter for excessive wear, grooves, metal transfer and discoloration from overheating. If necessary, replace the shaft, gear and bearings.
4. Check the idler gear teeth for excessive wear, corrosion or rust and mechanical damage. Check the teeth for galling, chips, cracks, missing pieces, distortion or discoloration from overheating. If necessary, replace the gear.
5. Reassemble the intermediate shaft. Install a new O-ring on the shaft.

Output shaft

Refer to **Figure 15**.

1. Using a suitable puller (**Figure 16**), remove the bearing, spacer and reverse gear from the output shaft.
2. The retaining nut at the end of the shaft is staked. Use a chisel to cut away the staked portion so the nut will rotate. To hold the output shaft, position the coupling flange in a vise, then set the output shaft into the splines in the flange as shown in **Figure 17**.

NOTE
The retaining nut has left-hand threads.

3. Unscrew the retaining nut by rotating the nut clockwise (left-hand threads).
4. Using a suitable puller, pull the bearing, spacer and forward gear off the output shaft.
5. Remove the pin from the shaft.

NOTE
Mark the clutch cone in Step 6 according to forward or reverse end so it can be reinstalled in its original position.

6. While holding the clutch cone, tap the end of the shaft with a soft-faced hammer to remove the inner roller bearing race, spacer and cone clutch. A suitable puller or press may also be used. Remove the remaining inner bearing race and spacer.
7. Check the forward and reverse gear teeth for excessive wear, corrosion and mechanical damage. Check the teeth for galling, chips, cracks, missing pieces, distortion or discoloration from overheating. If necessary, replace the gears.

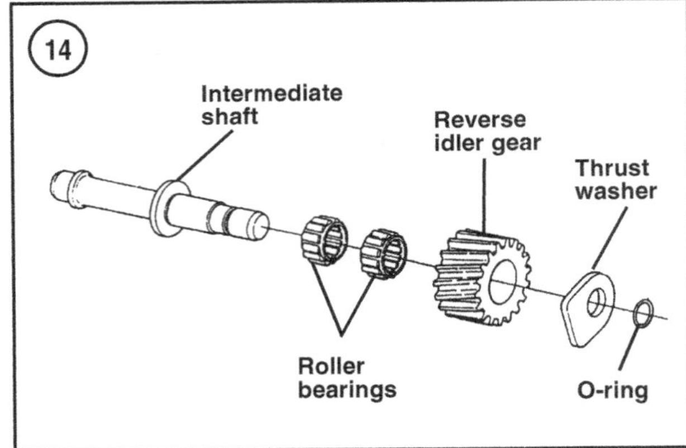

8. Inspect the forward and reverse gear inside diameters for excessive wear, grooves, metal transfer and discoloration from overheating. If necessary, replace the gears.
9. Install the cone clutch on the output shaft and check movement of the clutch on the output shaft. If the clutch does not move smoothly, inspect the splines on the clutch and shaft for burrs, scoring, galling or other signs of damage. If dressing will not correct the damaged splines, replace the clutch and/or shaft.
10. Inspect the tapered surface of the forward and reverse gears for galling, scoring or other damage that will prevent smooth cone clutch engagement. If necessary, replace the gears.
11. Install the cone clutch into the forward and reverse gears. Measure clutch depth as shown in **Figure 18**. Compare the measurement with the specification in **Table 3**. Replace the part, in necessary.
12. Measure the width of the shifter groove in the cone clutch (**Figure 19**) and compare with the specification in **Table 4**.
13. Inspect the roller bearings and inner bearing races for excessive wear, grooves, metal transfer and discoloration from overheating. If necessary, replace the bearings and inner races.
14. Measure the wear surface of the thrust washers. If wear exceeds 0.20 mm (0.008 in.) on the thin thrust washer, replace the washer. If wear exceeds 0.05 mm (0.002 in.) on the thick thrust washer, replace the washer.
15. On KM2P and KM3P transmissions—Measure the width of the spring cups and compare them with the specifications in **Table 5**.
16. On KM2P and KM3P transmissions—Measure the width of the spring cup retainers and compare them with the specifications in **Table 5**. If any surface wear on the retainer exceeds 0.10 mm (0.004 in.), replace the retainer.
17. Assemble the output shaft by reversing the disassembly procedure while noting the following:

(15)

OUTPUT SHAFT

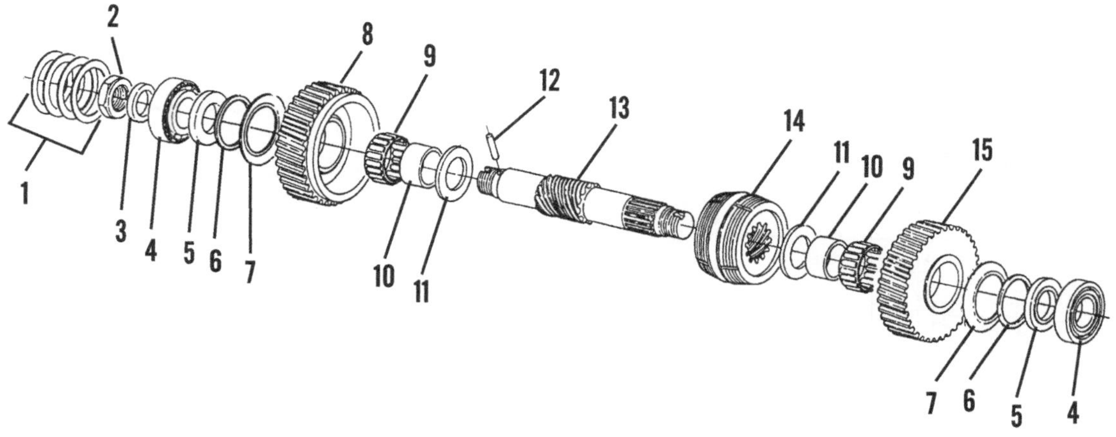

1. Shims
2. Nut (LH)
3. Washer
4. Roller bearing
5. Thrust washer
6. Retainer (KM2P and KM3P)
7. Spring cup (KM2P and KM3P)
8. Forward gear
9. Needle bearing
10. Inner bearing race
11. Thrust washer
12. Pin
13. Output shaft
14. Clutch cone
15. Reverse gear

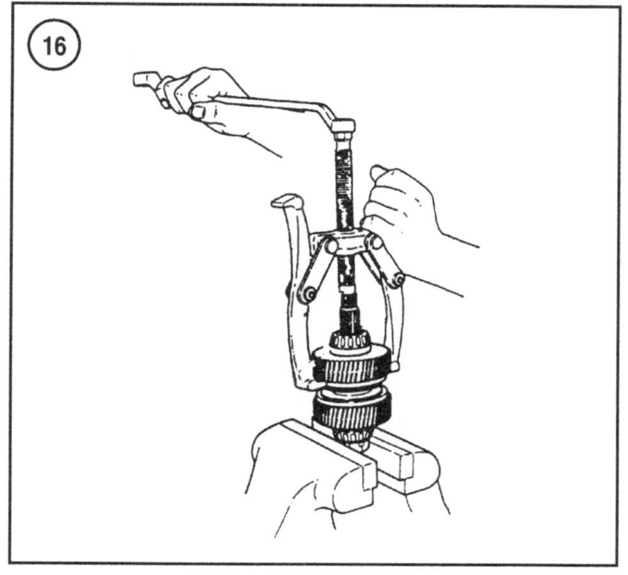

(16)

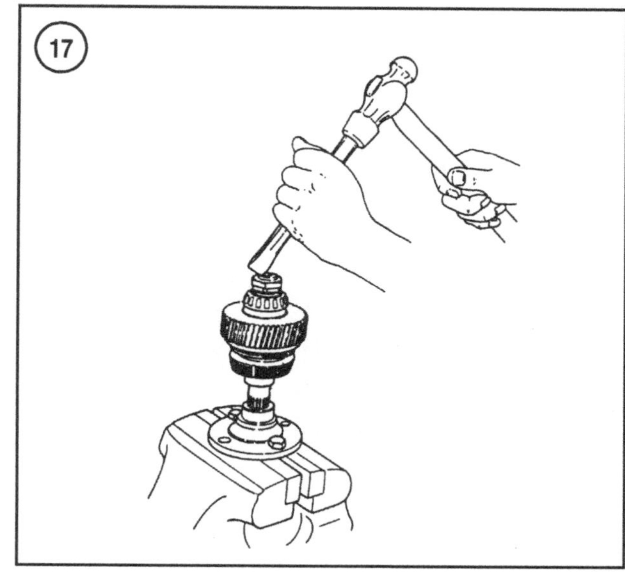

(17)

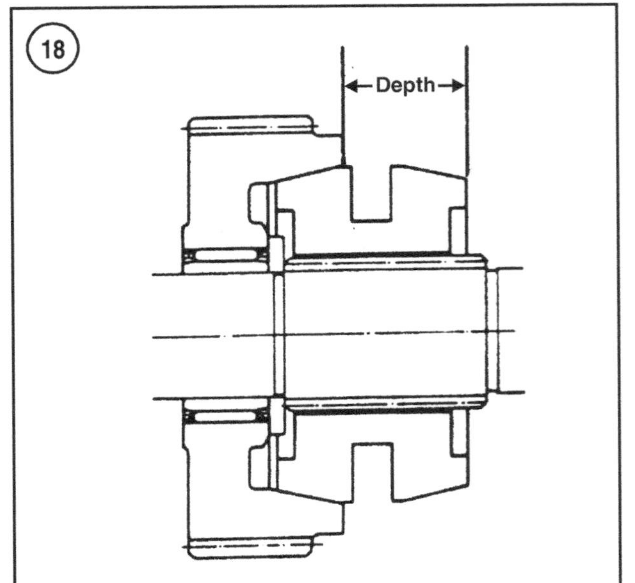

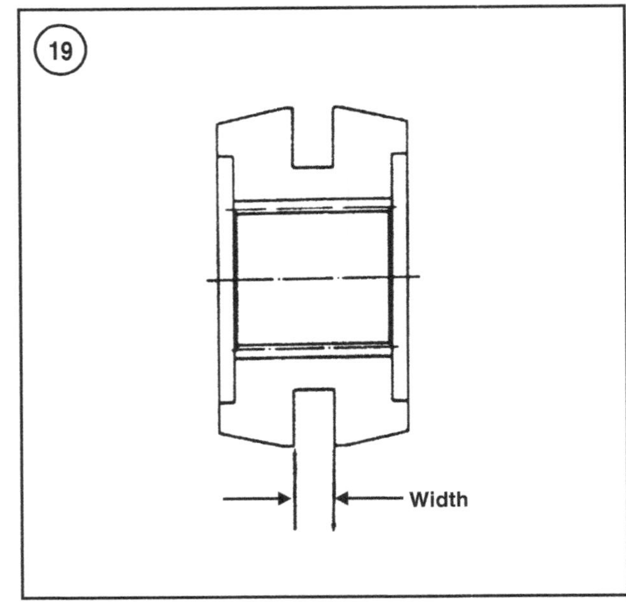

20

SHIFTER (KM2A, KM2C AND KM3A MODELS)

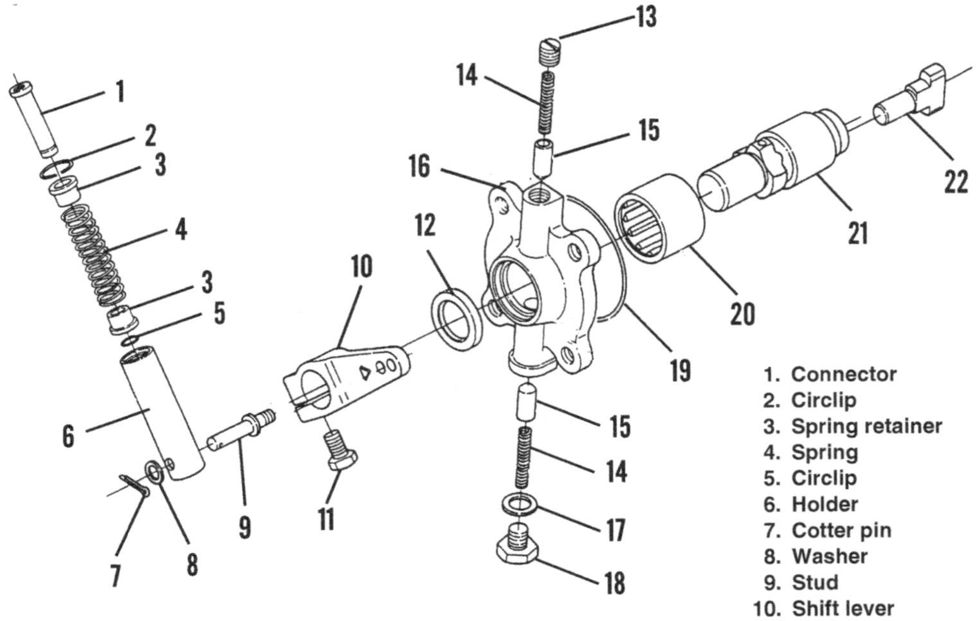

1. Connector
2. Circlip
3. Spring retainer
4. Spring
5. Circlip
6. Holder
7. Cotter pin
8. Washer
9. Stud
10. Shift lever
11. Bolt
12. Seal
13. Setscrew
14. Spring
15. Detent pin
16. Body
17. Gasket
18. Plug
19. O-ring
20. Bearing
21. Shift shaft
22. Shifter

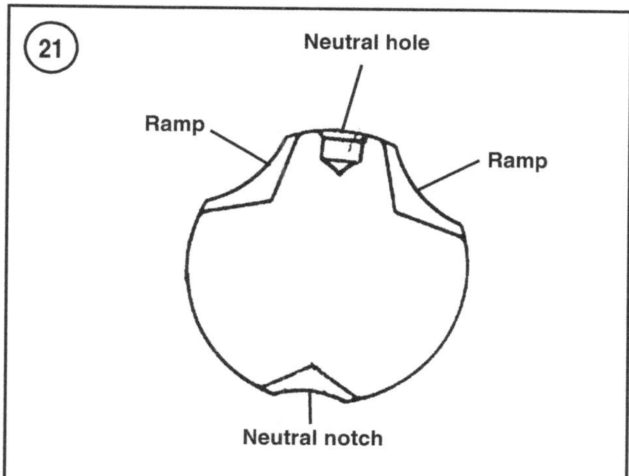

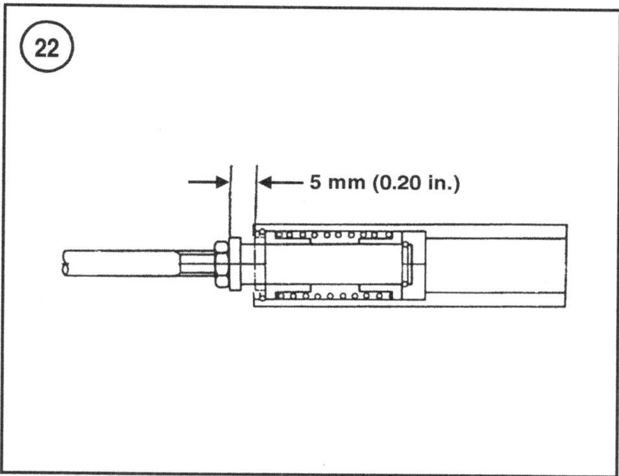

a. If reinstalling the original clutch cone, install it in its original position—forward end toward the forward gear.
b. Install the pin before installing the inner roller bearing race.
c. Use a suitable tool or sleeve to drive the inner roller bearing race onto the shaft. Do not use excessive force. Drive the race onto the shaft until it bottoms.
d. Use a suitable tool or sleeve to drive the tapered roller bearing onto the shaft. Do not use excessive force. Drive the bearing onto the shaft until it bottoms.
e. On KM2P and KM3P transmissions—Install the spring cups so the cupped side is toward the gear.
f. Install each thick thrust washer so the stepped side is toward the tapered roller bearing.
g. Install the washer so the pin in the output shaft fits in the groove in the washer.
h. Tighten the nut (left-hand threads) to the torque specified in **Table 2**.
i. Make sure the gears rotate freely.
j. Stake the nut to lock the nut in place.

Shifter (KM2A, KM2C and KM3A models)

Refer to **Figure 20**.

1. If not previously removed, detach the cotter pin and remove the actuator from the shift lever.
2. Remove the shifter.

NOTE
Make alignment marks on the shift lever and shift shaft so the shift lever can be reinstalled in its original position.

3. Loosen the clamp bolt and remove the shift lever.

NOTE
The setscrew and plug contain the springs and may fly out.

4. Remove the setscrew and plug, then remove the springs and detent pins.
5. Remove the shifter shaft.
6. Remove and discard the O-ring.
7. Use a screwdriver or suitable tool to pry out the seal. Be careful not to damage the bearing.
8. Inspect the bearing. If it is faulty, replace it as follows:
   a. Heat the shifter body to 212° F (100° C), then drive out the bearing.
   b. Install the new bearing with the stamped end out. Push in the bearing until it bottoms.
9. Inspect the shift shaft. Check the detent portion of the shaft for cracks or excessive wear that will allow poor clutch engagement. The ramps should be smooth and the neutral detent hole should be unworn (**Figure 21**).
10. Inspect the detent pins. Replace the pins if they are damaged or excessively worn.
11. Inspect the springs for deformation or other damage. Specified spring free length is 34 mm (1.34 in.).
12. Inspect the shifter for damage and excessive wear. Measure the shifter width and shaft diameter. Replace the shifter if the measurements exceed the specifications in **Table 6**.
13. Check the internal movement of the actuator. The actuator should slide without binding. To check spring tension, attach a spring scale to the threaded end of the actuator and measure the spring tension when the actuator rod is pulled 5 mm (0.20 in.) from the end of the tube (**Figure 22**). If the spring tension is not as specified in **Table 6**, replace the spring.

14. Reassemble the shifter by reversing the disassembly procedure. Note the following during reassembly:
   a. Apply sealant to the detent setscrew threads.
   b. Install the shift lever on the shift shaft while aligning the marks made during disassembly.
   c. If no alignment marks are available when installing the shift lever, rotate the shift shaft so the shifter bore is down as shown in **Figure 23**. The shift shaft should engage the neutral detent. Install the shift lever at a 45° angle as shown in **Figure 23**.
   d. Install the shift lever on the shift shaft so the side clearance between the lever and body is approximately 0.5 mm (0.020 in.).

Shifter (KM2P and KM3P models)

Refer to **Figure 24**.

1. If not previously removed, remove the control cable connector from the shift lever.
2. Remove the shifter and spring.
3. Remove the stop bolt and shims.
4. Loosen the clamp bolt and remove the shift lever.
5. Remove the shifter shaft.
6. Remove and discard the O-ring.
7. Use a screwdriver or suitable tool to pry out the seal. Be careful not to damage the bearing.
8. Inspect the shift shaft. Check the detent pin for damage and excessive wear. If necessary, replace the detent pin. Measure the shifter shaft bore in the shift shaft and compare with the specifications in **Table 7**.
9. Inspect the body for galling, scoring or other damage to the bore. Inspect the detents for damage and excessive wear that will cause poor clutch engagement (**Figure 25**).
10. Inspect the spring for deformation or other damage. Specified spring free length is 22.6 mm (0.89 in.). Minimum spring length is 19.8 mm (0.78 in.).
11. Inspect the stop bolt. Replace it if it is excessively worn.
12. Inspect the shifter. Measure the large diameter of the shifter shaft and compare it with the specifications in **Table 7**.
13. Reassemble the shifter by reversing the disassembly procedure, but do not install the stop bolt until final installation of the shifter assembly on the transmission.
14. Reassemble the shifter by reversing the disassembly procedure. Note the following during reassembly:
   a. Do not install the stop bolt until final installation of the shifter assembly on the transmission.
   b. Rotate the shift shaft so the detent pin engages the neutral detent (**Figure 25**). On the KM2P transmission, install the shift lever so the side with the triangle mark (A, **Figure 26**) is out. On the KM3P transmission, install the shift lever so the side with the triangle mark is toward the shifter body. With the shift shaft in neutral, position the shift lever at a 45° angle as shown in **Figure 26** and tighten the clamp bolt.

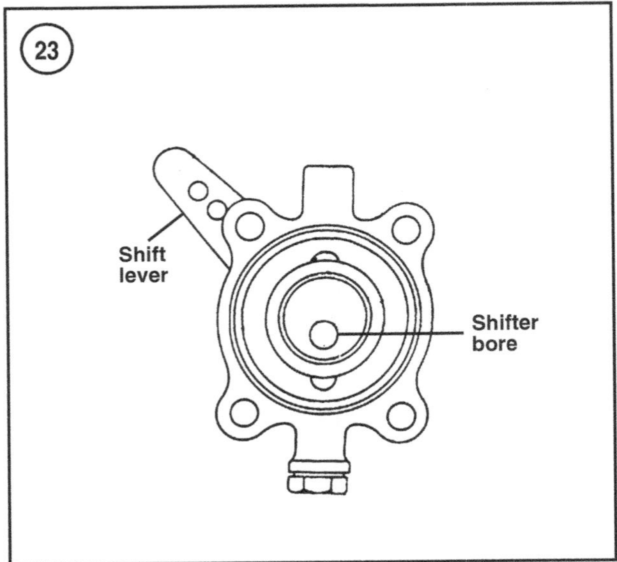

REASSEMBLY

NOTE

On KM2P and KM3P transmissions, refer to the ***Bearing Adjustment*** *section prior to reassembly if the following components have been replaced: input shaft, input shaft bearings, output shaft, thrust washers and output shaft bearings.*

1. If removed, install the outer bearing races into the transmission case and mounting flange.
2. Apply sealer to the outside diameter of the oil seals and install them into the transmission case and mounting flange with the open side to the inside.
3. Install the input shaft into the transmission case.
4. Install the intermediate shaft assembly into the transmission case. Install a new O-ring on the intermediate shaft. Use a soft-faced hammer to tap the shaft into the case.
5. While holding the input shaft out of the way, insert the output shaft assembly into the transmission case. Move the gears into mesh on the intermediate shaft, input shaft and output shaft while installing the output shaft.
6. If the following components have been replaced, refer to the *Bearing Adjustment* section: input shaft, input shaft bearings, output shaft, thrust washers and output shaft

24

SHIFTER (KM2P AND KM3P MODELS)

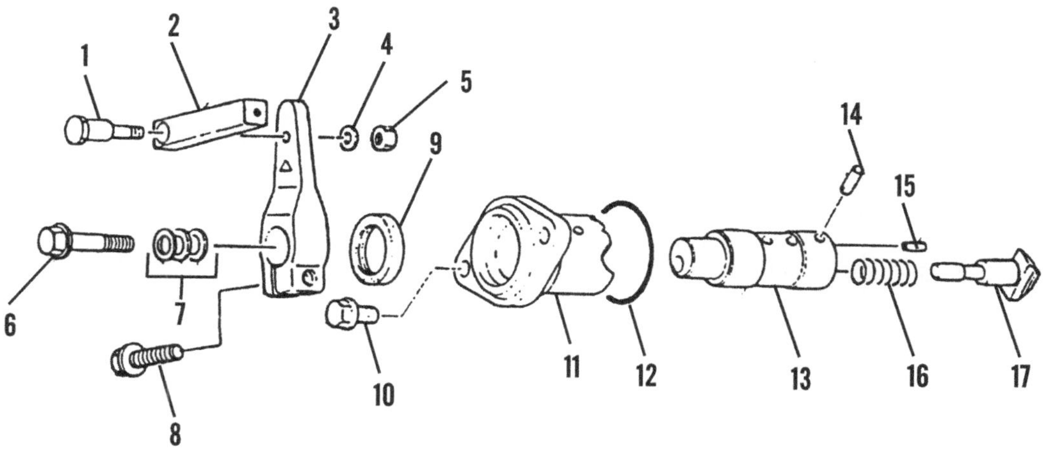

1. Shoulder bolt
2. Connector
3. Shift lever
4. Washer
5. Nut
6. Stop bolt
7. Shims
8. Bolt
9. Seal
10. Bolt
11. Shift body
12. O-ring
13. Shift shaft
14. Detent pin
15. Pin
16. Spring
17. Shifter

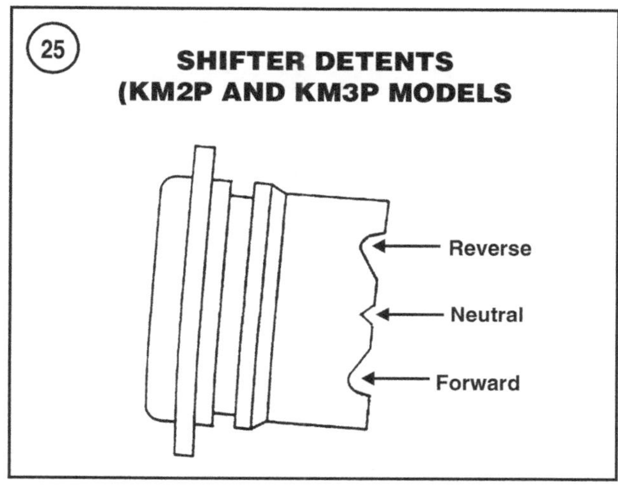

25

SHIFTER DETENTS (KM2P AND KM3P MODELS

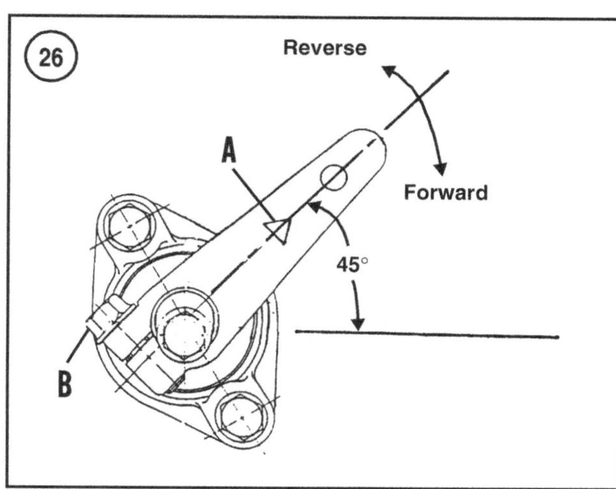

26

bearings. After adjusting the bearings, continue to reassemble the transmission as described in the following steps. If the preceding components have not been replaced, bearing adjustment is not necessary and the orginal shims may be reused. Proceed to the following step.

7. Position the transmission on a vise with soft jaws so the input shaft is held by the vise jaws.

8. Apply sealer to the mounting flange and install it onto the transmission case.

9. Tighten the mounting flange retaining bolts to the torque in **Table 2**.

10. Install the output flange on the output shaft.

11. Install the O-ring on the output shaft.

NOTE
The output flange retaining nut has left-hand threads.

12. Install the output flange retaining nut by rotating the nut counterclockwise (left-hand threads). Tighten the nut to the torque specified in **Table 2**.

13. Stake the nut to lock the nut in place.

14A. On KM2A, KM2C and KM3A transmissions—Install the shifter assembly on the transmission using the following procedure:

NOTE
Note that the bolt holes in the shifter mounting flange are sufficiently large to allow movement of the flange around the bolts.

a. Install the shifter assembly on the transmission and tighten the retaining bolts.
b. Measure the amount of shift lever travel from neutral to forward and from neutral to reverse (**Figure 27**). The measurement should be equal from neutral to either forward or reverse.
c. Loosen the shifter retaining bolts and slide the shifter assembly fore or aft as needed to obtain equal shift lever movement.

14B. On KM2P and KM3P—Install the shifter assembly on the transmission using the following procedure.

a. Position the shifter so its curvature is as shown in **Figure 28**.
b. Install the shifter assembly on the transmission and tighten the retaining bolts.
c. Move the shift lever 10-15° from the neutral position to either forward or reverse position.
d. Measure the depth of the end of the shifter shaft from the end of the shift shaft as shown in **Figure 28**. Measure the length of the stop bolt (**Figure 29**).

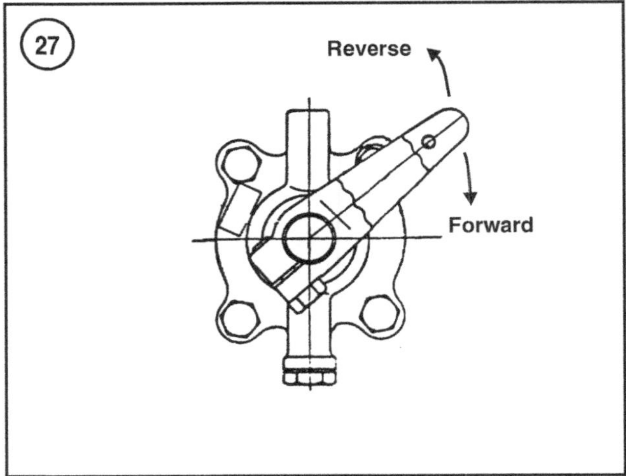

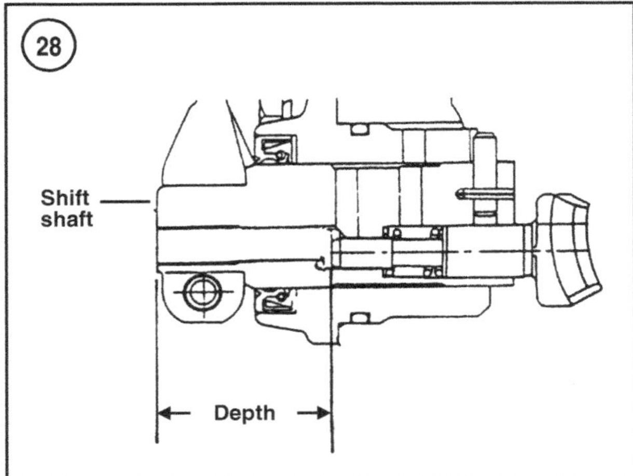

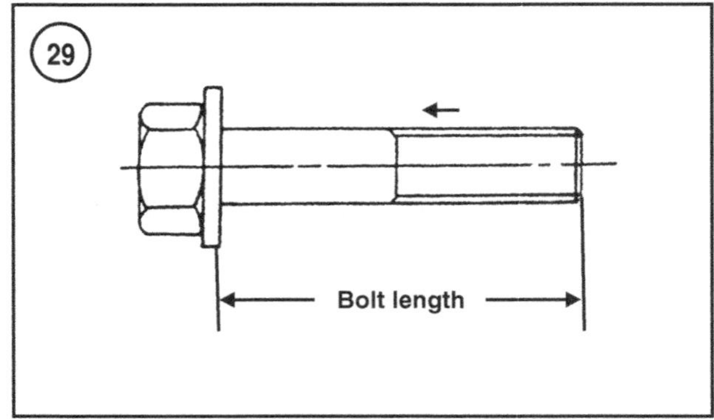

e. Subtract the length of the stop bolt from the shifter shaft depth.
f. Install shims on the stop bolt that equal the result of substep e.

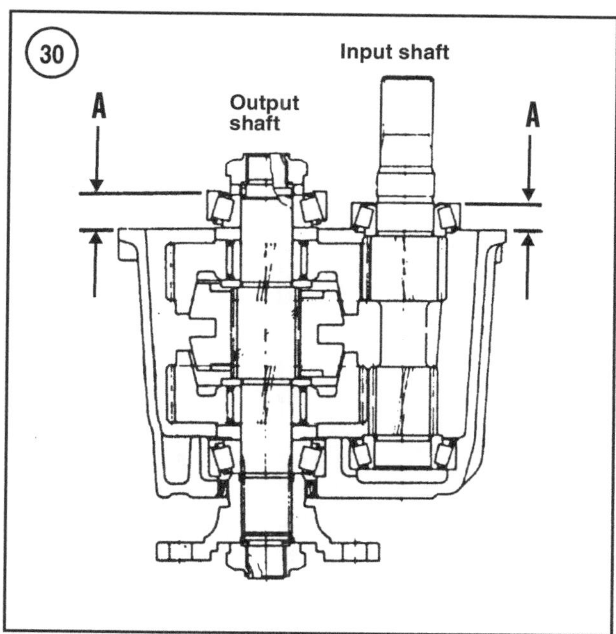

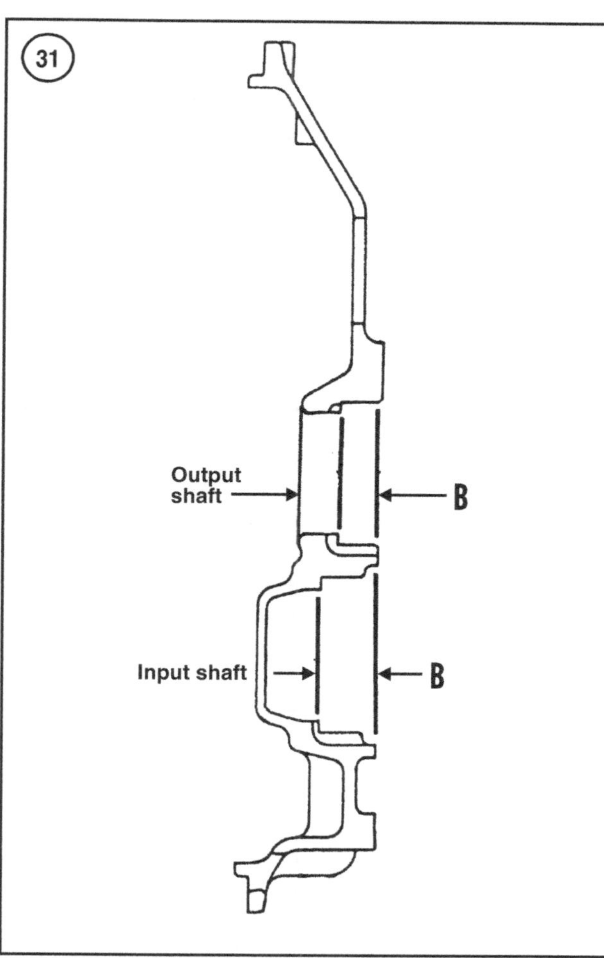

g. Apply sealer to the stop bolt threads, but not to the threads at the end of the bolt (approximately 0.20 in.). Install the stop bolt into the shifter.

BEARING ADJUSTMENT

Perform the following procedure if the following components have been replaced: input shaft, input shaft bearings, output shaft, thrust washers and output shaft bearings. This procedure determines the thickness of shims that must be installed so the tapered roller bearings properly contact the bearing outer races.

KM2A, KM2C and KM3A

1. Install the input shaft, intermediate shaft and output shafts as described in the *Reassembly* section.
2. Position the transmission case so the open end is up and no pressure is being applied to the splined end of the output shaft.
3. Install the outer bearing races on the input and output shaft tapered bearings.
4. Measure the distance (A, **Figure 30**) in millimeters from the mounting flange mating surface on the case to the top of each bearing race. Record the measurements.
5. Measure the distance (B, **Figure 31**) from the mounting flange mating surface to the bottom of the bearing race bore for both the input and output shaft bearings.
6. Subtract the A measurement from the B measurement for each shaft.
7. From the result obtained in Step 6, subtract 0.0-0.05 mm. This result equals the thickness of the shim(s) that must be installed in the bearing bores in the mounting flange.
8. Install the shim(s) in the bearing bores in the mounting flange, then press the bearing outer races into the mounting flange on top of the shims. Make sure the races are bottomed.

KM2P and KM3P

Input shaft

NOTE

*The following procedure for adjusting the input shaft bearings is similar to the procedure for the KM2A, KM2C KM3A transmissions, but only use the callouts in **Figure 30** and **Figure 31** that pertain to the input shaft.*

10

1. Install the input shaft assembly in the transmission case.
2. Position the transmission case so the open end is up.
3. Install the outer bearing race on the input shaft tapered bearing.
4. Measure the distance (A, **Figure 30**) in millimeters from the mounting flange mating surface on the case to the top of the bearing race. Record the measurement.
5. Measure the distance (B, **Figure 31**) from the mounting flange mating surface to the bottom of the bearing race bore for the input shaft bearing.
6. Subtract the A measurement from the B measurement.
7. From the result obtained in Step 6, subtract 0.0-0.05 mm. This result equals the thickness of the shim(s) that must be installed in the bearing bore in the mounting flange.
8. Install the shim(s) in the bearing bore in the mounting flange, then press the bearing outer race into the mounting flange on top of the shims. Be sure the race is bottomed.

Output Shaft

In the following procedure to adjust bearing preload, the neutral position of the clutch cone must be established for proper transmission operation. The desired clutch cone groove centerline on Model KM2P is 48.3 mm from the mating surface of the transmission case. On Model KM3P the desired clutch groove centerline is 47.3 mm from the mating surface of the transmission case.

NOTE
To perform the following bearing adjustment procedure, the output shaft must be out of the case and the outer bearing races must be on the bearings and not installed in the case or mounting flange.

1. Measure and record the distance (A, **Figure 32**) from the mounting flange mating surface to the bottom of the bearing race bore for the output shaft bearing.
2. Measure and record the distance (B, **Figure 33**) from the mounting surface of the case to the bottom of the bearing race bore for the output shaft bearing.
3. Measure and record the distance (C, **Figure 34**) from the faces of the output shaft bearing races.

NOTE
In Steps 4 and 5, force the gears toward the cone clutch.

4. Measure and record the distance (D, **Figure 34**) between the faces of the forward and reverse gears.

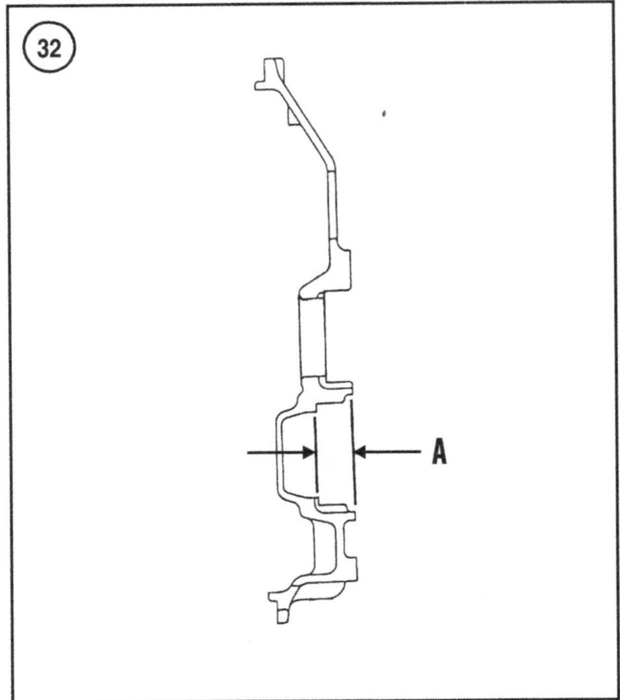

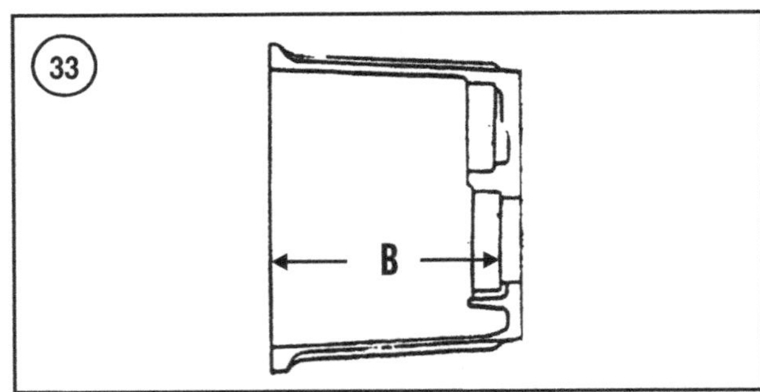

5. Measure and record the distance (E, **Figure 34**) from the face of the reverse gear and the face of the rear bearing race.

6A. On KM2P transmissions—To determine rear shim thickness (**Figure 35**), proceed as follows:

a. Subtract 48.3 mm from measurement (B, **Figure 33**).
b. Divide measurement (D, **Figure 34**) by 2.
c. Subtract substep b from substep a.
d. Subtract measurement (E, **Figure 34**) from substep c.
e. Subtract 0.0-0.05 mm from substep d. The result is the required rear shim thickness.

6B. On KM3P transmissions—To determine rear shim thickness (**Figure 35**), proceed as follows:

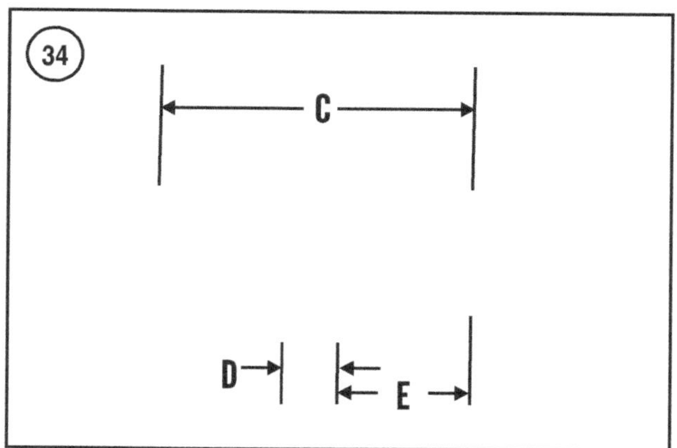

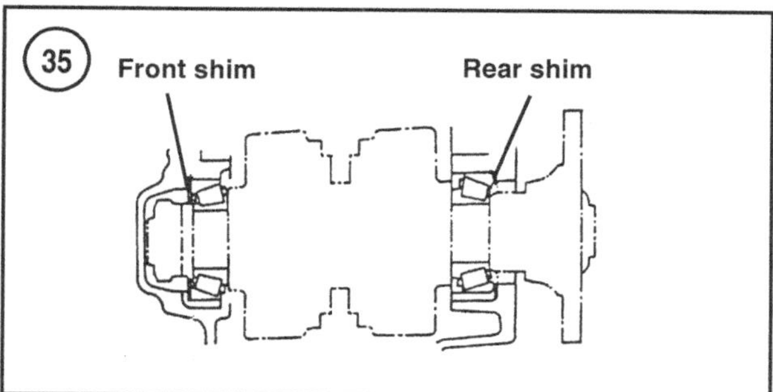

a. Subtract 47.3 mm from measurement (B, **Figure 33**).
b. Divide measurement (D, **Figure 34**) by 2.
c. Subtract substep b from substep a.
d. Subtract measurement (E, **Figure 34**) from substep c.
e. Subtract 0.0-0.05 mm from substep d. The result is the required rear shim thickness.

7. To determine front shim thickness (**Figure 35**), proceed as follows:
a. Add measurement (A, **Figure 32**) to measurement (B, **Figure 33**).

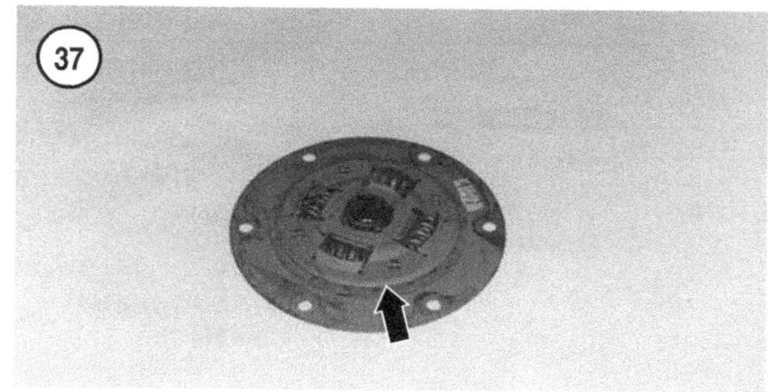

b. Subtract measurement (C, **Figure 34**) from substep a.
c. Subtract the rear shim thickness (determined in Step 6A) from Step b.
d. Subtract 0.0-0.05 mm from substep c. The result is the required front shim thickness.

8. Install the shim(s) in the bearing bores in the mounting flange and case, then press the bearing outer races on top of the shims. Make sure the races are bottomed.

DRIVE DISC

The drive disc attached to the engine flywheel transmits power from the engine flywheel to the transmission input shaft. Bolts secure the disc to the flywheel while the transmission input shaft engages the splined hub on the drive disc. The drive disc incorporates springs that dampen driveline shocks between the engine and transmission.

Removal/Installation

1. Remove the engine from the boat.
2. Remove the transmission.
3. Remove the drive disc (**Figure 36,** typical**).**
4. Install the drive disc by reversing the removal procedure. Install the drive disc so the side marked FLYWHEEL SIDE (**Figure 37**) is toward the flywheel. Tighten the drive disc retaining bolts to the torque specified in **Table 2**.

Inspection

Replace the drive disc if any of the following conditions exist:

1. Broken spring.
2. Worn or damaged splines in hub.
3. Damaged disc.
4. Damaged pins.

Table 1 ENGINE/TRANSMISSION MODELS

Model	Transmission	Transmission ratio (forward gear)
1GM	KM2A	2.21, 2.62 or 3.22
1GM10	KM2C or KM2P	2.21, 2.62 or 3.22
2GM	KM2A	2.21, 2.62 or 3.22
2GMF	KM2A	2.21, 2.62 or 3.22
2GM20	KM2C or KM2P	2.21, 2.62 or 3.22
2GM20F	KM2C or KM2P	2.21, 2.62 or 3.22
3GM	KBW10D	2.14, 2.63 or 2.83
3GMF	KBW10D	2.14, 2.63 or 2.83
3GMD	KM3A	2.36, 2.61 or 3.20
3GM30	KM3A or KM3P	2.36, 2.61 or 3.20
3GM30F	KM3A or KM3P	2.36, 2.61 or 3.20
3HM	KBW10E	2.14 or 2.83
3HMF	KBW10E	2.14 or 2.83
3HM35	KBW10E	2.14 or 2.83

Table 2 TIGHTENING TORQUES

Fastener	N•m	ft.-lb.
Transmission mounting flange	20-25	15-18
Output shaft nut	85-115	63-85
Output flange nut	85-115	63-85
Drive disc	25	18

Table 3 CLUTCH DEPTH

	Normal depth	Wear limit
KM2A, KM2C	24.4-24.7 mm (0.961-0.972 in.)	24.1 mm (0.949 in.)
KM2P	29.2-29.8 mm (1.150-1.173 in.)	28.1 mm (1.106 in.)
KM3A	29.9-30.2 mm (1.177-1.189 in.)	29.6 mm (1.165 in.)
KM3P	32.7-33.3 mm (1.287-1.311 in.)	32.4 mm (1.276 in.)

Table 4 CLUTCH GROOVE WIDTH

	Standard width	Wear limit
KM2A, KM2C and KM3A	8.0-8.1 mm (0.315-0.319 in.)	8.3 mm (0.327 in.)

Table 5 OUTPUT SHAFT

	Standard width	Wear limit
Thrust washer		
Thin washer	–	0.20 mm (0.008 in.)
Thick washer	–	0.05 mm (0.002 in.)

(continued)

Table 5 OUTPUT SHAFT (continued)

Spring cup (KM2P, KM3P)	2.8-3.1 mm (0.110-0.122 in.)	2.6 mm (0.102 in.)
Spring cup retainer (KM2P, KM3P)	2.92-3.08 mm (0.115-0.121 in.)	2.8 mm (0.110 in.)

Table 6 SHIFTER (KM2A, KM2C AND KM3A)

Shifter width	
Standard	7.80-7.85 mm (0.3071-0.3091 in.)
Wear limit	7.7 mm (0.303 in.)
Shifter shaft diameter	
Standard	9.986-9.995 mm (0.3931-0.3935 in.)
Wear limit	9.95 mm (0.392 in.)
Detent spring free length	34 mm (1.34 in.).
Actuator spring tension	
Standard	2.8 kg (6.2 lb.)
Min.	2.5 kg (5.5 lb.)

Table 7 SHIFTER (KM2P AND KM3P)

Shifter spring free length	
Standard	22.6 mm (0.89 in.)
Min.	19.8 mm (0.78 in.).
Shifter shaft diameter	
Standard	11.966-11.984 mm (0.4711-0.4718 in.)
Wear limit	11.95 mm (0.470 in.)
Shift shaft bore	
Standard	12.0-12.018 mm (0.4724-0.4731 in.)
Wear limit	12.05 mm (0.474 in.)

Chapter Eleven

Transmission—KBW Series

This chapter covers the Kanzaki Hurth KBW10D and KBW10E marine transmissions that are attached to Yanmar 3GM, 3HM and 3HM35 engines. Refer to **Table 1** for a cross-reference of engine and transmission models. The identification plate (**Figure 1**) located on the transmission case specifies the transmission model.

The KBW10 series transmissions covered in this chapter are inline transmissions that provide forward and reverse direction. All gears are constant mesh. A plate-type clutch engages the gears to transmit power to the output shaft. Oil contained in the transmission case lubricates the internal transmission components.

Refer to Chapter Three for maintenance information.

Tables 1-3 are located at the end of this chapter.

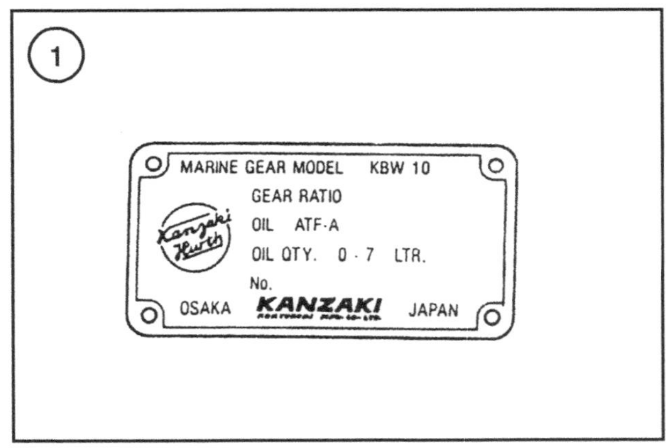

OPERATION

The input shaft on the transmission engages the drive disc attached to the engine flywheel. Because this is a constant-mesh transmission, engine power is transmitted to all gears. Power flows to the output shaft when the clutch engages either the forward gear or the reverse gear. The clutch contacts a clutch pack of several discs adjacent to the forward and reverse gears. In **Figure 2**, the clutch is shown engaged with the forward gear. Because power flows from the input shaft gear through the reverse idler gear to the reverse gear, the reverse gear rotates in the opposite direction of the forward gear. When the clutch engages the reverse gear, the output shaft rotates in reverse.

Moving the shift lever rotates the shift shaft. When the shift shaft rotates, the shifter fork slides the shift ring into engagement with the forward or reverse gear clutch. The drive hub on the output shaft transfers power from the selected clutch to the output shaft.

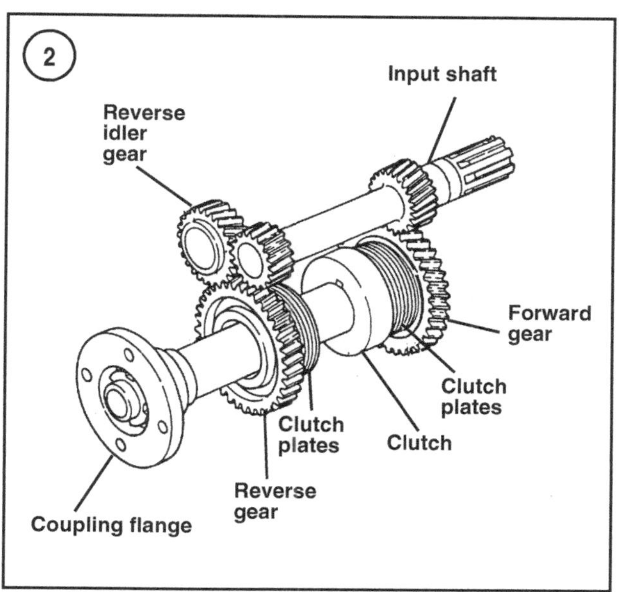

REMOVAL/INSTALLATION

The following procedure addresses units that are accessible. In some cases, it may be necessary to remove the engine and transmission as a unit before removing the transmission from the engine. Refer to Chapter Six if engine removal is necessary.

1. If not previously disconnected, disconnect the remote control cable from the transmission shift lever.
2. If not previously disconnected, disconnect the drive coupling from the transmission drive flange.
3. Remove the bolts that secure the transmission to the engine bellhousing.
4. Remove the transmission from the engine.
5. Reinstall the transmission by reversing the removal procedure. Make sure to align the splines on the transmission input shaft and the drive disc during installation. Tighten the transmission retaining bolts to the torque specified in **Table 2**.

OVERHAUL

Refer to **Figure 3**.

NOTE
Overhaul of the KBW transmission requires special tools, which can be obtained from Yanmar or fabricated. If the special tools are not available, have a Yanmar dealership overhaul the transmission.

Disassembly

1. Remove the drain plug and drain the transmission oil.
2. Position the transmission in a vise with soft jaws so the input shaft is held by the vise jaws.
3. The output flange retaining nut is staked. Use a chisel to cut away the staked portion so the nut will rotate.
4. Install a tool that will prevent rotation of the output flange.
5. Unscrew the output flange retaining nut.
6. Remove the oil dipstick.
7. Make match marks on the shifter cover and the transmission case so the shifter can be installed in its original position.
8. Remove the shifter retaining bolts and remove the shifter assembly.
9. Remove the transmission from the vise.
10. Using an 8 mm Allen wrench, remove the shift bar retaining plug (68, **Figure 3**) in the rear of the case.
11. Install a 10 mm bolt into the end of the shift bar, then pull the shift bar (58, **Figure 3**) out of the case while also removing the shift fork (57).
12. Remove the transmission mounting flange retaining bolts.

NOTE
In Step 13, position the transmission so the transmission input shaft is up when removing the mounting flange so the transmission shafts will not fall out.

13. Tap on the mounting flange using a soft-faced hammer to dislodge the flange. Position the transmission with the input shaft up, then remove the flange from the transmission case.
14. Remove the output shaft assembly from the transmission case and set aside for disassembly.
15. Remove the intermediate shaft assembly from the transmission case and set aside for disassembly.
16. Remove the input shaft assembly from the transmission case and set aside for disassembly.
17. Using a large screwdriver, pry out the oil seal in the transmission case. Be careful not to damage the case or the adjacent bearing race.
18. Using a large screwdriver, pry out the oil seal in the transmission mounting flange. Be careful not to damage the case or the adjacent bearing race.
19. If inspection indicates additional disassembly is necessary, refer to the following sections.

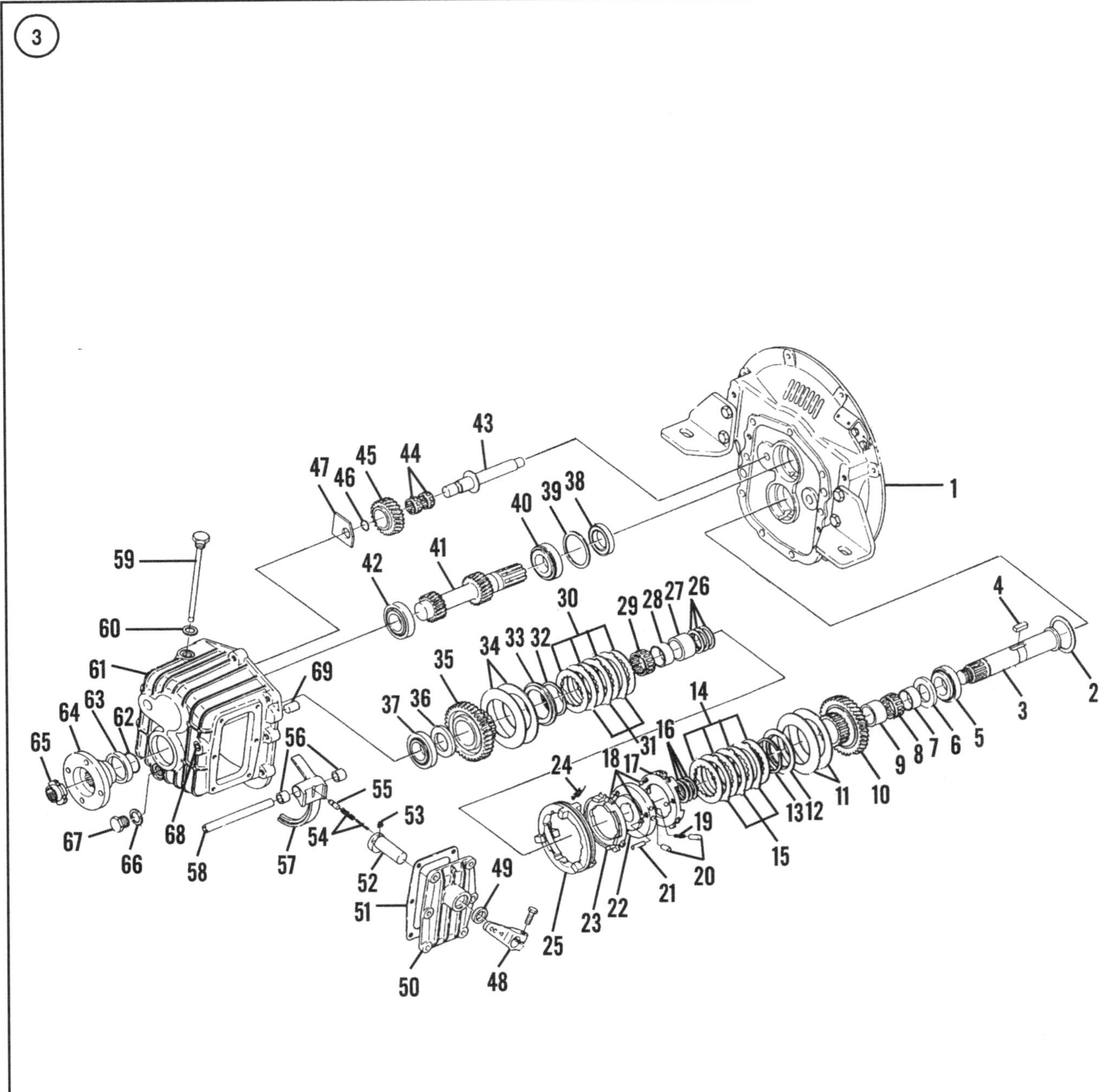
3
1
2
3
4
5
6
7
8
9
10
11
12
13
14
15
16
17
18
19
20
21
22
23
24
25
26
27
28
29
30
31
32
33
34
35
36
37
38
39
40
41
42
43
44
45
46
47
48
49
50
51
52
53
54
55
56
57
58
59
60
61
62
63
64
65
66
67
68
69

TRANSMISSION

1. Mounting flange
2. Shim
3. Output shaft
4. Key
5. Bearing
6. Thrust washer
7. Bearing inner race
8. Bearing
9. Spacer
10. Forward gear
11. Belleville springs
12. Retainer
13. Snap ring
14. Friction plates
15. Steel plates
16. Shims
17. Pressure plate
18. Balls (3)
19. Spring
20. Detent pins
21. Alignment pin
22. Driving plate
23. Pressure plate
24. Return spring
25. Shift ring
26. Shims
27. Spacer
28. Inner bearing race
29. Bearing
30. Friction plates
31. Steel plates
32. Snap ring
33. Retainer
34. Belleville washers
35. Reverse gear
36. Thrust washer
37. Bearing
38. Seal
39. Shim
40. Bearing
41. Input shaft
42. Bearing
43. Intermediate shaft
44. Roller bearings
45. Idle gear
46. O-ring
47. Thrust washer
48. Shift lever
49. Seal
50. Shifter cover
51. Gasket
52. Shift shaft
53. Snap ring
54. Springs
55. Detent pin
56. Bearings
57. Shift fork
58. Shift bar
59. Oil dipstick
60. Gasket
61. Case
62. O-ring
63. Seal
64. Flange
65. Nut
66. Gasket
67. Drain plug
68. Plug
69. Dowel pin

Input shaft

1. Check the gear teeth for excessive wear, corrosion or rust and mechanical damage. Check the teeth for galling, chips, cracks, missing pieces, distortion or discoloration from overheating. Replace the input shaft if the gears are damaged.
2. Inspect the input shaft bearings and seal surfaces for excessive wear, grooves, metal transfer and discoloration from overheating. Use a press to remove damaged bearings and to install new bearings.

NOTE
Shims (39, ***Figure 3****) behind the outer bearing race in the mounting flange determine bearing preload for the input shaft bearings. Save the shims and reinstall them if reusing the original parts.*

3. Inspect the input shaft bearing outer races in the transmission case and mounting flange. If either race is damaged or excessively worn, remove it using a suitable puller.

Intermediate shaft

1. Remove and discard the O-ring (46, **Figure 3**) at the end of the shaft.
2. Remove the thrust washer (47, **Figure 3**), idle gear (45) and roller bearings (44).
3. Inspect the bearings, shaft and reverse idler gear inside diameter for excessive wear, grooves, metal transfer and discoloration from overheating. If necessary, replace the shaft, gear and bearings.
4. Check the idler gear teeth for excessive wear, corrosion or rust and mechanical damage. Check the teeth for galling, chips, cracks, missing pieces, distortion or discoloration from overheating. If necessary, replace the gear.
5. Reassemble the intermediate shaft. Install a new O-ring on the shaft. Check that the idler rotates freely on the shaft.

Output shaft

NOTE
Exercise care when using the puller in Step 1. Make sure the threads on the output shaft are not damaged.

1. Using a suitable puller, remove the output shaft from the forward and reverse gear assemblies as shown in **Figure 4**. Do not mix the forward gear parts and reverse gear parts.

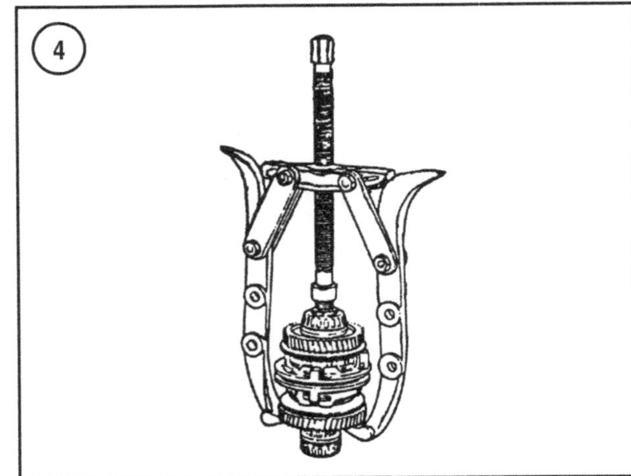

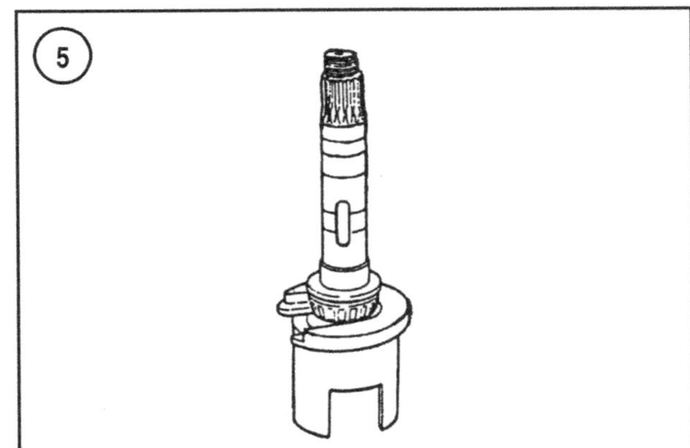

2. Remove the spacer (9, **Figure 3**) and the bearing inner race (7) from the output shaft.
3. Hold the threaded end of the output shaft so the threads are protected.
4. Place the outer race onto the front bearing inner race. Using a suitable bearing driver, gently drive the inner bearing race away from the shaft collar approximately 10 mm.
5. Place a pulling support plate (such as Yanmar special tool 17099-09030) between the collar of the output shaft and bearing.
6. Use Yanmar special tool 17095-09070, or a suitable equivalent tool, to press the bearing off the shaft, as shown in **Figure 5**.
7. Remove the clutch friction plates (14, **Figure 3**) and steel plates (15) from the forward gear (10).
8. Use Yanmar special tool 17095-09070, or an equivalent tool, to compress the Belleville springs (11, **Figure 3**) and remove the snap ring from the forward gear, as shown in **Figure 6**.

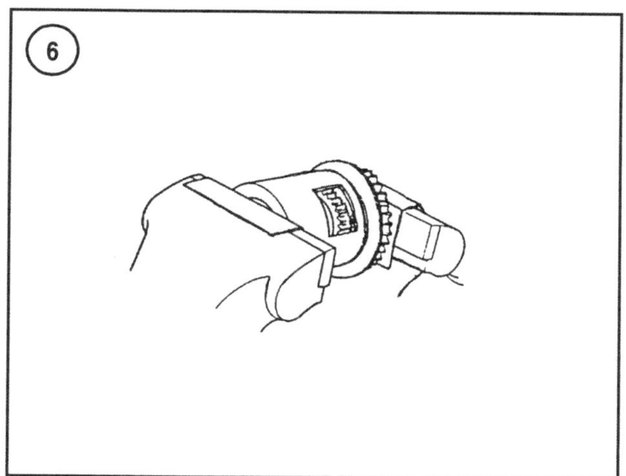

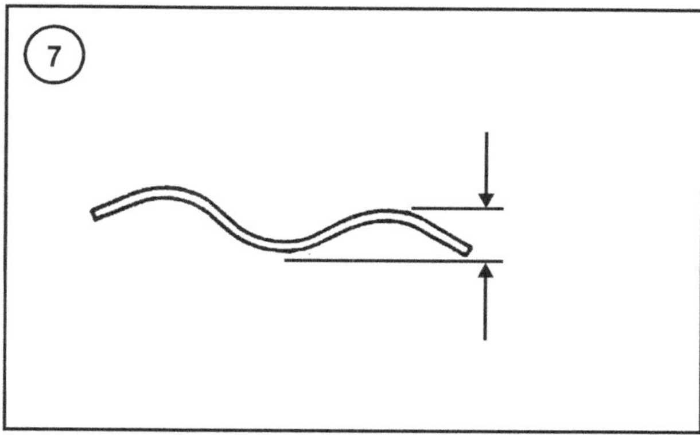

9. Refer to Steps 7 and 8 and disassemble the clutch components on the reverse gear.
10. Lay the shift ring and pressure plate assembly flat.
11. Remove the pressure plate return springs (24, **Figure 3**), then lift off the top pressure plate (17) and remove the steel balls (18).
12. Lift the shift ring (25, **Figure 3**) and driving plate (22) off the bottom pressure plate and remove the three remaining balls.
13. Slip the shift ring (25, **Figure 3**) off the driving plate (22).
14. Remove the alignment pins (21, **Figure 3**) and detent pins (20) with springs (19) from the driving plate (22).

Inspection

1. Check the gear teeth for excessive wear, corrosion or rust and mechanical damage. Check the teeth for galling, chips, cracks, missing pieces, distortion or discoloration from overheating. Check the splines for excessive wear or damage. Replace the gears if damaged.
2. Inspect the output shaft bearings and seal surfaces for excessive wear, grooving, metal transfer and discoloration from overheating.
3. Inspect the key and output shaft keyway for damage.

NOTE
Shims behind the outer bearing race in the mounting flange determine bearing preload for the output shaft bearings. Save the shims and reinstall them if reusing the original parts.

4. Inspect the input shaft bearing outer races in the transmission case and mounting flange. If either race is damaged or excessively worn, remove it using a suitable puller.
5. Measure steel plate warpage as shown in **Figure 7** and compare the result with the specification in **Table 3**.
6. Measure the width of the steel plates tangs and compare the result with the specification in **Table 3**.
7. Measure the width of the grooves in the pressure plates and compare the result with the specification in **Table 3**. The clearance between the tangs and the grooves should be 0-0.6 mm (0-0.024 in.).
8. Measure the width of the friction plates and compare with the specification in **Table 3**. Both sides of friction plates have a 0.35 mm (0.014 in.) copper sintered layer. Replace the friction plates when the copper layer is worn more than 0.2 mm (0.008 in.) on one side.
9. Measure four friction plates. The sum of wear of four friction plates (forward or reverse) must not exceed 0.8 mm (0.031 in.). If wear exceeds 0.8 mm (0.031 in.), replace all friction plates (forward or reverse).
10. Assemble each set of steel and friction plates. Compress the plates to remove steel plate warp. Measure the assembled plates. The assembled thickness must exceed 10.0 mm (0.394 in.).
11. Measure the backlash between the teeth on the friction plates and the gear splines. The backlash must not exceed 0.9 mm (0.035 in.).
12. Lay the shift ring and pressure plate assembly flat and remove the pressure plate return springs (24, **Figure 3**). Lift off the top pressure plate (17) and remove the steel balls (18).
13. Lift the shift ring (25, **Figure 3**) and driving plate (22) off the bottom pressure plate and remove the three remaining steel balls. Slip the shift ring (25) off the driving plate (22), remove the alignment pins (21) and detent pins (20) with the springs (19) from the driving plate (22).
14. Inspect the pressure plate (17 and 23, **Figure 3**) ball grooves for wear and renew the plate if wear is noticeable.
15. Measure the pressure plate thickness and compare the result with the specification in **Table 3**.

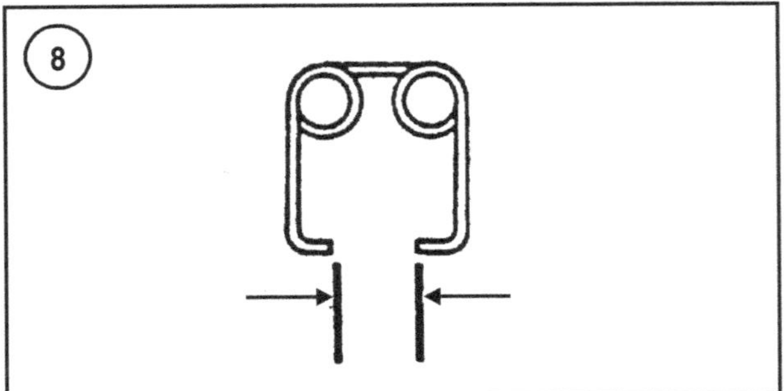

16. Measure the return spring end gap (**Figure 8**) and compare the result with the specification in **Table 3**.

17. Check the driving plate ball grooves (**Figure 9**), detent pin bores, detent pins (A) and keyway (B) for any noticeable wear.

18. Measure the driving plate hub outer diameter (C, **Figure 9**) and compare it with the specification in **Table 3**.

19. Measure detent pin spring (D, **Figure 9**) free length and compare it with the specification in **Table 3**.

20. Measure the plate spring retainer thickness (A, **Figure 10**) and compare the result with the specification in **Table 3**. Measure the plate spring inside diameter (B) and compare with the specification in **Table 3**. Measure the plate spring shoulder diameter (C) and compare the result with the specification in **Table 3**.

21. Measure the free width of the Belleville springs and compare it with the specification in **Table 3**.

22. Inspect the shift ring pressure grooves (A, **Figure 11**) and pin contact grooves (B) for any signs of excessive wear. Measure the width of the circumferential groove (C) and compare the result with the specification in **Table 3**.

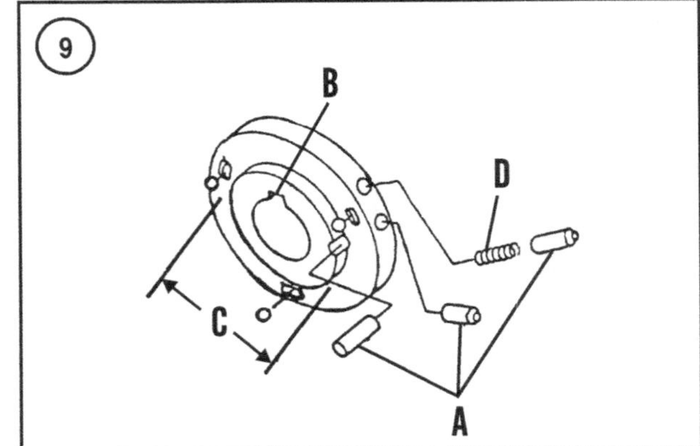

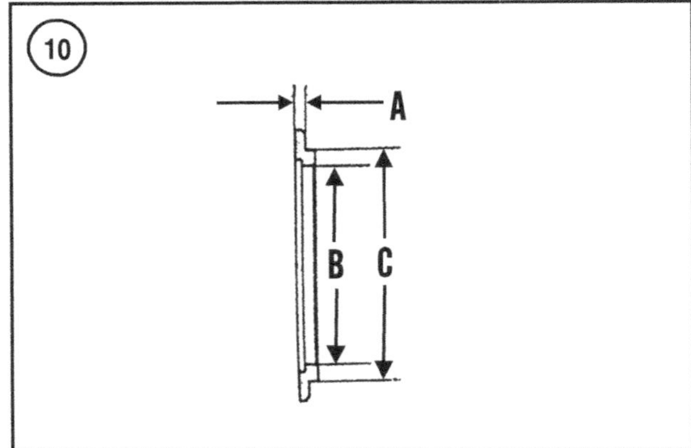

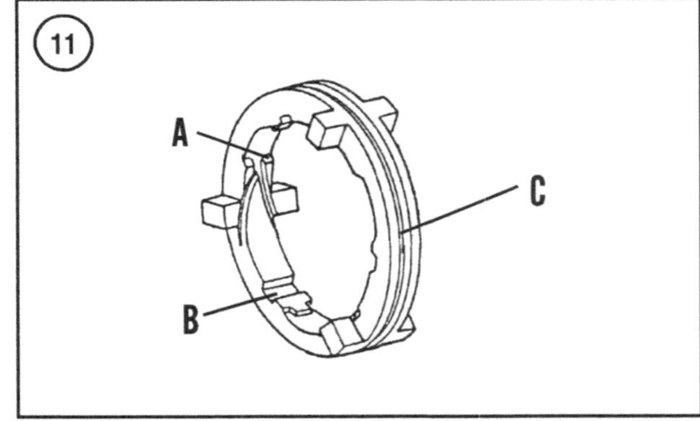

Reassembly

1. Install the Belleville springs on the forward gear so the concave sides face each other as shown in **Figure 12**. Position the retainer (12, **Figure 3**) over the Belleville springs and slide the snap ring onto the spline of the forward gear. Using Yanmar special tool 177095-09070, or a suitable equivalent tool, compress the forward gear assembly in a vise and engage the snap ring in the groove around the forward gear splines.

2. Refer to Step 1 and assemble the reverse gear, Belleville springs, retainer and snap ring.

3. To determine the correct thickness of shims (16 and 26, **Figure 3**), install the inner bearing race and spacer in their respective gears. Measure the depth (A, **Figure 13**) of the bearing race from the end of the gear as shown in **Figure 13**. Install shims equal to the depth.

4. Alternately install four friction plates (14, **Figure 3**) and three steel plates (15) on the forward gear (10) splines starting with a friction plate.

5. Refer to Step 4 and assemble the reverse gear, steel plates and friction plates.

6. Using a suitable bearing driver, install the output shaft front bearing onto the shaft. Be sure the bearing inner race contacts the collar on the end of the output shaft.

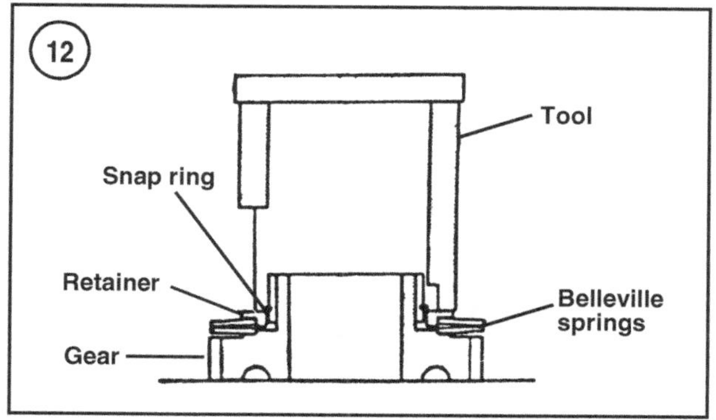

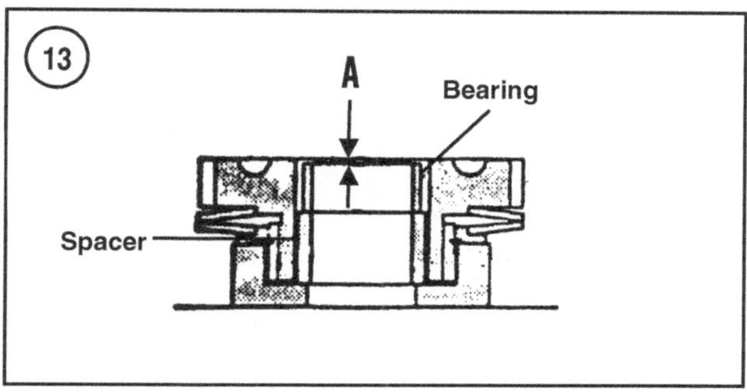

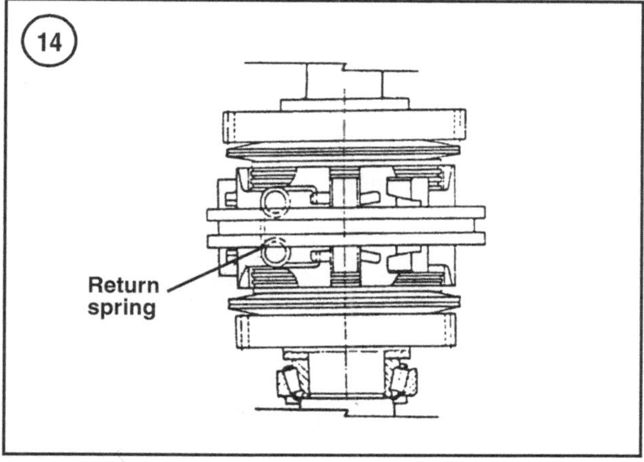

7. Install the thrust washer on the output shaft with the sintered copper surface facing away from the bearing.

8. Using a suitable bearing driver, install the needle bearing inner race on the output shaft. Be sure the race bottoms against the thrust washer.

9. Install the needle bearing, spacer and shim on the output shaft.

10. Install the forward gear assembly on the output shaft and align the steel plate tangs.

11. Fit the key (4, **Figure 3**) into the slot on the output shaft so the fillet side of the key faces the threaded end of the output shaft.

12. Install the pressure plate, with the ball slots facing up, so the steel plate tangs fit into the three slots in the pressure plate. Make sure the pawls of all three steel plates engage the pressure plate.

13. Install three steel balls into the slots on the pressure plate. Install the drive plate onto the output shaft so the side of the drive plate with concentric groove is facing the forward gear assembly. Make sure all three steel balls remain in place and the grooves of the pressure plate and the drive plate match when the drive plate is installed.

14. Insert both locating pins into the drive plate so they engage the torque limiter slots of the pressure plate.

15. Install the shim, spacer and inner needle bearing race on the ouput shaft using a suitable bearing driver.

16. Insert the detent pins and springs into the drive plate. Install the shift ring over the drive plate so the three legs with grooves are facing the forward gear and the detent pins in the drive plate properly engage the pin slots of the inside diameter of the shift ring.

17. Install three steel balls in the slots of the drive plate and place the pressure plate over the drive plate. Make sure the steel balls remain in position and the slots of both plates match.

18. Install the pressure plate return springs between the shift ring and the drive plate. Attach the spring ends to the small holes inside the pressure plates as shown in **Figure 14**.

19. Install the reverse gear assembly so the tangs of all three steel plates properly engage the slots in the pressure plate.

20. Install the needle bearing and thrust washer with the copper sintered side of the washer facing the reverse gear.

21. Using a suitable bearing driver install the rear output shaft inner race onto the output shaft. Make sure the race bottoms against the thrust washer.

22. Check for smooth rotation of both the forward and reverse gears. Check for correct operation of the shift ring.

Shifter

Refer to **Figure 3**.

NOTE

Make alignment marks on the shift lever and shift shaft so the shift lever can be reinstalled in its original position.

1. Loosen the clamp bolt and remove the shift lever.
2. Remove the shift cam.

3. Push in the detent pin, remove the snap ring and remove the pin and springs.
4. Use a screwdriver or suitable tool to pry out the seal.
5. Inspect the shift ring. Check the detent notch for excessive wear that will allow poor clutch engagement.
6. Inspect the detent pin. Replace the pin if it is damaged or excessively worn.
7. The shift ring contact surface of the shift fork is plated with molybdenum. Renew the shift fork if the plating is peeled or the shift fork base metal is exposed.
8. Reassemble the shifter by reversing the disassembly procedure. Install the shift lever so the triangle mark on the lever is out.

Reassembly

1. If removed, install the outer bearing races into the transmission case and mounting flange.
2. Apply sealer to the periphery of the oil seals and install them into the transmission case and mounting flange with the open side to the inside.
3. Install the input shaft into the transmission case.
4. Install the intermediate shaft assembly into the transmission case. Position the thrust washer so the beveled corner is toward the input shaft. Install a new O-ring on the intermediate shaft. Use a soft-faced hammer to tap the shaft into the case.
5. While holding the input shaft out of the way, insert the output shaft assembly into the transmission case. Move the gears into mesh on the intermediate shaft, input shaft and output shaft while installing the output shaft.
6. If the following components have been replaced, refer to the *Bearing Adjustment* section: input shaft, input shaft bearings, output shaft, drive plate, spacer, thrust washers and output shaft bearings. After adjusting the bearings, continue to reassemble the transmission as described in the following steps. If the preceding components have not been replaced, bearing adjustment is not necessary and the orginal shims may be reused. Proceed to the following step.
7. Install the input shaft oil seal.
8. Coat the case mating surface with RTV sealer.
9. Install the mounting flange and tighten bolts evenly.
10. Place the shift ring in neutral position and install the shift fork through the side opening.
11. Insert the shift bar through the hole in the rear of the case while installing the shift fork onto the shift bar.
12. Install the shift bar plug. Make sure the threaded end of the shift bar is installed toward the rear of the case.
13. Install the shifter assembly. Align the marks made during disassembly and tighten the retaining bolts securely. Loosen the shift lever clamp bolt and position the lever so it points up at a 45° angle toward the rear of the transmission. Retighten the clamp bolt.

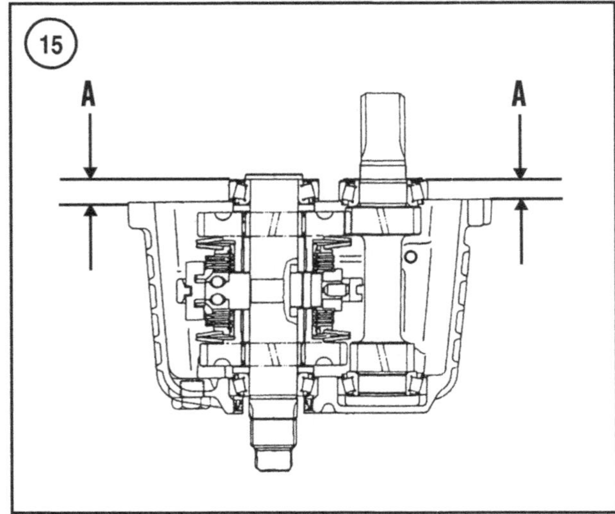

14. Check the operation of the transmission. A click should be audible when the gears are properly engaged. If the gears do not engage, loosen the shifter retaining bolts and reposition the shifter. If improper engagement continues, remove the shifter and check for improper assembly of the shifting components.
15. Install the O-ring on the output shaft.
16. If not previously installed, install the oil seal into the case.
17. Install the coupling flange onto the output shaft. Tighten the retaining nut to the torque specified in **Table 2**.
18. Install the drain plug and oil dipstick.
19. Fill the transmission with the recommended transmission fluid. Refer to Chapter Three.

BEARING ADJUSTMENT

Perform the following procedure if the following components have been replaced: input shaft, input shaft bearings, output shaft, drive plate, spacer, thrust washers and output shaft bearings. This procedure determines the thickness of shims that must be installed so the tapered roller bearings properly contact the bearing outer races.

1. Install the input shaft, intermediate shaft and output shafts as described in the *Reassembly* section.
2. Position the transmission case so the open end is up and no pressure is being applied to the splined end of the output shaft.
3. Install the outer bearing races on the input and output shaft tapered bearings.

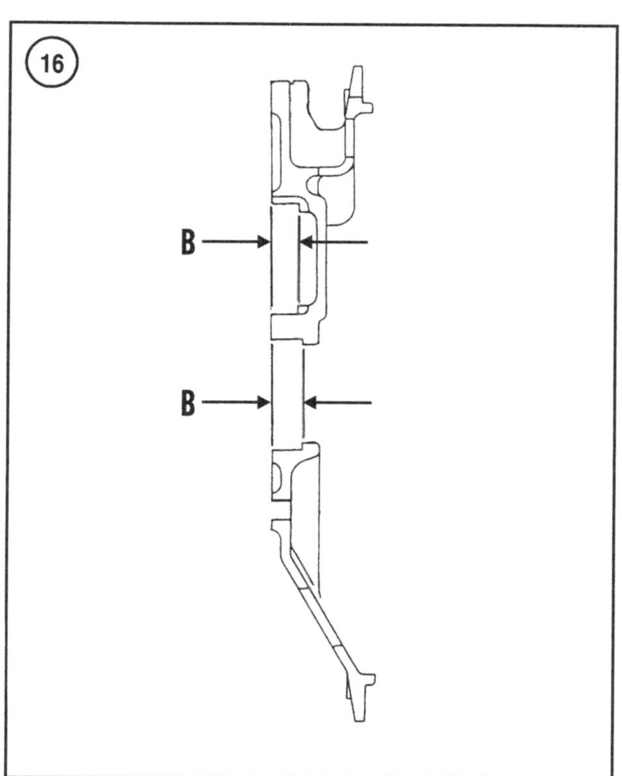

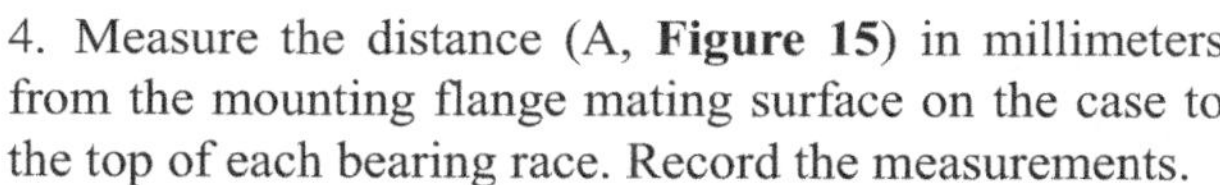

4. Measure the distance (A, **Figure 15**) in millimeters from the mounting flange mating surface on the case to the top of each bearing race. Record the measurements.
5. Measure the distance (B, **Figure 16**) from the mounting flange mating surface to the bottom of the bearing race bore for both the input and output shaft bearings.
6. Subtract the A measurement from the B measurement for each shaft.
7A. Input shaft—From the result obtained in Step 6, subtract 0.0-0.05 mm. This result equals the thickness of the shim(s) that must be installed in the bearing bore in the mounting flange.
7B. Output shaft—From the result obtained in Step 6, subtract 0.0-0.1 mm. This result equals the thickness of the shim(s) that must be installed in the bearing bore in the mounting flange.
8. Install the shim(s) in the bearing bore in the mounting flange, then press the bearing outer race into the mounting flange on top of the shims. Be sure the race is bottomed.

DRIVE DISC

The drive disc attached to the engine flywheel transmits power from the engine flywheel to the transmission input shaft. Bolts secure the disc to the flywheel while the transmission input shaft engages the splined hub on the drive disc. The drive disc incorporates springs that dampen driveline shocks between the engine and transmission.

Removal/Installation

1. Remove the engine from the boat.
2. Remove the transmission.
3. Remove the drive disc (**Figure 17,** typical).
4. Install the drive disc by reversing the removal procedure. Install the drive disc so the side marked FLYWHEEL SIDE (**Figure 18**) is toward the flywheel. Tighten drive disc retaining bolts to the torque specified in **Table 2**.

Inspection

Replace the drive disc if any of the following conditions exist:

1. Broken spring.
2. Worn or damaged splines in hub.
3. Damaged disc.
4. Damaged pins.

Table 1 ENGINE/TRANSMISSION MODELS

Model	Transmission	Transmission ratio (forward gear)
3GM	KBW10D	2.14, 2.63 or 2.83
3HM	KBW10E	2.14 or 2.83
3HM35	KBW10E	2.14 or 2.83

Table 2 TIGHTENING TORQUES

Fastener	N•m	ft.-lb.
Transmission mounting flange	20-25	15-18
Output shaft nut	85-115	63-85
Output flange nut	85-115	63-85
Drive disc	25	18

Table 3 CLUTCH SPECIFICATIONS

Steel plate warpage	1.4-1.7 mm (0.055-0.067 in.)
Steel plate tang width	11.8-12.0 mm (0.464-0.472 in.)
Pressure plate groove width	12.0-12.1 mm (0.472-0.476 in.)
Friction plate thickness	1.65-1.70 mm (0.065-0.067 in.)
Wear limit	1.5 mm (0.059 in.)
Pressure plate thickness	6.4-6.6 mm (0.252-0.260 in.)
Wear limit	6.3 mm (0.248 in.)
Return spring end gap	16.5-17.5 mm (0.650-0.690 in.)
Driving plate hub outer diameter-min.	58.8 mm (2.315 in.)
Detent pin spring free length	32.00-32.85 mm (1.260-1.293 in.)
Plate spring retainer thickness	2.72-2.80 mm (0.107-1.110 in.)
Wear limit	2.60 mm (0.102 in.)
Plate spring retainer inner diameter	65.9-66.0 mm (2.594-2.598 in.)
Wear limit	65.7 mm (2.587 in.)
Plate spring retainer shoulder diameter	57.56-57.606 mm (2.266-2.268 in.)
Wear limit	57.8 mm (2.276 in.)
Belleville spring width	6.15-6.35 mm (0.242-0.250 in.)
Min. width	6.0 mm (0.236 in.)
Shift ring circumferential groove width	6.0-6.1 mm (0.236-0.240 in.)
Wear limit	6.3 mm (0.248 in.)

Index

A

Alarm buzzer 197

B

Battery 56, 183-188
Bearing replacement. 18-23
Breather assembly
  multicylinder 101-102
  single-cylinder 71-72

C

Camshaft
  multicylinder 127-128
  single-cylinder 93-95
Charging system 189-190
  troubleshooting 31
    tests. 31-32
Cooling system 52-56, 159-165
  draining 64-66
  drive belts 169-170
  hose replacement 168-169
  maintenance
    freshwater 177-181
    seawater. 181
  pump
    freshwater. 177
    seawater 170-177
  thermostat 165-168
  troubleshooting. 34-35, 36
Crankshaft
  multicylinder 123-126
  single-cylinder 91-93
  block
    multicylinder. 128-131
    single-cylinder 95-97
  head
    multicylinder. 105-109
Cylinder
  head
    single-cylinder 73-76

D

Decompression mechanism
  multicylinder 102
  single-cylinder. 73
Diesel fundamentals
  engine
    single-cylinder 68-70
Drive belts 169-170
Drive disc
  multicylinder 123
  single-cylinder. 91

E

Electrical system
  alarm buzzer 197
  battery 183-188
  charging system 189-190
  protection 188-189
  senders. 195-196
  starting system. 190-195
  switches 195
  tachometer. 197-198
  warning lamps 197
  wiring diagrams 231-234

12

Engine
 emergency stopping 44
 exhaust smoke
  troubleshooting. 35
 maintenance and lubrication 44-52
 multicylinder 100-101
  breather assembly 101-102
  camshaft 127-128
  crankshaft 123-126
  cylinder
   block. 128-131
   head 105-109
  decompression mechanism 102
  drive disc 123
  exhaust manifold. 103-105
  flywheel 122-123
  lubrication system 120-122
  main bearings 126-127
  piston/connecting rod assembly 113-118
  push rods 113
  replacement parts 100
  rocker shaft assembly 109-110
  serial number and code 99-100
  timing gearcase. 118-119
  valve
   cover 101
   valves and seats. 110-113
 noises
  troubleshooting 35-36
 single-cylinder
  breather assembly. 71-72
  camshaft 93-95
  crankshaft. 91-93
  cylinder
   block. 95-97
   head 73-76
  decompression mechanism. 73
  diesel fundamentals. 68-70
  drive disc 91
  flywheel. 89-91
  lubrication system 86-89
  main bearings. 93
  piston/connecting rod assembly 79-85
  push rods 79
  removal precautions 70-71
  replacement parts. 70
  rocker shaft assembly 76
  serial number and code. 70
  timing gearcase 85-86
  valve
   cover 71
   valves and seats 77-79
 stopping the 44
 troubleshooting 36
 tune-up 57-60
Exhaust manifold
 multicylinder 103-105

F

Fasteners 4-8
Fitting out 66-67
Flywheel
 multicylinder 122-123
 single-cylinder 89-91
Freshwater
 cooling system, maintenance 177-181
 pump 177
Fuel
 injection
  fundamentals. 138-142
  injector 146-149
  lines 151-152
  pump 149-150
  system bleeding 142-144
  timing 144-146
  transfer pump 150-151
 requirements. 42
 system, troubleshooting 32-34

G

General information
 bearing replacement 18-23
 fasteners. 4-8
 lubricants 8-9
 mechanic's tips. 16-17
 parts replacement 4
 RTV gasket sealant 9
 seals 23
 threadlock 9
 tools
  basic hand 9-13
  precision measuring 13-16
 torque specifications 4
Governor systems. 152-157

H

Hose replacement. 168-169

L

Lay-up. 63-64
 cooling system draining 64-66

Lubricants 8-9
Lubrication system
 engine maintenance and 44-52
 multicylinder 120-122
 single-cylinder 86-89
 transmission 60-61
 troubleshooting. 36-40

M

Main bearings
 multicylinder 126-127
 single-cylinder. 93
Maintenance
 cooling system 52-56
 engine and lubrication 44-52
 fuel requirements 42
Mechanic's tips 16-17

O

Operation
 engine
  emergency stopping 44
  stopping the 44
 post-operational checks 44
 preoperational checks 42-43
 starting checklist 43-44

P

Parts replacement. 4
Piston/connecting rod assembly
 multicylinder 113-118
 single-cylinder 79-85
Post-operational checks. 44
Preoperational checks 42-43
Push rods
 multicylinder. 113
 single-cylinder. 79

R

Removal precautions
 engine
  single-cylinder 70-71
Replacement parts
 multicylinder. 100
 single-cylinder. 70
Rocker shaft assembly
 multicylinder 109-110
 single-cylinder. 76
RTV gasket sealant. 9

S

Seals. 23
Seawater
 cooling system maintenance 181
 pump. 170-177
Senders 195-196
Serial number and code
 engine
  multicylinder 99-100
  single-cylinder 70
Starting
 checklist 43-44
 system 190-195
  troubleshooting 27-31
Switches 195

T

Tachometer 197-198
Thermostat 165-168
Threadlock 9
Timing gearcase
 multicylinder 118-119
 single-cylinder 85-86
Tools
 basic hand 9-13
 precision measuring 13-16
Torque specifications. 4
Transmission 60-61
 KBW series
  bearing adjustment. 224-225
  drive disc 225
  operation 216
  overhaul 217-224
  removal/installation. 217
 KM series
  bearing adjustment. 211-213
  drive disc 213
  operation 199-201
  overhaul 202-208
  reassembly 208-211
  removal/installation. 201
Troubleshooting
 charging system 31
  tests 31-32
 cooling system. 36
 engine 36
  exhaust smoke 35
  noises 35-36
 fuel system 32-34
 lubrication system 36-40
 starting system 27-31

Tune-up
battery 56
engine tune-up 57-60

V

Valve
and seats
multicylinder 110-113
single-cylinder 77-79
cover
multicylinder 101
single-cylinder 71

W

Warning lamps. 197
Wiring diagrams 231-234

EARLY MODELS WITH LARGE INSTRUMENT PANEL

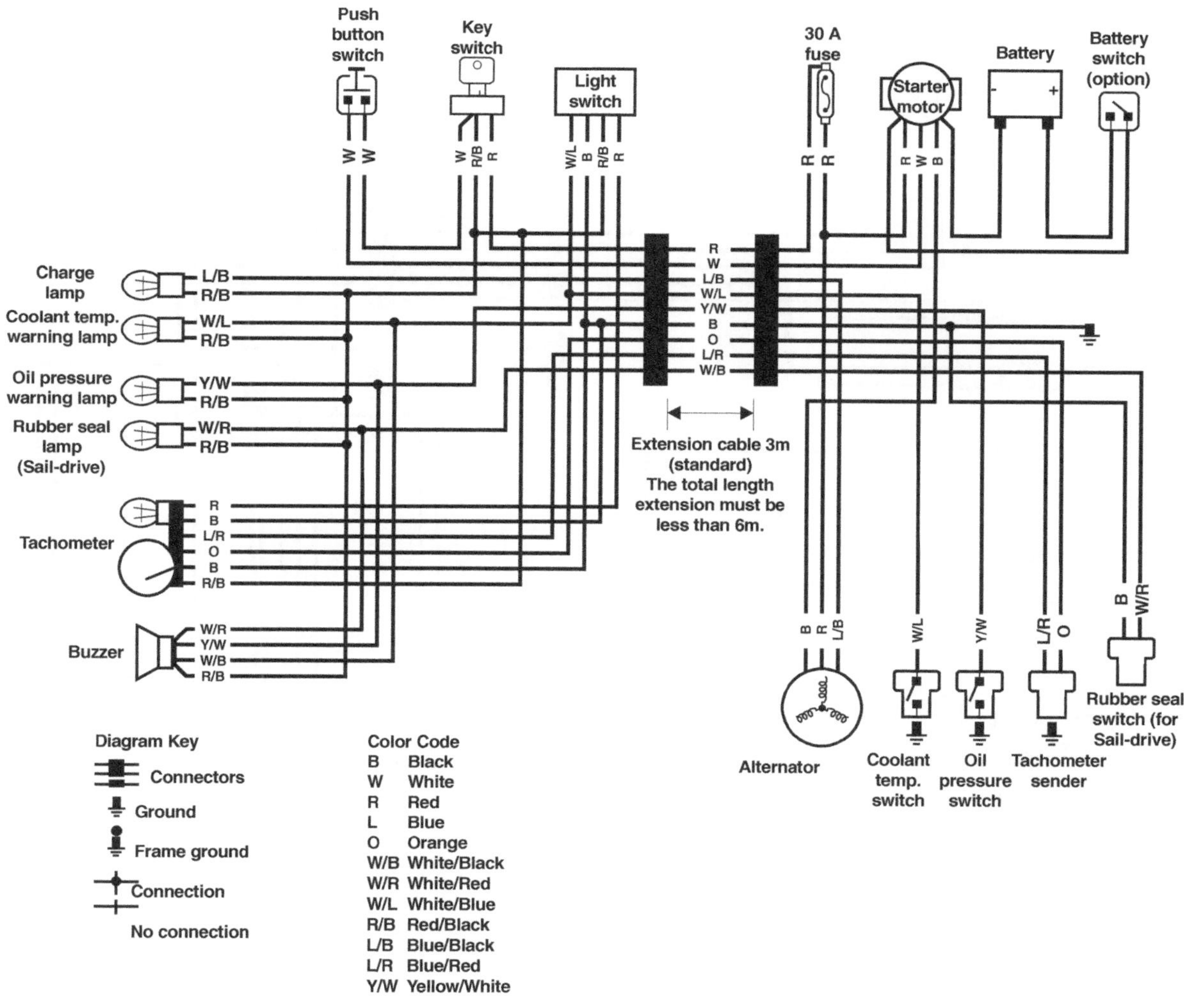

13

EARLY MODELS WITH SMALL INSTRUMENT PANEL (NO TACHOMETER)

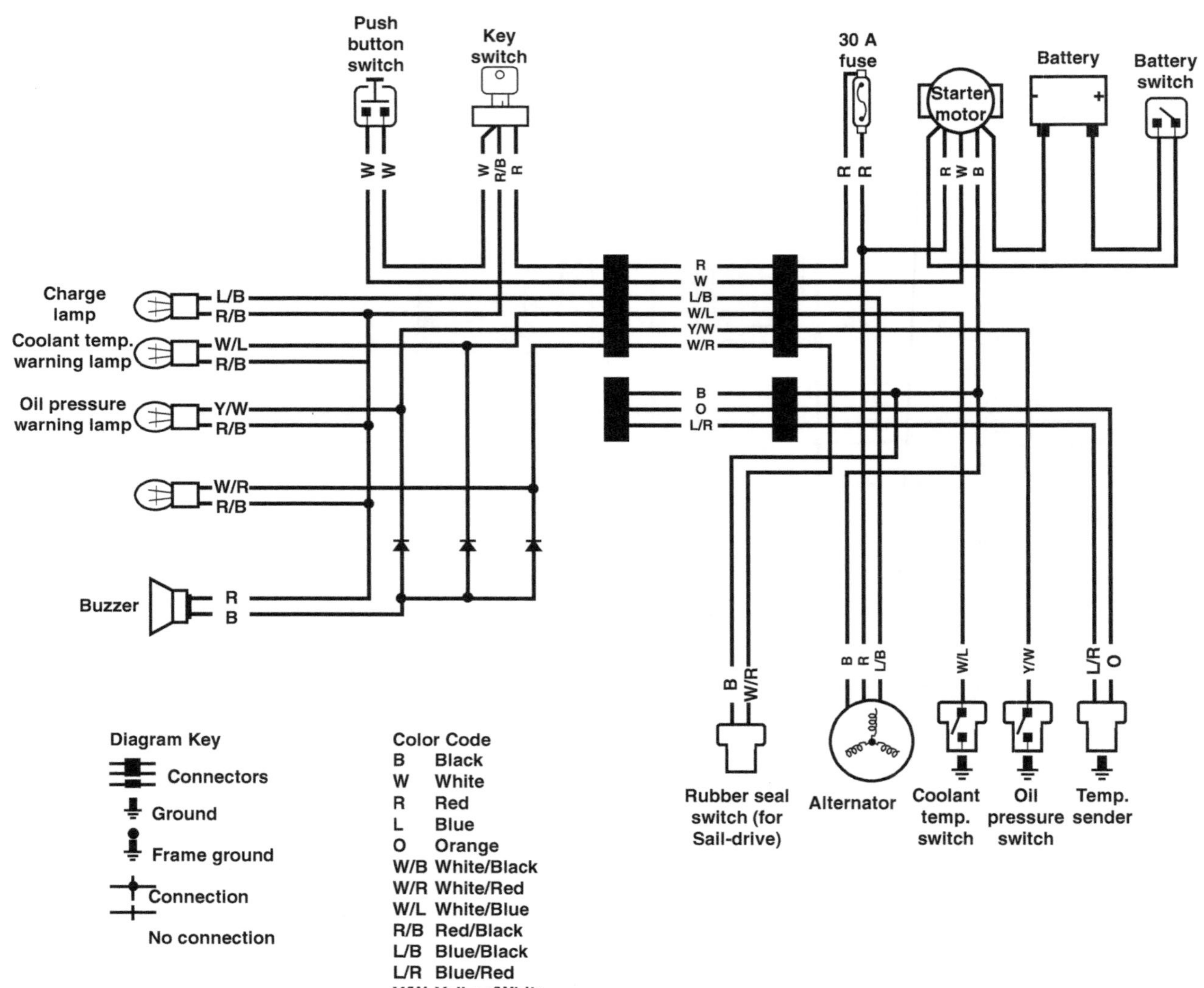

LATE MODELS WITH LARGE INSTRUMENT PANEL

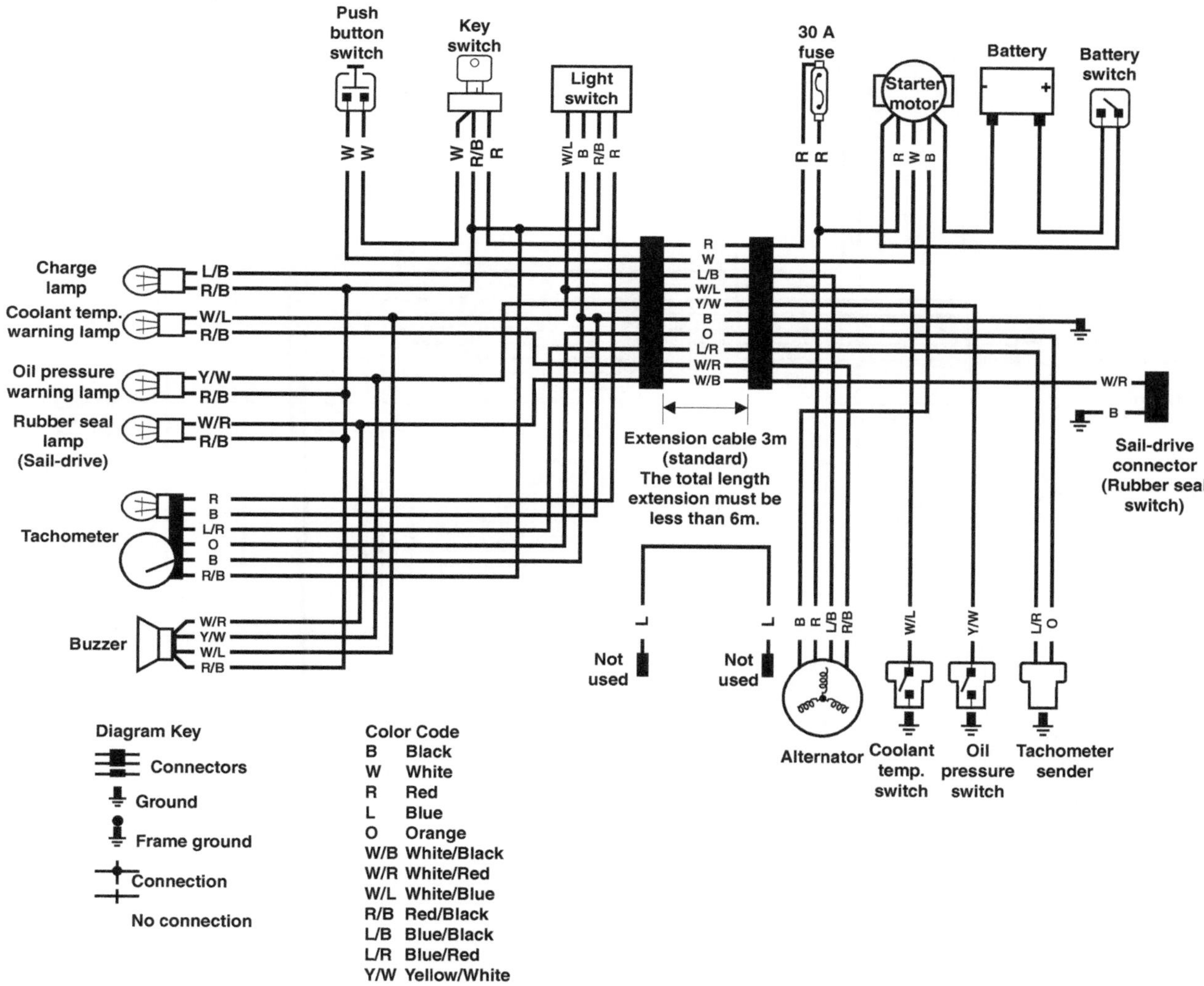

13

LATE MODELS WITH SMALL INSTRUMENT PANEL (NO TACHOMETER)

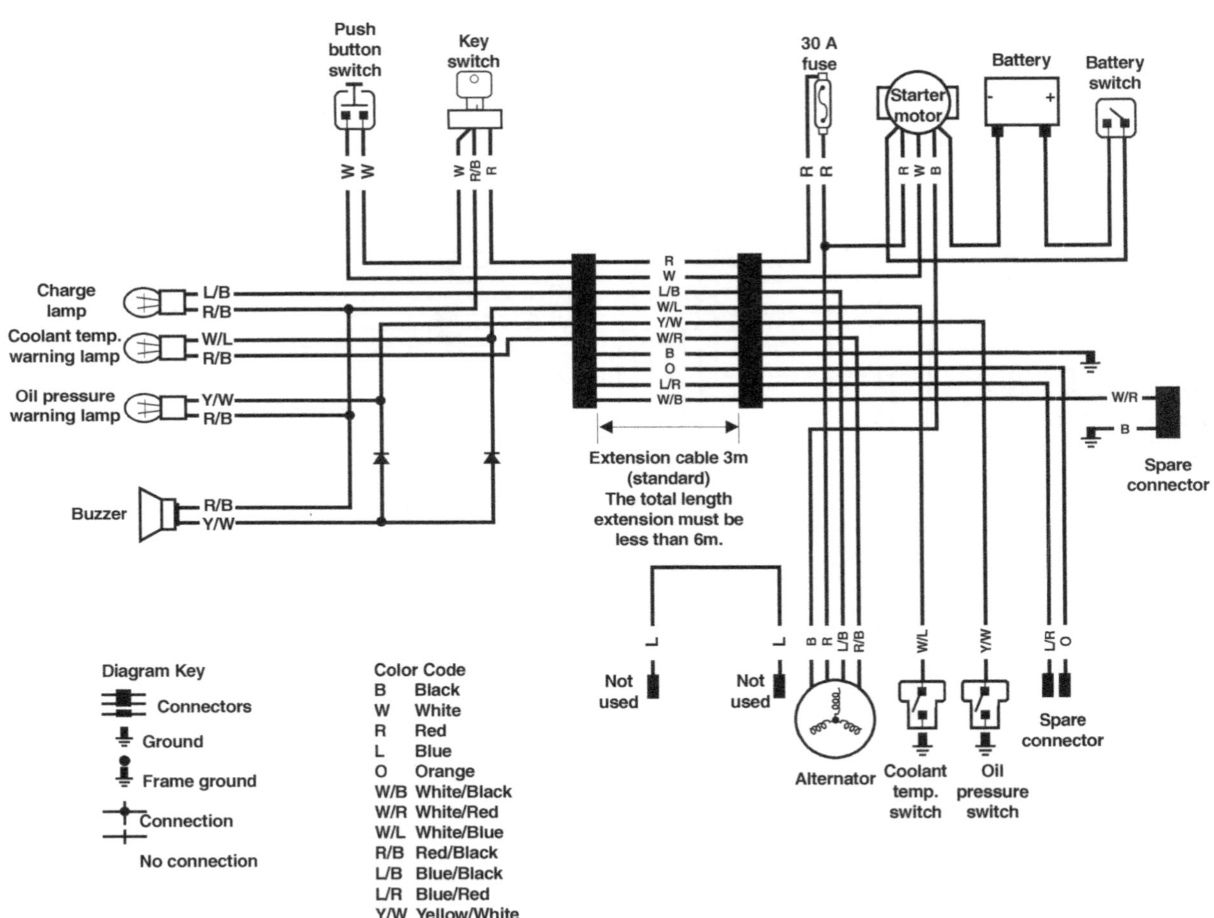

NOTES

NOTES

NOTES

MAINTENANCE LOG

Date	Maintenance Performed	Engine Hours